Iudith apibusque

CONTENTS

Abbreviations	ix
Citation of manuscripts	xi
Editorial principles	xi
Illustrations	xii
Acknowledgements	xiii
Introduction	xvii
1. The Latin passion of St Katherine in the print age	1
2. Greek texts	35
2.1 Sources and manuscripts	36
2.2 Katherine, Artemios, and Pansophios	52
2.3 Hymns	60
2.4 Calendars, menologia, and synaxaria	73
3. The story of Katherine moves west	87
3.1 Southern Italy	92
3.2 Calendars and other evidence from Italy	96
3.3 Latin translations and adaptations	103
4. The date and place of composition of BHL 1663	133
4.1 Sources and diction of BHL 1663	134
4.2 The early manuscripts of BHL 1663	170

5. BHL 1663 and Rouen	187
5.1 La Trinité-du-Mont de Rouen	188
5.2 Symeon of Trier: peddler of relics?	192
5.3 The passion of Katherine by Peter, Subdeacon of Naples, and BHL 1663	203
Conclusion	221
Appendix 1: The manuscript tradition of BHL 1663	237
Dissemination of the manuscripts	237
BHL 1663 and its epitomes	243
Katherine in the great legendaries	249
A check-list of manuscripts of BHL 1663	251
Appendix 2: Edition of the *Passio Sanctae Katerinae* (BHL 1661m)	275
The behaviour of Brussels KBR 4564-68	277
The epitomizer of BHL 1661m at work	283
The manuscripts of the *Passio Sanctae Katerinae* BHL 1661m	285
Editorial conventions and notes	290
Sigla of manuscripts	293
Edition and translation	296
Bibliography	377
General Index	417
Index of manuscripts	443

ABBREVIATIONS

AB	*Analecta Bollandiana*
AASS	*Acta sanctorum quotquot toto orbe coluntur*, ed. Heribert Rosweyde *et al.*, 1st edn (Antwerp and Brussels, 1643-1748); 2nd edn (Venice, 1734-1770); 3rd edn (Paris and Rome), 1863-
BBK	*Biographisch-Bibliographisches Kirchenlexikon*, ed. Friedrich W. Bautz and Traugott Bautz, 40 vols (Nordhausen, 1975-2019)
Bronzini	Giovanni B. Bronzini, *La leggenda di S. Caterina d'Alessandria: Passioni greche e latine*, Atti dell'Accademia Nazionale dei Lincei (Memorie: Classe di Scienze morali, storiche e filologiche, serie VIII) 9 (Rome, 1960)
CCSL	*Corpus Christianorum. Series latina*
CCCM	*Corpus Christianorum. Continuatio mediaevalis*
CSCO	*Corpus Scriptorum Christianorum orientalium*
ODB	*Oxford Dictionary of Byzantium*, ed. Alexander P. Kazhdan *et al.*, 3 vols (Oxford, 1991)
DOP	*Dumbarton Oaks Papers*
Dobson	*Seinte Katerine: Re-edited from MS Bodley 34 and the Other Manuscripts*, ed. Simonne R.T.O. d'Ardenne and Eric J. Dobson, EETS ss 7 (Oxford, 1981)

Ehrhard	Albert Ehrhard, *Überlieferung und Bestand der hagiographischen und homiletischen Literatur der griechischen Kirche von den Anfängen bis zum Ende des 16. Jarhunderts*, 3 vols (Leipzig, 1937-52)
LexMA	*Lexikon des Mittelalters*, ed. Robert Auty *et al.*, 10 vols (Munich/Zurich 1980-98)

MGH	*Monumenta germaniae historica*
	   AA: Auctores antiquissimi
	   Epp.: Epistolae
	   Poetae: Poetae latini medii aevi
	   SS: Scriptores
	   SSRG: Scriptores rerum germanicarum
	   SSRM: Scriptores rerum merovingicarum

ODNB	*Oxford Dictionary of National Biograpy*, ed. David Cannadine *et al.* (Oxford, 2004-20)
PL, PG	*Patrologia cursus completus,* ed. Jacques-Paul Migne; Series latina, 221 vols (Paris, 1844-64). Series graeca, 161 vols (Paris, 1857-66)
PMBZ Online	*Prosopographie der mittelbyzantinischen Zeit Online*, ed. Ralph-Johannes Lilie *et al.* (Berlin, 1998-2021), <https://www.degruyter.com/view/db/pmbz>
Viteau	Joseph Viteau, *Passions des Saints Écaterine et Pierre d'Alexandrie, Barbara et Anysia* (Bouillon: Paris, 1897)

CITATION OF MANUSCRIPTS

I cite manuscripts by location (anglicized), followed by the library's name and manuscript shelf-mark, date, and details of the folios when necessary (recto is assumed unless v for verso is given, a and b refer to columns). The first citation of a manuscript is written out in full while subsequent citations are shortened, consisting normally of the location, abbreviated library name, and shelf-mark, unless it is obvious through the context which manuscript is being discussed. I deviate from this rule for the Biblioteca Apostolica Vaticana in Vatican City/Rome, thus: BAV, MS Vat. gr. 807, s. x, fols 256-261v. Manuscript dates are given in Roman numerals, following 's.' for saeculum (for example, s. xii for the twelfth century). When a precise date is known, I give this in Arabic numerals. In the case of manuscripts from the Bayerische Staatsbibliothek in Munich, I omit the 'MS' since Clm stands for *codex latinus monacensis* and so on. The same is true for manuscripts held at the Stiftsbibliothek Klosterneuburg, where 'CCl' stands for *codex claustroneoburgensis latinus*.

EDITORIAL PRINCIPLES

I use modernized punctuation and spelling and have expanded abbreviations silently. Translations are my own unless otherwise noted. I cite medieval names by the conventional forms. I use the terms passion and life interchangeably.

ILLUSTRATIONS

Maps

1: The Mediterranean and Europe	xvi
2: Northern France	186

Figures

1: St Catherine's monastery, lithograph from 1830	85
2: St Catherine's monastery, photograph from 1862–63	86
3: Angers, Bib. Mun., MS 121, fol. 274	174
4: Angers, Bib. Mun., MS 121, fol. 278v	175
5: Brussels, KBR, MS 18018, fol. 26	177
6: Brussels, KBR, MS 18018, fol. 36	178
7: Paris, BnF, MS lat. 1970, fol. 54	180
8: Paris, BnF, MS lat. 1970, fol. 61	181
9: Paris, BnF, MS lat. 5343, fol. 135	183
10: Paris, BnF, MS lat. 5343, fol. 139v	184
11: Vita-icon of St Katherine	224
12: Icon of St Katherine with her relics	227
12: Relics of St Katherine (left hand and top of skull)	228
13: Relic of St Katherine (left hand)	228
14: Embroidery of Katherine's martyrdom	235

ACKNOWLEDGEMENTS

It is a happiness and privilege to be writing this section and reflect, with gratitude for the many connections made, on the extensive web of relationships that nourished me as a human and as a student and that made possible the research for and writing of this book.

The place that bore me is deeply saturated with history, the significance of which I have only been able to appreciate now that I no longer live there: mosaics made by Roman craftsmen, gardens and villages founded during the age of Charlemagne, vineyards and rivers Hildegard of Bingen looked upon centuries before I did – my parents showed it all to me, making sure I also never forgot my roots in a country where the olives and olive oil taste better than anywhere else. My gratitude, *danke & εὐχαριστώ*, knows no bounds.

Many teachers and mentors shaped or tried to shape my thinking and my approach to working with medieval Latin texts and manuscripts. To all of them, I am deeply grateful. This study began as a doctoral thesis at King's College London under the guidance of Carlotta Dionisotti, whose learning, vast and worn so lightly, and mentorship, warm and supportive, allowed me to find my own path, even when it seemed that there was none. It is hard to think of a teacher and scholar who can match her generosity, dedication, and care, and I am truly lucky to have been able to work with her. Moreover, she modelled a style of pedagogy, a compassion for others, and a sense of humour that I continually strive to emulate. David Ganz and Judith Herrin were also immensely helpful. The fine people of the Dictionary of Medieval Latin from British Sources (Theodore Christchev, David Howlett, Carolinne White) made me feel welcome and shared their time and knowledge willingly. In Paris and Brussels I was lucky enough to learn from François Dolbeau, Monique Goullet, Guy

Phillipart, and Patricia Stirnemann. Upon my arrival on the opposite side of the Atlantic, Frank Coulson helped me in adjusting to North American academia, as did Marilynn Desmond, Andrew Scholtz, and Dana Stewart. Thank you also to the teachers at conferences, seminars, and social gatherings whose names I forget but whose lessons are still with me.

Libraries and librarians made this work possible: I found quietude and belonging in the stacks of the Warburg Institute Library, where the unique arrangement of its holdings often led me to places I did not know I needed to go to. The staff and librarians at numerous libraries in London (the Institute of Classical Studies, the Institute of Historical Research, the Maughan Library at King's College, Special Collections at the Senate House Library, the British Library) as well as the many manuscript libraries across the UK and Europe provided help and access to their collections. There are too many of them to name individually and yet I am conscious of the often anonymous and invisible labour librarians and archivists undertake for researchers like me. More recently, the interlibrary loan department at Binghamton University, particularly Elise Thornley, has gone above and beyond in bringing books to me that I can no longer easily access in person.

Various institutions and fellowships provided financial assistance and I gratefully acknowledge them here: the (then) Arts and Humanities Research Council, the Erasmus Programme, Goodenough College, King's College London, Research Councils UK, and the University of London Convocation Trust. The Harpur College Dean's Office, the Institute for Advanced Studies in the Humanities, the Department of Middle Eastern and Ancient Mediterranean Studies, and the Center for Medieval and Renaissance Studies at Binghamton University also generously supported my work.

Compassionate and smart friends accompanied me on the journey towards this book and I am truly grateful for their presence: Anne Alwis, Jessica Bloom, Travis Bruce, Eileen

Campbell-Reed, Elizabeth Casteen, Isabelle Cochelin, Rachel Cornell, Albrecht Diehm, Janet Downie, Laura Franco, Stacey Graham, Anna Grotans, Alison Guenther-Pal, Susanne Hakenbeck, Daniel Hadas, Julian Harrison, Samantha Herrick, Jeffrey Kirkwood, John Kuhn, Sophie Lunn-Rockliffe, Drew Massey, Matthieu van der Meer, Kelly Murphy, Hildegund Müller, Costa and Margarita Sakellariou, Sarah Thomas, Marguerite Wilson, Justine Wolfenden, Mary Youssef, as well as, in particular, Thomas Canale and Allie French. The SALVI crowd welcomed me with open arms: I want to thank Andrew Morehouse, Justin Slocum-Bailey, and Evan Smith for showing me that Latin can be spoken by anyone and how healing and liberating it can be.

In the final stages, I received assistance with editing from Jeffrey Brubacker and Deirdre Riley while the editorial team at *Medium Aevum* were endlessly patient and helpful: very special thanks to Nigel Palmer for being a wonderful supporter of my work and an attentive editor and Anthony Lappin for his forbearance in tackling the huge task of typesetting.

xvi   The Passion of St Katherine of Alexandria

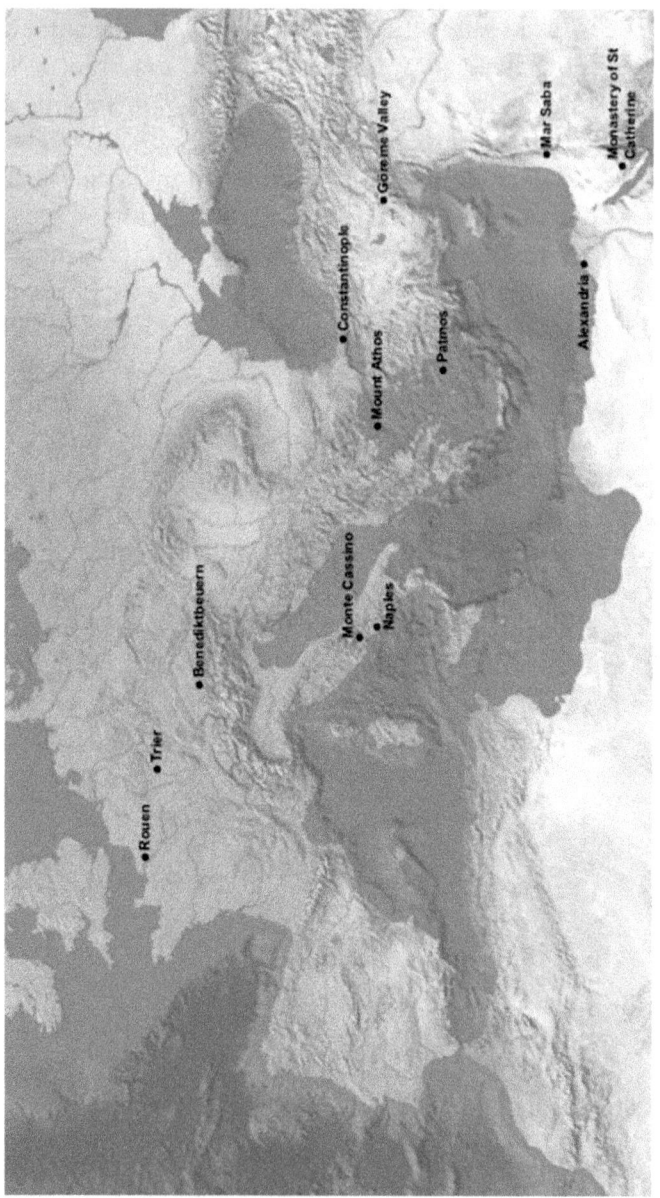

Map 1: The Mediterranean and Europe. Adapted on the basis of file: Mediterranean Basin and Near East before 1000 AD topographic map.jpg, © User: Flappiefh / Wikimedia Commons CC-BY-SA-4.0

INTRODUCTION

St Katherine of Alexandria is a curious example of an eastern saint whose cult rose to prominence in the West, having been brought to northern France through channels linking the region with Italy/southern Italy, and who was then re-introduced to the Greek East by travellers seeking relics and evidence of Katherine on Mount Sinai where her body was said to have been buried, and to the Crusader states by western Crusaders.[1] She was not especially significant in the eastern church compared to other saints, and had a rather universal appeal with no particular cult site before the turn of the millenium. Katherine's transformation from a relatively unimportant saint in the Greek pantheon of saints into one of medieval Western Christianity's most significant intercessors is predicated on a number of circumstances: (1) the telling of her story and this story's journey from the eastern part of the empire to Italy and from there to Normandy, (2) the deft adaptation of this story to the very specific needs of the reform movement in eleventh-century Normandy, (3) the foundation of a monastery along with the fortuitous acquisition of relics from a Greek monk from Sinai, allowing her cult to spread all across Europe, and (4) finally, the anchoring of her story to a

---

[1] See David Jacoby, 'Christian pilgrimage to Sinai until the late fifteenth century', in *Holy Image, Hallowed Ground: Icons from Sinai*, ed. Robert S. Nelson and Kristen M. Collins (Los Angeles, 2006), pp. 79–93 (p. 80 and 83). Nancy P. Ševčenko, 'St Catherine of Alexandria and Mount Sinai', in *Ritual and Art: Byzantine Essays for Christopher Walter*, ed. Pamela Armstrong (London, 2006), pp. 129–43 (p. 136 and 142). Ead., 'The Monastery of Mount Sinai and the cult of Saint Catherine', in *Bzyantium: Faith and Power (1261–1557)*, ed. Helen C. Evans (New York, 2006), pp. 118–37 (p. 124). On the liturgical diffusion in the wake of the Crusades, see James J. Blasina, 'Music and gender in the medieval cult of St Katherine of Alexandria' (unpublished doctoral dissertation, Harvard University, 2015), pp. 147–99.

remote and sacred location that was evocative and had deep biblical and historical roots.

After years of slowly gathering momentum and with a trajectory taking her from Byzantium across the Mediterranean to Italy, Katherine reached Normandy in the first half of the eleventh century. She arrived with a bang that was to reverberate across Europe in the following centuries, making her one of the most popular saints of the Middle Ages. This was made possible in part by an account of her passion, which clearly captured the imagination of her devotees.[2] It is commonly referred to as the '*Vulgate*' to explain its wide dissemination in western Europe and identified in the *Bibliotheca hagiographica latina* (BHL) with the number 1663. Katherine's passion has all the hallmarks of good hagiographical writing: a young, beautiful, and educated orphan comes face to face with an evil and misguided tyrant. He forces her into a public debate and thus affords her the opportunity to vanquish by argument fifty of the most gifted rhetors. However, blinded by pride and pagan wickedness, the tyrant does not accept Katherine's victory and subjects her to numerous punishments culminating in her death.[3] By the time of her decapitation, a

---

[2] There are three handlists for saints' lives put together by the Bollandists, a group of scholars dedicated to the study of saints' and hagiography: *Bibliotheca hagiographica latina* (BHL), *Bibliotheca hagiographica graeca* (BHG), and *Bibliotheca hagiographica orientalis* (BHO). Each saint's life carries its own BHL number within an alphabetical arrangement according to the names of the saints, with the assumed oldest life in first place. For a brief and accessible overview of the Bollandists' work, see David Knowles, *Great Historical Enterprises: Problems in Monastic History* (Edinburgh, 1963), pp. 1–32.

[3] Contrary to common belief, Katherine was never martyred on the infamous wheels, but only placed next to them in an attempt to threaten her. They are not unique to her story and also occur, for example, in the passions of Charitina of Amisus, Christina of Bolsena, Euphemia of Chalcedon, George of Cappadocia, Iuliana of Nicomedia, and Pantaleon. See the index in vol. 2 of Bonino Mombrizio's *Sanctuarium seu vitae sanctorum*, ed. monachi Solesmenses (Paris, 1910), s.v. *rota*.

great number of important protagonists have converted to the Christian faith, while thousands have suffered for clinging to their heathen gods.

She captured the imagination of eleventh-century monks in Normandy in part because they saw in her an exemplary early martyr who functioned as a vessel for their own preoccupations with matters of doctrine and conversion in the wake of the Viking incursions and their efforts to rebuild their monastic communities. A universal yet relatively obscure saint such as Katherine gave the Normans a stake in historical Christianity going back to its early days in the desert regions of Egypt, thus glossing over in some sense their relatively recent conversion to Christianity just a century earlier. From there, the saint's story continued to capture the imagination of increasingly diverse communities of Christians. Her masculine traits, such as her erudition, debating abilities, intelligence, bravery, steadfastness, and willingness to stand up to secular authority were initially more important for male audiences. The addition of the prequel materials in the thirteenth and fourteenth centuries that give an account of her conversion and marriage to Jesus tended to emphasize her virginity and beauty and made her an example also for virgins and women religious.[4]

In some ways, Katherine was surprisingly versatile with a wide appeal: her story resonated across the ages as various individuals and groups of people stood up to authoritarian representatives, secular or otherwise, to defend what they believed was the true Catholic faith. An excellent example of this is Jan Hus, the Czech preacher, heretic, and reformer who was the defendant in a heresy trial and a lenghty legal process

---

[4] Diane L. Mockridge, 'From Christ's soldier to his bride: Changes in the portrayal of women saints in medieval hagiography' (unpublished doctoral dissertation, Duke University, 1984), pp. 150–208 on Katherine. Ead., 'Marital imagery in six late twelfth- and early thirteenth-century vitae of female saints', in *That Gentle Strength: Historical Perspectives on Women in Christianity*, ed. Lynda L. Coon *et al.* (Charlottesville, VA, 1990), pp. 60–78.

that resulted in his death at the stake in 1415 in Constance. Hus can be seen as having 'fully accepted the eventuality of his own martyrdom, as he came to identify with figures like Jeremiah, Daniel, the Maccabees, Katherine of Alexandria, and John Chrysostom, who had suffered for their proclamation and persistent defence of divine truth'.[5] In a letter from prison, addressed 'to the faithful Bohemians', Hus writes:

> The virgin St Catherine ought to have renounced the truth and faith of the Lord Jesus Christ, because fifty philosophers opposed her; but the beloved virgin was faithful even unto death, and won the masters to God, which I as a sinner cannot do. I am writing this to you that you may know that they did not get the better of me by any scripture passage or any arguments.[6]

Hus, who took the stand to defend himself at his trial and who was offered numerous chances to reconsider his position during the process, is clearly drawing a parallel between Katherine and himself. Their positions, as dissenting underdogs engaged in a fight with the authorities, are strikingly similar even though the clergyman was technically part of the establishment he was trying to reform.

The defining feature of Katherine's story and, indeed, a defining feature of Katherine herself – her superpower, so to speak – is that she is a debating champion. The entire narrative is structured around the act of speech and the numerous, relatively long exchanges between the various protagonists. It also hinges on Katherine's extraordinary learning. As Susan Ashbrook Harvey has written, 'the saint's

---

[5] Phillip N. Haberkern, *Patron Saint and Prophet: Jan Hus in the Bohemian and German Reformations* (Oxford, 2016), pp. 15–16.

[6] Letter 76, 26 June 1415, originally written in Czech. See *The Letters of John Hus: With Introductions and Explanatory Notes*, Herbert B. Workman and R. Martin Pope (London, 1904), pp. 262–65 (p. 264).

activity makes the saint's identity'[7] and in Katherine's case this is manifest in the story itself – her initial act of interrupting the emperor's sacrifice with a speech is repeatedly enacted, giving her numerous opportunities to talk, thus solidifying her position as a public speaker and justifying her significant educational background. It is in the speeches in particular that the various authors and editors of the text(s) were able to intervene most and thus adapt the story to their needs. Here, especially, can be seen the connection between the text and its socio-cultural historical context: the author of BHL 1663 embedded into his version key debate treatises that were important to the reform movement in the eleventh century, and subsequently made BHL 1663 resonate with later generations as disputation and debate became an important aspect of medieval European education.[8]

Katherine's erudition and intellect are her weapons. She vanquishes her enemies not through physical strength or endurance, but by the keenness and power of her mind alone. The prologue that introduces the version known as BHL 1663 starts off with a simile – 'quid aliud agimus nisi, ut ita dicam, quoddam incentivum bellicum promovemus, per quod imbelles animos auditorum ad bella dominica accendamus' – and thus sets the tone for the rest of the prologue: the argumentative logic displayed here can almost be likened to a battle which, the author suggests, Katherine has fought already, and which his listeners ought to fight both now and in the future. The troops have been roused but are hesitant to follow. Katherine, the forerunner and prime example, attacks her enemies who come at her from all sides. She fights like a man and

---

[7] Susan Ashbrook Harvey, 'Women in early Byzantine hagiography: Reversing the story', in *That Gentle Strength*, ed. Coon *et al.*, pp. 36–59 (p. 37).

[8] See Alex J. Novikoff, *The Medieval Culture of Disputation: Pedagogy, Practice, and Performance* (Philadelphia, 2013).

overcomes them, while people such as the author ('nos barbati homines') do not even make an effort to emulate Christ when it is easy to do so, thus alluding to the *militia Christi*.[9]

Although Katherine is widely acknowledged as an influential medieval saint, and though recent years have seen an increased interest in her cult, depictions, and the later body of texts associated with her,[10] comparatively little work has been done on the Greek and Latin texts. While there has been great progress in examining the vernacular accounts of her passion,[11]

[9] Prologue in *Seinte Katerine: Re-edited from MS Bodley 34 and the Other Manuscripts*, ed. Simonne R.T.O. d'Ardenne and Eric J. Dobson (Oxford, 1981), pp. 144–45. Katherine A. Smith, *War and the Making of Medieval Monastic Culture* (Woodbridge, 2011).

[10] See for example Katherine J. Lewis, *The Cult of St Katherine of Alexandria in Late Medieval England* (Woodbridge, 2000). *St. Katherine of Alexandria: Texts and Contexts in Western Medieval Europe*, ed. Jacqueline Jenkins and Katherine J. Lewis (Turnhout, 2003). Gary Marker, *Imperial Saint: The Cult of St Catherine and the Dawn of Female Rule in Russia* (DeKalb, 2007). Christine Walsh, *The Cult of St Katherine of Alexandria in Early Medieval Europe* (Aldershot, 2007). Claire M. Waters, *Virgins and Scholars: A Fifteenth-century Compilation of the Lives of John the Baptist, John the Evangelist, Jerome, and Katherine of Alexandria* (Turnhout, 2008). Tracey R. Sands, *The Company She Keeps: The Medieval Swedish Cult of Saint Katherine of Alexandria and its Transformations* (Turnhout, 2010). Anne Simon, *The Cult of Saint Katherine of Alexandria in Late-medieval Nuremberg: Saint and the City* (Aldershot, 2012). Recent doctoral dissertations completed in North America include Blasina, 'Music and gender in the medieval cult of St Katherine of Alexandria', and Kristine M. Larison, 'Mount Sinai and the Monastery of St Catherine: Place and space in pilgrimage art' (unpublished doctoral dissertation, University of Chicago, 2016). See also Peter Schill, *Ikonographie und Kult der Hl. Katharina von Alexandrien im Mittelalter: Studien zu den szenischen Darstellungen aus der Katharinenlegende* (Munich, 2005).

[11] An indication of the sorts of angles from which Katherine has been studied in the past can be gleaned from the bibliography on Katherine in *BBK*, s.v. Katharina. See also Anna M. Valente Bacci, 'La leggenda di S. Caterina di Alessandria: Fonti e diffusione nell'area linguistica tedesca', *Cultura e Scuola*, 25 (1986), 75–87.

BHL 1663, from which many of them derive, has enjoyed little attention, not to mention the extant corpus of Greek and Latin texts. Two scholars have prepared editions of BHL 1663, but only as subordinate to their main interest, namely the Middle English version of Katherine's passion.[12] This has left the field open for a more intensive treatment of BHL 1663 in terms of its diction and style, but also as regards its transmission. Which are the oldest manuscripts, where do they come from, and how does BHL 1663 differ from other Latin accounts of Katherine's passion? Can one determine a text (or texts) that served as a model, and does this allow an insight into the author's purpose?

The Greek texts, in particular, have been neglected after a brief flurry of activity at the end of the nineteenth and beginning of the twentieth centuries, despite the fact that they represent the earliest accounts of Katherine's passion. The most recent examination of the corpus is Giovanni Bronzini's *La leggenda di S. Caterina d'Alessandria*,[13] to which scholars refer today and thus repeat its mistakes. Current misconceptions inherited from Bronzini among medieval historians concerned with Katherine's cult include the following statement:

> In the early 960s Simon Metaphrastes wrote a Greek life of the saint, generally held to be the earliest extant version; it is from this life that most later Latin versions trace their descent. Several other lives of St Katherine were written in Greek in the later

---

[12] Eugen Einenkel, *The Life of Sainte Katherine from the Royal Ms. 17A xxvii, etc., with its Latin Original from the Cotton MS. Caligula A. viii, etc.*, edited with introduction, notes, and glossary (London, 1884). Almost one hundred years later d'Ardenne and Dobson published an edition of BHL 1663 (based on 20+ manuscripts) in *Seinte Katerine: Re-edited from MS Bodley 34*.

[13] Giovanni B. Bronzini, *La leggenda di S. Caterina d'Alessandria: Passioni greche e latine*, Atti dell'Accademia Nazionale dei Lincei (Memorie: Classe di Scienze morali, storiche e filologiche, serie VIII) 9 (Rome, 1960). Reviewed by François Halkin, *AB*, 79 (1961), 178–79.

tenth century, the most famous of which is that contained in the *Menologium Basilianum* written for the Byzantine emperor Basil II (976-1025).[14]

As will become clear, none of this is true.

The preoccupation of scholars with the vernacular texts and the cult from the eleventh century onwards has obscured the fact that there is a significant amount of material from the earlier period, not all of which is as tenuous as has been assumed in the past. In order to arrive at a greater understanding of the early Greek and Latin textual corpus as well as that of BHL 1663, I have divided this study into the following chapters: I begin with an overview of the history of scholarship on Katherine and BHL 1663 from the print-age until the modern period to illustrate both the valuable insights of late medieval and early modern scholars, almost entirely ignored by their later successors, as well as the editing efforts of nineteenth-century intellectuals and academics. In the second chapter I bring together all extant material written in Greek and seek to place it within an historical context so as to clarify, as far as possible, the emergence of Katherine's passion and its early development. I consider parallels with other texts as well as a handful of early manuscripts. In Chapter 3, I take as my starting point the arrival of Katherine's passion in southern Italy and Carolingian Bavaria, in order to determine how far this was connected to the diffusion of the other Latin texts that tell her story, which were a product of southern Italy in the main. In Chapter 4, I concentrate on the compositional aspects of BHL 1663, the only text among the early Latin

---

[14] Thus the introduction to *St. Katherine of Alexandria*, ed. Jenkins and Lewis, pp. 7–8. This assessment is repeated in many studies. Equally erroneous and misleading is the entry on Catherine of Alexandria in the *Encyclopedia of Early Christianity*, ed. Everett Ferguson, 2nd edn (Oxford, 1999), p. 226, where one reads that 'her cult began in the ninth century at Mt Sinai and influenced the Crusaders, who brought it to the west'.

Introduction

passions of Katherine to have been written outside of Italy, and provide it with an historical and geographical framework. The final chapter focusses on the possible connection between BHL 1663, the arrival of Katherine's relics in Normandy, and the version of her passion written by Peter, Subdeacon of Naples (fl. 950-1000). The study ends with a number of appendices in which I gather important material not easily integrated into the main text: I present an examination of the manuscript tradition of BHL 1663 with a sketch of how it gave rise to a number of epitomes, followed by a checklist of manuscripts as far as I have been able to find them. I offer an edition along with a translation of an early epitome, BHL 1661m, that was composed soon after BHL 1663 was produced and certainly before the end of the eleventh century.

The principal method of investigation for this study has been the close scrutiny of manuscripts as regards their date and provenance as evidence for the origin of Katherine's cult and the progress of her story in its various forms across the Mediterranean into Northern France. Alongside data from the manuscripts, I have gathered as much information as possible for the historical context in which the various texts were written and/or circulated. Due to the wealth of material, the footnotes are richer and therefore more complex than initially expected. I have, however, chosen to keep them as they are because they allow the reader a more thorough understanding of how I have traced material, and in many cases bring together information otherwise not available in this form.

CHAPTER 1

THE LATIN PASSION OF KATHERINE IN THE PRINT AGE

Tracing the fortunes of BHL 1663, the most popular Latin version of Katherine's passion before the advent of the *Legenda aurea* in the medieval period and pre-printing would take up several books. One would have to account for the various epitomes and reworkings, as well as the text's inclusion in legendaries such as the *Magnum legendarium austriacum* or by named authors into their collections (e.g. Jean de Mailly, Jacobus de Voragine), not to mention the innumerable translations and adaptations that followed suit in many vernaculars. Thus, the following sketch of the fortunes of BHL 1663 and Katherine in the print age and beyond should be considered as an amuse-bouche, highlighting the paths that have already been cleared in this thick forest.[1]

Roughly twenty years after Johannes Gutenberg pioneered the printing press with movable types at Mainz in the 1450s, the first printed edition of BHL 1663 appeared in 1476 from the Cologne workshop of Johann Koelhoff the Elder, one of the city's most important printers in the early stages of

---

[1] 'Es gleicht einem dichten Urwalde, der sich endlos und lichtlos ins Ungemessene ausdehnt und in dessen Inneres kein Pfad hineinführt'. Albert Ehrhard, 'Die Legendensammlung des Symeon Metaphrastes und ihr ursprünglicher Bestand: Eine paläographische Studie zur griechischen Hagiographie', in *Festschrift zum elfhundertjährigen Jubiläum des deutschen Campo Santo in Rom*, ed. Stephan Ehses (Freiburg, 1897), pp. 46–82 (p. 46).

printing.² In this print the author of the text is given as Rabanus Maurus and the title as *Historia S. Catherinae*,³ so that the entry for BHL 1663 in the 1986 edition of the *Bibliotheca hagiographica latina: Novum supplementum* reads: 'Passio (interdum Rabano Mauro adscripta)'.⁴ Why this text should have been attributed to Rabanus is not quite clear, although misattributions to authors of his stature are not infrequent. He himself did not know of Katherine or her story, as he does not include her in his Martyrology that was finished around 843.⁵ Katherine only appears as a twelfth-/thirteenth-century marginal entry in some of its manuscripts.⁶ Perhaps the manuscript used by Koehlhoff identified its author as Rabanus, although he does not indicate from what source he printed the text. In Cologne there are now four fifteenth-

---

² Koehlhoff, born in Lübeck, worked in Venice and came to Cologne in 1471. He printed canon and civil law books for the university, and sold his books as far as the Baltic. From the 1480s onwards, professors also gave their works to him (and Peter Quentel, d. 1546) for printing. His son, Koehlhoff the Younger, printed saints' legends, including those of Margaret of Antioch, Barbara, Katharina, Dorothea, and Ursula. Both printed a large number of texts in German. See Wolfgang Schmitz, *500 Jahre Buchtradition in Köln: Von der Koehlhoffschen Chronik bis zu den Neuen Medien* (Cologne, 1999), p. 18.

³ In a copy at the British Library (call-mark IB.3501, p. g3) the title that precedes the Katherine text reads: 'Dive virginis sancte Katherine historia seu eiusdem passionis series Rabbani abbat. rei geste persuavis oratio eloquentie splendori plurimum alludens aminiculo. omnium cognitu et lectione fragrancissima'. The text includes the prologue.

⁴ *Bibliotheca hagiographica latina antiquae et mediae aetatis: Novum supplementum*, ed. Henryk Fros (Brussels, 1986).

⁵ John M. McCulloh, 'Hrabanus Maurus' Martyrology: The method of composition', *Sacris Erudiri*, 23 (1978/79), 417–61. Id., 'Das Martyrologium Hrabans als Zeugnis seiner geistigen Arbeit', in *Hrabanus Maurus: Lehrer, Abt und Bischof*, ed. Raymund Kottje and Harald Zimmermann (Wiesbaden, 1982), pp. 154–64.

⁶ See *Martyrologium Rabani Mauri*, ed. John M. McCulloh, CCCM44 (Turnhout, 1979), pp. xxxxvii–xxxix.

century manuscripts with a Cologne provenance that contain BHL 1663; the catalogue entries for these manuscripts do not mention Rabanus as a possible author.[7] A play from 1606 (*Catharinaria tragoedia*) appears to have made use of BHL 1663, based on its title which refers to Rabanus' Latin version: 'Catharina sive Tragoedia … eius res gestas ex Graecis edidit Metaphrastes, quas habet Lip[omanus] tom. V. et Surius tom. VI, ex Latinis Rabanus Abbas, alii'.[8]

In Koehlhoff's edition, BHL 1663 is preceded by a *Passio Jesu Christi necnon alius tractatus de Christi passione, sive collectura* by Johannes Kannemann. Kannemann (born *c.* 1400), a Franciscan preacher with a doctorate in theology from the University of Erfurt, was the *magister regens* at Magdeburg and a lector of theology in Berlin during the 1450s. He was a well-known reformer who strongly opposed the Waldensian rejection of the saints in his pastoral writings

---

[7] See Joachim Vennebusch, *Die homiletischen und hagiographischen Handschriften des Stadtarchivs Köln*, 2 vols (Cologne, 1993–2001). See Appendix 1 for a list of manuscripts.

[8] Stefan Tilg, *Die Hl. Katharina auf der Jesuitenbühne: Drei Innsbrucker Dramen aus den Jahren 1567, 1577, und 1606* (Tübingen, 2005), p. 298. Tilg's introduction provides a sense of the kind of interest accorded to Katherine by Catholic humanists and Jesuit teachers and poets. Under November 25 Lorenz Sauer (1523–78, Laurentius Surius in Latin) includes an otherwise unknown Latin passion of Katherine, which is in fact his own translation of Symeon Metaphrastes' version of Katherine's passion (reproduced in *PG* 116, cols 275–302, opposite the Greek text). See *De probatis sanctorum historiis ab Al. Lipomano olim conscriptis nunc primum a Laur. Surio emendatis et auctis* (Cologne, 1570–77), followed by another three editions. Also Paul Holt, 'Die Sammlung von Heiligenleben des Laurentius Surius', *Neues Archiv*, 44 (1922), 341–64. David J. Collins, *Reforming Saints: Saints' Lives and their Authors in Germany, 1470-1530* (Oxford, 2018), p. 134, noted that 'Surius indisputably shaped his writings to address the new Evangelical challenges, … . Sometimes he reinserted miracles that earlier humanists had excised; sometimes he added new ones'.

as can be seen in his *De oratione domini*.⁹ It is not known whether Kannemann was still alive by the time his treatise was printed by Koehlhoff in 1476; neither is it clear why it was followed by the passion of Katherine/BHL 1663. As far as I can tell there are no obvious or immediate parallels (e.g. borrowing of phrases and the like) between the two texts. Joining the two could have been a decision taken either by the printer or by the author himself. Nothing connects these the two texts, except perhaps that both are concerned with the untimely death of a sacred figure, so one may wonder if there was some link between them in Koehlhoff's source.

Kannemann may have come across Katherine while studying at Erfurt,¹⁰ and later he likely came across the saint in his capacity as theologian and preacher since her story at this time was circulating as part of the highly successful *Legenda aurea* or *Der Heiligen Leben*, its German language counterpart put together around 1400.¹¹ In German-speaking areas, Katherine was certainly used as an example in sermons from the

---

[9] These and more details in Livarius Oliger, 'Johannes Kannemann: Ein deutscher Franziskaner aus dem 15. Jahrhundert', *Franziskanische Studien*, 5 (1918), 39–67, and Johannes Schlageter, 'Franziskanische Theologie des Mittelalters in der Saxonia' in *Von den Anfängen bis zur Reformation*, ed. Volker Honemann, Geschichte der Sächsischen Franziskanerprovinz vol. 1 (Leiden, 2015), pp. 415–520 (pp. 489–501 on Kannemann).

[10] For example, the cathedral in Erfurt contains a Katherine-window depicting a cycle of thirteen scenes from her conversion and passion, dated to about 1375/80. See Schill, *Ikonographie und Kult der Hl. Katharina*, pp. 315–17 and Appendix A, pp. 131–33.

[11] *Der Heiligen Leben, vol. 2: Der Winterteil*, ed. Margit Brand *et al.* (Tübingen, 2004). *Iacopo da Varazze: Legenda aurea*, ed. Giovanni P. Maggioni, 2 vols (Florence, 1998). The bibliography on this important compilation of saints' lives, put together for preachers by the Dominican Jacobus de Voragine (*c.* 1229–1298) over several decades, is vast. See still Sherry L. Reames, *The Legenda Aurea: A Reexamination of its Paradoxial History* (Madison, 1985); Barbara Fleith, *Studien zur Überlieferungsgeschichte der lateinischen Legenda Aurea* (Brussels, 1991).

central Middle Ages onwards.¹² There is at least one fifteenth-century manuscript from Braunschweig (and another fifteenth-century manuscript now in Hildesheim), as well as an earlier manuscript from Chemnitz, that preserve BHL 1663, but it would be no more than guesswork to suppose that Kannemann may have seen them.¹³ Both Kannemann's *Passio Jesu Christi* and that of Katherine were reprinted a number of times.¹⁴

Glimpses of the importance of Katherine's cult in this period in Germany can be seen through the work, for example, of Anne Simon, who focuses on a close reading of a 1475-print of *Der Heiligen Leben* published by Johann Sensenschmidt in Nuremberg (*GW* M1141), which draws on a manuscript produced at the convent of St Katherine in Nuremberg.¹⁵ The nuns in this convent (founded in 1295) were drawn mostly from the upper classes of Nuremberg and

---

12 See David L. d'Avray, 'Katherine of Alexandria and mass communication in Germany: Woman as intellectual', in *Modern Questions about Medieval Sermons: Essays on Marriage, Death, History and Sanctity*, ed. Nicole Bériou and David L. D'Avray (Spoleto, 1994), pp. 401–08. On Katherine's passion in German-speaking areas see Bruce A. Beatie, 'Saint Katharine of Alexandria: Traditional themes and the development of a Medieval German hagiographic narrative', *Speculum*, 52 (1977), 785–800; Anna M. Valente Bacci, 'Sviluppo e diffusione della *Passio* di S. Caterina di Alessandria nell'area tedesca medievale', *Quaderni Catanesi*, 12 (1984), 435–63; Ead., 'Testi in volgare', *Quaderni Catanesi*, 13 (1985), 77–134; Ead., 'La leggenda di S. Caterina di Alessandria'.

13 Wolfenbüttel, Herzog August Bibliothek, MS Helmst. 396, s. xv; Hildesheim, Dombibliothek, MS 739f, s. xv; Leipzig, Universitäts-bibliothek, MS lat. 436, s. xiii.

14 Other early prints of BHL 1663 came out of Strasbourg (Martin Flach, 1478, M16062), Reutlingen (Michael Greyff, *c.* 1486, M16060), and Nuremberg (Peter Wagner, not after 15 June 1491, M16057); see *Datenbank Gesamtkatalog der Wiegendrucke (GW)*, ed. Falk Eisermann *et al.* (Berlin, 2020).

15 Simon, *The Cult of Saint Katherine of Alexandria*, p. 6.

produced many manuscripts that came to comprise a large and important library in the course of the fifteenth century.[16]

BHL 1663 was used and adapted also amongst Italian humanists and teachers – let me offer just one example:[17] with its 2000+ lines of hexameters, the poem *Parthenice secunda sive Catharinaria* (BHL 1675) composed by the Carmelite Battista Mantovano (1447-1516) is an ambitious retelling and clocks in at one quarter of Vergil's *Aeneid*.[18] It is part of a collection of seven hagiographic poems in honour of female saints, starting with Mary (followed by Katherine, Margaret, Agatha, Lucia, Apollonia, Caecilia). It combines Classical (think assembly of the gods) with Christian themes and, judging by the numerous reprints and a commentary written by Jodoco del Badia in 1499, it was received with enthusiasm by its intended audience.

The comparative silence surrounding Katherine and specifically BHL 1663 during the next 150 years or so is perhaps partly due to the Reformation. The ensuing theological but also political and social upheavals included the rejection of saints and their cults, so it is perhaps not surprising to find very little biographical or bibliographical

---

[16] Marie-Luise Ehrenschwendtner, *Die Bildung der Dominikanerinnen in Süddeutschland vom 13.–15. Jahrhundert* (Stuttgart, 2004). Karin Schneider, 'Die Bibliothek des Katharinenklosters in Nürnberg und die städtische Gesellschaft', in *Studien zum städtischen Bildungswesen des späten Mittelalters und der frühen Neuzeit*, ed. Bernd Moeller *et al.* (Göttingen, 1983), pp. 70–83.

[17] See also Alison K. Frazier, 'Katherine's place in a Renaissance collection: Evidence from Antonio degli Algi (*c.* 1400–1477), *De vitis et gestis sanctorum*', in *St Katherine of Alexandria*, ed. Jenkins and Lewis, pp. 221–40.

[18] Edited in Arpad P. Orbán, *Vitae sanctae* Katharinae, 2 vols (Turnhout, 1992), II, pp. 363–435, with a short introduction on pp. 353–61 and the commentary by Jodoco del Badia on pp. 437–583. Fifty-seven editions appeared between the first publication in 1489 and the year 1591. See Edmondo Coccia, *Le edizioni delle opere del Mantovano* (Rome, 1960).

The Latin Passion of Katherine in the Print Age   7

material on the saint or BHL 1663 during this period.¹⁹ A quotation from Jean Calvin (1509-1565) may perhaps serve as an example of the kind of view of saints taken by the reformers:

> Multa porro sunt templa Catharinae dedicata vel Christophoro vel aliis fictitiis nominibus. Catharinae aut Christophori precibus ut iuvetur plebs huius loci a Domino postulabit. Itane cum Deo ludetur ut qui nulli unquam fuerunt obtrudantur ad Deum exorandum patroni? Talibus monstris, qui fomenta suppeditant, gustumne aliquem unquam habuisse credendi sunt seriae sinceraeque Dei invocationis?²⁰

Another likely reason for BHL 1663 fading into the shadows somewhat is the increasing popularity of vernacular versions of Katherine's story and the proliferation of prequels such as her conversion and baptism or marriage to Christ, added for an audience ever hungrier for details of this saint's life before the events that lead directly to her martyrdom. Bonino Mombrizio's (d. *c.*1480) epic poem in Italian consisting of 1,405 lines, περὶ τῆς Αἰκατερίνης, composed for Bianca Maria Visconti-Sforza (Duchess of Milan, 1450-1468), is a late example of such a version.²¹ The poem offers a panoramic

---

[19] For a more nuanced examination of how fifteenth- and sixteenth-century German humanists in particular dealt with the topic of hagiography, see Collins, *Reforming Saints*; *Raccolte di vite di santi dal XIII al XVIII secolo: Strutture, messaggi, fruizioni*, ed. Sofia Boesch Gajano (Fasano, 1990).

[20] Jean Calvin, *Vera christianae pacificationis et ecclesiae reformandae ratio* (Geneva, 1549), p. 174.

[21] *Bonino Mombrizio: La légende de Sainte Catherine d'Alexandrie, poème italien du XVe siècle publié pour la première fois d'après le manuscrit unique de la Bibliothèque royale de Belgique*, ed. Alphonse Bayot and Pierre Groult (Gembloux, 1943). An example of an early vernacular adaptation of Katherine's passion is Clemence of Barking's (fl. 1163–*c.* 1200) Anglo-Norman adaptation. See *The Life of St. Catherine by Clemence of Barking*, ed. William MacBain, Anglo-Norman Text Society 18 (Oxford, 1964) and McBain and E.C. Fawtier-Jones, 'Les vies de

view of Katherine's life, starting with her genealogy (which links her to Constantine the Great), her birth, youth, and conversion, followed by her mystic marriage and eventually the events leading up to her death, clearly representing a combination of several sources.[22] It appears that Katherine was a saint for whom Bianca Maria had a special devotion: the single luxury manuscript of the poem contains a miniature of her kneeling in front of the saint and the preface describes her as 'la divota sua'. That these are not just rhetorical devices, as it were, is evidenced by a letter from Jacopo Ammannati Piccolomini to Bianca Maria indicating that she had made enquiries about an 'offitio de Sancta Catharina'.[23] Mombrizio was also involved in the production of an important collection of saints' lives known as the *Sanctuarium*, which includes a seemingly early Latin version of Katherine's passion (see Chapter 3).

Doubts about Katherine's existence were voiced by George Cassander (1513-1566), a Flemish theologian who was the first professor of Greek and Latin literature at Bruges.[24] In a letter from 1559 to Bonaventura Vulcanius, a fellow humanist and eventual professor of Classical literature at Leiden, Cassander writes:

> Vita autem illa ... neque veteribus nota fuit, et recentioris alicuius aliquot secula scriptoris est, ut ex stylo facile apparet, neque historiae a gravissimis et antiquis tam prophanis quam

Sainte Catherine d'Alexandrie en ancien français', *Romania*, 56 (193), 80–104.

[22] Alison K. Frazier, *Possible Lives: Authors and Saints in Renaissance Italy* (New York, 2005), pp. 101–67.

[23] Ibid., p. 159 and n. 253.

[24] Maria E. Nolte, 'Georgius Cassander en zijn oecumenische streven' (unpublished doctoral thesis, University of Nijmegen, 1951); Friedrich W. Kantzenbach, *Das Ringen um die Einheit der Kirche im Jahrhundert der Reformation: Vertreter, Quellen und Motive des 'ökumenischen' Gedankens von Erasmus von Rotterdam bis Georg Calixt* (Stuttgart, 1957), pp. 203–29.

> ecclesiasticis scriptoribus traditae fidem servat. ... Hunc autem scrupulum de vita Catharinae primus mihi iniecit, vel certe auxit auctor Florarii temporum ... ei nomen est Nicolaus Clopper ... . Ea autem, quae de Catharina scribit ad auctorem refert D. Gobelinum Decanum in Bilenvelde in libro quem Cosmodromium, id est, cursum temporum inscripsit.[25]

As is evident from the quotation, Cassander is drawing on the world chronicle *Florarium temporum* by the cleric Nicolaus Clopper (*c.*1432-1487), who spent most of his life in the Low Countries[26] and who himself used a book (the *Cosmidromius*) written by Gobelinus Person (1358-1420), a German cleric who worked at the Roman curia and eventually returned to Paderborn, the city of his birth, in the 1380s.[27] It is clear that uncertainty about the veracity of Katherine's existence already circulated among scholars at the end of the fourteenth century against the background of a continued devotion to the saints outside the ivory tower.

And yet, in Rome, cardinal Cesare Baronio (1538-1607) firmly believed that Katherine was an historical figure. In his *Annales ecclesiastici*, conceived of as the definitive history of the

---

[25] *Georgii Cassandri Belgae theologi ... opera quae reperiri potuerunt omnia* (Paris, 1616), p. 1093.

[26] *Florarium temporum (Bloemhof der tijden): Een laatmiddeleeuwse wereldkroniek door Nicolaas Clopper, geschreven in het Klooster Marienhage bij Eindhoven*, ed. Willem Erven *et al.* (Hilversum, 2018). Clopper evidently also had an interest in saints' lives, see Valerie Vermassen, 'Le *Floriarum sanctorum* de Nicolaus Clopper Jr et le martyrologe brabançon de Pièrre de Thimo: Deux martyrologes perdus, deux hagiographes brabançons méconnus', *AB*, 126 (2008), 119–50.

[27] '*Cosmidromius Gobelini Person*', *und als Anhang desselben Verfassers 'Processus translacionis et reformacionis monasterii Budecensis'*, ed. Max Jansen (Münster, 1900). Katherine is not listed in the index and does not appear in the text of this edition, which has many gaps.

church and aimed at bolstering the papacy's position within and without the church:[28]

> When assessing the historical testimonies of saints and martyrs and their cults, Baronio sought not only to write the history of the Roman church as a sacred institution, but also to demonstrate the historical origins of the cult of the saints and to validate and justify, for late sixteenth-century Church orthopraxis, the cults of the oldest saints and martyrs.[29]

According to Baronio, Katherine was the anonymous Christian who had to flee from Alexandria mentioned by Eusebius. He proposed that her pagan name was Hecaterine and that Dorothea was her Christian name, relying on an account by Rufinus, in whose *History* there appears a Dorothea who was apparently wealthy, educated, and a virgin and who was executed by the emperor Maximinus Daia in 320 (February) in Alexandria, thus ignoring most of the texts in which the name of the emperor, who is confronted by Katherine, is given as Maxentius, not to mention the fact that all texts of her passion indicate she was martyred in November. Baronio also adduces another famous woman from Alexandria's late antique intelligentsia, namely Hypatia, although he does not go so far as to identify her with Katherine.[30]

The Italian Costantino Gaetano (1560-1650) can be seen almost as a forerunner to the Bollandists. Called to Rome in 1603 by Baronio (who was then librarian of the Vatican

---

[28] Georgina Davidson, 'Divine guidance and the use of sources: A case from the *Annales* of Caesar Baronius', *Historical Reflections / Réflexions Historiques*, 15.1 (1988), 117–29.

[29] Guiseppe A. Guazzelli, 'Cesare Baronio and the Roman Catholic vision of the early Church', in *Sacred History: Uses of the Christian Past in the Renaissance World*, ed. Katherine van Liere, Simon Ditchfield *et al.* (Oxford, 2012), pp. 52–71 (p. 63).

[30] *Annales ecclesiastici*, ed. Antonio Pagi (Lucca, 1738), III, anno 307, ch. 31-33, pp. 444–46.

library) to assist the latter with the research for his *Annales*, Gaetano became a specialist in sacred literature and ecclesiastical history and enjoyed unlimited access to the vast collection of manuscripts at the Vatican (he was not, as often assumed, its librarian).[31] In honour of Gregory the Great, Gaetano founded the Biblioteca Aniciana (now part of the Bibliotheca Alessandrina), 'what must have been the best collection of hagiographical material in Rome besides that assembled by the Oratorians at the Biblioteca Vallicelliana'.[32] Gaetano is known for his edition of the works of Peter Damian, a fellow Benedictine who was venerated at Monte Cassino where Gaetano served as a monk. His writings include notes on the lives of a number of saints, such as Isidore of Seville and Gregory of Ostia.[33] Particularly significant for the story of BHL 1663 is a collection of saints' lives he put together, exactly when is not known, by visiting a number of libraries within easy reach of Rome, such as Monte Cassino and Rieti. When he transcribed a version of Katherine's passion from an old manuscript, he may unwittingly have preserved the sole witness to a main source of BHL 1663 (more on this in Chapter 3).

It is with the Bollandist enterprise, still active today, that a scholarly interest in Katherine and the corpus of texts about her resurfaced, in line with the aim of collecting and publishing the original sources for the lives of the saints. Jean Bolland (1596-1665) was inundated by information on saints'

---

[31] José Ruysschaert, 'Trois notes pour une biographie du benedictin C. Gaetano', *Benedictina*, 21 (1974), 215–23 (p. 218); Dante Baldoni, 'L'abate Costantino Caetani (1658–1650), editore delle opere di S. Pier Damiani (1604–1640)', in *Ascetica Cristiana e ascetica giansenista e quietista nelle regioni d'influenza avellanita: Atti del 1. convegno del Centro di studi Avellaniti* (Fonte Avellana, 1977), pp. 111–25.

[32] Simon Ditchfield, *Liturgy, Sanctity, and History in Tridentine Italy: Pietro Maria Campi and the Preservation of the Particular* (Cambridge, 1995), p. 151.

[33] Ibid.

lives as soon as he conceived of the *Acta sanctorum*.[34] Meanwhile, Daniel Papebroch and Godfrey Henschen, Bolland's collaborators, went on a two-year journey to collect saints' lives in 1660, criss-crossing Catholic Europe as they visited archives in their quest for sources.[35] The materials and texts they published included introductions which reveal the application of critical enquiry: 'pour la première fois, on essayait, sur une large échelle, de classer systématiquement les sources d'après l'âge des auteurs et la confiance qu'elles méritent'.[36]

A witness to this interest, indeed research, is a manuscript now at the KBR in Brussels (MS 8955-56) which is part of the collection of papers referred to as *Collectanea bollandiana*. The *Collectanea* consist of 127 volumes of archival materials gathered by the Bollandists and are made up of copies of manuscripts, letters, extracts from incunabula, etc., mostly from the seventeenth and eighteenth centuries. Forty-eight of these volumes comprise documents destined for the edition of saints' lives for the *Acta sanctorum* (from 16 October to the end of the year). MS 8955-56, put together between 1608-1792, reunites texts pertaining to Katherine and other saints commemorated on 25 and 26 November.[37] The majority of these texts consist of miracles, notes on her relics, and the discovery of her body. The principal text of her martyrdom is BHL 1663 (copied from a manuscript at the monastery of St.

---

[34] 'Il ecrivait partout, demandait des textes ou des renseignements, et de tous les coins de l'Europe on s'empressait de repondre à son appel', Hippolyte Delehaye, *À travers trois siècles: L'oeuvre des Bollandistes, 1615–1915*, 2nd edn (Brussels, 1959), p. 23.

[35] See a map and account of their travels in Bernard Joassart, 'Les voyages scientifiques' in *Bollandistes, saints et légendes: Quatre siècles de recherche*, ed. Robert Godding *et al.* (Brussels, 2007), pp. 60–73.

[36] Delehaye, *À travers trois siècles*, p. 26.

[37] See the catalogue by Joseph van den Gheyn, *Catalogue des manuscrits de la bibliothèque Royale de Bruxelles*, vol. 5: *Histoire—Hagiographie* (Brussels, 1905), # 3511, pp. 576–80.

Maximinus at Trier), alongside its epitome BHL 1661m (copied from a lectionary at Saint-Omer). Since the *Acta sanctorum* have yet to reach beyond 11 November (and may never do so),[38] one has to look elsewhere for a discussion in print of the saint and an (eventual) edition of BHL 1663.

Papebroch expressed his doubts on the historicity of Katherine in his *Responsio ad exhibitionem errorum*.[39] For example, amongst the many incongruities contained in her story, he notes that she is missing in the early historians and calendars:

> De Catharina, sive Aecaterina, constat, eius nomen in hunc usque diem abesse a Kalendaris Aegyptis et Abassinis, cum tamen passa dicatur Alexandriae in Aegypto. Deest etiam in genuinis et antiquioribus manuscriptis, Bedae, Adonis, atque Usuardi Martyrologiis, licet in recentioribus exemplis postea additum reperiatur.[40]

He also points out that the attribution of BHL 1663 to Rabanus Maurus cannot be correct since the editor of Rabanus' works was not persuaded by this either:

---

[38] François Dolbeau, 'Les sources manuscrites des *Acta sanctorum* et leur collecte (XVIIe–XVIIIe siècles): De Rosweyde aux *Acta sanctorum*', in *La recherche hagiographique des Bollandistes à travers quatre siècles: Actes du colloque international, Bruxelles* (5 octobre 2007), ed. Robert Godding *et al.* (Brussels, 2009), pp. 105–47 (p. 106).

[39] Written in response to a treatise by Sebastian de Saint Paul entitled *Exhibitio errorum quos P. Daniel Papebrochius Societatis Jesu suis in notis ad Acta sanctorum commisit* (Cologne, 1693) and echoed by the decree issued in November 1695 by the Spanish Inquisition against the volumes of March, April, and May of the *AASS*, forbidding their sale and purchase. The scholarly work of Papebroch and his colleagues threatened close-held beliefs about cherished and long-standing saints. See Delehaye, *À travers trois siècles*, pp. 120–40.

[40] *Responsio Danielis Papebrochii ... ad exhibitionem errorum*, 2nd edn (Antwerp, 1696) I, responsio ad art. XI, accusatio XIV, # 79–108, pp. 267–277 (# 78 and 83, pp. 253 and 255).

> non potuit persuaderi Georgio Calvenerio, qui non solum Rabani opera omnia quotquot reperire potuit tribus tomis edidit, sed etiam longam textui seriem aliorum quae aliquando extitisse vel alicubi adhuc extare noverat; et S. Catarinae nullam inter ea facit mentionem ... scilicet contemnens scriptionem, toto stylo a Rabani charactere diversam, quae tamen ut Rabani esset, non foret seculo non antiquior.

Papebroch is here making all kinds of astute observations and arguments concerning Katherine's passion 300 years before they resurfaced and were debated all over again by scholars who, almost without exception, ignored or did not cite his work.

Leaving aside the vagaries of Katherine's reception during the eighteenth century,[41] it is in nineteenth-century Britain that one must look for an interest in the textual corpus, amongst the publications of a number of bibliophiles and churchmen.[42] The Abbotsford Club, an elite group of bibliophiles, was founded in Edinburgh in 1833 one year after the death of the novelist and poet Sir Walter Scott.[43] In tune

---

[41] Some of which can be gleaned from Hermann Knust, *Geschichte der Legenden der Heiligen Katharina von Alexandrien und der Heiligen Maria Aegyptiaca, nebst unedirten Texten* (Halle a.S., 1890), pp. 188–89.

[42] The focus on producing editions and linguistic studies of national epics and other seminal or early medieval texts in nineteenth-century Britain is inextricably linked with English nationalism and the drive to prove and justify the racial and cultural superiority of the English. See Reginald Horseman, 'Origins of racial Anglo-Saxonism in Great Britain before 1850', *Journal of the History of Ideas*, 37 (1976), 387–410; Mary Rambaran-Olm, 'Medievalism and the "Flayed-Dane" myth: English perspectives between the seventeenth and nineteenth centuries', in *Flaying in the Premodern World: Practice and Representation*, ed. Larissa Tracy (Cambridge, 2017), pp. 91–115 (pp. 107–09); Ead., 'A wrinkle in medieval time: Ironing out the problems of periodization, gatekeeping, and "Others" in Early English Studies', *New Literary History*, 52 (forthcoming, autumn 2021).

[43] Sir Walter Scott built Abbotsford House in the Scottish Borders in the later years of his life, see *ODNB*, s.v. Scott, Sir Walter. See David

with the preoccupations of the Romantic movement, a number of books published for the club centred on native folklore and Old English poetry, and within the first decade of the club's foundation the passion of Katherine figured on its publication list: in 1841, James Morton (d. 1865), 'vicar of Holbeach, prebendary of Lincoln, chaplain to the Right. Hon. Earl Grey',[44] published an edition of Katherine's English passion, based on three manuscripts now kept in the British Library.[45] The purpose of his work was, in Morton's own words, the following: 'in presenting this volume to his associates of the Abbotsford Club, the Editor will be gratified if it should be considered by them to be of any value as *a contribution towards the history of the English language and literature* [italics mine]'.[46] The Middle English text is accompanied by a modern English translation as well as a glossary. In the preface Morton discussed what he saw as the historical and literary merits of the text;[47] he made no mention of the Latin version or manuscripts of it that he could have had the opportunity of knowing, since the British Museum at

---

Matthews, *The Making of Middle English, 1765–1910* (Minneapolis, 1999), pp. 88–90 for a brief overview of the club's founding and history.

[44] Frontispiece to James Morton, *The Legend of St Katherine of Alexandria: Edited from a Manuscript in the Cottonian Library* (London, 1841). A little more information on Morton can be found in Einenkel's preface to *Saint Katherine*, pp. v–vi, where he writes that 'the Revd. J. Morton's knowledge of Middle English was profound, and almost surprising, if one considers the then state of English Philology. As a proof of this may be cited his translations of the *Ancrene Riwle* and *St. Katherine*, which, apart from some slight mistakes, deserve to be called exact, and are still useful'.

[45] London, British Library, Cotton MS Titus D.xviii (*c.* 1250), with readings from London, BL, Royal MS 17.A.xxvii (1220–30), and London, BL, Cotton MS Nero A.xiv (s. xiii).

[46] Morton, *The Legend of St Katherine,* p. xv.

[47] Ibid., p. xi.

the time already possessed a Cotton manuscript containing BHL 1663.⁴⁸

In 1849, eight years after Morton's edition, Charles Hardwick (1821-1859) published *An Historical Inquiry Touching Saint Catherine of Alexandria, to which is Added a Semi-Saxon Legend*.⁴⁹ Hardwick was the archdeacon of Ely and a fellow of Katherine's Hall (now St Catharine's College), Cambridge, so that his membership of the latter explains his interest in the saint: 'the primary design in drawing up this paper was to put in order the results of an inquiry undertaken for my own satisfaction as a member of St Catharine's Hall'.⁵⁰ Hardwick's concern was mainly with Katherine as an historical figure. He concluded his overview of treatises that mention Katherine by writing that 'while the main features of the story are preserved throughout, we may trace a continual growth of information, – a gradual development (or deterioration) from the simpler to the florid'.⁵¹ Subscribing to the idea of needing to separate historical fact from fiction as generally practised by those engaged in the study of saints at the time, he meticulously went through ancient historians and other historical records that do

---

[48] London, BL, Cotton MS Caligula A.viii, s. xii. Following the fire in 1731 at Ashburnham House, a new catalogue of the Cottonian manuscripts was published in 1802, replacing that compiled by Smith in 1696.

[49] Charles Hardwick, *An Historical Inquiry touching Saint Catherine of Alexandria, to which is Added a Semi-Saxon Legend*, Publications of the Cambridge Antiquarian Society, Quarto ser. 15 (Cambridge, 1849).

[50] Ibid., p. 3. For details of his life see *ODNB*, s.v. Hardwick, Charles. St Katherine's Hall was founded in 1473 by Robert Woodlark and received its royal charter of incorporation in 1475 from King Edward IV. The college's arms display a wheel, a direct reference to Katherine's martyrdom. See Stanely C. Aston, 'Ad honorem sanctae Katerinae virginis', in *St Catharine's College Cambridge, 1473–1973: A Volume of Essays to Commemorate the Quincentenary of the Foundation of the College*, ed. Edwin E. Rich (Cambridge, 1973), pp. 33–58 (pp. 51–52).

[51] Hardwick, *An Historical Inquiry*, p. 8.

and do not mention Katherine,[52] and concluded his inquiry with the observation that 'we may hold ourselves ready to weigh any additional proofs from history, that there was in the fourth century an Alexandrian Virgin, who sacrificed not only her property but her life, for the sake of our holy religion'.[53] He did also offer his own edition of the 'semi-saxon' (as he called it) legend with a glossary, based on two of the three manuscripts used by Morton.[54] His reason for reprinting the text was that the exclusivity of the Abbotsford Club edition restricted its availability to the scholarly community. By pointing out that this Middle English passion is a translation from the Latin, he was the first to spell out that the English tradition depends on the Latin sources.

This conclusion does not seem to have been taken up by anyone until 1884, when the text of BHL 1663 itself was finally printed, though yet again secondary in importance, as the focus was still on the English text. This time it was not an English but a German national, and not a churchman but an academic scholar, who took an interest in the text. Eugen Einenkel (1853-1939), who taught English literature at the University of Münster until his death, had come into contact with Katherine while working on his doctorate in Leipzig.[55] The results of his thesis were published as 'Über den Verfasser

---

[52] The pertinent passages are those in Eusebius (Ἐκκλησιαστικὴ ἱστορία / *The Ecclesiastical History, books 1–5*, trans. Kirsopp Lake [Cambridge, MA, 1926], 8.14) and Rufinus (*Historia ecclesiastica*, ed. Theodor Mommsen [Leipzig, 1903], 8.14), and the latter's treatment of Dorothea, understood to be Katherine's Christian name.

[53] Hardwick, *An Historical Inquiry*, p. 20.

[54] Ibid., pp. 21–48. He disregarded London, BL Cotton MS Nero A.xiv.

[55] For over 30 years he was the editor of *Anglia: Zeitschrift für Englische Philologie*, founded in 1878 and still published today. See also the obituary notice by Viktor Langhans, 'Eugen Einenkel †', *Anglia*, 54 (1930), 209–12; and H. Joachim Neuhaus, 'Englische Philologie in Münster bis zur Gründung des Englischen Seminars im Jahre 1905', <http://www.anglistik.uni-muenster.de/1905/> [accessed 7 July 2021].

der neuangelsächsischen Legende von Katharina'.⁵⁶ Its main focus was the question of whether the Middle English life of Katherine was written by the author who composed the *Liflade* of Juliana and that of Margaret, or by the author of the *Hali maiðhad* (*Holy Maidenhood*).

These texts are part of 'The Katherine Group' (named after the first of the texts in the group), a set of texts written in the first centuries after the Norman Conquest, preserved in Oxford, Bodleian Libraries, MS Bodley 34, a manuscript small enough to be held in one hand.⁵⁷ The texts include (1) three saints' lives (Katherine, Margaret of Antioch, Juliana of Nicomedia), and two homilies, (2) *Hali maiðhad*, and (3) the *Sawles Warde* (*Guardianship of the Soul*). These texts have attracted the attention of scholars because they are some of the few surviving examples of literature composed in early Middle English, thus making them important for the historical study of the English language: the Katherine Group has come to be seen as an important stop-gap between Old English and Middle English literature. The saints' lives in particular portray the triumph of virginity over material wealth and power, allowing each of the saints to showcase her particular fortitude (Katherine: intellectual; Margaret: physical endurance; Juliana: spiritual discernment), and are thus appropriate reading material for young female readers.⁵⁸ By comparing the texts in terms of rare words and phrases as well as style, Einenkel concluded that the Katherine-author was not the

---

[56] *Anglia*, 5 (1882), 91–123.

[57] See Eric J. Dobson, *The Origins of Ancrene Wisse* (Oxford, 1976), pp. 163–66.; *The Katherine Group (MS Bodley 34): Religious Writings for Women in Medieval England*, ed. Emily R. Huber and Elizabeth Robertson (Kalamazoo, 2016).

[58] See Elizabeth Robertson, *Early English Devotional Prose and the Female Audience* (Knoxville, 1990), pp. 94–125. On the Katherine Group, see Julie B. Hassel, *Choosing Not to Marry: Women and Autonomy in the Katherine Group* (New York, 2002).

The Latin Passion of Katherine in the Print Age 19

same person as the author of the passions of Margaret and Juliana. Einenkel also drew on two manuscripts containing the Latin text in order to compare it with the English and thus show which passages, mostly the speeches, were omitted in the English version.[59]

Building on the material of his doctoral thesis, Einenkel spent the years 1883 and 1884 working in English libraries and published the results of his research on Katherine with the Early English Text Society.[60] Einenkel's primary concern was the Middle English text, of which he offered an edition with a modern English translation and detailed linguistic discussion. His reason for including the Latin text is as follows: 'but apart from the advantage of always having the chance of consulting the original in case of the many puzzles offered by the Middle English text, I hope to receive the thanks of many a scholar for printing the whole, as I have every reason to believe that MSS. as well as prints of this Latin text, are exceedingly scarce'.[61] Just as Morton and Hardwick before him, Einenkel did not actively look for manuscripts containing BHL 1663 – the British Museum did at the time own several witnesses to the

---

[59] London, BL, Cotton MS Caligula A.viii, s.xii, and Leipzig, UB, MS Rep. II 64, s. xiii.

[60] Einenkel, *The Life of Saint Katherine from the Royal MS 17 A.xxvii*. The Early English Text Society was founded in 1864 in order to more widely disseminate the canon of early English texts, some of which had already been published under the aegis of such exclusive bibliophile societies as the Abbotsford Club, the Roxburghe Club or the Bannatyne Club. See Antony Singleton, 'The Early English Text Society in the nineteenth century: An organizational history', *The Review of English Studies*, n.s. 56, no. 223 (2005), 90–118. Kathleen Biddick, *The Shock of Medievalism* (Durham, NC, 1998), pp. 92–96 briefly illuminates how gender, class, national, and imperial colonialist identities fed into the ways in which the *EETS* distributed its publications.

[61] Einenkel, *Saint Katherine*, p. vi.

text –,⁶² but relied instead on Hardwick's information and a manuscript he had come across while studying at Leipzig. He would otherwise have known that BHL 1663 was not nearly as rare as he believed it to be.⁶³

Einenkel could not escape the need to place Katherine within an historical context. He pointed to the Neo-Platonist philosopher Hypatia, who taught in Alexandria at the turn of the fourth century CE and was much-admired by her student Synesius of Cyrene (*c.* CE 370-413), as a parallel figure.⁶⁴ He did not go so far as to actually claim they were both one and the same person, although he clearly meant for his readers to follow him in that respect:

> Now in the history of Christianity, we meet with very many cases where features and attributes of pagan gods or heroes have been transmuted into those of the persons of the Trinity, the holy mother, or the saints ... . And in a country like Egypt, where between the second and the fourth centuries the struggle of pagan worship was fiercest and most tenacious, the heated imagination of the people must have been particularly apt for transmutations of this kind. Now it so happens by a strange coincidence, that the figure which, in this time and in this struggle of worship against worship, plays the most important part, is that of a woman – of a woman whose character and intentions were as pure, her abilities as high, as her fate was tragic and melancholy. ... I scarcely need say that I mean the pagan philosopher Hypatia; and I cannot but express my astonishment

---

[62] The manuscripts collected by Robert and Edward Harley arrived at the British Museum in 1753; a catalogue of this collection had been published by 1812. The collection of the Royal manuscripts was transferred to the British Museum by George II in 1757.

[63] It was not until a couple of years later that the Bollandists produced their catalogues of hagiographical manuscripts of the big collections in Brussels and Paris: volumes 2–7 of the *Analecta Bollandiana* treat the manuscripts in Brussels, while those documenting the Paris collection appeared as volume 2 of the *Subsidia Hagiographica*.

[64] s.v. Hypatia in *LexMA*.

that no one before me thought of untwining the knot in such a simple and natural way; so striking are the similarities of the life of our saint with that of her pagan paragon.[65]

As Marie Dzielska has shown, Hypatia first appeared in European treatises and literature in the eighteenth century where she was depicted as the last survivor of the Hellenistic pagan world, murdered at the hands of cruel Christians, often the very badly disguised Catholic clergy.[66] The pinnacle of Hypatia's popularity is embodied by Charles Kingsley's *Hypatia, or the New Foes with an Old Face* (1853), written in turgid and overblown prose yet remarkably popular at the time. Kingsley uses the story to disparage Catholicism, as well as to portray northern Europeans as superior and Judaism as inferior to Christianity, a distasteful, racist, and yet rather ubiquitous view at the time.[67]

Before the end of the nineteenth century, Einenkel's English and Latin texts were reprinted twice: for the first time in the same year, 1884, as an appendix to Henry Gibbs' publication of Katherine's passion for the Roxburghe Club.[68]

---

[65] Einenkel, *The Life of Saint Katherine*, p. x–xi.

[66] Marie Dzielska, *Hypatia of Alexandria* (Cambridge, MA, 1995), pp. 1–17. See also Chapter 10 in Edward J. Watts, *Hypatia: The Life and Legend of an Ancient Philosopher* (Oxford, 2017), pp. 135–47.

[67] *ODNB*, s.v. Kingsley, Charles. 'The *New Foes* were J.H. Newman, now a Roman Catholic, and the other leaders of the Oxford movement, such as E.B. Pusey; the *old face* imputed to them was that of the fanatical (and of course celibate) monks of fifth-century Alexandria who murdered the Neoplatonist philosopher Hypatia, and whom Kingsley viewed as extreme and discreditable examples of the asceticism of the early church from which contemporary Catholic spirituality had drawn inspiration'.

[68] Henry H. Gibbs, *The Life and Martyrdom of Saint Katherine of Alexandria, Virgin and Martyr, now first printed from a manuscript of the early part of the fifteenth century in the possession of Henry Hucks Gibbs*, with preface, notes, glossary and appendix (London, 1884). Gibbs (1819–1907) was a merchant and merchant banker, and renowned for his library. See *ODNB*, s.v. Gibbs, Henry Hucks. On the Roxburghe Club see

The English manuscript in Gibbs' possession included not only Katherine's passion, but also her ancestry, life, and conversion. He was aware also of Morton's and Hardwick's publications, and concurred with the latter's conclusion about her historicity. In 1894 Einenkel's Latin text was printed above a French verse legend of Katherine.[69]

Another edition of BHL 1663 appeared as part of the *Acta sanctorum hiberniae ex codice salmanticensi nunc primum integre edita*, and thus presents a different text to that of Einenkel.[70] The sole manuscript used by the Bollandists Charles de Smedt and Joseph de Backer was the *codex salmanticensis*, so-called because at one point it had belonged to the Jesuit-run Irish College at Salamanca in Spain, and from there found its way into the library of the Bollandists. It is now kept at Brussels, KBR, under the call-mark 7672-74.[71] One reason for the interest accorded to this manuscript is the fact that it contains a good number of lives known from nowhere else.

In his 1965 study and edition of this manuscript, William Heist (1910-81) concluded that the manuscript was written in Ireland during the fourteenth century, in a religious community of English or Anglo-Norman monks, friars or canons.[72] Heist observed that most of the saints in this manuscript were Irish, apart from Katherine who is the sole

Nicolas J. Barker, *The Roxburghe Club: A Bicentenary History* (London, 2012).

[69] *Incipit*: 'cil ki le bien seit e entent / demustrer le deit sagement', as published by Jan U. Jarník, *Dve verse starofrancouzské legendy o Sv. Kateriné Alexandrinské* (Prague, 1894).

[70] *Acta sanctorum hiberniae ex codice salmanticensi nunc primum integre edita*, ed. Charles de Smedt and Joseph de Backer (Edinburgh, 1888), cols 681–734.

[71] A full description of the manuscript, its contents, arrangement, and history can be found in the introduction of William W. Heist, *Vitae sanctorum Hiberniae: Ex codice olim Salmanticensi nunc Bruxellensi* (Brussels, 1965), pp. i–lii.

[72] Ibid., p. xii, and pp. xxix–xxxviii for a history of the manuscript.

The Latin Passion of Katherine in the Print Age

'foreigner'. She appears within a group of saints who seem 'lost' in their current place in the manuscript.[73] Heist did not discuss Katherine at great length and chose not to present the text of her passion in his edition, so as not to detract from the otherwise undisturbed Irishness of the manuscript.[74]

The nineteenth century saw a change of methodology at the Bollandist house under the guidance of de Smedt, who arrived there in 1876, having previously taught ecclesiastical history at the theological seminary for Jesuits at Leuven. He was in favour of a sound text basis that included the entire corpus of texts available for each saint, over the previous interest in finding one particular account which appeared to be the most truthful or which seemed to contain a nucleus of truth.[75] Under his guidance the Bollandists began to try to edit their texts from as many manuscripts as possible, and to determine their relationships as far as they could.

In view of this new development, Narbey's treatment of Katherine's passion, published in 1900, might seem a welcome addition, and while it does include a small number of good observations, its overall outlook still smacks of the positivist school.[76] The Bollandists were quick to dissociate themselves

---

[73] Ibid, pp. xlvi–xlviii.

[74] Ibid., p. xlix: 'the present edition, which includes all the Lives of Irish saints in the manuscript that can be considered as belonging to Irish tradition, omits the Life of St. Catharine, which is clearly an outsider, and one for which our text is of no particular interest.' Dobson, p. 135, writes that this manuscript 'is too late and inaccurate to be of use' and, p. xxv, that it 'gives an inaccurate text, many of whose errors have been emended by the editors, but purely conjecturally ... the edition is really of no value for scholarly purposes.'

[75] Delehaye, *À travers trois siècles*, p. 149. He published *Principes de la critique historique* in 1883 (Liège). On de Smedt's work see also Bernard Joassart, 'De 1837 à la veille de la Seconde guerre mondiale' in *Bollandistes, saints et légendes*, pp. 127–43.

[76] *Supplément aux Acta sanctorum pour des vies de saints de l'époque mérovingienne*, vol. 2: *Contenant des documents sur les origines du christianisme en*

from Narbey's work (which carried a misleading title, in their opinion).⁷⁷ Narbey was bold enough to claim to complete and correct the Bollandists' past efforts by having unearthed and putting forward 'primitive' texts, as he called them: 'ce second volume continue à completer, à rectifier les Bollandistes, sur beaucoup de points, où ils ont reproduit des documents falsifiés ou interpolés'.⁷⁸ Already the section heading that precedes Narbey's discussion of Katherine hints at the editor's school of thought: 'Les actes de Sainte Catherine d'Alexandrie (dont le nom de chrétienne était Dorothée), martyrisée vers 309'.⁷⁹ Despite the silence of the *Martyrologium hieronymianum* he concluded that she is in fact identical with the virgin Dorothea mentioned by Rufinus.⁸⁰ But as Hardwick had already pointed out, the details given by both Eusebius and Rufinus are far too sparse to establish a direct link between the two historians and Katherine's passion.

Narbey then proceeded to examine the 'actes' of Katherine he knew of: citing only manuscripts from Paris, he divided them according to the quality of the text they contained.⁸¹

Espagne, en Angleterre, sur les martyrs de la Gaule et des bords du Rhin avec de nombreux dessins d'antiquités, ed. C. Narbey (Paris, 1905).

⁷⁷ See also Delehaye, *À travers trois siècles*, under the heading 'publications pseudo-Bollandiennes', p. 189: 'Nous pouvons difficilement reconnaître ce recueil comme un complément des *Acta sanctorum*. Il n'est destiné à en combler aucune lacune déterminée, et les principes qui ont guidé son auteur sont singulièrement déroutants. ... L'ouvrage répond d'ailleurs si mal à son titre qu'on peut feuilleter tout le premier volume sans rencontre un seul saint mérovingien'.

⁷⁸ Narbey continued: 'Nous avons donc recherché avec soin les textes primitives. ... Là où l'original fait défaut, nous avons encore attaché de l'importance aux copies les plus anciennes, les moins chargées d'inventions fabuleuses', *Supplément*, I, p. 1.

⁷⁹ Narbey, *Supplément*, II, p. 317.

⁸⁰ Ibid., p. 317.

⁸¹ This chapter is titled 'Les deux sortes de grands Actes de Sainte Catherine sont pleins d'erreurs et de fables légendaires.' Ibid, p. 318.

First, the 'grands actes' (BHL 1663),[82] preserved in Paris, Bibliothèque nationale de France, MS lat. 5308, s. xii; Paris, BnF, MS lat. 5343, s. xii (but in reality s. xi); Paris, BnF, MS lat. 5365, s. xii; and Paris, BnF, MS lat. 12259, s. xii.[83] Then a second text, shorter than the 'grands actes' (Paris, BnF, MS lat. 14293, s. xiii) and finally an even shorter one (Paris, BnF, MS lat. 3809, s. xiii [but in reality s. xiv]). He edited the text preserved in Paris, BnF, MS lat. 14293, and prefaced it with the prologue contained in Paris, BnF, MS lat. 12259. While Narbey seemed to suggest that the shorter the text the more truthful it was, he did not at all take into consideration a) the dates of the manuscripts he was using or b) the relationships between the various texts. By comparing the vocabulary of BHL 1663 with other saints' acts from antiquity, he quickly established that it has very little in common with these, and that it was in fact a product of someone working after Charlemagne's revision of the Bible. Narbey further concluded that its author was a hagiographer of the ninth century on the basis of style and the numerous speeches.[84] These observations cannot be taken as conclusive, although they are the first steps towards considering BHL 1663 as a literary text in its own right.

While Hardwick, Narbey, and a few others still subscribed to the historicity of Katherine, the Bollandist Hippolyte Delehaye (1859-1941) very carefully suggested otherwise in his essay *Les légendes hagiographiques* (later turned into a book). According to him, Katherine's legend could not be placed in the category of saints whose cult was documented by their (official) acts, or in the category of saints who are known to

---

[82] Ibid., p. 318.

[83] In reality, Paris, BnF, MS lat. 12259 preserves an epitome.

[84] 'Le genre de la rédaction est bien aussi ce qu'étaient la plupart des récits laissés par les hagiographes de la seconde moitié du ixe siècle, c'est-à-dire une phraséologie délayée sans fin, des discours fréquents et qui sont souvent des dissertations, avec de longues descriptions, et des recherches de cadences sonores'. Ibid., p. 319.

have existed. Although he did not say so, he implied she was fictitious.[85] Delehaye could thus almost be seen to have anticipated the decision of the Second Vatican Council that led to the reform of the Roman calendar in 1969, and entailed the suppression of a number of saints' feast days, including those of Katherine and Barbara.[86] But already during the last decade of the nineteenth century, two German scholars came to the passion of Katherine with an interest rooted in the manuscripts rather than in her historicity. They were working in the field of comparative philology.

Hermann Knust published an historical overview of the legends of Katherine and Mary of Egypt in 1890.[87] The two saints have in common that they excelled even men in their respective virtues: Katherine in wisdom and learning, Mary in renouncing the world. But since Knust died before his book went to print, it lacks a prologue and introduction, so that one cannot know why he was interested in Katherine and Mary. Although Knust included a text of BHL 1663 (from London, BL, Cotton MS Caligula A.viii), his principal interest concerned two translations into French and Spanish.[88] After a cursory

---

[85] Hippolyte Delehaye, 'Les légendes hagiographiques', *Revue des questions historiques*, 38 (1903), 56–122 (117): 'Il n'est pas probable que l'on trouve jamais un argument décisif permettant de placer sainte Barbe et sainte Catherine dans la première ou dans la seconde catégorie des saints'.

[86] See *The Oxford Dictionary of the Christian Church*, ed. Frank L. Cross and Elizabeth Livingstone (Oxford, 2012), s. vv. Barbara, Katherine. *Calendarium Romanum, ex decreto sacrosancti oecumenici concilii Vaticani II instauratum: auctoritate Pauli PP. V promulgatum* (Rome, 1969), p. 147: 'Memoria S. Catharinae, saeculo XIII in Calendario romano ascripta, deletur: non solum Passio S. Catharinae est omnino fabulosa, sed de ipsa persona Catharinae nihil certum affirmari potest'.

[87] Knust, *Geschichte der Legenden*.

[88] Ibid., on pp. 231–314. BHL 1663 is printed at the top of the page, the French (Paris, BnF, MS fr. 412) and the Spanish (El Escorial, Real Biblioteca de San Lorenzo de El Escorial, MS h.I.13, s. xiv) beneath it.

The Latin Passion of Katherine in the Print Age 27

overview of the Greek texts of her passion, Knust examined those written in the Latin West. He proceeded by grouping the texts according to centuries, and within that category according to the language they were written in, citing many manuscripts for the first time.[89] Knust was a staunch supporter of those who saw in Katherine no more than a fiction, and in those who believed in her, superstitious backwoodsmen:

> Jahrhunderte sind seit diesen Worten [Calvin's], deren Wahrheit nicht bestritten werden kann, dahingegangen, ohne daß der Aberglaube seine Kraft verloren. Wahrscheinlich werden daher auch noch manche andere ihnen folgen, ehe wahre Religiosität überall sich Bahn bricht. Millionen und Millionen, welche sich über Kannibalen weit erhaben glauben, sehen wir noch heute ohne Gewissensbisse Theile ihres eigenen Gottes anbeten. Warum also die h. Katharina in ihrer Ruhe stören?[90]

Current events also found their way into Knust's book, and thus allow a glimpse into the last gasps of the *Kulturkampf* that

---

Parts of BHL 1663 are printed in italics; these are the passages that are left out by Paris, BnF, MS lat. 5278, which contains an epitome.

[89] Ibid., p. 7–11: Monte Cassino, Archivio della Badia, MS 139, s. xi; Monte Cassino, MS 187, s. xi; Paris, BnF, MS lat. 1970, s. xi; Paris, BnF, MS lat. 5371, s. xiii; Paris, BnF, MS lat. 5371, s. xiii; Paris, BnF, MS lat. 1864, s. xiv; Paris, BnF, MS lat. 5333, s. xiv; Paris, BnF, MS lat. 5336, s. xiv; Paris, BnF, MS lat. 5360, s. xiv; London, BL, Harley MS 12, s. xi (Katherine's passion 1080–1100). Paris, BnF, MS lat. 5278, s. xiii, on p. 17. Paris, BnF, MS lat. 5373, s. xv, on p. 42, and London, BL, Royal MS 12.E.1 on p. 44. Knust also makes reference to a lost verse legend by a monk Ainard (p. 11, see Chapter 5 below), and a number of printed books (p. 8). He did not use the Bollandists' catalogue of the hagiographical manuscripts at Paris (both his book and their work appeared in the same year, and he actually makes reference to the 1744 catalogue of the Royal Library at the then British Museum). His interest in delineating how the various Latin texts are related to each other (if only in a cursory manner) predates the attempts at categorization in the BHL which was to appear in 1898.

[90] Ibid., p. 191.

28   The Passion of St Katherine of Alexandria

had raged between the Vatican and Protestant governments,[91] caused by Pope Pius IX's publication of the *Syllabus errorum* in 1864 until the crisis was brought to an end under his successor Leo XIII in 1887. This same Leo can be credited with opening the Vatican Archives in 1883, thus making them accessible to scholars (in principle) and trying to instil confidence among non-Catholics that the Catholic Church was prepared to play with open cards.[92]

A year after Knust, Hermann Varnhagen (1850-1925) also published an historical study of the Katherine legends.[93] He

---

[91] On page 41 Knust's feelings get the better of him and he produces some fiery lines that show him to be a Protestant *Kulturkämpfer* through and through: 'endlich müssen wir auch, und das zeigt für die Ausbreitung der Legendenliteratur in diesem Zeitraum, auf eine arabisch geschriebene Katharinenhistorie, welche die Vaticansbibliothek sorgfältig verschließt, hinweisen. Wer aber ihren Inhalt zu sehen wünscht, muß sich an den päpstlichen Stuhl wenden. Der Augenblick für ein solches Wagnis ist ja günstig und nicht zu besorgen, der Bittsteller werde abfahren wie weiland so viele andere. Kommt es doch gerade jetzt darauf an, daß Mutter Kirche ihr feuriges Racheschnauben bis auf Weiteres unter der Maske liebender Sorge "für das ewige Seelenheil" ihrer Kinder verbirgt, so daß der h. Vater oder, wie er richtiger genannt wird, der Pontifex Maximus, der schlaue Leo, von "väterlicher Milde" und "versöhnlichem Herzen" schier überfließt und ein Verfechter des Scheiterhaufens, Cardinal Manning, sich einer christlichen Versammlung aufdrängt, um eine Deklamationsübung zu Gunsten der von seinem Meister bei Gelegenheit der Erbauung einer protestantischen Kirche in Rom als Teufelswerk verschrieenen Toleranz loszulassen—gegen eine schismatische Regierung'.

[92] For an account of events see Owen Chadwick, *Catholicism and History: The Opening of the Vatican Archives* (Cambridge, 1978). In contrast to the Archives, the Vatican Library had been open to readers from 1475 onwards. See Carmela Vircillo Franklin, '*Pro communi doctorum virorum comodo*: The Vatican Library and its service to scholarship', *Proceedings of the American Philosophical Society*, 146.4 (2002), 363–84.

[93] Hermann Varnhagen, *Zur Geschichte der Legende der Katharina von Alexandrien, nebst lateinischen Texten nach Handschriften der Hof- und Staatsbibliothek in München und der Universitätsbibliothek in Erlangen* (Erlangen, 1891).

was an Anglicist at the University of Erlangen from 1881 until 1920; his studies centred mainly on Old and Middle English texts, the results of which appeared in *Anglia: Zeitschrift für Englische Philologie*. His main gripe against Knust was that his colleague had failed to examine thoroughly the relationships between the many versions he had taken the trouble to list, that he had not considered the Greek versions which were the basis for the Latin texts and, finally, that he had grouped the texts according to the date of the manuscripts and their language. Despite these criticisms, Knust's book remains a treasure-trove for those interested in the development of Katherine's legend and story more generally in the vernacular languages.

Varnhagen was the first to use the term '*Vulgate*' in relation to Katherine's passion BHL 1663, a term taken up by Bronzini, for example.[94] He also looked at the relationship between the longer (BHL 1663) and the shorter text (as published by Knust and contained in Paris, BnF, MS lat. 5278, BHL 1663a), and concluded that the shorter one was a pared-down version of the longer text, rather than the longer one an elaboration of the shorter text. His argument was that it would be very unlikely for someone to elaborate a shorter text by simply adding new material without otherwise interfering with the text even once. True to his criticism of Knust, he tried to work out if and how the various Latin versions are related to the Greek texts, but dealt with the matter in less than three pages. Varnhagen published the text of a passion contained in Munich, Bayerische Staatsbibliothek, Clm 1133 (s. xii-xiv), beginning 'regnante igitur Maxentio cesare, Maximiani Augusti filio', which has most recently been attributed to Peter, Subdeacon of Naples (BHL 1659, see Chapter 4).[95]

---

[94] Ibid., p. 3: 'Ich bezeichne diese Bearbeitung als die Vulgata'.

[95] Varnhagen mentioned a further five manuscripts as witnesses to this text: Brussels, KBR, MS 9810-14; Saint-Omer, Bibliothèque publique, MS 27; Orléans, Bibliothèque publique, MS 330 and MS 334;

By the turn of the twentieth century, therefore, the text of BHL 1663 had appeared in print several times and was based on the following manuscripts:

1884 – Einenkel: London, BL, Cotton MS Caligula A.viii (s. xii) + Leipzig, Universitätsbibliothek, MS Rep. II 64 (s. xii^{ex})

1888 – de Smedt and de Backer: Brussels, KBR, MS 7672-74 (s. xiv)

1890 – Knust: London, BL, Cotton MS Caligula A.viii + Paris, BnF, MS lat. 5278 (s. xiii)

1900 – Narbey: Paris, BnF, MS lat. 12259 (prologue) (s. xii) + Paris, BnF, MS lat. 14293 (s. xiii).

Compared to the many manuscripts that had been mentioned by Narbey or Knust, only a very small number was used by the various editors for preparing their editions. In most cases they drew on material that was close at hand, understandable in an age when travelling and manuscript reproductions were costly, though surprising because London and Paris, where they worked for the most part, had many more manuscripts on offer.

While the passion(s) of Katherine began appearing in print, none of the texts (or, better, versions) were ever presented in a fashion that would satisfy modern scholarly needs: the apparatus remained scant and there was little, or no interest, in assembling a complete or as near as complete list of all the witnesses. This was due in part to the prevailing attitude towards saints' lives as curios rather than serious texts, highlighted by Knust's effort to show the progression of the legend through the ages and countries. Another reason is that

---

Montmorot, Archives départementales du Jura, MS 11; edited by Edoardo D'Angelo, *Pietro Suddiacono napoletano: L'opera agiografica*, (Florence, 2002). Varnhagen also published Katherine's conversion as conserved in Munich, BSB, Clm 7954, s. xiii, and three miracles from Erlangen, Universitätsbilbiothek, MS 712.

BHL 1663 was always seen or presented as subordinate to the Middle English version of the passion.

At the beginning of the twentieth century, the Bollandists themselves undertook some editing work on Katherine-related texts, which were short and not extant in too many manuscripts. In 1903, Albert Poncelet published the translation (BHL 1679b,c) and miracles of Katherine's relics from a manuscript now at Rouen (Bibliothèque municipale, MS 1410 [U.22]).[96] Four years later, Paul Peeters edited an Arabic version of Katherine's passion.[97] Since then, although her name has appeared in almost every index of the *Analecta Bollandiana*, the only major works undertaken that included BHL 1663 were Bronzini's monumental study of the Greek and Latin texts, and Simonne d'Ardenne and Eric Dobson's edition of the text.

In 1959, Bronzini (1925-2002) published a comparative study of the Greek and Latin passions of Katherine. He was the first to draw together the Greek and Latin accounts of Katherine's passion, an almost superhuman task. He presented an overview of the corpus, starting with the Greek accounts, on which he had comparatively little to say, and moving on to the Latin texts, which he examined in much greater detail. Bronzini's study fits in with the comparative approach practised by Knust and Varnhagen, although it is he who can be credited with bringing the Greek and Latin texts to the fore, and scrutinizing them comparatively. The inevitable problem with Bronzini's approach was the wealth of material he had sought to tackle. While there is something to be said for mapping the texts in a global way, there are many questions that must necessarily remain unanswered, because there was no time for the sort of detail that is required. Moreover, Bronzini

---

[96] Albert Poncelet, 'Sancta Catharinae virginis et martyris translatio et miracula rotomagensia saec. XI', *AB*, 22 (1903), 423–38.

[97] Paul Peeters, 'Une version Arabe de la Passion de Sainte Catherine d'Alexandrie', *AB*, 26 (1907), 5–32.

constructed stemmata for the relationships between the versions not on the basis of philological reasoning (despite his claims to the contrary), but on the basis of presence/absence of episodes. He also attributed much attention to the dates on which the protagonists of Katherine's passion were martyred and concluded that the *Menologion of Basil* contained the text that was closest to the original, now lost, passion.[98]

It was not until 1981 that BHL 1663 found an editor willing to collate more than a handful of manuscripts. The text appears as an appendix to a re-edition of the Middle English (ME) version published again under the aegis of the Early English Text Society. Two Oxford-based scholars, d'Ardenne and Dobson, undertook the job.[99] Dobson wanted to improve on Einenkel's edition of the Latin, and argued for a fuller use of more manuscripts. He proceeded to collate and use for his edition 23 manuscripts in total, choosing mainly early witnesses and one later one (Paris, BnF, MS lat. 15149, s. xiii-xiv), because of a connection between Saint-Victor in Paris, whence this later manuscript originates, and Wigmore Abbey in Herefordshire, the area in which the Katherine Group is thought to have been composed. Dobson was guided in this by

---

[98] In 1978 Gabriele Giamberardini tried to isolate the nucleus of truth/historicity in Katherine's passion, a saint he treats as an historical figure who underwent martyrdom in 307 CE. See *S. Caterina di Alessandria*, Quaderni della Terra Santa (Jerusalem, 1978).

[99] Simonne R.T.O. d'Ardenne (1899–1986) had studied at Oxford with J.R.R. Tolkien in the 1930s, under whose direction she worked on the *Liflade ant te Passiun of Seinte Iuliene*. Following its publication and d'Ardenne's appointment as Professor of Comparative Grammar at the University of Liège in 1938, they started corresponding about a similar study of the ME life of Katherine but World War II interrupted their efforts and the collaboration never came to fruition. In 1977, d'Ardenne published a transcription of *Seinte Iuliene* and *Seinte Katerine* from Oxford, Bodleian, MS Bodley 34, see *The J.R.R. Tolkien Companion and Guide*, vol. 2: *Reader's Guide*, ed. Christina Scull and Wayne G. Hammond (Boston, 2006), vol. 1, pp. 202–04. Eric J. Dobson (1913–84) was a Professor of English at Jesus College, Oxford.

his search for the model of the ME text, which is an abbreviation of BHL 1663 but not based on its epitome BHL 1663a. Thus, whenever the ME text does not offer a particular passage of 1663, this is printed in italics in Dobson's edition. He hypothesized that the ME text derived from an intermediary text. Since Dobson's interest in the Latin text was necessarily limited by his interest in the ME version, there is no real discussion of BHL 1663, its diffusion or what might have caused its extraordinary success in the Middle Ages. More serious are a number of Dobson's interventions in the text which are plainly wrong (see Chapter 4), and which he described as 'deep-seated corruptions [of] the archetype of all the copies that we have collated'.[100]

How little impact Dobson's edition has had can be seen in the fact that neither MacBain nor Orbán, two scholars who edited vernacular and Latin versions of Katherine's passion, made reference to it. In 1987 Knust's text was reprinted as an appendix to William MacBain's edition of the Picard version of Katherine's legend, despite availability of Dobson's edition.[101] More surprising perhaps is Orbán's silence: he edited a number of metrical Latin lives of Katherine in 1992.[102] None

---

[100] Dobson, p. xxvi.

[101] *De Sainte Katerine: An Anonymous Picard Version of the Life of St. Catherine of Alexandria*, ed. William MacBain (Fairfax, VA, 1987), pp. 177–216. MacBain also edited *The Life of St Catherine by Clemence of Barking* (Oxford, 1964), a poem in Anglo-Norman octosyllabic rhymed couplets, written in the second half of the twelfth century. *ODNB*, s.v. Clemence of Barking.

[102] Arpad P. Orbán, *Vitae Sanctae Katharinae*, CCCM 119-119A (Turnhout, 1992), edited: *Floruit insignis*, no BHL; *Palma triumphalis*, BHL 1666; *Sepius in sexu fragili*, no BHL; *Ricardus, Ut super omne melos*, no BHL; Pietro Carmeliano, *Numina si veteres*, BHL 1666a; *Hic Constantino patri*, BHL 1665, fragmentum upsaliense; Battista Mantovano, *Parthenice secunda sive Catharinaria*, incipit: *Costidis aggressi pugnam*, BHL 1675; Jodoco del Badia's commentary on Mantovano's poem.

of these poems predates the twelfth century (with the exception of that composed by a certain Ricardus),[103] and only two of them are based, directly or indirectly, on BHL 1663 or one of its epitomes. It was Knust's edition that served Orbán as a basis for comparison.

In 2001 the Catholic Church officially restored Katherine's cult for local use. In contrast, the revised edition of *Butler's Lives of the Saints* has no knowledge of her.[104] During all this time the Greek Orthodox Church has continued to see in her a powerful intercessor and many of the pilgrims and visitors to St Catherine's monastery on Sinai come from Russia.[105] What began in all likelihood as a local cult has survived, and indeed thrived, until today. I will start my survey precisely at the moment at which this cult emerged, or, more correctly, at which point it becomes readable.

---

[103] Cambridge, Corpus Christi College (CCC), MS 375, s. xii, contains on fols 1–54 Ricardus' poem on Katherine, and on fol. 57–118 his poem on Alphege of Canterbury. The latter is based on Osbern's life of Alphege (BHL 2518). Both poems are exceptionally long; that on Katherine comprises 3413 verses. Orbán hypothesized that the Ricardus who names himself in the epilogue to the Katherine poem could be the same as the *Ricardus monachus*, the scribe of Cambridge, CCC, MS 184, s. xii, prov. Christ Church Canterbury. See Orbán, pp. 156–57. James thought Cambridge, CCC, MS 375 was written at St Albans from where it was sent to Canterbury, see Montague R. James, *A Descriptive Catalogue of the Manuscripts in the Library of Corpus Christi College, Cambridge*, 2 vols (Cambridge, 1912), II, p. 221.

[104] See *Butler's Lives of the Saints*, ed., rev. & suppl. Herbert Thurston and Donald Attwater, 4 vols (Allen, TX, 1965), IV, pp. 420–21.

[105] The special attitude of Russia towards the monastery can be seen in a charter of Tsar Mickhail Fyodorovich from 1630, which gives the monks the 'right to travel to our state of Moscow for assistance in monastery building and for alms'. *Sinai, Byzantium, Russia: Orthodox Art from the Sixth to the Twentieth Century*, ed. Yuri Piatnitsky *et al.* (London, 2000), p. 234.

CHAPTER 2

GREEK TEXTS

The passion of Katherine belongs to a group of hagiographical creations centred on fictitious saints with novelistic or literary aspirations. These 'passions [were] aimed at a relatively cultivated audience which enjoyed the picturesque, the prodigies and even scenes of cruelty, as well as fictitious speeches that sounded impressively theological or philosophical'.[1] The protagonists of these stories were cast by their authors as epic heroes who, as champions of God, fight against the powers of darkness.[2] The action and tension is increased by extending speeches or descriptions of narrative scenes, by repeating things, usually by three, and by alternating speeches with interrogations and bodily tortures.[3] In addition, 'the number of persons who come into contact with the hero can be extended so as to create a lengthy concatenation of converts'.[4] In Katherine's case, the most important and final martyrdom

---

[1] Guy Philippart and Michel Trigalet, 'Latin hagiography before the ninth century: A synoptic view', in *The Long Morning of Medieval Europe: New Directions in Early Medieval Studies*, ed. Jennifer R. Davis and Michael McCormick (New York, 2008), pp. 111–29 (p. 119).

[2] Hippolyte Delehaye, 'L'amphithéâtre Flavien et ses environs dans les textes hagiographiques', *AB*, 16 (1897), 209–52 (pp. 236–52) for a definition of epic *passiones martyrum*; also id. *Les Passions des martyrs et les genres littéraires*, 2nd edn (Brussels, 1966), pp. 172–3.

[3] Christodoulos Papavarnavas, 'The role of the audience in the pre-metaphrastic passions', *AB*, 134 (2016), 66–82 (p. 71). See also Delehaye, *Les Passions des martyrs*, pp. 173–218 for a description of the various topoi one might find in these texts.

[4] Michael Lapidge, *The Roman Martyrs: Introduction, Translations, and Commentary* (Oxford, 2018), p. 20.

is obviously that of the saint herself; in the process, however, secondary characters also undergo martyrdom. The first to die are the fifty rhetors on 17 November, whose perfectly preserved bodies after having been burnt lead the crowd to believe in God. The second and third martyrdoms occur on 23 November: the queen is beheaded, as is the general Porphyrius with his soldiers. Finally, on the way to her death, Katherine is accompanied by a large crowd of mostly women. Katherine's story and martyrdom can thus be seen as a work of 'opulent fiction and rather unreliable theology', making those who read and hear it feel good about their faith.[5]

1. Sources and manuscripts

There are separate traditions of Katherine's passion in four languages: Greek, Arabic, Georgian,[6] and Latin, with the greatest number of variations in the Latin. In each case, a Greek version is at the origin of the tradition. The texts of Katherine's Greek passion are accessible through a bilingual (Latin and Greek) edition undertaken by Joseph Viteau (1859-1949) at the end of the nineteenth century.[7] A new edition is

[5] Philippart and Trigalet, 'Latin hagiography', p. 120 and p. 124.

[6] The Georgian version of Katherine's passion appears to be a translation of BHG 30 and has been preserved in at least three manuscripts. The oldest of these is Sinai, Monastery of Saint Catherine, MS georg. 6, in which the hand of John Zosimos has been identified. This provides a date for its transcription and binding of between 981 and 983. See Gérard Garitte, *Catalogue des manuscrits géorgiens littéraires du mont Sinai* (Leuven, 1956). John Zosimos was based at Mar Saba in Palestine and moved to Sinai in the early 970s. See Donald Rayfield, *The Literature of Georgia: A History*, 2nd rev. edn (London, 2000), pp. 32–33. The other two manuscripts are: Sinai, MS georg. 71 (s. xiii, fols 201v–215); Sinai MS georg. 91 (s. xiv, fols 106a–115b).

[7] Joseph Viteau, *Passions des Saints Écaterine et Pierre d'Alexandrie, Barbara et Anysia* (Paris, 1897). Karl Krumbacher wrote a damning review of it in *Byzantinische Zeitschrift*, 7 (1898), 480–83, which he began thus: 'Die vorliegende Ausgabe ist ein sehr brauchbares Mittel für Seminarübungen, wenn der Professor seinen Schülern an einem

needed because Viteau used a very small number of manuscripts and hence did not provide a full critical apparatus, and also because the texts are only available in a Latin translation. Moreover, as the following discussion will show, a careful examination still needs to be made of the sources used for the composition of these texts, their linguistic content, and their relationships with each other. Viteau published three texs: BHG 30, BHG 30a, and BHG 31, which he labelled A, B, and C, respectively. This arrangement brings out the chronology, as he saw it, of the texts, with A being the oldest. He argued that B, with its long and incomprehensible speeches, was a re-elaboration of A. He took it for granted that the shorter version, A, was the primitive and therefore the original one. The only reasoning he adduced for this was that, faced with the more or less curt exchanges in A, the soon-to-be redactor of B could not but have the idea to make the protagonists a little more talkative.[8]

An example of Katherine's volubility occurs towards the beginning of her first speech in BHG 30a: she is not simply overly loquacious, much of what she says is downright strange and incomprehensible (underlined): 'Ἀλκιμωτάτην λέξιν ἀναλαβοῦσα σφιρμιγγίλιόν τι ῥῆμα λέγω πρὸς σέ ἐν ὑψικαρήνῳ λέξει, πολυποίκιλον νεῦμα, ἀκτινοβόλον ἔδρασμα σφιρμιγγιλιορύθμιστον ἐρκολεκτρεώτατον λεπτοποίκιλον ἐκτροφωστῆρσι πανοπλίαν ἀλκιμοτάτως σκαμανδρόθεν ... etc'.[9] By using such unusual and downright made-up words, the author obviously wants to highlight Katherine's vast learning and bring home to his readers who, just as her adversaries, would not be able to understand her, exactly how comprehensive Katherine's victory had been. The

konkreten Beispiele alle Fehler klar machen will, die man bei der Veröffentlichung hagiographischer und verwandter Texte begehen kann und heute nicht mehr begehen sollte'.

[8] Viteau, p. 23.
[9] Ibid., p. 27, § 6.

rhetors reply in a similarly contorted speech. These unintelligible words are clearly not, for instance, a phonetic transcription, bereft of meaning, from another language. Instead, they derive their meaning from their incomprehensibility.[10] In a separate study, Viteau provided a brief analysis of the texts.[11] He thought that the quality of the Greek of BHG 30 is decent (and the speeches in BHG 30a 'extravagants et extraordinaires'), while he saw in the author of BHG 31 a skilled or learned rhetorician who moulds the speeches into something more reasonable with the help of a number of secondary sources. He proposed either the eighth or ninth century for its composition, since it must have already been in existence by the time Symeon Metaphrastes used it (see below).

Another of Viteau's concerns was the historical accuracy of the date on which Katherine was martyred. Using historical calendars and the various dates and days mentioned in the three texts, he determined that Katherine was martyred on Saturday, 24 November 305. Viteau also tried to establish the date of origin for Katherine's passion. He argued that BHG 30 cannot be earlier than the second half of the sixth century because this text already uses the 'common era' for the date: 'ἐτελειώθη δὲ ἡ κυρία μου Αἰκατερίνη μηνὶ νοεμβρίῳ, εἰκάδι τετάρτῃ, ἡμέρᾳ παρασκευῆς'.[12] Finally, Katherine's profession of faith[13] seems to accord in some of its ideas and

---

[10] In a forthcoming essay tentatively titled 'Ineffable speeches in the Greek Passion of St Katherine of Alexandria', I examine these speeches in more detail.

[11] Joseph Viteau, 'La Légende de Sainte Catherine (Ecaterine)', *Annales de Saint-Louis-des-Français*, 3.1 (1898), 5–23.

[12] Ibid., 'La Légende de Sainte Catherine', 9. This text is BHG 30.

[13] 'Αὐτός ἐστιν ὁ ἀληθινὸς θεός, ὁ πέμψας τὸν μονογενῆ αὐτοῦ υἱὸν Ἰησοῦν Χριστόν· ὃς ἐλθὼν καὶ ἐνανθρωπήσας ἐκ τῆς ἁγίας παρθένου καὶ θεοτόκου Μαρίας, ἴσος τε ἡμῖν γενόμενος πλὴν ἁμαρτίας, καὶ κηρύξας βασιλείαν οὐρανῶν τοῖς πιστεύουσιν αὐτῷ, σταυρωθείς τε καὶ ταφεὶς καὶ ἀναστάς, καὶ τὸ ἡμέτερον ἐκλυτρωσάμενος γένος ἐκ τῆς διαβόλου τυραννίδος καὶ τῆς παμφάγου ἁμαρτίας, καὶ κηρύξας

language with various decrees issued by a number of Church councils that took place in the fifth and sixth centuries (Council of Ephesus, 431; Council of Chalcedon, 451; Second Council of Constantinople, 553), leading Viteau to propose the second half of the sixth century as the earliest possible date, and the first half of the seventh as more likely.

In an essay from 1907, in which he published an Arabic version of Katherine's passion (BHO 26), Peeters demonstrated that this version is based on BGH 30a. However, a number of overlaps with BHG 30 lead him to propose a now lost Greek version.[14] Peeters also pointed out Viteau's error of supposing that BHG 30 was composed before BHG 30a: he demonstrated that the longer version, with its extensive and sometimes unintelligible speeches came first, and that BHG 30 was a modified version thereof, streamlining the speeches and excising the incomprehensible parts.

BHG 31 is a rewriting of BHG 30a and was used by Symeon Metaphrastes (d. c. 1000) to produce the passion of Katherine that features in his liturgical collection of Greek saints' lives; his version is identified by the tag BHG 32. A close analysis of this text has yet to be undertaken, not to mention a comparison with its source text.[15] Symeon, a writer and high official in Constantinople, systematized the lives of the saints in his monumental menologion, of which there are

βασιλείαν, ἀνῆλθεν εἰς οὐρανούς. Κτίστης γάρ ἐστιν πάντων καὶ σωτὴρ τῶν πλανωμένων καὶ θεὸς τῶν θεῶν καὶ κύριος τῶν κυριευόντων, ᾧ πρέπει τιμὴ καὶ δόξα εἰς τοὺς αἰῶνας. Ἀμήν'. Viteau, p. 9, § 6.

[14] Peeters, 'Une version Arabe de la Passion de Sainte Catherine'. This text features short speeches.

[15] Printed in *PG* 116, cols 275–302, from Paris, BnF, MS gr. 1525 with a translation into Latin by Lorenz Sauer. An initial attempt has been made by Stavroula Constantinou, 'The authoritative voice of St. Catherine of Alexandria', *Acta Byzantina Fennica*, 2 (n.s.) (2003–04), 19–38.

more than 800 extant copies.[16] His hagiographical collection consists of 148 saints' lives presented in ten volumes, most likely made for use at the imperial court.[17] Most of the texts he gathered were reworked orally before being written down in short-hand and then copied into longhand.[18] Soon after they were assembled, these lives 'were being read in monasteries ... by the early eleventh century. Their place at this time was at orthros, usually before the beginning of the poetic canon(s). The reading of the Metaphrastian lives must have gradually shifted to the refectory (at any rate they have no place in contemporary Menaia) and in their place, short Synaxarion texts were introduced after the sixth ode of the canon'.[19]

Albert Ehrhard showed that Katherine was part of Symeon's original plan for the collection, and that the text at the basis of his Katherine-version was BHG 31.[20] It is difficult to explain why Symeon did not use BHG 30a or BHG 30 as models for his version of Katherine's passion. Ehrhard concluded that Symeon used the 'old November martyrology' for the compilation of the lives of the saints for the month of November. This martyrology does not contain BHG 30a in its original conception, although later manuscript witnesses for this collection of saints' lives do preserve BHG 30a.[21] Ehrhard

---

[16] It is generally agreed that Symeon was a contemporary of Basil II, see *PMBZ Online*, #27504.

[17] Christian Høgel, *Symeon Metaphrastes: Rewriting and Canonization* (Copenhagen, 2002), p. 112.

[18] Ibid., p. 92.

[19] Nancy P. Ševčenko, *Illustrated Manuscripts of the Metaphrastian Menologion* (Chicago, 1990), p. 26.

[20] Ehrhard, 2.393.

[21] Ehrhard, 2.468: 'da Symeon sich zur Aufgabe stellte, die alten hagiographischen Texte zu verdrängen, leuchtet ein, daß die erhaltenen Exemplare des alten Novembermenologiums die Hauptfundgruben für die Gewinnung der von ihm überarbeiteten Martyrien und Heiligenleben darstellen. Sie enthalten in der Tat fast alle ... Vorlagen der meta-

provisionally concluded that its sources have been lost, so one cannot determine when and from where Katherine entered it.[22]

In 1902 Joseph Bidez demonstrated that the author of BHG 31 bolstered Katherine's speeches by drawing on a number of passages from the *Chronography*, a world history from the Creation to Justinian I by John Malalas (*c.* 490-*c.* 570) or a text used by Malalas.[23] Since Malalas himself used many sources and was employed extensively by later authors, a study of BHG 31 is badly needed to disentangle the threads and establish a better understanding of the relationships between the two texts.[24] Bidez also pointed to similarities between two passages in BHG 31 and two verses from the *Iliad*.[25]

---

phrastischen Novembertexte'. Also p. 469 n. 8: '... [BHG 31] fehlt in den Exemplaren des Novembermenologiums, wohl infolge der Verluste die es erlitten hat. ... BHG 30 steht in V1 und P1', = Vatican City, Biblioteca Apostolica Vaticana (BAV), MS Vat. gr. 807, s. x$^{1/4}$ and Paris, BnF, MS gr. 1539, s. x, both used by Viteau for his edition of BHG 30a.

[22] Ibid., 2.469 and 508–9.

[23] Joseph Bidez, 'Sur diverses citations, et notamment sur trois passages de Malalas retrouvés dans un texte hagiographique', *Byzantinische Zeitschrift*, 11 (1902), 388–94. In particular, the author more or less quotes, without saying so, parts of chapters 2.18, 4.7, and 2.14 of the *Chronography* (in this order). Katherine's opening speech to the emperor (Viteau, p. 45, § 6), especially the long passage of erudition in which she mentions Diodorus and Plutarch, corresponds to *Chronography* 2.18. The rhetor's address to Katherine in which he mentions Orpheus (Viteau, p. 51, § 11) seems to correspond to *Chronography* 4.7. At the end of Katherine's immediate response (Viteau, p. 53, § 11), a number of parallels point to *Chronography* 2.14, including the reference to Sophocles.

[24] See *Ioannis Malalae Chronographia*, ed. Johannes Thurn (Berlin, 2000), esp. p. 3*.

[25] The rhetor's mention of Homer's reference to Zeus as the greatest of the gods and the other immortal gods ('Πρῶτων μὲν Ὅμηρος ὁ σοφώτατος ποιητῶν ταῦτα ἐπευχόμενος οὕτωσὶ τῷ Διί· Ζεῦ κύδιστε μέγιστε καὶ ἀθάνατοι θεοὶ ἄλλοι'; Viteau, p. 51, § 11) comes from the

Following the discovery of Aristides' *Apology* inside the Greek version of *Barlaam and Ioasaph* (BHG 224) at the end of the nineteenth century, the Biblical scholar James Rendel Harris imagined that a similar, now lost, 'detached' Euhemerus-inspired apology could be traced in the passion of Katherine.[26] He connected the two legends because the festivals of Barlaam and Ioasaph (27 Nov.) and that of Katherine (25 Nov.) occur close to each other.[27] Finally, Harris observed that 29 November is the feast day of John of Damascus, whom he considered to be the author of the *Barlaam*. This proximity of festivals, along with the similar storyline in both legends which, in reality, does not go beyond the fact that the connection between the two protagonists is their steadfastness in adhering to their Christian faith, prompted Harris to compare the two texts.

Reading Katherine and *Barlaam and Ioasaph* side by side, Harris supposed that 'we arrive at the surprising result that a great part of the Catherine story is reproduced [!], with slight variation, in the story of the Indian prince and his teacher – and a careful examination will show that Catherine is the

---

Iliad 3.298, namely the beginning of the oath sworn by the Greeks and Trojans ('ὧδε δέ τις εἴπεσκεν Ἀχαιῶν τε Τρώων τε: / 'Ζεῦ κύδιστε μέγιστε καὶ ἀθάνατοι θεοὶ ἄλλοι ...'). Katherine's direct response hones in on the fact that there are a number of stories recounted by Homer that show Zeus being humiliated (Viteau, p. 51, § 11), which correlates to *Iliad* 1.399f, where Achilles reminds his mother of how she saved Zeus after Hera, Poseidon, and Athena had planned to tie him up.

[26] *The Apology of Aristides on Behalf of the Christians: From a Syriac Manuscript Preserved on Mount Sinai*, ed. James Rendel Harris (with an appendix containing the main portion of the original Greek text by Joseph A. Robinson) (Cambridge, 1891). See the introduction to *Aristide: Apologie*, ed. Bernard Pouderon *et al.* (Paris, 2003). On euhemerism, see Nickolas P. Roubekas, *An Ancient Theory of Religion: Euhemerism from Antiquity to the Present* (New York, 2017) with the review by Greta Hawes for *Bryn Mawr Classical Review* 2017.09.52.

[27] 26 August in the Greek tradition and 27 November in the Roman Martyrology.

earlier story of the two'.²⁸ As the basis for his investigation he took the metaphrastic text (BHG 32). This is problematic for his argumentation because the latter is a late tenth-century rewriting, and even the source text of the Metaphrast is a rewriting of BHG 30a. The problem arises from the fact that Harris saw in John of Damascus (d. *c.* 750) the author of the *Barlaam*. Thus, according to Harris, John authored first the Katherine legend and then, having written that, produced the *Barlaam*, recycling part of the Katherine-legend in doing so. In any case, Harris rather exaggerated when he wrote that 'a great part' of material from Katherine's passion is reproduced in the *Barlaam* – a number of parallels he cited are actually quotations from John Malalas (shared by both *Barlaam* and Katherine), and the rest are a couple of loosely similar sentences.²⁹

Upon Harris' publication, Erich Klostermann and Erich Seeberg responded that 'die Passio Catharinae von der Chronik des Malalas abhängig ist, und zwar gerade in den Stücken, die R. Harris als Bestandteil einer altchristlichen Apologie ansehen wollte'.³⁰ They did not accept the existence of the putative euhemerist apology put forward by Harris, and instead assigned Katherine's overarching belief-system, as evident from her speeches in BHG 31, to the sixth/seventh centuries. This belief-system, they pointed out, resembles the teachings of Sophronios and John II of Jerusalem (the former held to monophysitism), leading them to conclude that both BHG 31 and BHG 32 were written in Palestine. This con-

---

28 J. Rendel Harris, 'A new Christian Apology', *Bulletin of the John Rylands Library Manchester*, 7 (1922–23), 355–83.

29 Ibid., 377. To get a sense of the kind of textual discoveries Harris was used to making see Alessandro Falcetta, *The Daily Discoveries of a Bible Scholar and Manuscript Hunter: A Biography of James Rendel Harris (1852–1941)* (London, 2018) and Janet Soskice, *Sisters of Sinai: How Two Lady Adventurers Found the Hidden Gospels* (London, 2010).

30 Erich Klostermann and Erich Seeberg, 'Die Apologie der Heiligen Katharina', *Schriften der Königsberger Gelehrten Gesellschaft*, 2 (1924), 31–87 (p. 64).

clusion is as problematic as that of Harris, because BHG 32, at least, was produced by Symeon Metaphrastes at the end of the tenth century. Klostermann and Seeberg tried to circumvent this by positing that Symeon came upon the text ready-made and included it as it was in his collection.[31]

More recently, Robert Volk has undertaken an extensive study of fifteen texts from the Metaphrastic corpus including that of Katherine, in order to determine whether or not they contain evidence for Symeon's use of the *Barlaam*.[32] Volk showed that twelve of the texts contain snippets from the *Barlaam*, with Symeon seemingly preferring redaction B of the novel; that the author of the *Barlaam* most definitely did not use the Katherine text; and that BHG 31 is not the product of the *Barlaam* author. Further, he concluded that the *Barlaam* author used bits and pieces of BHG 31.[33] This is not the place to delve into the problems of authorship of *Barlaam and Ioasaph* and the dependence between the many versions to

---

[31] See Delehaye's review of Klostermann and Seeberg in *AB*, 45 (1927), where he writes on page 153 that Symeon's passion of Katherine is, 'sans le moindre doute, un remaniement d'un texte plus ancien. Il est possible, il est vrai, que les parties communes à Barlaam et à Catherine proviennent d'une rédaction de la *Passio Aecaterinae* intermédiaire entre les anciens textes et la métaphrase'. He does, however, point out that such a conclusion can only be reached after a thorough examination of the Greek Katherine corpus.

[32] Robert Volk, 'Symeon Metaphrastes: Ein Benutzer des Barlaam-Romans', *Rivista di studi bizantini e neoellenici*, n.s. 33 (1996), 67–180. Id., 'Das Fortwirken der Legende von Barlaam und Ioasaph in der byzantinischen Hagiographie, insbesondere in den Werken des Symeon Metaphrastes', *Jahrbuch der Österreichischen Byzantinistik*, 53 (2003), 127–69.

[33] The latter exists in some tenth-century manuscripts; for example, Paris, BnF, MS gr. 1180 (s. x, fols 332–40, see François Halkin, *Manuscrits grecs de Paris: Inventaire hagiographique* [Brussels, 1968], pp. 130–31) contains the kinds of mistakes in the transcription that indicate an exemplar written in Greek uncial. See Volk, 'Symeon Metaphrastes: ein Benutzer', 110.

which this story has given rise. Already the manuscripts disagree on who wrote the Greek version: both John of Damascus and Euthymios the Iberian have been promoted since medieval times.[34] Volk has produced an edition and commentary on the text, and laid to rest the debate over the authorship. He came to the conclusion that the work should be ascribed to Euthymios the Georgian (or Hagiorite, c. 955–1028), who translated the Georgian version into Greek in 985 at a monastery on Mount Athos.[35]

So far, what is more or less certain is that BHG 30 is a redaction of BHG 30a, that BHG 31 is an adaptation of the former two, and that BHG 31 was turned into BHG 32 by Symeon Metaphrastes. BHG 31 makes use of several sources, including John Malalas, providing it with a *terminus post quem* of c. 540. It also shares a number of narrative elements with the Greek *Barlaam and Ioasaph*. Based on Volk's arguments, BHG 31 predates the *Barlaam* and can be provided with a *terminus ante quem* of about 985, when Euthymios translated the *Barlaam* into Greek.

What is less certain is the geographical origin of these texts. Symeon was active in Constantinople and clearly BHG 31 was available to him there. This text was part of a two-volume collection of saints' lives written out by Methodios I, patriarch of Constantinople (d. 847), copies of which served as exemplars for Symeon's work.[36] Another tenth-century witness for BHG 31 is Sinai, MS gr. 526. Despite the presence in this

---

[34] See the overview of the various arguments by Alexander P. Kazhdan, 'Where, when and by whom was the Greek Barlaam and Ioasaph not written', in *Zu Alexander der Grosse: Festschrift G. Wirth zum 60. Geburtstag am 9.12.86*, ed. Wolfgang Will and Johannes Heinrichs, 2 vols (Amsterdam, 1988), II, pp. 1187–1207.

[35] Robert Volk, *Die Schriften des Johannes von Damaskos*, vol. 6.1: *Historia animae utilis de Barlaam et Ioasaph (spuria): Einführung* (Berlin, 2009); vol. 6.2: *Historia animae utilis de Barlaam et Ioasaph (spuria): Text und zehn Appendices* (Berlin, 2006).

[36] Ehrhard, 1.234.

manuscript of western saints such as Martin of Tours and Agatha of Catania, Ehrhard saw no good reason to group this manuscript with other Italo-Greek exemplars of the old martyrology.[37] Decades later, Vittorio Peri proposed a southern-Italian provenance for the three texts edited by Viteau.[38] He based his conclusions on two points: the first redaction of Katherine's martyrdom, BHG 30 and BHG 30a, is preserved, by Peri's count, in thirteen manuscripts from southern Italy, out of a total of twenty.[39] His other argument, which I will tackle first, rests on the differentiated use of the word βιργίλιος. It occurs mainly in BHG 30a but also in BHG 30, where, on the one hand, it refers to the Roman author Vergil,[40] and on the other hand, it is employed as a noun and adjective to denote someone as a wise person.

Peeters had already pointed out that knowledge of Vergil in Greek may have led hagiographers to use the term as synonymous with someone who is wise or a public speaker.[41] This is clearly the way the word is being used in the title of Katherine's passion where it balances the noun ῥήτορος: 'Μαρτύριον τῆς ἁγίας Ἀικατερίνης τῆς βιργίλιου καὶ ῥήτορος' (BHG 30a).[42] Peri detailed further uses of the word in BHG 30a, which are unique to this text and do not appear

---

[37] Ibid., 1.246.

[38] Vittorio Peri, 'ΒΙΡΓΙΛΙΟΣ = Sapientissimus: Riflessi culturali latino-greci nell'agiografia Bizantina', *Italia Medioevale e Umanistica*, 19 (1976), 1–40.

[39] Peri, 'ΒΙΡΓΙΛΙΟΣ', 9 and note 1.

[40] Vergil also figures as himself in the text: 'Ἦν γὰρ μεμαθυκυῖα πᾶσαν βίβλον Ἀσκληπίου καὶ Γαληνοῦ ... καὶ ὅσα ὁ Βιργίλιος ἔλεξεν ...' = BHG 30a, Viteau, p. 26, § 4.

[41] Paul Peeters, 'Une légende de Virgile dans l'hagiographie grecque', *Mélanges Paul Thomas: Recueil de mémoires concernant la philologie classique dédié à Paul Thomas* (Bruges, 1930), pp. 546–54 (p. 552).

[42] Viteau, p. 25. Slightly different in BHG 30: 'Μαρτύριον τῆς ἁγίας Ἀικατερίνας τῆς ἐκβιργίλιου καὶ ῥήτορος'. Viteau, p. 5.

in BHG 30. Many of these appear to create an equivalency with the noun 'rhetor', so for example: 'παρεγένοντο πρὸς αὐτὸν ῥήτορες καὶ βιργίλιοι'.[43] The word is also used as an adjective to describe a person as learned or wise. It is applied twice to Katherine, once to Homer, and once to Asclepius.[44]

Peri saw the usage of the adjective and noun βιργίλιος as typical of Byzantine southern Italy, in particular because knowledge of Vergil in the eastern part of the Empire was not in evidence in the Byzantine period. Despite the fact that Vergil was indeed known in the eastern part of the Empire in the fifth and sixth centuries,[45] Peri thought that the extreme rarity of the adjectival form of the word, in addition to very few references to Vergil in Byzantine texts, makes it hard to believe that eastern Christian authors would have created such a neologism. He would rather look for this innovation in southern Italy, arguing for a 'rimaneggiatore italogreco' for Katherine's passion BHG 30a, while allowing that the story

[43] Ibid., p. 29, § 9.
[44] 'ἀπάξω σέ πρὸς τὴν βιργίλιον Αἰκατερίναν', Viteau, p. 35, § 15. In BHG 30, the adjective in the corresponding paragraph for Katherine is 'πανσόφῳ κόρῃ' (ibid., p. 15), in BHG 31 it is 'σοφωτάτῃ' (ibid., p. 57).
[45] John Malalas seems to be alluding to and/or referencing the *Aeneid*, see Barry Baldwin, 'Vergil in Byzantium', in *Antike und Abendland: Beiträge zum Verständnis der Griechen und Römer und ihres Nachlebens*, vol. 28, ed. Werner v. Koppenfels *et al.* (Berlin, 1982), pp. 81–93 (pp. 84–85). Egyptian and Palestinian papyri of the fifth and sixth centuries CE contain fragments of and glossaries to Vergil. For knowledge of Vergil and other Classical authors in Egypt, see Roger A. Pack, *The Greek and Latin Literary Texts from Greco-Roman Egypt*, 2nd edn (Ann Arbor, 1965). On Milan, Biblioteca Ambrosiana, MS L 120 sup., which contains the Latin (with a Greek translation in the same hand, written out between the fourth and sixth centuries CE) of *Aeneid* 1.588–748 underneath Arabic hagiographical texts see Johannes Kramer, 'Der lateinisch–griechiche Vergilpalimpsest aus Milan', *Zeitschrift für Papyrologie und Epigraphik*, 111 (1996), 1–20. Maria C. Scappaticcio, 'Appunti per una riedizione dei frammenti del Palinsesto Virgiliano dell'Ambrosiana', *Archiv für Papyrusforschung*, 55 (2009), 96–120.

itself probably originates in sixth- or seventh-century CE Palestine/Syria.

Peri's second point, namely that the manuscripts that preserve BHG 30a and BHG 30 originate predominantly from southern Italy, deserves attention, although it is worth bearing in mind that the classification of the manuscripts according to BHG numbers is messy and unreliable. According to the *PINAKES* Greek manuscripts database, there are thirty-six combined witnesses for these two versions.[46] Of those, the database singles out seven as transmitting BHG 30a, whilst classifying other manuscripts as containing BHG 30 when in fact they contain BHG 30a. It is also worth pointing out that, already during the tenth century (and earlier), translations of Katherine's passion from Greek into Latin were being undertaken in Italy, so that the number of early manuscripts from this geographical area need not be an indication for the origin of a particular version. Finally, the feast of Katherine is not included in any of the 'early' martyrologies from Italy (see Chapter 3), whereas there is evidence for a cult of the saint in Byzantium, perhaps as early as the eighth century.

I shall limit myself to a brief mention of the very earliest manuscripts only and will not include manuscripts squarely dated to the eleventh century. Unsurprisingly, there are no manuscripts that predate the tenth century and very few from the tenth or eleventh centuries. Santo Lucà has pointed out that some of the manuscripts broadly ascribed to southern Italy by Peri are not actually from there.[47] The earliest of these

---

[46] *Pinakes / Πίνακες: Textes et manuscrits grecs*, Institut de recherche et d'histoire des textes, François Bougard (Paris, 2016).

[47] 'Le diocesi di Gerace et Squillace: Tra manoscritti e marginalia', in *Calabria bizantina: Civiltà bizantina nei territori di Gerace e Stilo*, ed. Claudio Sabbione *et al.* (Soveria Mannelli, 1998), pp. 245–343 (p. 249, n. 20). The manuscripts singled out by Lucà as not originating from southern Italy are: Paris, BnF, MS gr. 1539; BAV, MS Vat. gr. 807; and BAV, MS Vat. gr. 544. See also Delehaye, *Les Passions et les genres*, p. 224–25.

manuscripts, a witness for BHG 30a, is BAV, MS Vat. Gr. 807, s. x, fols 256-261v.[48] This manuscript, used by Viteau, was donated to the monastery of Theotokos Hodigitria (unidentified), according to an entry on folio 134v.[49] It contains a menologion for the month of November. Maria Luisa Agati listed it as a manuscript written out in the bouletée script and described the hand as 'scrittura Constantinopolitana'.[50] Another earlyish manuscript is Paris, BnF, MS gr. 1539, s. x or x-xi, fols 162-174. This manuscript is the second volume of a two-volume menologion for November and contains a collection of saints' lives from the end of the ninth century. It is one of the closest examples to the archtype of the collection.[51] The manuscript was used by Viteau for his edition of BHG 30a. Having initially suggested that this manuscript is not from southern Italy, Lucà seems to have revised his opinion in an essay from 2007, in which he reassigned it to the region, albeit without citing a reason for doing so and,

---

[48] According to Ehrhard, I.477–80, this manuscript was written out in the early tenth century.

[49] Santo Lucà, 'Il Diodoro Siculo Neap. B.N. gr. 4* e italogreco?', *Bollettino della Badia Greca di Grottaferrata*, 44 (1990), 33–79 (p. 57, n. 100): 'il codice venne donato al monasterio della Theotokos Odigitria, fol. 134v τῆς ἐν τῷ ὄρει τῆς Φανωμάτης', by an unnamed married couple.

[50] Maria Luisa Agati, 'Lista provvisoria dei manoscritti copiati in minuscola "bouletée"', *Scriptorium*, 42 (1988), 108. See also ead., *La minuscola "bouletée"* (Vatican, 1992).

[51] The date is given as tenth century by Ehrhard, 1.499: 'Ich datiere ihn unbedenklich in das 10. Jahrhundert'; and tenth-eleventh century by Halkin, *Manuscrits grecs de Paris*, p. 203. A description can be found in *La vie d'Etienne le Jeune par Étienne le diacre*, ed. Marie-France Auzépy (London, 2016).

admittedly, also not citing reasons for doubting Peri's initial localization.[52]

An additional two manuscripts dated either to the tenth or the beginning of the eleventh centuries are: (1) BAV, MS Vat. gr. 544, s. x/xi[in.] (palimpsest). The original hand can perhaps be assigned to the end of the tenth or the beginning of the eleventh century. This manuscript contains saints' lives from September to January and features Katherine on 25 November.[53] Lucà did not believe it to be from southern Italy.[54] (2) Paris, BnF, MS gr. 1538, s. x/xi[in], fols 43v-55v.[55] This manuscript contains a collection of saints' lives and was used by Viteau for his edition of BHG 30a. It appears that, according to some notes in the manuscript that perhaps were written out in the thirteenth century, this manuscript belonged to the monastery of St George of Rhinia (ἔγγιστα τῶν 'Ρινίων) and also was at the Megas Agros monastery on the Sea of Marmara at the time that Manuel Holobolos (d. 1310-1314) was in exile there.[56] Ehrhard dated it to the tenth century and thought it originated from southern Italy, giving the 'usual palaeographical criteria' for assigning it thus: parchment, clumsy handwriting, ornamental technique for the decorations and initials, while François Halkin deemed it to be

---

[52] Santo Lucà, 'Dalle collezioni manoscritte di Spagna: Libri originari o provenienti dall'Italia greca medievale', *Rivista di studi bizantini e neoellenici*, 44 (2007), 39–96 (p. 43, n. 7).

[53] Ehrhard 1.249–51. Folios 198v, 162, 172, 169, 164, 191, 200, 249, 254, 217r–v.

[54] Lucà, 'Le diocesi del Gerace', 249, n. 20.

[55] Date in Halkin, *Manuscrits Grecs de Paris*, p. 202.

[56] Raymond Janin, *Les églises et les monastères des grands centres byzantins* (Paris, 1975), p. 199 and p. 201. The notes were edited by Jean Darrouzès, 'Notes d'Asie Mineure', *Ἀρχεῖον Πόντου*, 26 (1964), 28–40 (p. 35 and 37–38). On Holobolos s.v. in *ODB*. The Megas Agros monastery was founded by Theophanes the Confessor (d. 817).

from the following century.⁵⁷ Other earlyish manuscripts from southern Italy seem to originate from the communities connected to Neilos, either at Rossano or Grottaferrata.⁵⁸

If any conclusion can be drawn from the above, other than that the localization of the Greek manuscripts preserving Katherine's passions BHG 30a and 30 still needs to be sorted out, it is that the earliest known witness for BHG 30a originates from Constantinople and was written out in the tenth century. However, given that the hymnographer referred to as the 'humble monk' already knew the text in the ninth century, a specific pocket of manuscripts from a particular region does not help much in determining where this particular version might have been written originally.⁵⁹

---

[57] Ehrhard, 3.77; Halkin, *Manuscrits Grecs de Paris*, p. 202.

[58] (1) Milan, BA, MS D 92 sup., s. x–xi, fols 106–111v (mentioned by Peri, 'ΒΙΡΓΙΛΙΟΣ', p. 7, n. 3, pp. 8–9, n. 1). Contains a collection of saints' lives from across the year. Ehrhard 3.782–83. It contains BHG 30a.
(2) Milan, BA, MS F 144 sup., s. x–xi, fols 66–71v. This manuscript, containing a pre-metaphrastic menologion for the whole year, was written out in the style of Rossano. See Santo Lucà, 'Rossano, il Patir e lo stile rossanese: Note per uno studio codicologico-paleografico e storico-culturale', *Rivista di studi bizantini e neoellenici*, 22 (1985), 93–170 (p. 161). It contains BHG 30a and not BHG 30. It is mentioned by Peri, 'ΒΙΡΓΙΛΙΟΣ', 7, n. 3 and 8–9, n. 1. Ehrhard 1.347.
(3) BAV, MS Vat. gr. 866, s. xi^{1/4}, fols 106–110v. This manuscript is an example of the old martyrology for use during the entire year. Its script is close to the 'minuscola niliana', see Lucà, 'Rossano', 48, n. 255. It was used by Viteau for BHG 30a. Ehrhard 1.342.
(4) BAV, MS Vat. gr. 1631, s. xi, fols 87–97v. This manuscript contains a half-year collection of saints' lives for the winter, as well as some saints whose feast days are in e.g. March. It is mentioned by Peri, 'ΒΙΡΓΙΛΙΟΣ', 7, n. 3. It used to belong to Grottaferrata and, based on palaeographical criteria, was copied in southern Italy. Ehrhard 1.323–5. It contains BHG 30.

[59] On the 'humble monk', see pp. 64–66.

2. Katherine, Artemios, and Pansophios

To return to Vergil: Katherine's passion is not the only hagiographical text in which he makes an appearance. As already mentioned by Peeters, two other saints' lives feature the Roman poet: that of Artemios of Antioch and that of Pansophios of Alexandria. Peeters used the term 'passions apologétiques' to describe these three texts since all of them are more or less structured around protracted logomachies between the respective saint and their adversaries.[60] He suggested that there might be a possible link between these saints' lives, though without offering much in the way of evidence. In turn, Peri proposed that the three texts are the product of the same hagiographic circle but did not go so far as to suggest that they were produced by the same author. He based this hypothesis on three points: (1) all three saints are connected to and/or located at some point in Alexandria; (2) all three texts contain convoluted and enigmatic ideas; (3) the authors deploy the same rhetorical technique of arguing that Christian ideas are equal to pagan philosophy by using arguments derived from pagan authors. Finally, Peri suggested that these texts were imitating the pagan milieu of Alexandria or harkening back to a 'giovane e tumultuosa cultura Cristiana' of Alexandria.[61]

The passion of Artemios (BHG 170, 20 October) was written by a John of Rhodes.[62] This version is a later elaboration of a version that is thought to have been 'composed

---

[60] Peeters, 'La Passion de Saint Pansophios d'Alexandrie', *AB*, 47 (1929), 307–37 (p. 318).

[61] Peri, 'ΒΙΡΓΙΛΙΟΣ', 15.

[62] And also attributed to John of Damascus, under whose name it can be found in *Die Schriften des Johannes von Damaskos*, vol. 5: *Opera homiletica et hagiographica*, ed. Bonifatius Kotter (Berlin, 1988), p. 193ff.

before the year 500'.⁶³ The author appears to have used the church histories of Philostorgios, Eusebius, Sokrates, Theodoretos and others. There also exists a miracle collection, likely put together during the second half of the seventh century – Artemios' intervention was sought by those suffering from hernias as well as testicular problems.⁶⁴ His relics were preserved in Constantinople, in the church of St John Prodromos, which stood near a busy commercial neighbourhood.⁶⁵ Artemios is mentioned in historical sources: he became *doux* of Egypt in 360 CE, where he was involved in anti-pagan activities such as destroying idols/statues and died in around 363 CE under emperor Julian, who was a pagan.⁶⁶

There are a number of overlaps between Katherine's and Artemios' passions that go beyond the standard repetition of hagiographical writing. It is noticeable that, just as Katherine, Artemios positions himself in his speeches as learned in Greek (and in Latin!) so that he can better attack pagan reasoning.⁶⁷

---

⁶³ Albert Dufourcq, 'Gestes d'Artemius', in Id., *Étude sur les gesta martyrum romains*. Vol. 5: *Les légendes grecques et les légendes latines* (Paris, 1988), pp. 183–90.

⁶⁴ Vincent Déroche, 'Porquoi écrivait-on des recueils de miracles? L'exemple des miracles d'Artémios', in *Les saints et leur sanctuaire: Textes, images et monuments*, ed. Catherine Jolivet-Lévy et al. (Paris, 1993), pp. 95–116. See also Virgil S. Crisafulli and John W. Nesbitt, *The Miracles of St Artemios: A Collection of Miracle Stories by an Anonymous Author of Seventh-Century Byzantium* (Leiden, 1997). Samuel N.C. Lieu, 'From villain to saint and martyr: The life and afterlife of Flavius Artemius, Dux Aegypti', *Byzantine and Modern Greek Studies*, 20 (1996), 56–76.

⁶⁵ Crisafulli and Nesbitt, *Miracles of St Artemios*, p. 8. See also Cyril A. Mango, 'On the history of the templon and the martyrion of St Artemios at Constantinople', *Zograph*, 10 (1979), 40–43.

⁶⁶ Crisafulli and Nesbitt, *Miracles of St Artemios*, p. 1.

⁶⁷ Kotter, *Die Schriften des Johannes von Damaskos*, vol 5, p. 221, § 34: Ἐγὼ δέ, ὦ ἀνόσιε, τῆς Ἑλληνικῆς τε καὶ Ῥωμαϊκῆς παιδείας ἄκρον ἐπειλημένος καὶ ταῖς τῶν παλαιῶν ἀνδρῶν θεολογίαις, Ἑρμοῦ τέ φημι καὶ Ὀρφέως καὶ Πλάτωνος, ἐξησκημένος, οὐχ ἥκιστα δὲ καὶ

One instance in particular makes me wonder: the combination of knowledge of the Sibyl and Vergil strikes me as more than a mere hagiographical topos:

Artemios[68]	Katherine[69]
Τὸν Χριστὸν ἄνωθεν οἱ προφῆται προκατήγγειλαν, ὡς καὶ αὐτὸς κρεῖττον ἐπίστασαι. Καὶ πολλαὶ τῆς αὐτοῦ παρουσίας αἱ μαρτρυρίαι κἀκ τῶν παρ' ὑμῖν σεβομένων θεῶν καὶ τῶν <u>χρησμῶν</u> αἱ προαγορεύσεις τά τε <u>Σιβύλλεια γράμματα</u> καὶ ἡ τοῦ <u>Βιργιλίου</u> τοῦ Ῥωμαίου ποίησις, ἣν ὑμεῖς Βουκολικὴν ὀνομάζετε, καὶ αὐτὸς ὁ παρ' ὑμῖν θαυμαζόμενος Ἀπόλλων ὁ μαντικὸς τοῖον δή τινα περὶ Χριστοῦ ἐξεφώνησε λόγον.	Ἦν γὰρ μεμαθηκυῖα πᾶσαν βίβλον Ἀσκληπίου καὶ Γαληνοῦ, Ἀριστοτέλους τε καὶ Ὁμήρου καὶ Πλάτωνος καὶ Φιλιστίωνος καὶ Εὐσεβίου καὶ Ἰαννοῦ καὶ Μαμβροῦ καὶ Διονυσίου καὶ <u>σιβυλλῶν νεκρομαντείας</u> καὶ ὅσα ὁ <u>Βιργίλιος</u> ἔλεξεν καὶ ὁ Ὀρίων. Καὶ ἅπαξ ἁπλῶς πᾶσα διήγησις ῥητόρων καὶ βιργιλίων καὶ πᾶσα λέξις τῶν ἑβδομήκοντα δύο γλωσσῶν τῆς γῆς ἐν τῷ στόματι αὐτῆς ἐλαλεῖτο.

The phrase *writings* or *necromancies of the Sibyl* likely refers to a collection (or collections) of Sibylline oracles, although its brevity makes it impossible to determine which collection is being referenced. Sibylline oracles prophesize woes and disasters that will befall humanity and are uttered by an old woman.[70] These prophesies, written out in Greek hexameter, were collected into several books; they are pagan in origin and were revised and adapted by Jewish and Christian authors.

ταῖς Ἰουδαϊκαῖς γραφαῖς ἐξωμιληκὼς καὶ τὴν τούτων τερθείαν πεπατηκὼς πάλιν ἐπὶ τὸ πατροπαράδοτον καὶ ἀρχαιότατον καὶ θεοφιλὲς τοὺς ἀνθρώπους ἔθος τε καὶ σέβας μένειν διακελεύομαι ἢ ταῖς τῶν ἀπαιδεύτων καὶ νεωτεριζόντων ἀνοίαις ἀκολουθεῖν.

68 Ibid., p. 228, § 45.
69 Viteau, p. 26, §4.
70 Several Sibyls are said to have existed in Antiquity: Varro, for example, knew of ten, see Lactantius, *Divinae Institutiones*, 1.6: 'M. Varro ... in libris rerum divinarum ... Sibyllinos libros ait non fuisse unius Sibyllae, sed appellari uno nomine Sibyllinos, quod omnes feminae vates Sibyllae sint a veteribus nuncupatae vel ab unius Delphidis nomine vel a consiliis deorum enuntiandis. ... ceterum Sibyllas decem numero fuisse'.

The various books range in date from the middle of the second century CE to the seventh century CE – some originate in Egypt, others perhaps in Syria, Asia Minor, or somewhere in the region.[71] Clearly, the authors of Katherine's and Artemios' passions at least knew of the existence of Sibylline prophecies, although the mere mention of them does not in itself prove that these two hagiographical texts were produced by the same atelier or even the same person, only that perhaps they were part of the same cultural milieu. Having said that, the oracles were known to authors such as Clement of Alexandria, Lactantius, and Augustine so this putative cultural milieu cannot easily be tied to a particular time or place. A deeper study, both of the references to the Sybillyne oracles as well as their manuscript traditions and the ways they intersect with that of Katherine and Artemios, if at all, is needed.[72]

Another tantalizing parallel to Katherine is the figure of the Christian philosopher Pansophios of Alexandria. Unlike Artemios and much like Katherine, Pansophios is not an historical saint. The Constantinopolitan synaxaria and some recensions of the Armenian calendar commemorate his passion on 15/16 January. Aside from these short entries, a fuller account of his exploits has survived in a Georgian manuscript from the

---

[71] For an overview of the development of the tradition of these oracles see Emilio Suárez de la Torre, 'Sibylles, mantique inspire et collections oraculaires', *Kernos*, 7 (1994), 179–205; Jean-Michel Roessli, 'Catalogues de sibylles, recueil(s) de *Libri Sibyllini* et corpus des *Oracula Sibyllina*', in *Recueils normatifs et canons dans l'Antiquité*, ed. Enrico Norelli (Lausanne, 2005), pp. 47–68.

[72] For example, the *Chronicon Paschale*, a Byzantine universal chronicle from the seventh century (*c.* 630s), contains a list of twelve Sybils, see the edition by Ludwig Dindorf, 2 vols (Bonn, 1832), I, pp. 201–02. The gobbledygook being uttered by Katherine, and some of the other speakers in BHG 30a, could perhaps be interpreted as an attempt by the author to imitate divinely-inspired visions.

thirteenth century.⁷³ Peeters suggested that the Georgian is a translation from the Greek, via an intermediary Arabic version. More recently, the Greek text has been published from a palimpsest contained in a manuscript copied during the thirteenth century. Numerous Greek and Hebrew manuscripts were recycled to produce this thirteenth-century one; one of the Greek manuscripts was a collection of saints' lives, written out in a hand that does not appear to feature Italo-Greek or 'provincial' traits and that Paul Canart and Rosario Pintaudi assigned to the tenth century.⁷⁴ What survives of this manuscript is the end of the miracles of Demetrios (26 October), the life of Pansophios (29 October),⁷⁵ and a large part of the passion of Artemios (20 October). There is some reason to suppose that these texts were perhaps part of a menologion for the second half of October, or, perhaps more likely, a collection of saints' lives for private use.⁷⁶ On the style of Pansophios' passion, Canart and Pintaudi comment that it is:

> un misculgio di parole e di costruzioni ora rare e ricerate, ora banali e perfino maldestre. Cio e dovuto, pensiamo, al fatto che il redattore atinge a fonti di livello linguistico e stilistico 'alto' ma, lasciato alle proprie forze, rivela i suoi limiti. Cio detto, la

---

⁷³ Peeters, 'La Passion de Saint Pansophios', 307–09. The Georgian text was published by Korneli Kekelidze, 'წამება წმიდისადა ყოვლად ქებილისა მოწამისა პანსოფი ალექსანდრიელისა' (Ts'ameba ts'midisada q'ovlad kebilisa mots'amisa p'ansopi aleksandrielisa) in *Monumenta hagiographica georgica*, vol. 1: *Keimena* (Tbilisi, 1918), 48–59, based on Sinai, MS georg. 6.

⁷⁴ Paul Canart and Rosario Pintaudi, 'Le Palimpseste hagiographique grec du Laurentianus 74,17 et la passion de S. Pansophius d'Alexandrie', *AB*, 104 (1986), 5–16 (pp. 7–8).

⁷⁵ Although Canart and Pintaudi noted that Greek synaxaria commemorate Pansophios on 15/16 January, while the Armenian ones commemorate him on January 22.

⁷⁶ Canart and Pintaudi, 'Le palimpseste', 10.

morfologia et la sintassi sono quelle normali nei testi agiografici della tarda antichita o del primo medio evo.[77]

There are a number of parallels between Pansophios and Katherine: both can look back on a deep and thorough education,[78] they deploy an eheumeristic doctrine in their arguments, they refute pagan beliefs with pagan arguments,[79] and, perhaps most interestingly, they both mention Jannes and Mambres (Katherine does so only in BHG 30a and 30), as already pointed out by Peeters. Who are Jannes and Mambres? They are magicians who appear in the book of Exodus 7.10-12, opposing Moses during his encounter with the Pharaoh. While they are not named there, II Timothy 3.8 gives their names 'as Ἰαννῆς and Ἰαμβρῆς in a remark that suggests that a considerable tradition had already arisen concerning them'.[80] They seem to have made appearances in 'stories centered on Moses'[81] and 'certainly by 3 AD and perhaps considerably earlier a book about our two magician's altercations with

---

[77] Canart and Pintaudi, 'Il martirio di San Pansofio', 193.

[78] Pansophios (the all-knowning) was, as his name reveals, well educated: ἐπαίδευσεν οὖν αὐτὸν ὁ πατὴρ αὐτοῦ πᾶσαν γραμματικὴν ἐπιστήμην, ῥητορικήν τε καὶ φιλοσοφίαν; ibid., 195, §1.

[79] Pansophios: 'Λικίνιος λέγει: 'πάντως ἔχεις περὶ ἀναστάσεως, καὶ οἱ Ἕλληνες περὶ τούτων διηγήσαντο. οἶδας ὅτι παραγραφῇ Βιργίλιος διηγήσατο ὅτι μετὰ τὸ κατελθεῖν εἰς τὸν Ἅιδην καὶ μετὰ τὸ παρελθεῖν τὸν τρικέβηρον κύναν.' ὁ ἅγιος Πανσόφιος λέγει: 'Ναί, σχολαστικέ, καὶ ἐγὼ ἀνέγνων. ἀλλ᾽ εἰπέ μοι, τὸν Βιργίλιον τὸν διηγησάμενον τίς ἐγέννησεν?' ἠπόρει δὲ περὶ τούτων ὁ Λικίνιος λέγων: 'εἴ τινα ἄν μοι σὺ διηγήσῃ, τοῦτο σαφές ἐστιν.' ὁ ἅγιος Πανσόφιος λέγει: 'ἄκουσον καὶ ἐρῶ σοι. οὗτος ὁ Βιργίλιος ἐγένετο ἐκ πορνείας καὶ ἐρρίφη ὑπὸ τῆς ἰδίας μητρὸς αὐτοῦ'; ibid., 205, § 11.

[80] Frederick M. Biggs and Thomas N. Hall, 'Traditions concerning Jamnes and Mambres in Anglo-Saxon England', *Anglo-Saxon England*, 25 (1996), 69–89.

[81] Albert Pietersma, *The Apocryphon of Jannes and Jambres the Magicians: P. Chester Beatty XVI* (Leiden, 1994), p. 25.

Moses was in circulation'.[82] Origen (d. *c.* 253) refers to an apocryphal text called *The Book of Jannes and Jambres*, which contains details of their exploits, and also mentions that Paul the Apostle was quoting from it.[83] In his commentary on Matthew 27.9 and with reference to II Tim. 3.8, Origen writes: 'item quod ait: "sicut Iamnes et Mambres restiterunt Moysi" non invenitur in publicis libris, sed in libro secreto qui suprascribitur liber Iamnes et Mambres'.[84]

Today, this 'secret book' survives in fragments only. The oldest surviving texts of this book are in Greek, and although a number of different languages have been proposed as the original, Albert Pietersma and Theodore Lutz write that 'there is as yet no good reason to believe that the original language of the composition was other than Greek'.[85] They go on to say that 'the earliest texts of Jannes and Jambres [Mambres] were found in Egypt and since our book is first mentioned by an Alexandrian author, the burden of proof may be assumed to lie with those who wish to advocate a Palestinian origin for the composition'.[86] While these two individuals are usually referred to as magicians, the passion of Katherine is the only text in which they are described specifically as necromancers.

This is what Pansophios has to say about the two brothers:

τοίνυν ἀποθνῄσκουσιν οἱ περὶ Ἰαννὴν καὶ Ἰαμβρὶ καὶ ἀπεκρύβη τούτων ὁ παράδεισος. Αἱ δε βίβλοι αὐτῶν οὐκ ἀπεκρύβησαν, ἀλλ' ἐξ αὐτῶν ἐλάμβανον καὶ ἐμάνθανον οἱ ἄνθροποι πᾶσαν τερατολογίαν, ἐπαοιδίαν καὶ φαρμακείαν, ἐξ

---

[82] Ibid., p. 43.

[83] Albert Pietersma and R. Theodore Lutz, 'Jannes and Mambres', in *Old Testament Pseudoepigrapha*, ed. James H. Charlesworth, 2 vols (New York, 1983–85), II, pp. 427–42 (p. 430).

[84] *Origenes Matthäuserklärung II: Die lateinische Übersetzung der Commentariorum series*, ed. Ursula Treu *et al.* (Berlin, 1976), p. 43.

[85] Pietersma and Lutz, 'Jannes and Mambres', 432.

[86] Ibid., 434.

ὧν Ζεὺς ὁ καὶ Δίας ὁ υἱὸς Κρόνου τὴν ἀφορμὴν δεξάμενος πᾶσαν ἀσέλγειαν εἰργάσατο.[87]

The author of this text is suggesting that Jannes and Mambres had written books relating to magic and that, having received these books from them, humans had learned everything about wondrous natural occurrences, enchantments, and the use of potions.

In version BHG 30a, Katherine says: 'Ἀλλὰ δὴ καὶ ὁ τιμογλύφιος Ἰαννῆς καὶ Μαμβρῆς τῇ προυμαΐδι (?) τῆς νεκρομαντείας τῆς δυνάμεως τῶν βίβλων καραξιώδους ὀπτρίζουσιν ἀπὸ τῶν αἰώνων κεκοιμημένα πρόσωπα ἐν τῇ γῇ τοῖς ζητοῦσιν θεάσαθαι'.[88] While this sentence is obviously difficult to understand, it seems the author is referencing books written by the two brothers, books seemingly used in the performance of necromancy. It is unclear whether the books were in the brothers' possession or whether the books told their tale, neither can one deduce from this whether knowledge of these books goes beyond mere awareness of their existence. The later Greek versions of Katherine's story (BHG 31 and BHG 32), as well as the Latin tradition, do not reference Jannes and Mambres. These snippets are not enough to establish a link between the two hagiographical texts; their authors could easily have learned about Jannes and Mambres independently from each other. And yet, this is a tantalizing connection and merits further investigation into the manuscript tradition of Pansophios and Katherine.[89]

---

[87] Canart and Pintaudi, 'Il martirio di San Pansofio', 201, §6.

[88] BHG 30a, Viteau, p. 30, § 11; this is not in BHG 30. In sections 4 of BHG 30a and BHG 30, Jannes and Mambres are names in the list of authors Katherine has learned, with no specific reference to their book(s).

[89] Aside from the passion of Pansophios and Katherine, the brothers also make an appearance in the passion of Margaret/Marina of Antioch (BHG 1165–66): 'οἱ δὲ πρῶτοι ἀρχιδαίμονες λέγονται ἐν Αἰγύπτῳ καὶ Αἰθιοπίᾳ γεγονέναι, καθὼς εἰς τὴν Ἔξοδον Μωυσέως περὶ Ἰαννῆ καὶ

3. Hymns

As Eva Catafygiotu Topping remarked, 'the orthodox church annually celebrates a galaxy of female and male saints'.[90] The two powerhouses for hymnographical production in the Byzantine realm were the monastery of Mar Saba near Jerualem during the seventh century and the Constantinopolitan monastery of St John Stoudios during the ninth, 'a period of intense hymnographical activity in Constantinople'.[91] Byzantine hymns were (and are) scripture-based and orthodox, and thus inform and teach, as well as uplift the faithful during church services, although the increasing production of hymns by monastics meant that hymns tended to speak to their interests and were less didactic. While they do not necessarily imply an official or centralized cult, their existence coupled with the fact that hymns are normally sung on a particular saint's feast day, indicates that someone somewhere was celebrating a given saint's memory.[92]

'Ἰαμβρῆ περιέχει' in Hermann Usener, 'Acta S. Marinae et S. Christophori', *Festschrift zur fünften Säcularfeier der Carl-Ruprechts-Universität zu Heidelberg* (Bonn, 1886), p. 35. This text, whose manuscript tradition goes back to the eighth/ninth centuries, was written during the fifth–seventh centuries. See Nikolaos Kälviäinen, '"Not a few of the martyr accounts have been falsified from the beginning": Some preliminary remarks on the censorship and fortunes of the demonic episode in the Greek passion of St Marina (BHG 1165–1167c)', in *Translation and Transmission: Collection of Articles*, ed. Jaakko Hämeen-Anttila and Ilkka Lindstedt (Münster, 2019), pp. 107–37 (p. 119). See also Juliana Dresvina, 'The significance of the demonic episode in the legend of St Margaret of Antioch', *Medium Aevum*, 81 (2012), 189–209 (pp. 192–93).

[90] Eva Catafygiotu Topping, *Sacred Songs: Studies in Byzantine Hymnography* (Minneapolis, 1997), p. 5.

[91] Ibid., p. 7.

[92] For a (slightly outdated) overview see Egon Wellesz, *A History of Byzantine Music and Hymnography*, 2nd edn, rev. & enlarged (Oxford, 1961) with the review by Kenneth Levy in *Speculum*, 37 (1962), 467–69.

BHG 30a and BHG 30 indicate that Katherine died on 24 November (the day of her martyrdom in BHG 31 is recorded as 25 November), thus providing clear guidance for when to venerate the saint's death. In fact, before Katherine is beheaded, she is granted the opportunity to pray, allowing the author(s) to embed some important information as regards her commemoration into the text. The saint repeats three times the request that her name be remembered. She promises that those who do this will benefit from bounty, health, and lively beasts of burden; they will be forgiven their sins at the time of their death; and finally, they will benefit from fertile produce. In version BHG 30, the third entreaty includes not only a request that 'her name be remembered' but also that 'her memory be kept/celebrated', perhaps an indication that some sort of cult of the saint has already taken hold.

BHG 30a[93]	BHG 30[94]
Ἀλλὰ δός, Κύριε, τῷ μνημονεύοντι τοῦ ἐλαχίστου ὀνόματος μου Αἰκατερίνας εὐθηνίαν ἐν τῇ γῇ. ...	Ἀλλὰ δός, Κύριε, τοῖς μνημονεύουσιν τοῦ ἐλαχίστου ὀνόματος Αἰκατερίνας εὐθηνίαν ἐν τῇ γῇ. ...
Δός, Κύριε, τῷ μνημονεύοντι τοῦ ὀνόματός μου Αἰκατερίνς ἄφεσιν ἁμαρτιῶν... ...	Δός, Κύριε, τῷ μνημονεύοντι τοῦ ὀνόματος μου ἄφεσιν ἁμαρτιῶν ... ...
Δός, Κύριε, πάντα τὸν μνημονεύοντα τῷ ὀνόματί μου ἵνα μὴ γένηται ἀφορία καρπῶν ...	Δός, Κύριε, πᾶσι τοῖς μνημονεύουσιν τοῦ ὀνόματος μου καὶ <u>ἐκτελοῦσιν τὴν μνήμην μου</u> ἵνα μὴ γένηται ἀφορία καρποῦ ...

In the two later versions, the request has been slightly altered. Katherine has changed into a saint whose role is that of intercessor, indicating that she is already being venerated:

---

[93] Viteau, p. 38, § 24.
[94] Ibid., p. 21, § 24.

BHG 31[95]	BHG 32[96]
Δὸς δέ, Κύριε, καὶ <u>τοῖς σε καλοῦσιν</u> ἐν καιρῷ περιστάσεως <u>δι' ἐμοῦ</u> πάντα τὰ πρὸς τὸ συμφέρον αἰτήματα.	Δίδου δὲ καὶ <u>τοῖς δι' ἐμοῦ</u> καλοῦσι τὸ σὸν ἅγιον ὄνομα τὰ πρὸς τὸ συμφέρον αἰτήματα, ἵνα διὰ πάντων ὑμνῆται τὰ σὰ μεγαλεῖα νῦν καὶ εἰς τοὺς αἰῶνας.

The Arabic version also includes the prayer with the request for her name to be invoked. Peeters' Latin translation of it reads: 'Qui mei memoriam scriptis persequentur, qui meam historiam auscultabunt, qui eam legent, iis omnibus clemens esto, Domine'.[97] This is a meta-reference by the saint to the existence of a written text of her martyrdom and a desire, on the part of the author, that it be both heard and remembered. Simultaneously, the saint is, through the author's pen, asking that those who record her memory be received with clemency by God.

The Greek hymns in honour of Katherine, which have received little scholarly attention, can help in dating the text(s) of her passion. Two seventh-century hymnographers, a certain Anatolios and a similarly obscure Babylas, each wrote a relatively short hymn on the saint.[98] The one by Anatolios

[95] Ibid., p. 65, § 24.

[96] *PG* 116, col. 301A.

[97] Peeters, 'Une version Arabe', section 21, p. 31: 'Wa-taghfir yā rabbī lil-kātib tidhkārī wa-lil-sāmi'īn bi-qiṣṣatī wa-li-qāri'īhā wa-li-ajma'īn āmīn'; Forgive, oh my Lord, all those who write out my memoirs and who hear and read my story. Amen.

[98] They have been edited on the basis of twelfth- and thirteenth-century manuscripts by Henry J.W. Tillyard, *The Hymns of the Sticherarium for November* (Copenhagen, 1938), pp. 133–38.
Anatolios' hymn: Χαρμονικῶς τῇ πανηγύρει / τῆς θεοσόφου μάρτυρος Αἰκατερίνας / συνδράμωμεν ὦ φιλομάρτυρες / καὶ ταύτην τοῖς ἐπαίνοις / ὡς ἄνθεσι καταστέψωμεν. / Χαίροις βοῶντες αὐτῇ / ἡ τῶν φληνάφων ῥητόρων / τὴν θρασυστομίαν ἐλέγξασα / ὡς ἀπαιδευσίας ἀνάπλεων / καὶ τούτους πρὸς πίστιν θείαν χειραγωγήσασα. / Χαίροις ἡ τὸ σῶμα πολυπλόκοις βασάνοις ἐκδοῦσα / δι' ἀγάπην τοῦ ποιητοῦ

concentrates on Katherine's victory over the chattering rhetors and her suffering under complicated tortures, without betraying knowledge of a particular version of her passion. The hymn attributed to Babylas is half the length of Anatolios' hymn and mentions both the dogmatic emperor and the defeated rhetors.

Although there are more than one hundred Byzantine hymns that claim Anatolios as their author, it is difficult to determine when he may have lived. Casimir Émereau proposed two solutions: either an Anatolios who was a pupil of Theodore (d. 826) of the Stoudios monastery in Constantinople or an Anatolios who was archbishop at Thessalonika in the ninth century. Hans-Georg Beck favoured a suggestion by Wilhelm Christ who proposed a date before the middle of the eighth century.[99] Even more obscure is Babylas, apparently a hymnographer from Mar Saba in Palestine.[100] He has a couple of idiomela to his name, but Émereau declined to give a date

σου / καὶ μὴ καταβληθεῖσα / ὡς ἄκμων ἀνήλατος. Χαίροις ἡ ταῖς ἄνω μοναῖς / ἀντάξια τῶν πόνων εἰσοικισθεῖσα / καὶ δόξης αἰωνίου κατατρυφήσασα / ἧς ἐφιέμενοι οἱ ὑμνῳδοί σου / τῆς ἐλπίδος μὴ ἐκπέσωμεν.

Babylas' hymn: Βίον ἄυλον ἐξησκημένη / βῆμα ἄθεον καταλαβοῦσα / ἔστης τροπαιοφόρος Αἰκατερίνα σοφή / ἀνθηφοροῦσα τοῦ Θεοῦ τὴν λαμπρότητα / καὶ τὸ θεῖον σθένος ἐνδεδυμένη / δόγμα τυράννου κατεμυκτήρισας / καὶ ῥητόρων ἔπαυσας / τὰς φληνάφους ῥήσεις πολύαθλε.

[99] Casimir Émereau, 'Hymnographi byzantini', *Échos d'Orient*, 21 (1922), 258–79 (p. 265). Hans-Georg Beck, *Kirche und theologische Literatur im byzantinischen Reich* (Munich, 1959), p. 472, referring to *Anthologia graeca carminum christianorum*, ed. Wilhelm Christ and Matthaios K. Paranikas (Leipzig, 1871), pp. xli–xlii. Nothing new in Josef Szövérffy, *A Guide to Byzantine Hymnography: A Classified Bibliography of Texts and Studies* (Brookline, MA, 1978), p. 257.

[100] Joseph Patrich, *Sabas, Leader of Palestinian Monasticism: A Comparative Study in Eastern Monasticism, Fourth to Seventh Centuries* (Washington, D.C., 1995), p. 329.

while Beck added him to his list of seventh-century liturgical poets without giving a reason for doing so.[101]

The hymn 'χορείαν σεπτὴν' edited by José Grosdidier de Matons, an expert on Romanos the Melode, provides perhaps a better lens through which to look at the Greek Katherine texts.[102] It was written by a certain 'humble monk' as the acrostic informs us: 'τοῦ μόνου ταπεινοῦ ἡ ᾠδή' – and has been transmitted in its entirety in an eleventh-century manuscript from Patmos (Monê tou Hagiou Iôannou tou Theologou, MS 212) and in a further six manuscripts of eastern origin which more or less only contain the first three strophes. The oldest of these, Sinai, MS gr. 925, dated to the tenth century, is misleading because here the first strophe only has been added at a later stage to the manuscript. The first three strophes do, however, figure in a tenth-/eleventh-century manuscript from Athos (Monê Batopediou, MS 1041).[103]

This 'humble monk' also wrote a hymn in honour of Peter of Alexandria and another on Eustratios and companions.[104] Grosdidier remarked that the kind of acrostic used by this author was typical of the hymnographers working in a loose circle around Theodore of the Stoudios monastery, who was at the centre of the iconophile resistance at the end of the eighth century and maintained connections with sympathizers

---

[101] Émereau, 'Hymnographi Byzantini', 277; Beck, *Kirche und Literatur*, p. 472.

[102] 'Un hymne inédit à Sainte Catherine d'Alexandrie', *Travaux et Mémoires*, 8 (1981), 187–207.

[103] Sophronius Eustratiades and Arkadios Vatopédinos, *Catalogue of the Greek Manuscripts in the Library of the Monastery of Vatopedi on Mt. Athos*, Harvard Theological Studies XI (Cambridge, MA, 1924), p. 186. Most of the manuscript contains hymns by Romanos the Melode.

[104] Peter of Alexandria (25 Nov.), acrostic: 'ἔπος τοῦ μόνου ταπεινοῦ'. Eustratios and companions (13 Dec.), acrostic: 'τὸ ὕφος μόνου ταπεινοῦ'. Neither of these has been edited. Grosdidier de Matons, 'Un hymne inédit', 187.

throughout the Byzantine realm.¹⁰⁵ The style of this particular hymnographer, as gleaned from his three hymns, places him in the first half of the ninth century, if not before.¹⁰⁶ Interestingly, and in contrast with the two shorter hymns by Anatolios and Babylas, the 'humble monk' appears to follow a specific text, namely BHG 30a rather than BHG 30:¹⁰⁷

Hymn	BHG 30a + 30
Strophe 5, line 7: ἰδοὺ γὰρ ἔστιν ἐνταῦθα <u>ἀλκιμώτατον</u> γύναιον καὶ σοφόν.	The author of BHG 30a uses the adverbs ἀλκίμως and ἀλκιμωτάτως which the redactor of BHG 30 does not. For example, in BHG 30a Katherine begins her first speech to the emperor thus: '<u>ἀλκιμωτάτην</u> λέξιν ἀναλαβοῦσα'.¹⁰⁸
Strophe 7, line 6: χρήματά τε ὑπισχνεῖτο διδόναι, εἰ πείσωσι τὸ γύναιον μεταστῆναι.	This loosely corresponds to BHG 30a ('ἐκέλευσεν ... συναχθῆναι πᾶν τὸ πλῆθος τῆς πόλεως ἐπὶ τῇ θεωρίᾳ τῆς λέξεως τῶν ῥητόρων πρὸς τὴν μακαρίαν')¹⁰⁹ and is not found in BHG 30.

There is only one, small, instance that points to the possibility of the author having also known BHG 31: in the phrasing of 'Μέγας ὁ Θεὸς τῶν χριστιανῶν' the hymn is closer to BHG 31 ('Μέγας ὁ Θεὸς τῶν χριστιανῶν') than either BHG 30a or BHG 30 ('Εἷς ὁ θεὸς τῶν χριστιανῶν'), although this apprars to be a common phrase.¹¹⁰ If the dating of the hymn by

---

¹⁰⁵ Grosdidier, 'Un hymne inédit', 187–89. On Theodore see Roman Cholij, *Theodore the Stoudite: The Ordering of Holiness* (Oxford, 2002).

¹⁰⁶ Grosdidier, 'Un hymne inédit', 188.

¹⁰⁷ Ibid., 200–02, where he offered a commentary on the text and discussed possible parallels with the various versions of the passion.

¹⁰⁸ Viteau, p. 27, § 6.

¹⁰⁹ Ibid., p. 29, § 9.

¹¹⁰ Ibid., p. 61, § 20 and p. 37, § 20 respectively.

Grosdidier is correct, and I have no reason to doubt his expertise, then it follows that the hymnographer's source text had already been committed to parchment in time for him to make use of it during the 800–850s, broadly speaking, and was available in Constantinople.

Grosdidier also mentions a kanon on Katherine attributed to Theophanes Graptos (d. 845), a pupil of Michael Synkellos at Mar Saba before coming to Constantinople.[111] In a thesis on the life and work of Theophanes Graptos, Alexandra Zervoudaki presented information on this kanon, which was attributed to Theophanes by Bartholomaios Koutloumousianos in the *Menaion of November*.[112] The majority of manuscripts preserving it do not indicate an author, except for three, and none of these predate the twelfth century.[113] Most likely, the kanon on Katherine was ascribed to Theophanes owing to his reputation as a hymnographer.

Since Theodore of the Stoudios monastery was active in Constantinople, Grosdidier suggested that Katherine's passion originated in that city. However, just because at least one hymn that seems to have used BHG 30a was probably written in Constantinople does not mean that BHG 30a itself

---

[111] This kanon forms part of the office of Katherine, see Grosdidier, 'Un hymne inédit', 202: 'l'office actuel de Sainte Catherine nous offre encore un canon attribué à Théophane (Graptos)'. The kanon begins: 'Αἰκατερίνης τῆς πανσόφου μάρτυρος / ταῖς ἱκεσίαις, Χριστέ ... '. There is an acrostic that reads: 'ΑΙΚΑΤΕΡΙΝΑ ΤΗΝ ΠΑΝΑΟΙΔΙΜΟΝ ΑΣΜΑΣΙ ΜΕΛΠΩ'. In the *Menaion* (see following note) the kanon is recorded under 25 November and not 24.

[112] Bartholomaios Koutloumousianos, *Menaion of November* (Venice, 1843). See also Alexandra Zervoudaki, 'Θεοφάνης ὁ Γραπτός: Βίος καὶ ἔργο' (unpublished doctoral thesis, University of Crete, 2002), pp. 214–15. I am grateful to Alexandra Zervoudaki for being willing to share her research with me.

[113] Paris, BnF, MS gr. 13, s. xiii, fol. 147; Athos, Lavra, MS Δ 14, s. xii, fol. 90v; Athens, National Library of Greece, MS 629, 1386, fol. 277. The entry on Theophanes Graptos in *PMBZ Online*, #8093, which mentions the kanons written by him, does not include the one on Katherine.

originated from there. Grosdidier's remark that Constantinopolitans had a penchant for learned saints is equally true for the monks at Mar Saba, who would have enjoyed Katherine's learning as much as their colleagues in the capital.[114] During the eighth and ninth centuries, this monastery was far from being an unimportant outpost in the south: it was rich and powerful, and a great number of Palestinian bishops of the period had first been monks there. John of Damascus is one of its best known residents,[115] followed by Kosmas the Hymnographer and Theodore Abū-Qurrah (d. 820).[116] Indeed, it was seen as an iconophile stronghold during the eighth and ninth centuries, with those in Constantinople often turning to their Sabaite brethren for support.[117] For example, Theodore of the Stoudios monastery adopted the early Sabaitic liturgical

---

[114] See Marie-France Auzépy, 'De la Palestine à Constantinople (VIIIe – IXe siècles): Étienne le Sabaïte et Jean Damascène', *Travaux et Mémoires*, 12 (1994), 186.

[115] But see Marie-France Auzépy, 'Les Sabaites et l'iconoclasme', in *The Sabaite Heritage in the Orthodox Church from the Fifth Century to the Present,* ed. Joseph Patrich (Leuven, 2001), pp. 305–14 (p. 305, n. 4), who argued that John was more likely a clerical member of the Anastasis in Jerusalem.

[116] Extensive copying of manuscripts and translating from Greek into Arabic and Georgian, as well as from Syriac into Greek took place there. See Patrich, *Sabas, Leader of Palestinian Monasticism,* p. 329. See also Aristarchos Peristeris, 'Literary and scribal activities at the monastery of St. Sabas', in *The Sabaite Heritage in the Orthodox Church,* ed. Patrich, pp. 171–94. John C. Lamoreaux, 'The biography of Theodore Abū Qurrah revisited', *DOP,* 56 (2002), 25–40. Kosmas was born in Jersualem *c.* 675 and was a contemporary of John of Damascus. The vita of John and his adoptive brother Kosmas (BHG 884) is printed in *PG* 94.429–90. See Theocharis Detorakes, 'Vie inédite de Cosmas le Mélode', *AB,* 99 (1981), 101–16; Alexander P. Kazhdan and Stephen Gero, 'Kosmas of Jerusalem: A more critical approach to his biography', *Byzantinische Zeitschrift,* 82 (1989), 122–32.

[117] Patrich, *Sabas, Leader of Palestinian Monasticism* p. 330.

typikon for use in Constantinople, attesting to the influence of the monastery's traditions beyond its confines.[118]

There is evidence that monks left Mar Saba and travelled to Constantinople: in *c.* 813 Michael Synkellos and the brothers Theodoros and Theophanes Graptos arrived in the capital. It is likely that disagreements over theological matters with the patriarch of Jerusalem, as well as the ongoing attacks of the Arabs, contributed to their decision to leave Palestine.[119] They could have brought with them Katherine's legend – at that time BHG 30a seems to have already existed. Marie-France Auzépy came to the conclusion that what mattered in Syria and Palestine during the first half of the ninth century was not so much the debate on icon-worship, but the question of dyotheletism and the pressures exerted by the Islamic occupiers.[120] Auzépy has also argued that the monks at Mar Saba were perhaps less preoccupied with icon worship and more interested in questions around conversion to Christianity.[121] If the origin of Katherine's passion is to be sought in Palestine, then this background combined with the Arab occupation might explain why it is lacking in any obvious iconophile or iconoclast elements. Perhaps Katherine's story was written to strengthen the faith of those in the direct line of Saracen and Arabic attacks?

Christine Walsh suggested that Katherine's prayer for her body not to be found can be read as 'making a statement against relics in keeping with the Iconoclast viewpoint', although she did not go so far as to argue that the passion is an iconoclast work.[122] In both BHG 30a and BHG 30, Katherine begins her prayer thus (with a slight variation in BHG 30):

[118] Ibid., p. 358.
[119] Auzépy, 'De la Palestine à Constantinople', 209–11.
[120] Ibid., 197 and 203.
[121] Auzépy, 'Les Sabaites et l'iconoclasme', p. 306
[122] Walsh, 'The early development', p. 55.

'Ἐπειδήπερ πολλοί εἰσιν ἑστῶτες καὶ ἐκδεχόμενοι μέρος τοῦ σώματός μου, διό, Κύριε, εὐδόκησον μὴ εὑρεθῆναι μέρος τοῦ σώματός μου ἐν τῇ γῇ.'[123] This request regarding her body cannot be taken as evidence for or against an iconoclast author because it is a hagiographical topos already present in Athanasius' life of Anthony of Egypt and Jerome's life of Hilarion the Great.[124] The detail of the translation of Katherine's body to Sinai occurs in all four versions of the passion. That it cannot have been a later addition is evident from the hymn edited by Grosdidier, where it is included. The scheme and overall balance of the hymn suggest that the transfer of Katherine's remains is part of its original composition, and hence likely was already in its source text. In keeping with a comment by Delehaye about saints' lives that omit any reference to the location of the saint's body, it could be argued that the Sinai detail in the early passions of Katherine has some sort of significance.[125] Is it not more likely that this prayer and the body's journey to Mount Sinai at the hands of angels point to the fact that, from the start, there were no physical remains? Mount Sinai, outside the sphere of direct Byzantine political rule from the seventh century onwards, was likely seen as being remote enough so no-one could easily go on a quick journey to verify the saint's body's whereabouts. It also has a plausible geographical connection to Alexandria, a city of deep and ancient learning and known as a place where Christians were martyred, and biblical accounts of

---

[123] Viteau, p. 38, § 24.

[124] See *Early Christian Lives*, tr. Carolinne White (London 1998), p. xxviii.

[125] Hippolyte Delehaye, *Sanctus: Essai sur le culte des saints dans l'antiquité* (Brussels, 1927), pp. 148–49: 'lorsqu'on prend soin de nous dire que le corps d'un saint a été miraculeusement englouti dans le sol, qu'il a disparu dans la fente d'un rocher ... c'est que pour les anciens eux-mêmes le culte d'un saint dont personne ne connaissait le tombeau avait un coté anormal dont il fallait rendre raison', by adding a prayer on behalf of the saint asking for their body not to be found, for example.

Moses' encounters with God ensure a strong aura of holiness.[126]

BHG 30a and BHG 30 both end with a colophon that contains information about their author: 'Ταῦτα ἐγὼ Ἀναστάσιος [BHG 30: Ἀθανάσιος], ὁ ταχύγραφος, ἅμα δοῦλος ὑπάρχων τῆς κυρίας μου Αἰκατερίνης, συνεγραψάμην τὰ ὑπομνήματα τῆς κυρίας μου ἐν πάσῃ ἀσφαλείᾳ'.[127] It would be futile to try to identify who this Anastasius/Athanasius might have been, not only because the list of possible candidates is extensive and an identification would be pure conjecture, but also because the colophon is likely to be an addition either by the author himself or a copyist in order to validate the events of the passion. Who would be able to dispute Katherine's martyrdom if it was actually witnessed and written down by a member of her household? Homonymity with Athanasius, the author of the life of Anthony, who actually lived in Alexandria at the time of Katherine's purported martyrdom, probably also played a role in the choosing of the name.[128]

There are another two more or less narrative hymns on Katherine that were published by Jean Baptise Pitra: the hymn 'Ῥητορεύει σήμερον' occurs in eastern as well as western manuscripts, while the hymn 'Σοφίαν Θεοῦ ἐκ βρέφους

---

[126] The scene of Moses receiving the stone tables (Exodus 31.18) is depicted in a mosaic in the basilica at St Catherine's monastery on the Sinai. See George H. Forsyth and Kurt Weitzmann, *The Monastery of Saint Catherine at Mount Sinai: The Church and Fortress of Justinian* (Ann Arbor, 1973), plate CXXVII

[127] Viteau, p. 39, § 26.

[128] If one had to cast about for an historically attested author, then Anastasius Sinaites would be a perfect candidate: he was a monk at Sinai towards the end of the seventh century and wrote an important handbook for the fight against monophysitism, as well as saints' lives. See *PMBZ Online*, #268. Daniel D. Caner's *History and Hagiography from the Late Antique Sinai* (Liverpool, 2010) includes 'Tales of the Sinai Fathers' and 'Edifying Tales', both ascribed to Anastasius.

χαριτώσασα' is particular to Italo-Greek kontakaria.[129] This latter hymn, of which only the beginning survives, lists a number of authors Katherine had read: 'πᾶσαν γραφὴν Ἀσκληπίου, Ὁμήρου καὶ Πλάτωνος μαθοῦσα, καὶ Βιργιλίου, Γαληνοῦ, Εὐσεβίου τὰ δόγματα, Ἀριστοτέλους διδάγματα, τοῦ Χριστοῦ ἀνεδείχθης μαθήτρια'.[130] Both BHG 30a and BHG 30 include such a list, but only the former features Vergil. Finally, Athanasios Kominis published a kanon of nine odes on Clement of Rome, Peter of Alexandria, Mercurius, and Katherine, six of which contain a strophe on Katherine.[131] The kind of information given about Katherine here, including her knowledge of Vergil, again points to knowledge of version BHG 30a. Unfortunately, none of these hymns have an acrostic that would help in determining when and where they were written.

Last but not least, there exists a lengthy encomium on Katherine, attributed to Anastasius the Stammerer, who served in the civil administration of Emperor Leo VI (886-912).[132] This Anastasius composed both secular and religious texts, and is known to have written an encomium on Agathonicus (BHG

---

[129] Jean Baptiste Pitra, *Analecta sacra spicilegio solesmensi parata*, vol. 1 (Paris, 1876; repr. Westmead, 1966–67), pp. 639–41. The manuscripts are (1) BAV, MS Vat. gr. 2, s. xi (from Grottaferrata?). This manuscript contains liturgical material by Theophanes Graptos, Joseph the Hymnographer, and John of Damascus. (2) Grottaferrata, Biblioteca Statale del Monumento Nazionale, MS Δ.α.27 (gr. 339), s. xiii. On this manuscript see Vadim B. Krysko, 'Nuove fonti greche di testi innografici slavi nei manoscritti di Grottaferrata', *Bollettino della Badia greca di Grottaferrata*, 2 (2005), pp. 43–55.

[130] Pitra, *Analecta sacra*, third strope, p. 641.

[131] Athanasios D. Kominis, *Analecta hymnica graeca*, vol. 3: *Canones novembris* (Rome, 1972), pp. 489–505. He used the same manuscripts as Pitra. See note 129 above.

[132] *PMBZ Online*, #20297. He was also referred to as Anastasius 'ὁ Τραυλός' (the stutterer, the lisper).

42) as well as one on Katherine (BHG 32b).[133] The text of the encomium on the latter was edited by George Metallinos from three manuscripts.[134] It is 'a typical example of the genre',[135] written in a lofty style, and seemingly based on BHG 30a and BHG 30, although the author's knowledge of BHG 31 cannot be entirely ruled out.[136] Dirk Krausmüller states that it 'appears to be a bland text that does not engage in contemporary debates',[137] except perhaps the brief exchange between the emperor and Katherine, wherein the former offers to make her empress and have her statue be venerated. She rejects this offer and continues to explain that she knows her struggle on behalf of God will result in her being 'depicted and honoured as a martyr' ('καὶ διὰ τῆς ὑπὲρ αὐτοῦ ἀθλήσεως εἰκονίζεσθαί τε καὶ μαρτυρικῶς τιμᾶσθαι εὖ οἶδα').[138] As already noted by Metallinos, the use of the verb εἰκονίζω points towards a period in which the depiction of saints in icons was acceptable, which fits with Anastasius' time in office.[139]

---

[133] Dirk Krausmüller, 'The encomium of Catherine of Alexandria (BHG 32b) by the *Protasecretis* Anastasius, a work of Anastasius 'the Stammerer'', *AB*, 127 (2009), 309–12. Edition of the text by George Metallinos, 'Ἀναστασίου πρωτασηκρήτις Ἐγκώμιον εἰς τὴν Ἁγίαν Αἰκατερίνην', *Ἐκκλησιαστικὸς Φάρος*, n.s. 54 (1972), 237–74.

[134] Istanbul, Patriarchikê Bibliothêkê, MS Hagia Trias 99, s. xi, fols 177–194; Messina, Biblioteca Regionale Universitaria 'Giacomo Longo', MS S. Salv. 15, s. xi, fols 36v–51v; BAV, MS Ottob. gr. 415, s. xiv, fols 24v–42.

[135] Krausmüller, 'The encomium', 311.

[136] Metallinos, 'Ἀναστασίου πρωτασηκρήτις Ἐγκώμιον', 247.

[137] Krausmüller, 'The encomium', 312.

[138] Metallinos, 'Ἀναστασίου πρωτασηκρήτις Ἐγκώμιον', 264, §17. 19–20.

[139] Ibid., 249.

4. Calendars, menologia, and synaxaria

I now turn to evidence for Katherine's cult that can be gleaned from liturgical manuscripts, and will proceed in chronological order. Her name figures among a number of female saints ('Thecla, Barbara, Iuliana, [.]phthimia, Eupraxia, Melania, Maria, Catharina, Shamunith et septem eius filii supplicamini pro nobis peccatoribus') at the end of a Syriac litany in BAV, MS. Vat. syr. 77 published by Anton Baumstark in 1904.[140] According to the catalogue description, this litany is a translation from the Greek (now lost), and was written out from the eleventh century onwards.[141] Michael Lapidge pointed out that the *terminus post quem* for this litany is 620 CE, the year of the death of John the Almoner, who also features in the list.[142] By misinterpreting this information, Walsh assumed that this litany dates from the seventh century, cited this as the earliest written reference to Katherine's name, and posited that the saint was already being venerated at that point.[143] A comparison with a number of Syriac synaxaria shows that Katherine only starts appearing in these manuscripts during

---

[140] Anton Baumstark, 'Eine syrisch-melchitische Allerheiligenlitanei', *Oriens Christianus*, 4 (1904), 98–120.

[141] Giuseppe S. Assemani, *Bibliotheca orientalis Clementino-Vaticana* (Hildesheim, 2000, reprint of 1719 edition), I, p. 615. BAV, MS Vat. syr. 77 (*olim* XXXVI) belongs to a group of manuscripts which Assemani *advexit ex Oriente*, from places such as Aleppo and Mount Lebanon, as well as the monasteries of St Mary El-Sourian and of Our Lady of Saidnaya. I am indebted to Sebastian Brock for the reference and the dating. On Assemani (1687–1768), who searched for manuscripts in areas today known as Egypt, Syria, and Lebanon, and thus contributed to the important holdings of eastern manuscripts at the BAV, see Giorgio Levi della Vida, 'Assemani, Guisepe Simonio', in *Dizionario biografico degli italiani*, vol. 4 (Rome, 1962), s.v.

[142] Michael Lapdige, *Anglo-Saxon Litanies of the Saints* (London, 1991), p. 17.

[143] Walsh, 'The early development', p. 78.

the twelfth century at the earliest.[144] Moreover, the *terminus post quem* of 620 does not imply that BAV, MS Vat. syr. 77 was produced in the seventh century, even though the Greek original might have originated from the patriarchate of Antioch.[145] Most of the female saints who surround Katherine in this litany stem from Asia Minor, although Eupraxia (Thebes), Melania (Rome), and Maria (Egypt?) have a more universal appeal. These saints, as a group, do not suggest an origin from Antioch. I think it is more likely that the inclusion of Katherine in this litany occurred much later than Walsh would like to think, and thus cannot be taken as evidence for a cult in the seventh century.

The focus so far on Greek texts must not obscure the fact that Byzantium, and especially Syria and Palestine, were thriving with religious activity and attracted people from all over the Empire: monks were mobile and 'their international subculture was woven together in complex ways, aware of what was happening in other parts of the Christian world from the Euphrates to Ethiopia'.[146] Eastern Christianity encompassed a myriad of languages, including Coptic, Syriac, Georgian, Armenian, Persian, Slavic, and others, even though 'Greek was the dominant language of the ecclesiastical culture ... from the fourth century until well into the eighth century and

---

[144] See Joseph-Marie Sauget, *Premières recherches sur l'origine et les caractéristiques des synaxaires melkites (xie–xviie siècles)* (Brussels, 1969). Sinai, MS ar. 412 (s. xii): Katherine is a later addition; Sinai, MS ar. 418 (1237): Katherine is a later addition; Sinai, MS ar. 420 (1287), Katherine is a later addition; Sinai, MS ar. 421 (1237). Sauget (pp. 84–85) mentioned another manuscript that also contains the translation of Katherine's body to Mount Sinai: Harissa, Bibliothèque des Missionnaires de Saint Paul, MS ar. 70 (s. xvi). Sebastian Brock very kindly directed me in Sauget's direction.

[145] Lapidge, *Anglo-Saxon Litanies*, p. 17.

[146] John A. McGuckin, 'Poetry and hymnography (2): The Greek world', in *The Oxford Handbook of Early Christian Studies*, ed. Susan Ashbrook Harvey and David G. Hunter (Oxford, 2009), pp. 652–32.

beyond'.¹⁴⁷ Despite the political reality on the ground in the seventh and eighth centuries and the loss of territory in the wake of Arab conquests, Christian centres of learning and monasteries continued to exist in the areas of Palestine, Syria, and beyond, particularly in Palestine, 'in Jerusalem, and the neighbouring monasteries'.¹⁴⁸ Mar Saba was one of the monasteries where much copying and translation of religious texts took place.¹⁴⁹ The following is only an initial survey, but the kind of evidence I have come across suggests that many more Greek, Georgian, and Arabic manuscripts may contain lives or other accounts of Katherine.¹⁵⁰

For example, John Zosimos, whose hand has been identified in at least two Georgian manuscripts now at Sinai, was one of generations of Georgian monks who were active at the scriptorium of Mar Saba from the eighth until the tenth

---

¹⁴⁷ Sidney H. Griffin, 'From Aramaic to Arabic: The languages of the monasteries of Palestine in the Byzantine and early Islamic periods', *DOP*, 51 (1997), 11–31 (p. 11).

¹⁴⁸ Cyril A. Mango, 'Greek culture in Palestine after the Arab conquest', in *Scritture, libri et testi nelle aree provinciali di Bisanzio*, ed. Guglielmo Cavallo *et al.*, vol. 1 (Spoleto, 1991), pp. 149–60 (pp. 149–50).

¹⁴⁹ A very large number of translations (from Greek or Arabic, or occasionally from Syriac) are to be found in extant Georgian manuscripts of the eighth-tenth centuries, see Gérard Garitte, 'Géorgienne, littérature spirituelle', in *Dictionnaire de Spiritualité*, 6 (Gabriel-Guzman), ed. Marcel Viller (Paris, 1967), 247–55. Most of these would have been translated in Palestinian monasteries, among which would certainly have been that of Mar Saba. Such a provenance is especially likely in the case of the lives of Sabbas and Stephen the Sabaite, and the life of Romanos the Neomartyr by the Sabaite Stephen of Damascus. See also Robert Schick, *The Christian Communities of Palestine from Byzantine to Islamic Rule* (Princeton, 1995), pp. 98–100; Peter Charanis, 'Cultural diversity and the breakdown of Byzantine power in Asia Minor', *DOP*, 29 (1975), 1–20.

¹⁵⁰ The Synaxarion of the Coptic Church has no trace of Katherine's name or feast-day; see *The Coptic Encyclopedia*, ed. Aziz S. Atiya (New York, 1991), s.v. synaxarion.

centuries.¹⁵¹ Sinai, MS georg. 34, a manuscript that contains mainly liturgical texts such as offices and hymns, preserves on folios 25r-33v a calendar starting on 1 January, which includes Katherine on 24 November, the date for her martyrdom given in BHG 30a and BHG 30. Gérard Garitte showed that John wrote this part of the manuscript probably before 973 at Mar Saba. A colophon on folio 143 mentions his name,¹⁵² and John also indicates the sources he used for the composition of the calendar on folio 33v: 'haec synaxes [ex] 4 exemplaribus a me descriptae sunt: praecipue canonis [exemplari], et Graeciae [exemplari], et Hierosolymae, et Sancti Sabae'. John's principal source is the Lectionary of Jerusalem (partly transcribed by him in Sinai, MS georg. 37), a Byzantine Greek model, an exemplar from Jerusalem, and one from Mar Saba.¹⁵³ The interesting point here is that the calendar in Sinai, MS georg. 34, according to Garitte, on occasion bears resemblance to the calendar in Patmos, MS 266 for which Juan Mateos has suggested a Palestinian origin (see below).¹⁵⁴

There are also manuscripts now at Sinai which contain Katherine's martyrdom: they are Sinai, MS georg. 6, MS georg. 71, and MS georg. 91, of which georg. 6 is the earliest.¹⁵⁵ Again the hand of John Zosimos can be identified

---

[151] Gérard Garitte, *Le Calendrier Palestino-Géorgien du Sinaiticus 34 (Xe siècle)* (Brussels, 1958), p. 17.

[152] '... haec hymnaria menaea ... in quo (*sic*) scripta sunt festa omnia nova et antiqua integre, et horae 12 integre, iberice (= *Georgian*) et secundum Sancti Sabae [ordinem], et chronicon integre omnino, et aliae multae dispositiones, mihi gratificatus est Dominus describere in Laura et deserto sancti patris nostri, ... scriba huius [libri] Iohannes ... qui hoc scripsimus' (Garitte's translation of the Georgian), see Garitte, *Le Calendrier Palestino-Géorgien*, p. 16.

[153] 'Ce qu'il designe comme sa source principale et qu'il appelle 'canon' (*kanoni*) ne peut être que le lectionnaire hierosolymitain, qui était bien connu de Jean'. Garitte, *Le Calendrier Palestino-Géorgien*, p. 23.

[154] Garitte, *Le Calendrier Palestino-Géorgien*, p. 23 and pp. 31–32.

[155] Georg. 71, s. xiii, fols 201v–215. Georg. 91, s. xiv, fols 106a–115b.

in this manuscript, along with others, and a colophon on folio 224 dates the process of transcription and binding of the entire codex to 981, 982, and 983, while also indicating that the volume was destined for Michael, a 'decanus' at the monastery of Sinai.[156] The texts in this manuscript, and the other two manuscripts, are entirely hagiographical, and are all Georgian translations from the Greek; in the case of Katherine the Greek text used is BHG 30.[157] Another, relatively early, manuscript from Sinai, MS ar. 542 (late ninth/early tenth century), was said by Atiya to contain a tract on the skull of Katherine.[158] However, as André Binggeli has shown, the 'skull' (*jumjumat*) mentioned in the text refers to the summit of Mount Sinai, as is usual in contemporary Arabic hagiography. The rubric reads 'Panégyrique de la cime du Mont Sinaï' [*hādhihi madḥat jumjumat ṭūr sīnā*]. This is a homily on the occasion of the dedication of the church of the Holy Summit of Mount Sinai.[159] There is also at least one other

---

[156] Gérard Garitte, *Catalogue des manuscrits géorgiens littéraires du mont Sinaï* (Leuven, 1956), p. 26.

[157] BHG 30 here still refers to both version 30 and 30a. The distinction of the two versions was not reflected in the BHG until 1969, see François Halkin, *Novum auctarium bibliothecae hagiographicae graecae* (Brussels, 1969).

[158] Aziz S. Atiya, *The Arabic Manuscripts of Mount Sinai: A Hand-list of the Arabic Manuscripts and Scrolls Microfilmed at the Library of the Monastery of St Catherine, Mount Sinai* (Baltimore, 1955), p. 22. Other Arabic manuscripts at Sinai preserving texts of Katherine are Sinai, MS ar. 533, 1237 CE (life of John the Theologian, Mimar [homily] of Andrew Bishop of Crete, martyrdom of Cyricus and Julitta, life of Katherine) and Sinai, MS ar. 548, 1306 CE (selection from the Paradise of the Fathers with several interpolations including two Mimars [homilies] by Ephraem and an encomium to Katherine), see Atiya, *The Arabic Manuscripts,* p. 20 and 22. The skull and hand are still at the monastery today according to Nancy P. Ševčenko, 'The *vita* icon and the painter as hagiographer', *DOP,* 53 (1999), 165.

[159] André Binggeli, 'L'hagiographie du Sinaï en arabe d'après un recueil du IXe siècle', *Parole de l'Orient,* 32 (2007), 163–80 (pp. 166–67).

Arabic manuscript, used by Peeters for his edition of the Arabic version of Katherine's passion (BHO 26). Unfortunately, Peeters did not provide the call-mark or date of the manuscript in question, although he indicated that it was probably written c. 1750.[160] As in the case of the Georgian manuscripts, the Arabic is a translation from the Greek, BHG 30a.[161] Well before the monastery of the Theotokos changed its name to reflect the growing importance of Katherine, the manuscripts indicate that she must have been known by the Sinai monks at least during the tenth century, if not before.[162]

---

[160] Peeters, 'Une version Arabe', 11–12. To be fair, Peeters could not have provided more information on the manuscript, since none was provided by Louis Cheikho in 'From Riaq to Hama: A modern journey for Father Louis Cheikho, Jesuit' [Min Riyāq ilā Ḥamā: Riḥla ḥadītha lil-ab Lūyis Shaykhū al-Yasū'ī], *Al-Mashriq: Révue Catholique Orientale: Sciences, Lettres, Arts* (*al-Mashriq: Majallah Kāthūlīkiyah sharqīyah tabḥathu fī al-'ilm wa-al-adab wa-al-fann*), 5 (1902), 904–09 (pp. 908–09). Cheikho described how he found numerous manuscripts in Homs such as commentaries on the Gospels, sermons, hagiographical texts, and ten illuminated pages from the Gospel of Luke. He said that he found the latter at the home of a deacon, that it was written in 1344, and that it belonged to the church of Saints Sergius and Bacchus in Bosra. Cheikho believed the hagiographical manuscript was about 150 years old. The manuscript is thus more or less contemporaneous with BAV, MS Vat. ar. 696 (92), which also contains a life of Katherine according to Peeters, 'Une version arabe', p. 12. I am grateful to Mary Youseff and Omid Ghaemmaghami for providing assistance with the Arabic.

[161] 'Variété de forme plutôt que de fond, car il ne se distingue du récit traditionnel que par des traits insignifiants et par les maladresses du traducteur', Peeters, 'Une version arabe', 5.

[162] Historical sources show that the monastery still bore the name of the Theotokos during the thirteenth century: in a letter of privilege from 12 January 1226 from Pope Honorius III to Bishop Symeon of Mount Sinai (starting 'regularem vitam eligentibus') the monastery was referred to as *ecclesiam s. Mariae montis synai*, see Georg Hofmann, 'Lettere pontificie edite ed inedite intorno ai monasteri del monte Sinai, *Orientalia Christiana Periodica*, 17 (1951), 283–303 (p. 248). A letter from 1517 and addressed by Pope Leo X to the monastery is often cited

The shortest prototype of what was to become the Synaxarion of Constantinople is preserved in fragmentary form in a ninth-century manuscript written in Greek uncial.[163] Ehrhard printed the contents as he found them in a previous description of the manuscript, and 'Aikaterine' is listed on 25 November (which corresponds to the date of her martyrdom as reported in BHG 31). While this evidence must be treated with the necessary caution because a reappraisal of the manuscript's date is needed, the inclusion of Katherine's name in a manuscript of this prototype which emerged between the middle of the seventh and the first half of the eighth centuries points to some sort of cult of the saint at least by the time the manuscript in question was copied.[164]

The fully-fledged synaxarion as it was used at Constantinople and preserved in Jerusalem, Patriarchikê bibliothêkê, MS Timiou Staurou 40 (s. x/xi) does not feature Katherine's name either on 24 or 25 of November.[165] There is, however, an earlier manuscript that does include the same text with slight variations and contains a brief summary of Katherine's passion,[166] alongside the names of Clement of Rome, Peter of

as the earliest piece of evidence for the monastery officially changing its name to that of Katherine, see Georg Hofmann, 'Sinai und Rom', *Orientalia Christiana Analecta*, 9.3, no. 37 (1927), 270: 'Gloriosae virginis Catherinae, quae fide fulta et sapientia ornata doctores gentilium doctissimis argumentis confu[n]dens terra'.

[163] Ehrhard, 1.28–29 and 33: Athos, Skêtê Hagiou Andreou, MS 2.
[164] Ibid., 1.33.
[165] Juan Mateos, *Le Typicon de la Grande Eglise: Ms. Sainte-Croix n. 40, xe siècle*, vol. 1: *Le cycle des douze mois* (Rome, 1962), p. ix. See also Andrea Luzzi, *Studi sul Sinassario di Constantinopoli* (Rome, 1995).
[166] The contents of this typikon have been edited by Aleksej Dmitrievskij, *Opisanie liturgitsekich rukopisej*, 3 vols (Hildesheim, 1965, reprint of Kiev 1895 edition), I, pp. 1–152, Katherine on p. 26: 'Καὶ τῆς ἁγίας μάρτυρος Αἰκατερίνης. Αὕτη ὑπῆρχεν τῆς μεγαλωνύμου πόλεως Ἀλεξανδρείας θρέμμα, θυγάτηρ βασιλίσκου τινὸς, ὀνόματι Κόστου, πάνυ οὖσα ὡραία καὶ τῷ κάλλει ἀμώμητος, καὶ ὑπερμεγέθης τῇ ἡλικίᾳ, καὶ ὅλῳ τῷ σώματι ἀστεία, καὶ χριστιανὴ πιστοτάτη ἐπὶ τῆς

Alexandria, and Mercurius under 25 November. This is Patmos, MS 266 (s. xi/xii), which provides a snapshot of the sanctoral going back to around 900 CE and preserves 'un Tipico-Sinassario' used at Patmos, and might have been written out by a scribe somewhere in Palestine.[167] This synaxarion is essentially Constantinopolitan but has been adapted for usage at a monastery outside the capital. On the basis of the possible provenance it is tempting to stipulate that the Palestinian scribe had inserted Katherine into the synaxarion of this typikon because he had encountered her cult in that region. The presence of Vergil in the list of authors that Katherine rattles off is suggestive of knowledge of BHG 30a.[168]

> βασιλείας Μαξεντίου τοῦ τυράννου. Αὔτη πᾶσαν παιδείαν ἑλληνικὴν καὶ ῥωμαϊκὴν ἀκριβῶς ἐγγυμνασθεῖσα, φημὶ δὴ Ὁμήρου σοφοῦ καὶ Βηργιλίου τοῦ Ῥωμαίων μεγίστου ποιητοῦ, Ἀσκληπιοῦ τε καὶ Γαληνοῦ τῶν ἰατρῶν, Ἀριστοτέλους καὶ Πλάτωνος, Φιλιστίωνος καὶ εὐσεβίων φιλοσόφων, Ἰαννῆ καὶ Ἰαμβρῆ τῶν μάγων, Διονυσίου καὶ Συβίλλης, καὶ ὅσοι ῥητορικοὶ ἐφευρέθησαν τῷ κόσμῳ οὐ μὴν, ἀλλὰ καὶ πᾶσαν γλῶσσαν τῶν οβ´ἐθνῶν τὴν διάλεκτον μαθοῦσα, εἰς ἔκπληξιν ἔφερεν οὐ μόνον τοὺς ὁρῶντας αὐτὴν, ἀλλὰ καὶ τοὺς ἀκούοντας τὴν φήμην τῆς παιδείας καὶ τῆς σοφίας αὐτῆς'. This summary, primarily of the authors Katherine knew, could have been drawn either from BHG 30a or BHG 30; the order of the authors as listed here is not quite the same as that in the martyrdom text. The mention of Vergil suggests an affinity with BHG 30a where he is explicitly referenced as a writer in the list of authors (see Viteau, p. 26, § 4). Vergil does not figure in the author-list in BHG 30. There is no list of authors in BHG 31 or BHG 32.

[167] Luzzi, *Studi*, p. 5 and Id., 'Il Patmiacus 266: un testimone dell' utilizzo liturgico delle epitome premetafrastiche', *Rivista di studi bizantini e neoellenici*, 49 (2012), 239–61 (p. 243 and p. 260). The monastery of St John the Theologian at Patmos was founded by Christodoulos (who had also been a monk at Latros near Miletus from 1076–79) on the Palestinian model in *c*. 1088. It saw its heyday during the twelfth century, when it also had its own scriptorium. *ODB*, s. vv. Patmos, Christodoulos of Patmos.

[168] Another earlyish manuscript of the Constantinopolitan synaxarion, Paris, BnF, MS gr. 1590, 1062/3 CE, includes a short paragraph on Katherine's exploits, with an emphasis on her knowledge of Greek

The *Menologion of Basil,* so-called because it was created for the Emperor Basil II (976-1025), is a version of the Synaxarion of Constantinople.[169] It survives in a number of manuscripts: 'three of these date from the eleventh century and have been adorned with miniatures; the rest date from the twelfth to fourteenth centuries, or from the late sixteenth century, and are without miniatures'.[170] BAV, MS Vat. gr. 1613 is one of the best kown examples of this menologion, written out perhaps as early as after 979 and possibly in *c.* 1005. This manuscript consists of 272 folios and contains 430 saints' lives (fifteen miniatures lack text, and two miniatures lack both text and title), and covers the first six months of the ecclesiastical year, from September to February.[171] The layout and decoration of this manuscript is almost without equal: the 'absolute balance ... between text and image is unparalleled in any other calendar cycle: each occupies half a page, and just as each miniature, regardless of content, has been composed to fit

authors and Vergil. The detail of the debate with the rhetors and their death has been left out. This manuscript contains a synaxarion for the months from September to February (the month of November is represented on folios 54–102) and belongs to the F family. Some of the members of this group of manuscripts originate from Palestine or Cyprus, and some from southern Italy. This particular manuscript is either from Cyprus or from Palestine. See Costas N. Constantinides and Robert Browning, *Dated Greek Manuscripts from Cyprus to the Year 1570* (Washington, DC, 1993), p. 49 with plates 1 and 171a.

[169] BAV, MS Vat. gr. 1613. The entire manuscript is available as a facsimile: *Il menologio di Basilio II (cod. vaticano greco 1613)* (Turin, 1907), vol. 1 (testo) + vol. 2 (tavole). For the date: 'The miniatures are often signed by their painters of whom one, Pantoleon, could be the same painter attested elsewhere. This would make the Menologion contemporary with the Psalter of Basil II (Venice, Biblioteca Nazionale Marciana, MS gr. 17, dated to *c.* 1005)'. *ODB,* s.v. Menologion of Basil II.

[170] Nancy P. Ševčenko, 'The imperial menologia and the "Menologion" of Basil II', in *The Celebration of the Saints in Byzantine Art and Liturgy,* ed. ead. (Farnham, 2013), pp. 1–32 (p. 4).

[171] Ihor Ševčenko, 'The illuminators of the menologium of Basil II', *DOP,* 16 (1962), 243 + 245–276 (p. 245).

a prescribed space, so each Synaxarion text has been modified so as to take up exactly sixteen lines'.[172] The texts used were shortened in order to fit them on the page, so that the omission of certain episodes was necessitated by the lack of space. In contrast to Patmos, MS 266, but just as Paris, BnF, MS gr. 1590, this manuscript provides not only Katherine's name on 25 November, but also some details on her martyrdom. The short paragraph mentions her beauty and erudition, and that she argued with the emperor when she noticed animal sacrifices were being conducted. The fifty rhetors are included, as well as the emperor's command for them to debate with Katherine or be burned. The paragraph ends with their baptism and death, and Katherine's beheading. All other details have been left out.[173]

To summarize the findings of this chapter: Grosdidier's study of the hymn 'χορείαν σεπτὴν', dated to the first half of the ninth century, is suggestive of the existence of a Greek version before the end of the eighth century; in all likelihood this was version BHG 30a. If the hymnographer Babylas was indeed a monk at Mar Saba in the seventh century, then his hymn on Katherine would be the earliest piece of written

[172] *ODB,* s.v. Menologion of Basil II.
[173] Transcribed from BAV, MS Vat. gr. 1613, p. 207: 'τῇ αὐτῇ ἡμέρα ἄθλησις τῆς ἁγίας μεγαλομάρτυρος Ἀικατερίνης. ἡ μάρτυς Ἀικατερίνα ἐγένετο ἀπὸ Ἀλεξανδρείας· θυγάτηρ βασιλίσκου τινός· πλουσίου καὶ ἐνδόξου· εὔμορφος πάνυ· εὐφυὴς δὲ ὑπάρχουσα, ἔμαθεν ἑλληνικὰ γράμματα, καὶ ἐγένετο σοφή. λαλοῦσα καὶ γλώσσας, πάντων τῶν ἐθνῶν· ἐπετελεῖ τὸ δὲ ἑορτὴ τοῖς εἰδώλοις, παρὰ τῶν ἑλλήνων· καὶ θεωροῦσα τὰ ζῶα ἀφαξόμενα, ἐλυπήθη· καὶ ἀπῆλθεν εἰς τὸν βασιλέα Μαξεντίου, καὶ ἐφιλονείκησεν αὐτόν· εἰποῦσα ὅτι διὰ τι ἐγκατέλιπες Θ(εὸ)ν ζῶντα, καὶ προσκυνεῖς εἰδώλοις ἀψύχοις· ἐκεῖνος δὲ ἐκράτησεν αὐτήν, καὶ ἐτιμωρήσατο ἰσχυρῶς· καὶ μετὰ τοῦτο, ἔφερεν ὁ βασιλεὺς πεντήκοντα ῥήτορας καὶ εἶπεν αὐτοῖς· ὅτι διαλέχθητε πρὸς τὴν ἁγίαν Κατερίνα(ν) καὶ πείσατε αὐτήν· ἐὰν γὰρ μὴ νικήσατε αὐτήν, πάντας ὑμᾶς κατακαύσω πυρί· ἐκεῖνοι δὲ ἰδόντες ὅτι ἐνικήθησα(ν) ἐβαπτίσθησαν καὶ οὕτως ἐκάησαν. ἀπεκεφαλίσθη δὲ κ(αὶ) αὐτή.'

evidence I am aware of for the existence of her story or cult but, unfortunately, the evidence for this is somewhat tenuous. In addition, the inclusion of Katherine's name in a manuscript of the prototype for the Synaxarion of Constantinople, which emerged between the middle of the seventh and the first half of the eighth centuries, points to some sort of cult of the saint at least by the time the manuscript in question was copied.

By the end of the ninth/beginning of the tenth century, Anastasius the Stammerer has produced an encomium in her honour. Meanwhile, a tiny shift in Katherine's final prayer between BHG 30a and BHG 30 is perhaps an indication that people were beginning to celebrate her feast-day. In BHG 31 and 32 her role as intercessor is fully fledged. Indeed, that at least religious women carried her name is evidenced by the existence of an abbess of the Loukas monastery in Thessalonike who went by the name of Αἰκατερίνα in the first half of the ninth century.[174]

Once the tenth century is in full swing, the evidence for a more widely spread and established cult of Katherine, though not anchored to a specific site, is plentiful, and particularly strong for the eastern part of the Empire. Paul the Younger, a monk at the monastic centre of Latros near Miletus where he died in December 955, had a soft spot for the saint according to his life,[175] which was written around twenty years after his death.[176] Its author thus knew of Katherine in 975, and it is

---

[174] *PMBZ Online*, #148.

[175] 'Καὶ τῶν ἄλλων μὲν ἁγίων αἱ μνῆμαι εὐφροσύνης ἀφορμαὶ τῷ Παύλῳ· ἡ δὲ τῆς μάρτυρος Αἰκατερίνης οὐχ ἡδονῆς μόνον ἐπλήρου τὸν ὅσιον, ἀλλὰ μικροῦ καὶ σκιρτήματος· ἐπεὶ καὶ ἑώρταζε ταύτην οὐ σωματικῶς ἁπλῶς, ἀλλὰ παρακιρνῶν αὐτῇ καὶ πνευματικὴν ἀγαλλίασιν, μᾶλλον δὲ τὸ πλεῖον διδοὺς τῷ πνεύματι. Hippolyte Delehaye, 'Vita S. Pauli Iunioris in monte Latro', *AB*, 11 (1892), 5–74 & 136–82, ch. 39. *PMBZ Online*, #26337.

[176] The earliest manuscripts date from the eleventh century, see Hippolyte Delehaye, 'La vie de Saint Paul le Jeune et la chronologie de Métaphraste', in *Revue des Questions Historiques*, 54 (1893), 49–85 (p.

likely that Paul did too. His life contains many references to contemporary events that can be cross-checked with parallel documents.[177] In the *Souda*, the name Αἰκατερίνα is listed as an ὄνομα κύριον, thus indicating popular currency of the name in around 1000, when this lexicon was compiled.[178]

By the end of the tenth century, the passion has been translated into Georgian and Arabic, and into Latin (see the next chapter), attesting to the growing appeal of this saint and her story. In the case of the Georgian and Arabic translations the text used by the translators was always BHG 30 (whether 30a or 30 is still uncertain) which clearly illustrates the success of this version, and can also be taken as evidence for the later emergence of BHG 31. The inclusion of Katherine's name in some of the early manuscripts of the Synaxarion of Constantinople, albeit with uncertainty over the date, also indicates that her cult was gaining traction at this point. Some of these manuscripts, with potential connections to or origins in Palestine, put her feast day on 24 November, as recorded in BHG 30a and BHG 30.

Frustratingly, the passion lacks any details that would allow it to be placed in a particular time period or geographical context, nor does it contain enough evidence to suggest it was written as an iconoclast text. Since it does not read as a pro- or anti-iconoclastic work, it perhaps predates this mostly Constantinopolitan phenomenon, which took place in two phases (730-87 and 815-43). It also does not seem to bear the obvious stamp of the experience of a particular religious community or region. While one might be able to point to the

---

54). For the manuscripts, see Delehaye, 'Vita S. Pauli Iunioris', 8–10: Paris, BnF, MS gr. 1490; Paris, BnF, MS suppl. gr. 916; Paris, BnF, MS Coisl. 148.

[177] Delehaye, 'La vie de Saint Paul', 57.

[178] Ada Adler, *Suidae Lexicon*, 5 vols (Leipzig, 1928–38), alphaiota 163. The *Souda* is a lexicon compiled from other lexica and contains mostly ancient or biblical material. *ODB*, s.v. *Souda*.

difficulties of Christian and monastic communities in Palestine/Syria during the fifth and sixth centuries and link Katherine's story to their experiences and need for models of resistance, this is no more than tenuous or wishful thinking.[179] I see potential avenues for further investigation into the origin of BHG 30a by deepening an analysis of the nonsensical speeches and the sources used, as well as the overlaps with the lives of Pansophios and Artemios.

Figure 1: St Catherine's monastery, lithograph from 1830: 'Vue du couvent de Sainte-Catherine, prise du nord (Mont Sinaï) (1830)', General Research Division, The New York Public Library, *New York Public Library Digital Collections*.
<https://digitalcollections.nypl.org/items/510d47d9-61ef-a3d9-e040-e00a1 8064a99> [accessed 7 July 2021]

---

[179] The absence of Katherine in the Syriac synaxaria could pose a problem to this conclusion.

Figure 2: St Catherine's monastery, photography from 1862-1863: 'The Convent of Sinai, at the foot of Mount Horeb (1862-1863)', The Miriam and Ira D. Wallach Division of Art, Prints and Photographs: Photography Collection, The New York Public Library, *New York Public Library Digital Collections.*
<https://digitalcollections.nypl.org/items/510d47d9-6132-a3d9-e040-e00a18064a99> [accessed 7 July 2021]

CHAPTER 3

THE STORY OF KATHERINE MOVES WEST

An intriguing and rather early appearance of Katherine's name in a manuscript produced outside the Greek-speaking world has given rise to some speculation as to when her passion might have been composed originally. The manuscript in question is Munich, BSB, Clm 4554, containing one of the earliest collections of saints' lives known in the Latin West.[1] Both Elias Lowe and Bernhard Bischoff have provided a precise date and provenance for Clm 4554, assigning it to the end of the eighth and the first quarter of the ninth century (i.e. around 800 + 800-825).[2] Bischoff identified the three hands of the manuscript as belonging to the scriptorium at Benedikt-

---

[1] Albert Siegmund, *Die Überlieferung der griechischen christlichen Literatur in der lateinischen Kirche bis zum zwölften Jahrhundert* (München–Pasing, 1949), p. 206. Guy Philippart, *Les légendiers latins et autres manuscrits hagiographiques* (Turnhout, 1977), pp. 31–32. Hippolyte Delehaye, 'Martyrs d'Egypte', *AB*, 40 (1922), 124–27.

[2] Elias A. Lowe, *Codices latini antiquiores: A Palaeographical Guide to Latin Manuscripts prior to the Ninth Century*, vol. 9: *Germany, München – Zittau* (Oxford, 1959), no. 1242. Bernhard Bischoff, *Die südostdeutschen Schreibschulen und Bibliotheken in der Karolingerzeit*, vol. 1: *Die bayrischen Diözesen*, 2nd edn (Wiesbaden, 1960), p. 22. On page 27 (n. 3), Bischoff referred to the index as 'ein Inhaltsverzeichnis ... das an hagiographischen Seltenheiten kaum seinesgleichen haben dürfte'. The dating is the same in Bernhard Bischoff, *Katalog der festländischen Handschriften des neunten Jahrhunderts (mit Ausnahme der wisigotischen)*, ed. Birgit Ebersperger (Wiesbaden, 2004), vol. 2, no. 2970.

beuern, thus making it one of the oldest surviving manuscripts produced in that monastery.³

The index of this collection, written in the first hand, contains more than ninety saints' names. Only about one third of these saints is represented with an actual text in the codex. Katherine is one of the saints for whom there is no text; her name appears in the index in its Greek form ('lxxxi Passio ecatarine virginis dei', fol. 1v). Most of the saints who are assigned a text occur at the beginning of the index, although a handful, whose names occur much further down, also have a text to their name. These omissions are the result of incomplete copying, rather than a loss of folios. In fact, Maximilian Diesenberger has argued recently that the initial and very ambitious plan for this large-scale collection, based on saints from the Mediterranean (North Africa, Asia Minor, Greece, Italy, southern France) and thus gesturing towards Benediktbeuern's contacts with Italy, was changed to reflect political realities. Following Charlemagne's gains in Bavaria, the scriptorium adapted to the monastery's new possessions within this changed landscape: different scribes in the first quarter of the ninth century oriented themselves more towards Frankish saints and finally also some local ones and thus abandoned the original plan.⁴

---

3   Bischoff, *Schreibschulen*, I, p. 23. Bierbrauer labelled the script 'a pre-carolingian minuscule of several hands (fols 1–159), Carolingian minuscule of several hands (fols 160–164)'. The manuscript was written, following Bischoff, in three separate stages (fols 1r–96r, 96v–159v, 160r–164v). See Katharina Bierbrauer, *Die vorkarolingischen und karolingischen Handschriften der Bayerischen Staatsbibliothek*, Textband (Wiesbaden, 1990), no. 85 p. 49. See also Günter Glauche, *Katalog der lateinischen Handschriften der Bayerischen Staatsbibliothek München: Die Pergamenthandschriften aus Benediktbeuern: Clm 4501–4663* (Wiesbaden, 1994), p. 80.

4   Maximilian Diesenberger, '*Le manuscrit Bayerische Staatsbibliothek CLM 4554, témoin de lectures*', in *Les manuscrits médiévaux: Témoins de lectures*, ed. Catherine Croizy-Naquet *et al.* (Paris 2015), pp. 89–106 (pp. 103–04).

Delehaye supposed that Clm 4554 derives from a Greek menologion where the saints were arranged in calendrical order but, following François Dolbeau and a close examination of the index, it is clear that the saints are instead arranged in an hierarchical order starting with the apostles, popes, bishops, priests, and followed by martyrs.[5] At the same time, it is more likely that the collection compiles various translations made in Rome or southern Italy of scattered Greek passions, rather than translating an earlier menologion, since no equivalent Greek collection has yet emerged.[6] As Clare Pilsworth has pointed out, all of the surviving early Latin legendaries, the earliest of which date from the mid-eighth century, are Frankish in origin. Using Italian martyrs as the focus of her essay, Pilsworth demonstrated that the narratives of the saints often travelled across the Alps in 'small scale "booklet" style manuscripts'.[7]

Clm 4554 is evidence for links between Bavaria and Italy at the end of the eighth century, demonstrating how eastern or Mediterranean saints might be transmitted into northern Europe.[8] In the words of Sven Meeder, 'Carolingian northern Italy ... undoubtedly worked as the region of connection

---

[5] Delehaye, 'Martyrs d'Egypte', 125. François Dolbeau, 'Fragments de manuscrits provenant de Saint-Rambert-en-Bugey', *Scriptorium*, 54 (2000), 317. Id., 'Notes sur l'organisation interne des légendiers latins', in *Hagiographie, cultures et sociétés (IVe – XIIe siècles)*, actes du colloque organisé à Nanterre et à Paris (2–5 mai 1979) (Paris, 1981), pp. 11–31 (p. 17).

[6] Philippart and Trigalet, 'Latin hagiography', pp. 125–26.

[7] Clare Pilsworth, 'Vile Scraps: "Booklet" style manuscripts and the transmission and use of the Italian martyr narratives in early medieval Europe', in *Zwischen Niederschrift und Wiederschrift: Hagiographische und historiographische Texte im Spannungsfeld von Kompendienüberlieferung und Editionstechnik*, ed. Richard Corrardini *et al.* (Vienna, 2010), pp. 175–96.

[8] The manuscript contains about fifteen passions of saints from Egypt, see Delehaye, 'Martyrs d'Egypte', 123–24.

between the territories north of the Alps and southern Italy. Through the learned centres there, notably Nonantola and Verona, Monte Cassino's network stretched to the intellectual powerhouses around Lake Constance (Reichenau and St-Gall) and further into eastern Francia'.[9] The transalpine route from Italy to Bavaria involved crossing either the Brenner or the Great St Bernard Pass. These passes were heavily used over millennia by merchants, armies, pilgrims, and even relics.[10] The Brenner Pass in particular was a good option since, owing to its lower elevation, it could be crossed in the winter if necessary.[11] The connection between Benediktbeuern (founded in 739) and Italy is also reflected in Ambrose Autpert's (d. 784) dedication of one of his works, the *Conflictus vitiorum et virtutum*, to Landfrid, its first abbot. Finally, some northern Italian influence can also be seen in some of the earliest manuscripts from St. Emmeram in Regensburg, another early Benedictine monastery about 170 km north of Benediktbeuern.[12]

---

[9] Sven Meeder, 'Monte Cassino's network of knowledge: The earliest manuscript evidence', in *Writing the Early Medieval West: Studies in Honour of Rosamond McKitterick*, ed. Elina Screen and Charles West (Cambridge, 2018), pp. 131–45 (p. 145).

[10] *Über die Alpen: Menschen, Wege, Waren*, ed. Gudrun Schnekenburger (Stuttgart, 2002). Veronica Ortenberg, 'Archbishop Sigeric's journey to Rome in 990', *Anglo-Saxon England*, 19 (1990), 197–246. Julia M.H. Smith, 'Old saints, new cults: Roman relics in Carolingian Francia', in *Early Medieval Rome and the Christian West: Essays in Honour of Donald A. Bullough*, ed. Julia M.H. Smith (Leiden, 2000), pp. 317–39. Irmtraut Heitmeier, 'Zur Kontinuität der Raumorganisation in Nordtirol von der Spätantike bis ins hohe Mittelalter', in *König, Kirche, Adel: Herrschaftsstrukturen im mittleren Alpenraum*, ed. Rainer Loose and Sönke Lorenz (Lana, 1999), pp. 267–89.

[11] John E. Tyler, *The Alpine Passes: The Middle Ages (962–1250)* (Oxford, 1930), p. 43.

[12] See Bischoff, *Schreibschulen*, I, p. 173 (perhaps Verona?) and pp. 188–9, and Bischoff, 'Italienische Handschriften des neunten bis elften Jahrhunderts in frühmittelalterlichen Bibliotheken außerhalb Italiens',

Which version of Katherine's passion might have been included in this manuscript? Given that the index likely was copied in about 800, the absent text cannot have been BHL 1659, as suggested by Friedrich Wilhelm, who pointed out that there is a manuscript, now at Augsburg (Universitätsbibliothek, MS I.2.4° 16), which shares a number of saints' lives with Clm 4554.[13] The Augsburg manuscript dates from the last quarter of the twelfth century, and was probably written in Tegernsee.[14] It is a witness to BHL 1659, the Katherine passion attributed to Peter, Subdeacon of Naples, who was active in the second half of the tenth century.[15] The Bollandists stated, without explaining why, that the Katherine passion referred to in the index of Munich, BSB, Clm 4554 was BHL 1657 (printed *c.* 1480 by Mombrizio).[16] The simple and frustrating answer is that it is impossible to know, at this stage, which passion prompted the indexer of Clm 4554 to enter Katherine's name into the index.

The presence of Katherine's name in the index of Munich, BSB, Clm 4554 means that, by the turn of the eighth century at the latest, a text of her passion must have made its way

---

in *Il libro e il testo: Atti del convegno internazionale*, ed. Cesare Questa and Renato Raffaeli (Urbino, 1984), pp. 169–94.

[13] Friedrich Wilhelm, 'Lateinische Akten des hl. Psotius', *Münchener Museum für Philologie des Mittelalters und der Renaissance*, 1 (1911), 193. At the time, the manuscript in question was still at the Bibliothek Fürst von Oettingen-Wallerstein in Maihingen, MS. H.B.I.2. (lat.) 4° 16.

[14] See Hardo Hilg, *Die Handschriften der Universitätsbibliothek Augsburg: Die lateinischen mittelalterlichen Handschriften Cod.I.2.4° und Cod. II.1.4°* (Wiesbaden, 2007), pp. 70–71.

[15] D'Angelo, *Pietro Suddiacono napoletano: L'opera agiografica*. Peter used BHG 30, as well as a derivative of BHG 30a, see Bronzini, 342.

[16] *Propylaeum ad acta sanctorum decembris: Martyrologium romanum*, ed. Hippolyte Delehaye *et al.* (Brussels, 1940), p. 544: 'sed libellus sic in elencho designatus alius esse non potest atque passio BHL 1657'. Mombrizio, *Sanctuarium*, vol. 1, pp. 283–87.

north of the Alps.¹⁷ Thus the original must have been in circulation at least by the end of the eighth century, if not several decades before. This projects backwards the potential date of composition for the Greek passion to well before 800, chiming with the humble monk's hymn and the admittedly rather tenuous evidence from the otherwise unknown hymnographers Anatolios and Babylas discussed in Chapter 2. This tiny scrap of evidence also serves as a salutary reminder that the vagaries of transmission can skew both the evidence and its interpretation – the mention of Katherine in Clm 4554 antedates almost all textual and iconographic sources for her cult that are known to exist.¹⁸

1. Southern Italy

If Katherine's passion had made its way to the south of Italy by about 800, how might it have arrived there, and when? Greek-speaking monastics had been travelling through – and then also emigrating and fleeing from – Syria, Palestine, Egypt via North Africa to Italy over centuries in order to escape violence generated by incursions of Arab raiders into the Byzantine territories and the persecutions as a result of Iconoclasm. From North Africa, these monastics journeyed to

---

[17] There is no compelling reason to suppose with Bronzini (229), that the exemplar of Clm 4554 was translated into Latin in Carolingian Gaul.

[18] A fragment apparently containing a Latin passion of Katherine from the second quarter of the ninth century turns out to be part of a passion of Euphemia of Chalcedon instead. Holter had labelled it as *Vita S. Katharinae* but its contents, which include a reference to animals ('bestiae autem ut viderunt eam ceciderunt'), clearly show this not to be part of Katherine's story. See Kurt Holter, 'Zu einem Verzeichnis der frühmittelalterlichen Handschriften', in *Karolingische und ottonische Kunst: Werden, Wesen, Wirkung*, ed. Hermann Schnitzler (Wiesbaden, 1957), pp. 434–42 (pp. 440–41, plate 185). Maximilian Diesenberger included an edition of Euphemia's passion in his *Predigt und Politik im frühmittelalterlichen Bayern: Arn von Salzburg, Karl der Große und die Salzburger Sermones-Sammlung* (Berlin, 2016), pp. 436–38.

Sicily and Calabria, and from there to Campania and Latium. For example, in 645, a group of monks from Mar Saba founded a monastery in Rome on the Aventine.[19] Other connections between Rome and the eastern part of the Byzantine realm are exemplified by a number of popes of Syrian and Palestinian origin during the seventh and eighth centuries.[20] Many of the resulting and long-standing Greek-Christian communities in Italy continued to exist into the twelfth century and beyond and produced materials for their own worship.[21] These communities also maintained contacts with a variety of religious centres. As Paul Oldfield has shown, 'the key nodes within this network were Rome, Constantinople, Jerusalem, Athos, Sinai, and southern Italy itself, particularly … the … monastery of Montecassino. This movement established a climate of exchange and respect, most visibly between eastern and western monastic traditions'.[22]

---

[19] Jean-Marie Sansterre, *Les moines grecs et orientaux à Rome aux époques byzantine et carolingienne (milieu du VIe s. – fin du IXe s.* (Brussels, 1983), pp. 22–29, 149. Richard Krautheimer, *Rome: Profile of a City, 312–1308* (Princeton, 1996), p. 104.

[20] Andrew J. Ekonomou, *Byzantine Rome and the Greek Popes: Eastern Influences on Rome and the Papacy from Gregory the Great to Zacharias, A.D. 590–752* (Lanham, MD, 2007), with reviews *passim*. Other travellers from east to west include Sophronios, patriarch of Jerusalem (634–38), who is known to have journeyed widely in Egypt, Palestine, and even Rome, *ODB*, s.v. Sophronios. Theodore of Tarsus arrived in Canterbury in 669 via Constantinople and Rome. For an overview of Theodore's life and achievements, see *Archbishop Theodore: Commemorative Studies on his Life and Influence*, ed. Michael Lapidge (Cambridge, 1995).

[21] For a brief and useful overview of Greek monasticism in southern Italy see Vera von Falkenhausen, 'Greek monasticism in Campania and Latium from the tenth to the fifteenth century', in *Greek Monasticism in Southern Italy: The Life of Neilos in Context*, ed. Barbara Crostini and Ines Angeli Murzaku (New York, 2018), pp. 78–95.

[22] Paul Oldfield, *Sanctity and Pilgrimage in Medieval Southern Italy, 1000–1200* (Cambridge, 2017), p. 110.

These exchanges included the transmission of hagiographical texts from east to west (and from west to east).[23] Eastern saints who were venerated here include traditional saints, such as apostles, martyrs, and confessors. That they were venerated in southern Italy 'earlier and with deeper resonance than elsewhere in western Europe'[24] is perhaps not surprising if one considers the deep connections between the Greek Christian communities in southern Italy and those in the eastern part of the Empire. The Typikon of Constantinople was in use here too, but was augmented with local saints. The 'peculiar landscape of parts of southern Italy'[25] was perhaps not exactly reminiscent of the desert spaces in Palestine or Egypt, but it did offer similar opportunities for saints to seclude themselves from the world in caves and grottos, just as the early ascetics had done in Late Antiquity. These local Greek southern-Italian saints included Nicholas the Pilgrim of Trani,[26] Neilos of Rossano, and Bartholomew of Simeri. Non-local saints with a strong southern-Italian cult include, famously, Nicholas of Bari and, much earlier, Restituta.[27]

[23] Enrica Follieri, 'I rapporti fra Bisanzio e l'Occidente nel campo dell'agiografia', *Proceedings of the 13th International Congress of Byzantine Studies (Oxford, 5–10 September 1966)*, ed. Joan M. Hussey *et al.* (London, 1967), pp. 355–62. On the transmission and translation of hagiographical texts from Latin into Greek see Xavier Lequeux, 'Latin hagiographical literature translated into Greek', in *The Ashgate Research Companion to Byzantine Hagiography*, vol. 1: *Periods and Places*, ed. Stephanos Efthymiadis (London, 2016), pp. 385–99.

[24] Oldfield, *Sanctity and Pilgrimage*, p. 115.

[25] Ibid., p. 124.

[26] Stephanos Efthymiadis, 'D'Orient en Occident mais étranger aux deux mondes: Messages et renseignements tirés de la vie de Saint Nicolas le Pèlerin (*BHL* 6223)', in *Puer Apuliae: Mélanges offerts à Jean Marie Martin*, ed. Errico Cuozzo *et al.* (Paris, 2008), vol. 1, pp. 207–23.

[27] Holger A. Klein, 'Eastern objects and western desires: Relics and reliquaries between Byzantium and the West', *DOP*, 58 (2004), 283–314. Stacey Graham, 'The dissemination of North African Christian

Oldfield has described how this kind of transmission might have taken place by using the example of Peter the Deacon (1107-1159), who, in the *Acta S. Placidi* 'concocted a backstory to explain the manuscript transmission of this text', which Peter had actually written himself.[28] When a 110-year old man by the name of Simeon brings Placidus' passion to the monastery of St Laurentius in Salerno, a dependency of Monte Cassino, in 1115, he explains that it had been written in Constantinople by Gordianus, Placidus' alleged companion after the former had escaped the massacre in which Placidus was killed. Supposedly, Simeon's ancestors had taken in this Gordianus who, at the request of the emperor Justinian, wrote the account in Greek.[29] Gordianus left the account with Simeon's family and returned to Sicily. Fast forward to the beginning of the twelfth century: Simeon decides to visit Sicily and the place where Placidus was martyred, and then travels on to Salerno, bringing with him the Greek passion. He swears on the Cross that his account of how he got into possession of the text is true and is urged to translate the text into Latin. Simeon hopes that John, the suspicious prior of St Laurentius,

and intellectual culture in Late Antiquity' (unpublished doctoral dissertation, University of California, Los Angeles, 2005).

[28] Oldfield, *Sanctity and Pilgrimage*, p. 109: 'While the subjects are fictional, the framework within which Peter the Deacon placed them undoubtedly represents a familiar pattern of textual transmission'. See also Erich Caspar, *Petrus Diaconus und die Monte Cassineser Fälschungen: Ein Beitrag zur Geschichte des italienischen Geisteslebens im Mittelalter* (Berlin, 1909), pp. 47–72.

[29] 'Ibique iussu Iustiniani imperatoris enucleatius vitam atque miracula, necnon Passionem beatissimi martyris Placidi et Sociorum eius notificare, atque ad posteritatis memoriam Graecis litteris, quibus apprime imbutus fuerat, latius annotare curavit', in *AASS* Oct. III, *Acta SS. Placidi et Fratrum*, p. 138B.

will take the text to Monte Cassino, where it finally arrives after 1137.³⁰

Many of the Greek hagiographical accounts that reached southern Italy were translated into Latin so that the non-Greek speaking community could participate in the liturgical celebration of a given saint.³¹ Thus, the aim in translating these saints' lives from one language to another was first and foremost to make these texts accessible. During the ninth and tenth centuries, translators and their readers could be found in papal Rome, in the southern Duchies, particularly Naples and also Monte Cassino, as well as at the Carolingian royal court.³²

2. Calendars and other evidence from Italy

That the cult of Katherine only reached Italy during the ninth or tenth century is corroborated by martyrologies and calen-

---

30 Herbert Bloch, 'Peter the Deacon's vision of Byzantium and a rediscovered treatise in his "Acta S. Placidi"', in *Settimane di Studio – Centro Italiano di Studi sull'Alto Medioevo*, 34.2 (1988), pp. 797–847 (pp. 817–18).

31 Réka E. Forrai, 'The readership of early medieval Greek-Latin translations', *Settimane di Studio – Centro Italiano di Studi sull'Alto Medioevo*, 59 (2012), 293–311.

32 Edoardo D'Angelo, 'Agiografia latina del Mezzogiorno continentale d'Italia (750–1000)', in *Hagiographies: Histoire internationale de la littérature hagiographique latine et vernaculaire en Occident des origines à 1550*, ed. Guy Philippart (Turnhout, 2006), vol. 4, pp. 41–134. Réka E. Forrai, 'Byzantine saints for Frankish warriors: Anastasius Bibliothecarius' Latin version of the passion of Saint Demetrius', in *L'héritage byzantin en Italie (VIIIᵉ–XIIᵉ siècle)*, vol. 3: *Décor monumental, objets, tradition textuelle*, ed. Sulamith Brodbeck *et al.* (Rome, 2016), pp. 185–202. Of note here is Lifschitz' suggestion that the translation, adaptation, and diffusion of Greek texts also occurred in women's communities: Felice Lifshitz, *Religious Women in Early Carolingian Francia: A Study of Manuscript Transmission and Monastic Culture* (New York, 2014), p. 195. See also Dorothy de F. Abrahamse, 'Byzantine asceticism and women's monasteries in early medieval Italy', in *Medieval Religious Women 1: Distant Echoes*, ed. John A. Nichols and Lillian T. Shank (Kalamazoo, 1984), pp. 31–49 (pp. 35–36).

dars from previous centuries. For example, the *Martyrologium hieronymianum* (fifth century, northern Italy) and the *Martyrology* attributed to Bede (d. 735) both celebrate Peter of Alexandria on 25 November but have no knowledge of Katherine.[33] In Rabanus Maurus' *Martyrology*, Katherine's name only appears in one manuscript as a marginal entry from the twelfth/thirteenth centuries.[34] The Calendar of Naples, chiseled on two marble slabs on the basis of Greek and Latin sources perhaps between 847 and 877 at Naples, similarly does not reference Katherine.[35] She is also absent from the ninth-century sanctoral from Milan, which still followed the Ambrosian rite.[36] The earliest evidence from calendars for the celebration or perhaps emerging cult of Katherine's feast in southern Italy is to be found in two tenth-century manuscripts: one from Rossano and the other from Monte Cassino.

---

[33] On the martyrology attributed to Jerome see Jacques Dubois, *Les martyrologes du Moyen Âge latin* (Turnhout, 1978), pp. 29–37. For Bede see Jacques Dubois and Geneviève Renaud, *Édition pratique des martyrologes de Bède, de l'anonyme lyonnais et de Florus* (Paris, 1976), p. 215: the only entry on 25 November is Peter of Alexandria: 'Maximini praecepto capite obtruncatur: cum quo simul et alii plures ex Aegypto episcopi'.

[34] St Gall, Stiftsbibliothek, MS 458, s. ix⁴; 'et natale Sancte Katerine virginis et martyris'. See *Martyrologium Rabani Mauri*, pp. xxxvii–xxxix.

[35] Date proposed by Domenico Mallardo, *Il calendario marmoreo di Napoli* (Rome, 1947), p. 44. Also in Nicola Cilento, 'La chiesa di Napoli nell'alto medioevo' in *Storia di Napoli*, ed. Ernesto Pontieri, vol. 2.2 (Naples, 1969), pp. 641–735. Hippolyte Delehaye, 'Hagiographie Neapolitaine', *AB,* 57 (1939), 5–64 (p. 59) proposed a date of 849–872. Both dates are essentially based on the fact that this calendar does not contain a commemoration of Bishop Athanasius I of Naples (15 March 849 – 15 July 872, translated in 877).

[36] Odilo Heiming, 'Die ältesten ungedruckten Kalender der mailändischen Kirche', in *Colligere Fragmenta: Festschrift Alban Dold zum 70. Geburtstag*, ed. Bonifatius Fischer (Beuron, 1952), pp. 214–35. Judith Frei, *Das Ambrosianische Sakramentar D 3-3 aus dem mailändischen Metropolitankapitel* (Münster, 1974).

The first manuscript is a lectionary contained in Athens, NLG, MS 74. It includes a menologion which lists four saints for 25 November: Clement of Rome, Peter of Alexandria, Mercurius, and Katherine. This group of saints is not particular to the south of Italy: early manuscripts of the Typikon of Constantinople (such as Patmos, MS 266) commemorate exactly the same saints on that date. The Greek lectionary under consideration here was in all likelihood copied between 965 and 1000, by a scribe called Leo who was a member of a Greek monastic community in southern Italy, perhaps the Patir Monastery in Rossano.[37] However, it may be more accurate to refer to it as the monastery of the Theotokos Nea Hodigitria, at least during this early period, since the name 'Patir' is tied to the monastery's re-founding at the very end of the eleventh/beginning of the twelfth century by Bartholomew of Simeri.[38] The second manuscript/calendar with evidence for Katherine was written at Monte Cassino, in Latin and in Beneventan script, c. 969-987 (Monte Cassino, MS 230).[39]

It is possible, therefore, that knowledge of Katherine reached Monte Cassino through contacts with the Greek monastic communities in the south of Italy. Neilos of Rossano, also known as Neilos the Younger (born in Rossano/Calabria, c. 910, d. 1004) lived with his brethren at the monastery of Vallelucis (Valeloukion), a dependency of Monte Cassino, following an invitation of Abbot Aligernus

---

[37] Maria Zolota, 'A study of Athens, National Library Ms. 74, with an edition of its Menologion (fols. 203–214)' (unpublished M.A. dissertation, University of London, 2000), pp. vii–viii and p. 10, cited by permission of the author and the Chair of the MA Board of Late Antique and Byzantine Studies. I am grateful to Charalambos Dendrinos for bringing this study to my attention.

[38] Cristina Torre, 'Italo-Greek monastic typika', in *Greek Monasticism in Southern Italy*, ed. Crostini and Murzaku, pp. 44–77 (p. 50).

[39] Virginia Brown, 'A new Beneventan calendar from Naples: The lost *Kalendarium Tutinianum* rediscovered', *Mediaeval Studies*, 46 (1984), 395 and 418–19.

after Saracen attacks in Calabria (*c.* 979-994) necessitated their departure.[40] Neilos, who was bilingual, celebrated the liturgy in Greek at Monte Cassino and also composed a Greek hymn in honour of Benedict at the request of the abbot.[41] Following the abbot's death and a deterioration of monastic discipline at Monte Cassino, Neilos left the monastery. Since the Greek communities of Calabria had strong contacts with the Christian East, and monks from that region regularly visited Constantinople, Jerusalem, Sinai, and Mount Athos, Neilos and his predecessors could have been a possible channel of transmission for Katherine's Greek passion to Monte Cassino, Naples, and beyond, although there are many others who undertook these journeys.[42] Indeed, two of the early southern-Italian Greek manuscripts that preserve BHG 30a originate from the circle around Rossano and Neilos (BAV, MS Vat. gr. 866 and BAV, MS Vat. gr. 1631). In addition, there is evidence that her cult was being celebrated at this important monastery before the turn of the eleventh century.[43]

---

[40] See Patricia M. McNulty and Bernard Hamilton, 'Orientale lumen et magistra latinitas: Greek influences on Western monasticism (900–1000)', in *Le Millénaire du Mont Athos, 963–1963: Études et mélanges* (Venice, 1963–64), pp. 181–216. On Neilos s.v. Neilos 1 in *LMA*.

[41] Olivier Rousseau, 'La visite de Nil de Rossano au Mont-Cassin', in *La chiesa greca in Italia dall'VIII al XVI secolo: Atti del convegno storico interecclesiale (Bari 30 apr. – 4 magg. 1969)*, 3 vols (Padua, 1973), III, pp. 1111–37; Jean-Marie Sansterre, 'Saint Nil de Rossano et le monachisme latin', *Bollettino della Badia greca di Grottaferrata*, n.s. 45, (1991), 339–86. *The Life of Saint Neilos of Rossano*, ed. and trans. Raymond L. Capra *et al.* (Cambridge, MA, 2018), ch. 73.4–74.1.

[42] McNulty and Hamilton, 'Orientale lumen', p. 182.

[43] A number of Beneventan calendars and martyrologies written at Monte Cassino towards the end of the eleventh century include Katherine's name in the original script:
(1) BAV, MS Urb. lat. 585, 1099-1105, fols 14–10v. For a plate of this manuscript see Francis Newton, *The Scriptorium and Library at Monte Cassino, 1058–1105* (Cambridge, 1999), plate 41 and description of the plate on p. 341.

During the abbacy of Desiderius (1058-1087), the monastery was the recipient of donations that increased its property holdings immeasurably and, as a result, Desiderius set out to construct new buildings. In September 1075 a number of these were consecrated, including the tower chapel of the archangel Michael.[44] The chronicle of the monastery records that some relics were sealed in the altar of that chapel, among them those of Katherine: 'Sane in altari beati archangeli Michahelis reliquias condidit sanctorum Nicandri et Marciani, Iohannis et Pauli, Viti, Mercurii et Caterine et vocabula sanctorum Apollinaris episcopi, Proti et Iacinthi'.[45] Of the nine saints named as having their relics thus fixed in place, with the exception of John and Paul, only Mercurius and Katherine are foreigners to either Monte Cassino or southern Italy.

Slightly before the above entry, the chronicler describes Desiderius' basilica of St Martin and its decorations: 'absidam autem musivo decenter vestivit. In qua etiam aureis litteris hos

(2) BAV, MS Borgia lat. 211, 1094–1005, fols 1v–13. Brown, 'A new Beneventan calendar', mentions Hartmut Hoffmann's edition 'Der Kalender des Leo Marsicanus', *Deutsches Archiv für Erforschung des Mittelalters*, 21 (1965), 99–126.
(3) Monte Cassino, MS 444, 1075–1090, pp. 1–12. See a plate of p. 228 ('Kalendarium et regula sancti Benedicti') in Newton, *The Scriptorium*, plate 36 and description of the plate on p. 340.
(4) BAV, MS Vat. lat. 4958, *c.* 1087, fols 2v–93 (*Martyrology* of Usuard with adaptations).
(5) Naples, Biblioteca Nazionale, MS VIII.C.4, s. xi^{ex}, fols 2v–90v (*Martyrology* of Usuard with adaptations). All these in Brown, 'A new Beneventan calendar', 394–95 and 396–97.

[44] See Herbert E.J. Cowdrey, *The Age of Abbot Desiderius: Montecassino, the Papacy, and the Normans in the Eleventh and Early Twelfth Centuries* (Oxford, 1983), pp. 12–17. Drawings of the reconstructed late eleventh-century monastic complex of Monte Cassino can be found in Henry M. Willard and Kenneth J. Conant, 'A project for the graphic reconstruction of the Romanesque abbey at Monte Cassino', *Speculum*, 10 (1935), pp. 144–46, plate 1; and Newton, *The Scriptorium*, p. 14.

[45] *Chronica Monasterii Casinensis*, ed. Hartmut Hoffmann, MGH SS 34 (Hannover, 1980), 3.34 (p. 410).

versus describi praecepit: cultibus extiterat quondam locus iste dicatus'.[46] It is generally accepted that the poem referred to here was composed by Alfanus, archbishop of Salerno (1058-1085).[47] Alfanus and Desiderius had met in 1055, when Alfanus seems to have joined the monks at Monte Cassino, and the two men remained friends until his death in 1085.[48] Alfanus, whose writings include a passion of Christina (BHL 1759) as well as a number of medical texts, has also been identified as the author of three hymns in honour of Katherine. They were published in the sixteenth century by Tito Martinengo (d. 1594), a Casinese monk from Bressanone, as part of a larger group of poems on the basis of a manuscript from Monte Cassino, now lost.[49] None of the poems published by Martinengo are transmitted in Monte Cassino, MS 280, a manuscript that transmits the collected

---

[46] Ibid., 3.34 (p. 409).

[47] *I carmi di Alfano I, arcivescovo di Salerno*, ed. Anselmo Lentini and Faustino Avagliano (Monte Cassino, 1974), pp. 37–38. Alfanus was present at the basilica's consecration by Pope Alexander II, see *Chronica Monasterii Casinensis* 3.29 (p. 398). A full list of his works can be found in *Compendium auctorum latinorum medii aevi*, ed. Michael Lapidge *et al.* (Florence, 2000), I.1, pp. 179–80. For biographical details see *LexMA*, s.v. 2 Alfanus; and Pietro Caiazza, 'Aspetti e problemi dell'opera di Alfano I, arcivescovo salernitano', *Benedictina*, 22 (1975), pp. 347–58.

[48] *Chronica Monasterii Casinensis*, 3.7 (p. 368).

[49] Tito P. Martinengo, *Pia quaedam poemata, at theologica, odaeque sacrae diverso carminum genere conscriptae* (Rome, 1590), p. 168: 'exscripti sunt autem ex pervetusto codice, Longobardicis litteris exarato monasterii Casinensi'. For the poems on Katherine see pp. 189–192. A number of these poems overlap with a list of Alfanus' poems given by Peter the Deacon in his *De viris illustribus casinensibus*, according to Monte Cassino, MS 361, s. xii. This manuscript is written 'mainly in Peter's hand', see Newton, *Scriptorium*, p. 285, n. 266.

works of Guaiferius of Monte Cassino and Alfanus and seems to have been produced shortly after Alfanus' death in 1085.[50]

The three hymns on Katherine do not include enough detail to allow their assignation to a particular tradition:[51]

Poem 42, lines 22-4:

Sanguineas vulnus dum mittere debuit undas,
lac dedit, egregio corpusque dedere sepulcro
turba supernorum, guttas funditque salubres.

Poem 43, lines 30-33:

Vulnus illatum laticem dat album.
Coelicae turbae sepelivit ossa
puritas; manant oleum salubre.

Poem 44, lines 28-31:

Et lac consequitur vulnera candidum.
Montanoque locant vertice funera
dextrae coelicolum, quis refluit liquor
reddens debilibus membra valentia.

The double miracle of the milk and the angels carrying Katherine's body to Sinai is already present in the Greek accounts. The only versions of Katherine's passion to mention explicitly her relics and the healing capacities of the oil they exude are some of the Latin ones (BHL 1657, BHL 1662b,

---

[50] '... the manuscript ... MC 280, gives the impression of belonging to the latest part of Desiderius' rule or to the Oderisian period. This impression is strongly confirmed by ... Hoffmann's discovery that three of the hands in MC 280 also served as scribes in the Munich manuscript [Clm 4623] of the Chronicle, a manuscript written later in the rule of Oderisius, and specifically within the years 1099–1103. In fact, in both manuscripts the master scribe who begins the copying is the *bibliothecarius* of the abbey and author of the oldest part of the Chronicle, Leo Marsicanus himself'. Newton, *Scriptorium*, p. 78.

[51] Lentini, *I carmi*, pp. 196–200.

BHL 1663).⁵² Thus the textual evidence, at least, indicates that the oil motif entered Katherine's passion in the Latin West. This seems to support Charles Jones' point, who argues that the myroblitic power of Katherine's relics was introduced to the text/cult in Normandy in the eleventh century on the basis that Nicholas also shared this trait, and was, moreover, a foreign saint to Normandy just like Katherine.⁵³

3. Latin translations and adaptations

A number of Latin translations, adaptations, and reworkings of Katherine's passion began to appear in Italy as early as the tenth century. While the Greek versions behave in a fairly straightforward way, that is to say, it is relatively easy to identify a version from which all others descend, the same is not true for the Latin texts. There are numerous elaborations with a significant degree of variation within each strand as well as contamination between some of them. The system of classification developed by the Bollandists in the *BHL*, which relies on similarities and differences in the *incipit* and *explicit* of each text to define each strand, becomes cumbersome once one turns instead to the main body of the texts for identifying relationships between them. Sorting out these relationships is made more difficult by the unavailability of reliable modern editions – something that seriously hampered Bronzini's findings, a situation that has not changed much since he undertook his study.

The following pages are not intended as a detailed or comprehensive study of the relationship between the Greek and Latin texts, but are to be seen more as an afterthought to Bronzini's work and an indication of how much still needs to

---

[52] Whether or not it is part of BHL 1658 is not known since an edition of this text has yet to appear.

[53] See Charles W. Jones, 'The Norman cult of Sts Catherine and Nicholas, saec. xi', *Hommages à André Boutemy*, ed. Guy Cambier (Brussels, 1976), p. 218.

be done. Many of his findings are still being cited today; some of them are plainly mistaken, such as his undue concentration on the *Menologion of Basil*. While Bronzini can be credited for bringing together all the extant texts of Katherine's passion, not all of his conclusions on the relationships among the texts are fine-tuned in a satisfactory way. Based on the variation of the dates on which the different characters die, Bronzini concluded that these are later additions to the nucleus of the story. This nucleus comprises, according to him, the initial sacrifice to the gods, the debate with the rhetors, their death, and that of Katherine. He argued that everything else in the story is typical hagiographic elaboration. It is not at all likely that the short paragraph in the *Menologion of Basil* contains the nucleus from which all Greek (and Latin) versions derive.[54] As already discussed, the process of compiling a collection such as the *Menologion of Basil* entailed synthesizing already existent saints' lives rather than commissioning a particular version for inclusion, not to mention the fact that, based on the manuscripts and textual evidence, BHG 30a/30 antedate this collection.

While Bronzini can be credited with attempting a classification of these texts, he did not succeed in satisfying philological standards.[55] His principal error was to assume two branches from which the Greek texts descend, with γ, i.e. the *Menologion of Basil*, representing the tradition that has no knowledge of Katherine's translation to Sinai, and β standing in for all those texts in which angels waft her off to her final resting place.[56] Of the four Greek versions, only BHG 30a and

---

[54] See pp. 81–82 above.

[55] See the review by François Halkin, *AB*, 79 (1961), 179–80.

[56] Bronzini, 288. Hans R. Seeliger's article on Katherine in *Lexikon für Theologie und Kirche* still followed this view of two branches, s.v. Katharina von Alexandrien. Christine Walsh, 'The Role of the Normans in the development of the cult of St Katherine', in *St Katherine of Alexandria*, ed. Jenkins and Lewis, pp. 19–35, in turn focused her

BHG 30 seem to have had a significant influence on the development of the tradition in the Latin West, particularly in terms of translations and adaptations. This is corroborated to some extent by the diffusion of the manuscripts: BHG 30a and BHG 30 are preserved in a number of southern-Italian manuscripts, whereas BHG 31 and BHG 32 had a more restricted and Byzantine diffusion. One difficulty here is that the determination of provenance for Greek manuscripts is still lagging behind that of Latin manuscripts, and the existence of a large number of manuscripts in Italian libraries does not, per se, imply that they originated in southern Italy. In the absence of critical editions, any statements about the relationships between the Greek and Latin texts, as well as among the different Latin texts, must necessarily remain provisional. Another serious problem is the very likely fact that some versions have not survived, as will become clear below. Just as Peeters posited a lost Greek version between the Arabic and the Greek, it is very possible that some of the variations and incongruities are due to a lost version or versions.

As Dolbeau has shown, the process of translation occurs in several stages.[57] The first stage usually involves a direct word-for-word translation from the Greek, often keeping the Greek word order intact. If it has not been revised, the translation will likely also mimic the use of grammatical cases employed in the Greek, as well as feature more particles and present participles (instead of a finite form of the verb). The second stage is an attempt to turn the word-for-word text into something more idiomatic (*renovatio*), perhaps shuffling words around into a more nimble Latin order, as well as using subjunctives where they are required or using pluperfect for

---

attention on BHG 32 in Symeon's menologion as the earliest datable text (pp. 20, 22, & 79).

[57] François Dolbeau, 'Le rôle des interprètes dans les traductions hagiographiques d'Italie du sud', in *Traduction et traducteurs au Moyen Age*, ed. Geneviève Contamine (Paris, 1989), pp. 145–62 (p. 152).

the synthetic Greek forms. Paolo Chiesa identified a third stage of engagement with the translated text, practitioners of which include Bonitus Neapolitanus and Peter, Subdeacon of Naples: both are very free in their treatment of whatever text they are rewriting.[58] This final stage retains the narrative elements and is otherwise (and usually) unbound by the linguistic choices of its predecessor(s). At this stage the reviser likely did not have access to the original Greek. In the second and third stages, as it were, the 'translators' were looking to adapt the text to their particular context, thus omitting or adding episodes to fit with 'religious interests, political incentives, ecclesiastical necessities, and requests by patrons'.[59] In the case of the Latin versions of Katherine's passion, it is not always clear what exactly the relationships are because the texts do not just progress in a straight line from (1) the Greek to a Latin translation, (2) a Latin reworking of an earlier translation, and (3) further adaptation of an already exisiting Latin redaction.

A literal translation can help to determine whether a Latin text derives from a Greek text. A large number of literally translated sentences, combined with an accumulation of specific details found nowhere else, can also help to cement a relationship. Not so useful is the presence or absence of particular episodes, speeches, and the like; this can often be coincidental. When the idiosyncrasies of the translated text have been smoothed over to make it more pleasing to the reader of Latin, this represents a text that is removed from the Greek at one stage. A text that bears no resemblance to a translation as regards vocabulary/sentence structure but does

---

[58] Paolo Chiesa, 'Le traduzioni dal Greco: L'evoluzione della scuola napoletana nel X secolo', in *Lateinische Kultur im X. Jahrhundert*, ed. Walter Berschin (*Mittellateinisches Jahrbuch* 24–25 [1990–91]), pp. 67–87.

[59] Réka E. Forrai, 'Translation as rewriting: A modern theory for a premodern practice', *Renaessanceforum: Tidsskrift for Renaessanceforskning*, 14 (2018), 25–49 (p. 34).

retain the storyline with its details, is removed from the Greek by at least two stages. It is worth bearing in mind that 'linguistic revisions of translations, usually made without reference to the Greek text, but with the aim of rescuing them from translationese', are relatively frequent phenomena.[60]

The bewildering variety in BHL numbers is partly the result of differing prologues and epilogues being accounted for and does not imply some sort of chronological order. In the case of Katherine's portfolio, the numbers range from 1656x to 1700h. 1680 and onwards refer to miracles, with one number assigned to each miracle, while 1668-1672p were assigned to texts that recount Katherine's birth and conversion to Christianity. In what follows, I concentrate on those Latin texts that can, in some way, be linked to Italy in the period before her cult takes off in Rouen. I will focus on the following texts:[61]

---

[60] A. Carlotta Dionisotti, 'Translator's Latin', in *Aspects of the Language of Latin Prose*, ed. Tobias Reinhardt *et al.* (Oxford, 2005), pp. 357–75 (p. 368). Ead., 'Translated saints: Wisdom and her daughters', *Journal of Early Christian Studies*, 16 (2008), 165–80.

[61] There are two other Latin versions, identified by the tags BHL 1662d and 1662e respectively. Seeing that these two texts have had a very narrow diffusion, with only one surviving manuscript for each text and having had no apparent influence on BHL 1663, I do not treat them here.
BHL 1662d: One manuscript: Brussels, KRB, MS 944, s. xii. Bronzini thought this version descended from the separate tradition he had identified for the *Menologion of Basil* (Bronzini, 321–27.). However, it appears to be in some relationship with BHG 30a and 30 (or perhaps a now lost intermediary text); in places, it reads like a translation. In particular, it keeps the speeches short. Also, it retains the gruesome detail of the queen's punishment, which has been altered in BHL 1662 and BHL 1663, and which is not present at all in BHL 1657 or Peter's version BHL 1659. Certain episodic details present in BHL 1663 are missing from this version, so that a relationship between the two appears unlikely. However, the existence of this text in a twelfth-century manuscript now in Belgium shows that it was plausible for such a translation to travel north from Italy (where it was likely to have been

(a) BHL 1662 ('Monte Cassino Version')

(b) BHL 1657 ('Mombrizio Version')

(c) BHL 1658

(d) BHL 1662b

I am leaving aside for now the polished Latin version attributed to Peter, Subdeacon of Naples, BHL 1659 (with epilogues BHL 1660 and BHL 1661), since I will treat it in more depth in Chapter 5. Likewise I am passing over for now BHL 1661 b, d, e, f, m, although see Appendix 2 for a discussion and an edition of 1661m which is essentially an epitome of 1663.

(a) BHL 1662

BHL 1662 is a version of Katherine's passion very obviously associated with Monte Cassino, since its manuscript tradition is restricted to that monastery. It features an ending not found anywhere else: Katherine's body is not wafted off to the holy mountain on the Sinai by angels but instead buried by the faithful close to the city of Alexandria:

> produced). One would of course need to examine the provenance of Brussels 944, as well as its contents, in order confirm this hypothesis.
> BHL 1662e: One manuscript: Ivrea, Biblioteca Capitolare, MS 104 (CV), s. xiv. This account begins: 'igitur Constantinus cum rempublicam strenue in Galliis procuraret'. Although its *incipit* reads like that of BHL 1663, this version reveals itself to be a witness to the *Legenda aurea*, or at least to be a contaminated version. See *Inventario Manoscritti della Biblioteca Capitolare di Ivrea*, ed. Alfonso Professione, rev. Ilo Vignono (Alba, 1967), s.v. 104; Albert Poncelet, 'Catalogus codicum hagiographicorum latinorum Bibliothecae Eporidiensis', *AB*, 41 (1923), 326–36 (p. 339): 'igitur Constantinus cum rempublicam strenue in Galliis procuraret, Maxentius vero praetorium Romae gubernaret, inter eos bellum civile exortum est'. *Des*[*init*]: 'haec autem omnia insimul fuerunt in beata Katherina. Ultima pars totidem paene verbis legitur in *Legenda Aurea*, ch. 172 (167)'. See also *Legenda Aurea*, ed. Maggioni, II, p. 1215.

Expleta oratione cervicem tetendit, et iuxta quod tyrannus iusserat decollationis sententiam laetanter excepit, sicque ad sponsi sui regis aeterni thalamum perenniter cum ea (*sic*) regnatura conscendit. Consummavit autem cursum certaminis sui beata Ecaterina septimo kalendas Decembris, et reconditum est corpus eius a fidelibus iuxta civitatem Alexandriam in loco optimo et condigno meritis eius. Ad laudem et gloriam dei omnipotentis qui trinus et unus vivit et regnat in saecula saeculorum. Amen.[62]

This version was thus not likely to have been the basis of Alfanus' Hymn 44 (at least), where 'montano vertice' must refer to Mount Sinai. It is preserved in two Cassinese manuscripts,[63] namely Monte Cassino, MSS 139 and 149.[64] Lowe assigned MS 139 to the period between 1070 and 1100 and MS 149 to the second half of the eleventh century.[65] In his study of the Cassinese scriptorium, Francis Newton was able to be a little more precise; in his opinion MS 139 was either written during the last years of Desiderius' abbacy (1058-1087) or during the time of Oderisius (1087-1105), while MS

---

[62] *Bibliotheca Casinensis seu codicum manuscriptorum qui in tabulario Casinensi asservantur monachorum Ordinis S. Benedicti*, vol. 3 (Monte Cassino, 1877), Florilegium, p. 187 [henceforth *Florilegium*]. The edition of this version and BHL 1658 (see below) contains a great number of impossible readings.

[63] And also in Brussels, KBR, MS 8955-56, s. xvii [Collectanea Bollandiana].

[64] Katherine is at fols 172–175 in MS 139, and fols 142v–145v in MS 149. In both cases the saint immediately following is Peter of Alexandria (BHL 6693). For the contents see *Codicum casinensium manuscriptorum Catalogus* (Monte Cassino, 1915), I, pp. 222–24 and 238–39 (though there is no mention of Katherine in the description provided here of MS 149).

[65] MS 139 = s. xi ex., MS 149 = s. xi^2, see Elias A. Lowe, *The Beneventan Script: A History of the South Italian Minuscule*, 2nd edn prepared by Virginia Brown, vol. 2: *Hand List of Beneventan Manuscripts* (Rome, 1980), pp. 71–72.

149 was definitely produced under the latter.⁶⁶ The resulting *terminus ante quem* for the composition of this passion is 1070-1100. Since its medieval diffusion was restricted to Monte Cassino, it is likely this text may have been written for in-house use only, or perhaps the legendaries that it was part of were considered too precious to be lent to other houses for copying. Certainly the presence of Katherine's relics as well as the existence of Alfanus' hymns in honour of the saint point towards a cult, or at least an increased interest in her at Monte Cassino. It is of course impossible to determine who took the trouble to produce this account of Katherine's passion. She may have been known to such hagiographers as Alberic the Deacon and Guaiferius, who were active at Monte Cassino during Desiderius' abbacy.⁶⁷

BHL 1662 contains details that are present in no other known version, Greek or Latin, such as naming the emperor Maximinus rather than Maxentius and locating the burial of the saint just outside Alexandria.⁶⁸ The possibility that they are derived from a Greek tradition which is now lost is at least an option. However, the presence or absence of particular episodes and the like is not a reliable tool for determining relationships. In this regard, Bronzini was mistaken in his

---

⁶⁶ 'MS 139 dates from the 1080s, and perhaps falls in the era of Oderisius, and MS 149 is definitely Oderisian. This latter volume was lavishly decorated with gold ..., and the vivid colors and sometimes bizarre designs could serve as a textbook for study of Oderisian experimentation'. Newton, Scriptorium, p. 72, see also pp. 123, 165, 224 (MS 149 has the medieval shelf-mark 'O', and medieval page numbering), and 257. Plate 44 shows the beginning of the passion of Katherine, the description is on p. 342: 'the scribe wrote the saint's name ecaterina; the first e was erased'.

⁶⁷ See *LexMA*, s. vv. Alberich v. Montecassino, Guaiferius v. Montecassino.

⁶⁸ The text of Katherine's passion preserved in MS 149 was included in the *Florilegium*, pp. 184–87. Both Bronzini and Walsh appear to have ignored the existence of MS 149, yet cite MS 139.

assumption that the *Menologion of Basil* served as the foundation for this version.[69] He associated the two texts on the basis of the emperor's name, given in both as Maximinus. The occurrence of this overlap in names as evidence for derivation from a particular Greek text is problematic. Both Maxentius and Maximinus were historical emperors in charge of African provinces at the beginning of the fourth century: Maxentius in the West (306-312 CE) and Maximinus Daia in the East, including Egypt and thus Alexandria (305-313 CE). All that would have been necessary for the substitution of the 'wrong' emperor Maxentius (who is so named in all four Greek versions)[70] for the 'correct' Maximinus was an author or scribe who had a keener sense of history, and this is exactly what seems to have happened in the case of BHL 1662: unlike any of the other Greek and Latin accounts, with the exception of BHL 1663, this version begins by providing a short historical context, describing the division of power between the senior and junior emperors and alluding to the persecution of Christians in Alexandria under Maximianus (usually referred to as Galerius):

> Constantinus sacratissimus et christianissimus imperator cum post mortem Constantii patris in Galliis et Britannia imperare caepisset, et Maximianus cognomento Galerius cum filio Maximino Caesare in orientis partibus pariter imperaret, Romae Maxentius Maximiani Herculii filius tyrannide assumpta regnabat. Sed postquam divinae virtutis auxilio a Constantino in congressione pontis Molvii idem tyrannus summersus est, et Romanae urbis imperium prefatus Augustus obtinuit, Maximianus Galerii filius Constantini gloriae invidens, apud Egyptum maximeque

---

[69] Bronzini, '319–20: 'ora non si tratta ... di omissioni pure e semplici ... ma di vere e proprie varianti che provengono certo dalla fonte di cui egli si servì. ... [C]i orienta verso la stessa più genuina ramificazione della leggenda ... a cui appartiene MB'.

[70] Here an up-to-date edition of the Greek texts could help to determine whether there are any manuscripts that have Maximinus instead of Maxentius.

apud Alexandriam adversus Christianos persecutione commota, omnium scelerum et flagitiorum auctor imperii sibi nomen arripiens, in Christianos saevire modis omnibus caepit.[71]

A possible source for this sort of historical detail could have been Paul the Deacon's *Historia romana*. Paul, a monk at Monte Cassino in the second half of the eighth century, had written his *Roman History* on the basis of Eutropius' *Breviarium* for Adelperga, the wife of Arechis II of Benevento.[72] A direct link between the two texts is not apparent, but the availability of Paul's work could have provided the necessary historical background.

The many exchanges between the saint and her adversaries that act as centerpieces for and, in some way, define the early Greek version, have been drastically shortened in this rendering. For example, Katherine's initial reproach to the emperor is given as indirect speech and is much shortened: 'Et ut erat oratorum ac philosophorum studiis vehementer accensa; cur tantus ac talis vir tantis ac talibus flagitiorum illecebris deserviret; constanter et libere cum palam omnibus redarguere caeperit'.[73] Similarly, her learned and long attack on pagan sacrifices against the rhetors is summarized in one sentence: 'Sed quoniam sapientia saeculi stultitia est ad sapientiam dei, ita eos sancta virgo suis propositionibus et conclusionibus superavit ut neque quid quaererent neque quid responderent possent aliquatenus invenire'.[74]

Smaller details suggest that this version is a translation or adaption of a Greek text, although one cannot know whether the speeches were already short in the originating Greek version. For instance, Katherine's name is always given as 'Ecaterina', close to the Greek form Αἰκατερίνα, an indication

---

[71] *Florilegium*, p. 184.

[72] *LMA*, s.v. Paulus Diaconus.

[73] *Florilegium*, p. 185.

[74] Ibid., p. 185.

perhaps that this version was at one remove from a Greek text. Other evidence for this can be found in the phrase 'probemus, ait, constantiam pessimae huius', which is not very elegant Latin. Another snippet that seems to have escaped polishing is the phrase 'simul et erubescens superari posse se a puella', where *posse se* is not the normal word order in Latin.[75] Yet, at the very end of the text the author/scribe ends with the following phrase: 'qui trinus et unus vivit et regnat in saecula saeculorum'. A parallel to this can be found in a sermon by Peter Damian, as well as in an eleventh-century manuscript containing Latin papal benedictions.[76]

Overall, this version reads like a competent translation that has not undergone a polishing effort to render it into a higher style of Latin. It is terse and to the point; certainly, none of the extant Greek versions contain so few and such short speeches. The focus on narrative rather than speech while retaining the major episodes makes this a relatively readable text. The absence of long theological discussions also makes it more digestible. The major martyrdoms of Porphyrius and his soldiers, the queen, and Katherine are all present, and there is, interestingly, significant focus on the emperor's feelings in the face of Katherine's superiority.

---

[75] Ibid., p. 186 and p. 187 respectively.

[76] Peter Damian, Sermon 17 bis, line 394: 'Qui trinus et unus vivit et gloriatur per infinita saecula saeculorum'. A similar phrase can also be found in a pontifical manuscript from the eleventh century: 'Quod ipse praestare dignetur, qui trinus et unus vivit et gloriatur Deus et regnat in saecula saeculorum'; Paris, Bibliothèque Sainte-Geneviève, MS 2657; see Fernand Combaluzier, 'Un bénédictionnaire épiscopal du Xe siècle (Ms 2657 Bibl. Sainte-Geneviève, Paris)', *Sacris Erudiri*, 14 (1963), 286–342, although the part of the manuscript containing the blessings was assigned by Bischoff to the second third of the eleventh century. It was likely written at Lorsch. See Bernhard Bischoff, *Die Abtei Lorsch im Spiegel ihrer Handschriften* (Lorsch, 1989), pp. 114–15.

(b) BHL 1657

Another account of Katherine's passion, BHL 1657, is often identified by its association with Bonino Mombrizio, a humanist scholar from Milan, who printed the text around 1477 as part of his *Sanctuarium seu Vitae Sanctorum*, a collection of 334 legends of martyrs and confessors.[77] This work is more widely accessible through an annotated reprint from the early twentieth century.[78] The ascription to Mombrizio as the printer probably oversimplifies what is actually known about his involvement in the production of this collection: it is likely that he was part of a collective that funded the project and he may also have acted as an editor, but it is unclear whether he gathered manuscripts for the enterprise.[79]

The collection remains an important tool for hagiographers, both because of its useful index and because it is in some cases the sole witness for legends otherwise lost. Antonia Frazier, who examined this collection of saints' lives, concluded that the *Sanctuarium* is, 'in some fundamental ways, an unfinished or hastily finished edition. Mombrizio used highly authoritative sources in some cases; in other cases, he seems to have used such texts as came to hand. This eclecticism may indicate carelessness, or a greater concern to fill gatherings than to present valuable texts, or a hasty change

---

[77] For an overview of Mombrizio's activities see Serena Spanò Martinelli, 'Bonino Mombrizio e gli albori della scienza agiografica', in *Erudizione e devozione: Le raccolte di vite di santi in età moderna e contemporanea*, ed. Gennaro Luongo (Rome, 2000), pp. 3–18, and ead., 'Mombrizio (Montebretto), Bonino', in *Dizionario biografico degli Italiani*, (Rome, 2011), vol. 75, pp. 471–75. For the printing-date of the *Sanctuarium* see Tino Foffano, 'Per la data dell'edizione del *Sanctuarium* di Bonino Mombrizio', *Italia medioevale e umanistica*, 22 (1979), 511.

[78] Mombrizio, *Sanctuarium*; Katherine is at vol. 1, pp. 283–87. Reviewed by Albert Poncelet, *AB* 29 (1910), 442–44.

[79] Alison Frazier, *Possible Lives*, p. 165.

The Story of Katherine Moves West 115

of plan.'[80] Some of the texts in the *Sanctuarium* are taken from late medieval compilations of saints' lives such as Vincent de Beauvais' *Speculum historiale* or Jacobus de Voragine's *Legenda aurea*.[81]

BHL 1657 begins 'temporibus Maxentii impiissimi imperatoris anno quinto imperii' and thus appears to stand, at least on the basis of the *incipit*, in some sort of relationship with BHL 1658 (on which, see below). I have only made a cursory comparison of the two versions, but I believe that the two are indeed related in some way. The number of parallel passages is too great to be coincidental. As a first guess, and this is what it must remain, I would suggest that BHL 1658 precedes BHL 1657, for in BHL 1658, or at least in Monte Cassino, MS 117 which preserves it, Katherine's name is always spelled *Ecaterina*, suggesting a close relationship with a Greek text. Bronzini was right to point out that BHL 1658 reproduces, in its own way, the gargantuan and convoluted speeches of BHG 30a, an indication that it derives from that account. These have been touched down in BHL 1657, making them short and succinct. As Frazier has noted, the redactor of the Mombrizio text 'often completely rewrites them, reducing ecstatic nonsense to rational discourse'.[82] To what extent and

---

[80] Ibid., p. 152.

[81] For about 183 of the texts the source is unknown and/or may have been a thirteenth- or fourteenth-century legendary of northern Italian origin, see Gerhard Eis, *Die Quellen für das Sanctuarium des Mailänder Humanisten Boninus Mombritius: Eine Untersuchung zur Geschichte der großen Legendensammlung des Mittelalters* (Berlin, 1933). Reviewed by Hippolyte Delehaye, *AB*, 53 (1935), 412–22. See also pp. 120–22 below.

[82] Frazier, *Possible Lives*, p. 163. In Como, Biblioteca del Seminario Vescovile, MS 5, however, the speeches have been retained. This manuscript was thought to have served as a source for the *Sanctuarium* by Baudouin de Gaiffier, 'Deux passionaires de Morimondo conservés au séminaire de Côme', *AB*, 83 (1965), 142–56. See also pp. 120–22 below.

how these two versions are related to the Greek texts is difficult to determine, partly because they share a great number of parallels which can only have occurred through the use of a common translation. I have looked at some of the parallels cited by Bronzini, and contrary to what he concludes from this comparison, namely that BHL 1657 is closest to BHG 30, I can show that this is simply not true.[83]

BHG 30a[84]	BHG 30[85]	BHL 1657[86]
τῶν δὲ γραμμάτων ἐκπεμφθέντων, παραγίνεται πρὸς αὐτὸν πλῆθος πολὺ τῶν κατοικούντων ἐν τῇ ὑποτεταγμένη αὐτῷ βασιλείᾳ.	τῶν δὲ γραμμάτων τοῦ βασιλέως ἐκπεμφθέντων κατὰ πάσης τῆς οἰκουμένης, παραγίνεται πρὸς αὐτὸν πλῆθος πολὺ τῶν κατοικούντων ἐν τῇ ὑποτεταγμένη αὐτῷ βασιλείᾳ.	missis vero litteris convenit ad eum multitudo copiosa, quae sub imperio eius erat constituta.

Here BHL 1657 clearly follows BHG 30a: the first part of the sentence up to *copiosa* replicates exactly the word order of the Greek. It does not translate τοῦ βασιλέως or κατὰ πάσης τῆς οἰκουμένης found only in BHG 30.

Another comparison, this time between BHG 30a, BHG 30, BHL 1657, and BHL 1658:

BHG 30.[87]	BHG 30a[88]	BHL 1657[89]	BHL 1658
Ἦν γὰρ τῷ κάλλει ἀμώμητος, πᾶσαν φύσιν γυναι-	Ἦν γὰρ τῷ κάλλει ἀμώμητος ὑπὲρ πᾶσαν	erat autem Catherinae irreprehensibilis forma praem-	erat enim irreprehensibilis forma preminens ultra

---

[83] Bronzini, 306–07.
[84] Viteau, p. 25, § 2.
[85] Ibid., p. 5, § 2.
[86] Mombritius, *Sanctuarium* 2, p. 284, line 1.
[87] Viteau, p. 7, § 5.
[88] Ibid., p. 26, § 5.
[89] Mombritius, *Sanctuarium* 2, p. 284, line 23.

κῶν ὑπερβάλ-λουσα. Ἦν δὲ καὶ ὑπερμεγέθης τῇ ἡλικίᾳ σφόδρα, καὶ ὥσπερ κυπάρισσος εὐθαλής, τὴν ἑωθινὴν δρόσον βαστάζουσα, ἀνατεταμένη ἐν τῷ ἀέρι καὶ ὑπερμεγέθης ὑπὲρ πᾶν δένδρον τῆς γῆς τῷ κατακόμῳ τῆς κεφαλῆς, ἵσταται εὐπρεπῶς, οὕτως καὶ ἡ μακαρία, προαγούσης αὐτῆς τῆς χάριτος τοῦ Κυρίου, ἐφαίνετο τοῖς ὁρῶσιν.	φύσιν γυναικῶν. Ἦν δὲ καὶ ὑπερμεγέθης τῇ ὄψει τῆς ἡλικίας σφόδρα. Ὡς κυπάρισσος παμποίκιλος τὴν ἑωθινὴν δρόσον βαστάζουσα, ἀνατεταμένη ἐν τῷ ἀέρι, ὑπερμεγέθης παρὰ πᾶν δένδρον τῆς γῆς τῷ κατακόμῳ τῆς κεφαλῆς, ἵσταται εὐπρεπῶς, οὕτως καὶ ἡ μακαρία, προαγούσης αὐτὴν τῆς χάριτος τοῦ Κυρίου.	<u>inens</u>que ultra omnes mulieres cum florida <u>spetie</u> sicut <u>excelsa cipressus</u> portans matutinum rorem et sicut palma quae circumadsistit decorata super omnes arbores.	omnes mulieres cum florida <u>specie</u>, sicut <u>excelsa cypressus</u>, portans matutinum rorem, que circa comam existit decorata super omnes arbores. Sic et beata cum precedente gratia domini radiabat.

Praeminens: agrees with ὑπερβάλλουσα = BHG 30

Specie: renders τῇ ὄψει (τῆς ἡλικίας) = BHG 30a

Excelsa cypressus: neither κυπάρισσος εὐθαλής (BHG 30) nor κυπάρισσος παμποίκιλος (BHG 30a).

In this section, the relationships are not as straightforward as suggested by Bronzini.[90] Both BHL 1657 and BHL 1658 agree with BHG 30 and BHG 30a once, but also retain (at least) one feature which is present in neither of the two Greek texts.

---

90 Bronzini, 308.

One more comparison, between BHL 1657 and BHL 1658:

BHL 1657[91]	BHL 1658[92]
Temporibus Maxentii impiissimi imperatoris anno quinto imperii eius erat multa insania idolorum. <u>Et sedens imperator pro tribunali in civitate Alexandrinorum posuit preceptum ubique sacrificare diis</u>, *et huiusmodi scripsit epistolam.* <u>Omnes convenite</u> ad nostram praesentiam, ut cognoscatis <u>praeceptum, quod positum est a nobis</u>. Si quis vero obedierit huic nostrae iussioni, habebit gratiam nostram, qui vero non obedierit, statim eum faciam gladio et diversis penis corruere.	Temporibus Maxentii impiissimi imperatoris anno tricesimo quinto regni eius erat multa insania idolorum colentes (*sic*). <u>Et sedens pro tribunali in civitate Alexandrinorum, posuit preceptum ubique sacrificare diis</u>, et *misit epistolam habentem hanc figuram.* <u>Omnes convenite</u> (ut) agnoscatis <u>preceptum quod positum est a nobis</u>. Si quis non obedierit huic nostre iussioni statim faciam eum corruere gladio et diversis suppliciis.

The Greek version BHG 30a reads:

ὅθεν προκαθίσας ὁ βασιλεὺς Μαξέντιος ἐπὶ τοῦ βήματος, ἐν τῇ πόλει τῶν Ἀλεξανδρέων, ἔθετο πρόσταγμα πάντῃ τε καὶ πανταχοῦ θύειν τοῖς θεοῖς καὶ ἀπολύεσθαι, γράψας *ἐπιστολὴν περιέχουσαν τὸν τύπον τοῦτον*: «Βασιλεὺς Μαξέντιος πάσῃ τῇ οἰκουμένῃ χαίρειν. Πάντες συνέλθετε μέχρις ἡμῶν ὅπως γνῶστε τὸ ἐκτεθέν. Εἴ τις οὖν μὴ ὑπακούσῃ τοῦ θεσπίσματος τούτου, αὖθις παραστήσεταί μοι ἐν τῷ βήματι, ὑφιστάμενος τὴν διὰ τοῦ ξίφους καὶ πυρὸς τιμωρίαν.[93]

BHG 30 starts in the same way, although the sentence beginning 'Πάντες συνέλθετε μέχρις ἡμῶν' reads like this: 'Πάντες συνέλθατε μέχρις ἡμῶν ἐν τῇ μεγάλῃ τῶν Ἀλεξανδρέων πόλει, ἔκθεσις γὰρ γίνεται περὶ τῶν μεγάλων θεῶν κατὰ πασῶν πόλεων καὶ χωρῶν, ὅπως γνῶτε τὸ

---

[91] Mombritius, *Sanctuarium* 2, p. 283.

[92] *Florilegium*, p. 74.

[93] Viteau, p. 26, § 1.

ἐκτεθέν'.⁹⁴ Thus, it looks as though the two Latin texts are adhering more closely to BHG 30a in this instance. In BHL 1658 the phrase 'misit epistolam habentem hanc figuram' is a translation from Greek that has not been touched up, while 'huiusmodi scripsit epistolam' in BHL 1657 is a fully 'latinized' version of the same phrase. By the same token, 'statim faciam eum corruere gladio et diversis suppliciis' in BHL 1658 retains the word order of the Greek original; in BHL 1657 the verb has been moved to the end of the sentence. These are only snippets, but they suggest that perhaps Bronzini was not as meticulous in his comparisons as he could have been and that a lot of work still needs to be done. Certainly one explanation for the overlap of BHG 30a and BHG 30 in the Latin versions would be an (intermediary) Greek version, combining elements of the published versions BHG 30a and BHG 30.⁹⁵

As regards the compilation of the *Sanctuarium*, Tino Foffano stated that Mombrizio used old manuscripts, employed sound philological criteria to establish the text, and

---

⁹⁴ Ibid., p. 5, § 1.

⁹⁵ As regards the witnesses listed by the *BHLms* for 1657, I can add one more: Bergamo, Biblioteca Civica, MS MAB.64, s. xiii–xiv. Further, MS C.400 at the Universitetsbiblioteket in Uppsala (*c.* 1375, Constance?, fols 74–81v) appears at first sight to be a witness for BHL 1657 on the basis of its *incipit*: 'Temporibus Maxencii inpiisimi imperatoris anno xxxv imperii eius erat multa insania ydolorum'. The *explicit*, however, differs significantly from the ending as printed in Mombrizio's *Sanctuarium* and, unless it is a later addition, suggests that this manuscript is in fact a witness for 1658: 'decollata est autem sancta Katherina mense novembris ... ex cuius ossibus indesinenter oleum manat et cunctorum debilium membra sanat. Passa est autem sub tyranno maxencio circa annos domini cccmo xmo'. See Margaret Andersson-Schmitt *et al.*, *Mittelalterliche Handschriften der Universitätsbibliothek Uppsala: Katalog über die C-Sammlung*, vol. 4: HSS C 301–400 (Stockholm, 1991), s.v. C.400. This proves once more that *incipits* and *explicits* are rather unreliable tools for determining relationships and dependencies between texts.

did not indulge in humanistic rewritings, although he cited no direct evidence for this.[96] In a comparative study gone terribly wrong, Gerhard Eis claimed to have discovered that Mombrizio relied heavily on the *Magnum legendarium austriacum* (*MLA*) for a great number of the legends in his collection.[97] Eis' method was one of comparing more than 120 saints from the two collections, citing as proof in his publication never more than one or two 'representative' parallels and not necessarily for each saint. In the case of Katherine, the two passages could not be further removed from each other.[98]

BHL 1657	MLA
Veniens autem spiculator amputavit cervicem eius, et pro sanguine lac emanavit in terra. Angeli vero venientes tulerunt corpus eius et portaverunt illud in montem Sinai et posuerunt in monumentum novum.	Mox ille insurgens decollavit eam. Duae res dignae memoria apparuerunt. Una quia lac pro sanguine in testimonium virginalis pudicitiae de corpore eius effusum terram uberius irrigavit. Altera quia mox angeli accesserunt et assumptum corpus per altum in aera subvehentes in montem Sinai deposuerunt, qui mons a loco occisionis distat viginti et eo amplius itineris dierum.

[96] 'Compose con validi criteri filologici pubblicando integralmente testi agiografici desunti da antichi codici, senza indulgere a rifacimenti umanistici', in Foffano, 'Per la data', 509. Mombrizio's reputation as a printer/editor of classical texts may well have prompted this comment. It remains to be seen whether the account printed in Mombrizio was his reworking or whether it is thus preserved in the manuscripts. If so, then this would would suggest that the 'adaptor' was active much earlier.

[97] Eis, 'Die Quellen'. The *MLA* is a collection of saints' lives put together towards the end of the twelfth century in a Cistercian context. Baudouin de Gaiffier, 'Au sujet des sources du *Sanctuarium* de Mombritius', *Mittellateinisches Jahrbuch,* 14 (1979), 278–81. On the *MLA*, see now Diarmuid Ó Riain, 'The *Magnum Legendarium Austriacum*: A new investigation of one of medieval Europe's richest hagiographical collections', *AB*, 133 (2015), 87–165.

[98] Eis, 'Die Quellen', 41–42.

Eis comments: 'Das Verhältnis des Mombritianischen Textes zu dem des *MLA* ist ein recht nahes. ... Er hält alles Wesentliche bei und übergeht unwichtiges Beiwerk. ... ständig merkt man die sinnvoll [!] eingreifende Hand des Humanisten. ... Trotz aller glättenden und kürzenden Arbeit des Gelehrten ist jedoch das *MLA* ganz deutlich als seine Quelle zu erkennen. Die Verwandtschaft springt in die Augen [!]' and so on. Dobson relied on Eis' work when he wrote: 'the Austrian collection (the *MLA* into which the epitome 1663a was incorporated) in its turn was the source of the *Sanctuarium* (1480) of Boninus Mombritius, in which the text of the *Passio beatae Catherinae virginis* underwent further shortening'.[99] The passion of Katherine in the *MLA* is in fact BHL 1663a – the so-called 'shorter *Vulgate*' (see Appendix 1).

Using a hypothesis put forward by Baudouin de Gaiffier, namely that a number of rare texts in the *Sanctuarium* can be traced back to two manuscripts at the Episcopal seminary in Como, Frazier undertook a comparison between the text of Katherine's passion in the *Sanctuarium* and the two manuscripts noted by de Gaiffier. The manuscripts in question, Como BSV MS 5 and MS 6, 'are partial witnesses to ... the *Magnum legendarium austriacum*'.[100] MS 6 does not preserve a passion of Katherine, but MS 5 does. Frazier found that, whether or not Como MS 5 was at the basis of the *Sanctuarium* text, a number of changes were made. They include orthographical changes, word order and vocabulary adjustments, as well as touching up to render phrases 'more mellifluous'.[101] And while Katherine's prayer at the end of the passion seems to point towards a relationship with the *MLA* in some way, Frazier noted that 'other forms of direct discourse ... represented in the *Sanctuarium*'s account of Katherine

---

[99] Dobson, p. xviii.
[100] Frazier, *Possible Lives,* p. 160.
[101] Ibid., pp. 161–62.

deviate more radically from the manuscript'. In particular, she observed that the exchanges between Katherine and the rhetors, which she described as representing 'a mystical excess of meaning, if not an intermediary's simple incomprehension of a Greek original', have been rewritten in the *Sanctuarium* version so as to make them less nonsensical and more comprehensible.[102] Overall, however, Frazier characterized the interventions undertaken by Mombrizio and/or his collaborators as typically humanist in that 'they touch on classicizing orthography, direct address, and minor points of fact', yet without intervening drastically in the narrative.[103]

(c + d) BHL 1658 and 1662b

BHL 1658 is preserved in a manuscript from Monte Cassino (MS 117) and begins: 'temporibus Maxentii impiissimi imperatoris anno tricesimo quinto regni eius erat multa insania idolorum colentes (*sic*). Et sedens pro tribunali in civitate Alexandrinorum, posuit preceptum ubique sacrificare diis, et misit epistolam habentem hanc figuram'.[104] It bears no resemblance at all to BHL 1662, the Monte Cassino version, and enjoyed a much wider diffusion. MS 117 remains its earliest witness so far: most recently it has been assigned to the twelfth century.[105] This text has not yet been published in full

---

[102] Ibid., p. 163.

[103] Ibid., p. 164.

[104] *Florilegium*, p. 74.

[105] 'This Desiderian *homiliarium* [MC Compact. IX, set 10], when complete, must have been nearly in competition with another volume in the Monte Cassino collection, [which was, however,] not written in Beneventan and later than our period [1058–1105], the huge lectionary Monte Cassino 117 (twelfth-century, in ordinary minuscule), which measures 570 x 375 (470 x 285), 2 cols, 50 lines'. Newton, *Scriptorium*, p. 123. Bronzini, 301: 'della fine dell' XI o del principio del XII secolo'. For the contents see *Codicum Casinensium ... Catalogus*, vol. 1, pp. 186–98. The other witnesses for BHL 1658 are: Como, MS 5 [xiv-2], s. xii/xiii; Novara, Biblioteca Capitolare, MS 23, s. xiii/xiv; Novara, MS

so that a discussion of its relationship with the Greek and/or Latin versions remains preliminary.[106] Of note is the fact that this version is also preserved in Como MS 5, a manuscript used by Frazier in her discussion of the Mombrizio version BHL 1657 cited above.

At first sight, this version looks like a translation from Greek that has not yet been turned into polished Latin (Katherine's name is *Ecaterine*). For example, the turn of phrase 'epistulam habens hanc figuram' is based on 'ἐπιστολὴν περιέχουσαν τὸν τύπον τοῦτον'.[107] Other examples given by Bronzini are further support for his conclusion that 1658 is ultimately derived from BHG 30a rather than BHG 30. This can be seen in particular in the speeches of Katherine and the rhetors, which are mostly retained in this version. From the example below it is clear that BHG 30a (rather than BHG 30) was the model. The translator made a valiant effort to render the unrenderable into Latin – while there are individual words and small phrases that make sense, such as references to *Aristoteles splendidissimus rhetor*, the overall effect on the reader is one of confusion.

BHL 1658[108]	BHG 30a[109]
Ex aquoso elemento consistunt maria fucate robuste, et multum laetantes (*sic*) repetunt et congregantur in invio pelago hoc est maximum Omeri. Ait enim	ἐξ ἀμυήτου πελαγίσματος ὑποκείμενα βάθη σφιρμιγγιλιοτρύπτως ἀλκιμωτάτως νηκτῶν πολυκύδων σαφῶς ἐν ἀβάτῳ πελάγει πελματίζουσιν ἄβατον

29, s. xiv; Stuttgart, Württembergische Landesbibliothek, HB MS XIV 19, 1439–1442.

[106] The *Florilegium* (pp. 74–76) contains the text of Katherine's passion as preserved in Monte Cassino, MS 117, but this manuscript is defective, breaking off in mid-debate. Bronzini provided extracts from Novara, MS 23 on 314–17.

[107] *Florilegium*, p. 75, col. 1. For BHG 30a see Viteau, p. 5, § 1, and BHG 30, Viteau, p. 26, § 1.

[108] *Florilegium*, p. 75, col. 2.

[109] Viteau, p. 30, § 11.

124 The Passion of St Katherine of Alexandria

Aristotiles splendidissimus rethor, ita evidenter affero erupata in maxima visione solantem acerrime solatum in calcabilibus voraginum, subterraneum et in tractum laetanter reptant in plenitudine draconis. Secundum capitulum est insultatoris virgilii, sed et radiatus scilicet Dionisius calcabiles semitas rethorum sciens affatus est dicens. Robuste liquido inpudenter et in conpendiosa, et fundo dictione subtiliter variatum, invisibles directiones plane discurrunt impalpabilis semita etc.

Mention is made also of Asclepius (Scolapius), Philistion, Plato, then the manuscript breaks off.

τρίβον. Τοῦτο τοῦ μεγίστου Ὁμήρου βιργιλίου πρῶτον κεφάλαιον. Ἔλεξεν δὲ καὶ Ἀριστοτέλης, ἀκταιότατος ῥήτωρ, οὕτως· Γομφοτάτῳ σιδήρῳ γεργένομα ἐν μεγίστῃ ὀπτασίᾳ ἀποπελματιζόμενα δριμυτάτως πελματιζόμενα ἐν ἀβύθοις ἕλιξιν ὑπὸ γαιῶνα συρόντων σφιρμιγγιλιοδαπῆ νηκτὰ εἰς πλήρωσιν δράκοντος. Τοῦτο δεύτερον κεφάλαιον τοῦ πολυκύδου βιργιλίου Ἀριστοτέλους. Ἀλλὰ δὲ καὶ ὁ ἀκταιότατος Διονύσιος, ὁ ἀβάτους ἄβακας ῥητόρων ἐπιστάμενος etc.

Mention is made also of Asclepius, Galen, Philistion, Plato, Iannes and Mambres, Eusebius and the Sibyl.

The reason I cite this particular passage is the expression *fucate robuste*; something similar occurs a little earlier in Katherine's speech to the emperor: 'robustam et fuco verborum plenam dictionem suscipiens, ita fucatum quoddam sublime verborum quod loquar ad te in sublimi dictione etc'.[110] The combination of *robustus* with *fucatus* recurs in BHL 1663 and also in yet another version, identified by the tag BHL 1662b. In this version Katherine begins her first speech to the emperor thus:

BHL 1663[111]	BHL 1662b[112]
robustas et fuco verborum plenas dictiones quibus vos fultos ad instantem pugnam video occurrere.	robusta et fuco verborum plenam dictionem suscipiens, ita fucatum quoddam verbum loquor ad te, in sublimi dictione multiplice.

[110] *Florilegium*, p. 74, col. 2. Also: 'sicut obscurus sermo in vobis et fuco plenum dicite mihi' (p. 75, col. 1), and in BHL 1657: 'si est in vobis obscurus sermo et fusco plenus, dicite mihi'.

[111] Dobson, l. 353.

[112] Bronzini, 334.

What has happened? Does BHL 1663 derive from 1658 or from 1662b, or from both, or does the derivation work the other way round? A closer look at BHL 1662b and its tradition can help to raise the curtain a little. The text is preserved in a unique manuscript from the seventeenth century: Rome, Biblioteca Universitaria Alessandrina, MS 96. Bronzini, who published the text, suggested that it is 'antica'.[113] On the basis of parallel passages there seems to be a relationship with BHL 1658:

BHG 30a[114]	BHL 1662b[115]	BHL 1658[116]
Τότε θαμβηθεὶς ὁ βασιλεὺς εἶπεν <u>αὐτῇ</u>: 'Ἐγὼ μὲν οὐκ ἰσχύω ἀνταποκριθῆναί σοι. Ἐλεύσονται δὲ ἄνδρες ῥήτορες καὶ <u>βιργίλιοι</u>, ὅπως δυνήσωνται ἀνταποκριθῆναί σοι <u>κατὰ πάντα σου λόγον</u> ὑψικαρίζοντα, ὅπως πταίσασα ὑπ' αὐτῶν καὶ παντελῶς πέσασα τότε ἐν τῇ πολλῇ αἰσχύνῃ σου ἔλθῃς ἐπὶ τὸ συμφέρον καὶ σπείσῃς τοῖς θεοῖς.'	Tunc stupefactus imperator dixit <u>ad eam</u>: 'Ego non valeo respondere tibi, sed venient philosophi <u>virgiliani</u> et rhetores qui ad omnes tuos figuratos sermones respondebunt tibi <u>per omne verbum tuum.</u> Tunc in multa confusione venies quod congruum est tibi et credes diis.'	Tunc stupefactus imperator dixit: 'Ego non possum respondere tibi; venient autem rethores et ceteri sapientes ut confundant te cum magna confusione, et sic credas diis.'

From this initial example it would seem that 1658 is using 1662b and is shortening it, rather than also directly translating from the Greek – it is not very common for two translators of the same or similar passages to produce the same result. One

---

[113] Ibid., 328–41.
[114] Viteau, p. 28, § 8.
[115] Bronzini, 335.
[116] *Florilegium*, p. 75 col. 1.

can also see that 1662b is closer to the Greek than 1658: it reproduces Greek idiosyncracies, including the noun βιργίλιοι/*virgiliani*, describing the wise men.

Another example: take the prophecy of the Sibyl about the wood/cross on which Christ died – this only occurs in BHG 30a:

BHG 30a[117]	1662b[118]	1658[119]
Περὶ δὲ τοῦ ξύλου ἡ σιβύλλα εἶπεν: ὦ ξύλον τρισμακάριστον ἐν ᾧ Χριστὸς ἐκτετάνυσται, ὀπτριζομένη τὸ ξύλον τοῦ σταυροῦ.	de ligno autem crucis Sibylla dicit: o lignum ter beatum in quo Christus estensus [*sic*] est, perspiciens lignum crucis.	de ligno autem Sibilla prospitiens lignum sancte crucis dixit: o lignum ter beatum in quo Christus extensus est.

The phrase 'perspiciens lignum crucis' (rendering: ὀπτριζομένη τὸ ξύλον τοῦ σταυροῦ) stands in 1662b where it is in the Greek, while in BHL 1658 it has been moved to the beginning of the sentence so that it now stands next to the *Sibilla* whose action it describes.[120] Clearly BHL 1658 is brushing up BHL 1662b.

There seems to be a parallel between these two Latin versions and the additions Landolfus Sagax made to Paul the Deacon's *Historia romana* during the third quarter of the tenth century at Benevento.[121] Since his method of expansion was

---

[117] Viteau, p. 32, § 11.

[118] Bronzini, 336.

[119] Monte Cassino 117 has a lacuna, but Novara, MS 23 contains the full text. See Bronzini, 316.

[120] The variation between *perspiciens* and *prospiciens* could be as simple as a scribe (or the editors) choosing to resolve the abbreviated *per/pro* differently.

[121] Thus Michel Festy in the introduction to his edition of the *Epitome de caesaribus* (*Abrégé des Césars*) (Paris, 1999), p. lxxv. Landolfus' amplification survives in two manuscripts: BAV, MS Pal. lat. 909, s. x[ex],

one of relying on a great number of earlier historians it is not possible, at this stage at least, to determine how he came to include the following in his work: 'De hoc ligno Sibylla dixit apud paganos: "o ter beatum lignum in quo deus extensus est"'.[122] This is certainly much closer to what the Sibyl says in Katherine's Greek passion than the original verse-line from the *Oracula sibyllina*.[123] How this Sibyl-quotation in Landolfus is related to what the prophetess says in BHL 1662b and BHL 1658 is not clear. It is tempting to see in Landolfus someone who may have had something to do with the translation of BHL 1658, for what his Sibyl says is a little closer to BHL 1658 than BHL 1662b, but that is pure conjecture.

Bronzini also compared passages from BHG 30a with BHL 1662b, but I have found at least one case where the passage in question is actually closer to BHG 30.[124]

BHG 30[125]	BHL 1662b[126]
Αὑτὴ ἦν μεμαθηκυῖα <u>πᾶσαν βίβλον ῥητορικὴν τῆς ἐκβιργιλίων</u> καὶ δημοσθενικῶν δογμάτων [ἐπιστήμης], πᾶσαν <u>τέχνην</u> Ἀσκληπίου καὶ Ἱπποκράτους καὶ Γαληνοῦ, Ἀριστοτέλους τε καὶ Ὁμήρου καὶ Πλάτωνος, Φιλιστίωνος καὶ Εὐσεβίου καὶ Ἰαννοῦ καὶ Μαμβροῦ, καὶ σιβύλλης νεκρομαντείας, καὶ ἁπλῶς πᾶσα διήγησις ῥητόρων φιλοσόφων ...	didicerat enim <u>omnes libros Virgilii atque rhetoricae artis</u> nec non Eusculapii et Galeni, Aristotelis et Homeri, Platonis et Philistionis et Eusebii, Iannes et Mambres, Dionisii et Sybille et quanta Virgilius protulit et Origenes et quantum glorioso genere tantum inclita sagacitate pollebat.

and Bamberg, Staatsbibliothek, MS Hist. 2 (E. III. 13), s. xi, a *codex descriptus*.

[122] Landolfus Sagax, *Additamenta ad Pauli Historiam romanam*, ed. Hans Droysen, MGH AA 2 (Berlin, 1879), p. 327, l. 33.

[123] VI.26: 'ὦ ξύλον ὦ μακαριστόν, ἐφ' οὗ θεὸς ἐξετανύσθη'. *Die Oracula Sibyllina*, ed. Johannes Geffcken (Leipzig, 1902).

[124] Bronzini, 329.

[125] Viteau, p. 7, § 4.

[126] Bronzini, 333.

The clinch is 'omnes libros Virgilii atque rhetoricae artis'.[127] However, seeing that there are parallels in BHL 1662b with both BHG 30a and BHG 30 it is possible that an intermediary Greek text, now lost and posited by Peeters for the Arabic, was used. This would then also explain the parallels between BHL 1662b and BHL 1658.

As already mentioned, BHL 1663 (the most successful Latin version before the appearance of the *Legenda aurea*) seems to be in some sort of relationship with BHL 1658 and BHL 1662b over the beginning of Katherine's speech to the rhetors.[128] On closer inspection, BHL 1662b shares many more parallels with BHL 1663 than any of the other versions. Bronzini thought that these were interpolations that occurred at a later stage.[129] While this is possible, the contamination could well have happened the other way round, namely that BHL 1662b served as a template for BHL 1663. By comparison with BHL 1663, BHL 1662b is much closer to the Greek. At the same time, it has already been tampered with: for example, a number of verses from the *Disticha Catonis* (s. iii[ex]) have been inserted into the text:[130]

---

[127] Cf. BHG 30a: 'ἦν γὰρ μεμαθηκυῖα πᾶσαν βίβλον Ἀσκληπίου καὶ Γαληνοῦ, Ἀριστοτέλους τε καὶ Ὁμήρου καὶ Πλάτωνος καὶ Φιλιστίωνος καὶ Εὐσεβίου καὶ Ἰαννοῦ καὶ Μαμβροῦ καὶ Διονυσίου καὶ σιβυλλῶν νερκομαντείας καὶ ὅσα ὁ Βιργίλιος ἔλεξεν καὶ ὁ Ὁρίων'. Viteau, p. 26, § 4.

[128] 'robustas et fuco verborum plenas dictiones quibus vos fultos ad instantem pugnam video occurrere'. Dobson, l. 353.

[129] '... questi tratti, che ritroviamo in parte nella *Vulgata*, possono essere entrati successivamente nella tradizione di R [Rome, Alessandrina, MS 96], che a noi è giunta senza dubbio notevolmente ampliata', Bronzini, 332.

[130] The same quotations resurface in Peter, Subdeacon of Naples' version at exactly the same place in the story. See D'Angelo, *Pietro Suddiacono*, II.33 and II.49.

The Story of Katherine Moves West

BHL 1662b[131]	*Disticha Catonis*[132]
nec te collaudes, nec te vituperes[133] ipse; hoc faciunt stulti quos gloria vexat inanis.	nec te conlaudes, nec te culpaveris ipse; hoc faciunt stulti, quos gloria vexat inanis.
nam tu si te animo rexeris rex es, si corpore servus.	tu si animo regeris, rex es; si corpore, servus.

Aside from the *Disticha*, there are several passages that have been touched up to produce a much smoother text compared to the 'translationese' still present elswhere in the text. Some of these touched-up passages recur verbatim in BHL 1663.

Bronzini saw in the author of BHL 1663 a translator who was working on the basis of BHG 30 (but who was also amplifying it), citing as an example a parallel between the two texts.[134] Could not the apparent closeness of BHL 1663 to a Greek account be due to its relationship with BHL 1662b, which is a translation that is still unpolished in places? This would, for example, account for the list of philosophers Katherine refers to in her initial speech to the rhetors, already present in the Greek accounts, but also present in BHL 1662b. Another passage cited by Bronzini in support for his supposition that BHL 1663 was a translation of BHG 30 is the description of the rhetors' death in the fire – true, the parallel between the two texts is there, but yet again this is also present in BHL 1662b.[135]

This potential model for BHL 1663 survives in a single manuscript: Rome, Biblioteca Alessandrina, MS 96 is a collection of saints' lives for November and December, put

---

[131] For the text, see Bronzini, 334 and 335.

[132] *Disticha Catonis*, ed. Marcus Boas and Henry J. Botschuyver (Amsterdam, 1952). bk. 2, *distichon* 16, p. 224 and *monostichon*, 7, p. 237.

[133] In 1662b *vituperes* does not scan – the original *culpaveris* does.

[134] Bronzini, 363–64.

[135] Ibid., 372.

together by Costantino Gaetano.[136] Gaetano bequeathed his prodigious collection of manuscripts to the Collegium Gregorianum de Urbe which he founded in 1621 as a place of study for the Benedictine order and whose manuscript holdings, known as the Bibliotheca Aniciana, passed, more or less intact, to the university La Sapienza.[137] Gaetano provided clues for his method of collecting manuscripts and texts: in the margins of his manuscripts he often indicated in which library he had found and copied a particular text.[138] In the case of Alessandrina MS 96, the marginal comment reads: 'ex ms. perant.[iquo] cathedralis Reatinae'.[139] Other libraries visited for the same collection include Monte Cassino (MS 70), Mantua, and the Vatican.[140]

On the basis of Gaetano's marginal note referring to Rieti cathedral, it seems reasonable to suppose that the manuscript from which he copied Katherine's passion was indeed an old one. Given that he had access to the Vatican's collection of

---

[136] Enrico Narducci, *Catalogus codicum manuscriptorum praeter orientales qui in bibliotheca Alexandrina Romae adservantur* (Rome, 1877), pp. 55–61. See also Albert Poncelet, *Catalogus codicum hagiographicorum latinorum bibliothecarum Romanarum praeter quam Vaticanae* (Brussels, 1909), p. 181.

[137] José Ruysschaert, 'Costantino Gaetano, O.S.B.: Chasseur de manuscrits: Contribution à l'histoire de trois bibliothèques romaines du XVIIe s.: L'*Anciana*, L'*Alessandrina* et La *Chigi*', in *Mélanges Eugène Tisserant*, vol. 7: *Biblioteche Vaticane* (Vatican City, 1964), pp. 261–326. See also *Dizionario biografico degli Italiani*, vol. 51 (Rome, 1998), s.v. Gaetani, Costantino.

[138] 'Souvent est indiquée nommément la bibliothèque où se trouvait le texte original reproduit. À part le Mont-Cassin et la Vaticane, cités pour de nombreux manuscrits, la plupart du temps, ces bibliothèques n'ont été visitées que pour un seul manuscrit'. Ruysschaert, 'Costantino Gaetano, O.S.B.', 265.

[139] Poncelet, *Catalogus*, p. 181 and Narducci, *Catalogus*, p. 57.

[140] See Narducci, *Catalogus*, pp. 55–61. The life of Barbara, fols 369a–373b (in Rome, Alessandrina, MS 96) (BHL 917p–q), was also copied from a manuscript at Rieti.

manuscripts and given his own personal interest in manuscripts,[141] he would not have called a fourteenth- or fifteenth-century manuscript very old, so Gaetano's judgement with regard to the lost Rieti manuscript can be considered sound, although it is of course impossible to be any more precise. It also seems reasonable to suppose that Gaetano copied the text of Katherine's passion as he found it. If this was the case, the 'interpolations' with BHL 1663 as Bronzini described the parallels between the two texts, must date from the time when the Rieti manuscript was produced (at least).[142]

It is probably due to the recentness of the witness that Bronzini thought the parallels between BHL 1662b and BHL 1663 were due to later interpolations, but what matters here is not the date of the manuscript but its contents. Bronzini himself demonstrated that 1662b is a translation, but he was mistaken in seeing in BHL 1663 yet another translation. As I will show in the following chapter, BHL 1663 is very obviously the work of someone who had some skill in composing, in Latin, a relatively long saint's life such as that of Katherine. At the same time, he must have been working from some kind of model or template, because it is impossible otherwise to explain the various parallels discussed above. The missing link could well have been a text that looked something like 1662b, in which case this would certainly be an outstanding example of how a recent manuscript can help to disentangle an early stage in a text's tradition.

---

[141] At the time of his death, Gaetano's library comprised 527 manuscripts. See Ruysschaert, 'Costantino Gaetano, O.S.B.', 266.

[142] The Fonte Colombo of the Biblioteca Comunale Paroniana at Rieti preserves eleven manuscripts, none of them contain any saints' lives. See Guiseppe Mazzatinti, *Inventari dei manoscritti delle biblioteche d'Italia*, vol. 2 (Forlì, 1892), pp. 166–70. Of the twelve manuscripts described in Lidia Buono *et al.*, *I manoscritti datati delle provincie di Frosinone, Rieti, e Viterbo*, in *Manoscritti datati d'Italia* 17 (Florence, 2007), none contain saints' lives.

Katherine's emerging cult in Italy was preceded by the arrival there of her Greek passion, particularly BHG 30a and 30, which resulted in a number of translations and adaptations into Latin. The earliest, now lost, example of this is the entry of her name in the index of Munich, BSB, Clm 4554. As is abundantly clear from my brief comparative study, there is a huge amount of contamination between the various Latin versions. Definite conclusions as to their relationships can only really be drawn once all of them have received their own investigation and edition. This relatively unstable corpus of texts could also be an indication for a cult that was still comparatively young, and had not yet gained a foothold in the congregation of saints. Two accounts of Katherine's passion emerge as the most successful: BHL 1659 (that of Peter, Subdeacon of Naples) and BHL 1663. The reason for their success partly lies in the way the two authors composed their texts: neither of the two are direct translations from Greek or are reworkings or adaptations of a more literal translation. But while Peter's account belongs to a higher literary sphere, that of BHL 1663 steers a middle course. The identification of BHL 1662b (Rome, Alessandrina, MS 96) as a potential model for BHL 1663 could be the missing link between Italy and Normandy. The conspicuous lack of early Italian manuscripts for BHL 1663 and a handful of Norman manuscripts point towards the possibility of this version having been composed in France. I will seek confirmation of this hypothesis in the next chapter.

CHAPTER 4

THE DATE AND PLACE OF COMPOSITION OF BHL 1663

I begin by examining the sources used for the composition of BHL 1663 as well as the earliest surviving manuscripts in order to gain a better understanding of its origin. I then turn to Rouen, where Katherine's relics surfaced in the eleventh century, in order to consider the context within which BHL 1663 was composed.[1] This version, which includes a prologue, proved to be the most popular of the Latin versions before the *Legenda aurea* emerged and is thus also sometimes referred to as the '*Vulgate*'; it survives in about 260 manuscripts.[2] Among the great number of epitomes of Katherine's passion, there are two that are clearly related to BHL 1663:[3] BHL 1663a is a version of BHL 1663 in which the speeches have been shortened, but not cut, and which has the same prologue. It

---

An earlier version of this chapter and the next appeared as 'The date and place of composition of the Passion of St Katherine of Alexandria (BHL 1663)', *AB* 130 (2012), 40-88 — I am grateful to the Society of Bollandists for permitting me to reproduce it here with changes.

[1] BHL 1663 was edited by Dobson in 1981 on the basis of twenty-three manuscripts, see Dobson, *Seinte Katerine*, pp. 132–203 and 287–293. An English translation by Nancy Wilson van Baak is available in *La festa et storia di Sancta Caterina: A medieval Italian Religious Drama*, ed. Anne Wilson Tordi (New York, 1997), pp. 249–91.

[2] For a checklist of the manuscripts see Appendix 1.

[3] I have been unable to determine the relationship of BHL 1664b (Trier, Seminarbibliothek, MS 98, s. xiii, fols 118r-120v) or of BHL 1664d (Verdun, Bibliothèque publique, MS 1, s. xii¹, fols 119r-120) to BHL 1663. Having said that, Douai, Bibliothèque Marceline Desbordes-Valmore, MS 151, s. xiv, fols 178r-180r, listed on the *BHLms* site as containing BHL 1664d, in fact contains BHL 1663 with the prologue.

has its own significant transmission and is available in Dobson's edition of BHL 1663 where he calls it the 'shorter *Vulgate*'. He recorded the readings for BHL 1663a on the basis of four manuscripts in the second apparatus.[4] It survives in at least twenty-two manuscripts. In addition, BHL 1661m, an early epitome of BHL 1663, has its own significant transmission in at least eleven witnesses (see Appendix 2). In some of the manuscripts, the text has been divided into readings, indicating that Katherine's cult was beginning to be officially marked by inclusion in the liturgy.

1. Sources and diction of BHL 1663

While BHL 1663 preserves many, if not all, elements of standard hagiographical texts or early *acta*, Katherine's many speeches and subsequent triumph over a huge crowd of rhetors as well as a great number of converts are a good opportunity for the hagiographer to buff up his text by drawing on external sources. This was a common hagiographical technique but contrary to Delehaye's disparaging comment, the author required skill and knowledge to bring it off successfully.[5] Delehaye plays down what remains a creative process since the speeches are not strictly necessary for the story to stand. The central theme of BHL 1663 is Katherine's repeated debates with the emperor and the rhetors, which the hagiographer uses to throw into relief her learning and his own by choosing texts that work well in context. For example, a large part of the dialogue between Katherine and the emperor Maxentius, and the debate between her and the rhetors, is based on the anonymous *Consultationes Zacchei Christiani et Apollonii*

---

[4] Dobson, pp. 144–203.

[5] 'L'hagiographe n'a souvent pas pris la peine de composer la harangue qu'il fait prononcer par son héros; il trouve plus commode de transcrire un chapitre ou des extraits de quelque traité convenablement choisi', in Hippolyte Delehaye, *Les légendes hagiographiques*, 3rd edn (Brussels, 1927), pp. 88–89.

Philosophi (*CZA*). This is a fictional dialogue in which Zaccheus, a Christian, tries to persuade Apollonius, a pagan, to become a Christian, and ultimately succeeds in doing so. In much the same way, Katherine manages to convince the rhetors to convert.

Consider an extract from Katherine's first speech before the emperor:

BHL 1663 (Dobson, ll. 116-34)[6]	CZA, Book I[7]
KATHERINE	ZACCHEUS
	29.11
Etenim malorum omnium inventor diabolus, <u>inter omnes scelerum suorum artes, nulla dubios perniciosius appetit, nec alias a Dei cultu subtilius avocat, quam ut, cum sciamus nos Deo</u> soli <u>debere quod formamur et nascimur</u>, haec omnia elementis mundi ascribi <u>debere suadeat</u> –	Inter omnes enim <u>scelerum suorum artes nulla dubios perniciosius appetit, nec alias a dei cultu subtilius</u> homines <u>avocat, quam ut, cum sciamus</u> omnes <u>deo nos debere quod formamur et nascimur</u>, fato nos <u>suadeat debere</u> quod vivimus.
	25.16
quibus <u>vos</u> divinitatis numen attribuitis et, <u>appositis nominibus, pro Deo singula atque universa veneramini</u>,	Haec <u>vos appositis nominibus pro deo singula atque universa veneramini</u>.
	25.3-5
nulla alia ratione in hanc erroneam opinionem traducti nisi quod <u>coeternam</u> Deo essentiam in se servare videntur; quae plane a Deo <u>ex nichilo facta sunt, et in hanc mundi formam mirabili conspiratione sociata; quae, sicut initium ex Dei creatione</u>	Omnia igitur elementa, quae vos deo velut <u>coaeterna</u> numeratis, ab ipso, sicut iam dixi, et <u>ex nihilo facta sunt, et in hanc mundi formam mirabili conspiratione sociata</u>. Quae, sicut initium ex dei creatione sumpserunt, ita

---

[6] References are to line numbers in Dobson's edition of BHL 1663 in *Seinte Katerine*.

[7] References are to the chapter divisions in *Questions d'un païen à un chrétien*, ed. Jean-Louis Feiertag and Werner Steinmann (Consultationes Zacchei christiani et Apollonii philosophi) (Paris, 1994).

sumpserunt, ita perennitatem eius beneficio consequentur.

perennitatem eius beneficio consequentur.

Et ideo coeterna Deo non sunt, quia impossibile est creaturam, temporaliter factam, creatori suo, qui est sine tempore, coaevam esse et consempiternam;

Et ideo ei coaeterna non sunt a quo facta sunt, quia nulli dubium est, auctori quaelibet non solum paria non esse, sed esse subiecta.

25.19

ille enim solus est sine initio a quo rerum omnium processit exordium. Talibus ergo divinitas non est ascribenda, quae, sub Dei dispositione posita, non quae suae voluntatis sunt faciunt, sed a Deo imposite serviunt rationi.

Vides ergo deo soli initium non apponendum, a quo omnium processit exordium, nec consempiterna maiestati illius aestimanda quae, ut aeterna sint, sicut de homine, ipse facturus est.

25.18

Dii ergo non sunt plures, sed unus nascentium et viventium formator est Deus, qui, sicut omnia creavit, ita imperio suo omnia coercet atque disponit.

Dii enim plures non sunt, sed unus nascentium viventiumque formator, sicut fecit omnia, et regit, parique imperio vel mansura efficit, vel casura decernit.

From the above it is apparent that the author of BHL 1663 has cobbled together various phrases from his source text, although without following the order of the text, at least as it survives, to form a more or less coherent whole. Possibly, his main concern was not so much a theologically coherent argumentation as the appearance of learning in his protagonist.

Consider also the rhetors' second question to Katherine and her answer:

BHL 1663
(Dobson, ll. 480-502)
RHETOR

CZA, Book I

APOLLONIUS
14.1-2

Si praedicta miracula, ut credi iubes, manens in homine Deus praestitit, numquid suscipere et pati crucem debuit? Aut quam ob causam, alios erepturus a morte, ipse etiam morte non caruit? Vel

1. Si praedicta miracula, ut credi studes, manens in homine deus praestitit, numquid suscipere et pati crucem voluit? Aut quam ob causam erepturus a morte alios morte non caruit? Vel

certe quomodo <u>aliis proderit qui sibi prodesse non potuit</u>, <u>cum in</u> sua <u>libera</u>tione etiam <u>aliis</u> spem <u>liberatio</u>nis contuli<u>sset</u> ?

quemadmodum <u>aliis proderit qui sibi prodesse non potuit?</u>
2. <u>Cum in</u> hoc magis fidem de se ambigentibus munire debuerit, <u>libera</u>turum et <u>alios</u> fore, quo hoc primum in sua <u>liberatio</u>ne monstra<u>sset</u>. Qua in re aut rationem prodi necesse est, aut credulitatem non exigi satis iustum.

KATHERINE

Et <u>in hoc etiam estimatio tua fallitur, si in crucis affixione</u> impassibilem Deum passionem doloris et mortis sustinuisse arbitraris. Non enim natura caelestis crucis sensit iniuriam, sed assumptae in Deum infirmitas carnis. Nam, <u>incomprehensibilis et liber</u> ab omni passione, Deus <u>nec pati potuit nec teneri; sed quendam de diabolo per assumptum hominem egit triumphum cum, in ligno</u> materiam <u>carnis imponens, eum sine sui iniuria per hominem superavit qui hominem cum Dei iniuria egerat in delictum.</u>
<u>Homo ergo, non divinitas,</u> *cruci affixus*[8] <u>est, et qui peccaverat per lignum fixus in ligno est.</u>
<u>Haec Deo fuit assumendi</u>

ZACCHEUS
14.3-5
3. <u>Etiam in hoc aestimatio tua fallitur, ut in crucis adfixione</u> divinitatem credas iniuriam pertulisse, quae <u>incomprehensibilis et libera nec pati potuit, nec teneri. Sed quendam de diabolo per adsumptum hominem egit triumphum, cum in ligno</u> victoriam <u>carnis imponens, eum sine sui iniuria per hominem superavit, qui hominem cum dei iniuria egerat in delictum.</u>
4. <u>Homo ergo, non divinitas</u> *trucidata* <u>est. Et qui per lignum peccaverat, fixus in ligno est.</u>
5. Atque <u>haec deo fuit adsumendi</u>

---

8 The reading 'cruci affixus' is not merely an alternative to 'trucidata'. It is plausible that the author of BHL 1663 was working from a *CZA*-manuscript that carried 'cruci data' (as attested in MSS *L* or *T* of the *CZA*). He emended 'data', previously in agreement with 'divinitas', to 'affixus' to agree with 'homo', not paying attention to the argument in *CZA* where a distinction is being made between the human and the divine nature of Jesus.

hominem praecipue ratio vel voluntas, ut peccatum ab homine contractum per hominem tolleretur, et ab illo fides resurrectionis inciperet quem primum resurgere debuisse constaret. Potens equidem erat Deus, per angelum quemvis aut per aliquam caelestem virtutem, prostrato diabolo hominem eripere, si voluisset, sed, omnia cum ratione agens, Deus sic modum statuit victoriae ut qui hominem subiugarat per hominem ipse vinceretur.	hominem praecipua ratio vel voluntas, ut peccatum ab homine contractum per hominem tolleretur, et ab illo fides resurrectionis inciperet, quem primum resurgere debuisse constaret. Purus enim et ab omni immunis delicto pati pro omnibus voluit, ut non sola potestate, sed merito omnibus praeferretur.

The *CZA* has been used twice more in BHL 1663: Katherine's first speech, in which she takes on the role of Zacchaeus, is answered by the emperor, who takes on the role of Apollonius. His answer, as well as Katherine's second speech (Dobson, ll. 149-166 + 171-202), are based on *CZA* book 1.1.2-3, and then book 1.25.6 + 1.25.9-17. The rhetor's first question (Dobson, ll. 396-402), where he takes on the role of Apollonius and Katherine's lengthy reply (Dobson, ll. 403-466) in the 'guise' of Zacchaeus are based on *CZA* book 1.2.1 and then 1.2.3 + 1.4.3 + 1.6.4-7 + 1.5.4-5 + 1.6.3 + 1.4.4-9.[9] The author of *BHL* 1663 only used book one of the *CZA*, even though there are three. The explanation lies in the overall structure of the *CZA*: in book one Zacchaeus expounds the fundamental questions of the Christian faith and Apollonius converts to Christianity.

[9] In her study of Clemence of Barking's twelfth-century Anglo-Norman verse life of Katherine, Annegret Hilligus showed that the author of BHL 1663 incorporated passages from the *CZA* into his text. While she clearly set out the parallels, she did not consider the implications of her discovery as regards the dissemination of the *CZA* or the origin of BHL 1663. See Annegret Hilligus, *Die Katharinenlegende von Clemence de Barking: Eine anglo-normannische Fassung aus dem 12. Jahrhundert* (Tübingen, 1996).

Very little is known about the origin of the *CZA*: it was in all likelihood composed between 375-8 (or 409) and 489, either in Gaul or northern Africa. It may have been known to Evagrius (Gaul, flourished 430), but was certainly read by Victor of Vita (end of the fifth century) and Isidore of Seville (d. 636).[10] It is preserved in only seven manuscripts, most of which originate from Benedictine monasteries in the Frankish kingdom, with the majority dating from the tenth and eleventh centuries.[11]

[10] For an exhaustive discussion of the date and place of composition see: Germain Morin, 'Ein zweites christliches Werk des Firmicus Maternus: Die Consultationes Zacchaei et Apollonii', *Historisches Jahrbuch*, 37 (1916), 229–66; August Reatz, *Das theologische System der* Consultationes Zacchaei et Apollonii, *mit Berücksichtigung ihrer angeblichen Beziehung zu J. Firmicus Maternus* (Freiburg i. Br., 1920); Bertil Axelson, *Ein drittes Werk des Firmicus Maternus?: Zur Kritik der philologischen Identifizierungsmethode* (Lund, 1937), pp. 107–32; Ferdinand Cavallera, 'Un exposé sur la vie spirituelle et monastique au ive siècle', *Revue d'ascétique et de mystique*, 16 (1935), 132–46; Pierre Courcelle, 'Date, source et genèse des *Consultationes Zacchaei et Apollonii*', *Revue de l'histoire des religions*, 146 (1954), 174–93; García M. Colombás, 'Sobre el autor des las *Consultationes Zacchaei et Apollonii*', *Studia Monastica*, 14 (1972), 7–15; Jean-Louis Feiertag, *Les* Consultationes Zacchaei et Apollonii: *Étude d'histoire et de sotériologie* (Fribourg, 1990). For the parallels with Isidore of Seville (as well with Victor of Vita) see A.C. Lawson, 'Consultationes Zacchaei Christiani et Apollonii philosophi: Source of S. Isidore of Seville', *Revue Bénédictine*, 57 (1947), 187–95. A convenient list of the parallels can also be found in Christopher M. Lawson's edition of *Sancti Isidori Episcopi Hispalensis: De ecclesiasticis officiis*, CCSL 113 (Turnhout, 1989), p. 154.

[11] *T* Paris, BnF, MS lat. 2667A, s. x, prov. Fleury, but not written there; *P* Paris, BnF, MS lat. 2968A, s. x, passed through Fleury [?]); *M* Metz, Bibliothèque municipale, MS 141, s. xi, prov. Saint-Arnould/Metz, destroyed during WWII but used by Morin; *L* Paris, BnF, MS lat. 2400, s. xi, prov. Saint-Cybard/Angoulême?, then Saint-Martial/Limoges; *B* Leiden, Universiteitsbibliotheek, MS Voss. Lat. Q. 113, s. xi, apparently the second part of BAV, MS Reg. lat. 252, s. x–xi: according to André Wilmart, *Codices reginenses latini*, vol. 2 (Città del Vaticano, 1937–45), it comes from a scriptorium at Tours; *V* variants from manuscripts from La Trinité at Vendôme (taken from the first

Although the evidence of shared readings between BHL 1663 and specific manuscripts of the *CZA* is scant, it seems the former follows the *β*-branch of the manuscript transmission, which includes two manuscripts from northern France.[12] As regards the question of the direction of the borrowing, the fact that the *CZA* was available to Victor of Vita and Isidore of Seville excludes the possibility that BHL 1663 served as its source-text. In addition, none of these authors use the same passages of the *CZA* as the author of BHL 1663, which means that the latter was working from the *CZA* itself, though not necessarily a complete copy. However, all the extant manuscripts preserve the full text of the *CZA*.

I have discovered that, in the prologue, the author of BHL 1663 makes use of another dialogue-based text, the *Conflictus vitiorum et virtutum* (*Conflictus*) by Ambrose Autpert (d. 784), the abbot of San Vincenzo near Benevento:[13]

BHL 1663 (Dobson, ll. 15-28)	*Conflictus* Ch. 1.1-6:
Et, quia Christianitas in suis principibus iam religiosa iamque fidelis est, iam persecutionis procella detumuit, iam vincula et verbera, carceres et eculeos et cetera suppliciorum genera procul cessisse	Apostolica vox clamat per orbem, atque in procinctu fidei positis, ne securitate torpeant, dicit: Omnes qui pie volunt vivere in Christo Iesu persecutionem patientur. Et ecce quia Christianitas in suis

edition of Jean-Luc d'Achéry in vol. 10 of *Veterum aliquot scriptorium qui in Galliae bibliothecis maxime Benedictorum latuerant spicilegium* [Paris, 1671], pp. 1–125); *C* Bernkastel-Kues, St. Nikolas Hospital, MS 52, s. xii, prov. St. Eucharius-Matthias/Trier (?); another manuscript belonged to Zacharias Conrad von Uffenbach († 1734) but appears now to be lost. Two manuscripts were also mentioned in medieval catalogues of the abbeys Saint-Èvre/Toul and Saint-Martin/Massay, but are now lost. See the list of manuscripts in Feiertag, *Questions d'un païen*, vol. 1, pp. 43–54.

[12] Feiertag, *Questions d'un païen*, indentified two groupings (see vol. 1, pp. 53–63): *β* = ***BVLT*** and *κ* = ***CMP***.

[13] *Libellus de conflictu vitiorum et virtutum* in *Ambrosii Autperti Opera* vol. 3, ed. Robert Weber (Turnhout, 1979), pp. 907–31.

manifestum est, et ideo Christicolis iure non potest imputari si, his nostris temporibus, penalibus tormentis non probantur, quia persecutionis occasio, sedata pace, iam quievit.

principibus iam religiosa, iamque fidelis est, desunt pie viventibus in Christo Iesu vincula, verbera, flagra, carceres, eculei, cruces, et si qua sunt diversorum genera tormentorum.

Ch. 1.14-19:

Huic, quisquis ille est, tale damus responsum: virgo haec non uniformi persecutionis genere impugnabatur, cui a fronte externus hostis, a tergo incumbebat domesticus et occultus; alia enim intelligenda est persecutio, quae immanior et magis noxia est et quam non materialis intorquet severitas, sed vitiorum gignit adversitas.

Istane est illa generalis persecutio, quam Apostolus omnes pie viventes pati descripsit? Non facile dixerim, cum sint quidam religiosi quibus nemo pravorum audeat in faciem derogare. Alia ergo intellegenda est, quae immanior et magis noxia est, quamque non materialis intorquet severitas, sed vitiorum gignit adversitas.

Ch. 1.34-36:

Porro haec generosa virago, gemina oppugnantium acie circumsepta, et furentem persequentium rabiem constanter evicit et conglobatas vitiorum acies viriliter debellavit.

... quid aliud quam crudelis pie viventium persecutio adversus conglobatas virtutum acies desaevit?

Autpert was an author very much in vogue during his lifetime and shortly after. Among his literary output, the ten-book commentary on the Apocalypse was the most important, yet the *Conflictus* enjoyed a much wider circulation. This can be explained in part by homonymy with Ambrose of Milan.[14] Autpert's works circulated mainly in France and Italy in the eighth to tenth centuries; the *Conflictus* survives in more than one hundred manuscripts. It was addressed to Landfrid, the

---

[14] In a number of manuscripts, the *Conflictus* is attributed to him. The *PL* features it among the works of Ambrose and Augustine. It also circulated under the names of Leo I, Gregory the Great, and Isidore of Seville. Jacques Winandy, 'L'œuvre littéraire d'Ambroise Autpert', *Revue Bénédictine*, 60 (1950), pp. 93–119, lists the authors and the manuscripts.

first abbot of Benediktbeuern; thus emerges the likely audience for the dialogue, namely Benedictine monks.[15]

In the eighteenth century, Autpert and the *Conflictus* were brought into association by Antoine Rivet.[16] Robert Weber, in turn, put forward two reasons for Autpert's authorship of the dialogue: 1) the oldest manuscritps all carry his name;[17] 2) the twelfth-century *Chronicon vulturnense* and the anonymous monk of Melk (*De scriptoribus ecclesiasticis*) attribute the dialogue to Autpert.[18] For his edition of the *Conflictus*, Weber

[15] See Winandy, 'L'œuvre littéraire', p. 99, and Claudio Leonardi, 'Spiritualità di Ambrogio Autperto', *Studi Medievali*, 3rd series, 9 (1968), 1–131.

[16] He pointed out that a manuscript at Saint-Évroult (Normandy) attributed the dialogue to Autpert, cf. Antoine Rivet *et al.*, *Histoire littéraire de la France*, vol. 4 (Paris, 1738), p. 148. But already in 1685, the Maurists had restored Autpert's authorship of the dialogue in the appendix of their Augustine edition, on the basis of a number of parallels with the commentary on the Apocalypse (*PL*, vol. 40, cols 1091–92), see Winandy, 'L'œuvre littéraire', p. 98.

[17] *M* Munich, BSB, Clm 14746, s. xi, prov. St. Emmeram/Regensburg: 'Incipit libellus Autperti presbyteri de conflictu vitiorum atque virtutum: missus ad Landefredum presbyterum et abbatem in Baioaria constitutum'. Bischoff, *Schreibschulen*, I, p. 196: the *Conflictus* is followed by Autpert's *Sermo in purificatione Mariae*. The two works were copied by two different, but probably contemporary, hands. *N* Munich, BSB, Clm 14500, s. ix, prov. St. Emmeram/Regensburg: Autpert's name is on fol. 2, and the dedicatee is also mentioned: 'Lantfredum presybterum et abbatem in Baioaria constitutum'. For the date and provenance see Bischoff, *Schreibschulen*, I, p. 38. For details on Autpert's name see Morin, 'Le *Conflictus*', pp. 204–12. *P* Paris, BnF, MS lat. 2731A, s. xi^{ex} from France. Date and provenance: personal comment by Bischoff to Weber. Its previous call-marks were Colbert 4085 and Regius 4533^{55}, see *Catalogue général des manuscrits latins*, vol. 3: Paris BnF (Paris, 1958), pp. 40–41. Paris, BnF, MS lat. 2732 is described on pp. 41–42; it is a libellus containing the *Conflictus*, s. xii, and belonged to Jacques Auguste de Thou.

[18] Weber, *Libellus*, p. 878. The *Chronicon vulturnense* also contains Autpert's life of Paldo, Tato and Taso (BHL 6415), as well as his own life (BHL 368) written by the monk John, the author of the *Chronicon*.

only used three manuscripts, although there are a good number of other early witnesses.[19]

As regards the transmission of the *Conflictus*, it is clear that the earliest witnesses come from ninth/tenth-century Bavaria, mainly Regensburg as well as Schäftlarn. Moreover, it survives in four manuscripts from Jumièges in Normandy, one of which has been dated to the tenth century.[20] Hubert Silvestre's study of the manuscripts of the *Conflictus* includes three from the eleventh century, with northern French and Flemish provenances.[21]

See Hartmut Hoffmann, 'Das *Chronicon Vulturnense* und die Chronik von Montecassino', *Deutsches Archiv*, 22 (1966), 179–96.

[19] In addition to the three manuscripts *M*, *N*, and *P*, Weber collated: α = S. Augustini liber de conflictu uiciorum et virtutum [Argentorati, G. Husner 1474?] and μ = S. Augustini Opera, ed. Maurinorum, vol. 6, 1685, Appendix, cols 219–28. The manuscripts for the latter edition came from Corbie, Lyre, Saint-Victor in Paris and Saint-Germain-des-Prés, as well as a manuscript described as *regius* by its editors. See Weber, *Libellus*, p. 879. Other early manuscripts include: Munich, BSB, Clm 14757, fols 100–127, written at St. Emmeram, Regensburg at the time of bishop Baturich (817–47); Munich, BSB, Clm 27059, s. ix/x, prov. Schäftlarn; Munich, BSB, Clm 17059, s. ix (Schäftlarn); Paris, BnF, MS lat. 2843, s. x/xi (*Conflictus* = s. xi), prov. Saint-Martial, Limoges.

[20] Rouen, MS 1378 (U.40), written between 942 and 973, see François Avril, *Manuscrits normands XI–XIème siècles* (Rouen, 1975), p. 8; Rouen, MS 670 (A.592), s. xiii; Rouen, MS 1468 (U.136), s. xiii; Rouen, MS 933 (I.60), s. xv. The thirteenth-century catalogue from Lyre lists the *Conflictus*, as does the seventeenth-century catalogue for Saint-Évroult. See Geneviève Nortier, *Les bibliothèques médiévales des abbayes bénédictines de Normandie: Fécamp, Le Bec, Le Mont Saint-Michel, Saint-Évroul, Lyre, Jumièges, Saint-Wandrille, Saint-Ouen* (Paris, 1971), p. 197.

[21] Hubert Silvestre, 'Notes sur les manuscrits de Bruxelles du *De conflictu vitiorum atque virtutum* d'Ambroise Autpert', in *Calames et cahiers: Mélanges de codicologie et de paléographie offerts à Léon Gilissen*, ed. Jacques Lemaire and Émile Van Balberghe (Brussels, 1985), pp. 162–65: Brussels, KBR, MS 8344-46, s. xi$^{med.}$, prov. Saint-Laurent/Liège (?); Brussels, KBR, MS 8714-19, s. xi, prov. Sainte-Rictrude, Marchiennes;

Given the author's penchant for using literary texts to buff up his version of Katherine's passion, one might expect him to use Autpert's *Conflictus* more than once. And, indeed, it turns out that he saw in it a useful source for the prison scene, during which Katherine once more extols the Christian faith and succeeds in converting the queen and the general of the army, Porphyrius. In her answer to the latter's question about the nature of God's gifts, Katherine slips from her own words into the role of the *amor patriae caelestis* of Autpert's *Conflictus*:

BHL 1663	*Conflictus*
(Dobson, ll. 775-800)	26.17-39
KATHERINE	AMOR PATRIAE CAELESTIS
Quod si ita est – immo quia ita est – nunc in adversum mentis defige intuitum et, quia interrogando sciscitaris quae sunt et quanta illa praemia quae suis Christus pro transitoriis rependit, sic accipe: porro, <u>si</u> haec <u>quae sub caelo sunt</u> tam fluxa atque fugitiva aliquo modo forent expetenda, <u>cur non</u>[22] multo <u>magis quae super caelos sunt</u> firma et stabilia mentes humanas non <u>oblectant</u>, prasertim cum illa nec ad votum possunt retineri, ista, semel accepta, ultra non possunt amitti? Mundus iste velut <u>carcer</u> est tenebrosus, in <u>quo</u> <u>nullus ita nascitur ut non</u>	Si te ita delectant <u>quae sub caelo</u> <u>sunt</u>, <u>cur non magis delectent</u> ea <u>quae super caelos sunt</u>? Si <u>carcer</u> ita pulcher est, <u>patria</u>, <u>civitas</u> et domus qualis est? Si talia sunt quae incolunt peregrini, qualia sunt quae possident filii? Si mortales et miseri in hac vita taliter sunt remunerati, inmortales et beati qualiter sunt in illa vita ditati? Quapropter recedat amor

Paris, BnF, MS lat. 10400, fol. 138 + Brussels, KBR, MS 9398-99 + 9361-67, s. xi$^{1/2}$, prov. Saint-Laurent/Liège.

[22] Dobson emended *non* to *enim*, although the manuscripts agree on *non*. Dobson's justification, p. 292: 'all copies read *non* where we emend to *enim*, but their text seems impossible in view of *non* before *oblectant* in the next line; we assume that in the archetype the abbreviation ·N· for *enim* had been replaced by ñ for *non*'. The parallel in the *Conflictus* shows that *non* is correct in terms of the source text, but becomes nonsensical in BHL 1663 due to the repeated *non* in front of *oblectant*.

moriatur; illa superna <u>patria</u>, pro qua fit mundi contemptus, velut <u>civitas</u> est, sole numquam indigens, <u>ubi nulla turbat adversitas, nulla necessitas angustat, molesia nulla inquietat, sed perennis laetitia</u>, iocunditas aeterna, felicitas <u>regnat</u> sempiterna. <u>Si quaeris quid ibi sit ubi tanta et talis beatitudo</u> consistit, <u>aliter dici non potest nisi</u> 'Quicquid boni est ibi est, et quicquid mali est nusquam est.' 'Quod', inquis, '*bonum*?' 'Illud est', dico, '<u>quod oculus non vidit nec auris audivit nec in cor hominis *ascendit*, que praeparavit Deus diligentibus se</u>. Ad hanc felicitatem quidam, <u>divitiis constipatus, anhelabat, dicens</u> 'Usque quo me, Deus, in hoc mundi squalentis pulvere reprimis?' 'Usque adeo sitientem ad te spiritum intra carnis ergastulum reprimis?' 'Usque quo prolongatur incolatus meus?' Haec est illa desiderabilis patria ubi non est luctus neque clamor neque dolor, sed absterget Deus omnem lacrimam ab oculis sanctorum; de qua dicit unus ex suis, '<u>Satiabor *dum* manifestabitur gloria tua</u>.' Parva quidem sunt quae dico ad ea quae visu et rerum veritate experieris si fidelis usque in finem perseveraveris.

praesentis saeculi, <u>in quo nullus ita nascitur, ut non moriatur</u>, et succedat amor saeculi futuri, in quo sic omnes vivificantur, ut deinceps non moriantur, <u>ubi nulla adversitas turbat, nulla necessitas angustat, nulla molestia inquietat, sed perennis laetitia regnat. Si quaeris, quid ibi sit, ubi tanta et talis beatitudo</u> perstitit, <u>aliter dici non potest nisi, quicquid boni est, ibi est et quicquid mali est, nusquam est</u>. Quod, inquis, *illud bonum* est? Quid me interrogas? A Propheta et apostolo definitum est: '<u>Quod oculus</u>', inquiunt, '<u>non vidit, nec auris audivit, nec in cor hominis *ascenderunt*, quae praeparavit Deus his qui diligunt eum</u>.' <u>Ad hanc felicitatem</u> multis saeculi <u>divitiis constipatus</u> David <u>anhelabat</u> cum <u>diceret</u>: 'Quid mihi restat in caelo, et a te quid volui super terram?' Multis regalium dapibus abundans dicebat: '<u>Satiabor cum manifestabitur gloria tua</u>.' Et rursum: 'Sitivit anima mea ad Deum vivum, quando veniam et parebo ante faciem Dei?' Et rursum: 'Sitivit anima mea ad Deum vivum, quando veniam et parebo ante faciem Dei?' Rursumque: 'Heu me, quod incolatus meus prolongatus est?' Hinc et Paulus: 'Cupio dissolvi et esse cum Christo, multo autem melius.'

Apparatus – *BHL 1663*
cur non multo magis quae super caelos sunt] **Codd**.
oblectant] oblectent *CDLN*
bonum illud] **Codd**.

Apparatus – *Conflictus*
cur non magis delectent ea quae super caelos sunt] om. *P*
delectent] delectant *a*
illud bonum] bonum illud *P*

ascendit] *Codd.*	ascenderunt] ascendit *P α μ*
dum	cum] dum *P*

The comparison of the two apparatus reveals that in three instances BHL 1663 follows the Paris manuscript: the inversion of *bonum illud* and the reading of *dum* instead of *cum* are not very strong evidence. However, the agreement of BHL 1663 over *ascendit* (rather than *ascenderunt*) with *P*, as well as *α* and *μ* suggests that BHL 1663 is following the French tradition of the *Conflictus*, especially if one considers the fact that *μ* represents at least four manuscripts of French provenance. The omission by *P* of more than a mere word (i.e. the phrase 'cur non magis delectent ea quae super caelos sunt') need not pose difficulties since *α* and *μ* preserve it, so that the conclusion must be that BHL 1663 was not based on the text preserved in *P*. Since Weber only used a limited number of the available manuscripts, these observations must remain provisional.

In light of the manuscript evidence, it seems likely that the author of BHL 1663 borrowed from the *Conflictus*, rather than the other way round: the latter can claim at least four pre-900 CE manuscripts while BHL 1663 survives only in manuscripts from the eleventh-century onwards, all of which originate in northern France.[23] At the same time, the date of Autpert's death, 784, serves as the *terminus post quem* for the composition of BHL 1663.

On a compositional level, the effect of the word *carcer* is rather skillful ('mundus iste velut carcer est tenebrosus', Dobson, l. 783).[24] The setting of Katherine's encounter with

---

[23] It is highly unlikely that the lost text from Munich Clm 4554 was that of BHL 1663. See Chapter 3.

[24] In his *sermo de adsumptione Sanctae Mariae*, 8.1, Autpert writes: 'quaecumque igitur anima sancta talibus fuerit incitamentis occupata, nihil concupiscit terrenum, nihil transitorium, nihil quod ad tempus arridet, nihil quod ad praesens delectat; quae risum luctum deputat, et gaudium in maerorem commutat; cui mundus carcer, caelum vero

the queen and Porphyrius is her prison cell, while the short exchanges in the *Conflictus* have been set neither in time nor space. This actual setting in BHL 1663 echoes one of the arguments put forward by the *amor patriae caelestis*. Towards the beginning of its speech it asks: 'si carcer ita pulcher est, patria, civitas et domus qualis est?' The *carcer* here clearly refers to the world in which the *amor saeculis praesentis* feels so comfortable, and it is contrasted with the *patria caelestis*, referred to not only as *patria*, but also by decreasing entities of *civitas* and *domus*. One can easily imagine Katherine making a sweeping gesture as she points to the dark walls of her surroundings that are illuminated only by the glimmer emanating from her and the holy men sitting around her.

It is clear, therefore, that the author had thought carefully about which passages of the *Conflictus* he was going to use and where in his text he was going to use them. The role-play that is created is also striking, because, although he does not get to speak in this passage, Porphyrius is described as 'primae cohortis praefecturam agebat et magnis rerum possessionibus pollebat' (Dobson, l. 763) and thus silently assumes the role of the *amor saeculi praesentis*. Finally, the author of BHL 1663 reveals himself as someone who seems to enjoy debating questions of faith and observance, and as someone who had something to say and took the trouble to sit down and piece together a new version of Katherine's passion.

Lastly, I have detected a third source. Hagiographers often turned to historical accounts to historicize their subjects and range them among the early martyrs of the Christian church when they were writing about saints whose existence was in

---

habitatio est, cui exultatio de praesentibus nulla est, quia in illo tantum gaudere appetit, qui super omnes est'. Other authors who equate the world with a prison are, for example, Augustine, *Enarrationes in Psalmos*, Ps. 141.17.13, and Paschasius Radbertus (d. *c.* 860), *Expositio in Matthaeo Libri xii*, ed. Paulus Beda (Turnhout, 1984), 3.1751 and 7.3878.

doubt. Use of this technique began in the ninth century.²⁵ A particular favourite was the early fifth-century apologetic historian Paulus Orosius. His *Historiarum adversus paganos libri vii* was used as a universal text-book during the Middle Ages, 'and no monastic, school, or university library could afford to be without a copy'.²⁶ An indication of its popularity can be seen in the surviving 245 manuscripts.²⁷ The earliest manuscripts, from the sixth to the eighth centuries, mainly come from Irish foundations in northern Italy and France.²⁸

---

25 I owe this information to Monique Goullet. Passages from Orosius' seventh book, but not the passage here under consideration, have been incorporated into the accounts of the following saints, without actually making reference to the source: Helena BHL 3772, passim; Genulfus BHL 3358, ch. 2; Marcella BHL 5222, ch. 4; Patroclus BHL 6521, ch. 2; Theodoros of Heraclea BHL 8086, introduction. In the life of Salaberga (BHL 7463), the author names his source: 'nam cum illo in tempore gens Baïcariorum, quam Orosius vir eruditissimus et historiarum cognitor Boïos prisco vocabulo appellat', *Passiones vitaeque sanctorum aevi Merovingici*, ed. Bruno Krusch and Wilhelm Levison, MGH SSRM 5 (Hannover, 1910), p. 51, l. 2. In the prologue to Walafrid Strabo's life of Gallus *scriptores authenticos* refers to Orosius and Solinus (I owe this reference to Monique Goullet); *Passiones vitaeque sanctorum aevi Merovingici*, ed. Bruno Krusch, MGH SSRM 4 (Hannover, 1902), p. 281.

26 David J.A. Ross, 'Illustrated manuscripts of Orosius', *Scriptorium*, 9 (1955), p. 35.

27 Janet M. Bately and David J.A. Ross, 'A check list of manuscripts of Orosius' "Historiarum adversum paganos libri septem"', *Scriptorium*, 15 (1961), 329–34. The *Histories* was also abbreviated many times and translated, for example, into Old English and Arabic. The list of manuscripts is available online: <www.tertullian.org/rpearse/manuscripts/orosius_history.htm> [accessed 3 July 2021]

28 For a detailed description of the early manuscripts see Marie-Pierre Arnaud-Lindet ed., *Orosius: Histoires (contre les Païens)* (Paris, 1990), vol. 1, pp. lxx–lxxx; Karl Zangemeister ed., *Pauli Orosii historiarum adversum paganos libri VII*, CSEL 5 (Leipzig, 1882), also provides descriptions on pp. vi–xviii. Orosius was available at Fécamp, Le Bec, Saint-Évroult, and Lyre in the twelfth century, see Nortier, *Les bibliothèques médiévales*, p. 223.

For the most part, anyone writing a saints' life during the ninth/tenth centuries in the Latin West would have had access to a copy of Orosius. The editor of Orosius' *Histories* distinguished three groupings within the manuscript tradition, but BHL 1663 does not seem to be following a particular one; there are no decisive readings in either apparatus to allow a rapprochement:

BHL 1663 (Dobson, ll. 33-44)	*Orosius*, Book VII
Tradunt annales historiae quod Constantinus, qui gubernacula imperii a patre Constantio suscepit, quae uno et triginta annis moderator egregius tenuit, pacem ecclesiis, post decem annos a persecutoribus vexabantur, indulsit.	26.1: Anno ab Urbe condita MLXI, Constantinus tricensimus quartus gubernacula imperii a Constantio patre suscepit, quae uno et triginta annis felicissime tenuit. *Intervening passages deal with the persecutions suffered by the Christians under Nero until Maximian.*
Hic Constantinus cum rempublicam strenue in Galliis procuraret, praetoriani milites Romae Maxentium, Herculii filium, qui privatus in Lucania morabatur, Augustum nuncupaverunt.	28.5: Constantino in Gallis strenuissime rempublicam procurante, praetoriani milites Romae Maxentium, filium Herculii, qui privatus in Lucania morabatur, Augustum nuncupaverunt
Inde inter Constantinum et Maxentium bellum civile exortum est. Maxentius, siquidem proelio fugatus, Alexandriae partibus sese recepit.	28.15-16: Constantinus pacem ecclesiis post decem annos quam a persecutoribus vexabantur indulsit. Deinde inter Constantinum et Maxentium bellum civile exortum est. Maxentius, saepe multis proeliis fatigatus, ultime ad pontem Mulvium victus et interfectus est.
Audiens autem Constantinum	28.17: Maximinus, persecutionis

intra Illiricum sinum bellis undique consurgentibus detineri	Christianorum incentor exsecutorque infestissimus, apud Tharsum, dum civile bellum contra Licinium disponit, interiit. 28.18:
ipse, <u>repentina rabie</u> in<u>citatus</u>, ecclesiam Christi zelo idolatriae persequi instituit et ad profana sacrificia Christianos aut praemiis aut tormentis incurvare.	Licinius, <u>repentina rabie</u> sus<u>citatus</u>, omnes Christianos e palatio suo iussit expelli.

Chapters 26 and 28 from Book 7 deal with the period at the beginning of the fourth century during which many of the first Christian martyrs met their deaths. The author of BHL 1663 not only sought to historicize Katherine's passion, he also ranged the saint among the early martyrs of the Christian church. At the same time, he imbued his account with an air of learning. Having said that, the historian who looks to BHL 1663 for any other historical references will be disappointed: all persons and episodes are typical of hagiographic accounts and only allow insight into the author's preoccupations with theological debate and with portraying Katherine as an edifying example.

In sum, there are three literary sources, mostly of apologetic nature, found cited verbatim in BHL 1663: the anonymous *CZA*, which survives in a small number of French manuscripts mostly from the tenth and eleventh centuries. Then there is Ambrose Autpert's *Conflictus virtutum vitiorum*, also in dialogue form just as the *CZA*. Finally, the author has used Orosius' *Histories* to historically legitimize his account of Katherine's exploits. The presence of these three major sources in BHL 1663 also enables a firm conclusion about the development of one of the epitomes, BHL 1663a. This version was first identified by Knust as an abbreviation of BHL 1663, a hypothesis confirmed by Dobson.[29] A brief examination of this epitome reveals that, like its originating text, it contains the

---

[29] Knust, *Geschichte der Legenden,* pp. 17–18. Dobson, pp. xix–xxi.

historical introduction based on Orosius, as well as a number of remnants from the *CZA* and Autpert's *Conflictus*. However, since the epitomator was not aware of the sources embedded in the text he was working with, he ended up cutting wherever he thought the material was superfluous.

Besides the use of literary texts, the choice of words can also provide clues for where and when BHL 1663 might have been written. Two rare words, the adverb *celeranter* (a variant for *celeriter*) and the noun *tarinca*, suggest an initial localization for the composition of the text. First, the adverb: towards the beginning of the story, Katherine hears the noise of the sacrificial animals and various musical instruments emanating from the emperor's palace. She sends someone to find out what the fuss is about: 'stupens itaque causam celeranter iubet inquiri' (Dobson, l. 92). The polysyllabic adverb *celeranter* is not very common: the late fourth/early fifth-century grammarian Nonius Marcellus cites the second-century BCE grammarian Lucius Accius as using *celeranter*.[30] Nonius' dictionary survived due to interest accorded to it by Carolingian scholars: Leiden, MS Voss. Lat. F. 73, the manuscript regarded by Nonius' twentieth-century editor as the most faithful, was 'written at Tours in the early years of the ninth century, probably while Alcuin was still Abbot of St Martin's'.[31] On the basis of the first manuscript-family out of three, all derived from one archetype, 'the valley of the Loire' emerges as 'the centre of Nonius' transmission'.[32] Nonius'

---

[30] Book 11 (*De indiscretis adverbis*), in *Nonii Marcelli De compendiosa doctrina libros XX*: 'celeranter, pro celeriter. Accius Antenoridis (123): sed quis est qui matutinum cursum huc celeranter rapit?', p. 513, ed. Wallace M. Lindsay (Leipzig, 1901).

[31] Leighton D. Reynolds, 'Nonius Marcellus', in Id., *Texts and Transmission: A Survey of the Latin Classics* (Oxford, 1983), p. 250.

[32] Ibid., p. 251. After an examination of the manuscripts Reynolds reiterates, on p. 252, that Nonius circulated mainly in one area. The other main witnesses for *De compendiosa doctrina* are: Florence, Biblioteca Medicea Laurenziana, MS Laur. 48.l, s. ix¹, corrected by Lupus of

work is mentioned in only two medieval library catalogues: one from the eleventh century compiled at Saint-Vincent, Metz, and one from the twelfth put together at Saint-Amand.³³ The only other authors who used *celeranter*, as far as the evidence goes, were Ermoldus Nigellus, Milo of Saint-Amand, and John the Scot, although the latter is perhaps less compelling here since he employed the adverb to gloss *properanter* in a manuscript of Martianus Capella.³⁴

Ermoldus, 'the court poet manqué of his generation',³⁵ wrote a panegyrical poem entitled *In honorem Hludovici imperatoris* in 826 to effect his release from exile for having been a negative influence on Louis' son Pippin. Max Manitius pointed to his penchant for Grecisms and archaizing words such as *induperator/induperatrix*, first (probably) coined by Ennius, while Edmond Faral signalled his indebtedness to other Carolingian poets.³⁶ Despite his literary efforts, Ermoldus and his poems are not mentioned by any of his

---

Ferrières; London, BL, Harley MS 2719, s. ix/x, prov. Brittany; El Escorial, MS m.III.14, s. ix²/³, prov. Auxerre?; Geneva, Bibliothèque publique et universitaire, MS lat. 84, s. ix, prov. Fulda; Bern, Burgerbibliothek, MS 83, s. ix, prov. Reims (during Hincmar's tenure of the archbishopric); Cambridge, University Library, MS Mm.5.22, s. ix^ex, prov. Bourges; Paris, BnF, MS lat. 7667, s. x, prov. Fleury.

33 Ibid., p. 252 n. 17.
34 Glos. Mart. 479,7, p. 192, 2, *Iohannis Scotti annotationes in Marcianum*, ed. Cora E. Lutz (Cambridge, MA, 1939). *Celeranter* is not included in *Latinitatis italicae medii aevi lexicon: saec. V ex. – saec. XI in.*, ed. Francesco Arnaldi *et al.*, (Florence, 2001).
35 Peter Godman, *Poetry of the Carolingian Renaissance* (London, 1985), p. 45.
36 Max Manitius, *Geschichte der lateinischen Literatur des Mittelalters*, vol. 1: *Von Justinian bis zur Mitte des zehnten Jahrhunderts* (Munich, 1911), p. 556. Edmond Faral, *Poème sur Louis le Pieux et épîtres au roi Pépin* (Ermold le Noir) (Paris, 1932), p. xxv.

contemporaries, and there are only two surviving manuscripts of his work.³⁷ He used *celeranter* twice in his poem.³⁸

Milo wrote a metrical life of Amand (BHL 333) in four books between 845 and 855. A pupil of Haimin of Saint-Waas in Arras, who also taught Heiric of Auxerre, Milo initially dedicated the life to his teacher. The intended audience 'was the monastic community of St Amand'.³⁹ The language of his poetry is simple, and his principal models were Vergil and Sedulius.⁴⁰ Like Ermoldus, Milo always places *celeranter* in the same *sedes* in the verse, but he used it five times and at least once in each book of Amand's life.⁴¹

The witnesses to Milo's poem suggest that it circulated mainly in the area around Saint-Amand,⁴² while medieval

---

37 Vienna, Österreichische Nationalbibliothek, MS 614, s. x (poem on Louis only); London BL, Harley MS 3685, s. xv, probably a copy of the Vienna manuscript; see Georg H. Pertz, *Ermoldi Nigelli Carmina*, MGH SS 2 (Hannover, 1829), pp. 464–66; Ernst Dümmler, *Ermoldi Nigelli Carmina*, MGH Poetae 2 (Berlin, 1884), pp. 1–93; Id., 'Die handschriftliche Überlieferung der lateinischen Dichtungen aus der Zeit der Karolinger II', *Neues Archiv der Gesellschaft für ältere deutsche Geschichtskunde*, 4 (1878), 260–61.

38 'Mittantur missi, qui celeranter eant?' (l. 432); 'Laudibus et donis pergit celeranter onustus' (l. 611).

39 Godmann, *Poetry of the Carolingian Renaissance*, p. 62.

40 Manitius, *Geschichte*, vol. 1, p. 579. Milo also wrote a didactic poem entitled *De sobrietate*, modelled on Prudentius' *Psychomachia* and Aldhelm's *De virginitate*.

41 'subditus obsequio famulus celeranter in omni' (1.175); 'sanctum sed enim celeranter Amandum/ unanimes adeunt' (2.237); 'incolumes udas nautae celeranter harenas / impressere suis plantis' (2.261); 'Aspirante deo describens carmine vitam / praesulis egregii sanctam celeranter / Amandi' (3.2); 'horum celeranter adivit / belliger insignis terras' (4.61).

42 Ludwig Traube identified the following in his edition, *Milonis carmina*, MGH Poetae 3 (Berlin, 1896), p. 559: Valenciennes, Bibliothèque municipale, MS 414, s. ix^(ex), prov. Saint-Amand; Valenciennes, MS 502, s. xi, prov. Saint-Amand; Douai, BMD-V, MS 857, s. x + xii, prov. Marchiennes, as well as Brussels, KBR, MS 8721-28, s. xii, and a

catalogues attest that it was available at Saint-Bertin and Anchin.[43] As with the manuscripts preserving the account of his life, Amand's cult in the ninth century was limited to the area of northern France and Belgium, and it remained a fairly local one.[44] Given that Milo was a relatively well known and influential poet and the poem in which he used the adverb *celeranter* is a hagiographical text, it seems likely that the author of BHL 1663, himself engaged in an hagiographical task, came across the word in this way. In addition, there is also a more or less direct link between Milo and Nonius in the shape of a twelfth-century catalogue from Saint-Amand, which shows that the grammarian was available there.

From the above it emerges that *celeranter* was favoured by two ninth-century poets active in Francia and that it has a somewhat archaizing flavour. Of course, the more common *celeriter* is not usable in dactylic verse, but ancient poets had managed well enough with forms of *citus*, *cito*, *citius*, etc., and verbal forms from *celero*, *propero*, *festino*, etc. Its occurrence in BHL 1663 implies some sort of literary activity (wider reading, etc.) on the part of its author. Interestingly, the adverb also appears once in the miracle collection of Ouen (Audoenus) of Rouen (BHL 760), written by one Fulbert before 1092.[45] This

---

manuscript containing fragments at Copenhagen, Det Kongelige Bibliotek, MS 520 (*olim* Tottiniana).

[43] Manitius, *Geschichte*, vol. 1, p. 580.

[44] *LexMA*, s.v. Amandus. The monastery he founded (Elnone = Saint-Amand-les-Eaux) was just north of Valenciennes.

[45] 'Vos igitur, quia pars impia abscessit, vos, inquam, filii nolite deficere; Patris vestri sacrum loculum <u>celeranter</u> attollite. Ecce vobis adstat ad iuvandum paratus, qui vos ingrato otio remorabatur immotus'. Text at *AASS* Aug. IV, Dies 24, pp. 825–37 (p. 832D). The date is according to the *Hagiographies* database, s.v. Audoenus, BHL 760. See also Elisabeth M.C. van Houts, 'L'oralité dans l'hagiographie normande aux xie et xiie siècles', in *Les saints dans la Normandie médiévale*, ed. Pierre Bouet and François Neveux (Caen, 2000), p. 88; and Lucien Musset, 'Recherches

text is preserved in one single manuscript: Rouen, BM, MS 1406 (Y.41), s. xi (fols. 181-209v), from Saint-Ouen in Rouen.[46] Fulbert's use of *celeranter* in prose thus clinches the presence of a local preference, as it were, for this particular form.

Besides *celeranter*, there is one more word in BHL 1663 that can be localized. It occurs as a descriptive detail of the wheels amongst which Katherine is placed by the emperor as a last attempt to get her to renounce the Christian faith: 'Has inter media Christi famula, exposita inter serras et tarincas ferreas, ex rotarum membratim discerperetur misero mortis genere (Dobson, ll. 948-50)'. *Tarinca*, a noun signifying 'nail' or 'spike' as suggested by the context, is extremely rare.[47] A latinization of a vernacular word of Gallic origin, it originates from a particular region, as is evident from the texts in which it occurs.[48] BHL 1663 aside, it is found in only three texts,

sur les pélerins et les pélerinages en Normandie jusqu'à la Première Croisade', *Annales de Normandie*, 12 (1962), 127–50 (p. 132).

[46] This manuscript is also known as the *Livre Noir* and is a witness for the *Acta archiepiscoporum Rothomagensium*, see Louis Violette, 'Le problème de l'attribution d'un texte Rouennais du XIe siècle: les *Acta archiepiscoporum Rothomagensium*', *AB*, 115 (1997), 113–29. The greater part contains lives and miracles of and readings about Ouen, as well as lives of other saints associated with Rouen or Normandy, such as Romanus (BHL 7310–20) and Vulganius (BHL 8746–b). See Henry Omont, *Catalogue général des manuscrits des B.P. de France*, vol. 1: Rouen (Paris, 1886), pp. 404–09. Avril, *Manuscrits Normands*, dated it to the end of the eleventh century, pp. 46–47.

[47] It is not included in the *Oxford Latin Dictionary*, *Lewis and Short Latin Dictionary*, *PL*, *Library of Latin Texts*, *Monumenta Germaniae Historia*, or the *Bibliotheca Teubneriana Latina*. The *Dictionary of Medieval Latin from British Sources* yields three quotations for *taringa*, of which the earliest is from the *Vita Haroldi* [d. 1066], written in England before 1216, ed. Walter de Gray Birch, *The Romance of the Life of Harold, King of England* (London, 1885), p. 60.

[48] It has been postulated that *tarinca* is related to *tarare*, also a Gallic word, from which is derived the modern French word *taranche*, 'a large nail of iron'. See *Französisches etymologisches Wörterbuch: Eine Darstellung des*

namely the passion of Quintinus (BHL 7000; BHL 7009) and in that of Fuscianus and Victoricus.

BHL 7000, an early account of Quintinus' life, is preserved in an eighth/ninth-century manuscript, probably written at Corbie.[49] An alternative form, *taringas*, occurs in BHL 7009, a ninth-century version of Quintinus' life: 'Tunc Rictiovarus, cernens eum constantia validius roborari, eius cruciatus adhuc augeri truculentis sitiens, iussit vocari fabrum ferrarium, praecipiens ei ut faceret duas sudes ferreas, quae Gallica lingua <u>taringae</u> vocantur, quibus beatus Quintinus a cervice usque ad crura transfigeretur'.[50] The 'spikes' recur in these two accounts because they were used as a means to torment Quintinus. The cult of Quintinus, or Quentin, was already active in the sixth century, particularly at Saint-Quentin in Picardy, where the saint is said to have been martyred. Bede includes him in his

galloromanischen Sprachschatzes, ed. Walther v. Wartburg *et al.*, vol. 13 (Basel, 1966), s. v. '*tarinca*'. Under the lemma *tero*, Alois Walde and Johann B. Hofmann (*Lateinisches Etymologisches Wörterbuch*, Heidelberg, 1965) cite Isidore *Orig*. 19, 19.14: 'taratrum, quasi teratrum', and also compare Irish *tairnge* [*taringia] 'nail'. Also in Georges Dottin, *La langue gauloise: Grammaire, textes et glossaire* (Paris, 1920), p. 291, and Xavier Delamarre, *Dictionnaire de la langue gauloise: Une approche linguistique du vieux-celtique continental* (Paris, 2003), p. 291.

[49] Turin, Biblioteca Nazionale, MS D.V.3, s. viii–ix, north-east France, probably Corbie. See *CLA*, vol. 4, no. 446. On Quintinus see *LexMA*, s.v. Quintinus.

[50] *AASS* Oct. XIII, Dies 31, p. 799A and also p. 783A. It is not entirely clear what is meant by 'Gallica lingua'. When Cassiodorus employs the phrase (*Vivarium libri duodecim*, ed. Åke J. Fridh [Turnhout, 1973], 8.12), he is contrasting the Latin language with what he considers the Celtic language. Isidore of Seville (*Etymologiarum sive originum libri xx*, ed. Wallace M. Lindsay [Oxford, 1911], 11.1) is probably echoing Cassiodorus, or making an inherited statement. More interesting is its use by Gregory of Tours, who was living in the middle of Francia. He uses the phrase to refer to the local, in other words vernacular, language spoken in the area: *Historiarum libri x*, ed. Bruno Krusch and Wilhelm Levison, MGH SSRM 1.1 (Hannover, 1951), 1.32, p. 25: 'Arvernus, delubrum illud, quod Gallica lingua Vasso Galate vocant'.

Martyrology and Gregory of Tours provides a short account of how his body was found.[51]

Fuscianus and Victoricus were martyred at about the same time, under the emperor Maximianus according to the account, in the same geographical area; they had been missionaries to the Morini and were beheaded at Amiens.[52] Their entry in Usuard's *Martyrology* reads:

> Civitate Ambianis, sanctorum martyrum Gentiani et Fusciani. In horum naribus vel auribus iussit iudex <u>tarincas</u> immitti, et clavis candentibus capita transfigi, deinde oculos evelli ac postremum per eorum corpora iaculari; sicque una cum sancto Victorico, hospite suo, capitibus amputatis migraverunt ad Dominum.[53]

Their feast day (11 December) appears in Florus' *Martyrology*, from which Usuard took the names, although the latter's entry is longer and more detailed.[54] There is no trace of the two saints in Bede's *Martyrology*. This may furnish a period of roughly between 735 (Bede's death) and *c.* 860 (death of Florus) for the emergence of their cult.[55] One of the versions of

---

[51] See Dubois and Renaud, *Édition pratique*, p. 197: 'In Galliis, sancti Quintini, qui sub Maximiano imperatore martyrium passus est: et post annos quinquaginta quinque inventum est, revelante angelo, corpus eius et sepultum, viii kal. jul.'. Gregory of Tours, *Liber in gloria martyrum*, in Id., *Miracula et opera minora*, ed. Wilhelm Arndt and Bruno Krusch, MGH SSRM 1.2 (Hannover, 1885), cap. 72.

[52] See Butler, *The Lives of the Saints*, ed. Thurston and Attwater, vol. 4, p. 539 (see also new revised edition, *Butler's Lives of the Saints*, ed. David H. Farmer *et al.* [Tunbridge Wells, 1999], vol. 2, p. 94).

[53] *Le martyrologe d'Usuard: Texte et commentaire*, ed. Jacques Dubois, Subsidia Hagiographica 40 (Brussels, 1965), p. 357.

[54] Ibid., p. 357. In the first version of Florus: 'In Galliis, civitate Ambianensis [*sic*], natale sanctorum martyrum Victorici et Fusciani', p. 222 in Dubois and Renaud, *Édition pratique*.

[55] A much closer study of Florus', Ado's, and Usuard's martyrologies than has been possible here is required in order to establish firmly the date of the emergence of their cult. The fact that Ado enlarged Florus' martyrology and that there are various recensions of both makes a conclusive

their passion (BHL 3226) is preserved in Paris, BnF, MS lat. 12598, s. viii-ix, which was 'written in the Lowlands or north-east France'.[56]

The existing evidence shows that the noun *tarinca* occurs only in two saints' lives besides that of Katherine: Quintinus on the one hand and Fuscianus and Victoricus on the other, both of which are based in northern France/the Low Countries and were probably also written there. This suggests that anyone using the word either had read one of these two accounts and/or was himself living in that area. Unlike *celeranter*, *tarinca* is a word that 'lived' in or originated from a particular region. On might say that it seeped into BHL 1663 almost by an unconscious slip of the author's pen into the vernacular, while the use of *celeranter* clearly involved some literary activity on his part.

BHL 1663 is full of episodic and literal allusions to earlier hagiographical accounts, a list of which would be too long to present here.[57] But perhaps one instance can be considered.

---

answer difficult. The absence of Fuscianus and Victoricus from Bede does not, of course, preclude the emergence of their cult in a local context during his lifetime (or even before).

[56] *CLA*, vol. 5, no. 644b: 'early Carolingian minuscule, ... certainly at Corbie soon after it was written, as suggested by the entries in Maurdramnus minuscule'. I have not been able to verify whether *tarinca* occurs in this account, although the notes to BHL 7000 in the *AASS* Oct. XIII, Dies 31, p. 785C, suggest that it is included in at least one of the lives of Fuscianus and Victoricus.

[57] For the practice see, for example, Baudouin de Gaiffier, 'Les "doublets" en hagiographie Latine', *AB*, 96 (1978), pp. 262–69. Phrases from BHL 1663 were incorporated into the life of Vincentius of Collioure (BHL 8656), martyred in the south-eastern corner of the French Pyrenees: the passage that describes the death of the rhetors at Dobson, ll. 535–57 was used to portray the death of Vincentius at *AASS* Apr. II, Dies 19, pp. 612F–622A, a life written in the sixteenth or seventeeth centuries. It has been suggested that its author was the Spaniard Tamayo de Salazar: see Baudouin de Gaiffier, 'Sub Daciano preside: Étude de quelques passions espagnoles', *AB*, 72 (1954), p. 393.

The passage describing Katherine's familial and monetary situation is also found in the life of the Belgian widow Amalberga (BHL 321).[58] Compare the two:

BHL 1663 (Dobson, ll. 71-84)	Life of Amalberga[59]
Hac in urbe Alexandrinorum erat quaedam puella, annorum duo de viginti, speciosa valde sed quod pluris est religiosa fide, quae regis quondam filia unica, patre iam defuncto filiae nomen amiserat, nomine Katerina. *Haec,* <u>parentum orbata solatio, tenera licet aetate familiam quae successione hereditaria sibi inhaeserat pervigili cura</u> *gubernabat,* <u>non quia servorum aut ancillarum numerosa turba, quod inter prim</u>*a* <u>mortales puta</u>*nt,* delecta*batur,* <u>sed quia</u> non sine crimine <u>esse putabat si paternum censum avide retinens, fame et inedia quemlibet eorum perire pateretur,</u> quippe quae nichil cum mundo habere commune decreverat; de his tantum sollicita, ex omni substantia patris paululum sibi reservabat, cetera in usus pauperum consumendo patrios thesau-	Beata Amalberga illustrissimis exorta natalibus, sed moribus elegantioribus adornata, Sanctas oppidum excoluit: cuius ductrix et Domina usque ad assumptam religionis beatitudinem iure hereditario extitit. *Quae* <u>parentum orbata solatio, tenera licet aetate familiam, quae successione hereditaria sibi inhaeserat, pervigili cura,</u> *suaviterque tractabat,* <u>non quia servorum aut ancillarum numerosa turba, quod inter mortales prim</u>*um* <u>puta</u>*tur,* delecta*retur,* <u>sed quia</u> *iniustum* <u>esse putabat, si paternum censum avide retinens, fame et inedia quemlibet eorum</u> pateretur perire. <u>Non ipsa puellares iocos, non amatoria carmina,</u> *non ludicra quaelibet, ac frivola* <u>audire,</u> *vel* <u>videre</u> curabat, sed quasi Maria secus pedes Domini residens, quod actura fuerat, actu

---

[58] This is a very short life, just a little more than one page in the *AASS*. The widow Amalberga is not to be confused with the virgin Amalberga (BHL 322–325d). The question of whether Goscelin of Saint-Bertin was the author of BHL 323 has been taken up by Rosalind Love, 'Et quis me tanto oneri parem faciet?': Goscelin of Saint-Bertin and the life of St Amelberga', in *Latin Learning and English Lore: Studies in Anglo-Saxon Literature for Michael Lapidge*, ed. Katherine O'Brien O'Keeffe *et al.*, 2 vols (Toronto, 2005), II, pp. 232–52. The author concluded that the life of Amalberga (BHL 323) is an early work by Goscelin. See also Albert Poncelet, 'Les biographes de Ste Amalberge', *AB*, 31 (1912), 401–09.

[59] *AASS* Jul. III, Dies 10, p. 67A.

rus penitus exhauderat. <u>Non ipsa</u> et habitu praemonstrabat.
<u>puellares iocos, non amatoria car-
mina, videre</u> aut <u>audire</u> volebat,
divinis tantummodo, et his atten-
tius, scripturis insistebat.

Amalberga's life was written by a monk at Lobbes sometime before the end of the eleventh century; its editor suggested a date of composition after the third quarter of the eleventh century, in other words the years between 1075 to 1100. The monk in question also used a number of passages from the life of Raineldis of Hainaut (BHL 7082) for its composition.[60] If the composition of BHL 1663 were to predate that of BHL 321 the former must have been at Lobbes while Amalberga's life was being written. Evidence for this can be found in a catalogue which records the books at Lobbes library from *c.* 1049 until *c.* 1158-60: it includes a legendary that contains both *BHL* 1663 and the passion of Raineldis, but not that of Amalberga.[61]

---

[60] Léon van der Essen, *Étude critique et littéraire sur les* Vitae *des saints mérovingiens de l'Ancienne Belgique* (Leuven, 1907), pp. 301–02. The author suggested that Amalberga's life was to be dated after the third quarter of the eleventh century because the life of Raineldis had been written first. According to the *Hagiographies* Database at Namur University, Amalberga's life was written between 1051 and 1100 and that of Raineldis between *c.* 1015 and 1035. See also François de Vriendt, 'La vie de sainte Renelde, martyre à Saintes (BHL 7082), in '*Scribere Sanctorum Gesta*': Recueil d'études d'hagiographie médiévale offert à Guy Philippart, ed. Étienne Renard *et al.* (Turnhout, 2005), pp. 399–415 (p. 409). Frans J. van Droogenbroeck, 'Hugo van Lobbes (1033–1053), auteur van de Vita Amalbergae viduae, Vita S. Reinildis en Vita S. Berlendis', *Eigen Schoon en de Brabander* 94, (2011), 649–84 argued that the monk in question was Hugo of Lobbes, abbot of the monastery during the first half of the eleventh century.

[61] This manuscript is now Brussels, KBR, MS 18018, s. xi^{ex}. François Dolbeau, 'Un nouveau catalogue des manuscrits de Lobbes au xie et xiie siècles', *Recherches Augustiniennes,* 13 (1978), 3–36 (p. 29); Id., 'Un nouveau catalogue des manuscrits de Lobbes aux xie et xiie siècles, II: commentaire et tables', *Recherches Augustiniennes,* 14 (1979), 191–248.

Since BHL 1663 and BHL 321 overlap only once, as demonstrated above, it is tricky to establish which text borrows from which, although some initial observations can be made. The first sentence shared by the two texts contains a short aside about the importance mortals attach to having a large number of servants: 'quod inter prima mortales putant'. BHL 321 retains the idea, but instead one reads: 'quod inter mortales primum putatur'. It turns out that two of the manuscripts collated by Dobson for BHL 1663 have inverted the order of *prima* and *mortales*, thus: 'quod inter mortales prima putant'.[62] An unattentive reader might think that *mortales* is an accusative after *inter*, seemingly leaving *putant* without a subject, and so requiring *primum* to become *prima* and *putant* to become *putatur* in the life of Amalberga. One of the witnesses for BHL 1663 that reports this inversion is Brussels KBR 18018, which was copied at Lobbes towards the end of the eleventh century and also includes the list of books held at that monastery mentioned above, thus establishing a geographical link between BHL 1663 and BHL 321.

Secondly, the reason Katherine did not want to keep her father's inheritance is, according to BHL 1663, 'non sine crimine esse putabat fame et inedia quemlibet eorum perire pateretur'. In BHL 321, *sine crimine* has been replaced by *iniustum*; one could argue here that the lectio difficilior is the more original one and thus the text that came first, in this case BHL 1663. Thirdly, the balanced description (*non* + an adjective + noun) of Katherine's dislike of girlish jokes and love songs in BHL 1663 ('non ipsa puellares iocos, non amatoria carmina videre aut audire volebat') is amplified by a third pair (*ludicra quaelibet*) and a fourth noun on its own (*frivola*), thus disrupting the otherwise neat description.

---

[62] *G* (Brussels, KBR, MS 18018, s. xi, prov. Lobbes; not 18108 as reported by Dobson) and *W* (Paris, BnF, MS lat. 15149, s. xiii–xiv, prov. Saint-Victor, Paris).

The potential incorporation of BHL 1663 into Amalberga's life could thus furnish the former, for the first time, with a *terminus ante quem* of 1075 to 1100. Not only was BHL 1663 known at Lobbes by the end of the eleventh century, but it seems that it had also gained sufficient momentum to make the passage to Lobbes and be deemed good or important enough to act as a source for another hagiographical text. However, it is impossible to determine exactly at which point in the eleventh century BHL 1663 had been completed, although the earliest manuscripts can help to shed light on the question (see below).[63]

As one would expect, there are also echoes to and citations from the Bible, most of which were identified by Knust.[64] The author of BHL 1663 also alludes to Vergil's *Aeneid* at least three times.[65] The fact that snippets from Vergil crop up in

---

[63] A sobering reminder of how fast and far texts could travel is the example of Benedict Biscop, who lugged books back from Rome to Northumbria during several visits to Rome. See Bede's *Historia abbatum*, ch. 4 in *Venerabilis Bedae opera historica*, ed. Charles Plummer, vol. 1.364–87 (Oxford, 1896). See also Eric Fletcher, 'Benedict Biscop', *Jarrow Lecture 1981* (Jarrow on Tyne, 1981), pp. 7 and 9–10.

[64] Knust, *Geschichte der Legenden*, pp. 231–314.

[65] (1) 'puella ... in qua ... non animalis homo loquitur sed divinus quidam spiritus, qui sane haud mortale sonans' (Dobson, l. 521). This description of Katherine is reminiscent of Vergil's description of the Cumaean Sibyl (*Aen.* 6.50, 'nec mortale sonans'). See Knust, *Geschichte der Legenden*, p. 319. BHL 1663 is not the only hagiographical text to echo this line: it also appears in the life of Gaugericus, bishop of Cambrai (d. *c.* 625) (BHL 3287), *AASS* Aug. II, Dies 11, p. 673A: 'sed vir Domini Gaugericus ... nec mortale sonans, coepit verbum Dei leproso praedicare'.
(2) 'Audiens regina ferale coniugis edictum, licet gentili errore teneretur, tamen animi ingenita bonitate tenere aetatis sortem miseratur iniquam' (Dobson, l. 682). This is perhaps the strongest of the three Vergil-echoes: the Laurentines and Latins are taking pity on Turnus at Vergil *Aeneid*, 12.243: 'infectum et Turni sortem miserantur iniquam'. This line-ending is echoed in the metrical life of Germanus, bishop of Auxerre (d. *c.* 448) (BHL 3458), *AASS* Jul. VII, Dies 31, p. 234C:

BHL 1663 does not necessarily imply that its author had read the Aeneid or used a text of it for his composition. It is equally possible that these quotations are part of the cultural fabric of the time, as is clear from the parallels in the lives of Gaugericus and Germanus.[66] Having said that, there are instances where the author reveals himself to have read or absorbed a number of medieval authors, such as Eugenius of Toledo, Eusebius Gallicanus, Petrus Chrysologus, and Augustine. What follows is a brief listing of the parallels:

BHL 1663 (Dobson, l. 814)	Eugenius of Toledo[67]
Ipse est <u>Deus</u> et dominator omnium saeculorum, in cuius potestate <u>constat</u> universalis <u>machina mundi</u>.	rex <u>deus</u>, immensi quo <u>constat machina mundi</u>, / quod miser Eugenius posco, tu perfice clemens.

Although the expression 'machina mundi' was first coined by Lucretius,[68] who was known at least by some individuals in northern France and the Low Countries from the end of the eighth century onwards, it seems unlikely that the author of

'praesul Iugentis sortem miseratus iniquiam / posse reformari spondet dispendia fisci'.
(3) 'Ad haec tyrannus <u>dolos in pectore versans</u>, ne a circumstantibus tamquam iniquus et implacabilis accusaretur, ait puellae' (Dobson, l. 853). The tyrant Maxentius is likened to Mercury's description of Dido at *Aeneid* 4.563 ('illa <u>dolos</u> dirumque nefas <u>in pectore versat</u>'). Narbey, *Supplément aux Acta sanctorum*, p. 319.

[66] See note 65 above.
[67] Cyr U.J. Chevalier, *Repertorium hymnologicum: Catalogue des chants, hymnes, proses, séquences, tropes en usage dans l'Eglise latine depuis les origines jusqu'à nos jours* (Leuven, 1892–1920), no. 17442a. It is not entirely clear whether the Eugenius in question was the second or the third; in any case, he was bishop of Toledo in the middle of the seventh century; s.v. 4. Eugenius II, *LexMA*; see the preface to Eugenius' life in *PL*, vol. 87, cols 347–348. The full prayer, and a number of Eugenius' shorter poems are printed in the same volume, cols 359B ff.
[68] Lucretius, *De rerum natura*, 5.91: 'sustentata ruet moles et machina mundi'.

BHL 1663 drew inspiration from him.[69] Rather, the combination of *machina mundi* with *constat* as it occurs in Eugenius of Toledo's prayer suggests an influence through the liturgical use of the latter. This prayer became part of the liturgy and was quoted by Alcuin and Bede.

As Katherine's dispute with the rhetors draws to a close, her speech is rounded off with a comparison:

BHL 1663 (Dobson, l. 474)	Eusebius Gallicanus, *Homilia II de Pascha*[70]
sed <u>est speciosa victoria</u> adversarium telis <u>suis, velut propriis laqueis, irretire et</u> auctorum <u>suorum</u> testimoniis <u>confutare</u>, quia quorum fidem aspernaris, eorum testimonia non recipis.	<u>Speciosa victoria est</u>, contrariam partem chartulis <u>suis velut propriis laqueis irretire et</u> testimoniorum <u>suorum</u> vocibus <u>confutare</u> et aemulum telis suis evincere, ut pugnatoris tui argumenta tuis probentur utilitatibus militare.

This is based on the opening remarks of a sermon delivered at Easter from the collection of Eusebius Gallicanus, which acquired its present shape in the seventh century.[71] Sermon

---

[69] The abbey of Lobbes had acquired a text of *De rerum natura* by the first half of the twelfth century, see François Dolbeau, 'Un nouveau catalogue des manuscrits', esp. no. 34 and p. 233. See also s.v. 'Lucretius' in Reynolds, *Texts and Transmission*, p. 220.

[70] *Eusebius 'gallicanus': Collectio homiliarum*, ed. Franciscus Glorie, CCSL 101–101B (Turnhout, 1970–1971), vol. 1, p. 155.

[71] The process by which this collection was formed is very complicated: what is generally agreed on today is that it includes sermons by authors such as Augustine and Hilarius of Arles, that it was used by Caesarius of Arles (the main representative of Gallic monasticism) and then Faustus of Riez, and that it was put into the shape known today by one Eusebius (from Gaul?) in the seventh century. Out of the sixty manuscripts that preserve parts of the collection, one ninth-century manuscript preserves almost the whole (except for sermons 1–16); it was perhaps written at the abbey of Longpont in northern France: Brussels, KBR, MS 1651-52 (1316), s. ix^{in}. A further four manuscripts supply the text for sermons 1–16 and in turn preserve large parts of the collection: Paris, BnF, MS lat. 2628, s. xi; Paris, BnF, MS lat. 2169, s. xii–xiii; BAV, MS Vat. lat.

thirteen belongs to the group of sermons (1-35) that form the beginning of the collection, within which they have been arranged according to the order of the ecclesiastical year. This particular sermon has been transmitted in eleven manuscripts, including ninth/tenth-century witnesses from places such as Fleury, Angers, Saint-Bertin, and Marchiennes in northern France.[72]

As the rhetors describe Katherine's effect on them to the emperor, their language is distinctly reminiscent of lyric poetry, and they use phrases that might describe the effect that the sight of the beloved has on the one in love: the author of BHL 1663 in this instance did not of course draw on Sappho herself, or any of the later imitations and adaptations of her poetry. Rather, the sermon-collection by Petrus Chrysologus was his inspiration, in particular the beginning of Sermon 127.1:

9882, s. ix–x; Geneva, BPU, MS 24, s. xii, prov. Fleury? For a list and discussion of all the manuscripts see Glorie's edition, vol. 1, pp. xviii–xxxvii.

[72] BAV, MS Reg. lat. 131, s. ix¹ (ca. 820–30); Geneva, BPU, MS 24, s. xii, prov. Fleury?; Berlin, Staatsbibliothek zu Berlin Preussischer Kulturbesitz, MS Theol. fol. 270, s. xii, prov. Maria Laach; Karlsruhe, Badische Landesbibliothek, MS Aug. Perg. 15, s. ix, prov. Reichenau; Troyes, Bibliothèque municipale, MS 154, s. ix; Angers, Bibliothèque municipale, MS 144 (136), s. x, prov. Saint-Aubin; Paris, BnF, MS lat. 2811, s. xii^{in}; Boulogne-sur-mer, Bibliothèque municipale, MS 106, s. x/xi, prov. Saint-Bertin; Douai, BMV-D, MS 201, s. xii, prov. Marchiennes, Saint-Sauveur d'Anchin; Paris, BnF, MS lat. 2169, s. xii–xiii.

BHL 1663 (Dobson, l. 525)	Petrus Chrysologus, *De natale sancti Iohannis Baptistae*[73]
Nam ut Christi nomen et divinitatis eius potentiam simulque crucis ipsius mysterium praedicari ab ea audivimus, <u>confusa</u> <u>sunt</u> <u>viscera</u>, <u>corda</u> nostra <u>tremuerunt</u>, <u>et omnes corporis sensus stupendo aufugerunt</u>.	hodie nobis Iohannis virtus, Herodis feritas dum refertur, <u>concussa</u> <u>sunt</u> <u>viscera,</u> <u>corda</u> <u>tremuerunt,</u> <u>caligavit</u> <u>visus,</u> <u>intellectus hebuit, aufugit auditus</u>. Aut quid constat in sensibus humanis, quando perdit virtutum magnitudinem criminum magnitudo?

The tradition of this collection of sermons is complex: in 724 Felix, archbishop of Ravenna, compiled Peter's sermons on the basis of an already existing collection. Felix also added a prologue and a list of contents. None of the manuscripts that preserve the 'collectio Feliciana' was written before the eleventh century, and within this tradition there is a German and a French branch. The manuscripts that preserve Sermon 127 reveal a diffusion in Italy, France, and Germany.[74] Two of these manuscripts come from northern France (Cambrai, BM,

---

[73] Beginning of the sermon. *Sancti Petri Chrysologi collectio sermonum*, ed. Alejandro Olivar, CCSL 24–24B (Turnhout, 1975–82). See also Sermon 143 (l. 67): 'turbata est caro, concussa sunt viscera, mens tremuit, tota cordis obstupuit altitudo, quia ingresso angelo virgo sensit divinitatis ingressum'.

[74] Tours, Bibliothèque municipale, MS 308, 1186, prov. Marmoutier; Cambrai, Bibliothèque municipale, MS 543, s. xii$^{2/3}$, prov. Vaucelles; Paris, BnF, MS lat. 16867, s. xii^{ex} (? xiii^{in}), prov. Saint-Martin des Champs; BAV, MS Vat. lat. 4952, s. xi, prov. Ravenna; Brussels, KBR, MS 683 vol. 2, s. xv; Todi, Biblioteca communale, MS 107, s. xiii, prov. Italy; Oxford, Balliol College, MS 163, s. xiii^{in}; Munich, BSB, Clm 23621, s. xiv, prov. Italy; Rome, Biblioteca Vallicelliana, MS B.20, s. xii, prov. Toscana; Vienna, ÖNB, MS 3759, s. xv, prov. Germany; Paris, BnF, MS lat. 2145, s. xiii, prov. Saint-Martin, Tournai?; Florence, BML, MS Sanctae Crucis plut. XXX sin. 2, s. xii. See Olivar, *Sancti petri Chrysologi Collectio Sermonum*, vol. 3, pp. 780–82. For a description of the manuscripts see vol. 1, pp. ix–xlviii.

MS 543 and Paris, BnF, MS lat. 2145). BHL 1663 follows four manuscripts in the reading of *confusa* for *concussa*, although this allows no further insight because at least two of them come from Italy and survival of the manuscripts likely skews the perspective.[75]

The combination of elements reminiscent of Psalm 113 with the mention of an ape and birds defiling a statue is modelled on Augustine's exposition of this same psalm: he argues that to worship man-made statues is absurd because they lack all the sensory qualities of their maker, who is superior to them.

BHL 1663 (Dobson, ll. 596-601 & 607-12)	Augustine, *Exposition of Psalm 113*[76]
Quae erit illa insignis materia – alens, vivificans, atque discernens – ex qua oculi ad videndum, aures ad audiendum, os lingua[que][77] ad loquendum, et cetera quaeque informentur, quae sensu vigentia salutationes hominum audiant, videant, et intelligant? Nam si haec ista defuerint, quid refert michi feminei vultus decorem dari an simiae turpem imaginem aptari? ….	Namque, cum superius dixisset: "os habent et non loquentur", quid opus erat, postquam a capite usque ad pedes membra decursa sunt, de faucium clamore repetere, nisi, credo, quia illa quae de ceteris membris commemorabat, communia esse hominibus belluisque sentimus? Nam et vident, et audiunt, et olfaciunt, et ambulant et quaedam, sicut simiae, manibus contrectant. (Sermon II.2.10-17)

[75] *J* = Todi, BC, MS 107. *O* = Oxford, Balliol College, MS 163. *Clm* = Munich, BSB, Clm 23621. *Chry* = Secundus tomus operum divi Iohannis Chrystomi, Basileae, apud Froben, 1558, cols 1190–92.

[76] *Sancti Aurelii Augustini enarrationes in Psalmos*, ed. Eligius Dekkers and Jean Fraipont, CCSL 38–40 (Turnhout, 1956), Psalm 113 – Sermon II.2. In his *Enarratio* of Psalm 96 (*Sermo ad populum* 19.31), Augustine again makes reference to a monkey: 'aut si quis simiam miraretur, diceres: non est ista pulchritudo'.

[77] Dobson emended *os lingua* to *os lingua[que]*. The majority of manuscripts he used agree on the reading without a connective (*DFNS*), only four read *os et lingua*.

Sed aves caeli haudquaquam istud verebuntur, dum milvus et corvus, undecumque avolantes,[78] sedem in me sibi usurpabunt et immunda digesti cadaveris proluvie faciem meam innotabunt. Quid interim pueri facturi sunt, qui, divinum causae mysterium venerari nescientes, huc simul egesturi convenient? Aut quid canes commincturos ego commemorem?

Quanto ergo melius mures atque serpentes, et id genus animantium cetera, de simulacris gentium si ita dicendum est, quodammodo indicant, in quibus quia non sentiunt humanam vitam, non curant humanam figuram? Itaque in eius plerumque nidificant, et nisi humanis motibus deterreantur, nulla sibi habitacula munitiora conquirunt. Movet ergo se homo, ut viventem bestiam a suo deo deterreat; et illum non se moventem, quasi potentem colit, a quo meliorem deterruit.

(Sermon II.2.39-47).

This is Katherine's main point of argument against Maxentius. She has already explicitly referred to this psalm in one of her previous speeches to him, and it thus reveals itself as being somewhat programmatic.[79] The athor of BHL 1663 is not the only hagiographer who made use of Psalm 113. A search in the *AASS* database reveals that there are more than 30 saints' lives that refer to it in some way or other, so that it can be counted among the tools of the trade. Because Augustine's *Enarrationes* survives in over 360 witnesses it would be a futile exercise to try to link BHL 1663 with a particular group of manuscripts from within that tradition.

After all this, it is opportune to reflect on the evidence gathered so far. First, the use of the disparate words *celeranter* and *tarinca*, and their localization in ninth-century Francia and/or the Low Countries, points to an author who was working in that same area. Fulbert's use of *celeranter* in the miracle collection of Ouen of Rouen (BHL 760, written before 1092)

---

[78] 'Undecumque avolantes' must mean 'to fly away from whatever direction' in the sense of 'flying away from many places towards one'. Four manuscripts (**DΘNS**) offer 'advolantes' which makes better sense.

[79] Dobson, l. 240ff.

establishes a connection with Rouen, where, as I delineate in Chapter 5, Katherine's relics began to perform miracles in the eleventh century. Second, the incorporation of passages from Ambrose Autpert's *Conflictus* into BHL 1663 furnish the latter with a *terminus post quem* of 784, the year of Ambrose's death. The incorporation of a significant passage from BHL 1663 into the life of Amalberga furnishes the former with a *terminus ante quem*: Amalberga's life was written in the fourth quarter of the eleventh century at the monastery of Lobbes.

Third, the author of BHL 1663 made use of three more or less apologetic texts in his account of Katherine's passion: the anonymous *CZA*, Autpert's *Conflictus*, and Orosius' *Histories*. While Orosius' and Autpert's works experienced a significant manuscript diffusion, the same cannot be said for the *CZA*. It survives in only a handful of tenth-century manuscripts from France, two of which passed through Fleury in northern/central France. This interest in an otherwise unknown text in tenth-century France might have something to do with the monastic reform movement kick-started by Cluny. It is plausible that the kind of exchange between Zaccheus and Apollonius could have appealed to the reformers: Book 3 of the *CZA* in particular talks about monastic life and its rules. Perhaps, then, BHL 1663 can be seen as displaying the kind of religious fervour that was widespread in eleventh-century northern France: 'La ferveur religieuse issue du mouvement de réforme gagnant du terrain, l'idéal de sainteté reprit vigueur. Les idéaux de l'*ecclesiae primitivae forma* et de la *vita apostolica* se firent jour, entraînant la réforme et la création d'abbayes'.[80] Finally, the author of BHL 1663 had read or had at his disposal the sermon collections of Eusebius Gallicanus and

---

[80] Ineke van 'T Spijker, 'Gallia du Nord et de l'Ouest: Les provinces ecclésiastiques de Tours, Rouen, Reims (950–1130)', in *Hagiographies: Histoire internationale de la littérature hagiographique latine et vernacularie en Occident des origines à 1550*, ed. Guy Philippart (Turnhout, 1994), vol. 2, pp. 239–90 (p. 245).

Petrus Chrysologus, as well as Augustine's *Enarrationes in psalmos*, and likely a number of additional texts. Just as other hagiographers, he had a predilection for Psalm 113, which talks about those pagans who worship idols.

The attentive study of the text of BHL 1663 has already yielded clues for its geographical and chronological contexts. An equally careful study of the manuscripts, in particular of the earliest witnesses, can reveal the plausibility of the conclusions arrived at on the basis of the text alone.

2. The early manuscripts of BHL 1663

Out of the total of about 260 manuscripts that preserve BHL 1663 and its derivatives, only four were written before 1100.[81] A close examination of these four manuscripts can yield further clues for localizing and dating BHL 1663.

Angers, Bibliothèque municipale, MS 121 (113) is a lectionarium copied for the abbey of St Nicholas at Angers (see Figures 3 and 4).[82] It consists of 289 folios, measures 33.5 x 24

---

[81] Bern, Burgerbibliothek, MS 133 has been assigned to the eleventh century (*Catalogus codicum bernensium: Bibliotheca Bongarsiana*, ed. Hermann Hagen [Bern, 1875], p. 182), but its provenance is not confirmed. The presence of a passion of Thomas Becket at the end of the manuscript (fols 128r–130v) suggests that this text, at least, was added after 1120. Most of the saints in this volume are more or less universal, although Benignus of Dijon fols 63v–66v, just in front of Katherine, gives it a French flavour, along with the passion of Aegidius (= Giles from Provence, fols 58v–63v). Cambrai, BM, MS 863 was written in the eleventh century, but fols 263–278 are a twelfth-century addition. Cambridge, Fitzwilliam Museum, MS McClean 100 was written in the tenth century, but the folios containing Katherine (fols 149–161 at the very end) are a twelfth-century addition. Trier, Stadtbibliothek, MS 388/1152 2° was written in the eleventh century, but the folios containing the text of Katherine (116v + 117–118v) were written in a twelfth-century hand and are a later addition.

[82] Jean Vezin, *Les scriptoria d'Angers au xie siècle* (Paris, 1974), pp. 76–78 and 232–33. See also Leslie W. Jones, 'The library of St Aubin's at Angers in the twelfth century', in *Classical and Medieval Studies in*

Date & Place of Composition of BHL 1663   171

cm, is written in two columns of thirty-one lines each, and contains saints' lives from December to January, all of which are divided into readings. The life of Katherine is on folios 274-280, between that of Lambertus (BHL 4679a) and Lucia (BHL 4992).[83] This text is an abbreviated version of BHL 1663 without the prologue and divided into twelve readings. It shares numerous errors with Paris, BnF, MS lat. 5343, but not all of them, and does not share any errors with the other two eleventh-century manuscripts.[84]

Nicholas takes centre stage in this manuscript, while the presence of saints such as Licinius, Albinus, Maurus, and Maurilius contributes to its Angevin flavour. The abbey of St Nicholas, St Jerome, and St Lazarus was founded in 1020 by

Honor of Edward Kennard Rand, ed. Leslie W. Jones (New York, 1938), p. 159, where he identified this manuscript as a likely candidate for one of the three lectionaries listed in the twelfth-century library catalogue of Saint-Aubin at Angers.

[83] For a detailed list of the contents see Joseph v. d. Straeten, *Les manuscrits hagiographiques d'Orléans, Tours et Angers* (Brussels, 1982), pp. 199–213.

[84] Whenever the Angers-epitome differs from Dobson's edition, it generally shares errors with other French manuscripts, mainly the two manuscripts *EO* when *JS* are correct. There are also a number of cases when *EO* are in error but Angers 121 is not. Angers 121 also has a number of individual errors not found in any of the other manuscripts recorded by Dobson; most of them are omissions or misreadings. See Dobson, *Seinte Katerine*, p. 135–36: '*EJOS* form a recognizable group. *O* .. has at least 140 non-original readings identical with, or clearly related to, those of *E*, and over 60 similarly shared with or related to those of *J* and/or *S*; *EO* form a subgroup within the larger *EJOS* group. *O* may represent, though imperfectly, an early stage in the development of the group, since it often retains original readings when one or more of the other three diverge, but it has its own peculiar errors where the others are correct [*There is no evidence for this in the apparatus. Dobson was perhaps influenced by the date of O.*]; and *J* and *S* often have original readings when *EO* agree on non-original ones'. *E*: Bern, BB, MS 137, s. xii, prov. Île-de-France(?). *J*: Rouen, BM, MS 1394 (U.119), s. xii, prov. Mortagne. *O*: Paris, BnF, MS lat. 5343, s. xi, prov. Vendôme. *S*: Paris, BnF, MS lat. 5365, s. xii, Limoges.

Fulk Nerra, Count of Anjou. Jean Vezin was able to pinpoint the copying of this manuscript to Angers due to the fact that Nicholas' name is the only one highlighted in vermilion throughout and traced in larger letters ahead of the text. He also pointed out that the translation of Nicholas at folios 157-166v is a later addition to the manuscript, to be dated after 1052, on the grounds that folios 162v-166v contain the account of the translation of Nicholas' arm, which took place in 1052 under Geoffrey Martel, Count of Anjou. The same scribe also transcribed folios 235-253v and 276-280v. Folios 68v-72 contain the translation of the body of Nicholas to Bari in 1087; the hand responsible for the writing on these folios appears to be a little later than those of the original manuscript and the first addition (at folios 162v-166v), which allows dating of the original and first addition to before 1087, and perhaps even to before 1052.[85] For the passion of Katherine on folios 274-280 this results in the following: folios 276r-280v can be dated to the period between 1052 and 1087. Folios 274r-275v were transcribed by a hand from the first half of the twelfth century.[86]

The epitome in Angers 121 is an example of how quickly BHL 1663 was subject to abbreviation, probably within decades of its composition, although this particular epitome did not engender its own tradition. BHL 1663 was too long to be read in its entirety at mass, during the office, or in the refectory and thus needed to be shortened.[87] The division into

[85] *Catalogue des manuscrits en écriture latine portant des indications de date, de lieu ou de copiste:* vol. 7: *Ouest de la France et Pays de Loire*, ed. Denis Muzerelle *et al.* (Paris, 1994), p. 19 and plate XVIII.

[86] The most likely explanation for the change of hand is that someone had erased so much of the text that it was easiest simply to recopy it or that the original leaves were damaged and needed to be replaced. Given that it looks as if the writing has been retraced at the bottom of fol. 274ab, and that at that same place parts of the text have been crossed out, it is likely that fols 274r–275v are supply-leaves.

[87] Philippart, *Les légendiers latins*, pp. 112–18.

twelve readings indicates that the text was meant to be read during the matins liturgy (matins or vigils, now known as the office of readings or the night office), which is characterized by an emphasis on reading longer extracts from scripture or lives of saints, for example, in a Benedictine monastery.[88] The fact that Katherine's shortened life has been divided into these readings indicates the importance of her cult since less important saints are not commemorated in this way.

Radical cutting of the full text has resulted in the suppression or omission of the centrepiece, the encounter between Katherine and the rhetors. In the same way, the construction of the wheels, another essential feature of Katherine's passion, has been omitted. This leaves the emperor's decision to have the queen tortured without an antecedent, and is thus another indication of the epitomizer's disinterest in a logical dénouement of the story. The presence of phrases such as 'sola contra quinquaginta viros pugnatura' (Dobson, l. 322) and 'expectat quam mox invitetur ad laborem certaminis' (Dobson, l. 322) supports this supposition. All unnecessary material has been eliminated and very few attempts have been made to smoothe over the gaps. The primary interest here was to shorten the text, with almost no intervention to make the new text transition easily from one passage to the next.

[88] Matins was the first service of the day, taking place after midnight and before daybreak. Matins has three parts: (1) an opening, (2) a middle section of one to three nocturns, and (3) a closing section. The nocturns vary in number and structure depending on the cursus, the rank of the feast, and the time of year. The monastic cursus (number and arrangement of elements of this service) includes, inter alia, three nocturns, each of which has four lessons/readings. See Lila Collamore, 'Charting the Divine Office', in *The Divine Office in the Latin Middle Ages: Methodology and Source Studies, Regional Developments, Hagiography*, ed. Margot Fassler and Rebecca Baltzer (Oxford, 2000), pp. 5–6: since 'the night is longer in winter than in summer', one could allow 'more time for Matins without loss of daylight hours for work'. Katherine's feast day falls towards the end of November, so there was a little more time.

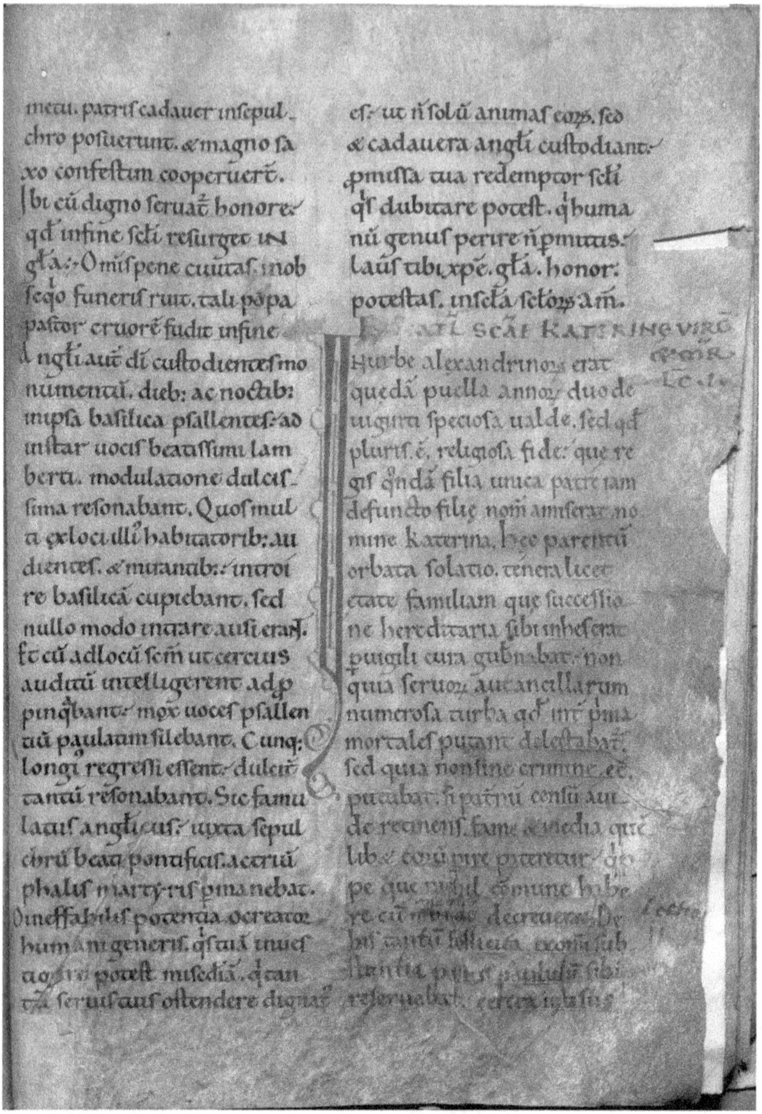

Figure 3: Angers, Bib. mun., MS 121, fol. 274, s. xii$^{1/2}$ hand, prov. Angers
© Ville d'Angers, site commulisse.angers.fr

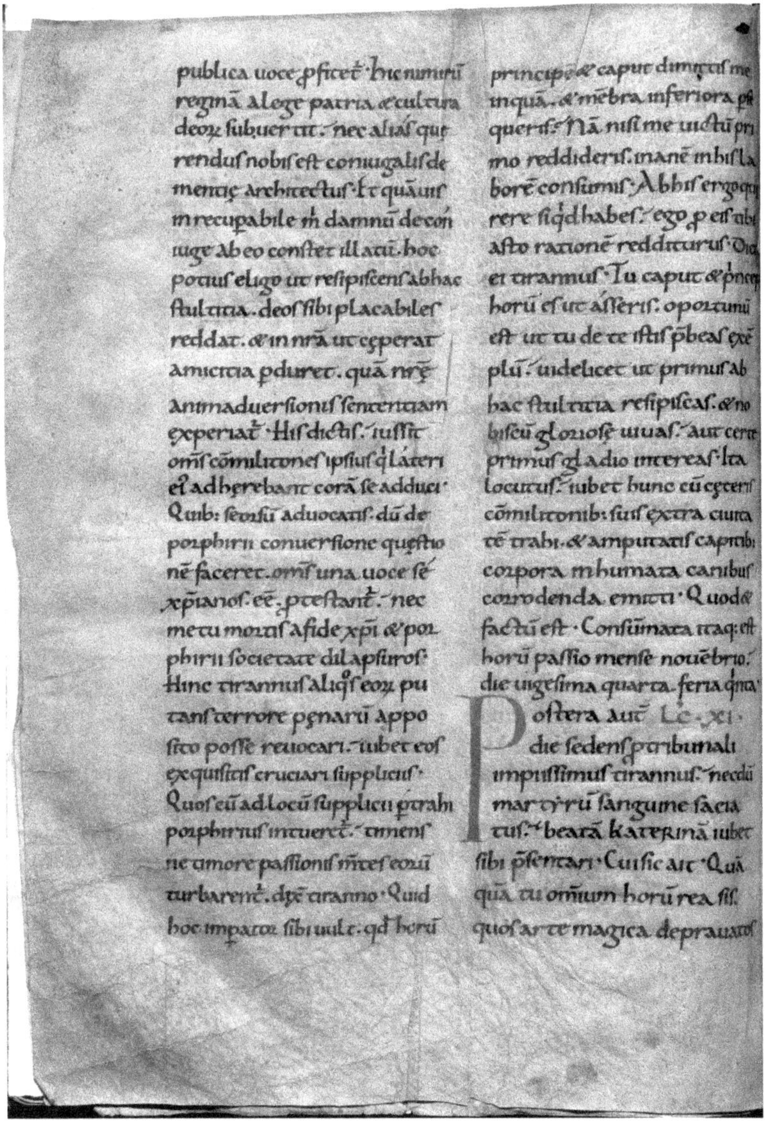

Figure 4: Angers, Bib. mun., MS 121, fol. 278v, s. xi$^{2/2}$ hand (between 1052 and 1087), prov. Angers
© Ville d'Angers, site commulisse.angers.fr

Brussels, KBR, MS 18018, is a *lectionarium* copied at the Benedictine abbey of St Peter at Lobbes (see Figures 5 and 6). It consists of 194 folios, measures 31.2 x 22.3 cm, is written in two columns of forty lines each, and contains saints' lives from all the months of the year. Many of the saints are universal (Ambrose, Barbara, George, Martin), but a good number betray a local flavour (Begga from Andenne, BHL 3885; Remaclus from Stavelot, BHL 8021; Servatius from Tongeren, BHL 5552; Raineldis from Hainaut, BHL 7082; and others). The passion of Katherine is on folios 25v-37r, sandwiched between Marinus and companions (BHL 5532) and Barbara (BHL 913).[89] The text is BHL 1663 with the prologue, although it lacks Dobson, ll. 96-187 due to a missing leaf between folios 26r and 27r. It was used by Dobson who assigned it the siglum *G*.[90]

The provenance for this manuscript rests on a twelfth-century note in the margin at the top of folio 56 which reads 'laubiensis mona[sterium]'. Léon Gilissen identified the hand of the scribe of folios 25v-26 as Goderan, who left Lobbes for the abbey of Stavelot in 1093. Goderan was one of the two scribes who signed the Stavelot Bible (London, BL, Add. MS 28196 and MS 28107), written in 1097, and the Lobbes Bible (Tournai, Bibliothèque du Grand Seminaire, MS 1), written out in 1084, as well as a manuscript of Josephus' *De bello judaico* (Brussels, KBR, MS II.1179), written before 1105.[91]

---

[89] For a detailed list of the contents see *Catalogus codicum hagiographicorum Bibliothecae Regiae Bruxellensis*, vol. 1.2 (Brussels, 1889), pp. 414–19, where the shelf-mark is erroneously given as 18108.

[90] Dobson, p. 133 also gave the shelf-mark as 18108, and followed the catalogue in dating the manuscript to s. xii^{in}.

[91] See Léon Gilissen, *L'expertise des écritures médiévales: Recherche d'une méthode avec application à un manuscrit du xie siècle: Le lectionnaire de Lobbes, Codex Bruxelensis 18018* (Ghent, 1973). See also Andrew G. Watson, *Catalogue of Dated and Datable Manuscripts, c. 700–1600, in the Department of Manuscripts, the British Library* (London, 1979), for a picture of the Stavelot Bible, pp. 70–71, no. 321, pl. 52.

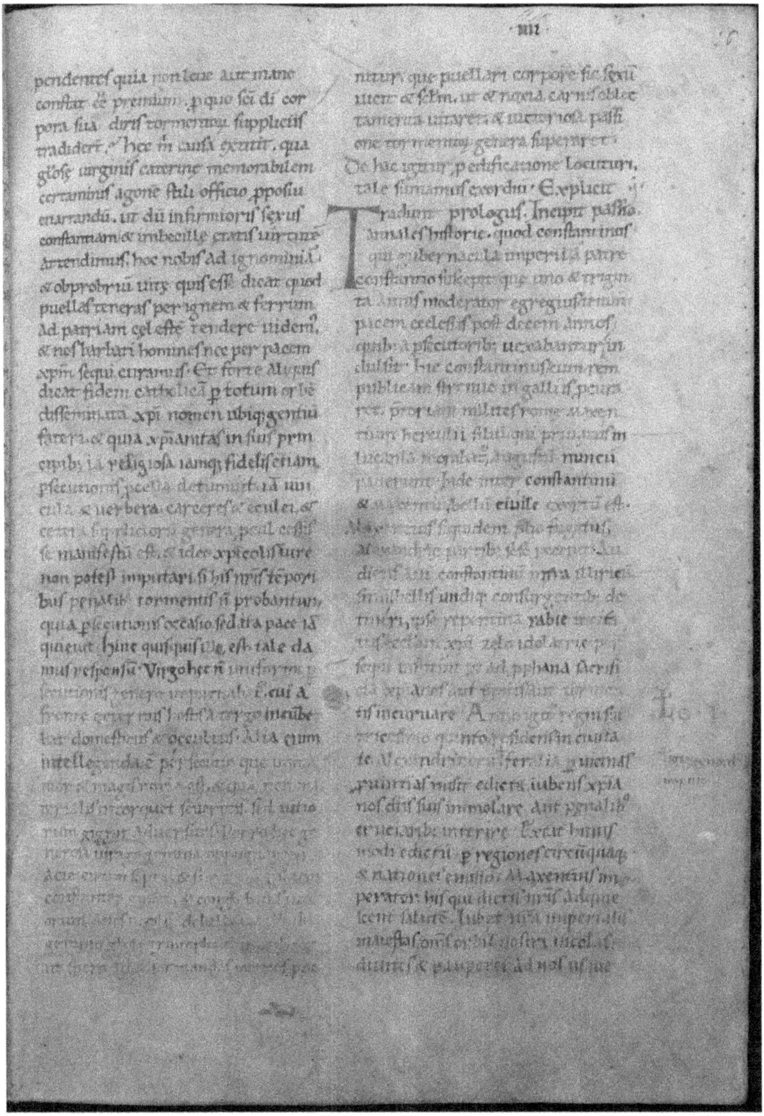

Figure 5: Brussels, KBR, MS 18018, fol. 26, 1084-1093
Goderan and the scribe of the Passionary of Lobbes
Copyright KBR

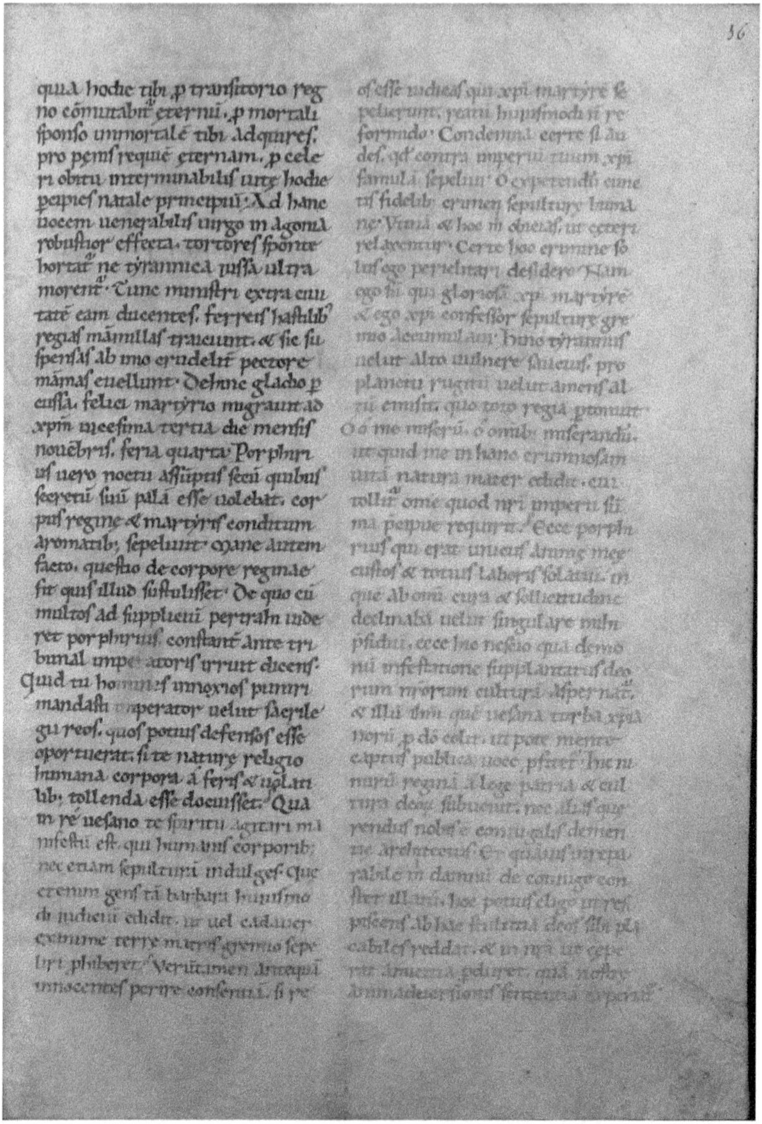

Figure 6: Brussels, KBR, MS 18018, fol. 36, 1084-1093
The scribe of the Passionary of Lobbes
Copyright KBR

Date & Place of Composition of BHL 1663   179

The remainder of Katherine's passion (folios 26-37) was transcribed by the 'scribe of the passionary of Lobbes', so called because he transcribed the greater part of that manuscript.[92]

Paris, Bibliothèque nationale de France, MS lat. 1970 (see Figures 7 and 8) consists of two parts: the first, folios 1-71, contains patristic texts including Augustine's *In epistolam Iohannis ad Parthos tractatus x* and Maximinus of Tours' *Sermones de S. Laurentio*, as well as Katherine's passion. The second part, folios 72-153, preserves Bede's *De tabernaculo*.[93] These two parts are attested, separately, in a twelfth-century catalogue of books belonging to Fécamp, although Katherine's passion is not mentioned.[94] The two parts were bound together at some point between the twelfth and fifteenth centuries. The manuscript in toto consists of 153 folios and measures 25.5 x 16.5 cm. The passion of Katherine, BHL 1663 with prologue, is on folios 54-70v and is part of the initial conception of the first part, i.e. it is not a later addition even though it occupies the last sixteen folios. This manuscript was used by Dobson (siglum *M*).

---

[92] Brussels, KBR, MS 14924-34, a passionary from Lobbes, was transcribed by the same hand. See Gilissen, *L'expertise des écritures*, p. 9, and also p. 10 for a table listing the scribes of Brussels, KBR, MS 18018.

[93] *Catalogue général des manuscrits latins*, ed. Philippe Lauer, vol. 2 (numbers 1439–2692) (Paris, 1940), p. 26, where the date is given as s. xii.

[94] The catalogue is preserved on fol. 180 in Paris, BnF, MS lat. 1928, 'Augustinus super Iohannem' and 'Beda De Tabernaculo', see François Dolbeau, 'Anciens possesseurs des manuscrits hagiographiques latins conservés à la Bibliotheque Nationale de Paris', *Revue d'Histoire des Textes*, 9 (1979), 190. See also Nortier, *Les bibliothèques médiévales*, pp. 9–10 and p. 235. A catalogue from the eleventh-century survives on fol. 55v of Rouen, BM, MS 1417 (U.45), which lists the 'De tabernaculo lib. I', see Henri Omont, *Catalogue général des manuscrits des bibliothèques publiques de France: Départements*, vol. 1: Rouen (Paris, 1886), p. xxiv.

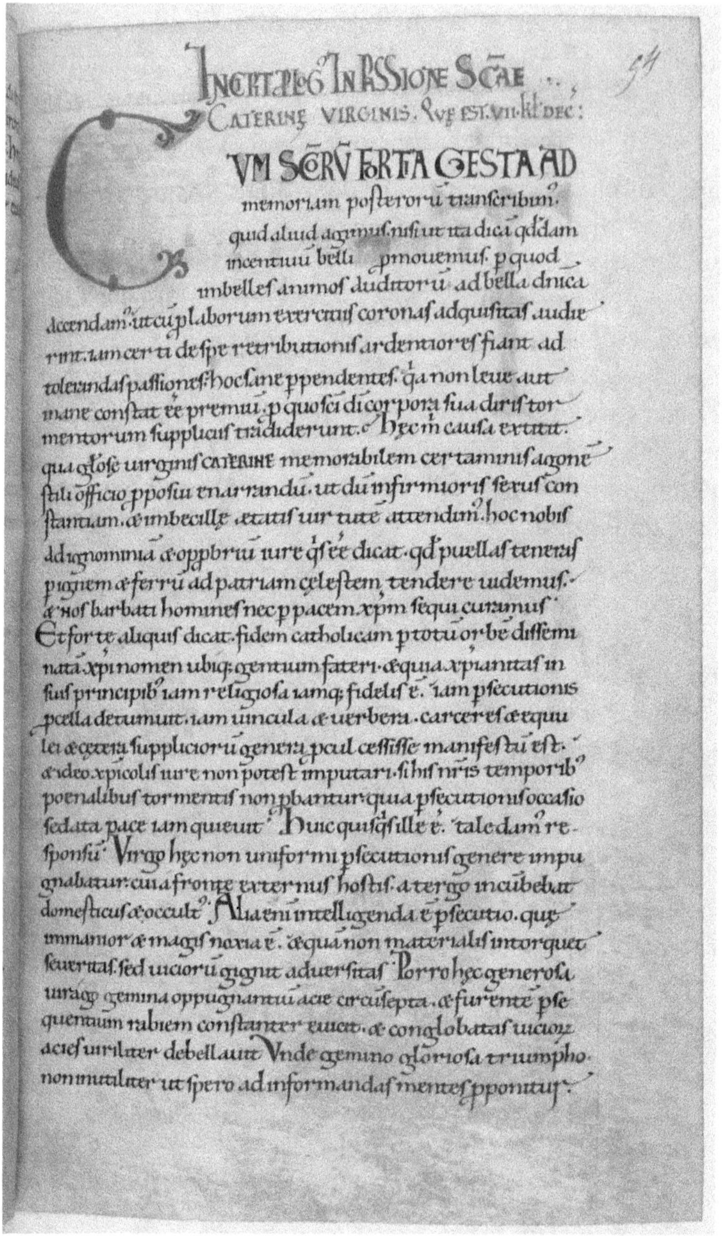

Figure 7: Paris BnF, MS lat. 1970, fol. 54, s. xi., prov. Fécamp

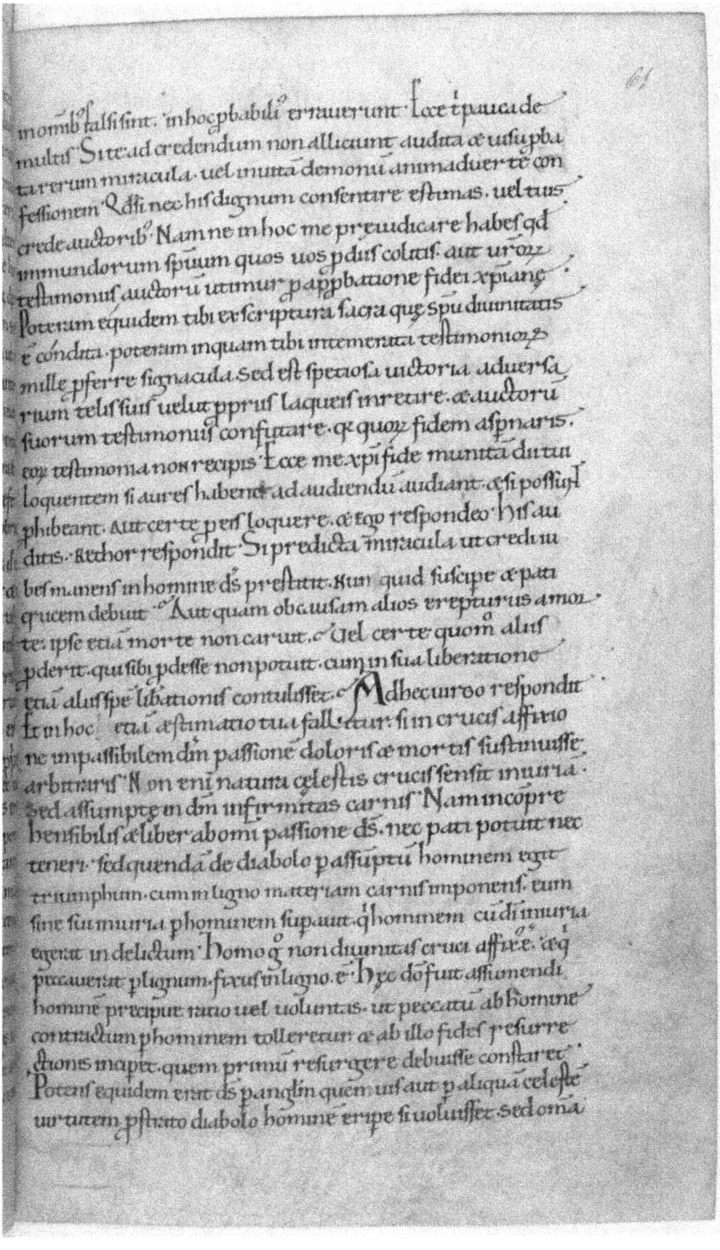

Figure 8: Paris BnF, MS lat. 1970, fol. 61, s. xi, prov. Fécamp

Paris, Bibliothèque nationale de France, MS lat. 5343 contains a *legendarium* copied at La Trinité de Vendôme, a monastery founded in 1034 by Geoffrey II, Count of Angers, and his wife Agnes (see Figures 9 and 10).[95] It consists of 156 folios, measures 29 x 20 cm, and was written out by several hands of the eleventh and twelfth centuries on thirty-seven long lines (s. xii = folios 84-91, and 103-116). The passion of Katherine, BHL 1663 with prologue, is on folios 135-137v and 140-148v. It is preceded by various tracts on the date of Easter (*homiliae variae de paschae*), interrupted by the life of Saturninus (BHL 7495 & 7507), and followed by Denis *et al.* (BHL 2175). It was used by Dobson who assigned it the siglum *O*. The saints contained in this manuscript have their feast days from May until November and range from the universal (Augustine, Benedict, Paul, Peter) and the more or less local (Denis/Paris, Photinus/Lyon, Radegunda/Poitiers, Saturninus/Toulouse, Sigismund/Burgundy), to the obscure (Reverentius/Bayeux BHL 7199).[96]

---

[95] Laurent H. Cottineau and Grégoire Poras, *Répertoire topo-bibliographique des abbayes et prieurés*, 3 vols (Mâcon, 1935–1970), II, col. 3317.

[96] For the contents see *Catalogus codicum hagiographicorum latinorum antiquiorum saeculo xvi qui asservantur in Bibliotheca Nationali Parisiensi*, ed. Hagiographi Bollandiani, vol. 2 (Brussels, 1890), pp. 269–70. On Reverentius see Jules Lair, 'Vie de Saint Révérend', *Bibliothèque de l'École des Chartes*, 23 (1862), 118–24, who edited the life based on Paris, BnF, MS lat. 5343, the only witness (I owe this reference to François Dolbeau). Guy Oury, 'Les pérégrinations de reliques: Saint Révérend de Nouâtre', *Bulletin Trimestriel de la Société Archéologique de Tourraine*, 35 (1968), 279–93.

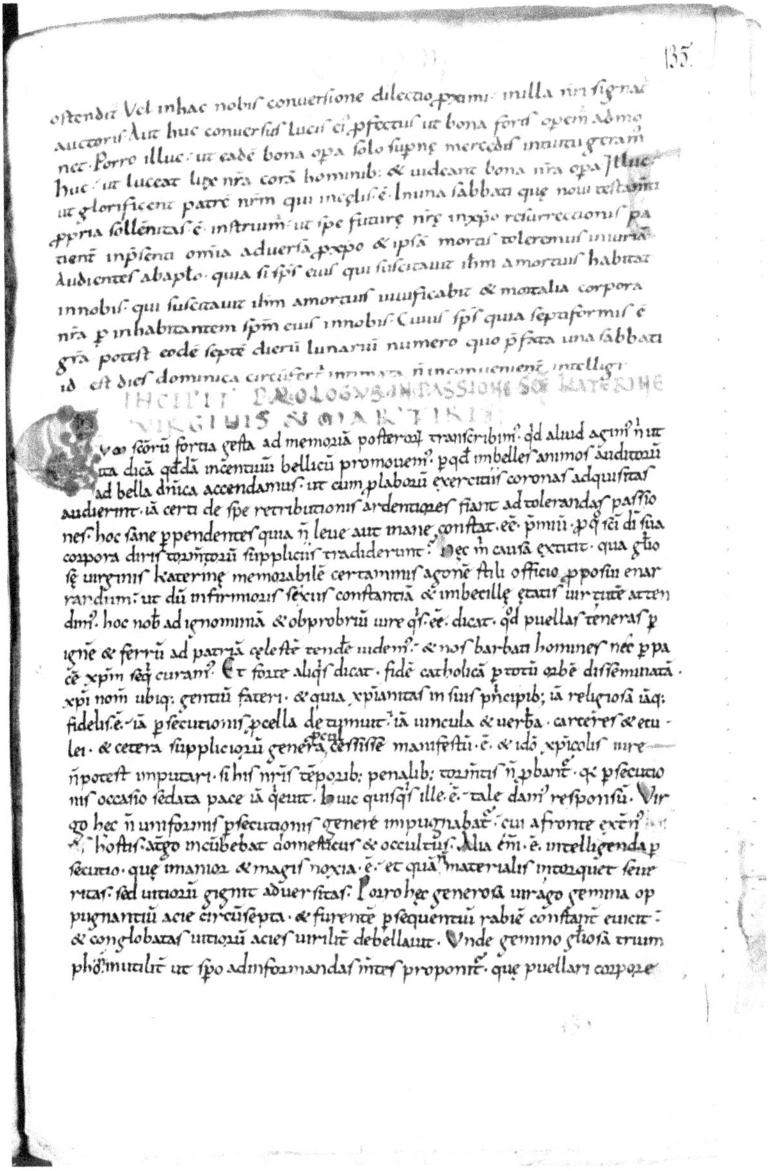

Figure 9: Paris, BnF, MS lat. 5343, fol. 135, s. xi, prov. Vendôme

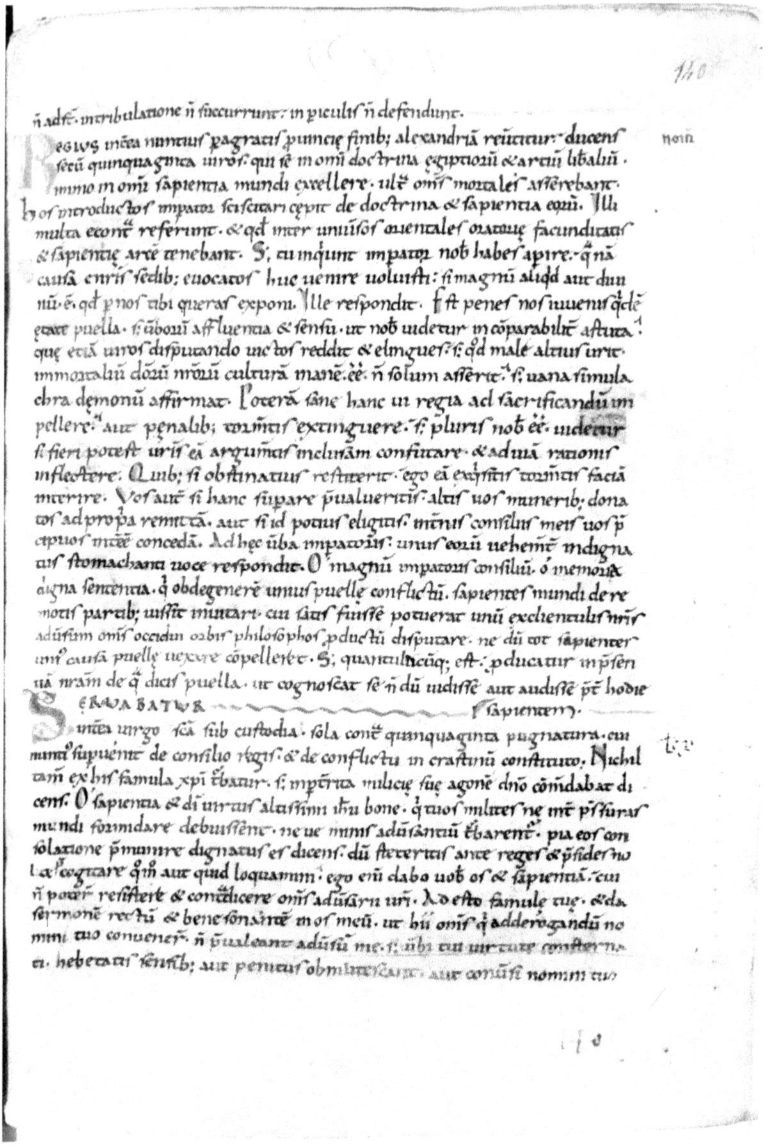

Figure 10: Paris, BnF, MS lat. 5343, fol. 139v, s. xi, prov. Vendôme

In sum, there are three witnesses to BHL 1663, including the prologue, from the eleventh century, and one eleventh-century witness to an abbreviated version of BHL 1663. The dates of likely copying at each provenance are as follows: Angers, 1052-1087; Fécamp, 1000-1100; Lobbes, 1084-1093; and Vendôme, 1034-1100. Their dissemination is clearly concentrated in northern France: there is an obvious geographical division between Fécamp (Normandy) and Lobbes (Hainaut) in the north, and Angers (Anjou) and Vendôme a little further to the south-west. The latter two are connected by the river Loir and about 140 kilometres apart.[97] The manuscript from Angers shares a number of errors with the manuscript from Vendôme, despite the fact that it contains an abbreviated version.[98] By superimposing the geographical localization of *celeranter* and *tarinca* on the above locations, two geographical pockets emerge: Fécamp and Rouen on the one hand, and Amiens, Corbie, Saint-Amand, Valenciennes, Saint-Quentin, and Lobbes on the other hand. Angers and Vendôme do not share a proximity with the localization of *celeranter* and *tarinca*. On the basis of this evidence, the localization of the composition of BHL 1663 could very well lie within the geographical area between Fécamp and Lobbes, which encompasses the cathedral city of Rouen just seventy kilometres south-east of Fécamp. The question now is, under what circumstances did Katherine's passion arrive in this geographical area?

---

[97] Not to be confused with the Loire.

[98] In error with *O* at Dobson, l. 82 (exhaurierat] exhauriret), l. 123 (coaeternam] aeternam), l. 124 (formam] *om.*), l. 314 (resistere] *om.*), l. 715 (hunc] *om.*), l. 722 (abhorruisset] abhorret *O*, abhorreret *Angers*), l. 745 (ab ipso] ab illo), l. 849 (corporalem] *om.*), l. 1039 (sepulture humane] humane sepulture), l. 1054 (irreparabile] irrecuperabile *O*, inrecuperabilem *Angers*), l. 1067 (dico] *om.*), l. 1093 (effatam] affatam), l. 1102 (Christum me] me Christum), l. 1145 (olei] *om.*).

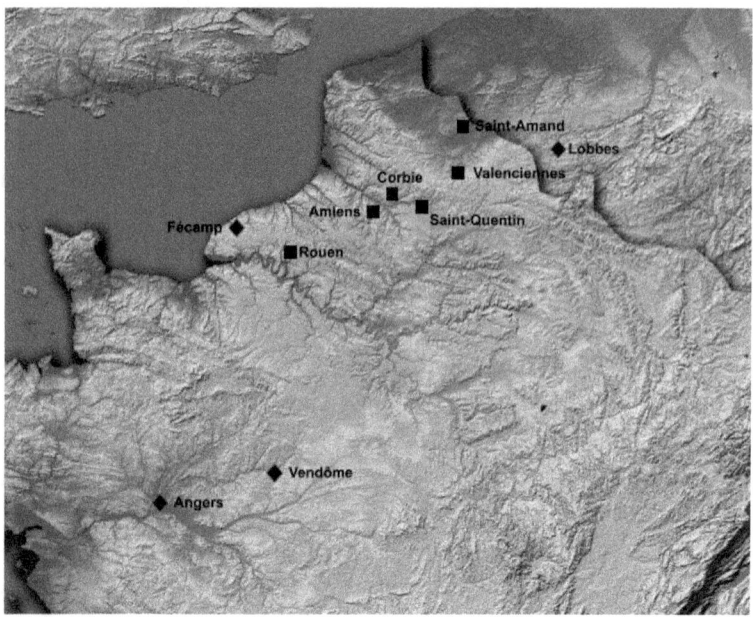

Map 2: Northern France. Diamonds: eleventh-century manuscripts of BHL 1663, squares: localization of *celeranter* and *tarinca*. Based on image PIA03393 by NASA/JPL/NIMA (https://photojournal.jpl.nasa.gov/catalog/PIA03393) [accessed 7 July 2021].

CHAPTER 5

BHL 1633 AND ROUEN

One potential story for the arrival in Normandy of Katherine's relics, at least, is that of Symeon of Trier, for which there is a rich documentary context. The role of Symeon in relation to the dissemination of Katherine's cult is often cited, although the contacts the Normans had with Italy are just as likely to have resulted in the arrival of Katherine's passion in northern France. For example, William of Volpiano, an Italian, is one possible channel for the arrival of Katherine in Normandy; even if he himself did not bring the story with him, he still maintained his connections with Italy. In 1001, Duke Richard II of Normandy (d. 1026) called to Normandy the reformer William of Volpiano, who was then based at Saint-Bénigne in Dijon. He arrived with twelve monks and quickly set about transforming the abbey of the Trinity at Fécamp into an intellectual centre, with an active scriptorium, school, and library; its twelfth-century catalogue lists 176 volumes.[1] Richard also assigned him to Saint-Ouen in Rouen (1006?), Jumièges (1015), and Mont Saint-Michel (1023).[2] William ended up establishing the reform movement of monasteries in Normandy: he not only was in charge of numerous abbeys, he also instructed 'a generation of monks whose reforms would

---

[1] *Dictionnaire d'histoire et de géographie ecclésiastiques*, vol. 16, ed. Alfred Baudrillart *et al.* (Paris, 1967), s.v. Fécamp (Sainte-Trinité). The Benedictine abbey of the Trinity at Fécamp was a Merovingian establishment, founded in *c.* 664. In 842 (or 876) it was destroyed by the Normans, but restored and given over to regular canons under Richard I of Normandy, who was born there.

[2] *LexMA*, s.v. Wilhelm v. Volpiano.

eventually extend throughout the region and the century'.[3] He brought with him to Fécamp another Italian, John of Fécamp, an administrator, scholar, and author of prayers and contemplative treatises.[4]

1. La Trinité-du-Mont de Rouen

In *c.* 1030 the Norman nobleman Goscelin, a confidant and nephew of Duke Robert I (1027-37), and his wife Emmeline founded the abbey of La Trinité-du-Mont at Rouen.[5] Their new foundation is the first in the duchy by members of the aristocracy, and the first in the capital.[6] Isembert, a German and a monk of Saint-Ouen at Rouen, became the abbot of La Trinité in 1033. He received the staff from the Duke and the blessing from the archbishop of Rouen, Robert.[7] During his

---

[3] Cassandra Potts, *Monastic Revival and Regional Identity in Early Normandy* (Woodbridge, 1997), p. 29.

[4] Walter Simons, 'New forms of religious life in medieval Western Europe', in *The Cambridge Companion to Christian Mysticism*, ed. Amy M. Hollywood and Patricia Z. Beckmann (Cambridge, 2012), pp. 80–113.

[5] The charter of Robert's confirmation of the foundation of La Trinité survives, see Achille Deville, 'Cartulaire de l'abbaye de la Sainte-Trinité-du-mont-de-Rouen', in *Cartulaire de l'abbaye de Saint-Bertin*, ed. Benjamin Guérard, *Collection de documents inédits sur l'histoire de France* 3 (Paris, 1840), pp. 421–23, charter 1. Goscelin and Emmeline also founded Saint-Amand at Rouen, a convent for women, at some point in the 1040s, see Jean-Marie Soyez, 'Les abbayes de Rouen au XIe siècle', in *La Normandie bénédictine au temps de Guillaume le Conquérant (XIe siècle)*, ed. Louis Gaillaird (Lille, 1967), pp. 69–81 (pp. 74–75).

[6] See Véronique Gazeau, 'Recherches autour des débuts de l'abbaye de la Trinité-du-Mont de Rouen', in *La ville médiévale en deça et au-dela de ses murs: Mélanges J.-P. Leguay*, ed. Philippe Lardin and Jean-Louis Roch (Rouen, 2000), pp. 151–59 (pp. 152–53).

[7] Véronique Gazeau, *Normannia monastica: Prosopographie des abbés bénédictins (X^e – XIIe siècle)*, 2 vols (Caen, 2007), II, pp. 263–65. Isembert was consecrated on the same day as the new church of Saint-Wandrille at Fontenelle, an event that is said to have taken place on 12 September 1033.

abbacy the monk Ainard, also a German, wrote an *historia* of Katherine's passion (according to Orderic Vitalis, d. *c.* 1142):

> Circa haec tempora reverendus Ainardus, Divensium primus abbas, in lectum decidit, et completis in eo quae servo Dei competunt, 19 Kal. Februarii obiit. Hic fuit natione Teutonicus, geminaque scientia pleniter imbutus, versificandi et modulandi cantusque suaves edendi peritissimus. Hoc evidenter probari potest in historiis Kiliani Guirciburgensis episcopi et Katerinae virginis, aliisque plurimis cantibus quos eleganter idem edidit in laudem Creatoris. In iuventute vero studio religionis flagrans venerabilem Isembertum abbatem expetiit eiusque disciplinis pro amore Dei se gratanter submisit et in coenobio sanctae Trinitatis, quod Goscelinus de Archis in monte Rotomagi ad orientalem plagam construxerat monachatum, suscepit.[8]

Orderic's description indicates that this *historia* of Katherine's passion was a prime example of Ainard's ability to compose chants.[9] Recently, James Blasina has proposed that the *historia Katerinae virginis* written by Ainard is in fact the so-called Norman-German office for that saint.[10] The earliest exemplar for this office can be found in a late eleventh-century breviary

---

[8] Orderic Vitalis, *Historia Ecclesiastica*, ed. and tr. Marjorie Chibnall (Oxford, 1969–1980), Book IV, pp. 352–54. A different Ainard was the teacher who wrote a glossary for his pupils at Saint-Èvre at Toul, and dedicated it to its abbot, Aprus, in the year 969 under Otto the Great. See *Ainardo: Glossario*, ed. Paolo Gatti (Florence, 2000). The sources refer to a third monk by name: Gradulph succeeded Gerard of Crépy as the abbot of Saint-Wandrille in 1031. See Elisabeth M.C. van Houts, 'Historiography and hagiography at Saint-Wandrille: The 'inventio et miracula Sancti Vulfranni'', *Anglo-Norman Studies*, 12 (1989), p. 234.

[9] Saara Nevanlinna and Irma Taavitsainen, *St Katherine of Alexandria: The Late Middle English Prose Legend in Southwell Minster MS 7* (Cambridge, 1993), p. 5, thought that 'Ainard's passion of St Katherine … came to be known as the *Vulgate* version [= BHL 1663] of the legend.'

[10] James J. Blasina, 'Ainard of Dives and the Ste-Catherine-du-Mont office for St Katherine of Alexandria: "Inter praecipuos cantores scientia musicae artis"', *Plainsong and Medieval Music*, 30 (2021), 55-83.

(Paris, BnF, MS n.a. lat. 1083), ascribed to Saint-Denis at Duclair in Normandy.[11] Given that there is a clear relationship between this manuscript and two manuscripts now at Rouen (BM, MS 670 [A.592] and MS 204 [A.591]), the only extant manuscripts of offices from the abbey of La Trinité which contain a version of the Norman-German office that is nearly identical to that in Paris, BnF, MS n.a. lat. 1083, Blasina argues that the latter may have originated at the abbey in Rouen, although a close study of the manuscript is needed before a definitive conclusion can be reached. In this manuscript, the office of Katherine is almost completely notated, indicating the importance of the saint's feast.

This office, which Blasina argues is the *historia* on Katherine by Ainard mentioned by Orderic, appears to have been deliberately composed by

> Ainard to create an archaizing aesthetic, implying the historicity and legitimacy of the (new) cult of St Katherine. ... The strategy is evident in the chant melodies, but also in the way in which Ainard builds his office around a repertory of common chants that would align Katherine with the most renowned women in heaven. This propagandizing agenda is evident, furthermore, in the multitude of antiphons and responsories that promote St. Katherine's relics and the healing power of their secreted oil.[12]

The text of this office is relatively short and only contains the barebones of the story, so it is difficult to draw definitive conclusions from a comparison with different versions of Katherine's story. In one instance, there seems to be a hint of some kind of relationship: following the emperor's final attempt to lure Katherine to his side, she rejects him, leading to the construction of the four-wheeled torture machine. His subsequent anger is described in BHL 1663 as such: 'tyrannus,

---

[11] Michael Gullick has informed me that this very small (218 x 120 mm) manuscript dates from or about the 1070s.

[12] Blasina, 'Music and Gender', p. 127.

ut leo violentus dentibus frendens, in vocem huiusmodi erupit'.[13] In BHL 1659 the text reads: 'iratus est rex vehementer'.[14] The text of the office has this: 'Caesar ut invictam penitus vidit Katharinam ut leo crudelis iubet hanc discerpere poenis'.[15]

By 1083 the abbey of La Trinité had acquired a reputation for healing, as attested by a charter, the first explicitly to make reference to Katherine, which records the gift by Fulco of Caldri and his wife Ita of the fourth part of a church in 'Behervilla' in gratitude for Fulco's healing through Katherine's relics.[16] The increasing popularity of Katherine's relics did seemingly not result in a full name change for the monastery, which continued to be referred to in the documentary sources as *Sancta Trinitas* (and variations thereof), mirroring the situation at the monastery on the Sinai.[17] There is, however, a gift that was made at some point (the charter does not carry a date) in which the saint's name is mentioned alongside that of the Holy Trinity: 'notum sit omnibus, quoniam Rainaldus, filius Viliberti Pain, et Eva et Auffrida, soror eius, dederunt Sanctae Trinitati et beatae Caterinae pratum unum'.[18] Based on the surviving charters, the monastery was the beneficiary of numerous gifts (money, land, etc.) from Norman aristocrats, mirroring the endowment of abbeys by other aristocrats and indeed by the Norman dukes as a way of assuring their

---

[13] Dobson, l. 886.

[14] D'Angelo, *Pietro Suddiacono Napoletano*, II.154, p. 140.

[15] Blasina, 'Music and Gender', p. 211. Maxentius is referred to three times as *caesar* in this office, which, as I note below on p. 216, is how he is described most often in 1659 but never in 1663.

[16] Deville, 'Cartulaire', pp. 466–67, charter 90: 'montem Sanctae Trinitatis Rotomagensis adii, ubi sacratissimae ac venerabilis virginis et martiris Caterinae miro miraculo cotidie ab omnibus longe lateque venerantur ossa, ipsiusque interventu ibidem sospitatis munus accepi'.

[17] Gazeau, 'Recherches autour des débuts', p. 152 and n. 3.

[18] Deville, 'Cartulaire', p. 469, charter 97.

spiritual wellbeing and establishing their power in the political arena.[19]

2. Simeon of Trier: Peddler of relics?

The life of Symeon of Trier (BHL 7963) written by Eberwin, abbot at St. Martin in Trier, at the behest of archbishop Poppo very soon after the saint's death in 1035, reveals that there existed connections between Sinai and Rouen at the beginning of the eleventh century. Eberwin's knowledge of his friend's life before arriving in Trier is based entirely on conversations with him or hearing others talk with him.[20] As the story goes, Symeon, 'instructus enim Aegyptiaca, Syriaca, Arabica, Graeca et Romana eloquentia', had travelled twice across the Mediterranean from the Holy Land to France and Trier. The son of a Greek father and a Calabrian mother, he was born in Syracuse, and taken by his father to Constantinople 'ibique eruditissimis viris sacris inbuendus litteris traditur et in timore Domini diligenter enutritur'.[21] As an adult he travelled to Jerusalem where he was a tour-guide for pilgrims for seven

---

[19] Giovanni Coppola, 'L'essor de la construction monastique en Normandie au XIe siècle: Mécénat, matériaux et moines-architectes', *Annales de Normandie*, 42–4 (1992), 335.

[20] 'Quae vel ipse ex eius ore audivi vel a fidelibus viris ab ipso audita, sive de miraculis visa, didici'; *Vita Sancti Symeonis*, *AASS* Junii, p. 89B. On Eberwin see Michele C. Ferrari, 'From pilgrim's guide to living relic: Symeon of Trier and his biographer Eberwin', in *Latin Culture in the Eleventh Century: Proceedings of the Third International Conference on Medieval Latin Studies* (Cambridge, 9–12 September 1998), ed. Michael W. Herren *et al.*, 2 vols (Turnhout, 2002), I, pp. 324–44; Klaus Krönert, 'Des interventions du saint au travail des hagiographes: Les miracles de Syméon de Treves', in 'Rerum gestarum scriptor': *Histoire et historiographie au Moyen Âge: Mélanges Michel Sot*, ed. Magali Coumert *et al.* (Paris, 2012), pp. 363–76.

[21] *Vita Sancti Symeonis*, *AASS* Junii I, p. 89.C.

years. He lived in monasteries in Bethlehem and Sinai,[22] and also spent time as a hermit in the desert.[23] At one point his brethren chose Symeon to travel to Normandy in order to bring back alms from Richard II:

> Interea fratres aliqui pro necessitatibus loci Occidentalibus partibus directi, moriuntur. Pecunia pro qua fratres abierant, quae de terra Richardi comitis Normanniae monasterio debebatur, ab ipso diligenter conservatur, et ut aliquis fidelis frater mitteretur, qui eam monasterio deferet, per legatos mandatur. Communi consilio ad hanc obedientiam, famulus Dei Symeon destinatur.[24]

After his ship was attacked by pirates, Symeon reached Antioch where he met the abbots Richard and Eberwin while they were on pilgrimage to the Holy Land.[25] He finally arrived in France via Rome,[26] and 'a quodam igitur sibi noto Comite

---

[22] 'Ad aliud monasterium, quod est situm ad radices Montis Sina, in eo scilicet loco ubi S. Moyses ardentem vidit non ardere rubum'. *Vita Sancti Symeonis, AASS* Junii I, p. 89.F. 'In vertice autem Montis Sinai, eo videlicet loco quo Moyses gloriam Domini vidit et legem in tabulis lapideis scripsit, aliud monasterium erat, quod propter Arabitas incursantes, qui per illam eremum semper vagantur, omni habitatore desertum remanserat'. Ibid., p. 90.A.

[23] Alfred Haverkamp, 'Der heilige Simeon (gest. 1035), Grieche im fatimidischen Orient und im lateinischen Okzident: Geschichten und Geschichte', *Historische Zeitschrift*, 290.1 (2010), 1–51, has offered an in-depth context-based analysis of Symeon's travels before his arrival in Trier.

[24] *Vita Sancti Symeonis, AASS* Junii I, p. 91.A.

[25] Richard of Saint-Vanne travelled to Palestine and then Sinai in 1026/27, all expenses paid for by Richard II, with a large group of pilgrims. Eberwin also went on this journey. See Hugh of Flavigny, *Chronicon Hugonis monachi virdunensis et divionensis abbatis flaviniacensis*, ed. Georg H. Pertz, MGH SS 8 (Hannover, 1848), book 2.18, p. 383. See also the *Vita Richardi Abb. S. Vitoni virdunensis*, ed. Wilhelm Wattenbach, MGH SS 11 (Hannover, 1854), ch. 17, pp. 280–290.

[26] 'Prosperumque iter faciens per Romam pervenit in Franciam'. *Vita Sancti Symeonis, AASS* Junii I, p. 91.E, although several of the eleventh-century manuscripts do not mention his sojourn in Rome, see Tuomas

Wilhelmo benigne suscipitur, et apud eum aliquamdiu moratur'.[27] While he remained there, his travelling companion Cosmas died.[28] Symeon then continued his journey to Rouen, but discovered that Duke Richard had died in the meantime – and so he went to visit Richard of Saint-Vanne instead.[29] He returned to Jerusalem in the company of archbishop Poppo of Trier, presumably with the aim of delivering whatever money he had collected to his brethren. In 1030 he came back with him to Trier where he had himself immured in the Porta Nigra, dying there in 1035.[30]

Heikkilä, *Vita S. Symeonis Treverensis: Ein hochmittelalterlicher Heiligenkult im Kontext* (Helsinki, 2002), p. 118.

[27] *Vita Sancti Symeonis, AASS* Junii I, p. 91.E.

[28] 'In illis ergo partibus quidam monachus Cosmas nomine, vir sanctissimus, quem secum de Antiochia adduxerat, moritur'. *Vita Sancti Symeonis, AASS* Junii I, p. 91.E. Another example of a Greek monk dying far from his monastery is a certain Jorius. According to Jan Vermeulen (d. 1585), Jorius (a corrupted form of the Greek Georgios?), who died on 26 July 1033 in Béthune in Belgium, was, apparently, an abbot of Sinai ('episcopus de monte Sinai'). While on pilgrimage to Boulogne-sur-Mer, he stopped to visit a former servant of his now living at Béthune, where he died suddenly. A hymn written in his honour records his connection to Sinai. See *Natales sanctorum Belgii et eorundem chronica recapitulatio* (Leuven, 1595).

[29] 'Solus venit Rothomagum ... ubi cum Richardum Comitem jam mortuum reperisset, et de pecunia et censu qui de terra illius pro eleemosyna suo monasterio debebatur, nullus sibi responsa daret, moestificatus aliquantulum, non pro suo labore, sed quod locus montis Sinai fustratus esset tanta utilitate: toto corde conversus ad Deum, quid ageret quaerit consilium. Occurrit autem animo ut suum carissimum Patrem, Richardum scilicet abbatem, nosque suos comites inviseret: quod et fecit'. *Vita Sancti Symeonis, AASS* Junii I, p. 91.E.

[30] Symeon of Trier was not the only Greek who came to live in the West: Symeon of Reichenau, a native of Achaea in Greece, had been given a jug by the patriarch of Jerusalem. It was stolen from him, so he set out to find it and eventually reached the monastery at Reichenau where it stood on the altar. The account of how the jug reached Reichenau is the *raison d'être* for the *Vita Symeonis Achivi* (BHL 7950) written before 985 and preserved in five manuscripts, the oldest of which was written

Almost immediately after his death and at the instigation of Poppo, Eberwin composed the life that eventually resulted in Symeon's canonisation before 1039 at the hands of Pope Benedict IX.[31] Symeon's life and miracles survive in about fifty manuscripts; the oldest of these date from the eleventh century and come from such places as Aulne (near Liège), St Gall, Trier, Echternach, Fécamp, Liège, Fulda, and Paderborn.[32] Two points in Eberwin's account are corroborated by contemporary sources, demonstrating that a) connections between Sinai and Rouen did indeed exist at the beginning of the eleventh century, and that b) Symeon probably passed through France in in the 1020s.

According to Radulfus Glaber, the dukes of Normandy, particularly Duke Richard II, were known for their generosity towards the monastery at Sinai as well as to the Church of the Holy Sepulchre at Jerusalem:

> Dona etiam amplissima sacris ecclesiis pene in toto orbe mittebant, ita ut etiam ab oriente, scilicet de nominatissimo

---

before the end of the tenth century. See Walter Berschin and Theodor Klüppel, 'Vita Symeonis Achivi', in *Die Abtei Reichenau: Neue Beiträge zur Geschichte und Kultur des Inselklosters*, ed. Helmut Maurer (Sigmaringen, 1974), pp. 115–24. Simeon of Polirone, or the Armenian, had lived in the desert as well as at Jerusalem until he arrived in Italy. Following his death in 1016, he was canonized by Pope Benedict VIII; the account of his life was written before 1024 by an anonymous Benedictine monk. See Paolo Golinelli, 'La *vita* di s. Simeone monaco', *Studi medievali*, ser. 3a, 20 (1979), 709–88. A detailed bibliography of this Simeon can be found in *BBK*, s.v. Simeon.

[31] See Heikkilä, *Vita S. Symeonis*, pp. 138–46. Eberwin also wrote the life of Magnericus (BHL 5149), a sixth-century abbot of Trier, who (re-)founded the abbey St. Martin of Trier, see *BBK*, s.v. Magnerich. He is also thought to be the author of a *De calamitate abbatiae S. Martini Treverensis*, which survives in one manuscript (Trier, Stadtbibliothek, MS 1413, s. xi, fols 8–12), ed. Georg Waitz, MGH SS 15.2 (Hannover, 1888), pp. 739–41.

[32] A description of the extant manuscripts can be found in Heikkilä, *Vita S. Symeonis*, pp. 148–66.

monte Sina, per singulos annos monachi Rotomagum venientes, qui a predictis principibus plurima redeuntes auri et argenti suis deferrent exenia. Hierosolimam vero ad sepulchrum Salvatoris centum auri libras secundus misit Richardus, ac quosque cupientes illuc devote peragrare donis iuvabat inmensis.[33]

Glaber, who died in 1047 and spent most of his life in various Burgundian monasteries, probably did not have a vested interest in linking Richard with Sinai or Jerusalem (unless for propaganda purposes), though it is likely that Richard's gifts to these churches were useful tools in promoting him as a Christian ruler. Thus, well before 1026 – the year of Richard II's death – it seems to have been established practice for monks to set out from Sinai on a regular basis to receive whatever Richard had in store for them.[34] Before reaching Rouen, Symeon and his travelling companion Cosmas stayed with one Count William (probably William IV Taillefer and Duke of Angoulême). Taillefer was away on pilgrimage to Palestine from 1026 to 1027; Eberwin's life of Symeon indicates that Symeon arrived in Rouen after the death of Richard II in 1026, so it seems likely that Symeon, if he did meet Taillefer, did so after the latter had returned home.

An indirect witness to Symeon's stay with Taillefer is Ademar of Chabannes (c. 989-1034), a monk of Saint-Cybard in Angoulême; he is known for his *Chronicon* as well as for his attempts to have Martial of Limoges recognized as an apostle, although this undertaking ultimately failed. In his efforts on behalf of Martial, Ademar even forged a decree in support of

---

[33] *Rodulfi Glabri historiarum libri quinque*, ed. and tr. John France (Oxford, 1989), book 1.27. Book 1 was originally written before 1030 and revised c. 1036–41, see p. xlv. One of the oldest manuscripts to preserve the text is Paris, BnF, MS lat. 10912 (alias suppl. lat. 1013), perhaps an autograph, see p. lxxxiv and p. xxxvi.

[34] Count William left in 1026 for a pilgrimage to Palestine, returned to Angoulême in 1027 and died in 1028. See *Ademari cabannensis Chronicon*, ed. Pascale Bourgain *et al.*, CCCM 129 (Turnhout, 1999), pp. vii–viii.

Martial's apostolicity and inserted it into the canons of the Council of Limoges (held on 18 and 19 November 1031).³⁵ At one point in the proceedings 'quidam eruditus ex ipsis Engolismensibus clericis' gives an account of how

> ante hos plures annos quidam ex fratribus de monte Sinai in hanc partem advenerunt occiduam Dei disponente nutu, moribus graves, doctrina catholicae fidei profluentes, vita per omnia honesti, utriusque linguae periti; qui, cum diu nobiscum Engolismae fuissent exspectantes principem civitatis, et litteris Graecis et Latinis eos videremus ad unguem imbutos, super hac re interrogare curavimus eos.³⁶ ... itaque illos conveni Graecos, sciscitans utrum Orientales Martialem nossent. Qui, alter Symeon, alter nomine Cosmas, consono ore responderunt, dicentes: 'nescimus praeter duodecim apostolos.³⁷

Robert Wolff pointed out that it would 'be absurd to imagine that two Greek monks of Sinai ... ever told the clerk of Angoulême what Ademar claimed to have heard from them about Martial'.³⁸ But the point is that Ademar probably did meet these two monks, that they were Symeon and Cosmas, and that they also provided him with information which he incorporated into his *Chronicon*.³⁹

---

35 These canons survive in one autograph manuscript: Paris, BnF, MS lat. 2469, *c.* 1030. They are available in print, see *PL* 142, cols 1354–1400.

36 Ibid., col. 1363C.

37 Ibid., col. 1364A.

38 Robert L. Wolff, 'How the news was brought from Byzantium to Angoulême; Or, the pursuit of a hare in an ox cart', in *Byzantine Style, Religion and Civilization: Essays in Honour of Sir Steven Runciman*, ed. Elizabeth M. Jeffreys (Cambridge, 1979), pp. 139–89 (p. 183).

39 One of the interpolated passages in the *Chronicon* occurs at book 3.47. Here Ademar recounts events that took place in September 1009: 'Ad monasterium quoque montis Sinai, ubi quingenti et eo amplius monachi sub imperio abbatis [*sic*] manebant, habentes ibidem proprium episcopum, venerunt Sarracenorum decem milia armatorum, ut monachos perimentes habitacula eorum cum ecclesiis diruerent. Propinquantes autem a quatuor fere milibus, conspiciunt totum montem ardentem

While Radulfus Glaber attests to links between the Normans and Sinai, and Ademar confirms Symeon's presence in France during the 1020s, neither they nor Eberwin know anything of the saint's participation in the arrival of Katherine's relics in Rouen. The likely reason for this is that at the time when they were writing these did not yet exist in Normandy. However, once they arrived, it was necessary to ensure they were seen as authentic. Both the author of the account of the arrival of Katherine's relics at Rouen (*Sanctae Catharinae virginis et martyris translatio et miracula rotomagensia* [henceforth *T&M*], BHL 1679b-c)[40] and Hugh of Flavigny realized the potential of Symeon, a *bona fide* saint by 1039 who had died in Trier, as a legitimizer for the cult, and thus added to their versions of the story what they claimed had been left out of the previous accounts.

Hugh expressed surprise that the life of Symeon did not mention such an important event, while the *T&M*, which

> et fumantem, flammasque in celum ferri, et cuncta ibi posita cum hominibus manere illesa. Quod cum renunciassent regi Babilonio, penitencia ductus tam ipse quam populus Sarracenus valde doluerunt de his quae contra Christianos egissent, et data preceptione, iussit reaedificari basilicam Sepulchri gloriosi. Tamen redincepta basilica, non fuit amplius similis priori nec pulchritudine nec magnitudine quam Helena mater Constantini regali sumptu perfecerat'. *Ademari Cabannensis: Chronicon*, ed. Bourgain *et al*. Ademar's *Chronicon* exists in three recensions, preserved in a number of manuscripts; Paris, BnF, MS lat. 5943A was written by Ademar himself, see Bourgain *et al*., pp. xiii–xxxix. Ademar can only have obtained from an outside source the detail of the abbot of Sinai also being its bishop (the abbot of Sinai first appears as a bishop in the Acts of the Photian Council of 869–70, see Hofmann, 'Sinai und Rom', 225), as well as the description of the monastery going up in flames as the Saracens approached it. See Wolff, 'How the news', pp. 142–50, for a discussion of this and another three passages that contain information about Byzantine and Levantine events.

[40] For an edition see Poncelet, 'Sanctae Catharinae virginis et martyris translatio et miracula'.

Hugh claims to have read in a book at Rouen, did.[41] So he proceeded to fill the gap and relied on the *T&M* for his account of Symeon's involvement. This means that during Hugh's lifetime a copy of the *T&M* of Katherine's relics was kept at a library in Rouen, perhaps even La Trinité, which had by this time acquired a reputation for healing. The *translatio* part of the *T&M* describes how the monks of Sinai, posted at the saint's tomb on a weekly rota, used to collect the oil that oozed from it. The one to strike lucky was Symeon who, by divine favour, was granted a special gift, although Symeon here is merely the passive receiver: 'nam cum illo salutaris olei liquore tria admodum minuta de sarcofago distillantia meruit ossa excipere' (*T&M*, Chapter 2). He stored the relics away safely for some future use, which sets up their conferral by Symeon on Goscelin's foundation when he passes through Rouen.

Thus it seems that Katherine's relics arrived at Rouen at some point in the second quarter of the eleventh century. Eberwin might well have blocked out all reference to Katherine in order to keep the focus on Symeon, whose canonization was at stake. At the same time, however, one could argue that Symeon's bestowal of the relics could have further added to his reputation. More likely is the scenario in which the *T&M* did not see the light of day until after Eberwin's writing of Symeon's life and his friend's canonization (between 1035 and 1039). In the end, Robert Fawtier concluded that Symeon probably had nothing to do with the arrival of Katherine's relics at Rouen, but that he was a useful legitimizer for their

---

[41] 'Igitur ad beatum Symeonem reflectentes articulum, quid apud Richardum Normaniae principem egerit, sicut in armario Rothomagensi continetur, licet libellus vitae eius hoc sileat, paucis explicemus.' *Chronicon Hugonis Monachi*, ed. Pertz, book 2.26, pp. 398–99. The *Chronicon* has been transmitted in only one manuscript, an autograph: Berlin, SBPK, MS Phill. 1870, s. xi^2, prov. Verdun.

existence there.⁴² In addition, Walsh proposed the following: the penultimate miracle in the *T&M* relates that Katherine's relics were taken to Caen where a council was being held under William II in 1047.⁴³ If this evidence is taken at face value it would then seem that the relics were at Rouen under Abbot Isembert, furnishing a *terminus post quem* of 1033, the year Isembert became abbot of La Trinité, and a *terminus ante quem* of 1047 for their arrival and the composition of the *T&M*.⁴⁴ But before anyone could successfully place the relics of a saint at an ecclesiastical centre, there must first have existed a demand for these. In other words, knowledge of Katherine and her passion probably preceded the acquisition of her relics by La Trinité, Rouen. If Symeon was not the bearer of Katherine's relics, or only an incidental one, how did the Normans become acquainted with Katherine?⁴⁵

⁴² Robert Fawtier, 'Les reliques Rouennaises de Sainte Catherine d'Alexandrie', *AB*, 42 (1923), 368.

⁴³ *T&M* 25: 'Ergo … Cadomis ducunt communi consilio, quod circumiacentium territoriorum limite videtur consistere medio. Tum inter cetera beatorum Normanniae suis meritis patrocinantium corpora reliquiarum sanctae virginis Caterine defertur capsula'.

⁴⁴ Poncelet proposed 1050 or shortly after as the date of its composition. He based this on the fact that Isembert, who is referred to in Chapter 5, seems to have died by 1050. See Poncelet, 'Sanctae Catharinae virginis et martyris translatio et miracula', p. 423. Fawtier fixed the *terminus post quem* at 1054, arguing that Poncelet's information on Isembert's death in 1050 was faulty, proposing instead the year 1090, based on a reference to a certain Odo towards the end of the account. See Fawtier, 'Les reliques rouennaises', p. 356, p. 363 n. 4.

⁴⁵ While Symeon may not have brought with him to Europe relics of Katherine, his satchel certainly contained at least one manuscript: besides Symeon's hat and shoe, the 'Domschatz' at Trier preserves a Greek Old Testament lectionary (*prophetologium*) (MS 72 [143 F]), which is said to have been Symeon's and is often referred to as the 'Codex Simeonis'. Its possible Sinai-provenance remains unresolved, although the dating to the turn of the eleventh century is confirmed. For a discussion of the manuscript see Sysse G. Engberg, 'Trier and Sinai: Saint Symeon's book', *Scriptorium*, 59 (2005), 132–46. The

Whatever the direct connections between Normandy and Sinai might have been,[46] it is in Italy that the first Latin accounts of Katherine appear. It is thus much more likely that knowledge of Katherine reached Rouen via Italians who travelled to Burgundy and Normandy, pilgrims returning from the Holy Land and/or via Italy, and the burgeoning Norman presence in southern Italy. A specific example of Norman pilgrims stopping in southern Italy on their way back to Normandy is given by Amatus of Monte Cassino. In his *History of the Normans*, probably finished in *c.* 1080 under

---

Stadtarchiv in Trier preserves a twelfth-century seal from the St. Simeon's Collegiate Church on which Symeon is depicted wearing his (woolly?) hat, holding a palm branch and a book in each arm. See an image of this seal in Alfred Haverkamp, 'Simeon von Trier in universalen Zusammenhängen', *Neues Trierisches Jahrbuch*, 44 (2004), 21–32 at 22. A(nother) Greek lectionary written out in western Europe is Paris, BnF, MS gr. 375, written out by the Greek monk and priest Elias in 1021 at Cologne. See Axel Bayer, 'Griechen im Westen im 10. und 11. Jahrhundert', in *Kaiserin Theophanu: Die Begegnung des Ostens und Westens um die Wende des ersten Jahrtausends*, ed. Anton von Euw and Peter Schreiner (Cologne, 1991), p. 341. According to his life (BHL 3431), Gerard of Toul had gathered a monastic community of Greeks and Irish in tenth-century Toul: 'coetum quoque Grecorum ac Scottorum agglomerans non modicu, propriis alebat stipendiis commixtum diversae linguae populum.' *Vita S. Gerardi auctore Widrico*, ed. Georg Waitz, MGH SS 4 (Hannover, 1841), pp. 490–505 (p. 501).

[46] Mahfouz Labib, *Pèlerins et voyageurs au Mont Sinai* (Cairo, 1961), pp. 23–24, told the story of Fromund and his brothers, who were punished for the murder of their uncle by being forced to travel to Rome, Jerusalem, and other holy sites in the ninth century. They stayed for three years at the monastery on Sinai before returning to Francia. He refers the reader to *AASS* Oct. X, Dies 24, pp. 847–848, where the Bollandists argue that this Fromund is not to be confused with Fromund of Cotentin. Duke Robert I departed on a pilgrimage to Jerusalem in 1034 where he died a year later, see *The Gesta Normannorum Ducum of William of Jumièges, Orderic Vitalis, and Robert of Torigni*, ed. Elisabeth M.C. van Houts (Oxford, 1992–1995), vol. 2, pp. 81 and 85. For connections between Normandy and Constantinople see ead., 'Normandy and Byzantium in the eleventh century', *Byzantion: Revue Internationale des Études Byzantines*, 55.2 (1985), pp. 544–59.

Abbot Desiderius, he records the arrival at Salerno of Norman pilgrims on their way back from Palestine in the year 1000.[47] It is likely that Amatus' account refers to the same group of Normans mentioned by William of Apulia as having paid a visit to Monte Sant' Angelo in 1016.[48] Other tenth-century Norman visitors to Italy include Odo of Cluny, who was accompanied by John of Salerno to France at least once, as well as Adalbero of Verdun, who had travelled to Salerno in 984.[49] Last but not least, one eminent example of those moving in the other direction is William of Volpiano, who is credited with reviving monasticism in Normandy.[50]

Besides people, books also undertook journeys. For example, in a study of manuscripts containing Beneventan and Carolingian minuscule, Caterina Tristano compared a number of Beneventan manuscripts with manuscripts from Rouen. She concluded that the Carolingian style of writing entered Italy also from the south, owing to Norman church and monastic

---

[47] 'Avan mille [*xvi. ans*] puis que Christ … prist char en la Virgine Marie, apparurent en lo monde xl vaillant pelerin. Venoient del saint Sepulcre de Jerusalem … . Et vindrent à Salerne, laquelle estoit assegé de Sarassin … .' *Storia de' Normanni di Amato di Montecassino: Volgarizzata in antico francese*, ed. Vincenzo de Bartholomaeis (Rome, 1935), ch. 17, p. 21. See also *The History of the Normans by Amatus of Montecassino*, trans. Prescott N. Dunbar, rev. with introduction and notes by Graham A. Loud (Woodbridge, 2004).

[48] Guillermi Apuliensis *Gesta Roberti Wiscardi a. 1009–1085*, ed. Roger Wilmans, MGH SS 9 (Hannover, 1851), pp. 239–98, esp. lines 1–27.

[49] John of Salerno, *Vita Sancti Odonis abbatis Cluniacensis secundi*, book II.6, *PL*, vol. 133, col. 64A. Baudouin de Gaiffier, 'Hagiographie Salernitaine: La translation de S. Mattieu', *AB*, 80 (1962), p. 102. See also *LexMA*, s.v. Adalbero II.

[50] See Pierre Bouet, 'Les Italiens en Normandie au XIe siècle', in *Les Italiens and Normandie: De l'étranger à l'immigré*, Actes du Colloque de Cerisy-la-Salle (8–11 Octobre 1998), ed. Mariella Colin and François Neveux (Caen, 2000), pp. 27–44. Véronique Gazeau, 'Guillaume de Volpiano en Normandie: État des questions', *Tabularia "Études"*, 2 (2002), 35–46.

foundations in Calabria: one manuscript in particular, Monte Cassino, MS 202, s. ix, contains Carolingian writing and decoration with distinct Norman characteristics.[51] Of course, books also travelled from Italy to Normandy.[52]

3. The passion of Katherine by Peter, Subdeacon of Naples and BHL 1663

While it is clear that there were several channels by which Katherine's story could have reached Normandy, it is a little more difficult to establish which account made which journey. An intriguing case is a version composed in tenth-century Italy: this is the text identified as BHL 1659-1661b, written by Peter, Subdeacon of Naples, who was active in that city from c. 930 until c. the early 960s.[53] Peter is a representative of the so-called Neapolitan school of hagiographers, which consisted of authors who translated texts from Greek into Latin and reworked Latin translations from the end of the ninth until the first half of the tenth century. This group included authors such as Paul the Deacon, Athanasius II, Guarimpotus, and others.[54] Edoardo D'Angelo, the editor of Peter's hagiographic works, regards the attribution of Katherine's passion to Peter

---

[51] Caterina T. Tristano, 'Scrittura benventana e scrittura carolina in manoscritti dell'Italia meridionale', *Scrittura e Civiltà*, 3 (1979), 8–150, (pp. 108–09 and p. 147).

[52] 'Quelques manuscrits italiens pénetrèrent en Normandie, apportés par les moines lombards ou par les pelerins'. Nortier, *Les bibliothèques médiévales*, p. 2.

[53] *Pietro Suddiacono napoletano: L'opera agiografica*, ed. D'Angelo.

[54] Chiesa, 'Le traduzioni dal greco', 67–86. Naples was, at the time, a bilingual city in which not just elite men but also an important fraction of the population knew Greek, although full mastery of Greek must not be assumed. Direct political links between Byzantium and Campania, as well as Greek-speaking minorities all over southern Italy ensured the continued existence and knowledge of Greek. See Chapter 3, above.

as 'molto probabile'.⁵⁵ What is more, and in stark contrast with Peter's other hagiographical works, Katherine's passion is the only one that had a significant diffusion outside of Italy, particularly in France/Normandy.

As Albert Siegmund observed in 1949, Peter was not so much a translator as he was a rewriter or adaptor.⁵⁶ In the epilogue to the passion of Katherine, Peter writes:

> Haec namque passio Greco famine scripta a prephato Athanasio variis translatoribus postmodum constat esse vitiata, adeo ut legi in cetu fidelium minime possit. Quam passionem ego Petrus, fidelium fratrum devotione compulsus atque amore ipsius sanctissimae martyris de inepto famine elevans, magis sensum quam verba sequens, incomposita resecans et necessaria addens, plenissime Latinis auribus tradere curavi, ad laudem et gloriam domini nostri Iesu Christi, qui cum patre et spiritu sancto vivit et regnat deus per omnia secula seculorum. Amen.⁵⁷

Peter clearly sees himself as improving on the work of Greek-to-Latin translators who corrupted the original account of Katherine's passion to such an extent that it could not be read during gatherings of the faithful. He explains that he improved the original translation by sticking to the *sensum* rather than the words, and by removing disordered material and adding what is necessary, in order to offer a text that is full of Latinity.⁵⁸

---

⁵⁵ Edoardo D'Angelo, 'Petrus Neapolitanus Subd.', in *La trasmissione dei testi latini del Medioevo*, ed. Lucia Castaldi and Paolo Chiesa (Florence, 2004), p. 349.

⁵⁶ With the exception of the life of Gregory of Nyssa, see p. cxix in D'Angelo, *Pietro Suddiacono*. Siegmund, *Die Überlieferung*, p. 276: 'es ist allerdings fraglich, ob er [Peter] unter die Übersetzer noch gerechnet werden kann; denn seine Arbeiten sind schon mehr Paraphrasen'. See pp. 255–77 for an overview of the Neapolitan "school".

⁵⁷ D'Angelo, *Pietro Suddiacono*, III.2, p. 146.

⁵⁸ The text of Peter's version of the passion follows the narrative elements already present in the Greek versions. It differentiates itself from BHL

Already in 1900, Fedele Savio saw in the epilogue to to BHL 1659 possible proof for attributing this version to Peter, both in the mention of him by name and in the triple occurrence of *famine* (twice in the epilogue and once in the main account).[59] It can also be found twice in the passion of George (BHL 3393, 3393b, 3394), a secure basis for attribution to Peter. In the passion of Margaret of Antioch (BHL 5308), a hypothetical attribution to Peter, it appears once in the prologue. D'Angelo has termed Peter's use of the noun *famen* a lexical quirk and also points out that his preferred sources keep turning up both in securely attributed and non-attributed texts.[60]

This neat conclusion is somewhat disturbed by the existence of a version of the epilogue in which the author's name is given as *Arechis*: in four manuscripts, the text reads *Arechis* rather than *Petrus*.[61] Dolbeau suggested that Arechis

---

1663 by lacking some of the longer exchanges between Katherine and the emperor and between Katherine and the rhetors. In general, all speeches are longer in BHL 1663. Peter's style is elevated, characterized by unusual or highly literary vocabulary (e.g. *amatrix*, II.121, p. 136; *nitor* a favourite verb II.145, p. 139; *aequiter*, II.148, p. 139; *conamen* II.187, p. 144; *argumentosus* II.156,p. 140, just sampling from a couple of pages) and by the insertion of verses/half-verses (pp. cxxv–cxxx in D'Angelo, *Pietro Suddiacono*), although there are not too many of them in this text. Peter's version lacks a prologue but does have a 16-line hexameter poem/epilogue in one of the manuscripts.

[59] Fedele Savio, 'Pietro Suddiacono Napoletano agiografo del secolo x', *Atti della R. Accademia delle scienze di Torino*, 36 (1900/01), p. 676.

[60] Other words Peter likes include *nectar, pestifer, stomacho, tandem aliquando*, see D'Angelo, *Pietro Suddiacono*, p. lii. Peter's preferred sources overlap with other texts securely attributed to him, e.g. Vergil, Ps–Cato, Paulinus of Nola, Gregor the Great, see D'Angelo, *Pietro Suddiacono*, p. lii. Peter also shows a predilection for inserting hexameter verses into his prose, something he does also in the passion of Katherine. See Edoardo D'Angelo, 'Prose et vers dans l'oeuvre de Pierre Sous-Diacre', *Archivum Latinitatis Medii Aevi*, 53 (1995), 187–99.

[61] Naples, BN, MS XIII.G.24, s. xii–xiii; Rouen, BM, MS 1382 (U.109), s. xi–xii; Rouen, BM, MS 1410 (U.22), s. xiii; Brussels, KBR, MS

might have been Peter's lay-name.⁶² This is possible: the name Arechis originates from Lombardy, as historical sources show.⁶³ D'Angelo, however, has suggested that his lay-name may have been Guiselgardus.⁶⁴ Yet, why would the author have issued two epilogues, almost identical, identifying himself as Peter in one and Arechis in the other? And why do three manuscripts of Norman provenance contain an epilogue with the distinct Lombard name Arechis?⁶⁵ The answer could be, perhaps, that the Arechis-epilogue was appended to the text when it was first translated, extending the epilogue already present in the Greek in which the ταχυγράφος Anastasios (Athanasios in BHG 30) claims to have written the account of his mistresses' martyrdom. Peter could then have substituted his own name when he reworked his text.⁶⁶ But there are also northern-French manuscripts for BHL 1659 that retain the Peter-

---

9810–14, s. xii or s. xiii. See pp. li and 119 in D'Angelo, *Pietro Suddiacono*. On the Brussels manuscript see Tino Licht, *Untersuchungen zum biographischen Werk Sigeberts von Gembloux* (Heidelberg, 2005), pp. 49 and 69. This manuscript contains a collection of passions/vitae of female saints put together over a long period of time at Saint-Laurent in Liège by copying and then binding together.

⁶² 'D'après la topique, il s'agit d'une œuvre de Pierre sous-diacre (dont Arechis serait le nom laïc?)', Dolbeau, 'Le rôle des interprètes', in *Traduction et traducteurs*, ed. Contamine, p. 152.

⁶³ Well-known bearers of the name were Arechis I (591–641), Duke of Benevento, and Arechis II, (758–774) Duke and (774–87) Prince of Benevento. A judge named Arechis was present at the election of the abbot Aligernus (948–85) of Monte Cassino (*Chron. Cas.* 1.60.3). Arechis, the son of Iannipertus, had possessions at Teano in Campania *c.* 968 (*Chron. Cas.* 2.6.12). The latest attestation for the name seems to be the son of Iannipertus.

⁶⁴ D'Angelo, *Pietro Suddiacono*, p. lxxi.

⁶⁵ Rouen, BM, MS 1382 (U.109); Rouen, BM, MS 1410 (U.22); and Naples, BN, MS XIII.G.24 are Norman.

⁶⁶ Bronzini, 303: 'hanc passionem graeco primum eloquio scriptam a praefato Athanasio ... ego Arechis ... de inepto famine elevans'. In the 'Peter-epilogue' *graeco* is replaced by another *famine*.

epilogue,[67] so that the Arechis-Peter attribution is not as interesting as it may seem. Still, the stylistic analysis conducted by D'Angelo seems to support the attribution of this version of Katherine's passion to Peter, furnishing the text with a *terminus post quem* of c. 930 and a *terminus ante quem* of c. 960.

Two of the earliest witnesses for Peter's account of Katherine were copied in northern France.[68] Thus Peter's version had travelled there from Italy by the eleventh century and within one-hundred years of composition. The manuscripts are, in order of relative age:

Orléans, Bibliothèque publique, MS 334
s. xi, prov. Fleury, fols 288-297 (not known to or used by D'Angelo).

Rouen, Bibliothèque municipale, MS 1382 (U.109)
s. xi-xii, prov. Jumièges, fols 112-118v (collated by D'Angelo).

Saint-Omer, Bibliothèque publique, MS 27
1150-60, prov. Saint-Bertin, fols 1-8 (known to but not collated by D'Angelo).

Rouen, BM, MS 1410 (U.22)
s. xiii, prov. Rouen, fols 103-109v (collated by D'Angelo).

The geographical origins of the above manuscripts overlap with those of the earliest manuscripts of BHL 1663 as well as the footprint of *celeranter* and *tarinca* (see Map 2). For

---

[67] Paris, BnF, MS lat. 11753, s. xii; Paris, BnF, MS lat. 3809A, s. xv; Paris, BnF, MS lat. 5373, s. xiv; Saint-Omer, BP, MS 27, s. xii.

[68] The only other eleventh-century manuscript is BAV, MS San Pietro in Vaticano A5, s. xi. Bronzini (303, n. 149) mentions Rome, Vallicelliana, MS 10, fols 200v–206. I am not taking into account the manuscripts now preserved outside Italy for which D'Angelo, *Pietro Suddiacono*, pp. xciii–xciv, has not furnished a provenance. They are: Brussels, KBR, MS 9810, s. xii or xiii; Cape Town, South African Library, MS 48b5; Montpellier, Bibliothèque de la Faculté de Médecine, MS 1 vol. 1, s. xii; Paris, BnF, MS lat. 3809A, s. xv; Paris, BnF, MS lat. 5373, s. xiv; Paris, BnF, MS lat. 11753, s. xii; Trier, Stadtbibliothek, MS 1155, s. xii.

instance, Jumièges was a Benedictine abbey founded in 631 by Philibert, destroyed by the Normans in 841 and 851, but restored *c*. 941 by William Longsword.[69] In the first decades of the eleventh century, Thierry de Montgommeri (1014-1028) was its abbot. A student of the monastic reformer William of Volpiano, he attracted a large number of students to Jumièges. Another of its abbots, Robert Champart (d. 1052 or 1055), eventually became bishop of London at the behest of Edward the Confessor.[70] Before taking up his post at Jumièges in 1037, Robert had been a monk and prior at Saint-Ouen in Rouen: he was a confidant of the Goscelin who founded La Trinité at Rouen and one of the signatories to its foundation charter. Fleury, with its links to Italy through Odo's hagiographer John of Salerno, and as a significant centre of learning under Abbo (d. 1004), who had himself travelled to Rome, could also easily have obtained a copy of Peter's account of Katherine's passion.

Three of these four manuscripts also transmit the text of Katherine's *Translatio et miracula (T&M)*; in each case, the text of the passion precedes it.[71] A logical link between the passion and the miracle collection seems to be Katherine's oil-oozing relics kept at Rouen. At first sight, the end of Peter's account does not contain any details of these, and the majority of the manuscripts end: 'Hoc cum audisset, beata Caterina laeta effecta de caelesti promissione surrexit ab oratione. Satel-

[69] Cottineau I, cols 1496–97.

[70] He gave to his old abbey a missal written at Winchester (Rouen, BM, MS 274 [Y.6]). Rouen, BM, MS 231 (A.44), an Anglo-Saxon psalter, was perhaps also a gift from Robert. See Nortier, *Les bibliothèques médiévales*, p. 146. Robert was the archbishop of Canterbury in 1051–52.

[71] Orléans, BP, MS 334, fols 298–303 (not known to its editor Poncelet); Saint-Omer, BP, MS 27, fols 8r–10v; Rouen, BM, MS 1410 (U.22), fols 109v–115v. The *T&M* survives in only these three manuscripts, not two as Walsh writes in *The Cult of St Katherine*, p. 79 and n. 96. She is unaware of the manuscript now at Orléans, as is D'Angelo.

lites autem accipientes illam secundum caesaris iussionem decollaverunt eam vicesima quinta die mensis Novembris'.[72]

However, two manuscripts used by D'Angelo continue in the following fashion:

> Statimque de corpore eius lac pro sanguine uberam [sic] defluxit in testimonio virginis [*R* virginei] pudoris ad laudem dei omnipotentis angeli quoque gloriosae martyris corpus accipientes exanimum in montem Synai detulerunt qui mons a loco occisionis ut fertur distat itinere viginti et eo amplius dierum [qui ... dierum) *om. R*] ubi per eam innumera divina virtus operari non desinit miracula siquidem de sepulcro eius fons olei indeficienter manare videtur quo peruncta debilium corpora optatae sospitatis reportant gaudia.[73]

They are Naples, BN, MS XIII.G.24, s. xii-xiii (= *N*), and Rouen, BM, MS 1382 (U.109) (= *R*). This is an indication for the separate tradition of *NR*, as well as *S* (Rouen, BM, MS 1410 [U.22], which also contains the miracle account), as hypothesized by D'Angelo and as apparent from the apparatus, especially in the case of *NR*.[74] Orléans, BP, MS 334, even though the text it preserves has huge gaps, shares the majority of its mistakes with *N* and *R*, thus making it a further witness to the Norman branch of Peter's version.

The Naples manuscript consists of eight folios and represents a single fascicle 'from what was once a larger booklet'.[75] The first six folios (1r-6v) contain Peter's version of Katherine's passion (BHL 1659), clearly divided into twelve

---

[72] D'Angelo, *Pietro Suddiacono*, II.195–96, p. 145.

[73] Ibid., apparatus to II.196, p. 145.

[74] Ibid., p. 119. Also, D'Angelo, 'Petrus Neapolitanus Subd.', p. 357, suggests an 'archetipo dinamico, date le caratteristiche "scivolose" delle varianti proposte dal gruppo *NRS*'.

[75] David Hiley, 'The *Historia sancte Caterine* in MS Napoli, Biblioteca Nazionale, XIII.G.24: The earliest proper office for St Catherine of Alexandria?', in *Musica e liturgica a Montecassino nel medioevo*, ed. Nicola Tangari (Rome, 2012), pp. 21–44 (p. 23).

readings, starting with the second reading.⁷⁶ This is followed on folio 6v by a sixteen-line hexameter poem in honour of Katherine and attributed in the manuscript to Athanasius.⁷⁷ This poem is succeeded by a song cycle: 'incipit historia eiusdem Sancte Caterine'.⁷⁸ This song cycle follows the Benedictine form of the Office and consists of Vespers and Matins. It breaks off in the middle of the second responsory in the second nocturne of Matins, leading David Hiley to estimate that another two folios/four pages would have contained what is missing. The texts are a mix of hexameters and prose. These chanted texts would have constituted their own narrative cycles while the lessons from the passio would have represented another.⁷⁹ Hiley suggested that this manuscript was copied in Normandy rather than in southern Italy on the basis of musical notations that are more commonly found in manuscripts from Normandy:

> Some of the signs in Naples XIII.G.24 have a relatively archaic shape, for example, the *clivis* just mentioned, which rises to a point (the older way of writing) rather than flattening out on top

---

⁷⁶ David Hiley, 'Liturgische Gesangszyklen zur Heiligenverehrung im Mittelalter: Das Beispiel der hl. Katharina', in *Roma quanta fuit: Beiträge zur Architektur-, Kunst- und Kulturgeschichte von der Antike bis zur Gegenwart: Festschrift für Hans-Christoph Dittsche*, ed. Albert Dietl (Augsburg, 2010), pp. 315–38 (p. 320): 'this text is rather long so it seems difficult to imagine that all twelve readings were recited during the Matins Office. There are notations in the margin that indicate much shorter readings, so that the first reading is in fact divided into three and the second into five sections (e.g. the first office contains 500+ words, the second 700+). ... This may indicate that the last four readings for the third nocturn were taken from a Homily, as was usual at the time in the monastic liturgy'.

⁷⁷ 'Explicit Passio Sancte Caterine virginis et martiris. Versus Sancti Atanasii in eius laudibus'. See reproduction of folio 6v in ibid., p. 337.

⁷⁸ See ibid. pp. 332–35 for an edition of this song cycle.

⁷⁹ Hiley, 'The *Historia sancte Caterine*', p. 26.

(the newer way). For this reason the manuscript should not be dated too late in the twelfth century.[80]

Blasina refers to the manuscripts preserving this office as 'the Norman-Neapolitan family, [which] present a monastic office with Norman origins that was known, at least in the fourteenth century, at Ste-Catherine's sister house in the heart of Rouen'.[81]

Orléans, BP, MS 334 contains a collection of saints' lives and was written out at the end of the eleventh century in Fleury.[82] This parchment manuscript of 308 pages seems to be the one referred to as *vitae sanctorum cum passionibus apostolorum* in another Fleury manuscript (Orléans, BP, MS 322), into which instructions for liturgical reading were added in the second half of the eleventh century.[83] On pages 288 to 297, it preserves a shortened version of Peter's version of Katherine's passion ('incipit passio sancte Cateline').[84] Towards the beginning, the text is broken up into five readings, although this stops on page 291. The text of the passion is followed by the *T&M* on pages 298 to 303, although less than the entire miracle collection published by Poncelet is preserved. It seems

---

[80] Ibid., p. 24.

[81] Blasina, 'Ainard of Dives'.

[82] See Élisabeth Pellegrin *et al.*, *Catalogue des manuscrits médiévaux de la bibliothèque municipale d'Orléans* (Paris, 2010), pp. 478–81.

[83] Ibid., p. 481. The contents are: (1) pp. 1–129: a number of saints' lives, e.g. Sulpitius of Bourges BHL 7930, 7931, Ursinus of Bourges BHL 8412, 8411. (2) pp. 130–225: this part has Apostles' lives, e.g. Matthew BHL 5690, Philipp BHL 6814, Simon and Judas. (3) pp. 226–87³: this part contains Constantius of Lyon's life of Germanus of Auxerre BHL 3454 with prologue BHL 3454. (4) pp. 288–303: this part contains the passion and miracles of Katherine. The cataloguers mention that folios are missing both from the passion and the miracle collection.

[84] The text ends mid-sentence towards the end of the passion, at II.192 'servile corpus assumere cru——', D'Angelo, *Pietro Suddiacono*, p. 144.

as though some of the text has been lost due to missing folios, while the absence of other miracles is harder to explain.[85]

It turns out that the alternative ending to Peter's version discussed above is shared, more or less, by BHL 1663 and by BHL 1662b.[86] In Peter's account proper, the story of Katherine's passion ends with her beheading. In BHL 1663, *NR*, and BHL 1662b, the beheading is followed by two miracles (milk and Sinai), which already form part of the Greek tradition.[87] What is new is the oil that oozes from Katherine's tomb, which is also in evidence in the *T&M*. Here is a side-by-side view of all four texts:

BHL 1659[88]	BHL 1663[89]	BHL 1662b[90]	*T&M*
	Quo ex facto duae res dignae memoria	Quo facto due res digne memoria	

[85] The text is truncated and starts on page 298 in the middle of the first miracle about Isembert, abbot of the monastery of La Trinité-du-Mont, who is suffering from a tooth-ache, see p. 431 of T&M '——inter alia minimum tamen'. The text ends, again in mid-sentence, on p. 303 '... idque adhuc ignora——' (see *T&M*, p. 437, miracle 17). The following miracles are preserved; section numbers taken from Poncelet's edition: miracle 7 – starts mid-sentence; miracle 8 – complete; miracle 9 – complete and ends at bottom of p. 301 in the manuscript; miracles 10, 11, 12, 13 absent; 13 – starts halfway through on p. 302 of the manuscript; 14 – complete; 15 – absent; 16 – complete, immediately after 14; 17 – ends mid-sentence at the bottom of p. 303.

[86] The ending of BHL 1663 does not fluctuate: all the manuscripts I have seen (at least those that contain BHL 1663 and its epitome 1663a) preserve it. BHL 1662b survives in a single manuscript, Rome, Alessandrina, MS 96.

[87] 'Προσελθὼν δὲ ὁ σπεκουλάτωρ ἀπέτεμεν αὐτῆς τὸν αὐχένα, καὶ εὐθέως ἀντὶ τοῦ αἵματος γάλα ἀπερρύη ἐπὶ τῆς γῆς. Καὶ εὐθέως κατελθόντες ἄγγελοι τέσσαρες ἀνεῖλαν τὸ σῶμα αὐτῆς καὶ ἀπέθεντο ἐν τῷ ὄρει Σινᾶ'. BHG 30a, Viteau, pp. 38–39, § 25.

[88] Apparatus to II.196, p. 145 in D'Angelo, *Pietro Suddiacono*.

[89] Dobson, ll. 1134–46.

[90] Bronzini, 314.

Statimque de corpore eius lac pro sanguine uberam [sic] defluxit in testimonio virginis [*R* virginei] pudoris ad laudem dei omnipotentis angeli quoque gloriosae martyris corpus accipientes exanimum in montem Synai detulerunt qui mons a loco occisionis ut fertur distat itinere viginti et eo amplius dierum [qui ... dierum) *om. R*] ubi per eam innumera divina virtus operari non desinit miracula.	apparuerunt: una, quia lac pro sanguine, in testimonium virginalis innocentiae de corpore eius effusum, terram uberius irroravit; altera, quia mox angeli accesserunt et assumptum corpus, per altum aera subvehentes, in monte Synai deposuerunt – qui mons a loco occisionis distat itinere viginti et eo amplius dierum; quo in loco innumera, ad laudem Domini, fiunt miracula. Inter quae et hoc unum insigne constat miraculum,	apparuerunt: una quod lac pro sanguine in testimonium virginitatis de corpore eius effusum in terra uberrime irrigavit; altera quod mox angeli accesserunt et assumpserunt corpus per altum aeres sublevantes in monte Synai posuerunt. Quo facto, innumerabilia ad laudem Dei fiunt miracula, inter quae unum insigne stat miraculum	
siquidem *DE SEPULCRO* eius *FONS* olei indeficienter manare videtur	quod *DE SEPULCRO* ipsius *RIVUS* olei indeficienter manare videtur; nam et *de minutis*	quod *DE SEPULCRO* de ipsius *RIVUS* olei indeficienter manare videtur,	Nam *AD* eius *TUMBA<M> RIVUS* olei indeficienter manare videtur, ex quo diversa corporum invalitudines divine virtute

	ossibus quae *de sarcophago cum oleo efflu*unt, ubicumque asportantur, *salutaris olei liquor stillare non desinit,*		curantur. *De* ipsis quoque *minutis ossibus cum oleo de sarcophago efflu*entibus, de quibus etiam et *salutaris olei liquor stillare non desinit.* ... . (l. 16-20, p. 426).
quo peruncta debilium corpora optatae sospitatis reportant gaudia.	ex quo peruncta, debilium corpora celeris medicinae opem reportant.	quo peruncta debilium corpora de liquore salutari, qui distillare non desinit de eius sepulchro, ubicumque asportentur celestis medicinae opem reportant.	In quo illud constat mirabile, quod non solum Christiani, sed etiam pagani beatae martyris suffragia expetentes, salutari eius oleo peruncti opem sibi medicinae reportant. (ll. 24-27, p. 427). ... Nam cum illo salutaris olei liquore tria admodum minuta de sarcofago distillantia meruit ossa excipere. (l. 26f, p. 427).

There are two readings here that can help to clarify the relationships between some of these texts.[91] BHL 1663 agrees with BHL 1659 over *de sepulchro* against *ad tumbam* found in the *T&M*. At the same time, BHL 1663 agrees with the *T&M* over *rivus* against *fons* of BHL 1659.[92] Clearly, BHL 1663 is related to both of them and neither of the other two are related to each other. A look back at the above table confirms this conclusion, for example: both BHL 1663 and *T&M* report that the tiny shards of bone that flow out from Katherine's tomb continue to ooze oil on their own. On the other hand, BHL 1659 and BHL 1663 share knowledge of how far Mount Sinai is from the place of Katherine's execution (20+ days: 'ut fertur distat itinere viginti et eo amplius dierum'). BHL 1659, as mentioned before, does not contain these details in the main tradition; they are present only in the northern French branch, i.e. the one manuscript copied at Jumièges in the eleventh/twelfth century and another copied at Rouen in the thirteenth, as well as a twelfth/thirteenth-century manuscript now in Naples, perhaps originating from northern France, according to Hiley. It seems appropriate to suggest that they were introduced to the tradition in northern France. This should not come as a surprise since the *T&M* in particular attests to the presence of Katherine's relics at Rouen by the middle of the eleventh century.

One likely scenario for the above situation is that Peter's account reached northern France, and that here it came to be used as a model for BHL 1663. At some point in the copying process the original ending of BHL 1659 was contaminated with that of BHL 1663. Once knowledge of Katherine existed in Normandy, her relics were discovered/found/acquired and it became necessary to authenticate them by writing an

---

[91] There is a very clear relationship between BHL 1663 and 1662b that I do not have space to discuss here. See p. 122ff above for some tentative remarks which I hope to expand on in a separate essay.

[92] The manuscripts for all three texts provide no alternative readings.

account of how they got there. The author of the *T&M* betrays knowledge of a booklet containing the text of her passion: 'sancta igitur Caterina, quemadmodum libelli passionis eius textus explanat, a Maxentio impio ac sacrilego caesare Alexandriae martyrio coronata est'.[93] This information, as well as the short summary of Katherine's martyrdom does not, at first sight, make it possible to determine which actual version was used, although perhaps a tiny hint can be detected.[94] In BHL 1663, Maxentius is almost always referred to as *imperator* (twice as *rex*), but never as *caesar*. At the beginning of this version of Katherine's passion, he is introduced as such: 'Maxentius, ..., anno igitur regni sui tricesimo quinto, ..., feralia per uicinas prouincias misit edicta ... : "Maxentius *imperator*, his qui edictis nostris acquiescent, salutem"'.[95] In BHL 1659, Maxentius is referred to most often as *caesar* (twenty-two times), followed by *rex* (ten times), and *imperator* and *augustus* twice each. This is how the story begins in this version: 'Regnante igitur Maxentio *cesare*, ...'. Peter's account also includes the summons to a public pagan sacrifice in which the emperor refers to himself as 'Maxentius *cesar*'. It is not much, but perhaps suggestive enough to allow the hypothesis that the author of the *T&M* knew of Katherine's story from Peter's account.[96]

Once the relics had begun to have miraculous effects on those seeking Katherine's help and her reputation grew, it was necessary to update Peter's version according to the tastes of the day and the socio-historical context of eleventh-century Normandy. The resulting version BHL 1663 thus steers a

---

[93] *T&M*, ch. 2, p. 426.

[94] The absence of an author's name is not surprising since not all manuscripts carry the epilogue in which Athanasius or Peter are named.

[95] Dobson, ll. 40–49.

[96] In BHL 1662b, Maxentius is predominantly an *imperator*, four times *caesar*, and once each *rex* and *tyrannus*. The text here begins: 'Regnante impio et iniquo *imperatore* Maxentio'.

middle ground in terms of diction and includes passages from a number of texts written primarily for a monastic audience, apt in the context of the renewal that was flourishing in the ecclesiastical province of Rouen in the first half of the eleventh century.[97]

Whether BHL 1663 precedes the *T&M* or not is not something that I can determine here conclusively. I do wonder about the absence of any specific mention of the relics' presence in Normandy in this particular version. The answer must be that at the time of its composition Katherine's relics had not yet surfaced at Rouen or that perhaps the author of BHL 1663 was not aware of their existence there, which seems less likely. From this, and on the basis of 1054 to 1090 as the time-frame for the composition of the *T&M*, results a first *terminus ante quem 'ex silentio'* for the composition of BHL 1663. The overlaps between the three versions of Katherine's passion seen above and the *T&M* could be no more than mere coincidence, and perhaps be an indication of the relative recency both of her cult and the written accounts. None of these texts had yet gained a strong foothold in Normandy so that the *T&M* could easily be joined to either BHL 1659 or BHL 1663. One thing is certain: the relics did not appear in a disconnect with the text(s), as a sort of *ex nihilo* defining feature of Katherine's cult in Normandy as suggested by Walsh, who posited that the relics preceded the texts; on the contrary, the texts were closely bound up in their arrival there.[98] A more likely scenario is the arrival of a new saint as part of a manuscript or booklet brought into the province, an interest in this saint taking hold as demonstrated by the existence of a newly composed passion, as well as the

---

[97] van 'T Spijker, 'Gallia du Nord et de l'Ouest', in *Hagiographies*, vol. 2, p. 241: '… surtout vers le milieu du XIe siècle, on peut parler de renaissance et restauration des communautés religieuses et des diocèses. Les écrits hagiographiques jouèrent en la matière un rôle important'.

[98] Walsh, *The Cult of St Katherine*, p. 150.

acquisition of relics and the subsequent production of a miracle collection. This was followed by an actual cult in the second half of the eleventh century, as can be seen, for example, by the epitome divided into readings in Angers, BM, MS 121.[99]

The examination of the sources and diction of BHL 1663, combined with the evidence provided by the earliest manuscripts, has yielded crucial information for its geographical origin and date. The localization of the eleventh-century manuscripts, together with the evidence gained from such distinct words as *celeranter* and *tarinca*, defines a radius of about 170 km with Corbie at its centre. Fécamp and Lobbes are the outer demarcations in the west and the east respectively. Between them lie such ecclesiastical centres as Saint-Ouen of Rouen, Jumièges, Saint-Quentin, Valenciennes, and Saint-Wandrille. The use of Autpert's *Conflictus* and the date of the manuscript from Angers furnish the following broad framework of dates within which BHL 1663 was composed: 784 (Autpert's death) and 1052/1087 (date of Angers, BM, MS 121). In addition, the *terminus ante quem* is strengthened by the incorporation of a passage from BHL 1663 into the life of Amalberga, composed in the last quarter of the eleventh century. Finally, the absence of any Crusader rhetoric is perhaps an indication, *ex silentio*, for a date of composition before the end of the eleventh century.

When it comes to the availability of the sources used for the composition of BHL 1663 in the geographical area delineated

---

[99] For example, the various catalogues of French breviaries, missals, and other liturgical manuscripts published by Victor Leroquais in the 1920s and 1930s indicate that Katherine's name is either a later addition in manuscripts from the eighth to the tenth centuries, or only starts appearing in the main hand in manuscripts from the end of the eleventh century onwards. See *Les sacramentaires et les missels manuscrits des bibliothèques publiques de France* (Paris, 1924); *Les bréviaires manuscrits des bibliothèques publiques de France*, 6 vols (Paris, 1934); *Les psautiers: Manuscrits latins des bibliothèques publiques de France* (Paris, 1941).

above, it is the *CZA* and Autpert's *Conflictus* that are the most interesting. As I have shown, BHL 1663 follows the branch of the tradition identified by the editor of the *CZA* as *β*. The manuscripts in this branch come from Tours (s. x-xi), Vendôme, Limoges (s. xi), and a manuscript that was kept but not written at Fleury (s. x). The oldest manuscripts of Autpert's *Conflictus* come from Bavaria, although the text was certainly available in tenth-century Jumièges, right in the heart of Normandy, as well as at Liège and Marchiennes in the eleventh century. In at least one instance BHL 1663 seems to be showing an affinity with the French manuscripts according to the apparatus constructed by Weber on the basis of one French and two Bavarian manuscripts.

In this geographical context, the use of *celeranter* in BHL 1663 and in BHL 760, the miracle collection of Ouen, is particularly striking. Both texts are hagiographic accounts written in prose, as opposed to other contexts for *celeranter* which are literary and written in metre. Not only that, but the cult of Ouen is firmly connected to Rouen, where the cult of Katherine took root in the second half of the eleventh century. Isembert, the first abbot of La Trinité, where Katherine's relics were kept, had previously been a monk at Saint-Ouen. Incidentally, the relics of Ouen were taken to the same council held at Caen in 1047 as those of Katherine.[100]

The connection between La Trinité, founded in 1030, and Katherine is beyond doubt: Isembert's pupil Ainard composed

---

[100] See the miracle collection of Ouen (BHL 760), *AASS* Aug. IV, Dies 24, pp. 834F–835A: 'Instabant causae, quibus episcoporum et abbatum provincialis conventus agebatur. Locus huic praefinitus erat sub Cadomensi territorio propter locu opportunitatem et frugum ubertatem. Huc sanctorum corpora reliquiasque sacras convehi universorum consilio decretum fuerat, inter quos venerabilis pater noster Audoenus allatus fuerat'. See also Lucile Trân-Duc, 'Les princes normands et les reliques (x[e]–xie siècles): Contribution du culte des saints à la formation territoriale et identitaire d'une principauté', *Pecia*, 8–11 (2005), 525–62 (p. 536).

an office in honour of the saint. By the end of the eleventh century, her relics are being credited with healing the sick Fulco, and, of course, the account of the relics itself explicitly mentions the abbey at Rouen. This latter text was composed between 1033 and 1047, and survives in three northern French manuscripts, among them one written in the eleventh century (Orléans, BP, MS 334). Not only that, but in this manuscript the account of the relics is preceded by BHL 1659, Peter's version of Katherine's passion, which was likely introduced to Normandy between between 970 (Peter's death?) and the middle of the eleventh century, either by Normans returning from Italy or Italians coming to Normandy.

The contrast between the very local origin of BHL 1663 and its subsequent success is notable. The combination of ideological and literary as well as narrative elements evidently appealed well beyond the circumstances of its composition or even of the original cult in France. This text stands apart from the corpus as a whole by virtue of its popularity and yet it is obviously indebted to the tradition. The kind of episodic detail as well as the overlaps with a number of versions of Katherine's passion mean that its author was working from a model, although it remains to be shown beyond doubt which one he used. I do not have the space here to delve into the specifics, nor is it possible to fully answer questions about why and how the author chose to re-write the passion of Katherine. However, now that the geographical and chronological contexts for BHL 1663 have been established, an examination of the text in its own right with a focus on its literary characteristics as well as the circumstances of its composition alongside a consideration of the social-cultural context is finally possible.

CONCLUSION

The geographical separation between the Sinai peninsula and the rest of the Bzyantine empire did not stop people from embarking on journeys: merchants, ambassadors, and travellers continued to go back and forth during the centuries after this and other areas came to lie outside the borders of Byzantine control.¹ It is not inconceivable that monks, who were travelling to and from the monastery on the Sinai, told their friends and brethren about this saint whose passion they had read and whose body was apparently buried on Mount Sinai and started venerating her, independently of what was happening in far-away Rouen. One instance that suggests the existence of a local cult of Katherine at Sinai comes in the shape of an Armenian inscription carved into a rockface on the eastern Sinai. Michael Stone, its editor, interpreted it as relating to a pilgrimage, based on the mention of Katherine and a prayer. The names of the authors of the inscription appear to be Yohan and Galen. On palaeographical grounds, Stone proposed that the inscription 'should be set after the ninth century, probably in the tenth or eleventh'.² Another

---

1 Dimitri Gutas, Anthony Kaldellis, and Brian Long, 'Intellectual exchanges with the Arab world', in *The Cambridge Intellectual History of Byzantium*, ed. Anthony Kaldellis and Niketas Siniossoglou (Cambridge, 2017), pp. 79–98.

2 See Michael W. Stone, *The Armenian Inscriptions from the Sinai* (Cambridge, MA, 1982), pp. 132–3. line 5: 'to St. Kathaṙ[ine'. This inscription is H Arm 42; an image of it can be found on p. 229. The inscription is on Rock III, area 3, 'on the northwestern side of the crevice … over 3m above ground level'. There is also a graffito mentioning Katherine in Greek from Göreme in Cappadocia: it was recorded by Guillaume de Jerphanion, who found it scratched into the dedicatory panel of the saint as well as her donor Anna: 'κ(υρι)ε *or* αγια Αικατερινα βοηθει τον δουλον σου (?) Γ]εοργιον πρεσβυτερον. Εκατερινα παντερπνε βωειθει μι τ(ον) δουλον σου Γε(ωργιον).

indication that Katherine had started to gain some traction elsewhere in the empire comes from Central Greece, in the Phokis region. There, a mosaic from the eleventh century (*c.* 1020) of Katherine standing between Irene and Barbara can be found in the church of Hosios Loukas (founded in the early tenth century). In the mosaic, Katherine is carrying a globe, the symbol of world domination, a harbinger of things to come.³

A more tangible sign of a cult dedicated to Katherine at the Sinai monastery comes in the shape of a liturgical typikon, newly composed by the abbot Symeon in 1214. He refers to her λάρναξ (coffin, tomb) as one of the stations within the monastery church.⁴ The manuscript containing this typikon, a redaction of the Typikon of St Sabbas of Jerusalem, is Sinai,

---

δ(ια)κο(νον) αμαρτουλον και (τα)πηνον (και) παντ (..) και τκ(ε.ο.) τ(..ο)'. These are inscriptions 59 and 60, underneath the image of Katherine and to the right of her image respectively. They come from the church of St Katherine (Church 21), which has been dated to the second half of the eleventh century on the basis of the frescos. See Guillaume de Jerphanion, *Une nouvelle province de l'art byzantin: Les églises rupestres de Cappadoce*, vol. 1 (Paris, 1925), pp. 474–8. Other images of Katherine in the rock-churches in Göreme Valley in Cappadocia range in dates from the early tenth to the late eleventh centuries, a time when this area was under Byzantine control. See Lyn Rodley, *Cave Monasteries of Byzantine Cappadocia* (Cambridge, 1985), p. 198, p. 205, p. 220. Marcell Restle, *Byzantine Wall Painting in Asia Minor*, tr. Irene R. Gibbons, 3 vols (Greenwich, CT, 1969), vol. 2, fig. 83, fig. 435.

3   Nicolas Oikonomides, 'The first century of the monastery of Hosios Loukas', *Dumbarton Oaks Papers*, 46 (1992), 245–55. Nano Chatzidakis, *Byzantine Mosaics* (Athens, 1994), fig. 73. Irina Andreescu-Treadgold, 'Some considerations on the eleventh-century Byzantine wall mosaics of Hosios Loukas and San Nicolo di Lido', *Musiva & Sectilia*, 5 (2008), 115–67, floor plan on 123.

4   Nancy P. Ševčenko, 'The Liturgical typicon of Symeon of Sinai', in *Metaphrastes, or, Gained in Translation: Essays and Translations in Honour of Robert H. Jordan*, ed. by Margaret Mullett and Robert H. Jordan (Belfast, 2004), pp. 274–86.

MS gr. 1097. In this text the monastery is still dedicated to the Theotokos, despite the increasing number of western pilgrims arriving there in the course of the twelfth and thirteenth centuries who had undertaken the journey specifically because of Katherine.[5] The commemoration 'Τῆς ἁγίας μάρτυρος Αἰκατερίνης καὶ τοῦ ἁγίου μάρτυρος Μερκουρίου' takes place on November 24. The monks sing stichera on Katherine, pray, and depart from her tomb ('καὶ γίνεται ἡ λιτὴ καὶ ἀπερχόμεθα ἐν τῇ λάρνακι τῆς ἁγίας, ψάλλοντες τὰ στιχηρὰ τοῦ Μηναίου'). Eventually, they read her martyrdom ('ἀναγιγνώσκομεν δὲ τὸ μαρτύριον τῆς ἁγίας').[6] Nancy Ševčenko pointed out that Katherine 'shares the day with St Merkourios, and though there is an Agrypnia (vigil) in her honour, it is not the Great Agrypnia awarded [to] Moses and the Sinai martyrs. This may be the earliest evidence we have for the presence of her relics inside the monastery', about 150+ years after they first showed up in Rouen.[7]

This burgeoning cult of Katherine at Sinai can perhaps also be seen reflected in the vita-icon of the saint, which depicts her standing in the middle of a panel surrounded by twelve major scenes from her passion. The icon has been dated to the end of the twelfth or the beginning of the thirteenth century.[8] It may have been produced at Sinai although, ultimately, the evidence is not conclusive. The narrative cycle surrounding Katherine does not include a panel or reference linking the saint to Sinai – there may not have been a need for this since the icon would have been displayed at the monastery in close proximity to her sarcophagus and/or relics.

---

[5] 'Τῇ πανσέπτῳ καὶ ἁγίᾳ μονῇ τῆς ὑπεραγίας Θεοτόκου, τῆς ἐν τῷ ἁγίῳ ὄρει Σινᾶ ἰδρυμένης in Dmitrievskij, *Opisanie liturgitseskich rukopisej*, III, p. 394.

[6] Dmimitrievskij, *Opisanie liturgitseskich rukopisej*, III, p. 411.

[7] Ševčenko, 'The Liturgical typicon of Symeon', p. 280.

[8] Larison, 'Mount Sinai', pp. 162–4. Ševčenko, 'The *vita* icon', 150–1.

Figure 11: Vita Icon of St Katherine. Sinai, St Catherine's Monastery, with permission.

The icon, with its narrative frame that does not require knowledge of a particular language, could be seen as responding to the needs of pilgrims from diverse language backgrounds.[9] As Ševčenko observed, vita-icons may have emerged at Sinai 'as a response to the particular multilingual, multi-ethnic environment of the region, as well as to the perceived role of Sinai in the fragmented political world of the Eastern Mediterranean in the first half of the thirteenth century'.[10]

It was the establishment of a cult of Katherine with an oil-oozing relic at Rouen in Normandy in the eleventh century that eventually compelled the monks at Sinai to present clamouring pilgrims, who had come to the monastery and the presumed location of her body's burial hoping to see the real thing, with their own version of the relics and oil.[11] The German cleric Thietmar, otherwise unknown, undertook a pilgrimage to the Holy Land between 1217 and 1218.[12] He

[9] Ševčenko, 'The monastery of Mount Sinai', 124. On the iconography of Katherine see Georgios Galavaris, 'Η Αγία Αικατερίνη στις εικόνες της Ι.Μ. Σινά', Σιναϊτικα Αναλεκτα, 1 (2002), 1–38.

[10] Ševčenko, 'The *vita* icon', 160–1.

[11] Jacoby, 'Christian Pilgrimage to Sinai', p. 80 and p. 83; Ševčenko, 'St Catherine of Alexandria and Mount Sinai', p. 136 and p. 142; and Ead., 'The Monastery of Mount Sinai and the cult of Saint Catherine', p. 124.

[12] 'Desiderio autem desiderans desiderantissime corpus beatae Katerinae, sacro sudans oleo, visitare, eoque ardentius, quod in animo meo proposueram diuturnius, totum me ... gratiae Dei et beatae Katerinae submisi auxilio, quaelibet pericula et casuales eventus non abhorrens'. *Mag. Thietmari Peregrinatio*, ed. Johann C.M. Laurent (Hamburg, 1857), ch. 8, p. 20. That the undertaking of reaching the monastery was not much easier at the end of the nineteenth century is clear from Soskice's account of Agnes and Margaret Smith's (Mrs Lewis and Mrs Gibson) travels to Cairo, Sinai, and Jerusalem. See *Sisters of Sinai*. On Thietmar see *Die deutsche Literatur des Mittelalters: Verfasserlexikon*, vol. 9: *Slecht, Reinbold – Ulrich von Liechtenstein*, ed. Burghart Wachinger *et al.* (Berlin, 1995), s.v. Magister Thietmar(us), cols 793–95.

describes how, owing to his great desire to see the relics of Katherine, he underwent considerable risks in order to fulfil his wish. Having finally arrived at the monastery, he provides a description of his encounter with the saint's remains:

> in eadem ecclesia iuxta chorum in eminenti versus meridiem tumba beatae Katerinae est locata. Tumba quidem brevis est et de marmore albissimo nobiliter praeparata. Cuius cooperculum elevatum est quemadmodum archa, et aperitur et clauditur. Cum episcopus loci illius intelligeret desiderium meum et causam adventus mei, praeparatus cum devotione et orationibus et cantu accensis luminaribus et thuribulis accessit ad sarcophagum beatae Katerinae virginis, et aperuit, et mihi introspicere praecepit. Et vidi perspicue facie ad faciem sine ambiguo corpus beatae Katerinae, et caput eius nudum deosculabar. Membra quidem et ossa nervis cohaerentia adhuc in ipso oleo natant, quia ipsum oleum de singulis resudat articulis, non de tumba; tamquam de corpore humano in balneo sudor de poris guttatim erumpit.[13]

Thietmar comes face to face (*facie ad faciem*) with Katherine and, *sine ambiguo*, sees her body floating in a pool of oil that is emanating speficially from her joints, not the tomb. The set-up is one of catering to pilgrims such as Thietmar: the marble casket has a lid that can be opened and closed, while the bishop is willing to put on a dazzling display of prayers, chants, lit candles, and incense.

---

[13] *Mag. Thietmari Peregrinatio*, ch. 19, pp. 42–3. See also Ulf Koppitz, 'Magistri Thietmari Peregrinatio: Pilgerreise nach Palästina und auf den Sinai in den Jahren 1217/1218', *Concilium medii aevi*, 14 (2011), 121–221 (p. 165), although this is not a new edition based on the collation of additional manuscripts (Laurent used only one manuscript, Koppitz scanned the text and added contextual notes).

Figure 12: Icon of St Katherine painted by Jeremias Pallada in 1612 with her relics (hand and skull) in the Katholikon of the Church of the Transfiguration at St Catherine's Monastery on Sinai. Credit: Boistesselin / KHARBINE-TAPABOR

228   The Passion of St Katherine of Alexandria

Figure 13: Relics of St Katherine (left hand and top of skull) in the Katholikon of the Church of the Transfiguration at St Catherine's Monastery on Sinai. Credit: Boistesselin / KHARBINE-TAPABOR

Figure 14: Relics of St Katherine (left hand) in the Katholikon of the Church of the Transfiguration at St Catherine's Monastery on Sinai. Credit: Boistesselin / KHARBINE-TAPABOR

Conclusion 229

Thietmar's desire and that of other travellers from western lands to see with their own eyes the spot where Katherine was laid to rest by the angels as well as encounter her relics was initially fanned by texts such as Peter's version (BHL 1659) and BHL 1663 in particular, as well as the many vernacular and ancillary texts that started to build up around the story of her passion. More or less 150 years after the arrival of the saint's relics in Rouen, her story is so compelling and the pull of her cult so strong that Thietmar specifically went out of his way during his pilgrimage to the Holy Land in order to journey to the monastery on the Sinai. Yet the origin of Katherine's passion itself is still somewhat shrouded in obscurity. Crucially, it is clear that the short paragraph on Katherine's martyrdom in the *Menologion of Basil* cannot be the original nucleus from which all versions of the story descend. While the evidence from Greek manuscripts only starts to come into focus towards the ninth century and more fully during the tenth, a Carolingian manuscript from Benediktbeuern from the eighth century serves as a reminder that Katherine's story was already circulating in Italy, likely first in the Greek religious communities in the south. It travelled north across the Alps through the channels connecting monasteries such as Monte Cassino and San Vinceno al Volturno with the newly established Benedictine monasteries in Bavaria, although apparently it did not fall on receptive ears or spark a special interest.

A Greek version of Katherine's passion thus already existed during the eighth century. The inclusion of the saint's name in a manuscript of the prototype for the Synaxarion of Constantinople, which emerged between the middle of the seventh and the first half of the eighth century, is highly suggestive of a cult. The Greek hymn 'χορείαν σεπτὴν' was probably written by a hymnographer from the circle around Theodore of the Stoudios monastery no later than the first half of the ninth century. He likely drew on BHG 30a for his composition which suggests that this version predates his period of activity.

The tantalizing parallels with the life of Pansophios ('the all-wise') and that of Artemios hint at the possibility that Katherine's passion belongs to the same cultural milieu in which their lives were produced. Given the current state of knowledge, however, it is impossible to determine whether the originating author of Katherine's story was based in Constantinople or in Syria/Palestine.

While BHL 1663 clearly stands apart from the Katherine corpus as a whole by virtue of its popularity, it is obviously indebted to the early tradition. The kind of episodic detail it contains implies that the author of BHL 1663 was working from a model; it is impossible for him to have dreamt up in a vacuum an account of Katherine's passion so similar to the others. I have mentioned above the possibility that BHL 1662b, preserved in a unique Latin manuscript (Rome, Alessandrina, MS 96) could have served as one of the models. That translations from Greek into Latin of saints' lives frequently travelled from Italy to France is proven, in Katherine's case, by the eleventh-century Norman witnesses to Peter, Subdeacon of Naples' passion of Katherine (BHL 1659) and the manuscript of another passion of Katherine in Brussels (KBR, MS 944, s. xii).

Symeon of Trier is always cited as the most obvious candidate for bringing knowledge and relics of Katherine to Normandy, especially because he was actually a monk from Mount Sinai, to which place Katherine's body was believed to have been carried by angels. But as the historical evidence reveals, his arrival in Normandy at the same time as Katherine's story (and relics) is in all likelihood coincidental. Especially as regards the diffusion of her passion, in addition to her appearance in calendars, it is much more plausible that the well-documented connections between Italy and Normandy are the answer. Italy was in many cases the first point of contact with the West for Greek saints' lives. There they were translated by their hundreds, in centres such as Rome and

Naples, and by people such as Anastasius Bibliothecarius and Paul the Deacon. These translations were then turned into more pleasing Latin prose: the account of Katherine's passion produced by Peter, Subdeacon of Naples is a case in point.[14]

In the tenth and eleventh centuries, connections between Normandy and Italy were good, and travel between the two countries went both ways. An outstanding example of someone who undertook this journey is Odo of Cluny, who brought his reform-movement to a number of Italian monasteries, among them the abbey of Monte Cassino. John of Salerno, his future biographer, accompanied him in Italy and appears to have travelled back with him to France (to Fleury?) at least on one occasion. Could not the two of them have brought back to Fleury or Cluny a manuscript containing a passion of Katherine? Another prominent monastic reformer from Italy was William of Volpiano, who took the Cluniac reform from Cluny to Dijon and then, famously, to Normandy where he was instrumental in transforming the abbey of Fécamp into a shining beacon for learning in the region.

---

[14] The lack of early depictions of Katherine from Italy is perhaps evidence, *ex silentio*, that her cult, while possibly practiced or acknowledged at places such as Monte Cassino, was still limited in its significance. For example, a depiction of Katherine in the church of San Lorenzo fuori le mura in Rome was probably painted either at the end of the eleventh or the beginning of the twelfth century. See John Osborne, 'Dating medieval mural paintings in Rome: A case study from San Lorenzo fuori le mura', *Roma Felix: Formation and Reflections of Medieval Rome*, ed. Éamonn Carragáin and Carol Neuman de Vegvar (London, 2007), pp. 191–206. The fresco, painted by a Crescentius in a subterranean section of the church for a monk named John, depicts Katherine standing next to three male saints, John the Evangelist, Andrew, and Lawrence. All are identified by painted inscriptions. See Walsh, *The Cult of St Katherine*, pp. 48–53 for a discussion of additional and potentially earlier depictions of Katherine from Italy.

Against the backdrop of the monastic reforms that swept through the Norman monasteries, the use by the author of BHL 1663 of texts such as Autpert's *Conflictus* and the *CZA* takes on a particular meaning. While the *Conflictus* is much more obviously a text aimed at those who are wavering in their religious resolve, the *CZA* is more rarefied. Crucially, its survival in only a handful of manuscripts from the tenth and eleventh centuries could be connected with the burgeoning reform: there was a need for texts that would strengthen the measures put in place in the monasteries and what better way to influence those vacillating than by giving them fortifying books. The Cluniac reform may thus be seen as a means of survival for the *CZA*; however, it could also be argued that it was the reason BHL 1663 came into existence. If its author was indeed a Benedictine monk, Katherine's intellectual prowess, already present in the Greek texts, became a means to an end. The composition of BHL 1663 was not undertaken solely to promote the cult of Katherine, but perhaps also to move forward the reform movement and to promote the sort of learning for which the Benedictine abbeys of Normandy were so renowned.

In the period after the Viking incursions and during the formation of the Norman principality, the new dukes embarked on a project of monastic restauration: this included the re-establishment of monasteries such as Fontelle (960) and Fécamp (1001), as well as the founding of new houses such as at Rouen such as Saint-Ouen (*c.* 920), Saint-Amand (1030), and La Trinité (1030) or the abbey of Le Bec just down the road (1034). All of these religious centres were abuzz with literary activity, which ranged from (re)building libraries to establishing schools and scriptoria, where saints' lives and ancillary texts were being copied and newly composed.[15]

---

[15] Lucile Trân-Duc, 'Le culte des saints en Normandie (IXe – XIIe siècle) : Enjeux de pouvoir dans les établissements bénédictins du diocèse de

These efforts went hand in hand with the re-establishment of the Norman church's 'hagiographical capital.'[16] This was done primarily in the form of acquiring or re-acquiring relics, as well as generating martyrdom and miracle accounts to give them credence. During the first half of the eleventh century, religious establishments in and near Rouen were able to obain relics of two foreign and far-away saints, namely Katherine and Nicholas, whose authenticity was difficult to dispute compared to the relics of local saints that had been stashed away at Norman dependencies further inland to protect them from being destroyed at the hands of marauding Vikings. The latter were being closely protected by churchmen who regarded the conversion to Christianity of the new Norman political elite with a healthy dose of scepticism.

The production of a new passion alongside the acquisiton of Katherine's relics took place against the backdrop of a larger project to bring back and outshine Normandy's eminent saintly past. Whoever had the idea of imbuing Katherine's relic(s) with myroblitic power was a genius: it enabled the monks at La Trinité to use the oil not only for curative and salvific purposes but opened up the possibility of also distributing it as a tertiary relic, thus enlarging the abbey's sphere of influence beyond Normandy.[17] The oil is introduced into the passion as a way of helping Katherine gain traction in a packed field of local saints and boost the newly established La Trinité, which needed to catch up with its sister houses in the region. Katherine's Norman cult and the report of her myroblitic

---

Rouen' (unpublished doctoral dissertation, University of Caen Basse-Normandie, 2015), vol. 1, p. 15.

[16] Lucien Musset, *Les translations de reliques en Normandie (IXe–XIIe siècles')*, in *Les saints dans la Normandie médiévale*, ed. Pierre Bouet and François Neveux (Caen, 2000), pp. 97–108.

[17] Jacques le Maho, 'Les lieux de pèlerinage rouennais au temps des ducs (X^e–XIIe siècles), in *Identités pèlerines*, ed. Catherine Vincent (Rouen, 2002), pp. 45–65 at 63–65.

relics are clearly connected to the account of her passion in BHL 1663 and the Norman manuscripts that preserve BHL 1659. Thus, the presence of the oil-oozing relic allows for an easy (and never-ending) distribution of the saints' healing powers, since the original bone can remain intact and Katherine herself can continue in her eternal sleep on Mount Sinai. It is not until her story reaches Normandy that she acquires myroblitic powers.[18] There is nothing particularly remarkable about the saint or her story, except perhaps the extraodrinary success it had soon after she was introduced in eleventh-century Normandy.

A saint such as Katherine, who is new to the region and whose life focused on faith and conversion, is a useful didactic example. Her Norman hagiographer had at his fingertips Autpert's *Conflictus* and the anonymous *CZA*, texts that held a particular appeal for monks looking for motivation and models for their own monastic communities and lives. It is thus perhaps not a surprise that Katherine's passion in the guise of BHL 1663 was as successful as it was. And even though Katherine is a foreign saint, her particular ability to convert pagans in their multiples perhaps also appealed to the Normans because they themselves were descendants of pagans not so long ago. It is worth keeping in mind that 'the Peace of God movement that flourished in the eleventh century looked for inspiration to the early Christian age'.[19] Her bona fides historical context, anchoring her firmly in the Egypt of the early martyrs, and being virtually unknown in Normandy at the time, made her rather attractive as a focal saint for the newly-established monastery at Rouen. One may well wonder

---

[18] Béatrice Caseau, 'Parfum et guérison dans le christianisme ancien: des huiles parfumées des médecins au *myron* des saints byzantins', in *Les Pères de l'Eglise face à la science médicale de leur temps*, ed. Véronique Boudon-Millot *et al.* (Paris, 2005), pp. 141–91 (p. 190).

[19] Samantha Herrick, *Imagining the Sacred Past: Hagiography and Power in Early Normandy* (Cambridge, MA, 2007), p. 123.

Conclusion

who, in eleventh-century Normandy, could have gone to the trouble to compose this medieval bestseller and, more intriguingly still, who his counterpart was across the Mediterranean and what circumstances compelled him to gift his community and Christians across the centuries with such a fine example of female strength and intellectual prowess.

Figure 15: Embroidery of Katherine's martyrdom. Stole, *c.* 1200, made in Rhineland or England, silk and gold on linen, 19.7 x 48.9 cm. The Metropolitan Museum of Art, New York, Gift of Irwin Untermyer, 1964, www.metmuseum.org

APPENDIX 1

THE MANUSCRIPT TRADITION OF BHL 1663

This appendix looks at the manuscript tradition of BHL 1663 from a number of angles: on the basis of the 250+ extant manuscripts of BHL 1663, one can get an idea of the popularity the text enjoyed during the Middle Ages.[1] The fact that, in large part, the manuscripts that exist today are survivors of fires, wars, and daily usage over the years further illustrates how popular BHL 1663 became, especially in comparison with the other available Latin accounts of Katherine's life, except for the *Legenda aurea*. The only other early version extant in more than a handful of manuscripts is that produced by Peter, Subdeacon of Naples in the course of the tenth century, of which at least twenty manuscripts are known to survive.

Dissemination of the manuscripts

While a specific and detailed study of the total of the manuscripts has not been possible, a preliminary look at their dissemination in terms of chronology and geography can give an indication of when and where BHL 1663 and its epitomes

---

[1] This popularity is confirmed by her inclusion in all of the thirteenth-century collections of saints' lives known as *legendae novae* (see Philippart, *Les légendiers latins*, p. 24) put together by Dominican authors. The most famous among them was Jacobus de Voragine's *Legenda aurea*, extant in more than 900 manuscripts (see Fleith, *Studien zur Überlieferungsgeschichte*, p. 1), as well as those of Bartolomeo da Trento, Jean de Mailly, Rodrigo de Cerrato, Peter Calo, and also Vincent de Beauvais.

were copied, and how the text was diffused throughout medieval Europe.

1. Number and dating of manuscripts[2]

11th century	4
12th century	55
13th century	75
14th century	50
15th century	69
16th century	3
Total	256

BHL 1663 and its derivatives enjoyed a particularly active diffusion from the twelfth to the fifteenth centuries, with a peak in the thirteenth. The comparatively small number of manuscripts from the eleventh century suggests that it was probably written during that century, as discussed in Chapter 4. The sudden leap from four manuscripts in the eleventh century to fifty-five in the twelfth is evidence for the appeal of 1663 and the spreading cult of Katherine.[3]

As already mentioned, BHL 1663 was subject to being shortened as early as the eleventh century as a way to incorporate it into the liturgy. The twelfth century saw the production of two distinct epitomes, each with their own diffusion, identified by the tags BHL 1663a and BHL 1661m,

---

[2] I have only included manuscripts for which I know the date. Whenever a manuscript falls between two centuries, I have counted the later date.

[3] See Guy Philippart and Michel Trigalet, 'L'hagiographie latine du xie siècle dans la longue durée: Données statistiques sur la production littéraire et sur l'édition médiévale', in *Latin Culture in the Eleventh Century*, ed. Herren *et al.*, vol. 2, pp. 281–301 (p. 291), who examined the distribution of 5120 hagiographic manuscripts and came to the preliminary conclusion that the twelfth and fifteenth centuries were the most important for the production of these manuscripts. Out of the eighteen most successful hagiographical works of the fifteenth century, only Katherine, along with Martin of Tours and Francis of Assisi, is the subject of texts not by or dedicated to Jerome, see p. 294.

Appendix 1: The Ms. Tradition of BHL 1663

although it seems that the latter may have in fact been produced in the eleventh century (on BHL 1661m see Appendix 2). BHL 1663a is represented by five twelfth-century manuscripts and BHL 1661m by two. There exist also a number of as yet unidentified epitomes, of which there are three manuscripts. During the thirteenth century, BHL 1663a and BHL 1661m continued to be copied, and are known from ten and six manuscripts respectively. Other unidentified epitomes account for a total of fourteen manuscripts. The fourteenth century saw a continued but already less committed interest in BHL 1661m with five extant copies, whereas BHL 1663a survives in only two. The manuscripts preserving other epitomes amount to seven witnesses. Despite the continuing downward trend, both BHL 1663a (with three manuscripts) and BHL 1661m (with four manuscripts) managed to survive into the fifteenth century. The still unidentified epitomes account for a total of nine manuscripts during that century. The above numbers are skewed by the huge interest accorded to the vernacular versions, as well as the *Legenda aurea* version and the vernacular translations it engendered. In summary, the greatest concentration of manuscripts containing epitomes derived from BHL 1663 dates from the thirteenth century, although the two most stable epitomes survive in earlier manuscripts and may have arisen relatively quickly after BHL 1663 was written.

2. Geographical diffusion[4]

Northern France and Low Countries

11th century	4
12th century	26
13th century	24
14th century	14
15th century	8

England and Ireland

12th century	8
13th century	4
14th century	2
15th century	1

German-speaking lands and Bohemia

12th century	9
13th century	25
14th century	12
15th century	29

Southern Europe (southern France, Portugal, and Italy)

12th century	1 (Portugal)
13th century	6 (Italy and S. France)
14th century	3
15th century	1 (Italy)

In the twelfth century, BHL 1663 was copied mainly in France. At the same time, it was also known in England. The

---

[4] I have not included manuscripts for which I do not know the provenance, although the place of conservation can sometimes be indicative (above all in local French libraries; the various card-catalogues at the Institut de Recherche et d'Histoire des Textes, Paris, tend to concentrate on French and Belgian manuscripts). Also, the varying degrees of cataloguing of different collections do not always include information on provenance. This will inevitably result in an unbalanced picture, but I have included whatever information was available.

witnesses from German-speaking lands in this period are due to the spread of the *Magnum legendarium austriacum*. The absence of Italian witnesses is remarkable, and perhaps further evidence although in itself not conclusive, that BHL 1663 originated from France. Having said that, there are a number of manuscripts with an Italian provenance from the twelfth century that contain epitomes of BHL 1663. In the thirteenth century, 1663 continued to be copied in France just as avidly as in the preceding century. It was equally popular in German-speaking lands. By contrast, it did not enjoy a large diffusion either in England or in Italy. During the fourteenth century, the number of witnesses from France and Germany drop from the twenties to fourteen and twelve respectively, while the witnesses from England and Italy remain very few.

The fifteenth century saw very little copying of the text, with the notable exception of Germany, where it enjoyed a renewed success. Why there are comparatively few fifteenth-century witnesses for BHL 1663 from France, in particular, is hard to explain. This could be a combination of cultural reasons, so that BHL 1663 was no longer the flavour of the day. It could also be due to the summative descriptions of legendaries in manuscript catalogues.

3. Institutional diffusion[5]

Benedictine:

11th century	4
12th century	16
13th century	20
14th century	13
15th century	15
16th century	2

---

[5] I have only included manuscripts for which I know the provenance, and therefore the religious institution.

Cistercian:

12th century	8
13th century	12
14th century	3
15th century	1

Augustinian/collegial:

12th century	3
13th century	8
14th century	2
15th century	7

The diffusion of BHL 1663 specifically within the Franciscan, Carthusian, and Premonstratensian orders was relatively limited.[6] A reason for this could be the impact of the *novae legendae,* such as Jacobus de Voragine's *Legenda aurea* or Jean de Mailly's *Abbreviatio de gestis et miraculis sanctorum,* whose aim was to provide preachers with an organized and canonical collection of saints' lives. In this light, the text preserved in Koblenz, Landeshauptarchiv, Best. 701 Nr. 150, s. xv, fols 121-125, is all the more fascinating: it is the only manuscript I know of to contain a macaronic version of BHL 1663, moving back and forth almost seamlessly from Latin to German throughout. The dialect of the German points to the Rhine area around Koblenz, and it is very likely to have issued from a Franciscan house.[7] One other text in this manuscript, on the passion of Jesus (fols 103-105), is explicitly labelled by the cataloguer as a 'Mischtext', switching from Latin and German

---

[6] Franciscan: one manuscript from the fourteenth, and one manuscript from the fifteenth century. Carthusian: three manuscripts from the fourteenth, and one manuscript from the fifteenth century. Premonstratensian: six manuscripts from the twelfth, and three manuscripts from the fourteenth century.

[7] I thank Stephen Mossman for this information.

just as the passion of Katherine.[8] It seems that BHL 1663 also circulated within university-circles, but this was, again, very limited.[9]

A certain pattern can be detected, in that BHL 1663 was copied largely within a monastic milieu. The Benedictines, above all others, played a crucial role in its transmission as well as composition. Their partiality towards intellectual endeavour found its match in Katherine, and 1663 with its patchwork of sources can in this light be seen as a showpiece for their learning.

BHL 1663 and its epitomes[10]

Already during the eleventh century it became apparent that the original text of BHL 1663 was both too long and too densely packed with theological content for inclusion in the liturgy. In parallel to its continued copying, various epitomizers went to work on it and produced a number of versions

---

[8] The manuscript consists of eleven disparate parts, all written out at various dates on paper in the fifteenth century in western Germany and the area around the Middle Rhine Valley (Bingen – Bonn). It contains materials for preaching: there are sermons on a variety of topics, including on the resurrection of Jesus and on Mauritius, along with examples and miracles of all kinds. See Christina Meckelnborg, *Mittelalterliche Handschriften im Landeshauptarchiv Koblenz, vol. 1: Die nichtarchivischen Handschriften der Signaturengruppe Best. 701 Nr. 1–190*, (Wiesbaden, 1998), pp. 271–80.

[9] Paris, BnF, MS lat. 16566 belonged to the library of the Sorbonne, and Paris, Bibliothèque Mazarine, MS 1713 belonged to the library of the Collège de Navarre. During the thirteenth century, the University of Paris adopted Katherine as one of its patrons, along with the Virgin and Nicholas, see André Tuilier, *Histoire de l'Université de Paris et de la Sorbonne*, vol. 1: *Des origines à Richelieu* (Paris, 1994), p. 173. The seal of the University and the Faculty of Arts, in use during the thirteenth century, is depicted on p. 68, showing the three patron saints, and below them scenes from university life.

[10] Details on the manuscripts mentioned in this section (such as folios and provenance) can be found in the check-list below.

that enjoyed varying degrees of success during the centuries that followed. The way in which the epitomizers proceeded in the main was to cut the lengthy speeches to varying degrees, or summarize them, as well as doing away with some of the repeat-passages (ie. different punishments, summaries of events, etc.). While it is possible to distinguish a number of 'fixed' versions, in the sense that they had their own more or less stable transmission, there are many others that simply elude classification.[11] The reason for this could be that a good number of them may have been produced for in-house use only, or failed to make a suitable impression. However, there are some observations that can usefully be made at this stage. I take as my starting point the classification of the BHL, although its flaws with regard to BHL 1663 and its derivatives will quickly become apparent.

BHL 1663
In the majority of cases the prologue is present, but a number of manuscripts omit it. This version is characterized by two sets of debates: the initial confrontation between Katherine and Maxentius, and the subsequent disputation between Katherine and the rhetors. All speeches are distinguished by their theological content, derived mostly from a number of literary sources. It is preserved in at least 130+ manuscripts.

BHL 1663a
Referred to by Dobson as the 'shorter *Vulgate*', this epitome retains many of the features of BHL 1663, even the prologue

---

[11] The classification of the textual corpus of Pelagia by a group of French scholars remains the pioneering and model example of how to dissect and classify hagiographic texts. See Pierre Petitmengin *et al.*, *Pélagie la Pénitente: Métamorphoses d'une légende*, 2 vols (Paris, 1981 and 1984). See also by the same author 'Les vies latines de sainte Pélagie: Inventaire des textes publiés et inédits', *Recherches Augustiniennes*, 12 (1977), 3–29; and 'Les vies latines de sainte Pélagie: Compléments à l'inventaire et classement des manuscrits du texte B', *Recherches Augustiniennes*, 15 (1980), 265–304.

(in some manuscripts).[12] The most significant difference is the extent of the speeches, which have been shortened but not entirely cut. A partial edition was undertaken by Dobson who recorded the readings of a handful of manuscripts in a second apparatus underneath the text of BHL 1663.[13] His apparatus reveals a number of idiosyncrasies only found in this epitome. The prologue that precedes it has been changed very slightly in a couple of places, a feature that is consistently present in its manuscripts. In particular, two deleted passages were restored at a different place in the text:

> a) Lines 223-60 have been cut from their original place and have been moved forward, in order to replace lines 147-202, which have been suppressed. The result is that the speech in which Katherine reveals her name takes the place of the short theological debate between the saint and Maxentius. At the same time, the messenger sent out to bring back the rhetors is no longer given time to do so by the interposition of events that take place at court.
>
> b) Lines 894-905 have been deleted from their original context and have been partially inserted after line 1095, where they replace lines 1095-1100. In other words, the passage describing a group of people following Katherine as she is being dragged off to be beaten as a punishment for having survived her incarceration is used instead to describe the group who follow her on the way to her execution. In the original, Katherine turns around to address specifically the *virgines* and *matronas* from that second group. Her speech includes the pronoun *ipsas* (Dobson, l. 1105). This has been changed to *ipsos* in BHL 1663a: Katherine

---

[12] Dobson, *Seinte Katerine*, p. 140.

[13] The contents of Aosta, Biblioteca Collegiata Sant' Orso, MS 27, s. xiii, were published by Maria Cattalano, 'Passio Sanctae Caterinae virginis', *Mélanges historiques et hagiographiques valdôtains* (Miscellanea Augustana), II (1953), 351–65. The folios that contain BHL 1663a seem to be in disorder: the queen is killed before the destruction of the wheels. Cattalano did not point this out, nor did she provide the call-mark of the manuscript she used.

begins her speech still in the context of line 903 ('deponite, o viri'), but continues at 1100 with her speech to the *virgines* and *matronas*. However, the new context requires the female pronoun to be changed to the masculine, present in the four manuscripts of BHL 1663a used by Dobson.

This epitome is extant in a good number of manuscripts from the twelfth century onwards, and has also been incorporated into the *Magnum legendarium austriacum (MLA)*; its earliest witness is Heiligenkreuz, Stiftsbibliothek, MS 14, 1190-1212. It remains to be seen whether it owes its existence to the inclusion in the *MLA* or whether it was an independent epitomization which was subsequently used by whoever compiled the *MLA*.

The *BHLms* also lists the following as containing BHL 1663a, although on examination these manuscripts prove to represent a great variety of epitomes, not yet classified: Bourges, Bibliothèque municipale, MS 34, s. xv$^{1/4}$; Paris, Bibliothèque Mazarine, MS 399, s. xiv; Rome, Biblioteca nazionale centrale, MS Sess. 147, s. xiv; Rouen, BM, MS 1388 (U.32), s. xii; Trier, Bischöfliche Seminarbibliothek, MS 33, s. xv; Trier, Stadtbibliothek, MS 388/1152 2°, s. xii; BAV, MS Pal. lat. 362, s. xv.

No BHL number (shorter 'shorter Vulgate')

Dobson referred to the epitome contained in Paris, BnF, MS lat. 14293 as the shorter 'shorter' *Vulgate* because it appears to be based directly on BHL 1663a (the 'shorter *Vulgate*').[14] It is divided into nine readings; it is possible that there are other witnesses for this text.

---

[14] Dobson, p. 140. The text is also printed by Narbey, *Supplément*, 2, pp. 321–27.

BHL 1664

A version of BHL 1663 which is followed by an epilogue that names an Athanasius as the *scriptor*, preserved in a least three manuscripts (according to the *BHLms*): Brussels, KBR, MS 7917, 1475; The Hague, Koninklijke Bibliotheek, MS L.29 (70.E.21), 1461; Vienna, ÖNB, MS s.n. 12754, s. xv. While Brussels, KBR, MS 7917 preserves the epilogue, The Hague, KB, MS L.29 does not and ends just like BHL 1663. I have not verified the Vienna manuscript. In any case, it appears that BHL 1664 merely reflects the addition of the epilogue to BHL 1663, as opposed to representing a truly different version. As in the case of the passion written by Peter, Subdeacon of Naples (whose text has been referred to variously as the Athanasius/Arechis/Peter version), the categorization according to epilogues (over and above the *incipit/explicit*) only breeds confusion.

BHL 1664b, c, d

The addition of the letters b, c, and d categorizes a number of manuscripts that contain epitomes with similar *incipits*. According to the *BHLms* these are:

> b: 'Maxentius tirannus anno tricesimo quinto regni sui residens in civitate Alexandrinorum feralia per vicinas provincias'. One witness: Trier, Seminarbibliothek, MS 98. The text in this manuscript is longer than both BHL 1661m and BHL 1663a, but I have been unable to place it within the corpus of texts. A relationship with the other two epitomes cannot be excluded at this stage.
>
> c: 'Maxentius imperator anno regni sui trigesimo quinto in civitate Alexandrinorum feralia per vicinas provincias misit edicta' One witness: Trier, Stadtbibliothek, MS 1050 (737). This is in fact a witness for BHL 1661m (see Appendix 2).
>
> d: 'Fuit in urbe Alexandrinorum quaedam puella'. Two manuscripts: Douai, Bibliothèque Marceline Desbordes-Valmore, MS 151 and Verdun, BM, MS 1. A comparison of the

two witnesses reveals that they do not preserve the same text. Verdun is much shorter, leaving out the debate with and death of the rhetors, the conversion of the queen and Porphyrius, their deaths, as well as the construction of the wheel.

BHL 1661m

The *incipit* of this text suggests that it is dependent on Peter, Subdeacon of Naples' version of the passion.[15] In reality, it is an epitome of BHL 1663 and extant in a good number of manuscripts, including at least three manuscripts dated to the twelfth century or earlier. It was first edited by Bronzini on the basis of two witnesses. I present a more detailed discussion and edition of this epitome in Appendix 2.

BHL 1673

This tag identifies an epitome of BHL 1663 in which mainly the speeches have been cut. It survives in Paris, BnF, MS lat. 810, a Proper of the saints for use at Saint-Martial, Limoges from the fifteenth century. The reason it was assigned yet another number is that the beginning of the text looks a little different: folios 124-128v contain a text that starts: 'Cum apud civitate Alexandriam Maxencius imperator advenisset, misit edictum', and which has been divided into nine readings. Folios 141v-144 contain a text that starts: 'Factum est autem cum traheretur ad supplicium' (Dobson, l. 894), and which has been divided into eight readings. While the first text broadly follows the storyline of BHL 1663 (cutting out undesired text without intervening otherwise), the second text seems to be without a context, containing as it does only Katherine's flogging, the building and destruction of the wheel, and the deaths of the queen and Porphyrius. Rather than assuming a maladroit scribe, it seems more likely that the

---

[15] BHL 1661m: 'Maxentius imperator anno regni sui tricesimo quinto residens in civitate Alexandrinorum'. BHL 1659: 'Regnante igitur Maxentio cesare, Maximiani augusti filio'.

first portion of the text was read to begin with – 'in natale sanctae Katherinae virginis et martyris' (fol. 124) – and that the part containing the episode of the wheels was read specifically during the night office (*noctibus*, fol. 141v).

As already indicated above, there are a number of epitomes that elude classification at this point. I wonder, also, how useful such an undertaking would be, seeing that many of the non-epitomes (so-to-speak) of Katherine's passion are still awaiting their editor. From the evidence I have seen, the only epitomes with any significant diffusion were BHL 1663a and BHL 1661m. Certainly one way of proceeding would be to scrutinize the early epitome-manuscripts in particular, and then move on to later witnesses.

Katherine in the great legendaries[16]

The success of BHL 1663, especially during the twelfth century, and the proliferation of legendaries particular to specific areas, resulted in its inclusion in a number of the great legendary collections of the Middle Ages. They were initially analyzed by Wilhelm Levison, although some of them have also been studied individually.[17] I only briefly mention the great collections that include BHL 1663:

Magnum legendarium austriacum = BHL 1663a.
This legendary was put together during the last decades of the twelfth century.[18] It derives its name from the fact that the

---

[16] This cursory overview cannot pretend to be inclusive of all the many collections that were put together. See Philippart, *Les légendiers latins*, pp. 122–28 for an initial bibliography.

[17] Wilhelm Levison, *Conspectus codicum hagiographicorum*, MGH SSRM 7 (Hannover, 1920), pp. 529–51.

[18] Albert Poncelet, *De magno legendario austriaco*, AB, 17 (1898), 98. See also Ó Riain, 'The *Magnum Legendarium Austriacum*', 87–165, and Id.

manuscripts which make up the collection are all conserved in Austrian monasteries, namely Heiligenkreuz, Lilienfeld and Zwettl (Cistercian), and Admont and Melk (Benedictine).[19] The only complete set, in seven volumes, is at Melk. The witnesses to Katherine's passion are: Heiligenkreuz, MS 14, s. xii; Melk, Stiftsbibliothek, MS 678 (M.8), s. xv; Zwettl, Stiftsbibliothek, MS 15, s. xii.

Legendarium flandrense = BHL 1663.

This collection was compiled in the middle of the twelfth century, and is preserved in a number of manuscripts, none of which make up a complete set.[20] The following are witnesses to BHL 1663, all of them from Cistercian monasteries except for Marchiennes: Bruges, Openbare Bibliotheek, MS 404, s. xiii, from Ter Doest Abbey in Flanders; Saint-Omer, BP, MS 716 vol. viii, s. xiii, from Clairmarais Abbey (near Saint-Omer); Brussels, KBR, MS 7461, s. xiii, from Vaucelles Abbey (near Cambrai); Douai, BMD-V, MS 838, s. xiii, from Marchiennes Abbey.

Liber de natalitiis

The *Liber de natalitiis* belongs to a collection of legendaries with many ramifications.[21] It is a six-volume work, compiled

'Neue Erkenntnisse zur Entstehung und Überlieferung des Magnum Legendarium Austriacum', *Mitteilungen des Instituts für österreichische Geschichtsforschung*, 128 (2020), 1–21.

[19] There is also a manuscript from St. Pölten now at Vienna, ÖNB, MS 337, see Joseph v.d. Straeten, 'Le "Grand Legendier Autrichien" dans les manuscrits de Zwettl', *AB*, 113 (1995), 321.

[20] See Levison, *Conspectus*, pp. 542–44; François Dolbeau, 'Nouvelles recherches sur le Legendarium Flandrense', *Recherches Augustiniennes*, 16 (1981), 399–455.

[21] Henri Rochais, *Un légendier cistercien de la fin du xiie siècle: Le* Liber de natalitiis *et de quelques grands légendiers des xiie et xiiie siècles* (Rochefort, 1975). François Dolbeau, 'Notes sur la genèse et sur la diffusion du

in the twelfth century, and of Cistercian origin. More than fifty manuscripts survive today. At least two manuscripts contain BHL 1663: Paris, BnF, MS lat. 16735 and Paris, BnF, MS lat. 17007.

A check-list of manuscripts of BHL 1663 (and its epitomes)

This is the most complete checklist of manuscripts containing 1663 (and its derivatives) so far. I started with the lists of manuscripts compiled by the Bollandists, available online, and Bronzini. I found additional manuscripts in the works of Dobson and Jennifer Bray,[22] as well as by browsing manuscript catalogues and manuscript databases (such as *In principio* and *Manuscripta mediaevalia*). Many of the provenances are based on the various card-catalogues of owners and places compiled by the Institut de recherche et d'histoire des textes in Paris, and, just as in the case of the dates, cannot in all cases be guaranteed to be certain, but are rather intended as a guide.[23]

I present here a list that will allow easy and quick overview of the manuscripts, without providing a full description of each witness. Moreover, given that there are reference-works to control the mass of manuscript catalogues, I have not included

---

Liber de natalitiis', *Revue d'Histoire des Textes*, 6 (1976), 143–95. Other French legendaries have been discussed by Dolbeau: 'Le légendier de l'abbaye cistercienne de Clairmarais', *AB*, 91 (1973), 273–86. 'Un légendier de la cathédrale d'Arras (Bruxelles, B. R., II. 2310)', *AB*, 107 (1989) 128. 'Les légendiers de Marchiennes', *AB*, 108 (1990), 336. 'Deux légendiers de Metz et de Châlons', *AB*, 108 (1990), 348. 'Deux légendiers démembrés du diocèse de Liège', *AB*, 109 (1991), 117–36. 'Le légendier de Châalis', *AB*, 117 (1999), 388–93.

[22] Dobson, pp. 132–43. Jennifer R. Bray, 'The legend of St Katherine in later Middle English literature' (unpublished doctoral thesis, University of London, 1984).

[23] In the case of the provenance, I give the earliest known origin, provenance or ownership.

references to the latter (here or in the bibliography).[24] The list accounts for manuscripts that preserve BHL 1663 and its epitomes as far as I have been able to identify them. In some cases, the catalogue descriptions were insufficient to allow a precise identification; when that was the case I have indicated this by a question mark. Due to the sheer number of manuscripts and the limited time available, I have not been able to take account of the other BHL numbers for Katherine.

The manuscripts are arranged in alphabetical order of the place where they are now kept. For each manuscript I give its location, call mark and folios containing BHL 1663 (or text in question) in the first column. I then give the date as found in the relevant catalogue or other publication. The third column contains information about what sort of account is preserved in the manuscript. The fourth column provides details about the contents of the manuscripts, as far as possible. The great number of categories is a result of varying degrees of accuracy in the catalogue descriptions and my own observations. As I have not been able to scrutinize all of the manuscripts and therefore classify them in the manner suggested by Guy Philippart,[25] I have chosen to keep the designations given in the catalogues (if not always strictly correct). In the fifth column I indicate the provenance and the religious order (if known).

It is likely that a number of witnesses are still lying dormant, particularly in eastern European libraries. The holdings of several monastic libraries in Austria and Switzerland are especially rich in mainly younger manuscripts, and are being progressively catalogued, although I have tried to include recent catalogues.

---

[24] See e.g. Paul O. Kristeller, *Latin Manuscript Books Before 1600: A List of the Printed Catalogues and Unpublished Inventories of Extant Collections*, revised and enlarged by Sigrid Krämer (Munich, 1993).

[25] Philippart, *Les légendiers latins*, pp. 21–26.

Appendix 1: The Ms. Tradition of BHL 1663

Abbreviations used in the check-list

Text

1663	
1663 prol:	1663 preceded by the prologue
1663 + LA:	text of 1663 apparently contaminated by the *Legenda aurea*
debate:	dispute between Katherine and the rhetors only
1663a:	epitome
1663a prol.:	epitome preceded by the prologue
1661m:	epitome
epit. (prol.):	an as yet unidentified epitome (preceded by the prologue)

Contents

Barl. & I:	Barlaam and Ioasaph
Becket:	Thomas Becket (life of)
Breviary	
fem.:	female saints only
Hom.:	homily, homiliary
Kath.:	Katherine
Lect.:	lectionary
Leg.:	legendary
LF:	*Legendarium flandrense*
Libellus:	contains only texts relating to Katherine
LM:	*Legendarium magdeburgense*
LN:	*Liber de natalitiis*
Misc.:	collection of various texts
Missal	
MLA:	*Magnum legendarium austriacum*
Off. Kap.:	office capitulary
Pass.:	passionary
Peter of Lond.:	Peter of London's *Liber revelationum* (d. 1221)
Serm. & Inst. Sct.:	sermons and *Instutiones sanctorum*
Serm. & Vit.:	sermons and saints' lives

VS: saints' lives
VV: lives of virgin saints

Abbreviations of religious orders:

aug.: Augustinian
ben.: Benedictine
carth.: Carthusian
can.: canons
cist.: Cistercians
coll.: Collegiate
dioc.: diocese
dom.: Dominican
franc.: Franciscan
jes.: Jesuit
prem.: Premonstratensian
reg.: regular

Check-list

	City, library, call-mark, folios	Date	Text	Contents	Provenance
1	Aberystwyth NLW, MS 21876A, fols 1v-24	xii	1663a	Misc.	France
2	Admont StiB, MS 552, fols 168-171	xii/xiii	epit.	Misc.	Admont, ben.
3	Alençon BM, MS 21, fols 144-156	xiv	1663	VS	La Trappe Abbey, cist.
4	Aosta Biblioteca Collegiata Sant' Orso, MS 8, fols 218-227v	xiii	1663a	Leg.	Sant' Orso, aug.
5	Aosta BC, MS 27, fols 57v-64v	xiii	1663a	Misc.	

Appendix 1: The Ms. Tradition of BHL 1663   255

6	Angers BM, MS 121 (113), fols 274-280	xi	epit.	Lect.		Saint-Nicolas, Angers, ben.
7	Angers BM, MS 308 (299), fols 123-144v	xii	1663	VS		
8	Angers BM, MS 813 (729), fols 46-72v	xii	1663	VS		Saint-Aubin, Angers?, ben.
9	Arras BP, MS 961 (344), fols 182a-183	xiv	1663	Lect.		Saint-Waast, Arras, ben.
10	Arras BP, MS 462 (573), fols 114a-121a	xiii	1663	VS		Saint-Waast, Arras, ben.
11	Aschaffenburg StiB, MS Perg. 4, fols 257a-264vb	xiii-xiv	1663?	Pass.		Aschaffenburg, ben./coll.
12	Bamberg SB, MS Q.VI.57, fols 258v-262	xv	?	Misc.		Bamberg, franc.
13	Berlin SBPK, MS theol.lat.fol. 482, fols 25vb-47b	*ante* 1179	1663	VS		Doberan Abbey, Pelplin, cist.
14	Berlin SBPK, MS theol.lat.fol. 267, fols 195a-199a	1150-1200	1663	Pass.		Springiersbach, Eifel, aug.
15	Berlin SBPK, MS theol.lat.fol. 719, fols 96b-104va	xiii	1663a	Leg.		Steinfeld, Eifel, prem.
16	Berlin SBPK, MS theol.lat.fol. 701, fols 1a-16va	xii/xiii	1663	Kath.		Kaisheim, Donauwörth, cist.
17	Berlin SBPK, MS Magdeburg. 138, fols 398-410v	*post* 1459		LM		Jacques Bongars, French (?)
18	Bern BB, MS 133, fols 65v-84v	xi-xii	1663 prol.	VS		France ?
19	Bern BB, MS 137, fols 158-178	xii	1663 prol.	VS		Île-de-France ?

20	Bourges BM, MS 34, fols 181b-190vb	1401-1425	epit.	Missal	Sainte-Chapelle, Bourges
21	Bruges OB, MS 34, fols 148a-167b	xiii	1663?	Misc.	Ter Duinen, cist.
22	Bruges OB, MS 113, fol. 1v	xii	prol.	Misc.	Ter Duinen, cist./St. Donatian, Bruges
23	Bruges OB, MS 404, fols 49-56	xiii	epit.?	LF	Ter Duinen, Ter Doest, cist.
24	Brussels Bib. Boll., MS lat. 5 (430), fols 101a-108a	xii	1663	VS	Grimberghen, prem.
25	Brussels Bib. Boll., MS lat. 433 (455), fols 156a-166va	xiii	1663	Vit. Sanct.	Heinsberg, Norbertines
26	Brussels KBR, MS 197, fols 206v-220	1465	1663?	Leg.	
27	Brussels KBR, MS 206, fols 114a-122b	xiii^{in}	1663 prol.	Pass.	Knechtsteden Abbey, prem.?
28	Brussels KBR, MS 4564-68, fols 34-45v	xiii	1661m	Misc.	Bruges, jes.
29	Brussels KBR, MS 4961, fols 1-31v	xv	1663 prol.	Libellus	Enghien, La Chapelle, carth.
30	Brussels KBR, MS 7461, fols 80b-91a	xiii	1663 prol.	LF	Vaucelles, cist.
31	Brussels KBR, MS 7672-74, fols 175a-186b	xiv	1663 prol.	Leg.	Irish
32	Brussels KBR, MS 7917, fols 4v-16	1475	1663 prol.	VV	St. Jerome, Utrecht
33	Brussels KBR, MS 8272-82, fols 236v-250v	xv	1663 prol.	VS	

Appendix 1: The Ms. Tradition of BHL 1663 257

34	Brussels KBR, MS 8690-8702, fols 14-42v	xii	1663 prol.	Leg.	Cornelius Duyn/Amsterdam, Bollandists
35	Brussels KBR, MS 8729-31, fols 43-75v	xv	1663 prol.	VV	Utrecht?, carth.
36	Brussels KBR, MS 8751-60, fols 52-67v	1442	1663 prol.	Leg.	Red Cloister, can.
37	Brussels KBR, MS 8955-56, fols 4-6v + 9-24	xvii	various	Collectanea Bollandiana	Bollandists
38	Brussels KBR, MS 9120, fols 92v-100	1180	1663	Pass.	Lille, jes.
39	Brussels KBR, MS 9810-14, fols 179-191v	xii	1663 prol.	Leg. Fem.	Saint-Laurent, Liège, ben.
40	Brussels KBR, MS 11550-55, fols 192-201	xiii	1663 prol.	Pass.	Park Abbey, prem.
41	Brussels KBR, MS 18018, fols 25v-37	xi^{ex}	1663	Lect.	Saint-Peter, Lobbes, ben.
42	Brussels KBR, MS 19071, fols 3-15v	1480	1663 prol.	Libellus	
43	Brussels KBR, MS 19080, fols 1-33v	1470	1663 prol.	Libellus	
44	Brussels KBR, MS 20374-77, fols 367-382v	xii	? prol.	Misc.	Leuven
45	Brussels KBR, MS II.1151, fols 99v-114v	xiii	?	Leg.	Cambron, cist.
46	Budapest OSK, MS lat. 40, fols 1v-2v	1457	epit.	VS (fem.)	
47	Budapest OSK, MS lat. 389, fols 90-106v	1400/1500	1663 prol.	Serm. & Vit.	Bohemia

48	Cambridge CCC, MS 405, fols 72v-79v	xiv^{in}	1661m	Misc.	Waterford, Ireland
49	Cambridge Fitzwilliam, MS McClean 100, fols 149-161	x+xii	1663 prol.	Pass.	German
50	Cambridge Gonville & Caius, MS 301/515, fols 141-150	xii	1663	VS & Misc.	Christ Church, Canterbury
51	Cambridge Trinity, MS 340, fols 75-109b	xv/xvi	1663 prol.	Lect.	English
52	Cambridge UL, MS Gg.I.26, fols 115-150	1421	1663	VS	English
53	Cambrai BM, MS 863 (767.i), fols 263-278	1076-92 + xii	1663 prol.	Leg.	Saint-Sépulcre, Cambrai, ben.
54	Carpentras BM, MS 72, fols 296-300	xii^{ex}	epit.	Breviary	
55	Charleville BP, MS 200, fols 117a-128b	xiii	1663 prol.	VS	Signy Abbey, cist.
56	Charleville BP, MS 254 vol.ii, fols 1-15	1151	1663	Leg. (fem.)	Belleval, ben.
57	Chartres BM, MS 190 (500 5/A), fols 269-274 [*destroyed*]	xii	?	Misc.?	Chartres
58	Chartres BM, MS 479 (516/B), fols 149v-152v [*destroyed*]	xv	epit.	Leg.	Chartres
59	Chartres BM, MS 92, fols 269-271 [*destroyed*]	xii-xv	1663	?	

Appendix 1: The Ms. Tradition of BHL 1663 259

60	Chartres BM, MS 51 vol. ii (1031 7/D), fols 197-198v [*destroyed*]	1373	?	Misc.?	Saint-Père, Chartres, ben.
61	Cividale MAN, MS XII, fols 177-179	xv	1661m	Pass.	Cividale (Capellini scribe), ben.
62	Cividale MAN, MS XXI, fols 197v-202	xii (xiii)	1661m	Pass.	Cividale, ben.
63	Cologne HA, MS GB.f.28, fols 150-165	1486		VS	St. Martin, Cologne, ben.
64	Cologne HA, MS GB.qto.110, fols 65-91	1409	1663 prol.	Misc.	Fratres sancte crucis, Cologne
65	Cologne HA, MS GB.qto.253, fols 96v-121	1450-60	1663 prol.	Misc.	Cologne
66	Cologne HA, MS W.f.164b, fols 175-189	*c.* 1463		Pass.	Corpus Christi, Cologne, aug.
67	Darmstadt HULB, MS 763, fols 388-409v	1400-1450	1663 prol.	Pass.	Wimpfen, dom.
68	Darmstadt HULB, MS 778, fols 222va-226va	1450-1500	epit.	Misc.	St. Salvator, Ewig, aug.
69	Darmstadt HULB, MS 896, fols 249va-vb	1200-1300	epit.	Misc.	Cathedral, Constance
70	Darmstadt HULB, MS 2766, fols 104a-106a	xiv	epit.	VS	Trier
71	Dessau StaB, MS Georg. 7, fols 225-285v	xv	1663	Misc.	Nienburg, ben. ?

72	Douai Bibliothèque Marceline Desbordes-Valmore, MS 434 vol. iii, fols 167v-169v	xiii	1663 prol.	Misc.	Anchin, ben.
73	Douai BMD-V, MS 151 vol. i, fols 178-180	xiv	1663 prol.	Lect.	Marchiennes, ben.
74	Douai BMD-V, MS 838, fols 15120	xiii	1663	LF	Marchiennes, ben.
75	Douai BMD-V, MS 854, fols 112-123v	xii	1663 prol.	VS	Anchin, ben.
76	Edinburgh UL, MS 23, fols 42-42v + 47-72v	xv	1663 prol.	VV	German or Dutch
77	Einsiedeln StiB, MS 251, fols 97-140	xii	1663 prol.	Barl. & I, Kath.	
78	Erlangen UB, MS 489, fols 90-90v + 94-109	1477	1663 + LA	Misc.	
79	Florence BNC, MS C.S.D.7 1158, fols 50-66v	xiii	1663 prol.	Misc.	Camaldoli
80	Frankfurt Sta & UB, MS Barth. 5, fols 148va-160va	1356	1663	VS	St. Bartholomäus, Frankfurt, can.
81	Frankfurt Sta & UB, MS Barth. 71, fol. 71	xiv	prol.	Misc.	St. Bartholomäus, Frankfurt, can.
82	Gent CBR, MS 245, fols 3a-48	xii-xiii+xiv	?	VS	Trier
83	Gent CBR, MS 423, fols 1a-91	xii-xiii	1663?	Libellus	

Appendix 1: The Ms. Tradition of BHL 1663

84	Gloucester Cathedral, MS I, fols 97v-105	xiiiⁱⁿ	1663 prol.	VS	St Peter, Leominster, ben. fem.
85	Gorizia BS, MS 9, fols 239v-244	xiii	1661m	Pass.	Aquileia
86	Gotha F&LB, MS Memb. I.64, fols 144-156v	xiv	?	VS	
87	Graz UB, MS 302, fols 274v-280	1384/85	1663	Misc.	Seckau, aug.
88	Graz UB, MS 412, fols 217-228v	xii	1663	VS	St. Lambrecht, aug.
89	Graz UB, MS 1069, fols 112-139v	1200	1663	Misc.	Seckau, aug.
90	The Hague KB, MS J.3 (78.A.31), fols 300-313	xiv	1663	VS	
91	The Hague KB, MS L.29 (70.E.21), fols 315v-325	1461	1663 prol.	Pass.	St. Catharina, Muiden
92	Heiligenkreuz StiB, MS 14, fols 13a-17vb	1190-1212	1663a prol.	MLA	Heiligenkreuz, cist.
93	Hereford Cathdral, MS P.VII.6, fols 103vb-115b	xii	1663 prol.	Pass.	Hereford, ben.
94	Herzogenburg StiB, MS 57, fols 270-276	1430	1661m	Misc.	Grein
95	Hildesheim Bischöfl. DomBib, MS 739f, fols 38vb-52va	xv	1663 prol.	Misc.	
96	Kassel GHB, MS 2° theol. 47, frg. 1, fols 2a-2vb	xii^{ex}	1663	Misc.	

97	Kassel GHB, MS 2° theol. 142, fols 151-157v	1367-89	1661m	Hom.	
98	Klosterneuburg StiB, CCl 79, fols 57b-58vb	1260/80	1661m	Off. Cap.	Klosterneuburg, aug.
99	Klosterneuburg StiB, CCl 193, fols 235a-236b	1420	1661m?	Misc.	Ybbs, cist. ?
100	Klosterneuburg StiB, CCl 574, fols 135v-139v	xiii	epit.	Misc.	Naumburg cathedral, ben. (A. Saxo von Hunoldesburch scribe)
101	Klosterneuburg StiB, CCl 709, fols 279-295	xiii	1663a prol.	MLA	Klosterneuburg, aug.
102	Koblenz LHA, Best. 701 nr. 141, fols 68va-81a	1465	1663 prol.	Misc.	Niederwerth, aug.
103	Koblenz LHA, Best. 701 nr. 150, fols 121-125	xv	mac.	Misc.	Central Rhine Valley
104	Koblenz LHA, Best. 701 nr. 113a, fols 334a-336b	1300-1350	1663	Leg.	Münstermaifeld, aug. can. (G. v. Andernach scribe)
105	Koblenz LHA, Best. 701 nr. 114, fols 242vb-257va		epit.	Leg. & Misc.	St. Castor, Karden, (can.?)
106	Koblenz LHA, Best. 701 nr. 115, fols 116b-124va	1250-1275	1663	Leg.	Diocese of Liège/Mainz cathedral?
107	Kremsmünster StiB, MS CC 309 (ii), fols 82-91	xii^{ex}	1663	Misc.	
108	Laon BM, MS 344, fols 135b-148a	xii	1663 prol.	Pass.	Cuissy, prem.
109	Leipzig UB, MS lat. 436, fols 15-28	xiii	1663 prol.	Misc.	Chemnitz, ben.

Appendix 1: The Ms. Tradition of BHL 1663   263

110	Leipzig UB, MS Rep. II 59a, fols 33-36v	xiii	epit.	VS	St. Mauritius, Altach
111	Leipzig UB, MS Rep. II fol. 64, fols 60v-100	xii^{ex}	1663 prol.	VS	
112	Liège UB, MS 58 (210, vol. ii), fols 161-172	1366	?	Leg.	
113	Liège UB, MS Wittert. 74, fols 1-14v	xiv	1663 prol.	Pass.	Visé
114	Lilienfeld StiB, MS 94, fols 64v-74v	1200/1300	1663a prol.	MLA	Kleinmariazell, cist.
115	Linz OöLB, MS 315 (78), fols 43-60	xii-xiii	1663?	Misc.	Garsten, Passau, ben.
116	Linz OöLB, MS 422 (18)	xiii	?	VS	
117	Linz OöLB, MS 20 (291)	xv	1663 prol.	?	Agnes Sampadin (scribe)
118	Lisbon BN, MS Alcobaça CCLXXXVI (420), fols 167a-179b	xii	1663a prol.	Leg.	Lisbon, cist.
119	Ljubljana UB, MS 17, fols 142-156v	xii	1663 prol.	Misc.	
120	London Lambeth Palace, MS 51, fols 766-769	1197-1221	epit.	Peter of Lond.	Holy Trinity, London, aug.
121	London BL, Arundel MS 330, fols 68va-69vb	xiv	epit.	Pass.	Mainz, carth.
122	London BL, Arundel MS 406, fol. 30v	xiii/xiv	epit.	Misc.	English?

123	London BL, Cotton MS Caligula A.viii, fols 169-191	xii	1663 prol.	Misc.	Ely, prem.
124	London BL, Royal MS 8.C.vi, fol. 160	xiv$^{2/2}$	prol.	Misc.	English?
125	London BL, Royal MS 12.E.I, fols 119v-121v	xiv^{in}	1661m	Misc.	John Theyer
126	London BL, Harley MS 12, fols 141-143v	1080-1100	1661m	VS	English
127	London BL, Harley MS 2345, fols 55va-56a	xiii/xiv	epit.	Serm. &Inst. Sct.	Winchcomb?, ben.
128	London BL, Add. MS 10933, fols 126b-134b	xv	1663 prol.	VS	Wiblingen, ben.
129	London BL, Harley MS 2800, fols 221va-228a	xiii	1663 prol.	Pass.	Arnstein, prem.
130	Mainz Wiss. StadtBi, MS I.106, fols 42-45v	1300	epit.	VS	Mainz, carth.
131	Mantua BCom, MS 57 (A.II.26), fols 174-199v	xvi	1663	VS	San Giorgio Maggiore, Venice, ben.
132	Melk StiB, MS 678, fols 214-222	xv	1663a	MLA	Melk, ben.
133	Melk StiB, MS 222, fols 79b-82a	xiii	1661m	Leg.	Melk, ben.
134	Melk StiB, MS 1706, fols 9v-11	xiii$^{2/2}$	?	Misc.	Vienna
135	Metz BM, MS 1149 (salis 3), fols 2va-19b	xii	1663 prol.	VS	Notre Dame, Tongerloo, prem.
136	Michaelbeuern StiB, MS Man.cart.67, fols 251vb-253b	xv$^{3/4}$	1661m	Misc.	Michaelbeuern, ben.

Appendix 1: The Ms. Tradition of BHL 1663

137	Metz BM, MS 305, fol. 1-?	xiii	1663	Misc.	Saint-Arnould, Metz, ben.
138	Mons BCU, MS R4/G 843 (olim A. Wine 3), fols 95-115v	xiv	1663	Kath. & 2 other saints	Saint-Ghislain or Notre Dame de Bonne Espérance (Tournai), ben./prem.
139	Mons BCU, MS R4/A 30/196 (213) (olim 301/968/439), fols 62-75v	xiii	epit.	VS	ND de Bonne Espérance, Saint-Foillan (*apud Reuxium*)
140	Montpellier FM, MS H.30, fols 1a-8va	xii	1663 prol.	Passionale	Saint-Bénigne, Dijon, ben.
141	Montpellier FM, MS H.78, fols 33vb-40a	xiii	1663a	Misc.	
142	Munich BSB, Cgm 1115, fols 1a-5va	xv	epit.	Misc.	
143	Munich BSB, Clm 701, fols 247v-253v	1280	Epit.	Lect.	Augsburg?
144	Munich BSB, Clm 2610, fols 16-26	xiii	1663 prol.	VS + Misc.	Alderspach, cist.
145	Munich BSB, Clm 2617, fols 127-153	c. 1248	1663	Misc.	Donauwörth, ben.?
146	Munich BSB, Clm 9506, fols 98v-100vb	xii & xiii	1663	VS	Oberaltaich, ben.
147	Munich BSB, Clm 5664, fols 1-1v + 7-33v	xv	1663 prol.	Misc.	Diessen, reg. can. aug.
148	Munich BSB, Clm 12389, fols 246-254	xiv-xv	1663	Misc.	

149	Munich BSB, Clm 14473, fols 94v-107v	xii + xiii	1663	VS	St. Emmeram, Regensburg, ben.
150	Munich BSB, Clm 15760, fols 169vb-176va	1450	1663? prol.	Misc.	Salzburg
151	Munich BSB, Clm 17140, fols 40-55	xii	1663	VS	Schäftlarn, prem.
152	Munich BSB, Clm 21549, fols 293-297	xiv	1661m	Misc.	Weihenstefan, ben.
153	Munich BSB, Clm 21658, fols 36a-b + 38va-48a	xv	1663 prol.	Misc.	Weihenstefan, ben.
154	Munich BSB, Clm 22279, fols 155-180	xii	1663	Misc.	Windberg, prem.
155	Namur MA, MS fonds ville 15, fols 270-275v	xiii-xiv	1663	VS	Saint-Hubert, Ardennes, ben.
156	Namur MA, MS fonds ville 2, fols 286v-290v	xiv	?	Lect.	
157	Nijmegen UB, MS 532, fols 27-45	xv	1663 prol.	VS	Witten
163	Oxford Bodleain, MS Fell 2, pp 199-224	xii^{ex}	1663	Leg.	St Augustine, Canterbury, ben.
158	Oxford Bodleian, MS Laud. Misc. sc. 75, fols 1a-9vb	xiii/xiv	1663 prol.	Misc.	Mainz, carth.
159	Oxford Bodleian, MS Laud. Misc. sc. 114, fols 164-184v	xii^{ex}	1663 prol.	VS	Pershore, ben.
160	Oxford Bodleian, MS Laud. Misc. sc. 430, fols 11a-20b	xiii	epit.? prol.	Misc.	Eberbach, cist. (Italian hand)

Appendix 1: The Ms. Tradition of BHL 1663 267

161	Oxford Bodleian, MS Lyell 5, fols 151a-163b	1200-1250	1663	Becket & Kath.	England, cist.
163	Paderborn Erzbischöfliche Akad. Bib., MS Ba.2, fols 241v-252	xv	?	Leg.	Böddeken, ben.
164	Paris Arsenal 233 [*item lost*]	xii	?	?	English?
165	Paris Arsenal, MS 938, fols 1v-8	xii-xiii	1663a	VS	Saint-Victor, Paris, reg. can. aug.
166	Paris Arsenal, MS 995, fols 104vb-118b	xiii	1663	Lect.	Saint-Jacques, Paris, dom.
167	Paris BnF, MS lat. 810, fols 124-128v + 141va-144b	xiv/xv	1673	Lect.	Saint-Martial, Limoges, ben.
168	Paris BnF, MS lat. 15149, fols 46-65v	xiii-xiv	1663	Misc.	Saint-Victor, Paris, reg. can. aug.
169	Paris BnF, MS lat. 1864, fols 85vb-101vb	xiv (xiii)	1663 prol.	Leg.	
170	Paris BnF, MS lat. 1970, fols 54-70v	xi	1663	Misc.	Fécamp, ben.
171	Paris BnF, MS lat. 3809, fols 145va-148a	xiv	epit.	Lect.	Moissac
172	Paris BnF, MS lat. 5278, fols 410b-416vb	xiii	1663a	Leg.	Moselle, Metz
173	Paris BnF, MS lat. 5308, fols 63v-72	xii	1663	Leg.	Lorraine (Metz)
174	Paris BnF, MS lat. 5333, fols 79a-101vb	1458	1663 prol.	Leg.	Sainte-Geneviève, Paris, reg. can.
175	Paris BnF, MS lat. 5336, fols 108v-119v	xii^{med}	1663	Leg.	English

176	Paris BnF, MS lat. 5343, fols 135-137v + 140-148v	xi/xii	1663 prol.	Leg.	Sainte-Trinité, Vendôme, ben.
177	Paris BnF, MS lat. 5360, fols 215vb-233va	xiv	1663 prol.	Leg.	Jouarre-en-Brie, ben. fem. ?
178	Paris BnF, MS lat. 5365, fols 163-171	xii	1663 prol.	Leg.	Saint-Martial, Limoges, ben.
179	Paris BnF, MS lat. 5371, fols 39a-51va	xii + xiii	1663 prol.	Leg.	Dioc. of Cambrai (= fols 55-231)
180	Paris BnF, MS lat. 8995, fols 118v-130	c. 1300	1663	Leg.	St. Barbara, Cologne, carth.
181	Paris BnF, MS lat. 11754, fols 213-221a	xiii + xiv	1663a prol.	Leg.	Saint-Germain-des-Prés, Paris
182	Paris BnF, MS lat. 11759, fols 251vb-258va	xiv	1663 prol.	VS	Saint-Ayoul, Provins, ben.
183	Paris BnF, MS lat. 12259, fols 267-286	xii	epit. prol.	Misc.	Saint-Germain-des-Prés, Paris (Soissons?)
184	Paris BnF, MS lat. 14293, fols 210a-217vb	xiii	1663a short	Misc.	Saint-Victor, Marseille, ben.
185	Paris BnF, MS lat. 14364, fols 150a-156a	xiii	1663a	Pass.	Saint-Victor, Paris, reg. aug. can.
186	Paris BnF, MS lat. 14651, fols 173-173v	xv	prol.	Leg.	Saint-Victor, Paris, reg. aug. can.
187	Paris BnF, MS lat. 15030, fols 25-41	xv	1663a prol.	VS	Saint-Victor, Paris?
188	Paris BnF, MS lat. 15149, fols 54-65v	xiii-xiv	1663	Misc.	Saint-Victor, Paris, , reg. aug. can.
189	Paris BnF, MS lat. 16566, fols 1-5v	xiii	epit.	VS	Sorbonne

Appendix 1: The Ms. Tradition of BHL 1663

190	Paris BnF, MS lat. 16735, fols 191a-197b	xii[ex]	1663 prol.	Leg. (LN)	Chaâlis, cist.
191	Paris BnF, MS lat. 17007, fols 203-210v	xii-xiii	1663 prol.	Leg. (LN)	Val Abbey (Val-d'Oise), cist.
192	Paris BnF, MS lat. 18309, fols 168vb-171vb	xiii	1663 end	Misc.	Jacobins de la rue Saint-Honoré
193	Paris BnF, MS n.a. lat. 2288, fols 1v-13v	1425	epit.	Leg.	Remiremont, ben.
194	Paris Mazarine, MS 399, fols 243va-247b	xiv	epit.	Lect.	Saint-Magloire, Paris, ben.
195	Paris Mazarine, MS 1713, fols 46va-57a	xiii	1663a prol.	Misc.	Collège de Navarre
196	Paris Sainte-Geneviève, MS 131, fols 287a-290a	xiii	?	Lect.	Saint-Lo, Rouen, aug.
197	Paris Sainte-Geneviève, MS 134, fol. 226	xii	1663a prol.	VS	Saint-Quentin, Belval, (ben.?)
198	Paris Sainte-Geneviève, MS 552, fols 202a-209vb	xii/xiii	1663a prol.	Lect.	Senlis cathedral
199	Pavia BS Legendarium Paviense, fol. G.4v-H.ij	1523	1661m	Leg.	San Felice, Pavia, ben.
200	Prague KMK, MS 263 (A.158), fols 63-82v	xiv			
201	Prague KMK, MS E.62.2, fols 68b-70a	xiv	debate	Misc.	Bohemia

202	Prague KMK, MS E.66, fols 231a-237a	xiv	epit. prol.	Misc.	
203	Prague NKČR, MS I.N.23, fols 220-221v	xv	?	Misc.	
204	Prague NKČR, MS I.B.17, fols 195a-201va	xv	epit.	Misc.	
205	Prague NKČR, MS I.E.18, fols 190a-192a	1395	epit.	Misc.	
206	Prague NKČR, MS 8.B.32 (1468), fols 198b	1405	?	Misc.	
207	Prague NKČR, MS 6.D.15 (1104), fols 337b-338b	xv	LA?	Misc.	
208	Prague NKČR, MS 6.E.1 (1114), fols 2-30b	xiii-xiv	1663 prol.	VS	
209	Prague NKČR, MS 8.D.29 (1524), fols 18v-24b	xiv	1663 prol.	Misc.	
210	Prague NKČR, MS 14.B.16 (2455), fols 108va-124a	xiii	1663	VS	
211	Reims BM, MS 299, fol. 266	xiii-xiv	epit.	Lect.	Saint-Thierry, Reims, ben. ?
212	Reims BM, MS 303 (F.467), fols 150b-152bis b	xii/xiii	epit.	Lect.	Saint-Remi, Reims, ben.
213	Rome Casanatense, MS 1055, fols 138-153v	xii	1663	Lect.	Hautefontaine, Marne, cist.

Appendix 1: The Ms. Tradition of BHL 1663

214	Rome BNC, MS Sessor. 147, fols 43-47	xiv	1663a	Libellus	Saint-Augustine, Cumis
215	Rome Vallicelliana, MS F.49, fols 52-71v	1441	1663	VS	
216	Rouen BP, MS 1388 (U.32), fols 163va-165va	xii	epit.	VS	Saint-Évroult, ben., or Fécamp?
217	Rouen BP, MS 1394 (U.119), fols 131-167	xii	1663 prol.	VS	Mortagne, aug.
218	Rouen BP, MS 1399 (U.2), fols 185m-n, 186-194	xii	1663 prol.	VS	Jumièges, ben.
219	Rouen BP, MS 1415 (U.17), fols 223vb-225v	xiv/xv?	epit.	Leg.	Fécamp, ben.
220	Sion Chapt., MS 10, fols 170-185v	xiii	1663	Misc.	
221	Sotheby's London, 7th Dec. 1982, Lot 55, fols 1b-23	1150-1180	?	Misc.	French?
222	Sankt Florian StiB, MS XI.252, fol. 234	xiii + xv	1663	Misc.	Wiblingen, ben.
223	St Gall StaB (Vad.), MS 70, fols 135-142v	xiv-xv	1663 prol.	Misc.	St Gall, ben.
224	Saint-Omer BP, MS 716 vol. viii, fols 182v-192v	xiii	1663 prol.	LF	Clairmarais, cist.
225	Saint-Dié-des-Vosges BM, MS 4, fols 218-225v	xii (xiv)	1663a	Lect.	Saint-Dié-des-Vosges, ben.
226	Stuttgart WLB, HB MS XIV 18, fols 97v-106	xiv	1663	Passionale	Weingarten, ben.
227	Turin BN, MS I.V.36, fols 17-23 [*destroyed*]	xii + xiii	1661m	VS	Staffarda, cist.

228	Treviso BC, MS 1818, fols 1a-22	xv	1663	Misc.		
229	Trier Bischöfliche Seminarbibliothek, MS 33 (olim R.I.8), fols 120-123v	xv	1663a	Leg.	St. Paul, Trier, coll.	
230	Trier BS, MS 34 (R.I.9), fols 190v-191	xv	?	Misc.	St. Eucharius-Matthias, Trier, ben.	
231	Trier BS, MS 36 (R.I.12), fols 163-177v	*post* 1235	1663	Leg.	St. Maximinus, Trier, ben.	
232	Trier BS, MS 98 (R.VI.I), fols 118-120v?	xiii	1664b	VS	St. Eucharius-Matthias, Trier, ben.	
233	Trier Bistumsarchiv, MS Abt. 95 Nr. 62, fols 126v-137v	xii-xiii	epit.	VS	Helmarshausen, then Abdinghof, ben.	
234	Trier StB, MS 388/1152 2°, fols 116v + 117-118v	xi-xii	epit.	Pass.	St. Simeon, Trier, priory	
235	Trier StB, MS 535/1531 8°, fols 187v-189	xiii/xiv	?	Misc.	St. Eucharius-Matthias, Trier, ben.	
236	Trier StB, MS 1050/1261 8°, fols 226v	1130-1170	1661m	Misc.	St. Eucharius-Matthias, Trier, ben.	
237	Trier StB, MS 1140/443 8°, fols 17-41	xv	1663	Leg.	Trier, jes.	
238	Trier StB, MS 2002/92 4°, fols 83-95	xv^{in}	1663	Leg.	Mettlach, Jesuits of Trier	
239	Troyes BM, MS 1876, fols 121v-140	xiii-xiv	1663 prol.	Misc.	Clairvaux, cist.	
240	Valenciennes BM, MS 513 (471A), fols 188vb-202a	1145-1169	1663 prol.	Lect.	Saint-Amand, ben.	

Appendix 1: The Ms. Tradition of BHL 1663   273

241	Vatican BAV, MS Pal.lat. 362, fol. 71	1401-1500	epit.	Misc.	Frankenthal, aug.
242	Vatican AC San Pietro, MS A.8 (olim G), fols 410-412	xv	epit. prol.	Lect.	San Pietro, Rome
243	Vatican AC San Pietro, MS A.9 (olim H), fols 220-221v	1339	epit. prol.	Lect.	San Pietro, Rome
244	Vercelli BCap, MS 12 (68), fols 284v-289v	xiv	1661m		
245	Verdun BM, MS 1, fols 119b-120	xiii	epit.	Lect.	Saint-Vanne, Verdun, ben.
246	Vienna ÖNB, MS 452 (Hist.eccl. 97), fols 1-3	xiii	1663 prol.	Libellus	
247	Vienna ÖNB, MS 1321 (Theol. 618), fols 100va-113a	xiii	1663	Misc.	
248	Vienna ÖNB, MS 1570 (Theol. 363), fols 39a-52a	xiii	epit.	Misc.	
249	Vienna ÖNB, MS s.n. 3610, fol. 131v	xii/xiii	1663	Misc.	Lambach, ben. ?
250	Vienna ÖNB, MS s.n. 12754, fols 265v-276	xv	1663?	Leg.	Corsendonk Abbey, Antwerp, aug.
251	Vienna ÖNB, MS s.n. 12835, fols 126-131v	xv	1663	Misc.	
252	Wolfenbüttel HAB August., MS 35.1.Aug.4°, fols 187-194	xv	?	Misc.	Strasbourg cathedral ?

253	Wolfenbüttel HAB, MS Helmst. 504, fols 10-40	xiv	1663	VS	
254	Wolfenbüttel HAB, MS Helmst. 396, fols 10-36	xv	1663?	Misc.	Braunschweig, ben.
255	Würzburg UB, MS M.p.th.f.122, fols 58va-67v	xiv	?	VV & Misc.	Ebrach Abbey, cist., Italy & Germany
256	Würzburg UB, MS M.ch.f.121, fols 260-261	1430	?	Misc.	St. Jacob, Würzburg, ben.
257	Zurich ZB, MS Rh. 18, fols 282-287v	1150-1200	1661m	Lect.	Rheinau, ben.
258	Zurich ZB, MS Rh. 101, fols 8v-29	1300	1663	Libellus	
259	Zwettl StiB, MS 15, fols 17va-21	xii^{in}	1663a prol.	MLA	Zwettl, cist.
260	Zwettl StiB, MS 71, fols 142b-145b	xii^{ex}	epit.	Pass.	Zwettl, cist.

APPENDIX 2

EDITION OF THE
PASSIO SANCTAE KATERINAE
(BHL 1661M)

This epitome is an example of how the relatively stable text of BHL 1663 engendered epitomes which in turn were to have their own more or less solid diffusions, alongside epitomes which were to be a one off (such as Angers, BM, MS 121, and no doubt many others). This is interesting – it means that there was a need for such epitomes, but more importantly, that some of them did their job so well that they were passed from one scriptorium to the next. One reason for editing this particular epitome is to illustrate the variety and interplay of epitomes, well into the period during which the *legendae novae* started to appear.

The earliest witness to this epitome of Katherine's passion is BL, Harley MS 12 where it occupies the three folios at the end of the manuscript. It was written out by the Great Domesday Book (GDB) scribe between 1080 and 1100, perhaps even after he had undertaken, between 1086 and 1088, the enormous task of assembling into a whole the disparate records of the Great Survey of England, undertaken at the behest of William the Conqueror.[1] The GDB scribe came from, worked, or was based in the West Country,

---

[1] Michael Gullick and Caroline Thorn, 'The scribes of the Great Domesday Book: A preliminary account', *The Journal of the Society of Archivists*, 8 (1986), 78–80. The survey took place under the aegis of Bishop of William of Durham, see Pierre Chaplais, 'William of Saint-Calais and the Domesday Survey', in *Domesday Studies*, ed. James C. Holt (Woodbridge, 1987), pp. 65–77.

somewhere west of a line running from Winchester to Oxford to Hereford (but certainly not Worcester).[2] This means that the date of writing of BHL 1661m is close to the date of composition of BHL 1663 which precedes it, turning the former into additional evidence for the dating of the latter.[3] Given that BHL 1663 itself is a product of northern France, knowledge of Katherine's passion must have reached England before 1080 or so. The other two twelfth-century witnesses were copied at Trier (Trier, Stadtbibliothek, MS 1050/1261 8°) and Rheinau (Zurich, Zentralbibliothek, MS Rh. 18). Witnesses from the thirteenth century onwards come from much further afield: on the basis of their provenances one can see the text moving westwards and southwards into Italy (Staffarda, Cividale) and Austria (Klosterneuburg).

The division into readings indicated in some of the manuscripts, particularly such early witnesses as BL, Harley MS 12 and Zurich, ZB, MS Rh. 18 (signposted by 'incipiunt lectiones de Sancta Katherina'), implies that the epitome was created as a response to the growing importance of Katherine's cult and her inclusion in the liturgy. In BL, Harley MS 12, each reading is followed by neumed responses, crowded into the margins and for the most part lost due to trimming. There are no such responses in Zurich, ZB, MS Rh. 18; instead the text there is followed by a single neumed response (fol. 287v:

---

[2] These observations were shared with me privately by Michael Gullick, who stressed that they are, at present, tentative and not conclusive. It is also he who alerted me to the fact that BHL 1661m was written out by the GDB scribe and that Chapelais' suggestion that this scribe came from or was trained at Durham or Winchester is not likely.

[3] Since Angers, BM, MS 121 contains an epitomized version of BHL 1663 that is divided into readings and its copying took place between 1052 and 1087, one may suppose that BHL 1663 was composed earlier than this, perhaps at some point in the first half of the eleventh century (after 1034, the date of the foundation of La Trinité of Vendôme, where Paris, BnF, MS lat. 5343 originates), although I cannot say with certainty exactly when.

'ex tumba sanctae Katherinae resudat oleum sacrum …'), a hymn (fol. 288: 'ave Katherina martyr et regina'), and a sequence (fol. 288: 'regi regum decantet fidelis chorus').

The behaviour of Brussels KBR 4564-68

What initially looked like a straightforward editing task turned into something a little more complicated when one witness (Brussels, KBR, MS 4564-68, [*B*]) revealed itself as containing passages not present in the other manuscripts. Moreover, it contains a large number of impossible readings, most of which are the result of the misinterpretation of abbreviations, and often due to the scribe. The aim, therefore, as regards *B* on its own, is to give the text of this version (of which there exists just one manuscript), eliminating careless errors of *B*'s exemplar. Of course, there can be cases where it is not so easy to distinguish between *B*'s redactor and its scribe. I have tried to carry this out but there will no doubt be cases where my choice is questionable. More careful scrutiny than I have been able to undertake is needed to arrive at a satisfactory understanding of how *B* came into being. There are, however, a few observations that can be made at this stage.

The most important question as regards the text in *B* is to establish if it is an unfinished version or an intermediary stage of the epitome. This would explain the additional passages not present in any of the other manuscripts. This scenario is a possibility, even though the diffusion of the epitome, with a more or less stable text, would suggest otherwise. But as seen in Appendix 1, an independent epitome that did not engender its own tradition is not without precedent. The other option is that *B* is an amplification of the epitome: someone took the trouble to insert back into the text passages which had previously been cut.

The first explanation, namely that *B* is an intermediary stage in the process of epitomization, is attractive and more immediately obvious. At first sight it looks like *B*, and BHL

1661m itself, were conceived on the basis of BHL 1663a (the only other epitome of BHL 1663 with its own significant diffusion). In many cases both epitomes cut exactly the same passages by jumping from one passage ahead to another. For example:[4]

> a) Following Katherine's assertion in section **7** that 'dii enim non sunt plures', both epitomes jump ahead to Dobson, l. 145, thus leaving out the end of her speech.
>
> b) At **39** both epitomes jump from Dobson, l. 562 to l. 570.
>
> c) Both epitomes leave out the description of Porphyrius: 'quia primae cohortis praefecturam agebat et magnis rerum possessionibus pollebat' (**64**, Dobson, ll. 763-64).
>
> d) At the end of **96** (Dobson, l. 988), BHL 1661m jumps ahead to Dobson, l. 998, in exactly the same way as BHL 1663a. However, the assertion that 'Christianorum aliquis subvertit' has been extended by 'et a cultura deorum avertit' in BHL 1661m.
>
> e) The detail of how God should look out for those who remember Katherine ('fugiat ab eis pestilentia et fames, morbus et clades, et universa aurarum intemperies; fiat in finibus eorum terrae fecunda messio, aer salubrior, et, secundum elementorum gratiam, iocunda fructuum ubertas', Dobson, ll. 1115-18), as the saint requests in her final prayer, has been left out from both epitomes (sections **116-17**)
>
> f) Both epitomes cut out 'stultum valde est te in hoc elaborare in quo laboris nullum poteris emolumentum acquirere' (Dobson, l. 624) at section **41**.

As is clear from this list of examples, both epitomes cut a number of identical passages. This cannot have been coincidental, and implies that there is a relationship between the two. However, a more careful scrutiny of both epitomes

---

[4] References in bold are to my section numbers of the edition, and to Dobson in the usual manner. He records the readings of 1663a in his second apparatus, where the consensus of the four manuscripts (P_1 P_2 H Z) he collated is designated by Σ.

reveals that BHL 1661m retains passages that have been cut from BHL 1663a. Consider the following:

BHL 1661m (sections 65-68)	BHL 1663a (Dobson, ll. 777-802)
Audi, inquit, Porphyri!	Audi inquit, Porphyri, et animadverte: Mundus iste velut <u>carcer</u> est tenebrosus, <u>in quo nullus ita nascitur ut non moriatur</u>; illa superna patria, pro qua fit mundi contemptus, velut civitas est, sole numquam indigens, <u>ubi nulla turbat adversitas, molestia nulla inquietat, sed perennis laetitia, felicitas regnat sempiterna.</u>
Illa superna patria pro qua fit mundi contemptus velut civitas est sole numquam indigens, <u>ubi nulla turbat adversitas, molestia nulla inquietat, sed perennis illic laetitia, *iocunditas aeterna*, felicitas regnat sempiterna. *Si quaeris quid ibi sit ubi tanta et talis beatitudo consistit, aliter dici non potest nisi quicquid boni est ibi est et quicquid mali est nusquam est. Quod inquis bonum? Illud est, dico, quod oculus non vidit nec auris audivit, nec in cor hominis ascendit quae preparavit deus diligentibus se.*'	
	Parva sunt quae dico ad ea quae visu et rerum veritate experieris si fidelis usque in finem perseverareris'.

<u>Underlined</u> = based on Ambrose Autpert
Italics = based on Ambrose Autpert *and* left out of 1663a

The presence of this passage in BHL 1661m, ultimately derived from Autpert's *Conflictus* but used in this way in BHL 1663, and its absence from BHL 1663a, implies that the latter was not at the basis of the epitome under discussion here. It is unlikely that the epitomizer of BHL 1661m would have come across the *Conflictus* independently. Another sizeable chunk of text that has been cut from BHL 1663a but stands in BHL 1661m is at sections **43-44**. Further, there are plenty of short phrases present in 1661m but absent from BHL 1663a that support the conclusion that BHL 1661m is not a shortening of BHL 1663a.[5]

The most likely explanation for this overlap between the two epitomes as well as their incongruous gaps would be an intermediary version, not yet identified, which conserves the passages not in BHL 1663a, and which, like BHL 1663a and BHL 1661m, omits the same passages. What then of the possibility that the text in *B* is amplifying BHL 1661m by adding passages from elsewhere? It is by scrutinizing the joints, the places where *B* departs from the text of the epitome and offers the deleted text, that the question can be answered. What is needed are cases where *B* can be shown to be following the epitome *and* its source-text both at the same time, which could result in grammatical or sense errors. Another behaviour useful for clinching the matter would be the presence in *B* of certain readings unique to BHL 1661m. A number of examples from the many on offer may suffice to illustrate the point.

A curious reading is 'concremari' at the end of 33; the epitomizer changed the original 'poenalibus incendiis cruciari' to the more definitive 'concremari': most likely because he omitted the whole narrative of the rhetors' martyrdom in the life, retaining only 'in quibus ... comparuit' (section 37)as a sufficient indication. *B* includes the narrative, yet has the epitome's innovation 'concremari'. This situation can only be

---

[5] The passages in question are: [1] anno regni sui tricesimo quinto; [26] philosophicas dissertiones + syllogisticas disputationes; [40] faciam ... erigam; [48] illi puellaribus ... noluisset; [49] teneretur ... iniquam; [51] prae claritate; [61] mox ... ierit; [64] qui pollebat; [78] in vocem ... magam istam et; [79] tunc deum ... auxilium; [63] ne verearis ... mansura; [67] si quaeris ... diligentibus se; [68] pro Christi nomine sustinenda; [76] sed ut michi ... diligo; [77] tu ergo ... holocaustum; [90] has inter media ... membratim; [95] quae te ... coegit; [104] vesano ... indulges; [107] ecce porphyrius ... confitetur; [107] conversa ... onerare.

the result of the redactor adding passages to the epitome from a fuller text.

A particularly interesting example is at section 77: here the epitomizer makes use of a phrase from a passage he has discarded. The phrase 'ipse deus meus, amator meus, ipse pastor et sponsus unicus meus' (Dobson, l. 851) is originally the firmly emphatic declaration of faith at the end of Katherine's assertion that she had not eaten any real food in prison. But since the description of this encounter and the exchange between the two main protagonists has been left out in the epitome, this declaration is now available for use, still within the same episode, but this time as an affirmation that Katherine is eager to suffer. *B*, which does offer the deleted passage (at sections 72-74), follows the epitome in displacing the phrase.[6]

After a large overlap with BHL 1663 (or an epitome) not present in BHL 1661m, *B* returns to the text of the epitome (sections 78-84). To bridge the gap created by this omission of Katherine's flogging, the epitomizer of BHL 1661m inserted a little explanatory phrase before the arrival of the wheel-builder Cursathes: 'cum ad haec tyrannus vehementissimo furore succenderetur superveniens' (section 85). In the epitome this makes sense, and while it does not feel completely out of place in *B*, it nevertheless is an indication of the interpolator's carelessness. In other words, he is happy to interpolate passages, and on occasion combine them with the epitome where the 'original' BHL 1663 gives him no reason to do so. And in so doing, he does not take the trouble to smooth over the, albeit small, incongruities he has created.[7]

---

[6] It has been completely cut out from the epitome BHL 1663a, see Dobson, l. 851. Another 'displaced' passage is at sections 27–28, as well as at section 109. The latter differs from the other two instances in that here the epitomizer inserted a phrase from further ahead in the text.

[7] Sections 80–82 contain a particularly decisive clue as to the 'source' text for *B*. In the epitome BHL 1663a this passage ('factum est autem ...

Another example is at 98. Here *B* is the only witness to retain 'tyrannus crudelis'; it seems unlikely that *B* could have arrived at exactly this constellation by pure conjecture (other possibilities: *Maxentius imperator,* or simply *tyrannus*). Much more plausible is the scenario that the redactor picked up the phrase from elsewhere. However, at the same time, he follows the epitome's toned down 'ad locum supplicii trahi', instead of the more gruesome 'transfixas clavis ferreis mamillas ab imo pectore extorqueri' (Dobson, l. 1005).

One last example, insignificant on its own but when set next to the others, is rather telling. At 112 the epitome reads: 'quae cum ad locum passion*is* duceretur, multae ... '. *B* preserves the following: 'quae cum ad locum praefixum passion*is* properaret, respiciens vidit ... , multae ... '. The corresponding passage in BHL 1663 (Dobson, l. 1094) has this: 'quae cum ad locum passion*i* praefixum properaret, respiciens vidit ... '. In the epitome, the genitive *passionis* is directly dependent on *locum*, there being nothing else on which it can depend. In BHL 1663 the reading is *passioni*, a dative which depends on *praefixum* (cut by the epitomizer of BHL 1661m). *B*, however, has clumsily conflated the two.

As these examples make abundantly clear, *B*'s redactor was using a text related to BHL 1663 to enlarge the epitome BHL 1661m, as opposed to the situation whereby 1661m is a shortened version of the text in *B*. Thus, a long text like BHL 1663 did not just shrink over time. *B* is an example that growth in the opposite direction was also possible. A similar

> voces', Dobson, ll. 894–905) has been moved from its original place in BHL 1663 to describe Katherine's final journey to the place of her passion (and thus fitting in much more neatly with similar crowds following Christ on the way to Golgotha at Luke 23.27–28: 'sequebatur autem illum mluta turba populi et mulierum quae plangebant et lamentabant eum. Conversus autem ad illas Iesus dixit: "filiae Hierusalem nolite flere super me, sed super vos ipsas flete et super filios vestros."'). However, *B* is following the original sequence of BHL 1663 by leaving the passage in its context.

sort of thing seems to have happened in the case of Paris, BnF, MS n.a. lat. 2288, with the difference that it adds passages not found anywhere else. A complete collation of all those manuscripts that appear to preserve epitomes of BHL 1663 could very well bring to light more witnesses that behave in a comparable way.

The epitomizer of BHL 1661m at work

What is attractive about epitomes is the insight they give into the way they were created, by virtue of the fact that one can compare them with the original if it survives. The epitomizer had at his disposal several mechanisms for creating a shorter text from the one he had chosen to tackle. Here are a few examples of how the epitomizer of 1661m went about his work.

Simple cuts: the most obvious way to shorten a text perceived as too long is to cut dispensable material, and making only minimal changes to the end bits left hanging. Episodes that have been left out include the prologue, the historical introduction, and Katherine's last exchange with the emperor.

Cutting and smoothing: this method can be seen at work already in the epitome's first sentence (section 1). The epitomizer has reduced the original three sentences (Dobson, ll. 45-52) to one by cutting out the content of the edict. He keeps the first sentence up to 'iubens', and then jumps ahead to 'omnes ... incolas'. In line with the new context, he changed 'nostri' (previously direct speech/content of the edict) to 'sui'. The episode of announcing the sacrifice to the assembled people has been suppressed ('iubet omnes introduci ...', Dobson, l. 55).

Pinning: in what could almost be termed a deliberate *saut-du-même-au-même*, the epitomizer uses little recurring constellations of words in one sentence or passages as pins or pegs, and cuts out the intervening text. An example of this process can be seen at section 63: after 'emercatur' the epitomizer suppresses the first peg – 'ne ergo verearis' – and moves straight to the second peg – 'ne verearis inquam' (Dobson, ll. 757-62). The emphatic 'inquam' perhaps indicates that the previous statement could be omitted. In the same way at section 85, the epitomizer ignores the first occurrence of 'imperator non' and moves ahead to its repetition (Dobson, ll. 921-22).

Cut and paste: this method, also familiar to modern authors, namely moving a passage from its original location to another, is not without examples in this epitome, for instance at section 77 (already alluded to above). Another instance is the description of the emperor's anger at section 42: 'hic tyrannus commotus furore'. This has been put together by using the original 'hic tyrannus' (Dobson, l. 648) and combining it with 'commotus furore' (Dobson, l. 841), which the epitomizer chose to cut at section 72, but which *B* is happy to use again in the reinstated passage. Similarly, at section 108, the description of the emperor's anger – 'ille insania et furore debriatus' – consists of the previously discarded 'ira et furore inebriatus' (Dobson, l. 648) in combination with 'debriatus' (Dobson, l. 1093).

Summarizing/simplifying: there is at least one instance in which the epitome makes better sense than it does in 1663. The description of Christ as someone 'qui est vera scientia et credentium beatituto sempiterna' (Dobson, l. 362) is rendered much clearer in the epitome by the addition of 'in se' before 'credentium' (section 26). The result is that what was previously understood is now explicitly stated, and reveals the epitomizer to be grammatically astute. The encounter between the queen and Porphyrius at sections 48-50 has been heavily cut: the justification for the queen's burning desire to see Katherine has been left out with the exception of the beginning of the sentence: 'pernotuerat vero reginae crudelissima viri sententia de beata Katerina' (Dobson, l. 675). Instead of going into details, the epitomizer simply writes 'unde' instead of 'fit', and makes the queen a more active protagonist by placing 'cupiebat' at the end of the sentence instead of 'fit'. Similarly, the epitomizer has dispensed with the unmediated appearance of Porphyrius (Dobson, l. 686). Instead, he moves ahead to 'evocans', and thus again makes the queen more active. The original 'Alexandrinorum redit ad urbem' becomes a more snappy 'Alexandriam redierat' at section 72.

Just as BHL 1663 was produced with care, so the epitomizer of BHL 1661m paid attention to detail. He created a text that retained the essence of Katherine's passion, without laying too much emphasis on the theological debate. Crucially, it was now short enough to be read in the liturgy.

The manuscripts of the *Passio Sanctae Katerinae* BHL 1661m

B

Brussels, KBR, MS 4564-68, fols 34-45v, s. xiii, prov. Jesuits of Bruges.

> A thirteenth-century collection of miscellaneous texts, including the *Computus gerlandi* (fols 2-22), and *mensurae medicinales* (fols 28-34). Three fragments of a charter dated to February 1229 by the abbess of Saint-Pierre at Laon, at fols 1v, 47, and 48v.[8]
>
> Parchment, 48 folios, 15.8 x 11 cm, long lines and 2 columns, ruling in lead, rubrics, several hands.

Bro

Bronzini, 'La leggenda', 379-83.

Readings from the printed legendary at Pavia, and a manuscript at Pavia:

> **LP** (collated from Bronzini)

---

[8] 'Catalogus codicum hagiographicorum Bibliothecae Regiae Bruxellensis, 1: Codices latini membranei, part. 1', Hagiographi Bollandiani, *AB* 2–5, Brussels 1886, 463–64.

Pavia, Biblioteca del Seminario, fol. G.4v-H.ij, 1523, prov. San Felice, Pavia.

This printed legendary contains twenty-three saints' lives.

Paper, 58 folios, quarto (height of printed page 18 cm), 2 columns, gothic letters, from the workshop of Bernardino de Garaldi. Poncelet observed that the same passion of Katherine also stood in a manuscript each at Turin and Vercelli. It is likely that Bronzini thus found the other two witnesses he included in his edition, although he cited no readings from the Turin manuscript.[9]

V (collated from Bronzini)

Vercelli, Biblioteca Capitolare, Fondo Manoscritti, MS 12 (68), fols 284v-289v, s. xiv.

A fourteenth-century collection of saints' lives, including a legend of the dedication of a church at Vercelli and that of Gaudentius of Novara (BHL 3278-a). Fol. 2v contains a bull by Pope Boniface IX (d. 1404) from the seventh year of his reign (1395?).[10]

Parchment, 301 folios, 45 x 30 cm, 2 columns.

---

[9] Albert Poncelet, 'Le Légendier de Saint-Felix de Pavie imprimé en 1523', *AB*, 23 (1904), 459–64. The Turin manuscript was destroyed in the fire that devastated the library in 1904. Bronzini counted this manuscript among the witnesses for 1661m probably on the basis of Poncelet's observation in the description of the Pavia legendary. A description of Turin BN, MS I.V.36, s. xii/xiii, prov. Staffarda, can be found in *AB*, 28 (1909), 450–51. Poncelet had seen the manuscript in October 1902. Bronzini (b. 1925) cannot have seen this manuscript: the fact that he did not include any readings from it in his apparatus makes this clear, although he did not point this out.

[10] See Mazzatinti, *Inventari dei manoscritti delle biblioteche d'Italia*, vol. 31: *Prato, Vercelli, Novara* (Florence, 1925), p. 79.

Appendix 2: Edition of the *Passio s. Katerinae*   287

C

Cambridge, Corpus Christi College, MS 405, fols 72v-79v, s. xiv[in], prov. St John of Jerusalem, Waterford.

> A fourteenth-century collection of charters, liturgical texts and poems. The liturgical texts (fols 17-93) are all divided into readings, each reading followed by responses. These lessons are the supplement to a Breviary, from the early fourteenth-century(?).[11]

> Vellum, ii + 251 folios, 22 x 15 cm, 24 long lines, ruling in crayon, rubrics, catchwords at bottom of folios for binding, proto-gothic hands. As regards Katherine's passion, the catalogue refers the reader to BHL 1658.[12] The text has a lacuna from section 69-111, and a slightly different ending.

K (collated from facsimile)

Klosterneuburg, Stiftsbibliothek, CCl 79, fols 57b-58vb, 1260/80, prov. Klosterneuburg.

> A thirteenth-century collection of liturgical texts, including Ado's *Martyrology* (fols 2a-47a), Augustine's *Regula secunda et tertia* (fols 49vb-56b), excerpts from homilies, and a necrology (fols 76v-107v).

> Parchment, i+136 folios, 40.5/41 x 30/30.5cm, two columns, signs of heavy usage, textualis formata and textualis.[13]

H

London, British Library, Harley MS 12, fols 141-143v, *c.* 1080x1100, prov. West Country.

---

[11] See James, *A Descriptive Catalogue*, II, pp. 277–88.

[12] Ibid.

[13] See Alois Haidinger, *Katalog der Handschriften des Augustiner Chorherrenstifts Klosterneuburg*, Teil I (Cod. 1–100) (Vienna, 1983), p. 171–76.

The greater part of this manuscript contains John the Deacon's life of Gregory the Great (BHL 3641-42) (fols 1-140v), likely written out in England soon after the Conquest, although it is unclear where (previously, Durham or Winchester had been proposed as likely copying locales). The life of Katherine, as mentioned above, is slightly later and was written out between 1080 and 1100, perhaps even after 1088.[14]

Parchment, i + 144 folios, fol. 141: 32 long lines, first line empty; fols 141va-143vb: 2 cols; fol. 141vb – 33 lines, fol. 142 – 36 lines, fol. 143 – 34 lines, 29.9 x 19.5cm, justified 23.3 x 16.4cm, above top line, Carolingian miniscule.

R

London, British Library, Royal MS 12.E.i, fols 119v-121v, s. xiv[in], belonged to John Theyer.

An early fourteenth-century collection of liturgical texts (saints' lives, prayers, etc.), bound with fifteenth-century material on arithmetic and other texts. There are also texts in English, such as a Latin-English list of synonyms of simple medicines (fols 69-107v); folios 193-195 contain sacred songs in English and French.[15]

Vellum, 197 folios, 13.5 cm x 10 cm, rubrics, several hands, occasionally minuscule in size, mostly long lines, signs of heavy usage, 26 long lines for the life of Katherine.

Mk (collated from facsimile)
Melk, Stiftsbibliothek, MS 222, fols 79b-82a, s. xiii[1/2], prov. Melk.

---

[14] See pp. 275–76 above. Chapelais, 'William of Saint-Calais and the Domesday Survey', p. 75, thought the GDB scribe was a scribe of Bishop William of Durham. Theyer sale-catalogue no. 275.

[15] See George F. Warner and Julius P. Gilson, *British Museum: Catalogue of the Western Manuscripts in the Old Royal and King's Collections*, vol. 2 (London, 1921), pp. 48–50.

A legendary commemorating saints from October to December in three parts: folios 1-12 and folios 13-86 are both from the first half of the thirteenth century, folios 87-98 are from the end of the thirteenth century.

Parchment, 99 folios, 30.5 x 22 cm, 2 columns, 36 lines, rubrics.[16]

M

Munich, Bayerische Staatsbibliothek, Clm 21549, fols 293-297, s. xiii/xiv, prov. Weihenstefan.

The catalogue describes the contents as 'Jacobi de Voragine, Nova legenda quam plures appellant passionale novum'.[17]

Parchment, quarto, s. xvi, 341 folios, 2 columns, 36 lines, rubrics, paragraph signs to indicate chapters throughout.

T

Trier, Stadtbibliothek, MS 1050/1261 8°, fols 226v-232v, *c.* 1130-70, St. Eucharius-Matthias/Trier.

The greater part of this manuscript contains works by Thomas Aquinas. The lives of Margaret of Antioch (BHL 5303) and Katherine are a later addition to the volume.[18]

Parchment, 232 folios, 15.5 x 10 cm, 19/20/23 long lines, several hands ranging from the twelfth to the fifteenth centuries.

The text of Katherine's passion has a lacuna from section 111 to the end.

---

[16] See Christine Glassner, *Inventar der Handschriften des Benediktinerstiftes Melk*, vol. 1: *Von den Anfängen bis ca. 1400* (Vienna, 2000), pp. 125–27.

[17] See Karl Halm and Wilhelm Meyer, *Catalogus codicum latinorum Bibliothecae Regiae Monacensis*, vol. 2.4 (Munich, 1881) p. 5.

[18] 'Catalogus codicum hagiographicorum bibliothecae civitatis Treverensis', *AB,* 51 (1934), 179.

Z (collated from facsimile)
Zurich, Zentralbibliothek, MS Rh. 18, fols 282-287v, s. xii$^{2/2}$, prov. Rheinau.

> This twelfth-century lectionary covers the period from Pentecost until Advent. The main part (fols 1-273v) was written by one scribe; the remaining folios are in different hands. The passion of Katherine is followed (on fols 288-288v) by a hymn ('Ave Katherina', [RH.1716]) and a sequence ('Regi regum decantet', [RH.17138]).[19]
>
> Parchment, 304 folios, 33 x 23.8 cm, Katherine: 23 long lines, rubrics.

Editorial conventions and notes

Presentation

The presence in *B* of passages absent from all other witnesses required a presentation that would account for *B*'s idiosyncrasies, without intruding unduly in the presentation of the text of BHL 1661m as preserved in all other witnesses. *B*'s additional passages have been demarcated from the rest of the text by italicization and a smaller font. In the majority of cases *B* preserves more text; whenever it preserves passages in parallel to the epitome this has been printed as two columns. Ideally some typographical means, perhaps more use of double columns, might have made it more immediately clear whether *B* opts for BHL 1663 or the epitome wording in the immediate neighbourhood of its additions from BHL 1663. For present purposes, cases where *B* opts for BHL 1663 beyond its additions are just registered in the apparatus. Any fuller study of the *B* text must of course take them into account.

---

[19] Leo C. Mohlberg, *Katalog der Handschriften der Zentralbibliothek Zürich*, vol. 1: *Mittelalterliche Handschriften* (Zurich, 1952), p. 168; for the hymn and the sequence see Chevalier, *Repertorium hymnologicum*.

Appendix 2: Edition of the *Passio s. Katerinae*

Division into sections, punctuation and capitalization

Rather than follow the division into liturgical lessons present in some manuscripts (see below), I have divided the text into sections, usually the length of a sentence, to allow easy cross-referencing with the apparatus. Punctuation and capitalization have been modernized.

Orthography

Only Harley 12 records 'ae' as e caudata, all the other manuscripts have 'e'. In the presentation of the text I have used 'ae', to facilitate the identification of forms. In most witnesses 'oe' is recorded as 'e'; in the text this is represented as 'œ'. I have indicated the phonetic use of 'u' before a consonant by printing 'v', but have not used 'j' to represent consonantal 'i'. Only two manuscripts, *M* and *C*, consistently use 'ci' instead of 'ti' before vowels (e.g. palacio). In the text I print 'ti'. All manuscripts have *michi* and *nichil* throughout, which has been adhered to in the text.

Lectiones and responses

A number of manuscripts divide the text into readings or sections. They do this by three different means:
- a) paragraph signs: the text in *M* is divided into 29 sections.
- b) by enlarged letter: *R* is divided into ten unequal sections.
- c) *lectiones*:

    Mk = roman numerals and enlarged letters = 9 (but not complete).

    B = roman numerals = 7 (but not complete).

    H = roman numerals = 12.

    C = written-out numbers and enlarged letters = 9.

    Z = roman numerals in margins and letters = 8.

    Bro = 9 readings (no further indication).

- d) no division: *K T*

The readings do not generally coincide with each other, as might be suggested by the fact that a number of manuscripts have the same number of readings. I have not recorded in the apparatus the various divisions of the text indicated by the manuscripts.

The following manuscripts offer responses:

> *H*: neumed responses in the margins, often incomplete due to trimming. From what is readable in *H*, it seems that the same responses (at least the first seven) are preserved in *C* where they have been integrated into the text to follow each reading. However, the responses in *C* are much longer than those in *H* so that they only coincide at the beginning of the sentence.
>
> *Bro*: it appears that there are responses only in *V*, because there are none present in the reproduction of *P*. Bronzini did not take them into account in his edition of the two witnesses.[20]

Apparatus

Given that there are manuscripts I have not seen, I have included as much information as possible, so that, in the light of other material turning up, this can be easily integrated into the existing apparatus. Whenever *B* offers text that is not present in the other manuscripts, I indicate this by a star (*) preceding the section number, as well as printing this in italics. Whenever a reading from the epitome is also present in Dobson's edition, or in manuscripts recorded by him in his apparatus, I have included them in my apparatus, differentiating them by underlining Dobson's sigla. <u>**Dob**</u> refers to Dobson's edition. I have not taken into account purely orthographic variants. In general, I have recorded inversions.

Stemma

For a text such as this epitome, particularly considering the presence of *B*, the stemma-model is not useful, since it is not a fixed text in the 'classical' sense. The undergrowth and interplay between the witnesses result in a kaleidoscope of manu-

---

[20] See Bronzini, p. 180 for the reproduction of *V* and p. 379 for the edition.

scripts rather than a tree. The witnesses to BHL 1661m do not fall into any obvious groups, nor does *B* systematically follow or share errors with any of them. However, a group of manuscripts used by Dobson keeps recurring in the apparatus: *P₂ Q H Z*. All four of them are witnesses to the epitome BHL 1663a, and thus clearly in a yet to be determined relationship with BHL 1661m.

Passio Sanctae Katerinae BHL 1661m – sigla of manuscripts

B	Brussels, KBR, MS 4564-68, fols 34-45v, s. xiii, belonged to the Jesuits of Bruges
Bro	Bronzini, 'La Leggenda', 379-83: Turin, BN, MS I.V.36, fols 1a-22, s. xii/xiii, prov. Staffarda, *destr.*
V	Vercelli, Biblioteca Capitolare, Fondo Manoscritti, MS 12 (alias 68), fols 284v- 289v, s. xiv
LP	Pavia, Biblioteca del Seminario, printed legendary, fol. G.4v-H.ij, 1523, prov. Pavia
C	Cambridge, Corpus Christi College, MS 405, fols 72v-79v, s. xiv[in], prov. Waterford
K	Klosterneuburg, Stiftsbibliothek, CCl 79, fols 57b-58vb, 1260/80, prov. Klosterneuburg
H	London, British Library, Harley MS 12, fols 141-143v, *c.* 1125-1150, prov. England/Normandy(?)
R	London, British Library, Royal MS 12.E.i, fols 119v-112v, s. xiv[in], belonged to John Theyer
Mk	Melk, Stiftsbibliothek, MS 222, fols 79b-82a, s. xiii[1/2], prov. Melk
M	Munich, Bayerische Staatsbibliothek, Clm 21549, fols 293-297, s. xiii/xiv, prov. Weihenstefan
T	Trier, Stadtbibliothek, MS 1050/1261 8°, fols 226v, *c.* 1130-1170, prov. St. Eucharius-Matthias, Trier
Z	Zurich, Zentralbibliothek, MS Rh. 18, fols 282-287v, *c. 1150-1200* (& hymn), prov. Rheinau

Manuscripts not used:

Cividale, Museo Archeologico Nazionale, MS XII, fols 177-179, s. xv, prov. Cividale

Cividale, MAN, MS XXI, fols 197v-202, s. xii, prov. Cividale (Capellini scribe)

Gorizia, Biblioteca del Seminario Teologico, MS 9 (Passionario iii), fols 239v-244, s. xiii, prov. Aquileia

Herzogenburg, Stiftsbibliothek, MS 57, fols 270-276, 1430, prov. Grein

Kassel, Gesamthochschul-Bibliothek, MS 2° Theol. 142, fols 151-157v, 1367-89, prov. Fritzlar

Klosterneuburg, Stiftsbibliothek, CCl 193, fols 235a-236b, 1420, prov. Ybbs

Michaelbeuern, Stiftsbibliothek, MS Man. cart. 67, fols 251vb-253b, s. xv$^{3/4}$, prov. Michaelbeuern

Dobson's manuscripts:[21]

<u>**Dob**</u> Dobson's edition

<u>C</u> London, BL, Cotton MS Caligula A. viii, fols 169-91, s. xii, Ely

<u>D</u> Bern, Burgerbibliothek, MS 133, fols 65v-84v, s. xi-xii, France? (Jacques Bongars)

<u>E</u> Bern, Burgerbibliothek, MS 137, fols 158-178, s. xii, Île-de-France?

<u>F</u> Brussels, KBR, MS 9120, fols 92v-100, 1180, Lille (jes.)

<u>G</u> Brussels, KBR, MS 18018,[22] fols 25v-37, s. xi^{ex}, Lobbes

<u>Θ</u> Brussels, KBR, MS 8690-8702, fols 13-41v, s. xii, Cornelius Duyn (Amsterdam)

<u>H</u> Heiligenkreuz, Stiftsbibliothek, MS 14, fols 13-17v, s. xii, Heiligenkreuz

---

[21] See *Seinte Katerine*, pp. 132–43.

[22] Erroneously cited by Dobson as 18108.

Appendix 2: Edition of the *Passio s. Katerinae*

I	Rouen, BM, MS 1399 (U.2), fols 185m-n + 186-194, s. xii, Jumièges
J	Rouen, BM, MS 1394 (U.119), fols 131-167, s. xii, Mortagne
L	Leipzig, Universitätsbibliothek, MS Rep. II 64, fols 60v-100, s. xii^{ex}
Λ	Paris, BnF, MS lat. 5336, fols 108v-119v, s. xii, English
Λ₂	corrector of Paris, BnF, MS lat. 5336
M	Paris, BnF, MS lat. 1970, fols 54-70v, s. xi, Fécamp
N	Paris, BnF, MS lat. 5308, fols 63v-72, s. xii, Lorraine (Metz)
O	Paris, BnF, MS lat. 5343, fols 135-137v, s. xi, Vendôme
Ω	Paris, BnF, MS lat. 8995, fols 118v-130, *c.* 1300, St. Barbara, Cologne
P₁	Paris, BnF, MS lat. 5278, fols 410-416v, s. xiii, Moselle/Metz
P₂	Paris, BnF, MS lat. 14364, fols 150-160, s. xiii, Saint-Victor, Paris
Q	Paris, BnF, MS lat. 14293, fols 210-217v, s. xiii, Saint-Victor, Marseille
S	Paris, BnF, MS lat. 5365, fols 163-171, s. xii, Saint-Martial, Limoges
Σ	agreement of *Ps P2 H Z*
U	Paris, BnF, MS lat. 12259, fols 267-286, s. xii, Saint-Germain-des-Prés, Paris
W	Paris, BnF, MS lat. 15149, fols 46-65v, s. xiii-xiv, Saint-Victor, Paris
Y	Paris, BnF, MS lat. 17007, fols 203-210v, s. xiii-xiv, Val Abbey
Z	Zwettl, Stiftsbibliothek, MS 15, fols 17v-21, s. xii^{ex}, Zwettl

Dobson
line nos

Passio Sanctae Katerinae

45-60

[1] Maxentius imperator anno regni sui tricesimo quinto residens in civitate Alexandrinorum, feralia per vicinas provincias misit edicta iubens omnes regni sui incolas divites et pauperes ad templum deorum suorum convenire et sollemne eis sacrificium offerre. [2] Fit itaque conventus universalis ad praetorium regis et astante ipso imperatore ante simulacra deorum iuxta possibilitatem suam divites quidem tauros et oves, pauperes vero volucres vivos offerebant.

71-73

[3] Hac in urbe Alexandria erat quaedam puella annorum duo de viginti, speciosa valde sed quod pluris est religiosa fide, regis quondam nomine Costi filia unica, liberalibus studiis ab annis puerilibus erudita, nomine Katerina.

Passio Sanctae Katerinae] *sic K*, incipiunt lectiones de sancta Katherina *Z*, passio sancte Katerine virginis *Mk*, incipit vitam sancta Katerine virginis et martiris *C*, vita s. Katherine *R*, *om. H T B Bro M*
1 per vicinas] pernicias *C* || omnes] *om. B* || regni sui] sui regni *B* || et¹] ac *B* || templum] templa *M* || suorum] *om. Bro*
2 conventus universalis] u. c. *T* || praetorium] praeceptum *C* || ipso] *om. B R* || imperatore] imperator *C* || deorum] *om. Z* || suam] *om. T Z* || quidem] quid *R*, vero quidem *C* || tauros et oves] o. et t. *B* || vero] *om. C* || volucres vivos] vivos v. *K M* || vivos] vivas *T N S*
3 hac] hic *R* || Alexandria] Alexandrina *M* || annorum] *om. T* || duo de] duodena *B* || viginti] viginti anni aetatis eius *T* || quod] quid *R* || religiosa] valde religiosa *B* || quondam] quondam egypti *add. in marg.* (*only the 2ⁿᵈ*) *Mk*, *om. C* || nomine¹] *om. T* || ab annis puerilibus erudita] e. ab a. p. *K M*

The Passion of St Katherine

[1] The emperor Maxentius, residing in the city of the Alexandrians in the thirty-fifth year of his reign, sent deadly decrees throughout the neighbouring provinces, ordering all the inhabitants of his kingdom, rich and poor, to come together at the temple of his gods and offer them a regular sacrifice. [2] And so a general assembly took place at the palace of the king and with the emperor himself standing before the images of the gods, each according to their ability, the rich sacrificed bulls and sheep while the poor sacrificed live birds.

[3] In this city of Alexandria there was a certain eighteen-year-old girl, very beautiful but, what is more, devout in her faith, the only daughter of a former king called Costus, educated in classical studies from a very young age, called Katherine.

90-102

[4] Haec itaque in palatio patris residebat cum ex templo idolorum hinc sonus animalium et tibicinum hinc multimodum genus organorum auribus ipsius insonuit. Quae causam requirens cum ex nuntio didicisset, assumptis secum aliquibus de familia ad templum usque properavit, ubi deplorantes quosdam inspexit qui se Christianos esse fatebantur, sed metu mortis ad profana sacrificia impellebantur. [5] Hinc vehementi dolore cordis sauciata, *tenens paululum intra se silentium, tacite quidem, sed ab alto, fudit orationem, dehinc* pectus et linguam Christi muniens signaculo audenter ad conspectum imperatoris prorupit.

4 itaque] *om. Z K Mk Bro,* itaque custos virginitatis suae *B,* illa custos virginitatis suae *Dob* ‖ residebat] residens *underlined R* ‖ ex templo] exemplo *Z H,* ex emplorum *C* ‖ idolorum hinc sonus] ydolo ‖ insonu *Z* ‖ multimodum] multimodorum *Mk p.c. L* ‖ genus] *om. M* ‖ ipsius] *om. Z,* suis *B U P₂ H Z,* eius *Mk D N* ‖ insonuit] *tr. post* auribus *C* ‖ requirens] inquirens *Mk Bro C* ‖ didicisset] didicisset *D,* dedicisset *C,* audisset *Dob* ‖ de familia] *om. B,* de familia sua *Bro* ‖ usque] *om. B* ‖ ubi] ibique *B* ‖ deplorantes quosdam] q. d. *B R* ‖ quosdam] aliquos *Mk* ‖ inspexit] aspexit *C* ‖ esse] *om. C* ‖ sed] et *Z K M, om. Mk,* ac *Bro* ‖ impellebantur] impellebant *M*

5 hinc] beata virgo *R* ‖ cordis] *om. Z* ‖ pectus] pectorem *Bro* ‖ et] *om. K Mk M* ‖ Christi] *om. B* ‖ audenter] audacter *Bro N E P₁* ‖ imperatoris] regis *C H Z*

*5 tenens] tenens itaque *Dob* ‖ tacite] tacito *B* ‖ dehinc] hinc *Dob*

[4] And so this girl lived in the palace of her father when, from the temple of the idols, there resounded in her ears the sound of animals and flute players on one side, and various kinds of instruments on the other. Inquiring into the reason for this, when she had found out from a messenger what it was, she took with her some persons from her househould and hurried all the way to the temple, where she saw certain people who were weeping bitterly and professing themselves to be Christians, but through fear of death were being forced to heathen sacrifices. [5] Wounded from this by a violent pain of her heart, *keeping silence within herself for a little while, indeed quietly but from deep within she poured out a prayer,* then, fortifying her heart and tongue with the sign of Christ, she burst forth fearlessly into the sight of the emperor.

105-11 [6] Cui sic ait: 'salutationem tibi imperator proferre nos et ordinis dignitas et rationis via promonebat, si haec ista quae cultibus demonum exhibes creatori tuo impenderes, et solam illius maiestatem adorandam intelligeres per quem reges regnant, per quem mundi elementa initium sumpserunt atque subsistunt. [7] Dii enim non sunt plures sed unus nascentium et viventium formator est deus qui sicut cuncta creavit, ita imperio suo cuncta coercet atque disponit.'

132-34

[8] Cum haec puella loquitur, imperator *iamdudum visum in virginem defixit* vultus ipsius claritatem et verborum constantiam admirans ait: [9] 'si nostrorum philosophorum gymnasiis, o virgo, erudienda persedisses, deorum nostrorum numina divinitatis honore vacua nequaquam astrueres.

145-46

204-07

6 cui ... nos] iuro vos *B* || ait] sancta virgo ait *C* || imperator] *om. Z K* || et¹] quia *Z*, *om. C* || ordinis dignitas] ordines dignitatis *B*, ordinis nostri dignitas *C* || via] viam *B* || promonebat] promonebat eadem *T*, promovebat *B F S W*, praemonebat *Bro J L N Y* || haec] *om. B* || ista] eadem *T*, *om.* Bro *D E J N O S Y Σ Q* || exhibes] exhibens *B* || illius] eius *B Mk P₂ Q H Z* || adorandam intelligeres] i. a. *B* || reges regnant] regnant reges *K* || quem¹] quam Bro || quem²] quam Bro || mundi elementa] e. m. Bro *C N* || sumpserunt] *ante* elementa *Mk*

7 dii] hii *B* || enim] *post* sunt *B*, *om. R* || non] *om. B*, *ante* dii *R* || sunt plures] p. s. *Z F* || et] atque *B C* || formator] creator *Z* || formator est] e. f. *T* || est deus] est Christus *post* viventium *B*, d. e. *M* || est] *om. R* || deus] *om.* Bro || sicut] sic *T Z* || cuncta¹] omnia *H Dob* || creavit ... cuncta²] *om. Z* || creavit] creavit ex nichilo *B* || ita] *om. Mk* || suo] *om. Mk* || atque] et *B K*

8 cum] dum *T H* || loquitur] prosequitur *B*, loqueretur *K Mk M R Σ Q* || imperator] *om. T* || ipsius] eius *C* || verborum] animi *B*

*8 visum in virginem defixit] visu in virginem defixo *Dob*

9 gymnasiis] gignasiis *C*, gynasiis *R* || divinitatis] diurnitatis *B*

[6] She spoke to him thus: 'Both the dignity of rank and the path of reason prompted me to offer a greeting to you emperor, if you were expending to your creator these things which you are displaying for the cults of devilish spirits, and if you understood that his sole majesty has to be worshipped, through whom kings reign, through whom the elements of the world have taken their beginning and continue to exist. [7] For there are not many gods but one god, the creator of things coming into existence and living, who just as he has created everything, so by his power he controls and arranges everything.'

[8] While the girl is speaking these words, the emperor *fixed his sight onto the virgin for a long while*, admiring the brightness of her face and the firmness of her words, he said: [9] 'O virgin, if you had sat through the schools of our philosophers for the purpose of learning, you would not at all accuse the majesty of our gods of being empty of the honour of divinity.

207-
21
[10] Dum ergo nos incepta sacra peragimus te interim nos opperire oportet, quia nobiscum itura es ad palatium et regiis honoranda muneribus si nostris acquiescis iussionibus.' [11] Haec dicens, accito clanculum nuntio misit litteras regio anulo signatas per infra iacentes provincias ad omnes rhetores et grammaticos, ut ad praetorium Alexandrinum eo studiosius occurrant, quo imperator altis illos honoribus donandos promittit, tantum si hanc temerariam contionatricem suis assertionibus superatam reddiderint *et hunc imperatori optatum reportaverint triumphum. [12] Quatinus blasphemias quas diis magnis irrogaverat, in suum caput refusas cognoscat, quia rationis ordo exigit ut primum arte oratoria, qua se iactanter extollit, revincatur, postmodum vero, si diis immolare detractet, pœnali cruciatu intereat.*

10 dum] cum *B* || nos¹] om. *T Z K Mk M G* || sacra] sacrificia *R* || te] et *H P₁* || interim]   interum *B*, iterum *Bro* || te interim] i. t. *K* || nos²] *post* opperiri *K*, nobiscum *C* || opperiri] opperire *H Z*, expectare te *B*, expectare *Bro G Q*, manere *C* || nobiscum itura] i. n. *C* || palatium] templum *Mk* || regiis] regis *K C Z* || acquiescis] acquieveris *Bro* || iussionibus] muneribus *B*, iudicibus *C*

11 accito] accercito *Bro*, accersito *C* || clanculum nuntio] clanculo *B*, clanculo nuntio *F H* || signatas] sigillatas *Bro* || ad¹] ut *M* || omnes rethores] r. o. *Bro* || et¹] om. *M* || ut] om. *M* || praetorium] praetorium regis *C* || occurrant] accurrant *C* || illos] *post* donandos *T*, eos *B* || honoribus] muneribus *B* || tantum] tamen *K P₁ Q*, om. *Bro* || si] ut *K M* || temerariam] om. *K* || reddiderint] reddierunt *a.c. M*, reddiderit *Bro*, reddiderunt *C*

*11 reportaverint] reportaverunt *B*

*12 irrogaverat] irrogaverit *E S*, inrogaverit *J Q* || cognoscat] agnoscat *Dob* || extollit] extollit *H Z*, attollit *Dob* || detractet] detractat *a.c. P₁ P₂*, de tractat *H*, detrectat *Dob*

[10] So while we bring to an end the commenced rites, you ought to wait for us in the meantime because you are about to go with us to the palace and you are to be honoured by royal gifts if you consent to our orders.' [11] Saying these things, and after he summoned a messenger in secret, he sent letters signed by the royal signet-ring through the provinces under his rule to all rhetoricians and grammarians, that they should hasten to the palace of Alexandria the more eagerly, because the emperor promised that they were to be given great honours, provided only that they cause this rash preacher-woman to be conequered by their affirmations *and earn the emperor his desired triumph. [12] So that she sees the blasphemies that she has laid on the great gods flow back onto her own head, because the order of reason demands that first she should be subdued by the art of oratory, with which she has raised herself arrogantly, but later, if she refuses to sacrifice to the gods, be killed by punishment of torture.*

221-
36

[13] Paruit nuntius regiis mandatis et expletis imperator sacrilegis officiis, virginem iubet comprehendi et ad palatium duci. Quam blando sermone primum cœpit affari: *[14]* 'nomen,' inquiens, 'tuum, puella, aut genus, et quos in studiis liberalibus magistros habuisti, penitus speciosa facta et decora protestareris, et loquendi peritia in laudem referatur magistrorum nisi in hoc uno oberrasses, quod diis omnipotentibus derogando et contumeliosa persistis. *[15]* Respondens puella, dixit tyranno: 'si nomen quaeris, Katerina dicor, Costi quondam regis filia. Liberalium non ignobiles doctores, quantum ad inanem mundi gloriam, habui, de quibus, quia nichil michi quod esset conducibile ad beatam vitam contulerunt, tota eorum memoria silescat. *[16]* Postquam enim michi sanctioris doctrinae lux emicuit, mox tenebrosam erraticae doctrinae sectam deserui. Audivi enim beatam vocem evangelii domini mei Iesu Christi, cui me sponsam et ancillam fœdere stabili devovi.'

*13 sermone primum] s. p. *E*, p. s. *Dob*
*14 penitus ... protestareris] penitus ignoro sed speciosa facies et decora te alto sanguine ortam protestatur *Dob* || referatur] refunderetur *Dob* || derogando et] derogando *Dob* || persistis] persisteris B
*15 respondens] respondit B, respondet a.c. *G*, respondens *Dob* || liberalium] liberalium *E O*, liberalium artium *Dob* || tota] tota haec *Dob*
*16 sectam] noctem *Dob*

[13] The messenger obeyed the royal orders, and when the emperor had finished the sacrilegious ceremonies, he ordered the virgin to be arrested and led to the palace. At first he began to address her with a flattering speech, [14] saying: 'You would be claiming very fine and honourable things in citing your name, girl, or your family, and which teachers you had in the liberal arts, and your skill of speaking would reflect the praise of your teachers if you had not erred in this one thing, inasmuch as you, insultingly, persist in diminishing the all-powerful gods.' [15] The girl answered and said to the tyrant: 'If you ask my name, I am called Katherine, the daughter of the late king Costus. I had very noble teachers of the liberal arts, as far as the vain glory of the world goes, about whom, because they did not provide for me what was useful for a happy life, my entire memory of them may become silent. [16] For when the light of the more holy teaching shone forth for me, then I deserted the dark teaching of false doctrine. For I have heard the blessed voice of the gospel of my lord Jesus Christ, to whom I have dedicated myself as wife and servant by a firm vow.

261-64

[17] Peragratis ergo provinciae finibus regius nuntius properanter Alexandriam revertitur, ducens secum quinquaginta viros qui se in omni sapientia mundi excellere ultra omnes mortales asserebant. Interea virgo sancta sub custodia servabatur *contra quinquaginta rhetores sola pugnatura,* cui consilium regis de conflictu imminenti nuntiatur. [18] *Nichil tamen ex his famula Christi turbatur,* ipsa sane imperterrita militiae suae agonem domino commendabat. *[19] Dicens: 'sapientia et Dei virtus altissimi, Iesu bone, qui tuos milites, ne inter pressuras mundi formidare debuissent nec minis adversariorum turbarentur, eos consolatione pia praemunire dignatus es, dicens "Dum steteritis ante reges et praesides, nolite praecogitare quomodo aut quid loquamini; ego enim dabo vobis os et sapientiam, cui non poterunt resistere et contradicere omnes adversarii vestri."*

292-302

17 ergo] *om. B,* igitur *C R* || provinciae] provincias *R* || regius] regis *K Mk* || regius nuntius] n. r. *C* || Alexandriam] Alexandrinam *K R, om. Mk Z* || quinquaginta¹] quinquagintos *B,* quinquagintas *C* || in] *om. Mk* || omni] *om. Z* || mundi] mundana *C P₂ Q* || excellere] *post* mortales *T* || ultra] *om. T Z B Bro M*
virgo sancta] s. v. *T C R,* beata virgo Katerina *B,* virgo *Bro* || custodia] custodia bona *M* || cui ... nunciatur] cui nuntius venit {venit *P₂ Q,* supervenit *Dob*} de consilio regis et de conflictu in crastinum constituto *B* || de] et de *C* || imminenti] *post* conflictu *C* || nuntiatur] imperatrix nuntiavit *K,* nuntiatum est *M*
17 contra ... pugnatura] sola contra quinquaginta pugnatura *Dob* || rhetores] rectores *B*
18 ipsa sane] sed *B Dob,* ipsa sancta *K,* ipsa sane et *C,* ipsa vero *Mk R* || agonem] aguonem *B*
19 et Dei] Dei et *B* || adversariorum] adversantium *Dob* || eos consolatione pia] p. e. c. *Dob* || enim] om. *B*

[17] So when the messenger had travelled through the territories of the province, he hastily turned back to Alexandria, leading with him fifty men who claimed that they excelled all mortals in all the wisdom of the world. Meanwhile the holy virgin was being kept under guard, about to battle alone against fifty rhetoricians, and the decision of the king about the imminent dispute was announced to her. [18] *None of this upset the servant of Christ*, she herself, quite undaunted, entrusted the test of her service to the lord. [19] *She said: 'O wisdom and virtue of the highest god, kind Jesus, who – so that your soldiers would neither have to fear the burdens of the world nor be thrown into disorder by the threats of enemies – thought fit to fortify them with pious consolation, saying "when you are standing before kings and governors do not premeditate how or what you will say; for I will give you a voice and wisdom which all your enemies will not be able to withstand or contradict."*

302-22

[20] *Adesto famulae tuae et da sermonem rectum et bene sonantem in os meum, ut hii qui ad derogandum nomini tuo convenerunt non praevaleant adversum me; sed verbi tui consternati virtute, hebetatis sensibus aut penitus obmutescant aut, conversi, nomini tuo dent honorem, qui solus es cum Patre et cum Sancto Spiritu et eris gloriosus in saecula, amen.'* [21] *Nec iam verba compleverat et ecce angelus Domini apparuit ei, cuius claritate vultus locus quo virgo clausa tenebatur mira coruscatione fulgurabat, ex qua virgo stupore et admiratione paene defecerat.* Cui angelus domini apparuit dicens: [22] '*ne paveas*', inquit, '*sed* constanter age grata deo puella, quia tecum est dominus pro cuius honore certamen inisti. Ipse affluentis verbi impetum fundet in os tuum, cui adversarii resistere non praevalebunt, sed per te insuper conversi ad Christum cum palma martyrii vitae ianua introibunt. [23] *Tu autem brevi tempore cursum certaminis tui victoriosa morte consummabis, et sic, inter choros virgineos suscepta, immortali sponso perenniter adhaerebis. Ego sum archangelus Michael testamenti Dei, missus haec tibi evangelizare.'* [24] *His dictis, continuo evasit ab ea. Ad hanc vocem virgo Dei in agonia roborata expectat quam mox invitetur ad laborem certaminis.*

*20 consternati virtute] v. c. **_Dob_** || honorem] honorem et gloriam **_Dob_** || es] post Spiritu **_Dob_** || cum²] om. **_Dob_**
21 cui] tunc *B* || domini ... dicens] om. *B*
*21 nec iam] necdum **_Dob_** || ei] ei **Σ** *Q*, illi **_Dob_** || claritate vultus] v. c. **_Dob_** || mira coruscatione] intra coruscationem *B*
22 grata deo puella] grata puella *post* inquit *B*, grata puella *R* || grata deo] d. g. **Mk** *M* **_C_** || honore] amore *T* || certamen inisti] certasti *B* || affluentis] confluentiae *Bro* || fundet] infundet *post* tuum *T*, infundet *M* **_G_** *P₂* **_Q_** **_H_** **_Z_** || in os tuum] in ore tuo *B* **_Dob_**, instantiam *Z* || praevalebunt] poterunt *B* || per te] *om. B M*, *post* insuper *R* || vitae] in te *C* || ianua] ianuam *K* **_Dob_**

[20] Be present to your servant and put a true and well-sounding speech into my mouth so that those who have come together to detract from your name may not prevail against me, but unsettled by the virtue of your word, with weakened sense may either become completely speechless or, converted, give honour to your name, you who alone are with the Father and with the Holy Spirit and will be glorious for ever, amen.' [21] She had not yet finished her words and behold an angel of the Lord appeared to her, by the brightness of whose face the place where the virgin was being kept enclosed was shining with an extraordinary brightness from which the virgin almost fainted in wonder and admiration. To whom appeared an angel of the Lord, saying: [22] 'Don't be afraid', he said, 'but act steadfastly, girl dear to god, because the Lord, for whose honour you have entered the contest, is with you. He himself will pour into your mouth a stream of the abundant word which your adversaries will not be strong enough to resist, but even converted by you to Christ they will enter the gateway of life with the glory of martyrdom. *[23] But in a short time you will achieve the course of your contest with a victorious death, and thus, taken up among the virgineal choirs, you will remain close to your immortal husband in perpetuity. I am the archangel Michael of the will of God, sent to proclaim these things to you.'* [24] Having said these things, he went away from her without delay. At this voice the virgin of God, strengthened in her trial, waits to be called in soon for the task of the dispute.

---

*23 inter] intra B **Δ** (p.c.) *E J O P₁ P₂ Q Z* || archangelus Michael] M. a. **Dob** || missus] missus a Deo **Dob**
24 his ... certaminis] haec angelus dicens recessit C
*24 evasit] discessit **Dob** || quam] quod B, quoad *H Z*

323-
31

344-
95

[25] Sedente itaque pro tribunali imperatore, adsunt oratores pomposo eloquentiae fastu tumentes, astat et puella fidens in domino. [26] Facto autem diuturno silentio, virgo Christi tandem conversa ad illos, 'ego', inquit, 'o seniores, Christi sacramentis imbuta, philosophicas dissertiones et syllogisticas disputationes penitus abrogans, iudico me inter vos nichil aliud scire nisi eum qui est vera scientia et in se credentium gloria, dominum meum Iesum Christum, qui est rerum omnium principium, fons et origo bonorum, per quem deus pater mundum cum non esset et omnia quae in eo sunt condidit, qui solus est ex quo omnia per quem omnia in quo omnia visibilia et invisibilia constant.

25 itaque] igitur *T* || pro tribunali imperatore] i. p. t. *R* || adsunt] adsistunt *B* || pomposo] pomposæ *Z L* || et] *om.* *K G P₂ Q H Z* || fidens] confidens *K Bro*
26 facto] peracto *Z* || diuturno] *om.* *B R* || virgo] sponsa *B* || tandem] *om.* *B R* || inquit] *post* illos *T* || Christi sacramentis] s. c. *B R* || imbuta] *post* Christi *C*, *post* seniores *R* || dissertiones] assertiones *Z*, dissertationes *B* || et¹] *om.* *B* || syllogisticas] sillegiticas *B*, silgisticas *C* || iudico] indico *C*, s.l. *R* || inter vos] *post* scire *T* || nichil] vel *C* || vera] summa et vera *M* || scientia] *p.c.* *K* || dominum] deum *C S* || Iesum Christum] C. I. *C* || qui] periti qui *T*, qui in præteritis *Dob* || est rerum] r. e. *C* || rerum omnium] o. r. *Z* || origo] horiguo *B* || pater] præter *C R* || cum non esset] *om.* *B*, cum non essent *R* || et⁴ ... sunt] et ea quæ in eo sunt *post* mundum *R* || sunt] sunt non essent *B* || ex quo omnia]   *ante* per *K Mk* || per ... omnia²] *om.* *B M* || in quo omnia] *om.* *T Z K Mk Bro F L U*

[25] And so with the emperor sitting on the dais, the orators are present, bursting with the arrogance of eloquence, the girl also stands by, trusting in the Lord. [26] But after a long silence, the virgin of Christ finally turned round to them and said: 'O elders, I – instructed in the sacraments of Christ, completely renouncing the philosophical discourses and the syllogistical disputations – judge myself among you to know nothing except him who is the true knowledge and glory of those who believe in him, my lord Jesus Christ, who is the beginning of all things, the fountain and origin of all good, through whom God the father, indeed founded the world and everything that is in it when it was not, who alone is the one from whom everything, through whom everything, in whom everything, visible and invisible, exists.

368-74 [27] Qui genus humanum per diabolum a paradisi deliciis dolens exclusum, his novissimis diebus cum esset invisibilis deus ex virgine carnem assumpsit per quam visibilis appareret, in qua etiam mortem pati dignatus est, resurrexit atque in caelum ascendit; mirabilibus quoque operum signis quia verus deus esset apparuit. [28] Hic est

503-06 deus noster, hic philosophia mea, hic victoria mea.'

[29] Dum haec et alia multa virgo de fide Christiana disseret, stupefacti cuncti oratores *quid contradicerent nesciebant* atque manifesta dei virtute perturbati, invicem se contuentes obmutuerunt.

27 dolens] *om. Mk M* || exclusum] expulsum *Mk* || dolens exclusum] e. d. *B* || cum] tum *R* || deus¹] *om. T* || deus¹ ... appareret] in nostra natura aparuit visibilis *Z* || ex] de *K Mk M R Dob* || assumpsit] sumpsit *C* || appareret] apparet *K* || qua] quam *H T Z R* || etiam] *om. K M* || atque] *om. K* || mirabilibus] mirabilis *K J*, mirabilium *Bro* || verus deus] d. v. *Z K R* || apparuit] aperuit *Mk Θ G Y Z*
28 deus] dominus *T P₁* || noster] meus *K M Σ Q* || hic²] hic est *T Dob*
29 dum] *post* multa *K Mk R*, cum *T Bro Z*, cumque *B C*, *om. Z M*, , || haec et alia] *om. B* || virgo] *om. B D* || Christiana] Christi sacratissima *B* || de fide Christiana] *om. K Mk R* || dissereret] disseret *H Mk*, asseret *K*, disceret *C* || atque] sed *B* || dei virtute] v. d. *Mk* || perturbati] confusi ac perturbati *B* || se] *om. B*

*29 contradicerent] contra discerent *Λ*, contra his dicerent *J*, contra haec dicerent *D*, contradicerent *E*, contrahiscerent *Dob*

[27] Who, grieving that the human race had been shut out by the devil from the delights of paradise, in these most recent days, though he was an invisible God, took on flesh from a virgin through which to appear visible, in which he even deigned to suffer death, rose up again and ascended into heaven; by miraculous signs of deeds he manifested himself as the true god. [28] He is our god, he is my philosophy, he is my victory.'

[29] While the virgin was declaring these and many other things about the Christian faith, all the orators were stunned with amazement *and did not know what to assert in opposition* and confused by the unmistakable virtue of God, gazing at each other in turn they fell silent.

506-34

[30] Quibus indignatus imperator cum furore nimio sic ait: 'quid vos ignavi et degeneres *hebetatis sensibus* sic obmutescitis? *Siccine vos, debilitatis viribus, virtus feminea perdomabit? Non superque satis esse poterat ad ignominiam omnium philosophorum si quinquagenae aut eo amplius feminae verbis unum e vobis evicissent? [31] Nunc autem, pro pudor!* quinquaginta robustos oratores, ab extremis mundi partibus electos, una puella verborum suorum turbine eos usque attonitos reddidit, ut hii quid vel contra nuntient prorsus non habent.' [32] Hic unus eorum maior natu *quem sibi magistrum et ducem praeesse ceteri fatebantur* tyranno respondit: 'hoc tibi imperator constanter fatemur, quia nisi aliam sectam probabiliorem ostenderis de diis quos hucusque coluimus, ecce omnes ad Christum convertimur, quia ipsum vere dominum et dei filium confitemur *per quem tanta mortalibus beneficia praestantur quae per virginem istam audivimus.*'

30 indignatus imperator] imp. i. *K Y* || degeneres] degeneres velud elingues *B R* || obmutescitis] obmutiscitis *H*
*30 siccine] si certe *B* || viribus] virtutibus *B* || perdomabit] perdomavit *B D* || non] num *B* || superque satis] sat. sup. *Dob* || unum e vobis] ex vobis unde *B*, unum ex vobis *O S* || evicissent] evicisset *B* , evicisset a.c. & evicissent p.c. *M*, evicisset *C Θ*
*31 pro] o pro *Λ₂*, pro *N*, o *Dob* || robustos] robustissimos *Dob* || verborum suorum turbine] t. v. s. *Dob* || eo] eos *B* || mutiant] nuntient *B*, unciant *W*

Appendix 2: Edition of the *Passio s. Katerinae* 315

[30] The emperor, offended by their behaviour, spoke thus with very great rage: 'Why do you, cowards and weaklings, with your senses dulled, keep silence in this way?' *Will a feminine ability weaken your strengths and subjugate you in this way? I suppose it is not possible that it would have been more than enough for the disgrace of all philosophers if fifty or many more women had utterly defeated one of you with words.* [31] But as it is, o shame, one girl with the whirlwind of her words has left fifty strong orators, chosen from the uttermost regions of the world, so dumbfounded that they now have altogether nothing to deliver in reply.' [32] Then one of them, more senior by birth *whom the others acknowledged to be superior to them as master and leader,* answered the tyrant: 'Emperor, we declare this to you steadfastly, that – unless you show us another more likely philosophy with regard to the gods which we have worshipped until now – behold we are all being converted to Christ, because we confess that he truly is the Lord and the son of God *through whom such great benefits are available for humans which we have heard from this virgin.*'

---

32 hic] tunc *B Mk*, tunc *s.l. J*, hinc *Bro R S Σ Q*, huic *C* || maior natu] n. m. *Mk* || respondit] respondit *P₂ Q H Z*, ita respondit *B D* tibi imperator] om. *B*, i. t. *Mk Δ* || imperator constanter] c. i. *M* || constanter] constanter igitur imperator *B* || probabiliorem] probabiliorem *D*, probabilioribus experimentis ventilatam *B Dob* || ostenderis] ostenderes *H*, ostenderis nobis *post* coluimus *B*, ostendas *Bro* || de diis] *ante* ostenderis *Mk* || hucusque] usque *K E*, usque huc *Mk U Q*, hactenus *Bro* || omnes] omnes quicquid (quodquod?) sumus *M*, omnes iam *C* || ad Christum convertimur] c. a. Chr. *B Mk Dob* || dominum] deum *K* || quia ... confitemur] om. *C* || vere] verum *Z B K Mk R E M N W Σ Q*
*32 fatebantur] fatiebantur *B*

535-
53
[33] Audiens haec tyrannus *praecipitibus furiis agitatus* accenso in medio civitatis vehementissimo igne, iussit omnes ligatis pedibus et manibus concremari.

[34] Qui dum traherentur ad ignem, unus eorum ceteros hortabatur, dicens: 'o socii mei et commilitones, quid agimus? Deus longos miseratus errores ad hanc suam gratiam nos vocare dignatus est, ut vel in finem sacro privilegio fidei et sancti nominis confessione non fraudaremur, cur non properamus ante vitae ipsius exitum signaculo et sacri fontis utero innovari?' [35] Cum haec diceret, rogabant unanimiter pretiosam virginem Christi ut lavacro salutifero perfunderentur. Quibus electa Dei ait: 'ne paveatis, o fortissimi milites Christi, sed constantes estote et de baptismo ne solliciti sitis. Erit enim vobis salutare baptismum sanguinis vestri perfusio, quam ignis iste cruciatorius flammeum Spiritus Sancti ignem vobis inferet.' [36] His dictis, adsunt ministri, et ex iussu imperatoris, ligatis manibus et pedibus, sanctos Dei martyres mediis flammis ingerunt; et sic, inter aestuantes flammas incendii Dominum confitentes, felici martyrio coronati ad Dominum migraverunt tertio decimo die mensis Novembris.

33   haec] hoc *C* || accenso] accenso protinus *M* || vehementissimo] copioso *Bro Σ Q* || vehementissimo igne] i. v. *B*, i.v. *post* accenso *Mk* || igne] igni *R* || pedibus et manibus] p. e. m. *G*, m. e. p. *Z B K Mk Bro M R Dob*

*34 mei] post commilitones **Dob** || Deus] postquam nostros Deus **Dob** || nos] nos **Λ₂ P₂ H Z**, vos *B* || est] om. *B* || finem] finem p.c. **Λ₂**, finem diei *E J O S* || sacro] sacrae **Dob** || fidei] post fine **Dob** || confessione] cognitione **Dob** || non¹] ne ut non *B* || ipsius exitum] e. i. **Dob** || sacri] sacro **Dob**

35   diceret] dicerent *B F L N* || sed] sed **Λ₂**, om. **Dob** || ne solliciti] n. s. *E G L O*, s. n. **Dob** || enim] enim **Λ₂**, om. **Dob** || vestri] nostri *B*, om. *H Z* || quam] *B P₂ H Z*, et **Dob**|| inferet] *B E J O Σ*, flammeum Spiritus Sancti ignem vobis inferet] **Dob**

*36 aestuantes] aestuantes *L*, aestuantis **Dob**

[33] On hearing these things the tyrant *was agitated by a rushing rage and* lit a very violent fire in the middle of the city, and ordered all of them to be burnt up with their feet and hands bound.

[34] While they were being dragged to the fire, one of them encouraged the rest, saying: 'O my colleagues and comrades, what are we doing? God took pity on our prolonged sins and deigned to call us to his grace so that at least at the end we would not be cheated of the sacred privilege of faith and the confession of the holy name, why don't we hurry to be renewed by his sign and the womb of the sacred fountain before the end of life itself?' [35] When he said these things, they unanimously asked the virgin precious to Christ that they be sprinkled with the redeeming water. God's chosen girl said to them: 'Don't be afraid, o most brave soldiers of Christ, but be steadfast and don't worry about the baptism. For the shedding of your blood will be your redeeming baptism, which this torturing fire will bring about. [36] After she said these things, servants appear and on the order of the emperor, they thrust the holy martyrs of God into the middle of the flames with their hands and feet bound; and thus, trusting in God among the burning flames of the fire and crowned by a blessed martyrdom, they passed to God on the thirteenth day of the month of November.

553-572

[37] In quibus illud mirabile contigit: quod nec in capillis eorum aut in vestimentis ulla ignis laesio comparuit. *Vultus autem illorum rosei coloris decore emicabant, ut dormientes potius quam extinctos putares, unde multi, conversi ad Deum, crediderunt.*

[38] His ita gestis tyrannus

iubet sibi sanctam virginem praesentari

<videns> beatam Katerinam immutabiliter fidei tenere constantiam nec minis aut terroribus turbari, arte quadam temptat animum illius emollire, ut ad profana sacrilegua officia vel promissis infractam valeat inclinare,

dixitque illi: [39] 'o virgo generosa, o digna imperiali purpura facies! Consule iuventuti tuae et sacrifica diis nostris et eris secunda post reginam in palatio meo, et adnutum tuum cuncta regni spectabunt negotia.

---

37 illud] hoc *Z*, *om*. *B* || mirabile] insigne miraculum *B* <u>Dob</u> || quod] quo *B*, quia *Mk* || in³] *om*. *T Z Bro R* || comparuit] apparuit *Bro*
*37 decore] colore *B*
38 ita] itaque *Z M C <u>D</u> <u>F</u> <u>P</u>₁ <u>H</u>* || iubet sibi] *post* virginem *Z* || sibi] *om*. *K Mk Bro* || praesentari] *post* sibi *C* || dixitque illi] dixit itaque illi *B* <u>Dob</u>, cui sic ait *Bro*
*38 videns] *om*. *B* || tenere] tenore *B* || sacrificia] sacrilegua officia *B* || inlinaret] valeat inclinare] <u>Dob</u>
39 o²] o virgo *Z*, *om*. *Mk Bro* || imperiali] imberabili *C* || purpura] honore purpurea *K M* || facies] *om*. *Bro* || iuventuti] iuventute *H* || tuae] tu *C* || eris] sis *B* || nutum] vultum *B* || nutum tuum] t. n. *Mk* || cuncta] *om*. *B* || regni] regis *Z* || spectabunt negotia] negotia spectabunt *R* <u>Dob</u>, negotia spectant *B*

[37] In them this marvelous thing happened: in that not a single injury of the fire appeared either in their hair or on their clothing. *But their faces were radiating with the blush of rose colour so that you might think they were sleeping rather than dead, from which cause many converted to God and had faith.*

[38] After these things were done in this way, the tyrant ordered the holy virgin to be presented to him *(seeing how) blessed Katherine immutably retained the steadfastness of the faith and was not troubled either by threats or fears, tries to soften her mind by some trick, so that he might succeed in weakening the girl by promises and so influence her to profane sacrifices,* and he said to her: [39] 'O noble virgin, o face worthy of the imperial purple! Consider your youth and sacrifice to our gods and you will be second after the queen in my palace, and all the affairs of the kingdom will look to your will.

580-85

623-29

648-9
+667

[40] Faciam perinde tibi sceptriferae imaginis statuam in medio civitatis erigi a cunctis civibus salutandam, ab omnibus adorandam. Postremo intra deas tibi templum de insigni marmore erigam.' [41] Ad haec virgo respondit: 'desine imperator talia suadere, quae sit scelus etiam cogitare. Christus me sibi sponsam adoptavit, ego me Christo sponsam indissociabili fœdere coaptavi. Ille gloria mea, ille amor meus, ille dulcedo et dilectio mea. Ab eius amore me non rerum blandimenta, non exquisita tormenta ab eius confessione poterunt revocare.' [42] Hic tyrannus commotus furore iubet eam expoliatam scorpionibus cedi, dehinc obscuro carceris ergastulo claudi ubi per duodenos dies fame et siti eam imperat cruciari.

40 faciam] faciam *D*, faciamque *B* || perinde] *post* tibi *C*, proinde *post* tibi *Z*, *om. B*, proinde *Mk M*, quoque *R* || sceptriferae] septiferae *B*, *del. K*, sceptrigerae *C* || a] et a *T* || ab] et ab *M L* || ab ... adorandam] *om. Mk* || postremo] preterea *T*, posttremum *B* || intra] inter *Bro*, infra *M* || deas] deos *B Bro L N* || tibi templum] t. tibi *H B Bro Dob*, tibi t. *T Z K Mk M*, templum *C*, templum dei tibi *(dei underlined) R* || marmore] vero marmore *M* || erigam] erigendum *M*

41 virgo] virgo beata Katherina *M* || talia] michi talia *M* || sit] sunt *T Z B Mk Bro M S E (a.c.)* || scelus] sceleris *Z* || scelus etiam] e. s. *C R H Z* || me¹] etiam me *B* || sibi] *post* adoptavit *K*, *om. B Bro* || sibi sponsam] sponsam s. *Z* || ego] et ego *Mk* || Christo sponsam] s. c. *Z* || indissociabili] indissolubili *K Mk Bro M E N Q H Z* || ille¹] Christus *C* || amor] honor *K* || dulcedo] dulcedo mea *T Mk D* || et dilectio mea] *om. C* || me³] *om. B C* || non¹] *om. Mk M* || non²] nec *C D P₂ Q H Z* || ab²] et ab *K* || confessione poterunt] p. c. *M* || poterunt] umquam poterunt *B Dob* || revocare] removere *M*

[40] In the same way I shall have erected for you the statue of a sceptre-bearing likeness in the middle of the city, to be greeted by all the citizens, to be worshipped by everybody. Finally, I shall erect for you a temple made of distinguished marble among the goddesses.' [41] To these words the virgin replied: 'Stop suggesting such things, emperor, that it is a crime even to contemplate. Christ has adopted me as his wife, I have joined myself to Christ as his wife with an unbreakable agreement. He is my glory, he is my love, he is my sweetness and my delight. From his love it is not blandishments of material things that can call me back, neither can choice torments call me back from his faith.' [42] Then the tyrant, shaken by anger, orders her to be stripped and beaten with lashes, then to be shut into a dark cell of the prison where he commends her to be tortured with hunger and thirst over twelve days.

---

42 hic] hinc *T Z Mk Bro R*, *om. B* || commotus furore] furore inebriatus *B Dob*, f. c. *K Mk M C R* || iubet eam] a ministris beatam virginem iubet *B*, iubet beatam virginem Caterinam *R* || expoliatam] spoliatam *Bro* || cedi] graviter cedi *M* || dehinc] deinde *C* || obscuro] in obscuro *Bro* || claudi] includi *C* || ubi ... cruciari] *om. B* || eam imperat] i. e. *Z*

650-75

[43] *Ubi dum duceretur constanter ait tyranno: 'ego plane in eius nomine libens flagellis cedi, ego carceris tenebrosi horrorem amplecti gaudeo, qui corpus suum pro me dedit ad flagella, qui mundum pugillo continens carceris angusti claustra non refugit. Tu michi tenebras ingeris; certum sit tibi quia per has lux perpetua michi paratur, tibi autem tenebrae aeternales succedent.'* [44] *Tunc iussa tyrannica ministri explentes, ferreis virgis corpus tenerum lacerabant et dum verberabant alii deficiebant, alii succedebant. Manet interim virgo laudans in verberibus et Deo gratias agens.* [45] *Clauditur virgo beatissima ex iussu regio in carcere tenebroso fame et siti bis senis diebus crucianda sub praefinito edicto, ne caeli lumen videat ne aliud quam tenebras horrentes inspiciat.* [46] *Sed nec in his Christus famulam suam deseruit; adsunt namque illi angeli de caelo confortantes eam et inaestimabili fulgore locum penitus irradiantes, adeo ut custodes qui a foris excubias observabant prae timore nimio in stuporem mentis converterentur; nullus tamen horum quid viderat tyranno nuntiare praesumpsit pro timore et feritate sua.*

[47] Accidit autem ut ipse pro causis instantibus extrema regionis confinia adiret.

43 dum] cum ***Dob*** || *ait tyranno]* t. a. ***Dob*** || *carceris tenebrosi]* t. c. ***Dob*** || *carceris]* vestris c. ***B*** || *michi]* tibi ***B*** || *tenebras]* tenebrae ***B***
44 verberabant] verberabant p.c. **Δ₂**, verberabant ***E J O S***, verberando ***Dob***
45 virgo beatissima ex iussu regio] ex iussu virgo regio ***C***, ex iussu regio virgo ***G***, ex iussu regis virgo regia ***Dob***
46 nec] nec ***D E F G N U W Y Σ Q***, ne ***Dob*** || *namque]* om. ***Dob*** || *inaestimabili]* inaestimabili ***D Q***, inaestimabili claritatis ***Dob*** || *a]* om. ***B L U*** || *observabant]* o. alii ***B*** || *nimio]* om. ***Dob*** || *stuporem]* timorem ***B D H Z*** || *viderat]* videat ***B*** || *tyranno]* post horum ***Dob*** || *nuntiare]* om. ***B*** || *feritate]* timore et feritate ***B***
47 ipse] ipse Maxentius imperator ***B*** || pro] om. ***Bro*** || extrema] extremae ***Bro***

[43] When she was being led there she resolutely said to the tyrant: 'I am entirely glad to be submitted to whips, I rejoice to embrace the horror of the shadowy jail in the name of the one who gave his body to the whips on my behalf, who – holding the world in his hand – did not flee the bars of his cramped prison. You are forcing shadows on me, you can be certain that through these shadows eternal light is being prepared for me, but for you eternal shadows will follow.' [44] Then the servants completed the tyrannical order and maimed the tender body of the virgin with iron rods, and while they were flogging [her], some lost strength and others took their place. The virgin kept on praising and thanking God during the flogging. [45] The most blessed virgin was shut in the gloomy jail on the royal order, to be tortured by hunger and thirst for twelve days under a fixed command so that she would not see the light of the sky nor look at anything else but the harrowing darkness. [46] But Christ did not desert his servant in this situation; for angels from heaven are there for her, comforting her and completely illuminating the place with an incalculable brightness, so much that the guards who were stationed outside the doors were turned to a bewilderment for the mind because of their fear; yet, because of his brutality and their fear, none of them took it on himself to announce what he had seen to the tyrant.

[47] But it happened that the tyrant himself went to the outermost borders of the region for pressing reasons.

675-86 [48] Pernotuerat vero reginae crudelissima viri sententia de beata Katerina, *qualiter innocentem virginem per sapientes saeculi tractasset et quomodo illi, puellaribus verbis evicti et ad fidem Christi conversi, gloriosa passione migrassent.* De quo facto vir eius indignatus, dum virgo diis libamina offerre noluisset, diris caesam scorpionibus sub arta custodia carceris iussit recludi ubi per duodenos dies iuxta crudelis regis sententiam puella innocens nullo cibi alimento frueretur. [49] *Audiens regina ferale regis coniugis edictum, licet gentili errore teneretur, tamen animi ingenita bonitate tenerae aetatis sortem miseratur iniquam.* Unde anxia videre faciem virginis et eam alloqui cupiebat *sed ne id pernoscat vir eius vehementer formidat. Talia meditando regiam domum solitaria deambulabat.*

48 vero] *om. B* || reginae] *om. C* || Katerina] Katerine virgine *M*
*48 innocentem virginem] *Dob*, om. *B* || passione] passione de mundo *Dob* || migrassent] migrassent *F*, emigrassent *Dob* || vir] ubi *B* || scorpionibus] corpionibus *B* || duodenos] duodenes *B* || cibi] sibi *B*
49 unde] fit *B Dob* || videre faciem] f. v. *B* || virginis] eius *H C* || et eam] eamque *Z* || eam alloqui cupiebat] *P₂ H Z*, colloqui cum ea *B*
*49 regis] om. *Dob* || ingenita bonitate] ingenua nobilitate *B*, ingenuitate *S* || sortem] sorte *B* || pernoscat] persentiat *A₂ E L*, percipiat *P₁*, persentiscat *Dob*

[48] Indeed, the very cruel sentence of her husband on blessed Katherine came to the knowledge of the queen, *how he had treated the innocent virgin at the hands of the pagan philosophers and how they were utterly defeated by the words of the girl and converted to the faith of Christ, and had died by a glorious martyrdom; for which reason her husband was angry, [and] since the girl had refused to offer libations to the gods, he ordered that, after she had been flogged with lashes, she should be shut up under the tight confinement of the prison where, for twelve days according to the sentence of the cruel king, the innocent girl was to enjoy no provision of food.* [49] *When the queen heard the deadly command of her husband, although she was possessed by pagan error, nevertheless by inherent goodness of her mind, she felt sorry for the unfair lot of the young girl,* which is why she was anxious and wanted to see the face of the virgin and to console her, *but she is terribly afraid her husband might find out about it. She was thinking such things while she was wandering around alone in the royal palace.*

686-96	[50] Evocans itaque ad se principem nomine Porphyrium postulat ut amotis aut placatis custodibus colloquio virginis potiretur.	*Fit illi optato eventu obviam militiae princeps quidam nomine Porphyrius, vir strenuus et quantum ad temporalem saeculi dignitatem consilio prudens fide promptus, amici secretum intra claustra silentii constantissime servans. Hunc ad se evocans imperatrix Augusta aperit ei voluntatem suam, simulque* postulat ut amotis aut placatis custodibus *carceris visu et* colloquio virginis potiretur.

'Nam ut,' inquit, 'tibi Porphyri, quae me sollicitant aperiam, multa hac in nocte per visum passa sum quorum ambigua revelatio me adeo suspensam reddit ut quocumque se horum exitus sive in adversum sive in prosperum vertat, eorum sane effectum mature superventurum certissime cognoscam.

50 evocans] convocans ***Bro***, advocans *C* || itaque] quippe *T Z K Bro M*, ergo ***Mk*** || quendam] quondam *H T Z Bro M C*
*50 militiae princeps] p. m. **Dob** || aut placatis] et iracastis B || visu] iussu B || inquit tibi] t. i. **Dob** || multa] multa L M C E F J N Δ O S Σ, multa michi **Dob** || vertat] vertar B || effectum] eventum **Dob** || superventurum] superventum B*

[50] And so calling to herself a certain leader of the army named Porphyrius, she demanded that, with the guards removed or placated, she might obtain a conversation with the virgin.	*Into her path came, by a lucky chance, a certain leader of the army by name of Porphyrius, a vigorous man and as regards his station in the world, prudent in counsel, ready in loyalty, keeping most loyally the secret of a friend inside the walls of silence. The empress Augusta summoned him to her and explained to him her wish, and at the same time* demanded that, with the guards *of the prison* either removed or placated, *she should gain sight and interview of the virgin.*

She said: 'For to reveal to you, Porphyrius, the matters that are troubling me, this night I have suffered many things in front of my eyes, things whose doubtful revelation has left me in such a state of suspense that – wherever their outcome may turn, whether to adversity or success – I shall find out most certainly the result of those things that are soon about to happen.

697-
718

[51] *Videbam hanc sane de qua loquimur puellam intra saepta domicilii sedentem inaestimabili claritate circumfultam et viros dealbatos circumsedentes quorum vultus inspicere prae claritate vix poteram. Illa autem me intuens iubet me propius accedere et de manu unius horum qui assistebant coronam auream accipiens capiti meo imponebat michi dicens haec uerba: "ecce tibi, o imperatrix, corona de caelo mittitur a domino meo Iesu Christo." [52] Qua ex visione suspensa nec somnum capere nec horae unius momento quiescere possum, ita cor tremulum me ad videndam virginem exagitat. Per te ergo michi viam ad puellam eundi et videndi facultatem dari precor, o Porphyri.' [53] Cui Porphyrius respondit: 'unde et me ipsum ad hoc promptum invenies famulum licet imperatoris iram sciam pro certo me non posse vitare si rescierit. [54] Nam de puella de qua loqueris crudeliter ab imperatore actum constat, quia et ego interfui quando ab extremis sapientes convocatos disceptare adversus puellam constituit et promissis muneribus si victam redderent vehementer incitavit. Illi autem adversus eam stare nec una hora praevaluerunt, sed ilico conversi deum quem puella praedicabat publice fatebantur. Unde et indignatus imperator omnes ignibus tradi imperavit in quibus illud mirabile contigisse vidi et ego, quod in his omnibus nec in capillis aut in vestimentis ulla ignis laesio comparuit.*

*51 hanc sane] s. h. **Dob** || saepta domicilii] secta domicilia B || inaestimabili] inaestimabile B || vix] haud **Dob** || me¹] om. **Dob** || manu] manus F || coronam] chororonam B || accipiens] accipere B, accipiebat **P₁** || michi dicens] post verba **W**, d. m. **Dob** || de] e **Dob**
*53 ipsum ad hoc] a. h. i. **Dob** || iram] non B || rescierit] rex rescierit B
*54 extremis] extremis finibus **D I L N Λ Ω Y**, externis finibus **Dob** || victam] victum B || incitavit] incitaret B || una hora] u. h. **I L**, h. u. **Dob** || praevaluerunt] praevalerent B || deum] deum **E J O S**, deum hunc **Dob** || ulla] nulla B **W**

[51] I truly saw this girl we are talking about sitting within the walls of her dwelling place, bathed in an unmeasureable brightness, and men dressed in white, whose faces I could hardly see due to the brightness, were sitting around her. But looking at me, she orders me to come closer and, receiving a golden crown from one of the men who were near her, she was placing it on my head, saying these words to me: "Behold, o empress, the crown is sent from heaven for you by my lord Jesus Christ." [52] Excited by this vision I am unable to go to sleep or rest for the space of a single hour, so much does my trembling heart urge me to see the virgin. Therefore I ask that you give me the way of going to the girl and the possibility of seeing her, o Porphyrius.' [53] Porphyrius answered her: 'whence you will find me also a ready servant in this matter, although I know that I certainly cannot avoid the anger of the emperor if he were to know of this. [54] For it is certain that the girl you talk about has been treated cruelly by the emperor, because I also was present when he set up the wise men, summoned from faraway frontiers, to dispute against the girl, and passionately encouraged them with promises of gifts if they subdued her. But they were not strong enough to withstand her even for an hour, but there and then they were converted and publicly accepted the god the girl was proclaiming. Whence indeed the angry emperor commanded all of them to be handed over to the flames, and I too saw that miracle happen to them, namely that no harm of the fire showed itself either in their hair or in their clothes.

719-27

[55] *Qua ex re fateor, o regina, ex illo die sic verba illius quibus ipsa deos nostros exprobavit – sic,' inquid, 'cor meum titillando sollicitant ut quicquid diis nostris exhibemus frivolum reputem et inane. Unde lex nostra nisi Christianorum sectam penitus abhorruisset, facile quis poterat me ad cultum Christi impellere. [56] Sed quoniam tu opportune ut puto consilium meum praeveniendo commones, quid restat nisi ut custodes carceris mercede ad consilium nostrum inflectamus ut ipsi celare hoc ipsum studeant?'* Nec mora: Porphyrius ad consensum custodes emollivit.

728-32

[57] Igitur de prima vigilia noctis regina simul et Porphyrius procedunt ad carcerem et introeuntes viderunt carcerem inaestimabili claritate undique coruscare cuius ex fulgore perterriti corruerunt in terram. Mox inaestimabilis odor suavitatis naribus infusus ad spem meliorem confortavit.

*55 qua ex re] quia ex re *B*, qua re *C*, quare *D*, qua ex re *Dob* || inquid] inquam *Dob* || nostris] om. *Dob* || frivolum] totum frivolum *Dob* || inane] inanum *B* || lex nostra nisi] nisi l. n. *Dob* || poterat] poterit *B* || impellere] pelle *B*

*56 quoniam tu] q. t. *L*, t. q. *Dob* || ut³] ut et *Dob*

56 mora] ipsa ora *B* || consensum] consensum eius *C* || emollivit] emollit *B*

57 de] in *Bro C* || prima vigilia] v. p. *Bro* || simul] om. *B* || viderunt] vident *H*, *post* undique *B Mk* || cuius] cui *R* || ex] om. *B* || ex fulgore] effulgore *C* || naribus] eorumnaribus *Bro N P₂*, naribus eorum *L P₁ H Z*, naribus ipsius *M* || spem] speciem *B* || confortavit] confortavit eos *B*, eos confortavit *S W*

[55] Because of this matter, o queen, I proclaim, from that day when she reproached our gods with such words,' he said, 'thus they stir my heart with tickling in such a way that whatever we are displaying to our gods I consider frivolous and empty. Whence, if our law had not totally shunned the sect of the Christians, someone could easily have persuaded me to the worship of Christ. [56] But since you opportunely, as I think, forestall me in my own plan, what remains except to persuade the prison guards of our plan with bribes so that they try to hide the matter?' There was no delay: Porphyrius softened the guards to agreement.

[57] Therefore at the onset of the first watch, the queen together with Porphyrius set out to the prison and, on entering, they saw that the cell was gleaming on all sides with an incalculably great brightness, and terrified of its brilliance they fell down on the ground. Soon an incalculably precious scent of sweetness poured into their noses and confirmed a kinder prospect.

732-
46

[58] 'Surgite', inquit virgo egregia, 'et ne paveatis quia et vos Christus vocat ad palmam.' Surgentes autem conspiciunt puellam sedentem, et angelos dei plagas et carnis scissuras aromatico unguine circumfoventes quibus caro et cutis superficies in admirabilem decorem convertebantur. *[59] Vident etiam et seniores circumsedentes quorum vultus candore emicabant. Horum ab uno qui astabat Christi uirgo coronam accepit velut aureo colore rutilantem, et reginae capiti imposuit dixitque circumsedentibus senioribus, 'haec est illa, domini mei, de qua postulaveram regina et quam militiae et coronae nostrae a Deo consortem depoposceram. Sed et hunc qui assistit militem in nostrae sortis numerum ascribi uolumus.' [60] Ad haec illi inquiunt: 'pretiosa Christi margarita, super his preces tuas ille suscepit pro cuius amore flagella et carceris horrorem non timuisti. Sed aeterno foedere ab ipso tibi collatum esse constat ut pro quibuscumque ipsius maiestatem interpellaueris impetratum reportabis.*

58 surgite] surge *B* || paveatis] paveas *B* || vocat ad palmam] a. p. v. *K* || autem] om. *Bro* || conspiciunt] contemplati sunt *H B M* || dei] om. *K* || plagas] plagas illius *B*, plagas eius *F N* || scissuras] illius scissuras *B* || unguine] unguento *Z Bro P₁ P₂ H*, ugine *M*, unguedine *C* || cutis] cutie *C* || superficies] superveniens *B* || convertebantur] vertebantur *B* R <u>Dob</u>, convertebat *Mk*

*59 candore] inedicibili lucis candore <u>Dob</u> || astabat] astabant *B H Z* || et³] om. <u>Dob</u> || coronae nostrae] coronam vitae *B* || depoposceram] depoposceram *I,* michi depoposceram <u>Dob</u> || numerum] militem et consortem *B*

*60 pretiosa] pretiosa *F,* o pretiosa <u>Dob</u> || sed] sed *N O W Σ,* sed et <u>Dob</u> || tibi collatum] c. b. <u>Dob</u> || reportabis] reportabit *B*

[58] The admirable virgin said: 'Get up and don't be afraid because Christ calls you too to the victory.' They got up and saw the girl sitting and the angels of god who were soothing round the wounds and tears of her flesh with an aromatic ointment by which her flesh and the surface of her skin were being turned into an admirable beauty. [59] *They also saw sitting around elderly men whose faces were shining with radiance. From one of these who was standing near, the virgin of Christ received a crown as though glowing with the colour of gold, and she placed it upon the queen's head and said to the elderly men who were sitting around: 'This is she, my lords, the queen I had demanded and had asked for from God as my consort to be my soldier and crown. But I also wish to add this soldier, who is standing by, to the squadron of my destiny.' [60] In response to these words they said: 'Precious pearl of Christ, as far as these people are concerned, he has accepted your prayers, he for whose love you did not fear lashes and the horror of the prison. But it is clear that it has been conferred on you by an eternal bond through himself, that for whomsoever you appeal to his majesty, you will obtain and win it.*

747-52

[61] *Hos interim qui visitationis gratia tibi assistunt scito inter primitias laborum tuorum iam ascriptos quos triumphali passione ante te caelica regna excipient coronatos.* Mox militiae agone peracto ille immortalis sponsus intra vitae aeternae ianuam te suscipiet ubi modulis dulcisonis caelica organa resonabunt, ubi clarissima turba virginum inter lilia roseis floribus vernantia sequuntur agnum quocumque ierit.'

753-77

[62] Tunc beata virgo reginam advocans blande consolari cœpit dicens: 'iam regina forti animo esto quia post hoc triduum itura es ad dominum. Ne ergo momentanea pœnarum genera formides quia *non sunt condignae passiones huius temporis ad* interminabilis gloria talibus pro Christo pœnis emercatur.

*61 interim] interum B, iterum <u>P₁</u> || tibi] iam <u>Dob</u> || ascriptos] abscriptos B || te] post ille <u>Dob</u> || ubi] ubi tibi <u>Λ₂</u>, ubi tibi <u>Dob</u> || dulcisonis] dulce sonoris <u>Dob</u> || resonabunt] resonant B || turba virginum] v. t. <u>Dob</u> || vernantia] verniatia B

62 tunc] his dictis B <u>Dob</u> || beata] om. M || reginam] regina B || advocans blande] adv. bl. eam Z, om. B, adv. ipsam blande M, b. a. R || consolari cœpit] cœp. cons. T B, cœp. alloqui H, cœp. eam alloqui C || hoc] om. B || hoc triduum] t. h. T || dominum] deum T M <u>Dob</u>, domini B || momentanea] momentaneorum B, momentanae M || pœnarum] pœnorum H, tormentorum Z || pœnarum genera] g. p. B || interminabilis gloria] interminabilem gloriam quae B <u>Dob</u> || pœnis] om. R

[61] Meanwhile these people who attend to you with the favour of visitation, know that they are already reckoned among the first fruits of your effort, who, crowned by a triumphant passion, will be received by the heavenly kingdom before you. Soon when the struggle of the battle has been completed, that immortal husband will receive you inside the doorway of eternal life, where heavenly instruments will resound with sweet-sounding tunes, where among the lilies flowering with rose-coloured flowers the most dazzling crowd of virgins follows the lamb wherever it may go.'

[**62**] Then the blessed virgin called forth the queen and gently began to comfort her, saying: 'Now, queen, be of strong spirit because two days from now you will be going to the Lord. Therefore do not fear the transitory kinds of punishments because *the sufferings of this time are not comparable to the* unending glory is that procured by such punishments on behalf of Christ.

759-67 [63] Ne verearis, inquam, regis temporalis et mortalis sponsi consortium aspernari pro rege aeterno et immortali sponso domino Iesu Christo, qui pro caducis honoribus donat aeterna praemia, pro transitoriis largitur sine fine mansura.' [64] Ad haec Porphyrius *qui primae cohortis praefecturam agebat et magnis rerum possessionibus pollebat* coepit rogando inquirere quaenam illa essent praemia quae suis Christus militibus pro damnis temporalibus recompensabit. [65] Cui virgo: 'audi', inquit, 'Porphyri!

784-92 [66] Illa superna patria pro qua fit mundi contemptus velut civitas est sole numquam indigens, ubi nulla turbat adversitas, molestia nulla inquietat; sed perennis illic laetitia, iocunditas aeterna, felicitas regnat sempiterna.

63 verearis] reveraris *Bro M* || inquam] inquit *R* || et¹] aut *B Dob* || regis temporalis et mortalis sponsi] temporalis sponsi *Z*, regis temporalis *K Bro*, regis temporalis sponsi *M*, t. r. et m. s. *C* || consortium] thorum *H T* || et²] *om. Bro* || domino] domino nostro *Z Mk Bro M G*, domino meo *D* || aeterna praemia] p. ae. *Bro G* || praemia] patria *B* || transitoriis] transitoriis *D (a.c.) E*, transituris *H R Dob*, || largitur] largitu *Bro*, largiatur *C*
64 haec] haec verba beatissimae virginis *B E I O S*, haec verba beatae virginis *Dob* || Porphyrius coepit] c. P. *M P₁* || coepit] incoepit *T* || illa essent] e. i. *T Z K Bro C D G Σ*, essent *B* || Christus militibus] Christus *Bro*, m. C. *K Mk M* || recompensabit] recompensabitur *Bro*
*64 qui] qui *B N W*, quia *Dob* || et] cum *B*
66 fit] sit *B* || est] *om. K* || sole numquam] n. s. *Z B Bro* || turbat] turbatio *Z* || adversitas] nulla adversitas *Z* || molestia ... inquietat] nulla angustia necessitas angustiat *B* || nulla²] numquam *K* || molestia nulla] n. m. *T Mk* || sed ... sempiterna] *om. T Z K Mk Bro M* || illic] *om. B R Dob*

[63] Do not be afraid, I say, to reject the companionship of the worldly king and the mortal husband on behalf of the eternal king and the immortal husband, the lord Jesus Christ, who gives eternal prizes instead of perishable honours, who lavishes things that will last without end instead of ones that are transitory.' [64] At these words Porphyrius, *because he was holding the command of the first cohort and was rich in great possessions of things*, began to inquire by asking what those prizes might be that Christ will measure out to his soldiers for temporal injuries. [65] The virgin said to him: 'Listen, Porphyrius! [66] That celestial land for the sake of which there is contempt for the world is a like a city never lacking in sunshine, where no adversity makes trouble, no distress disturbs, but in that place reigns constant happiness, eternal joy, and perpetual good fortune.

787-92 [67] Si quaeris quid ibi sit ubi tanta et talis beatitudo consistit, aliter dici non potest nisi quicquid boni est ibi est et quicquid mali est nusquam est. Quod inquis bonum? Illud est dico quod oculus non vidit nec auris audivit, nec in cor hominis ascendit quae preparavit deus

801-04 diligentibus se.' [68] His et aliis beatae virginis sermonibus exhilarati et supernorum civium praesenti visione laetificati regina simul et Porphyrius procedunt de carcere media nocte parati ad omnia *quae tortor insanus iubebat* pro

818-20 Christi nomine sustinenda. [69] Sed et ducenti milites Porphyrio obsequentes eius suasu et monitis idola respuentes ad Christum conversi sunt.

67 sit] est *R* || tanta et talis] talis et tana *C* || dici] dicit *C* || quicquid ... quod[1]] *om. B* || boni ... quicquid[2]] *om. M* || boni] bonum *Mk* || boni est] e. b. *K* || est[1]] es *Bro* || est[3]] et *C* || nusquam] non ibi usquam *T*, ibi non (nusquam *above* non) *J*, ibi nusquam *Z Bro* Θ, nusquam ibi *S* || quod[2]] quid *LP R* || inquis] inquit *post* bonum *B* || bonum] bonum est *V*, bonum et *C* || est dico] inquam bonum *T*, dico est *Z B* || oculus non] nec oculus *B* || nec[1]] et *H C* || audivit] non audivit *H C* || cor] cordis? *C* || ascendit] non ascendit *C* || quae] quod *T*

68 beatae virginis sermonibus] s. b. v. *T* || virginis] virginis Katherine *M* || sermonibus] *om. Z* || civium praesenti] civium *B*, *om. C* || civium] civium et *Z* || regina simul et Porphyrius] simul *T* || procedunt] recedunt *Bro* || de] a *Bro* || sustinenda] sustinenda(?) et *B*

*68 insanus] insanis *B*, insanissimus *F* || iubebat] poterit inferre] iubebat *Dob*

69 set et ... sunt] *om. C* || sed et] praeterea *T*, sunt *Bro* || ducenti] ducentes *B* || milites] homines milites *Bro* || Porphyrio] Porphyrius *B* || obsequentes] *post* Porphyrio *Z*, obsecruentes *B* || suasu] suasione *Bro* || monitis] monitu *T*, moni *Z* || respuentes] renuentes *B* || conversi] reversi *B*

[67] If you ask what there is where so much and so great blessedness exists, it cannot be explained otherwise than by saying that whatever is good is there, and whatever is bad is nowhere. What good?, you say. I say, it is that which the eye has not seen and the ear has not heard, and that which god has prepared for those who love him [and] does not rise in the heart of man.' [68] Cheered up by these and other words of the virgin, and gladded by the present vision of the heavenly citizens, the queen in the company of Porphyrius set out from the prison in the middle of the night, ready to suffer in the name of Christ everything *that the insane torturer ordered.* [69] And what is more, two hundred soldiers, under Porphyrius' command, by his advice and counsels rejected the idols and converted to Christ.

821-
32

[70] Servabatur interea in carcere *iuxta edictum imperatoris* innocens puella et quia bissenis diebus sine alimento eam esse tyrannus iusserat Christus per hos dies missa de caelo candida columba caelesti eam cibo refovebat. [71] Expletis vero diebus apparuit ei dominus cum multitudine angelorum quem sequebatur innumera turba virginum. Cui dominus: 'agnosce', inquit, 'filia, agnosce auctorem tuum pro cuius nomine laboriosi certaminis coepisti conflictum. Constans esto *et ne paveas* quia tecum sum nec te desero *est etenim non parva turba hominum per te nomini meo creditura.*' Haec dicens in caelum sese recepit *quem virgo euntem longo intuitu sequebatur.*

70 servabatur ... refovebat] *om. C* || interea] interim *T, post* carcere ***Bro*** || in carcere] *post* puella *T, om. R* || innocens puella] innocens virgo *B*, Christi virgo ***Dob*** || bis senis diebus] *om. T* || alimento] alimentis ***Bro*** || sine alimento eam esse tyrannus] eam sine a. t. e. *H* || per hos dies] *om.* *H Σ Q,* per hos *K* || missa de caelo] d. c. m. *T B* || caelo] loco *K* || candida columba] col. can. *T R P₂ Q H Z* || caelesti] *om. K Mk* || eam] *post* Christus *H* || caelesti eam cibo] e. ci. cae. *M* || refovebat] reficiebat *B*, refovebat quotidie ***Bro***

[70] In the meantime the innocent girl was kept in the prison *according to the command of the emperor*, and because the tyrant had ordered her to be without food for twelve days, Christ restored her with heavenly food through a white dove from heaven during those days. [71] But when the days were over, the Lord appeared to her with a multitude of angels and an innumerable crowd of virgins was following him. The Lord said to her: 'Recognize, daughter, recognize your maker in whose name you have begun the battle of a toilsome fight. Be unwavering *and don't be afraid*, because I am with you and do not forsake you *and indeed no small crowd of men is going to believe in my name because of you.*' He said these things and withdrew himself into heaven *and the virgin followed him with a long gaze as he was going*.

---

71 expletis ... recepit] post vero dies duodecim dum sollicita esset sancta virgo de regis presentia et metu penarum et deum suppliciter exoraret, ecce astitit dominus Christus in ea forma qua ab hominibus videri solet cum cetu angelico dicens ei: ne timeas neque paveas famula mea, ecce enim sum creator omnium Christus pro cuius amore talia sustines. Beata namque eris inter omnes mulieres et gaudia celorum recipient te. Hec cum audisset virgo domini gaudio magno exultans, cepid glorificare et collaudere deum et in femineo corpore virilem inserens vigorem parata erat pro Christi amore omnia sustinere *C* || dominus] dominus Iesu *H* || quem] quam *B* || inquit filia] f. i. *Bro* || agnosce²] agnosce inquid *B* || cuius] quo *Z* || nomine laboriosi certaminis] laboriosum *Z K Mk*, nomine laboriosum *Σ Q* || cœpisti conflictum] suscepisti conflictum *T*, conflictum *Bro*, cursum cœpisti *Dob P₁ P₂ Q*, certamen cœpisti *H Z* || tecum sum] ego sum *H B R*, ego tecum sum *Dob* || desero] deseram *T* || caelum] caelo *B* || sese] se *Z M R G U*
*71 etenim non] nec *B* || nomini] nomino *B* || euntem longo] e. l. *G W*, l. e. *Dob*

832-52 [72] At imperator expletis causis pro quibus ierat Alexandriam rediit. Postera die educitur de carcere virgo speciosa tribunali eius praesentanda. *Quae cum in eius staret praesentia vultumque illius quem tanto dierum spatio attenuatum ieiunio aestimarat, multo formosiorem et splendidiorem esse videret arbitrabatur clandestino officio ei subministrata alimenta. Unde furore commotus carcerarios iubet excruciari nisi fateantur a quo et per quem virgo in carcere cibis fuisset sustentata.* [73] Tunc Christi virgo ne custodes sui causa innocentes cruciarentur: [74] 'ego plane cibum ab homine corporalem nullum accepi, sed qui suos milites in tribulatione deserere nescit, ipse me, ancillam suam, per angelum suum caelesti alimento nutrire dignatus est.'

72 at imperator ... 111 inferre potueris] *om. C*
72 at] *om. Z* || expletis] impletis *B* || rediit] redierat *H T B K M C R,* reversus est *Mk* || postera] postea *B,* postera vero *M* || de] e *Z* || de carcere] *post* speciosa *Mk* || virgo speciosa] gloriosa virguo *B* || eius] regio *B Dob, om. M*
*72 carcerarios] carceratos *B* || in carcere cibis] cibis i. c. *Dob*
*73 tunc] at *Dob* || ne] nec *B,* non *F* || causa] causam *B* || innocentes] innocenter *Dob*
*74 in] in fame et *Dob* || suum] *om. Dob* || caelesti alimento] caelesti ibi alimento *W* (p.c.), caelestis cibi alimento *Dob*

[72] But the emperor returned to Alexandria when he had completed the matters for which he had gone. On the next day the beautiful virgin is led out of prison to be presented to his judgement. *When she came to a halt in his presence and he saw her face, which he had reckoned after such a long period of days would have been emaciated with the lack of food, to be a lot more beautiful and splendid, he thought that she had been supplied with provisions by a secret favour. Whence agitated by anger, he orders the prison-guards to be tortured if they do not confess from whom and through whom the virgin had been sustained with food in prison. [73] Then the virgin of Christ, so that the innocent guards would not be tortured because of her, said: [74] 'I have clearly not received corporeal food from any man, but he who does not know how to desert his soldiers in tribulation, he saw fit to nourish me, his maid-servant, through his angel with heavenly nourishment.*

859-66 [75] Ad quam tyrannus: 'licet', ait, 'te servare quam perdere maluissem, necesse est tamen praesenti deliberatione quod vis unum e duobus eligere – aut sacrificare ut vivas aut exquisitis tormentis dilacerari ut pereas.' [76] Cui Katerina respondit: 'vivere sane opto sed ut michi vivere Christus sit, mori autem pro eo non timeo sed potius diligo, quia moriendo pro eo interminabilis

873-78 vitae emolumentum lucrari me confido. [77] Tu ergo quaecumque tormentorum machinamenta potes excogitare ne differas, quia vocor a domino meo Iesu Christo cui carnem et sanguinem meum in sacrificium

851-52 offerre desidero, quia et ipse semetipsum pro me obtulit Deo patri in holocaustum. Ipse deus meus amator meus, ipse pastor et sponsus unicus meus.'

75 licet] licet autem Z || ait te servare] t. a. s. TZ, ait servare te B, ait te reservare R || maluissem] maluerim T || tamen] *post* maluerim T, tunc *Bro*, *post* necesse M, *om*. R || unum e duobus] *om*. Mk || e] de $B M$, est LP || eligere] elige T, elige *p.c.* K || aut] aut diis B *Dob* || tormentis dilacerari] d. t. *Bro* || dilacerari] corpus tenerum dilacerari B *Dob*

76 Katerina] beata Katerina $B \underline{\Delta}$, beata virgo $\underline{\Sigma} Q$ || respondit] ait T || ut] *om*. *Bro* || michi vivere] v. m. *Bro* $E \underline{W}$ || vivere Christus] vivam Christo B || mori] moriendo M || autem] *om*. $Mk \underline{N} \underline{S}$ || mori autem pro eo] p. e. a. m. M || non ... pro eo²] *om*. *Bro* || timeo] dubito Mk || quia ... confido] *om*. T || moriendo pro eo] p. e. m. Z || lucrari me] m. l. *Bro*

77 tu ... holocaustum] *om*. T || ergo] ergo tyranne B *Dob* || tormentorum] tormentor Mk || tormentorum machinamenta] m. t. B || carnem] carnem meam M || meum] nostrum B || et²] *om*. B || semetipsum pro me] p. m. s. B || obtulit Deo patri] d. p. o. $Z B K Mk$ *Bro* M || ipse² ... meus³] *om*. $H R$ || amator] adiutor $H T Z C R$ || pastor] pastor meus $K Mk M \underline{F}$ || meus³] *om*. Z

[75] The tyrant said to her: 'Although I would have preferred to keep you rather than lose you, yet it is necessary at the present consideration that you choose what you want from one of two: either to sacrifice so that you live or to be torn apart by choice torments so that you perish.' [76] Katherine answered him: 'Truly I choose to live, because to live for me is Christ, yet I do not fear to die for him but rather prefer it, because in dying for him I am confident to gain the reward of everlasting life. [77] You therefore, do not delay whatever devices of torments you can think of, because I am called by my Lord Jesus Christ to whom I wish to offer my flesh and blood in sacrifice, because he also gave himself up to God the father in an offering. He is my god, my lover, he is my shepherd, and my only husband.'

886- [78] Ad haec tyrannus ut leo violentus dentibus frendens in vocem
903 huiusmodi erupit: 'quid ignavi talia sustinemus? Usque adeo deos nostros tam contemptibiliter ab ista malefica incantatrice derogari patiemur? Cur non totum corpus eius discerpi non faciemus, ne et ceteri Christiani adversus deos nostros simili insultatione barbarizare praesumant? [79] Ergo omnes agite, quibuscumque deorum iniuria illata est! Apprehendite magam istam et diris suppliciis cruciatam morte crudelissima facite eam interire! Tunc deum suum de cuius se iactat praesidio, si fas est, provocet sibi ad auxilium.'

[80] Factum est autem cum traheretur ad supplicium, quidam miserantes formae virgineae decorem indigna morte perire, suadebant virgini ut imperatori potius obœdire deberet quam resistendo florem amitteret suae iuventutis; cui sic inquiunt: [81] 'o forma virginei decoris, o solaris species, quaenam tanta mentis obstinatio ista est ut generosi sanguinis puella cui divitiae et honores gratis offeruntur ultro mortem eligat? O virgo digna imperio, consule florentissimae iuventuti tuae et ne sinas pulchritudinis tuae vernantem speciem immatura morte perire!'

*78 ab] om. B || cur non] cur non E *J* *O* S, quin cur non **Δ**₂, quin **Dob** || eius] eius **Δ**, om. **Dob** || discerpi] membratim discerpi **Dob** || non faciemus] faciamus **Dob**, facimus E *O* || nostros²] om. **Dob**
*79 omnes agite] a. o. **Dob** || illata] curae **Dob** || cruciatam] cruciatam H *Z*, excruciatam **Dob** || facite eam] e. f. **Dob** || deum suum] deus suus B || fas] fax B || provocet] providet B
*80 formae virgineae] v. f. **Dob** || florem] sic E F *J* L **Δ** *O* S N, florentem **Dob** || suae] om. **Dob** || iuventutis] iuventutem E F *J* L **Δ** *O* S N, iuventam **Dob** || cui sic inquiunt] o inquiunt **Dob**
*81 o] om. B || specis] spes B || splendoris] decoris W E, candoris **Dob** || est] ista est **Dob** || puella cui] c. p. B || ultro mortem] uoluntarium mortis compendium **Dob** || sinas] negligas **Dob**

[78] *At these words the tyrant gnashed his teeth like a savage lion and broke into voice saying: 'Why do we sluggishly suffer such things? Shall we allow our gods to be reviled in such a contemptible way by this wicked witch to such a point? Why don't we have her whole body torn to pieces, lest the other Christians also presume to speak savagely with similar arrogance against our gods? [79] Therefore come all of you who suffer the injury to the gods! Seize this sorceress and torture her with dreadful punishments and make her undergo a most cruel death! Then, if it is proper, let her call out for help from the god about whose protection she boasts.'*

[80] *But it happened that when she was being dragged to her punishment some people, pitying the beauty of the virginal appearance that was to perish by an unworthy death, were persuading her that she should rather obey the emperor than lose the flower of her youth by resisting; they spoke to her in this way: [81] 'O ideal of virginal beauty, o sight of sunny radiance, what is such great obstinacy of the mind that a girl of noble blood, to whom riches and honours are being offered for free, should choose death of her own accord? O virgin worthy of the office of empress, take thought for your very flourishing youth and do not allow the blooming sight of your beauty to perish by an immature death!'*

903-
23

[82] *Quibus venerabilis virgo respondit: 'deponite, o uiri, planctus inania lamenta nec de pulchritudinis meae dispendio querulosas expendite voces, quia caro mea quae vobis velut florere videtur, velut fenum est et gloria eius tamquam flos feni, dum mox abeunte spiritu, marcescit et consumpta a vermibus reditura est in pulverem unde primordialem sumpsit originem.* [83] *De meo igitur interitu nolite flere neque solliciti esse, quia michi talis cruciatus non est interitus ad consummationem sed transitus ad vitam. Super vos potius tales expendite gemitus, quia vobis non transitus manet ad spem reparationis sed interitus ad aerumnam aeternae perditionis.'* [84] *His verbis beatae virginis quidam eorum compuncti subtraxerunt se ab idolorum cultura et imperatoris communione, non tamen id palam esse volebant.*

[85] Cum ad haec tyrannus nimio furore succenderetur superveniens quidam urbis praefectus nomine Cursathes et ipse vir Belial, exclamat: 'o magne', inquit, 'imperator, non videt adhuc Katerina tale genus tormenti quo exterreatur ut adquiescat tibi ad immolandum diis nostris.

*82 planctus] planctus *H Z*, planctus huius *Dob* || nec] ne *B* || expendite] deperdite *Dob* || velut] om. *Dob* || a] consumpta *Dob* || reditura] reducta *B* || primordialem] primordialis essentie *Dob*
*83 interitus] om. *B* || spem] speciem *B*
85 cum] cumque *T B*, om. *R* || ad haec] om. *B* , ad haec tunc *R*|| nimio] vehementissimo *H R* || succenderetur] succendetur *R* || urbis praefectus] p. u. *Z K Mk* || exclamat] furentem regem ad novam insaniam succendit (accendit insaniam *Dob*) et tormenta tormentis accumulat *B Dob*, exclamabat *Bro* || inquit] inquiens *T Z K Mk Bro M* || videt] vidit *Bro* || adhuc] om. *Mk* || tormenti] tormentorum *B* || exterreatur] exterreat *Mk*, terreatur *M* || ut] et *H B R* || diis] diis magnis *B Dob*

[82] The venerable virgin answered them: 'O men, put aside the vain weeping of lamentation and do not waste your querulous voices for the loss of my beauty because my flesh, which seems to be flourishing to you, is like grass and its glory is in the same way like the flower of grass while – as soon, with the spirit departing – it withers and, consumed by worms, it will be returned to dust whence it took its primordial origin. [83] Therefore do not cry over my premature death and do not be troubled, because such torture for me is not death leading to destruction but a journey leading to life. Rather confer such wailing on yourselves, because there awaits you not a journey leading to the hope of renewal, but death leading to the pain of eternal perdition.' [84] At these words of the blessed virgin some of them felt compunction and withdrew themselves from the worship of the idols and the association of the emperor, still they did not want this to be generally known.

[85] When the tyrant was inflamed by a very great anger at these words, a certain prefect of the city came along, by the name of Cursathes, himself a man of the devil, and he exclaimed and said: 'O great emperor, Katherine does net yet see such a kind of torment as to terrify her to give in to you and sacrifice to our gods.

924-44

[86] Iube ergo ut infra hoc triduum sint factae quattuor rotae quarum orbes et intimi circuli clavis prominentibus *et acutis* praefigantur, radii vero earum serris peracutis denso ordine *et mordaci acumine* imbuantur. [87] Has iuxta rotas Katerina exposita volventis machinae impetum sedens intueatur, ut ipso terrore ad culturam deorum incurvetur. Sin autem mox rotali impacta machinamento, *hinc inde serris et clavis mordacibus discerpta ad Christianorum terrorem* inaudito pereat exemplo.' [88] Nec mora: iubet tyrannus accelerari rotarum pœnale tormentum. Et iam dies tertia illuxerat et rotae in medio praetorii expositae terrorem circumspectantibus incutiebant. *At virgo nullo pœnarum apparatu terrebatur; mens eius namque a Christo fundata nec blandimentis mulceri poterat nec minis terreri.*

86 ergo] *om. B* || ut infra hoc triduum] i. h. t. u. *Bro* || sint] sunt *R* || quarum orbes] quorum extremi orbes *B* || radii vero] radioli *K M* || earum] articulares quibus altrinsecus rotarum orbes iuncti reguntur *B Dob* || serris] ferreis *Z*, syris *B*, ferris *K Bro M*, ferris *ante* preacutis *Mk* || imbuantur] ambiantur *B*
87 has iuxta] i. h. *Mk* || sedens] *om. R* || intueatur] intuetur *a.c. Mk* || ipso] ipsa *T Bro* || mox] *om. Mk Σ* || inaudito] *om. Bro*
*87 Christianorum terrorem] t. C. *Dob*
88 iubet tyrannus] t. i. *B* || accelerari] accelerare *T Z K Mk Bro M Z* || rotarum] *om. Mk M* || iam] cum iam *Bro* || dies tertia] t. d. *T* || tertia] tertius *V C N*, terram *LP*, *om. K Mk M* || illuxerat] illuxisset *Bro* || et²] *om. Bro* || praetorii] *om. K M* || circumspectantibus] circumspicientibus *Z*, circumstantibus *Bro D W P₂ Q* || incutiebant] incuebant *M*
*88 eius] om. *Dob* || terreri] exsterreri *O*, absterreri *Dob*

[86] Therefore order that within three days from now, four wheels be made whose outer and inner circumferences are pierced with projecting *and sharp* nails, indeed that their spokes are clustered with very sharp saws in tight arrangement *and cutting sharpness*. [87] When Katherine has been put right next to these wheels, as she is sitting let her watch the motion of the turning machine so that by the very fear she may be influenced to the worship of the gods. But if not, soon fixed to the wheeled instrument, *then hence torn apart by the sharp saws and spokes to the horror of the Christians*, she may die as an unheard-of example.' [88] There is no delay: the tyrant orders the penal torment of the wheels to be speeded up. And now the third day had dawned and the wheels, put out in the middle of the palace, were striking fear into the onlookers. *But the virgin was not alarmed by any instrument of punishment, because her will, strengthened by Christ, could not be softened by blandishments or deterred by threats.*

945-48 [89] Ipsa denique pœnalis machina hac arte expolita erat, ut duae uno ordine volverentur, duae autem contrario impetu agerentur, ut illae deorsum lacerando contraherent istae repugnantes sursum devorando impingerent.

948-60 [90] Has inter media exposita Christi famula inter serras et tarincas ferreas *ex motu rotarum membratim* horribiliter discerpenda, erectis in caelum oculis tacitae orationis verba ad deum fundebat: *[91] 'deus omnipotens qui te in periculis et necessitate invocantibus pia opitulatione subvenire non desinis, exaudi me in hac necessitate ad te clamantem et praesta ut pœnalis haec fabrica caelestis ictu fulminis attrita dissolvatur, ut manifestam potentiam tuam qui circumstant intuentes glorificent nomen tuum sanctum quod est benedictum in saecula. [92] Tu scis, Domine, quia non timore passionis haec obsecro, quae sitienti corde quovis mortis genere ad te venire et te videre desidero, sed ut hii qui per me credituri sunt, in te certiores de tuo adiutorio et constantiores in confessione tui nominis perseverent.'*

89 pœnalis] pœnale *R* || hac arte] ita *Bro* || expolita] exposita *K Bro M R W E H Z* || duae¹] duae rotae *Bro* || uno ordine] o. u. *R E N* || autem] *om. Bro* || contrario] ultra *B*, contrarie *K* || contraherent] contraherentur *K*, contrahentur *M* || istae] illae *Z R* || repugnantes sursum] repugnando sursum *B L*, *om. Bro*

90 inter] intus *Bro* || media] medias *H T Z B K Mk M Bro R* || exposita Christi famula] C. f. e. *K Mk R Dob* || tarincas] tahrincas *T*, troncas *Z*, zarinquas *B*, carincas *Bro*, tharincas *M*, taringas *R* || oculis] luminibus *Bro* || tacitae orationis] tacitam orationem *B* || verba ... deum] *om. B* || deum] dominum *K*, dominum deum *M* ||

*91 et²] om. *B Y* || potentiam tuam] p. t. *P₁ P₂ Q*, potentiam *H Z*, potentiae tuae virtutem *Dob* || circumstant intuentes] circumstent instuant *B*

*92 in te] om. *C D Z*, post *per me Dob*

[89] Moreover, that penal machine had been refined with such skill that two wheels were being turned in one direction, and two were being driven by an opposite motion so that the first set of wheels would tear by drawing together downwards, the other set would claw in and devour in an opposing motion.

[90] The maid of Christ in their midst, exposed among the saws and iron spikes, to be horribly torn apart *limb by limb by the movement of the wheels*, with her eyes lifted up to the sky poured out to God words of silent prayer: [91] '*All-powerful God who does not cease to stand by with pious help those imploring you in dangers and difficulty, heed me calling to you in this difficulty and grant that this construction of punishment be broken to pieces by a blow of heavenly thunder, so that those standing round see your unmistakeable power and glorify your holy name which is blessed forever. [92] You know, Lord, that I do not beseech you for this through fear of the passion, I who with thirsting heart long to come to you and see you by whatever kind of death, but so that those who are to believe in you through me may persist, more certain of your help and more steadfast in the confession of your name.*'

960-69 [93] *Necdum virgo verba finierat* et ecce angelus domini de caelo descendens molem illam vehementi impetu ita concussit ut partes avulsae super infusum populum tanta vi excuterentur ut quattuor milia de ipsa turba necarentur, *illa nimirum non degenerata ultione quam de Chaldeis Babylonica fornax olim exegerat.* Quid plura? Dolor et confusio gentilium, laus et exultatio Christianorum. Ipse tyrannus *dentibus frendens* mente turbatus quid agat excogitat.

93 et¹] *om. B* || de caelo descendens] descendens *K*, descendens d. c. *Bro* || descendens] descendit *Z*, descendebat *Bro* || molem] molemque *Z* || illam] istam *Bro* || vehementi ... partes] vehementi turbinis ictu impactam tanto [tanto: turbinis ictu toto *B*] impetu concussit ut ruptis compagibus partes *B Dob* || ita] *om. Mk* || impetu] impetu turbinis *R* || concussit] excussit *K*|| infusum] astantem *T*, visum *K*|| excuterentur] excuteretur *K H*, excuteretur *a.c. C*, excuterent *Z* || ut² ... necarentur] *om. B* || milia] milia hominum *K* || de²] ex *Z K Mk M* || gentilium] gentium *K M* || laus] vox *K Mk R Dob* || turbatus] confusus *Mk*, nimium turbatus *M* || quid agat] *post* tyrannus *T* || excogitat] ignorat *T*
*93 virgo verba] verba v. *Dob* || non] nunc *B*

[93] *The virgin had not yet finished her words* when behold an angel of the Lord, coming down from heaven, struck that structure with such a violent blow that the torn parts shot out over the streaming people with such force that four thousand of the crowd were killed, *evidently this was not a vengeance more unworthy than the one that the Babylonian furnace once carried out against the Chaldeans*. What then? There was pain and confusion among the pagans, praise and rejoicing among the Christians. The tyrant himself, *gnashing his teeth*, troubled in his mind, was thinking out what he should do.

970-88 [94] Erat regina desuper spectans divinae ultionis prodigium, quae protinus arrepto itinere se in conspectu belvae saevientis immersit, [95] 'quid tu', inquiens, 'miserande coniunx contra deum eluctaris? Quae te insania adversus factorem tuum insurgere coegit? *An tu prospero exitu finire arbitraris certamen quod adversus Deum et famulos famulasque ipsius sumpsisti?* Agnosce vel nunc in praesenti facto quam potens sit Christianorum deus et quia dii tui idola vana sunt, quae nec sibi nec cultoribus suis aliquid praestare possunt.' [96] Attonitus ad haec tyrannus et nimio furore succensus in hanc vocem erupit: 'quid tu, o regina, ita loqueris? Num te quoque magicis artibus seductam Christianorum aliquis subvertit et a cultura deorum avertit?

94 erat] erat autem *B*, erat dudum *Dob*, *om. R* || spectans] exspectans *K M* || protinus] mox *T K Mk Bro M* || quae protinus] et quae prius se occultabat propter metum viri sui nunc *B Dob*, *om. R* || arrepto ... se] *om. B* || belvae saevientis] s. v. *T* || immersit] ingessit *T B K Mk M*, iniecit *Bro*, inmisit *R Z*

95 tu] *om. Mk* || inquiens] inquid *B Mk R D H* || eluctaris] oblutaris *B* || quae ... coegit] *om. K M* || insurgere coegit] c. i. *Mk* || coegit] fecit *R F* || nunc] nec *H R* || facto] festo *Bro* || sit] est *H Z Dob* || tui] tui et *Bro* || idola vana sunt] s. v. i. *M* || cultoribus] scuptoribus *T* || cultoribus suis] s. c. *Bro* || possunt] *add. s.l. T*, poterunt *Mk*

*95 finire] furore *B* || Deum ... sumpsisti] factorem tuum insurgere cœpit contra famulos et famulas eius contra sumpsisti sanguinis ardore *B*

96 in] ad *Z* || erupit] erupit ut *T*, prorupit *Z K Mk R* || quid ... loqueris] *om. Bro* || o] o *D*, *om. K Mk* || ita] sic *R* || quoque] *om. Mk* || seductam Christianorum] c. s. *T* || aliquis] *post* quoque *T* || subvertit] fabritit *R*

[94] There was the queen, watching from above the miracle of the divine revenge, she immediately set out on the path and plunged herself into the sight of the raging monster, [95] 'why do you, pitiable husband, struggle against God? What madness has compelled you to rise up against your maker? *Can it really be that you think you can end with a favourable outcome the fight that you have taken up against God, his servants, and his maidens?* Recognize now at least, in the present deed, how powerful the god of the Christians is and that your gods are empty idols that cannot achieve anything either for themselves or for their worshippers.' [96] The tyrant was stunned at these words and kindled by a very great anger, he burst out with these words: 'O queen, why are you speaking in this way? Has one of the Christians also seduced you with magic tricks, ruined you, and turned you away from the worship of the gods?

998-1012

[97] Iuro ergo tibi per magnum deorum imperium quod nisi maturius *ab hac stultitia* resipiscens deos nostros adoraveris, extortis a pectore mamillis longo cruciatu torqueberis et sic caput tuum a cervice recidetur et carnes tuae feris et volatilibus dilacerandae reicientur.' [98] Iubet igitur *tyrannus crudelis* ministris eam contemptibiliter apprehendi et ad locum supplicii trahi. [99] Quae respiciens ad beatam Katerinam dixit: 'o veneranda virgo Christi, funde preces ad dominum *pro cuius nomine certaminis huius luctamen apprehendisti* ut infra instantem passionis articulum confirmet cor meum ne coronam ab eo promissam metu passionis amittam.'

97 iuro] iubeo *T* || ergo] *om. B P₁* || tibi] et tibi iuro *T*, tibi o regina *B* || deorum imperium] i. d. *B* || quod] *om. T* || resipiscens] resipisces *B*, resipicens *V*, respiciens *LP* || deos nostros adoraveris] diis immolaveris eosque adoraveris *B* || a pectore] primo *H Dob* || longo] longinquo *T* || torqueberis] torquebis *R* || et sic] *om. T* || caput] capudque *T* || et carnes ... reicientur] *om. B* || tuae] tuas *K* , *om. Dob* || volatilibus] volucribus *M* || dilacerandas] dilacerandas *Dob*, dilacerandae *H R*, *om. T Z K Mk Bro M*
98 igitur] ergo *T Mk E N O S P₂ H Z* || eam] *om. Z B* || apprehendi] regiam apprehendere matronam *B Dob*
98 tyrannus crudelis] t. crudelissimus *P₁*, c. t. *Dob*
99 quae] regina vero cum a ministris traheretur *R* || ad] *om. Bro* || virgo Christi] c. v. *Z K M* || dominum] filium *M* || infra] infra huius *B*, *om. R* || instantem] influentem *Bro*, instante *R L* || passionis[1]] p. meae *Mk* || articulum] hoc articulo *R* || confirmet cor meum] cor m. c. *B* || coronam] choronas *B* || ne ... amittam] habeam pro passionis articulo promissam amittere quiam *B* || passionis[2]] *om. R*
99 apprehendisti] apprehendit *S,* apprehendi *Dob*

[97] I therefore swear to you by the great power of the gods that, unless you repent at once *from this stupidity* and honour our gods, you will be tortured by a protracted torment as your breasts are pulled off from your chest, and then your head will be cut off from your neck, and your flesh will be flung aside to the wild animals and birds to be torn into pieces.' [98] Then *the cruel tyrant* ordered the attendants to seize her with contempt and to drag her to the place of punishment. [99] Looking back she said to Katherine: 'O venerable virgin of Christ, pour out prayers to the Lord *in whose name you have taken up the struggle of this fight* that, within the imminent moment of suffering, he make strong my heart lest I lose through fear of suffering the crown promised by him.'

1012-23 [100] Ad quam pretiosa virago: 'ne timeas', inquit, 'o deo dilecta regina sed viriliter age quia hodie tibi pro transitorio regno commutabitur aeternum,
hodie inquam immortalis vitae accipies praemium.' *pro mortali sponso immortalem tibi acquires, pro pœnis requiem permanentem, pro celeri obitu interminabilis vitae hodie percipies natale principium.*

[101] *Ad hanc vocem venerabilis matrona in agonia robustior effecta tortores sponte hortatur ne tyrannica iussa ultra implere morentur.* Tunc ministri extra civitatem eam ducentes ferreis hastilibus regias mamillas traiciunt, et sic suspensas ab imo pectore crudeliter mammas evellunt. Dehinc gladio percussa felici martyrio consummata est *vicesima tertia die mensis Novembris*. [102] Porphyrius autem noctu cum suis auferens corpus reginae et martyris conditum aromatibus sepelivit.

100 pretiosa] beata *T* || o] *om. K Mk Bro* || deo] adeo *Z*, a deo *Bro*, *om. K M* || tibi] *om. B* || aeternum] regnum aeternum *M* || inquam] inquit *K*, inquiens *Bro* ||
*100 acquires] tibi acquires *Dob* || percipies] participes *B*
101 eam] eam protinus *M* || regias] *om. Bro* || regias mamillas] m. r. *T* || traiciunt ... mammas] *om. Z* || traiciunt] eiciunt *B*, trahunt *K Mk M* || sic] *om. K* || suspensas] *post* pectore *Mk*, suspendentes *Bro* || pectore crudeliter] p. c. *D E*, pectore *B*, c. p. *Bro Dob* || mammas] *om. H B Bro*, mammas eius *K M* || evellunt] subtraxerunt *B*, evelliunt *R* || dehinc] dehunc *R* || felici martyrio] *om. H*, fideliter *B H*, felicissimo martirio *M*, martyrio *post* est *R* || consummata est] consumpta est *Z Bro*, migravit ad dominum *H*, migravit ad Christum *B Dob*

[100] The precious heroine said to her: 'Don't be afraid, queen dear to god, but act man-like because today for you the fleeting reign will be exchanged for an eternal one,

today, I say, you will receive the prize of immortal life.	*instead of a mortal one you will obtain an immortal husband, instead of punishments permanent peace, instead of a swift death you will receive today the primary beginning of eternal life.*

[101] In response to this voice, the venerable matron, strengthened in her sacrifice, deliberately encourages the torturers that they should no longer delay to carry out the tyrannical orders. Then the attendants led her outside the city and pierced the royal breasts with iron spears, and as the breasts were thus suspended, they cruelly tore them off from the depths of her chest. Then she was struck by the sword and she died a happy martyrdom on the twenty-third day of the month of November. [102] But at night, Porphyrius with his men carried off the body of the queen and martyr, embalmed it with perfumes, and buried it.

---

*101 sponte] sponsi B || implere] om. **Dob**
102 autem] igitur Z K Mk Bro M, om. B || noctu] noctum H, nocte R P₂, nocte post suis B, nocte post auferens K || cum suis] om. T || et martyris] om. B || sepelivit] honorifice sepelivit M

1026-44

[103] Mane autem facto fit quaestio de corpore reginae, quis illud sustulisset. De quo cum multos ad supplicium pertrahi Porphyrius videret, constanter ante tribunal irruit dicens: [104] 'vesano te spiritu, o Caesar, agitari manifestum est, qui humanis corporibus nec etiam sepulturam indulges. [105] Verumtamen si reos esse iudicas qui Christi famulam sepelierunt, hoc crimine solus ego periclitari desidero. Nam ego sum qui gloriosam Christi martyrem et ego Christi confessor sepelivi.' [106] Hic tyrannus velut alto vulnere saucius pro planctu rugitum velut amens emisit quo tota regia pertonuit. 'o, o me miserum, o omnibus miserandum, cui tollitur omne quod nostri imperii videtur subsidium.

103 quis] et quis *B* || illud] istud *K* || cum] *om. Z* || multos] militos *R* || pertrahi] protrahi *Bro* || Porphyrius] *post* supplicium *H R* || videret] videns *Z* || tribunal] tribunal imperatoris *B Dob* || irruit] irrupit *B*

104 te spiritu] s. t. *B* || agitari] *post* spiritu *B* || nec] nunc *B* || indulges] prohibes *B*

105 esse iudicas] i. e. *Bro* || Christi famulam] f. C. *K*, famulam Dei *Mk* || hoc] pro hoc *K M* || periclitari desidero] d. p. *K*, desidero pro te periclitari *M* || gloriosam] *om.* B, gloriosam ancillam et *Bro* || Christi martyrem] Christi famulam *B*, m. c. *Bro I*, Christi confessorem *K M* || martyr ... Christi] *erased Mk* || et ... confessor] *om. Z K* || Christi confessor] confessor C *T* || confessor] confessorem *Mk* || sepelivi] *post* famulam *B*

106 hic] hinc *T K M R G L W Σ*, ad haec autem *B*, tunc *Bro* || tyrannus] *post* vulnere *B* || alto] *om. Mk* || saucius] sauciatus *Z Mk Bro* || rugitum] rugitu *B* || amens] *om. M* || velut amens emisit] e. v. a. *K* || regia] regia domus *B*, regio *Bro*, regia aula *K Mk*, aula regia *M* || pertonuit] personuit *B*, sonuit *R* || o²] *om. T B K Mk Bro M D S A P₁ Z* || omnibus] me omnibus *Z*, hominibus *B* || videtur] praecipue summa *B Dob* || subsidium] praecipuum *T Z K Mk M Bro R*, requisium *B*, requirit *Dob*

[103] However, when the morning came, there was an inquiry about the body of the queen, [namely] who had carried it off. As a result, when Porphyrius saw that many people were being dragged off for punishment, he steadfastly rushed before the tribunal and said: [104] 'It is clear that you are driven by a frenzied spirit, o Caesar, you who do not even allow a burial for human bodies. [105] Still, if you judge those who buried the servant of Christ to be culprits, I desire to be tried alone for this crime. For it is I who buried the glorious martyr of Christ, and I am a believer in Christ.' [106] Hereupon the tyrant, as if injured by a deep wound, let out a demented bellow as lamentation, which resounded through the entire palace: 'O, o miserable me, o to be pitied by all, from whom everything is taken which is seen as the support of our kingdom.

1046-61 [107] Ecce Porphyrius qui erat unicus animae meae custos et totius laboris solatium in omni cura et sollicitudine singulare michi praesidium, ecce hic deorum nostrorum culturam pro dolor aspernatur et Iesum Christianorum deum publica voce confitetur!' [108] His dictis omnes commilitones eius seorsum advocans dum de Porphyrii conversione quaestionem faceret omnes una voce se Christianos esse fatebantur nec metu mortis a fide Christi et Porphyrii societate avelli se posse testabantur. [109] At *1093* ille insania et furore debriatus, iubet omnes una cum Porphyrio extra civitatem decollari et corpora eorum canibus corrodenda dimitti. Consummata est itaque et *1074-77* eorum passio *mense Novembrio die vicesima quarta, quarta feria* in sanctae fidei testimonio.

107 ecce] et ecce *M* || unicus] *om. Mk Bro* || meae custos et] *om. B* || laboris] *om. Z* || in ... sollicitudine] et solitudine *B* || cura] <u>cura</u> cura *R* || ecce] *om. B* || hic] hinc *B* || pro dolor] pro dolor <u>*D*</u>, pro hidolorum *Bro*, proch dolor *M*, pro hoc dolor *R* || et[3] ... confitetur] *om. Z* || deum] dominum *Bro* || publica] prophana *T B K Mk Bro M R* || confitetur] confitetur <u>*C*</u> <u>*D*</u> <u>*N*</u>, profitetur *B K Mk* <u>*Dob*</u>
108 omnes] *om. B Bro* || ipsius] eius *H* <u>*U*</u> || advocans] advocant *Mk*, convocans *M*, advocatis *R* || de] *om. K* || Porphyrii conversione] c. P. *Bro* || conversione quaestionem] q. conversatione *K*, conversatione q. *Mk*, q. c. *M* || quaestionem] quaestione *R* || faceret] facerent *K Bro* <u>*P₁*</u> || se[1]] *om. B* || se Christianos] C. s. *Z Mk* || fatebantur] fatebantur <u>*D*</u> <u>*Λ*</u>, protestabantur *B* <u>*Dob*</u> <u>*Λ₂*</u> || Christi fide] f. C. *H* || se[2]] *om. T Z* || testabantur] testantur *Z*, fatebantur *B*, <u>fateban</u> testabantur *R*

[107] Behold Porphyrius, who was the only guardian of my mind and the comfort of all trouble in every preoccupation and the help for me in every anxiety, behold, for shame, he rejects the worship of our gods and confesses to Jesus, the god of the Christians, with a public voice!' [108] After the emperor had spoken these words, he called forward all Porphyrius' fellow soldiers one by one, in order to ask them questions about the conversion of Porphyrius; all of them in one voice declared that they were Christians and they affirmed that fear of death could not tear them away from the faith in Christ or the company of Porphyrius. [109] But he, intoxicated with madness and anger, ordered them all to be beheaded outside the city together with Porphyrius, and their bodies to be abandoned and gnawed up by dogs. And so their suffering too came to an end *on the twenty-forth day of the month of November* in testimony to the holy faith.

---

109 ille] illa *B* || insania et furore] f. et i. *T* || debriatus] inebriatus *Z* || iubet] iussit *H R* || omnes] *om. B* || una] *om. T B* || decollari] produci et decollari *M* || et²] que *T*, *om. Mk* || canibus] canibus et avibus *M* || dimitti] *sic* <u>D</u> <u>L</u> <u>N</u> <u>Δ</u> <u>H</u> <u>Z</u>, demitti *B*, emitti *Dob* ||consummata] consummatum *T* || itaque et] qui et ita *T* || eorum] horum *H Bro R* <u>Dob</u>, illorum *T* || in] sub *H*, ubi in *B* || sanctae] sancta *H*, sententiae *B*

*109 mense Novembrio] menso Novembro *B*

1078-98

[110] Postera die Maxentius sedens pro tribunali beatam Katerinam sibi iubet praesentari. Cui sic ait: 'ne nos, o malefica deceptrix, amplius protrahas. Quod vis unum e duobus elige: aut maturius diis offer libamina aut hodie capitali plecteris sententia.' [111] Cui virgo: 'te', inquit, 'tyranne diutius protrahere non quaero. Fac quaecumque animo concepisti, paratam me videbis ad omnia sustinenda quae michi inferre potueris.' [112] Sic effatam tyrannus iubet eam extra portam civitatis decollari. Quae cum ad locum passionis duceretur, *respiciens vidit turbam multam virorum et mulierum sequentium se atque plangentium, inter quas* multae virgines et matronae nobiles eam persequentes lamentabantur.

110 postera] postera autem R *Dob* || Maxentius] *om.* B || sibi] *om.* B M P₁ Q H Z || praesentari] adduci B H Z || sic] *om.* K M || nos] vos M || o] *om.* K || malefica deceptrix] malefici deceptione K M || protrahas] decipias *Bro* || quod] quid H || unum] *om.* R || e] de B *Bro* F || offer] offeris H K R, inferas *Dob* || plecteris sententia] sententia punieris B
111 te] tunc K M || tyranne diutius protrahere] p. t. d. H, d. t. trahere B, p. d. t. R || protrahere *usque ad finem*] *om.* T || non quaero] nolo B || quaecumque] omnia quaecumque M || concepisti] cepisti R || paratam] parata H R || me] *om. Bro*, enim me K M || potueris] poteris M E N U Z
112 effatam] affata Z, affatam E J O S Q || tyrannus] *post* eam B || portam civitatis] civitatem Z *Mk* || decollari] pertrahi et caput eius decollari M || sic ... eam] postera vero die maxentius beatam katherinam C || quae] quam Z || ad] *om.* Z || locum passionis] passionis locum Z, locum praefixum passionis B, locum passioni praefixum *Dob*, locum passionis E J O S (and C *p.c.*) || duceretur] properaret B *Dob* || multae] *om. Bro* || persequentes] persequente K, prosequentes *Bro*, sequentes M
*112 virgines] praecipue virgines *Dob* || eam persequentes] *om. Dob*

[110] On the next day, Maxentius, sitting in his tribunal, orders blessed Katherine to be presented to him. He said to her the following: 'O wicked deceiving woman, do not put us off any longer. Choose whichever one you wish from these two: either offer libations to the gods at once or you will be punished today by execution.' [111] The virgin said to him: 'Tyrant, I do not seek to put you off any longer. Do whatever you have devised in your mind, you will see me ready to bear everything that you can inflict on me.' [112] When she had spoken thus, the tyrant ordered her to be decapitated outside the city. When she was being led to the place of suffering, *looking back she saw a great crowd of men and women following her and wailing, amongst whom* many virgins and noble matrons were following her and lamenting.

*1098-
1111* [113] Conversa igitur ad illas dixit: 'o generosae matronae, o virgines clarissimae, nolite obsecro passionem meam lamentabili planctu onerare, sed congaudete michi precor potius quia vocat me Christus deus et dominus meus qui est amor et sponsus unicus meus *qui est merces copiosa sanctorum, decus et corona virginum.* [114] *Vos vero planctum istum lacrimabilem quem inaniter in me deperditis in vos ipsas convertite, ne vos in hoc gentilitatis errore dies suprema deprehendat pro quo fletus aeternos subeatis.'*

[115] Haec locuta *a percussore orandi spatium indulgeri sibi poposcit. Quod cum spiculator annueret,* elevatis in caelum oculis oravit dicens: 'o spes et salus credentium, o decus et gloria virginum, Iesu bone, gratias tibi ago qui me intra collegium ancillarum tuarum connumerare dignatus es.

113 conversa ... dixit] om. *Z* || igitur] autem *B*, igitur virgo sancta *C*, ergo *K Mk M* || illas] eos *B* || generosae] gloriosae *K M* || nolite obsecro] o. n. *K* || obsecro] ergo *C* || lamentabili ... onerare] lamentari *Z* || congaudete] gaudete *Z P̲₂*, cum gaudere *B*, congaudere *Bro* || michi] om. *Z* || precor potius] potius p. *Z* || vocat me] *post* meus² *Z* || amor] amore *H*, amor meus *Z B Mk D̲o̲b̲* || unicus meus] u. m. *G̲*, m. u. *Mk Bro*
*113 virginum] vigilantium *B*
*114 deperditis] deperdistis *B* || ne] nec *B*
115 locuta] locuta gloriosa virgo Katerina *R* || elevatis] erectis *Z K Mk*, erecta *B*, erexit *M* || in] ad *Bro* || oculis] *ante* in *B D̲ L̲*, oculos *ante* in *M* || spes et salus] salus et spes *B* || credentium] omnium credentium *C* || Iesu] Iesu rex *Z K Mk Bro M* || gratias tibi] t. g. *B*
*115 a] om. *B*

[113] Therefore she turned round to them and said: 'O high-born matrons, o most noble virgins, do not, I beseech you, burden my suffering with a mournful lamentation, but I beg you, rather rejoice with me because Christ, my God and Lord, who is my love and my only husband, *who is the plentiful reward for saints, the glory and crown of virgins,* calls me. [114] *But turn this tearful lamentation which you are wasting for nothing on my behalf onto yourselves, lest the supreme day comes upon you unexpectedly in this error of paganism, for which you shall undergo eternal weeping.*'

[115] When she had spoken these words, *she asked the executioner that time to pray be granted to her. When the soldier on guard agreed,* she raised her eyes to heaven and prayed, saying: 'O hope and salvation of believers, o honour and glory of virgins, good Jesus, I thank you, you who have deigned to count me among the fellowship of your maid-servants.

1111-
21
[116] Fac ergo hanc cum ancilla tua obsecro misericordiam ut quicumque in laudem et gloriam nominis tui passionis meae memoriam egerint, sive in exitu animae suae aut etiam in quacumque angustia vel necessitate me invocaverint, celerem obtineant effectum tuae propitiationis. [117] Ecce pro tuo nomine domine Iesu Christe *expleto certaminis mei agone* ferientis expecto gladium, tu quod carnifex tollere non potest precor suscipe spiritum meum.'

116 obsecro] *om. K Mk Bro M* || obsecro misericordiam] m. o. *C* || gloriam] *om. B* || meae] mei *B* || memoriam egerint] e. m. *Bro* || egerint] fecerit *Z*, fecerint *B* || suae] *om. K C* || etiam] et in *R* || quacumque] qualicumque *Bro Q E* || angustia] tribulatione *Mk*, tribulatione vel a. *Σ Q* || necessitate] in necessitate *C* || me invocaverint] i. m. *Z* || celerem] celebre *B* || obtineant effectum] e. o. *K Bro* || tuae] tui *H*, *om. M*
117 Christe] *om. K Mk Bro* || expecto gladium] g. e. *B D* || tu ... meum] *om. C* || tu] et *Bro* || quod] quem *K Bro H Z* || carnifex] carnisex *corr.* carninex *R* || tollere] auferre *Bro* || potest] potes *B*, potuit *K* || precor] precor domine *Z*, *om. K Mk*, precor tu *Bro* || suscipe spiritum meum] spiritum m. s. *Z*

[116] And so I beseech you, have this mercy with your servant, that whoever remembers me in praise and glory of your suffering, whether they call upon me at the passing away of the soul or even in any difficulty or necessity, may they receive the swift fulfillment of your grace. [117] Behold in your name, Lord Jesus Christ, *I have come to the end of my struggle's fighting and* I await the executioner's sword, I pray, take up my spirit, which the executioner cannot take.'

*1123
-35* [118] Necdum orationem compleverat et ecce vox ad eam de caelo redditur: 'veni dilecta mea, speciosa mea, ecce tibi beatitudinis aperta est ianua, ecce *quietis eternae mansio tibi parata adventum tuum expectat iam* in occursum tuum chorus *ille virgineus* sanctorum *exultantibus animis* cum triumphali adventat corona. [119] Veni ergo et ne solliciteris de donis quae postulas, nam et his qui passionem tuam devotis mentibus celebraverint et qui in periculis et necessitatibus te invocaverint, optata praesidia promitto de caelis.' [120] Facta ergo hac voce Christi virgo lacteam cervicem protendens a spiculatore decollata est.

118 exultantibus] expectantibus B
118 necdum ... corona] cumque finisset orationem, vox e celo elapsa est dicens ad eam: exaudita est oratio tua. Veni ergo gloriosa, veni sanctissima virgo. Hec cum audisset beata Katerina leta effecta de celesti permissione {*sic*} surrexit ab oratione *C* || compleverat] finierat *Mk* || eam] eam est *Mk* || de caelo] *post* vox *B* || redditur] est emissa dicens *Z*, emissa *B K*, emissa est *Mk*, est missa *Bro*, est emissa *M* || veni] veni ergo *Mk*, *post* mea[1] *R* || dilecta] verum dilecta *R* || beatitudinis] beatitudinis tibi *B K* || aperta est] aperitur *Z B K Mk Bro M Dob* || tuum] *om. Z* || sanctorum] *ante* chorus *K M*, angelorum et sanctorum *Mk* || adventat] adveniet *Bro*, advenit *U*
119 veni ... caelis] *om. C* || solliciteris] sis sollicita *B* || postulas] postulasti *Mk*, a domino postulas *M* || et[2]] *om. K M* || devotis mentibus] *om. Z K Mk M* || celebraverint] *ante* devotis *B* || et[3] ... invocaverint] *om. Mk Σ Q* || necessitatibus] necessitatibus suis *M* || te] *post* qui[2] *Z* || optata] operata *Bro* || caelis] caelo *B* || promitto de caelis] et celerem de caelo opem promitto *Bro*, et opem celerem de caelo [caelis *U*] promitto *Dob*

[118] She had not yet finished her prayer when, behold, a voice spoke back to her from heaven: 'Come my beloved, my beautiful, behold, the door of happiness has been opened for you, behold *the house of eternal rest is ready for your arrival, already* the *virginal* choir of the saint advances with *rejoicing hearts and* a triumphant crown to meet you. [119] So come and do not worry about the favours you ask for, for both to those who celebrate your passion with devout minds and to those who call on you in dangers and difficulties, I promise the desired help from heaven.' [120] Therefore, when this voice had spoken, the virgin of Christ stretched out her milk-white neck and was decapitated by the executioner.

---

120 facta ergo ... 122 gloria] satellites vero accipientes eam secundum cesaris iussionem decollaverunt eam vigesimo quinto die mensis novembris. Statimque de corpore eius lac pro sanguine defluxit, angeli quoque gloriose martiris corpus accipientes exanime(?) in monte Synai detulerunt, ubi per eam innumera divina virtus operari non desinit miracula *C*

120 ergo] igitur *K* || Christi virgo] v. C. *B,* om. *Bro* || protendens] extendens *B*

1135-46 [121] Statimque de corpore eius lac pro sanguine effusum terram uberius irroravit. Angeli etiam assumptum corpus eius per altum aera subvehentes in montem Synai deposuerunt *qui mons a loco occisionis distat viginti et eo amplius dierum*, quo in loco innumera ad laudem domini fiunt miracula. [122] De sepulchro vero eius rivus olei indeficienter manare videtur; sed et de minutis ossibus, quae de sarcophago cum oleo effluunt ubicumque asportantur stillat oleum, ex quo peruncta debilium corpora celeri medicina sanantur, praestante domini nostri Iesu Christo cui est honor et gloria in saecula saeculorum amen.

121 eius[1]] *om. B K Mk* ‖ terram] *om. K Mk M* ‖ irroravit] irrigavit *Z N C L H Z*, irrogavit *Δ* ‖ etiam] quoque *Z B K Mk M R* ‖ eius[2]] eius *D*, *om. B M R Dob* ‖ per ... subvehentes] exaltam in aera sublevantes supportantes *Z* ‖ aera] in aere *B*, in aera *Bro M* ‖ montem] *sic W H Z*, monte *Z K M Dob* ‖ quo] *om. Z*, ecce *R* ‖ quo in] in quo *Bro M* ‖ innumera] innumerabilia *Bro* ‖ domini] dei *M D F G L P₂ Q H Z* ‖ miracula] mirabilia *Z K Mk*
121 occisionis] om. B D ‖ dierum] diebus *B*
122 vero] *om. Bro*, autem *R* ‖ indeficienter] incessanter *Z*, conficienter *B*, indesinenter *R* ‖ sed] nam *B Dob* ‖ de minutis] de minimis *K Mk*, diminutis *LP*, de minibus *M* ‖ de[2]] *om. B I Y* ‖ sarcophago] s. eius *R* ‖ cum] *om. R* ‖ ubicumque] et u. *R* ‖ ubicumque asportantur] *om. B* ‖ oleum quo] *om. B* ‖ ex] *om. H Bro C* ‖ quo *T Mk Dob* ‖ debilium] debilia *B* ‖ debilium corpora] c.d. *Bro* ‖ celeri] celeris *B* ‖ medicina sanantur] s.m. *H R* ‖ praestante ... amen] *om. R* ‖ praestante ... Christo] passa est beata Katerina mense Novembrio vicesima sexta, hora tertia, servans diem et horam qua Christus pro mundi redemptione ad passionem properavit *B* ‖ praestante] regnante *Bro* ‖ domino nostro Iesu Christ] domini nostri Iesu Christi *H* ‖ gloria] gloria cum patre et spiritu sancte *Bro* ‖ in ... amen] *om. H* ‖ in] per *B* ‖ saecula saeculorum] infinita saecula *B*

[121] And immediately milk instead of blood poured out of her body and moistened the ground abundantly. Indeed, angels took up her body, carried it through the lofty air, and put it down on Mount Sinai, *which mountain was more than a twenty-day journey from the location of her killing, and even more,* in which place innumerable miracles for the glory of the Lord are happening. [122] In fact, from her tomb a rivulet of oil is seen to flow incessantly; but even from tiny bones, which flow with the oil from the tomb, wherever they are taken, oil oozes and the bodies of the sick that are smeared with it are healed by a quick medicine, with the help of our Lord Jesus Christ, for whom honour and glory are forever, amen.

BIBLIOGRAPHY

Items cited in the list of abbreviations are omitted from the bibliography.

Databases

In Principio online – Incipit Index of Latin Texts (Brepols, 2021)
Manuscripta mediaevalia
    <http://www.manuscripta-mediaevalia.de/>
Biobliotheca hagiographica latina manuscripa (BHLms): Index analytique des catalogues des manuscrits hagiographiques latins publiés par les Bollandistes
    <http://bhlms.fltr.ucl.ac.be/>
Datenbank Gesamtkatalog der Wiegendrucke (GW), ed. Falk Eisermann et al. (Berlin, 2020)
    <https://www.gesamtkatalogderwiegendrucke.de/>
Hagiographies: Géographie et chronologie de l'hagioraphie latine, ed. Guy Philippart et al. (Namur, 1989-)
    <https://www.unamur.be/philo_lettres/histoire/h2220.htm>
Pinakes / Πίνακες: Textes et manuscrits grecs, Institut de recherche et d'histoire des textes, François Bougard (Paris, 2016)
    <https://pinakes.irht.cnrs.fr/>

Primary Sources

Acta sanctorum Hiberniae ex codice salmanticensi nunc primum integre edita, ed. Charles de Smedt and Joseph de Backer (Edinburgh, 1888)
Acta sanctorum quotquot toto orbe coluntur, ed. Heribert Rosweyde et al., 1st edn (Antwerp and Brussels, 1643-1748); 2nd edn (Venice, 1734-1770); 3rd edn (Paris and Rome), 1863-
'Acta S. Marinae et S. Christophori', ed. Hermann Usener, *Festschrift zur fünften Säcularfeier der Carl-Rupretchts-Universität zu Heidelberg* (Bonn, 1886)
Ademar of Chabannes, *Ademari cabannensis Chronicon*, ed. Pascale Bourgain et al., CCCM 129 (Turnhout, 1999)

Ainard, *Ainardo: Glossario*, ed. Paolo Gatti (Florence, 2000)
Alfanus of Salerno, *I carmi di Alfano, arcivescovo di Salerno*, ed. Anselmo Lentini and Faustino Avagliano (Monte Cassino, 1974)
Amatus of Montecassino, *Storia de' Normanni di Amato di Montecassino: Volgarizzata in antico francese*, ed. Vincenzo de Bartholomaeis (Rome, 1935)
——, *The History of the Normans by Amatus of Montecassino*, trans. Prescott N. Dunbar, rev. with introduction and notes by Graham A. Loud (Woodbridge, 2004)
Ambrose Autpert, *Ambrosii Autperti opera*, ed. Robert Weber, CCCM 27-27B (Turnhout, 1975-79)
Analecta hymnica graeca, ed. Athanasios D. Kominis, vol. 3: *Canones novembris* (Rome, 1972)
Analecta sacra spicilegio solesmensi parata, ed. Jean Baptiste Pitra (Paris, 1876-91; repr. Westmead, 1966-67)
Anastasios Protoasecretis, ed. George Metallinos, 'Ἀναστασίου πρωτασηκρῆτις ἐγκώμιον εἰς τὴν ἁγίαν Αἰκατερίνην', *Ἐκκλησιαστικὸς Φάρος*, 54 (1972), ii-iii, 237-74
Anthologia graeca carminum christianorum, ed. Wilhelm Christ and Matthaios K. Paranikas (Leipzig, 1871)
The Apocryphon of Jannes and Jambres the Magicians: P. Chester Beatty XVI, ed. Albert Pietersma, Albert (Leiden, 1994)
Aristides, *Aristide: Apologie*, ed. Bernard Pouderon *et al.*, Sources Chrétiennes 470 (Paris, 2003)
——, *The Apology of Aristides on Behalf of the Christians: From a Syriac Manuscript Preserved on Mount Sinai*, ed. J. Rendel Harris (with an appendix containing the main portion of the original Greek text by Joseph A. Robinson) (Cambridge, 1891)
Augustine, *Sancti Aurelii Augustini enarrationes in psalmos*, ed. Eligius Dekkers and Jean Fraipont, CCSL 38-40 (Turnhout, 1956)
Ps.-Aurelius Victor, *Epitome de caesaribus (Abrégé des Césars)*, ed. Michel Festy (Paris, 1999)
Baronio, Cesare, *Annales ecclesiastici*, ed. Antonio Pagi, vol. 3 (Lucca, 1738)
Bede, *Venerabilis Bedae opera historica*, ed. Charles Plummer (Oxford, 1896)

———, *Édition pratique des martyrologes de Bède, de l'anonyme lyonnais et de Florus*, ed. Jacques Dubois and Geneviève Renaud (Paris, 1976)

Butler, Alban, *The Lives of the Saints* (London, 1956), ed., rev. & suppl. Herbert Thurston and Donald Attwater, 4 vols (Allen, TX, 1965)

Butler's Lives of the Saints, ed. & rev. David H. Farmer *et al.* (Tunbridge Wells, 1999)

Calendarium romanum ex decreto sacrosancti oecumenici concilii vaticani II instauratum: Auctoritate Pauli PP. V promulgatum (Vatican City, 1969)

'Cartulaire de l'abbaye de la Sainte-Trinité du Mont de Rouen', ed. Achille Deville, in *Cartulaire de l'abbaye de Saint-Bertin*, ed. Benjamin Guérard, Collection de documents inédits sur l'histoire de France, vol. 3 (Paris, 1840)

Cassander, George, *Georgii Cassandri belgae theologi ... opera quae reperiri potuerunt omnia* (Paris, 1566)

Cassiodorus, *Vivarium libri duodecim*, ed. Åke J. Fridh (Turnhout, 1973)

Chronica monasterii casinensis, ed. Hartmut Hoffmann, MGH SS 34 (Hannover, 1980)

Chronicon Paschale, ed. Ludwig Dindorf, 2 vols (Bonn, 1832)

Clemence of Barking, *The Life of St. Catherine by Clemence of Barking*, ed. William MacBain, Anglo-Norman Text Society 18 (Oxford, 1964)

Clopper, Nicolas, *Florarium temporum (Bloemhof der tijden): Een laatmiddeleeuwse wereldkroniek door Nicolaas Clopper, geschreven in het Klooster Marienhage bij Eindhoven*, ed. Willem Erven *et al.* (Hilversum, 2018)

Consultationes Zacchei christiani et Apollonii philosophi, ed. Jean-Luc d'Achéry, *Veterum aliquot scriptorium qui in Galliae bibliothecis maxime Benedictorum latuerant spicilegium* (Paris, 1671), vol. 10

Consultationes Zacchei christiani et Apollonii philosophi / Questions d'un païen à un Chrétien, ed. Jean-Louis Feiertag and Werner Steinmann, Sources Chrétiennes 401-02 (Paris, 1994)

Disticha Catonis, ed. Marcus Boas and Henry J. Botschuyver (Amsterdam, 1952)

Dve verse starofrancouzské legendy o Sv. Kateriné Alexandrinské, ed. Jan U. Jarník (Prague, 1894)

Eberwin of Trier, *De calamitate abbatiae S. Martini Treverensis*, ed. Georg Waitz, MGH SS 15.2 (Hannover, 1888)

——, *Vita Sancti Symeonis, AASS* Junii I (Paris, 1867), pp. 86E-92F

Ermoldus Nigellus, *Ermoldi Nigelli carmina*, ed. Georg H. Pertz, MGH SS 2 (Hannover, 1829)

——, *Ermoldi Nigelli Carmina*, ed. Ernst Dümmler, MGH Poetae 2 (Berlin, 1884)

——, *Poème sur Louis le Pieux et epîtres au roi Pépin* (*Ermold le Noir*), ed. Edmond Faral (Paris, 1932)

Eusebius, Ἐκκλησιαστικὴ ἱστορία / *The Ecclesiastical History, books 1-5*, trans. Kirsopp Lake (Cambridge, MA, 1926)

Eusebius Gallicanus, *Eusebius 'gallicanus': Collectio homiliarum*, ed. Franciscus Glorie, CCSL 101-101B (Turnhout, 1970-71).

The Gesta Normannorum Ducum of William of Jumièges, Orderic Vitalis, and Robert of Torigni, ed. Elisabeth M.C. van Houts (Oxford, 1992-95)

Gobelinus, Person, *'Cosmidromius Gobelini Person', und als Anhang desselben Verfassers 'Processus translacionis et reformacionis monasterii budecensis'*, ed. Max Jansen (Münster, 1900)

Gregory of Tours, *Historiarum libri x*, ed. Bruno Krusch and Wilhelm Levison, MGH SSRM 1.1 (Hannover, 1951)

——, *Liber in gloria martyrum*, ed. Wilhelm Arndt and Bruno Krusch, in *Opera omnia*, MGH SSRM 1.2 (Hannover, 1885)

Der Heiligen Leben, vol. 2: Der Winterteil, ed. Margit Brand *et al.* (Tübingen, 2004)

Hugh of Flavigny, *Chronicon Hugonis monachi virdunensis et divionensis abbatis flaviniacensis*, ed. Georg H. Pertz, MGH SS 8 (Hannover, 1848), pp. 280-502

Hus, Jan, *The Letters of John Hus: With Introductions and Explanatory Notes*, Herbert B. Workman and R. Martin Pope (London, 1904)

'Un hymne inédit à Sainte Catherine d'Alexandrie', ed. Jean Grosdidier de Matons, *Travaux et Mémoires*, 8 (1981), 187-207

Jacobus de Voragine, *Legenda aurea*, ed. Giovanni P. Maggioni, 2 vols (Florence, 1998)

Isidore of Seville, *Sancti Isidori episcopi hispalensis: De ecclesiasticis officiis*, ed. Christopher M. Lawson, CCSL 113 (Turnhout, 1989)

——, *Etymologiarum sive originum libri xx*, ed. Wallace M. Lindsay (Oxford, 1911)

John of Damascus, *Die Schriften des Johannes von Damaskos*, vol. 5: *Opera homiletica et hagiographica*, ed. Bonifatius Kotter (Berlin, 1988); vol. 6/1: *Historia animae utilis de Barlaam et Ioasaph (spuria): Einführung*, ed. Robert Volk (Berlin, 2009) and vol. 6/2: *Historia animae utilis de Barlaam et Ioasaph (spuria): Text und zehn Appendices*, ed. Robert Volk (Berlin, 2006)

John Malalas, *Ioannis Malalae Chronographia*, ed. Johannes Thurn (Berlin, 2000)

John of Salerno, *Vita sancti Odonis abbatis cluniacensis secundi*, PL 133 (Paris, 1853), cols 43-86

John the Scot, *Iohannis Scotti annotationes in Marcianum*, ed. Cora E. Lutz (Cambridge, MA, 1939)

The Katherine Group (MS Bodley 34): Religious Writings for Women in Medieval England, ed. Emily R. Huber and Elizabeth Robertson (Kalamazoo, 2016)

La leggenda di S. Caterina d'Alessandria: Passioni greche e latine, ed. Giovanni B. Bronzini, Atti dell'Accademia Nazionale dei Lincei (Memorie: Classe di Scienze morali, storiche e filologiche, serie VIII) 9 (Rome, 1960)

Landolfus Sagax, *Additamenta ad Pauli Historiam romanam*, ed. Hans Droysen, MGH AA 2 (Berlin, 1879), pp. 227-376

The Legend of St Katherine of Alexandria: Edited from a Manuscript in the Cottonian library, ed. James Morton (London, 1841)

The Life and Martyrdom of Saint Katherine of Alexandria, Virgin and Martyr, now first printed from a manuscript of the early part of the fifteenth century in the possession of Henry Hucks Gibbs, with preface, notes, glossary and appendix, ed. Henry H. Gibbs (London, 1884)

The Life of Sainte Katherine from the Royal Ms. 17A xxvii, etc., with its Latin Original from the Cotton MS. Caligula A. viii, etc, ed. Eugen Einenkel, EETS o.s. 80 (London, 1884)

The Life of Saint Neilos of Rossano, ed. and trans. Raymond L. Capra *et al.* (Cambridge, MA, 2018)

'Il martirio di San Pansofio: Edizione critica', ed. Canart, Paul, and Rosario Pintaudi, *Analecta Papyrologica*, 16-17 (2004-2005), 191-245

Mag. Thietmari Peregrinatio, ed. Johann C.M. Laurent (Hamburg, 1857)

'Magistri Thietmari Peregrinatio: Pilgerreise nach Palästina und auf den Sinai in den Jahren 1217/1218', ed. Ulf Koppitz, *Concilium medii aevi*, 14 (2011), 121-221

Martyrologium romanum, ed. Hippolyte Delehaye *et al.*, Propylaeum ad AASS Decembris (Brussels, 1940)

Milo of St Amand, *Milonis Carmina*, ed. Ludwig Traube, MGH Poetae 3 (Berlin, 1896)

Il menologio di Basilio II (cod. vaticano greco 1613), BAV codices e Vaticanis selecti phototypice expressi, vol. 8 (Turin, 1907)

Mombrizio, Bonino, *Sanctuarium seu vitae sanctorum*, ed. monachi Solesmenses (Paris, 1910)

——, *La légende de Sainte Catherine: Poème italien du xve siècle publié pour la première fois d'après le manuscrit unique de la Bibliothèque royale de Belgique*, ed. Alphonse Bayot and Pierre Groult (Gembloux, 1943)

Nonius Marcellus, *Nonii Marcelli De compendiosa doctrina libros XX*, ed. Wallace M. Lindsay (Leipzig, 1901)

Die Oracula Sibyllina, ed. Johannes Geffcken (Leipzig, 1902)

Ordericus Vitalis, *Historia ecclesiastica*, ed. and trans. Marjorie Chibnall (Oxford, 1969-80)

Origen, *Origenes Matthäuserklärung II: Die lateinische Übersetzung der Commentariorum Series*, ed. Ursula Treu *et al.* (Berlin, 1976)

Orosius, *Histoires (contre les Païens)*, ed. and trans. Marie-Pierre Arnaud-Lindet (Paris, 1990-91)

——, *Pauli Orosii historiarum adversum paganos libri VII: Accedit eiusdem liber apologeticus*, ed. Karl Zangemeister, CSEL 5 (Wien, 1882)

Paschasius Radbertus, *Expositio in Matthaeo Libri xii*, ed. Beda Paulus, CCCM 56-56B (Turnhout, 1984)

'The martyrdom of Pansophios of Alexandria', 'წამებაჲ წმიდისაჲდა ყოვლად ქებილისა მოწამისა პანსოფი ალექსანდრიელისაჲ' (Ts'ameba ts'midisada q'ovlad kebilisa mots'amisa p'ansopi aleksandrielisa), *ed.* Korneli Kekelidze, in *Monumenta hagiographica georgica*, vol. 1: *Keimena* (Tbilisi, 1918), 48-59

'La Passion de S. Pansophios d'Alexandrie', ed. Paul Peeters, *AB,* 47 (1929), 307-37

'Passio sanctae Caterinae virginis', ed. Maria Cattalano, *Mélanges historiques et hagiographiques valdôtains* (Miscellanea Augustana), II, 1953, 351-65

Vita S. Pauli iunioris in Monte Latro', ed. Hippolyte Delehaye, *AB,* 11 (1892), 5-74 & 136-82

Pélagie la Pénitente: Métamorphoses d'une légende, ed. Pierre Petitmengin *et al.*, 2 vols (Paris, 1981-1984)

Petrus Chrysologus, *Sancti Petri Chrysologi collectio sermonum*, ed. Alejandro Olivar, CCSL 24-24B (Turnhout, 1975-82)

Peter the Deacon, *Acta SS. Placidi et Fratrum*, *AASS* Oct. III, pp. 114D-38D

Peter, Subdeacon of Naples, *Pietro Suddiacono napoletano: L'opera agiografica*, ed. Edoardo D'Angelo (Florence, 2002)

Rabanus Maurus, *Martyrologium Rabani Mauri*, ed. John M. McCulloh, CCCM 44 (Turnhout, 1979)

Rodulfus Glaber, *Rodulfi Glabri historiarum libri quinque*, ed. and trans. John France (Oxford, 1989)

Rufinus, *Historia ecclesiastica*, ed. Theodor Mommsen (Leipzig, 1903)

De sainte Katerine: An Anonymous Picard Version of the Life of St. Catherine of Alexandria, ed. William MacBain (Fairfax, VA, 1987)

St. Katherine of Alexandria: The Late Middle English Prose Legend in Southwell Minster ms 7, ed. Saara Nevanlinna and Irma Taavitsainen (Cambridge, 1993)

Sauer, Lorenz (Laurentius Surius), *De probatis sanctorum historiis ab Al. Lipomano olim conscriptis nunc primum a Laur. Surio emendatis et auctis* (Cologne, 1570-77)

Suidae lexicon, ed. Ada Adler, 5 vols (Leipzig, 1928-38)

Supplément aux Acta sanctorum pour des vies de saints de l'époque mérovingienne, vol. 2: *Contenant des documents sur les origines du christianisme en Espagne, en Angleterre, sur les martyrs de la Gaule et des bords du Rhin avec de nombreux dessins d'antiquités*, ed. C. Narbey (Paris, 1905)

Symeon Metaphrastes, Μαρτύριον τῆς ἁγίας καλλίνικου μεγαλομάρτυρος τοῦ Χριστοῦ Ἀικατερινῆς, *PG* 116 (Paris, 1891), cols 275-302
Usuard, *Le Martyrologe d'Usuard: Texte et commentaire*, ed. Jacques Dubois, Subsidia Hagiographica 40 (Brussels, 1965)
Vitae sanctae Katharinae, ed. Arpad P. Orbán, CCCM 119-119A (Turnhout, 1992)
'Vita S. Gerardi auctore Widrico', ed. Georg Waitz, MGH SS 4, (Hannover, 1841), pp. 490-505
Vita Haroldi in *The Romance of the Life of Harold, King of England*, ed. Walter de Gray Birch (London, 1885)
'Vita Richardi abb. S. Vitoni virdunensis', ed. Wilhelm Wattenbach, MGH SS 11 (Hannover, 1854), pp. 280-290
'Vita Salabergae abb. laudunensis', ed. Bruno Krusch and Wilhelm Levison in *Passiones vitaeque sanctorum aevi merovingici*, MGH SSRM 5 (Hannover, 1910), pp. 40-66
'Vita Symeonis Achivi', ed. Walter Berschin and Theodor Klüppel, in *Die Abtei Reichenau: Neue Beiträge zur Geschichte und Kultur des Inselklosters*, ed. Helmut Maurer (Sigmaringen, 1974), pp. 115-24
La vie d'Etienne le Jeune par Étienne le Diacre, ed. Marie-France Auzépy (London, 2016)
'La *vita* di s. Simeone monaco', ed. Paolo Golinelli, *Studi Medievali*, ser. 3a, 20 (1979), 709-88
'Une version Arabe de la Passion de Sainte Catherine d'Alexandrie', ed. Paul Peeters, *AB*, 26 (1907), 5-32
Walafrid Strabo, 'Vita Sancti Galli', ed. Bruno Krusch in *Passiones vitaeque sanctorum aevi Merovingici*, MGH SSRM 4 (Hannover, 1902), pp. 280-337
William of Apulia, *Gesta Roberti Wiscardi a. 1009-1085*, ed. Roger Wilmans, MGH SS 9 (Hannover, 1851), pp. 239-98

Secondary works

Abrahamse, Dorothy de F., 'Byzantine asceticism and women's monasteries in early medieval Italy', in *Medieval Religious Women 1: Distant Echoes*, ed. John A. Nichols and Lillian Thomas Shank (Kalamazoo, 1984), pp. 31-49

Agati, Maria Luisa, 'Lista provvisoria dei manoscritti copiati in minuscola "bouletée"', *Scriptorium*, 42 (1988), 104-9
——, *La minuscola "bouletée"* (Vatican, 1992)
Andersson-Schmitt, Margaret, *et al.*, *Mittelalterliche Handschriften der Universitätsbibliothek Uppsala: Katalog über die C-Sammlung*, vol. 4: HSS C 301-400 (Stockholm, 1991)
Andreescu-Treadgold, Irina, 'Some considerations on the eleventh-century Byzantine wall mosaics of Hosios Loukas and San Nicolo di Lido', *Musiva & Sectilia*, 5 (2008), 115-67
D'Angelo, Edoardo, 'Prose et vers dans l'oeuvre de Pierre Sous-Diacre', *Archivum Latinitatis Medii Aevi*, 53 (1995), 187-99
——, 'Petrus Neapolitanus Subd.', in *La trasmissione dei testi latini del Medioevo*, ed. Lucia Castaldi and Paolo Chiesa, vol. 1 (Tavarnuzze, 2004), pp. 349-63
——, 'Agiografia latina del Mezzogiorno continentale d'Italia (750-1000)', in *Hagiographies: Histoire internationale de la littérature hagiographique latine et vernaculaire en Occident des origines à 1550*, ed. Guy Philippart, vol. 4 (Turnhout, 2006), pp. 41-134
Alexander, Paul J., *The Oracle of Baalbeck: The Tiburtine Sibyl in Greek Dress* (Washington DC, 1967)
Aston, Stanley C., 'Ad honorem sanctae Katerinae virginis', in *St. Catharine's College Cambridge 1473-1973: A Volume of Essays to Commemorate the Quincentenary of the Foundation of the College*, ed. Edwin E. Rich (Cambridge, 1973), pp. 33-58
Atiya, Aziz S., *The Arabic Manuscripts of Mount Sinai: A Hand-list of the Arabic Manuscripts and Scrolls Microfilmed at the Library of the Monastery of St Catherine, Mount Sinai* (Baltimore, 1955)
Auzépy, Marie-France, 'De la Palestine à Constantinople (VIIIe – IXe siècles): Étienne le Sabaïte et Jean Damascène, *Travaux et Mémoires*, 12 (1994), 183-218
——, 'Les Sabaites et l'iconoclasme', in *The Sabaite Heritage in the Orthodox Church from the Fifth Century to the Present,* ed. Joseph Patrich (Leuven, 2001), pp. 305-14
d'Avray, David L., 'Katherine of Alexandria and mass communication in Germany: Woman as intellectual', in *Modern Questions about Medieval Sermons: Essays on Marriage, Death, History and Sanctity*,

ed. Nicole Bériou and David L. d'Avray (Spoleto, 1994), pp. 401-08

Avril, François, *Manuscrits normands XI-XIème siècles* (Rouen, 1975)

Axelson, Bertil, *'Ein drittes Werk des Firmicus Maternus?': Zur Kritik der philologischen Identifizierungsmethode* (Lund, 1973)

Baldoni, Dante, 'L'abate Costantino Caetani (1658-1650), editore delle opere di S. Pier Damiani (1604-1640)', in *Ascetica cristiana e ascetica giansenista e quietista nelle regioni d'influenza avellanita: Atti del 1. convegno del Centro di studi Avellaniti* (Fonte Avellana, 1977), pp. 111-25

Baldwin, Barry, 'Vergil in Byzantium', in *Antike und Abendland: Beiträge zum Verständnis der Griechen und Römer und ihres Nachlebens*, ed. Werner van Koppenfels *et al.*, vol. 28 (Berlin, 1982), pp. 81-93

Barker, Nicolas J., *The Roxburghe Club: A Bicentenary History* (London, 2012)

Bately, Janet M., and David J.A. Ross, 'A check list of manuscripts of Orosius' *Historiarum adversum paganos libri septem*', *Scriptorium*, 15 (1961), 329-34

Baumstark, Anton, 'Eine syrisch-melchitische Allerheiligenlitanei', *Oriens Christianus*, 4 (1904), 98-120

Bayer, Axel, 'Griechen im Westen im 10. und 11. Jahrhundert: Simeon von Trier und Simeon von Reichenau', in *Kaiserin Theophanu: Die Begegnung des Ostens und Westens um die Wende des ersten Jahrtausends*, ed. Anton von Euw and Peter Schreiner (Cologne, 1991), I, pp. 335-41

Beatie, Bruce A., 'Saint Katharine of Alexandria: Traditional themes and the development of a Medieval German hagiographic narrative', *Speculum*, 52 (1977), 785-800

Beck, Hans-Georg, *Kirche und Theologische Literatur im Byzantinischen Reich* (Munich, 1959)

Bibliotheca Casinensis seu codicum manuscriptorum qui in tabulario Casinensi asservantur monachorum Ordinis S. Benedicti, vol. 3 (Monte Cassino, 1877)

Bibliotheca hagiographia graeca, ed. François Halkin (Brussels, 1957)

Bibliotheca hagiographica latina, ed. Hagiographi Bollandiani (Brussels, 1949)

Bibliotheca hagiographica latina antiquae et mediae aetatis: Novum supplementum, ed. Henryk Fros (Brussels, 1986)

Bibliotheca hagiographica orientalis, ed. Paul Peeters (Brussels, 1970)

Bidez, Joseph, 'Sur diverses citations, et notamment sur trois passages de Malalas retrouvés dans un texte hagiographique', *Byzantinische Zeitschrift*, 11 (1902), 388-94

Biddick, Kathleen, *The Shock of Medievalism* (Durham, NC, 1998)

Bierbrauer, Katharina, *Die vorkarolingischen und karolingischen Handschriften der Bayerischen Staatsbibliothek*, Textband (Wiesbaden, 1990)

Biggs, Frederick M., and Thomas N. Hall, 'Traditions concerning Jamnes and Mambres in Anglo-Saxon England', *Anglo-Saxon England*, 25 (1996), 69-89

Binggeli, André, 'L'hagiographie du Sinai en arabe d'après un recueil du IXe siècle', *Parole de l'Orient*, 32 (2007), 163-80

Bischoff, Bernhard, *Die südostdeutschen Schreibschulen und Bibliotheken in der Karolingerzeit*, vol. 1: *Die bayrischen Diözesen*, 2nd edn (Wiesbaden, 1974)

——, 'Italienische Handschriften des neunten bis elften Jahrhunderts in frühmittelalterlichen Bibliotheken außerhalb Italiens', in *Il libro e il testo: Atti del convegno internazionale*, ed. Cesare Questa and Renato Raffaeli (Urbino, 1984), pp. 169-194

——, *Die Abtei Lorsch im Spiegel ihrer Handschriften* (Lorsch, 1989)

——, *Katalog der festländischen Handschriften des neunten Jahrhunderts (mit Ausnahme der wisigotischen)*, ed. Birgit Ebersperger (Wiesbaden, 2004)

Blasina, James J., 'Music and gender in the medieval cult of St Katherine of Alexandria, c.1050-1300' (unpublished doctoral dissertation, Harvard University, 2015)

——, 'Ainard of Dives and the Ste-Catherine-du-Mont office for St Katherine of Alexandria: "Inter praecipuos cantores scientia musicae artis"', *Plainsong and Medieval Music*, 30 (2021), 55-83

Bloch, Herbert, 'Peter the Deacon's vision of Byzantium and a rediscovered treatise in his "Acta S. Placidi"', *Settimane di Studio – Centro Italiano di Studi sull'Alto Medioevo*, 34.2 (1988), pp. 797-847

Boesch Gajano, Sofia, ed., *Raccolte di vite di santi dal xiii al xviii secolo: Strutture, messaggi, fruizioni* (Fasano, 1990).

Bouet, Pierre, 'Les Italiens en Normandie au XIe siècle', in *Les Italiens en Normandie: De l'étranger à l'immigré*, Actes du Colloque de Cerisy-la-Salle (8-11 octobre 1998), ed. Mariella Colin and François Neveux (Caen, 2000), pp. 27-44

Bray, Jennifer R., 'The Legend of St. Katherine in later Middle English Literature' (unpublished doctoral thesis, University of London, 1984)

Brown, Virginia, 'A new Beneventan calendar from Naples: The lost *Kalendarium Tutinianum* rediscovered', *Mediaeval Studies*, 46 (1984), 385-449

Buono, Lidia, *et al.*, *I manoscritti datati delle provincie di Frosinone, Rieti, e Viterbo*, in Manoscritti datati d'Italia 17 (Florence, 2007)

Caiazza, Pietro, 'Aspetti e problemi dell'opera di Alfano I, arcivescovo salernitano', *Benedictina*, 22 (1975), 347-58

Calvin, Jean, *Vera christianae pacificationis et ecclesiae reformandae ratio* (Geneva, 1549)

Canart, Paul, and Rosario Pintaudi, 'Le palimpseste hagiographique grec du Laurentianus 74,17 et la Passion de S. Pansophius d'Alexandrie', *AB*, 104 (1986), 5-16

Caner, Daniel F., *History and Hagiography from the Late Antique Sinai* (Liverpool, 2010)

Caseau, Béatrice, 'Parfum et guérison dans le christianisme ancien: Des huiles parfumées des médecins au *myron* des saints byzantins', in *Les Pères de l'Eglise face à la science médicale de leur temps*, ed. Véronique Boudon-Millot *et al.* (Paris, 2005), pp. 141-91

Caspar, Erich, *Petrus Diaconus und die Monte Cassineser Fälschungen: Ein Beitrag zur Geschichte des italienischen Geisteslebens im Mittelalter* (Berlin, 1909)

Catafygiotu Topping, Eva, *Sacred Songs: Studies in Byzantine Hymnography* (Minneapolis, 1997)

Catalogus codicum hagiographicorum Bibliothecae Regiae Bruxellensis, 1: Codices latini membranei, vol. 1, ed. Hagiographi Bollandiani (Brussels, 1886)

Catalogus codicum hagiographicorum Bibliothecae Regiae Bruxellensis, ed. Hagiographi Bollandiani, vol. 1.2 (Brussels, 1889)

Catalogus codicum hagiographicorum latinorum antiquiorum saeculo xvi qui asservantur in Bibliotheca Nationali Parisiensi, ed. Hagiographi Bollandiani, vol. 2 (Brussels, 1890)

'Catalogus codicum hagiographicorum bibliothecae civitatis Treverensis', *AB*, 51 (1934), 157-285

Cavallera, Ferdinand, 'Un exposé sur la vie spirituelle et monastique au ive siècle', *Revue d'ascétique et de mystique*, 16 (1935), 132-46

Chadwick, Owen, *Catholicism and History: The Opening of the Vatican Archives* (Cambridge, 1978)

Chaplais, Pierre, 'William of Saint-Calais and the Domesday Survey', in *Domesday Studies*, ed. James C. Holt (Woodbridge, 1987), pp. 65-77

Charanis, Peter, 'Cultural diversity and the breakdown of Byzantine power in Asia Minor', *DOP*, 29 (1975), 1-20

Chatzidakis, Nano, *Byzantine Mosaics* (Athens, 1994)

Cheikho, Louis, 'From Riaq to Hama: A modern journey for Father Louis Cheikho, Jesuit' ['Min Riyāq ilā Ḥamā: Riḥla ḥadītha lil-ab Lūyis Shaykhū al-Yasū'ī'], *Al-Mashriq: Révue catholique orientale: sciences, lettres, arts* (*al-Mashriq: majallah Kāthūlīkiyah sharqīyah tabḥathu fī al-ʿilm wa-al-adab wa-al-fann*), 5 (1902), 904-09

Chevalier, Cyr U.J., *Repertorium hymnologicum: Catalogue des chants, hymnes, proses, séquences, tropes en usage dans l'Eglise latine depuis les origines jusqu'a nos jours* (Leuven, 1892-1920)

Chiesa, Paolo, 'Le traduzioni dal Greco: L'evoluzione della scuola napoletana nel X secolo', in *Lateinische Kultur im X. Jahrhundert*, ed. Walter Berschin (*Mittellateinisches Jahrbuch* 24-25 [1990-91]), 67-87

Cholij, Roman, *Theodore the Stoudite: The Ordering of Holiness* (Oxford, 2002)

Chronopoulos, Tina, 'The date and place of composition of the Passion of St Katherine of Alexandria (BHL 1663)', *AB* 130 (2012), 40-88

Cilento, Nicola, 'La chiesa di Napoli nell'alto medioevo' in *Storia di Napoli*, ed. Ernesto Pontieri, vol. 2.2 (Naples, 1969), 641-735

Coccia, Edmondo, *Le edizioni delle opere del Mantovano* (Rome, 1960)

Codicum casinensium manuscriptorum Catalogus, vol. 1 (Monte Cassino, 1915)

Collamore, Lila, 'Charting the Divine Office', in *The Divine Office in the Latin Middle Ages: Methodology and Source Studies, Regional Developments, Hagiography*, ed. Margot Fassler and Rebecca Baltzer (Oxford, 2000), pp. 3-11

Collins, David J., *Reforming Saints: Saints' Lives and their Authors in Germany, 1470-1530* (Oxford, 2018)

Colombás, García M., 'Sobre el autor des las *Consultationes Zacchaei et Apollonii*', *Studia Monastica*, 14 (1972), 7-15

Combaluzier, Fernand, 'Un benedictionnaire episcopal du Xe siècle (Ms 2657 Bibl. Sainte-Geneviève, Paris)', *Sacris Erudiri*, 14 (1963), 286-342

Constantinou, Stavroula, 'The authoritative voice of St. Catherine of Alexandria', *Acta Byzantina Fennica*, 2 (n.s.) (2003-04), 19-38

Coppola, Giovanni 'L'essor de la construction monastique en Normandie au XIe siècle: Mécénat, matériaux et moines-architectes', *Annales de Normandie*, 42-4 (1992), 335-49

The Coptic Encyclopedia, ed. Aziz S. Atiya (New York, 1991)

Constantinides, Costas N. and Robert Browning, *Dated Greek Manuscripts from Cyprus to the Year 1570* (Washington, DC, 1993)

Courcelle, Pierre, 'Date, source et genèse des *Consultationes Zacchaei et Apollonii*', *Revue de l'histoire des religions*, 146 (1954), 174-93

Cowdrey, Herbert E.J., *The Age of Abbot Desiderius: Montecassino, the Papacy, and the Normans in the Eleventh and Early Twelfth Centuries* (Oxford, 1983)

Crisafulli, Virgil S., and John W. Nesbitt, *The Miracles of St Artemios: A collection of Miracle Stories by an Anonymous Author of Seventh-century Byzantium* (Leiden, 1997)

Crostini, Barbara and Ines Angeli Murzaku, ed., *Greek Monasticism in Southern Italy: The Life of Neilos in Context* (New York, 2018)

Darrouzès, Jean, 'Notes d'Asie Mineure', *Ἀρχεῖον Πόντου*, 26 (1964), 28-40

Davidson, Georgina, 'Divine guidance and the use of sources: A case from the Annales of Caesar Baronius', *Historical Reflections / Réflexions Historiques*, 15.1 (1988), 117-29

de Gaiffier, Baudouin, 'Sub Daciano preside: Étude des quelques passions espagnoles', *AB* 72 (1954), 378-96

——, 'Hagiographie Salernitaine: La translation de S. Mattieu', AB, 80 (1962), 82-110

——, 'Deux passionaires de Morimondo conservés au séminaire de Côme', AB, 83 (1965), 142-56

——, 'Les "doublets" en hagiographie Latine', AB, 96 (1978), 261-69

——, 'Au sujet des sources du Sanctuarium de Mombritius', Mittellateinisches Jahrbuch, 14 (1979), 278-81

De Jerphanion, Guillaume, *Une nouvelle province de l'art byzantin: Les églises rupestres de Cappadoce*, vol. 1 (Paris, 1925)

Delehaye, Hippolyte, 'L'amphithéatre Flavien et ses environs dans les textes hagiographiques', AB, 16 (1897), 209-52

——, 'La vie de Saint Paul le Jeune et la chronologie de Métaphraste', Revue des Questions Historiques, 54 (1893), 49-85

——, 'Les légendes hagiographiques', Revue des questions historiques, 38 (1903), 56-122

——, 'Les martyrs d'Egypte', *AB*, 40 (1922), 5-154

——, review of Erich Klostermann and Erich Seeberg, 'Die Apologie der Heiligen Katharina', *Schriften der Königsberger Gelehrten Gesellschaft*, 2 (1924), 31-87, AB, 45 (1927), 151-53

——, *Les Légendes hagiographiques*, Subsidia Hagiographica 18, 3rd edn (Brussels, 1927)

——, *Sanctus: Essai sur le culte des saints dans l'antiquité*, Subsidia Hagiographica 17 (Brussels, 1927)

——, review of Gerhard Eis, *Die Quellen für das Sanctuarium des Mailänder Humanisten Boninus Mombritius: Eine Untersuchung zur Geschichte der großen Legendensammlung des Mittelalters* (Berlin, 1933), in *AB* , 53 (1935), 412-22

——, 'Hagiographie Neapolitaine', *AB*, 57 (1939), 5-64

——, *À travers trois siècles: L'œuvre des Bollandistes: 1615-1915*, Subsidia Hagiographica 13.A2, 2nd edn (Brussels, 1959)

——, *Les Passions des martyrs et les genres littéraires*, 2nd edn (Brussels, 1966)

Déroche, Vincent, 'Porquoi écrivait-on des recueils de miracles? L'exemple des miracles d'Artémios', in *Les saints et leur sanctuaire: Textes, images et monuments*, ed. Catherine Jolivet-Lévy et al. (Paris, 1993), pp. 95-116

Detorakes, Theocharis, 'Vie inédite de Cosmas le Mélode', *AB*, 99 (1981), 101-16

Die deutsche Literatur des Mittelalters: Verfasserlexikon, vol. 9: *Slecht, Reinbold – Ulrich von Liechtenstein*, ed. Burghart Wachinger *et al.* (Berlin, 1995)

Dictionnaire d'histoire et de géographie ecclésiastiques, vol. 16, ed. Alfred Baudrillart *et al.* (Paris, 1967)

Dictionnaire de la langue gauloise: Une approche linguistique du vieux-celtique continental, ed. Xavier Delamarre (Paris, 2003)

Dictionnaire de Spiritualité, vol. 6 (Gabriel-Guzman), ed. Marcel Viller *et al.* (Paris, 1967)

Diesenberger, Maximilian, 'Le manuscrit Bayerische Staatsbibliothek CLM 4554, témoin de lectures', in *Les manuscrits médiévaux: Témoins de lectures*, ed. Catherine Croizy-Naquet *et al.* (Paris, 2015), pp. 89-106

——, *Predigt und Politik im frühmittelalterlichen Bayern: Arn von Salzburg, Karl der Große und die Salzburger Sermones-Sammlung* (Berlin, 2016)

Dionisotti, A. Carlotta, 'Translator's Latin', in *Aspects of the Language of Latin Prose*, ed. Tobias Reinhardt *et al.*, Proceedings of the British Academy 129 (Oxford, 2005), pp. 357-75

——, 'Translated Saints: Wisdom and Her Daughters', *Journal of Early Christian Studies*, 16 (2008), 165-80

Ditchfield, Simon, *Liturgy, Sanctity, and History in Tridentine Italy: Pietro Maria Campi and the Preservation of the Particular* (Cambridge, 1995)

Dizionario Biografico degli Italiani, ed. Alberto M. Ghisalberti (Rome, 1960-2020)

Dmitrievskij, Aleksej, *Opisanie liturgitseskich rukopisej*, 3 vols (Petersburg, 1917, reprinted Hildesheim, 1965)

Dobson, Eric J., *The Origins of Ancrene Wisse* (Oxford, 1976)

Dolbeau, François, 'Le légendier de l'abbaye cistercienne de Clairmarais', *AB*, 91 (1973), 273-86

——, 'Notes sur la genèse et sur la diffusion du *Liber de natalitiis*', *Revue d'Histoire des Textes*, 6 (1976), 143-95

——, 'Un nouveau catalogue des manuscrits de Lobbes aux xie et xiie siècles', *Recherches Augustiniennes*, 13 (1978), 3-36 & 14 (1979), 191-248

——, 'Anciens possesseurs des manuscrits hagiographiques latins conservés à la Bibliothèque Nationale de Paris', *Revue d'Histoire des Textes*, 9 (1979), 183-238

——, Notes sur l'organisation interne des légendiers latins', in *Hagiographie, cultures et sociétés (IVe – XIIe siècles)*, actes du colloque organisé à Nanterre et à Paris (2-5 mai 1979) (Paris, 1981), pp. 11-31

——, 'Nouvelles recherches sur le Legendarium Flandrense', *Recherches Augustiniennes*, 16 (1981), 399-455

——, 'Le rôle des interprètes dans les traductions hagiographiques d'Italie du sud', in *Traduction et traducteurs au Moyen Age: Actes du colloque international du CNRS organisé à Paris, IRHT (26-28 mai 1986)*, ed. Geneviève Contamine (Paris, 1989), pp. 145-62

——, 'Un légendier de la cathédrale d'Arras (Brussels, B. R., II. 2310)', *AB*, 107 (1989) 128

——, 'Les légendiers de Marchiennes', *AB*, 108 (1990), 336

——, 'Deux légendiers de Metz et de Châlons', *AB*, 108 (1990), 348

——, 'Deux légendiers démembrés du diocèse de Liège', *AB*, 109 (1991), 117-36

——, 'Le légendier de Châalis', *AB*, 117 (1999), 388-93

——, 'Fragments de manuscrits provenant de Saint-Rambert-en-Bugey', *Scriptorium*, 54 (2000), 309-18

——, 'Les sources manuscrites des *Acta sanctorum* et leur collecte (XVIIe-XVIIIe siècles): De Rosweyde aux *Acta sanctorum*', in *La recherche hagiographique des Bollandistes a travers quatre siècles: Actes du colloque international, Bruxelles (5 octobre 2007)*, ed. Robert Godding *et al.* (Brussels, 2009), pp. 105-47

Dottin, Georges, *La langue gauloise: Grammaire, textes et glossaire* (Paris, 1920)

Dresvina, Juliana, 'The significance of the demonic episode in the legend of St Margaret of Antioch', *Medium Aevum*, 81 (2012), 189-209

Dubois, Jacques, *Les martyrologes du Moyen Âge latin* (Turnhout, 1978)

Dufourcq, Albert, 'Gestes d'Artemius', in Id., *Étude sur les gesta martyrum romains. Vol. 5: Les légendes grecques et les légendes latines* (Paris, 1988)

Dümmler, Ernst, 'Die handschriftliche Überlieferung der lateinischen Dichtungen aus der Zeit der Karolinger II', *Neues Archiv der Gesellschaft für ältere deutsche Geschichtskunde*, 4 (1878), 241-322

Dzielska, Marie, *Hypatia of Alexandria* (Cambridge, MA, 1995)

Efthymiadis, Stephanos, 'D'Orient en Occident mais étranger aux deux mondes: Messages et renseignements tirés de la vie de Saint Nicolas le Pèlerin (*BHL* 6223)', in *Puer Apuliae: Mélanges offerts à Jean Marie Martin*, ed. Errico Cuozzo *et al.*, vol. 1 (Paris, 2008), pp. 207-23

Ehrenschwendtner, Marie-Luise, *Die Bildung der Dominikanerinnen in Süddeutschland vom 13.-15. Jahrhundert* (Stuttgart, 2004)

Ehrhard, Albert, 'Die Legendensammlung des Symeon Metaphrastes und ihr ursprünglicher Bestand: Eine paläographische Studie zur griechischen Hagiographie', *Festschrift zum elfhundertjährigen Jubiläum des deutschen Campo Santo in Rom*, ed. Stephan Ehses (Freiburg, 1897), pp. 46-82

Einenkel, Eugen, 'Über den Verfasser der neuangelsächsischen Legende von Katharina', *Anglia*, 5 (1882), 91-123

Eis, Gerhard, *Die Quellen für das Sanctuarium des Mailänder Humanisten Boninus Mombritius: Eine Untersuchung zur Geschichte der großen Legendensammlung des Mittelalters* (Berlin, 1933)

Ekonomou, Andrew J., *Byzantine Rome and the Greek Popes: Eastern Influences on Rome and the Papacy from Gregory the Great to Zacharias, A.D. 590-752* (Lanham, 2007)

Émereau, Casimir, 'Hymnographi Byzantini', *Échos d'Orient*, 21 (1922), 258-79

Engberg, Sysse G., 'Trier and Sinai: Saint Symeon's book', *Scriptorium*, 59 (2005), 133-46

Encyclopedia of Early Christianity, ed. Everett Ferguson, 2nd edn (Oxford, 1999)

van der Essen, Léon, *Étude critique et littéraire sur les Vitae des saints mérovingiens de l'Ancienne Belgique* (Leuven, 1907)

Eustratiades, Sophronius, and Arkadios Vatopédinos, *Catalogue of the Greek Manuscripts in the Library of the Monastery of Vatopedi on Mt. Athos*, Harvard Theological Studies XI (Cambridge, MA, 1924)

Falcetta, Alessandro, *The Daily Discoveries of a Bible Scholar and Manuscript Hunter: A Biography of James Rendel Harris (1852-1941)* (London, 2018)

von Falkenhausen, Vera, 'Greek monasticism in Campania and Latium from the tenth to the fifteenth century', in *Greek Monasticism in Southern Italy*, ed. Crostini and Murzaku, pp. 78-95

Fawtier-Jones, Ethel C., 'Les vies de Sainte Catherine d'Alexandrie en ancien français', *Romania*, 56 (193), 80-104

Fawtier, Robert, 'Les reliques Rouennaises de Sainte Catherine d'Alexandrie', *AB*, 42 (1923), 357-68

Feiertag, Jean-Louis, *Les* Consultationes Zacchaei et Apollonii*: Étude d'histoire et de sotériologie* (Fribourg, 1990)

Ferrari, Michele C., 'From pilgrim's guide to living relic: Symeon of Trier and his biographer Eberwin', in *Latin Culture in the Eleventh Century: Proceedings of the Third International Conference on Medieval Latin Studies,* (Cambridge, 9-12 September 1998), ed. Michael W. Herren *et al.*, 2 vols (Turnhout, 2002), I, pp. 324-44

Fleith, Barbara, *Studien zur Überlieferungsgeschichte der lateinischen Legenda aurea*, Subsidia Hagiographica 27 (Brussels, 1991)

Fletcher, Eric, 'Benedict Biscop', *Jarrow Lecture 1981* (Jarrow on Tyne, 1981)

Foffano, Tino, 'Per la data dell'edizione del *Sanctuarium* di Bonino Mombrizio', *Italia medioevale e umanistica,* 22 (1979), 509-11

Follieri, Enrica, 'I rapporti fra Bisanzio e l'Occidente nel campo dell'agiografia', *Proceedings of the 13th International Congress of Byzantine Studies* (Oxford 5-10 Sept. 1966), ed. Joan M. Hussey *et al.* (London, 1967), pp. 354-62

Forrai, Réka E., 'The readership of early medieval Greek-Latin translations', *Settimane di Studio – Centro Italiano di Studi sull'Alto Medioevo, 59* (2012), 293-311

——, 'Byzantine saints for Frankish warriors: Anastasius Bibliothecarius' Latin version of the Passion of Saint Demetrius', in *L'héritage byzantin en Italie (VIIIe-XIIe siècle),* vol. 3: *Décor monumental, objets, tradition textuelle*, ed. Sulamith Brodbeck *et al.* (Rome, 2016), pp. 185-202

——, 'Translation as rewriting: A modern theory for a premodern practice', *Renaessanceforum: Tidsskrift for Renaessanceforskning*, 14 (2018), 25-49

Forsyth, George H. and Kurt Weitzmann, *The Monastery of Saint Catherine at Mount Sinai: The Church and Fortress of Justinian* (Ann Arbor, 1973)

Französisches etymologisches Wörterbuch: Eine Darstellung des galloromanischen Sprachschatzes, ed. Walther v. Wartburg *et al.*, vol. 13 (Basel, 1966)

Frazier, Alison, 'Katherine's place in a Renaissance collection: Evidence from Antonio degli Algi (*c*.1400-1477), *De vitis et gestis sanctorum*', in *St Katherine of Alexandria*, ed. Jenkins and Lewis, pp. 221-40

——, *Possible Lives: Authors and Saints in Renaissance Italy* (New York, 2005)

Frei, Judith, *Das Ambrosianische Sakramentar D 3-3 aus dem Mailändischen Metropolitankapitel* (Münster, 1974)

Galavaris, Georgios, 'Η Αγία Αικατερίνη στις εικόνες της Ι.Μ. Σινά', *Σιναϊτικα Αναλεκτα*, 1 (2002), 1-38

Garitte, Gérard, Catalogue des manuscrits géorgiens littéraires du mont Sinai (Louvain, 1956)

——, *Le Calendrier Palestino-Géorgien du Sinaiticus 34 (Xe siècle)*, Subsidia Hagiographica 30 (Brussels, 1958)

Gazeau, Véronique, 'Recherches autour des débuts de l'abbaye de la Trinité-du-Mont de Rouen', in *La Ville médiévale en deça et au-dela de ses murs: Mélanges J.-P. Leguay*, ed. Philippe Lardin and Jean-Louis Roch (Rouen, 2000), pp. 151-59

——, 'Guillaume de Volpiano en Normandie: État des questions', *Tabularia "Études"*, 2 (2002), pp. 35-46

——, *Normannia monastica: Prosopographie des abbés bénédictins (X^e – XIIe siècle)*, 2 vols (Caen, 2007)

van den Gheyn, Joseph, *Catalogue des manuscrits de la bibliothèque Royale de Bruxelles*, vol. 5: *Histoire—Hagiographie* (Brussels, 1905)

Giamberardini, Gabriele, *S. Caterina di Alessandria*, Quaderni della Terra Santa (Jerusalem, 1978)

Gilissen, Léon, *L'expertise des écritures médiévales: Recherche d'une méthode avec application à un manuscrit du xie siècle: Le lectionnaire de Lobbes, Codex Bruxellensis 18018* (Ghent, 1973)

Glassner, Christine, *Inventar der Handschriften des Benediktinerstiftes Melk*, vol. 1: *Von den Anfängen bis ca. 1400* (Vienna, 2000)

Glauche, Günter, *Katalog der lateinischen Handschriften der Bayerischen Staatsbibliothek München: Die Pergamenthandschriften aus Benediktbeuern: Clm 4501–4663* (Wiesbaden, 1994)

Godman, Peter, *Poetry of the Carolingian Renaissance* (London, 1985)

Gutas, Dimitri, Anthony Kaldellis, and Brian Long, 'Intellectual exchanges with the Arab world', in *The Cambridge Intellectual History of Byzantium*, ed. Anthony Kaldellis and Niketas Siniossoglou (Cambridge, 2017), pp. 79-98

Graham, Stacey, 'The dissemination of North African Christian and intellectual culture in Late Antiquity', (unpublished doctoral dissertation, University of California, Los Angeles, 2015)

Griffin, Sidney H., 'From Aramaic to Arabic: The languages of the monasteries of Palestine in the Byzantine and early Islamic periods', *DOP*, 51 (1997), 11-31

Guazzelli, Guiseppe A., 'Cesare Baronio and the Roman Catholic vision of the early Church', in *Sacred History: Uses of the Christian Past in the Renaissance World*, ed. Katherine van Liere, Simon Ditchfield *et al.* (Oxford, 2012), pp. 52-71

Gullick, Michael, and Caroline Thorn, 'The scribes of the Great Domesday Book: A preliminary account', *The Journal of the Society of Archivists*, 8 (1986), 78-80

Haberkern, Phillip N., *Patron Saint and Prophet: Jan Hus in the Bohemian and German Reformations* (Oxford, 2016)

Hagen, Hermann, *Catalogus codicum bernensium: Bibliotheca Bongarsiana* (Bern, 1875)

Haidinger, Alois, *Katalog der Handschriften des Augustiner Chorherrenstifts Klosterneuburg*, Teil I (Cod. 1-100) (Vienna, 1983)

Halkin, review of Giovanni B. Bronzini, *La leggenda di S. Caterina d'Alessandria: Passioni greche e latine*, Atti dell'Accademia Nazionale dei Lincei (Memorie: Classe di Scienze morali, storiche e filologiche, serie VIII) 9 (Rome, 1960), in *AB*, 79 (1961), 178-79

——, *Manuscrits grecs de Paris: Inventaire hagiographique* (Brussels, 1968)

Halm, Karl, and Wilhelm Meyer, *Catalogus codicum latinorum Bibliothecae Regiae Monacensis*, vol. 2.4 (Munich, 1881)

Harvey, Susan Ashbrook, 'Women in early Byzantine hagiography: Reversing the story', in *That Gentle Strength: Historical Perspectives on Women in Christianity*, ed. Lynda L. Coon *et al.* (Charlottesville, VA, 1990), pp. 36-59

Hardwick, Charles, *An Historical Inquiry touching Saint Catherine of Alexandria, to which is Added a Semi-Saxon Legend*, Publications of the Cambridge Antiquarian Society, Quarto ser. 15 (Cambridge, 1849)

Harris, J. Rendel, 'A new Christian Apology', *Bulletin of the John Rylands Library Manchester*, 7 (1922-23), 355-83

Hassel, Julie B., *Choosing Not to Marry: Women and Autonomy in the Katherine Group* (New York, 2002)

Haverkamp, Alfred, 'Simeon von Trier in universalen Zusammenhängen', *Neues Trierisches Jahrbuch,* 44 (2004), 21-32

——, 'Der heilige Simeon (gest. 1035), Grieche im fatimidischen Orient und im lateinischen Okzident: Geschichten und Geschichte', *Historische Zeitschrift*, 290.1 (2010), 1-51

Hawes, Greta, review of Nickolas P. Roubekas, *An Ancient Theory of Religion: Euhemerism from Antiquity to the Present* (New York, 2017), in *Bryn Mawr Classical Review* 2017.09.52

Heikkilä, Tuomas, *Vita S. Symeonis Treverensis: Ein hochmittelalterlicher Heiligenkult im Kontext* (Helsinki, 2002)

Heiming, Odilo, 'Die ältesten ungedruckten Kalender der mailändischen Kirche', in *Colligere fragmenta: Festschrift Alban Dold zum 70. Geburtstag*, ed. Bonifatius Fischer (Beuron, 1952), pp. 214-35

Heist, William W., *Vitae sanctorum Hiberniae: Ex codice olim Salmanticensi nunc Bruxellensi* (Brussels, 1965)

Heitmeier, Irmtraut, 'Zur Kontinuität der Raumorganisation in Nordtirol von der Spätantike bis ins hohe Mittelalter', in *König, Kirche, Adel: Herrschaftsstrukturen im mittleren Alpenraum*, ed. Rainer Loose and Sönke Lorenz (Lana, 1999), pp. 267-89

Herren, Michael W. *et al*, ed., *Latin Culture in the Eleventh Century: Proceedings of the Third International Conference on Medieval Latin Studies*, (Cambridge, 9-12 September 1998) 2 vols (Turnhout, 2002)

Herrick, Samantha, *Imagining the Sacred Past: Hagiography and Power in Early Normandy* (Cambridge, MA, 2007)

Hiley, David, 'Liturgische Gesangszyklen zur Heiligenverehrung im Mittelalter: Das Beispiel der hl. Katharina', in *Roma quanta fuit: Beiträge zur Architektur-, Kunst- und Kulturgeschichte von der Antike bis zur Gegenwart: Festschrift für Hans-Christoph Dittsche*, ed. Albert Dietl (Augsburg, 2010), pp. 315-338

——, 'The *Historia sancte Caterine* in MS Napoli, Biblioteca Nazionale, XIII.G.24: The earliest proper office for St Catherine of Alexandria?', in *Musica e liturgica a Montecassino nel medioevo*, ed. Nicola Tangari (Rome, 2012), pp. 21-44

Hilg, Hardo, *Die Handschriften der Universitätsbibliothek Augsburg: Die lateinischen mittelalterlichen Handschriften Cod.I.2.4° und Cod. II.1.4°* (Wiesbaden, 2007)

Hilligus, Annegret Helen, *Die Katharinenlegende von Clemence de Barking: Eine anglo-normannische Fassung aus dem 12. Jahrhundert* (Tübingen, 1996)

Høgel, Christian, *Symeon Metaphrastes: Rewriting and Canonization* (Copenhagen, 2002)

Hoffmann, Hartmut, 'Der Kalender des Leo Marsicanus', *Deutsches Archiv für Erforschung des Mittelalters,* 21 (1965), 99-126

——, 'Das *Chronicon Vulturnense* und die Chronik von Montecassino', *Deutsches Archiv,* 22 (1966), 179-96

Hofmann, Georg, 'Sinai und Rom', *Orientalia Christiana Analecta*, 9.3, no. 37 (1927), 218-99

——, 'Lettere pontifice edite ed inedite intorno ai monasteri del monte Sinai', *Orientalia Christiana Periodica*, 17 (1951), 283-303

Holter, Kurt, 'Zu einem Verzeichnis der frühmittelalterlichen Handschriften', *Karolingische und ottonische Kunst: Werden, Wesen, Wirkung*, ed. Hermann Schnitzler (Wiesbaden, 1957), pp. 434-42

Horseman, Reginald, 'Origins of racial Anglo-Saxonism in Great Britain before 1850', *Journal of the History of Ideas*, 37 (1976), 387-410

van Houts, Elisabeth, 'Normandy and Byzantium in the eleventh century', *Byzantion: Revue Internationale des Études Byzantines*, 55.2 (1985), pp. 544-59

——, 'Historiography and hagiography at Saint-Wandrille: The 'inventio et miracula Sancti Vulfranni'', *Anglo-Norman Studies*, 12 (1989), 211231

——, 'L'oralité dans l'hagiographie normande aux xie et xiie siècles', *Les saints dans la Normandie médiévale*, ed. Pierre Bouet and François Neveux (Caen, 2000), pp. 83-94

Inventario dei manoscritti della Biblioteca Capitolare di Ivrea, ed. Alfonso Professione, rev. Ilo Vignono (Alba, 1967)

Jacoby, David, 'Christian pilgrimage to Sinai until the lafte fifteenth century', in *Holy Space, Hallowed Ground: Icons from Sinai*, ed. Robert S. Nelson and Kristen M. Collins (Los Angeles, 2006), pp. 79-93

James, Montague R., *A Descriptive Catalogue of the Manuscripts in the Library of Corpus Christi College, Cambridge*, 2 vols (Cambridge, 1912)

Janin, Raymond, *Les églises et les monastères des grands centres byzantins* (Paris, 1975)

Jenkins, Jacqueline, and Katherine J. Lewis, ed., *St Katherine of Alexandria: Texts and Contexts in Western Medieval Europe* (Turnhout, 2003)

Joassart, Bernard, 'De 1837 à la veille de la Seconde Guerre mondiale' in *Bollandistes, saints et légendes*, ed. Robert Godding *et al.* (Brussels, 2007), pp. 127-143

——, 'Les voyages scientifiques', in *Bollandistes, saints et légendes*, 61-73

Jones, Charles W., 'The Norman cult of Sts Catherine and Nicholas, saec. xi', *Hommages à André Boutemy*, ed. Guy Cambier (Brussels, 1976), pp. 216-30

Jones, Leslie W., 'The library of St. Aubin's at Angers in the twelfth century', in *Classical and Mediaeval Studies in Honor of Edward Kennard Rand*, ed. Leslie W. Jones (New York, 1938), pp. 143-61

Kälviäinen, Nikolaos, '"Not a few of the martyr accounts have been falsified from the beginning": Some preliminary remarks on the censorship and fortunes of the demonic episode in the Greek Passion of St Marina of Antioch (BHG 1165-1167c)', in *Translation and Transmission: Collection of Articles*, ed. Jaakko Hämeen-Anttila and Ilkka Lindstedt (Münster, 2019), pp. 107-37

Kantzenbach, Friedrich W., *Das Ringen um die Einheit der Kirche im Jahrhundert der Reformation: Vertreter, Quellen und Motive des 'ökumenischen' Gedankens von Erasmus von Rotterdam bis Georg Calixt* (Stuttgart, 1957)

Kazhdan, Alexander P., 'Where, when and by whom was the Greek Barlaam and Ioasaph not written', in *Zu Alexander d. Gr. - Festschrift G. Wirth zum 60. Geburtstag am 9.12.86*, ed. Wolfgang Will and Johannes Heinrichs, 2 vols (Amsterdam, 1988), II, pp. 1187-1207

——, and Stephen Gero, 'Kosmas of Jersualem: A more critical approach to his biography', *Byzantinische Zeitschrift*, 82 (1989), 122-32

Klein, Holger A., 'Eastern objects and western desires: Relics and reliquaries between Byzantium and the West', *DOP*, 58 (2004), 283-314

Klostermann, Erich, and Erich Seeberg, 'Die Apologie der Heiligen Katharina', *Schriften der Königsberger Gelehrten Gesellschaft* 2 (1924), 31-87

Knowles, David, *Great Historical Enterprises: Problems in Monastic History* (Edinburgh, 1963)

Knust, Hermann, *Geschichte der Legenden der Heiligen Katharina von Alexandrien und der Heiligen Maria Aegyptiaca, nebst unedirten Texten* (Halle a.S., 1890)

Koutloumousianos, Bartholomaios, *Menaion of November* (Venice, 1843)

Kramer, Johannes, 'Der lateinisch-griechiche Vergilpalimpsest aus Milan', *Zeitschrift für Papyrologie und Epigraphik*, 111 (1996), 1-20

Krausmüller, Dirk, 'The Encomium of Catherine of Alexandria (BHG 32b) by the *Protasecretis* Anastasius, a work of Anastasius 'the Stammerer'', *AB*, 127 (2009), 309-12

Krautheimer, Richard, *Rome: Profile of a City, 312-1308* (Princeton, 1996)

Kristeller, Paul O., *Latin Manuscript Books Before 1600: A List of the Printed Catalogues and Unpublished Inventories of Extant Collections*, revised and enlarged by Sigrid Krämer (Munich, 1993)

Krönert, Klaus, 'Des interventions du saint au travail des hagiographes: Les miracles de Syméon de Trèves', in Rerum gestarum scriptor:

Histoire et historiographie au Moyen Âge: Mélanges Michel Sot, ed. Magali Coumert *et al.* (Paris, 2012), pp. 363-76

Krumbacher, Karl, review of Joseph Viteau, *Passions des Saints Écaterine et Pierre d'Alexandrie, Barbara et Anysia* (Paris, 1897), in *Byzantinische Zeitschrift*, 7 (1898), 480-83

Krysko, Vadim B., 'Nuove fonti greche di testi innografici slavi nei manoscritti di Grottaferrata', *Bollettino della Badia greca di Grottaferrata*, 2 (2005), 43-55

Labib, Mahfouz, *Pèlerins et voyageurs au Mont Sinai* (Cairo, 1961)

Lair, Jules, 'Vie de Saint Révérend', *Bibliothèque de l'École des Chartes*, 23 (1862), 118-24

Lamoreaux, John C., 'The biography of Theodore Abū Qurrah Revisisted', *DOP*, 56 (2002), 25-40

Langhans, Viktor, 'Eugen Einenkel †', *Anglia*, 54 (1930), 209-12

Lapidge, Michael, *Anglo-Saxon Litanies of the Saints* (London, 1991)

———, *Archbishop Theodore: Commemorative Studies on his Life and Influence* (Cambridge, 1995)

——— et al., *Compendium auctorum latinorum medii aevi*, I.1 (Florence, 2000)

———, *The Roman Martyrs: Introduction, Translations, and Commentary* (Oxford, 2018)

Larison, Kristine M., 'Mount Sinai and the Monastery of St Catherine: Place and space in pilgrimage art' (unpublished doctoral dissertation, University of Chicago, 2016)

Lateinisches Etymologisches Wörterbuch, ed. Alois Walde and Johann B. Hofmann (Heidelberg, 1965)

Latinitatis italicae medii aevi lexicon: saec. V ex. – saec. XI in., ed. Francesco Arnaldi *et al.*, (Florence, 2001)

Lauer, Philippe, *Catalogue général des manuscrits latins*, vol. 2 (numbers 1439-2692) (Paris, 1940)

Lawson, A.C., 'Consultationes Zacchaei Christiani et Apollonii philosophi: A source of S. Isidore of Seville', *Revue Bénédictine*, 57 (1947), 187-95

Leonardi, Claudio, 'Spiritualità di Ambrogio Autperto', *Studi Medievali*, 3rd series, 9 (1968), 1-131

Lequeux, Xavier, 'Latin hagiographical literature translated into Greek', in *The Ashgate Research Companion to Byzantine hagiography*,

Volume 1: *Periods and Places*, ed. Stephanos Efthymiadis (London, 2016), pp. 385-99

Leroquais, Victor, *Les sacramentaires et les missels manuscrits des bibliothèques publiques de France* (Paris, 1924)

——, *Les bréviaires manuscrits des bibliothèques publiques de France*, 6 vols (Paris, 1934)

——, *Les psautiers: Manuscrits latins des bibliothèques publiques de France* (Paris:, 1941)

Levison, Wilhelm, *Conspectus codicum hagiographicorum*, MGH SSRM 7.2 (Hannover, 1920)

Levy, Kenneth, review of Egon Wellesz, *A History of Byzantine Music and Hymnography*, 2nd edn (Oxford, 1961), in *Speculum*, 37 (1962), 467-69

Lewis, Katherine J., *The Cult of St. Katherine of Alexandria in Late Medieval England* (Woodbridge, 2000)

Lexikon für Theologie und Kirche, ed. Walter Kasper *et al.*, 3rd & rev. edn (Freiburg, 1993-2001)

Licht, Tino, *Untersuchungen zum biographischen Werk Sigeberts von Gembloux* (Heidelberg, 2005)

Lieu, Samuel N.C., 'From villain to saint and martyr: The life and after-life of Flavius Artemius, Dux Aegypti', *Byzantine and Modern Greek Studies*, 20 (1996), 56-76

Lifshitz, Felice, *Religious Women in Early Carolingian Francia: A Study of Manuscript Transmission and Monastic Culture* (New York, 2014)

Lowe, Elias A., *Codices latini antiquiores: A Palaeographical Guide to Latin Manuscripts prior to the Ninth Century*, vol. 9: *Germany, München – Zittau* (Oxford, 1959)

——, *The Beneventan Script: A History of the South Italian Minuscule*, 2nd edn prepared by Virginia Brown, vol. 2: *Hand List of Beneventan Manuscripts* (Rome, 1980)

Love, Rosalind C., '"Et quis me tanto oneri parem faciet?': Goscelin of Saint-Bertin and the life of St Amelberga', in *Latin Learning and English Lore: Studies in Anglo-Saxon Literature for Michael Lapidge*, ed. Katherine O'Brien O'Keeffe *et al.*, 2 vols (Toronto, 2005), II, pp. 232-52

Lucà, Santo, 'Rossano, il Patir e lo stile rossanese: Note per uno studio codicologico-paleografico e storico-culturale', *Rivista di studi bizantini e neollenici*, 22 (1985), 93-170

——, 'Le diocesi di Gerace et Squillace: Tra manoscritti e marginalia', in *Calabria bizantina: Civiltà bizantina nei territori di Gerace e Stilo*, ed. Claudio Sabbione *et al.* (Soveria Mannelli, 1998), pp. 245-343

——, 'Il Diodoro Siculo Neap. B.N. gr. 4* e italogreco?', *Bollettino della Badia Greca di Grottaferrata*, 44 (1990), 33-79

——, 'Dalle collezioni manoscritte di Spagna: Libri originari o provenienti dall'Italia greca medievale', *Rivista di studi bizantini e neoellenici*, 44 (2007), 39-96

Luzzi, Andrea, *Studi sul Sinassario di Constantinopoli* (Rome, 1995)

——, 'Il Patmiacus 266: un testimone dell' utilizzo liturgico delle epitome premetafrastiche', *Rivista di studi bizantini e neoellenici*, 49 (2012), 239-61

le Maho, Jacques, 'Les lieux de pèlerinage rouennais au temps des ducs (Xe-XIIe siècles')', in *Identités pèlerines*, ed. Catherine Vincent (Rouen, 2002), pp. 45-65

Mallardo, Domenico, *Il calendario marmoreo di Napoli* (Rome, 1947)

Mango, Cyril A., 'On the history of the templon and the martyrion of St Artemios at Constantinople', *Zograph*, 10 (1979), 40-43

——, 'Greek culture in Palestine after the Arab conquest', in *Scritture, libri et testi nelle aree provinciali di Bisanzio*, ed. Guglielmo Cavallo *et al.*, vol. 1 (Spoleto, 1991), pp. 149-60

Manitius, Max, *Geschichte der lateinischen Literatur des Mittelalters*, vol. 1: *Von Justinian bis zur Mitte des zehnten Jahrhunderts* (Munich, 1911)

Marker, Gary, *Imperial Saint: The Cult of St Catherine and the Dawn of Female Rule in Russia* (DeKalb, 2007)

Martinengo, Tito P., *Pia quedam poemata, at theologica, odaeque sacrae diverso carminum genere conscriptae* (Rome, 1590)

Mateos, Juan, *Le Typicon de la Grande Eglise: Ms. Sainte-Croix n. 40, xe siècle*, vol. 1: *Le cycle des douze mois* (Rome, 1962)

Matthews, David, *The Making of Middle English, 1765-1910* (Minneapolis, 1999)

Mazzatinti, Giuseppe, *Inventari dei manoscritti delle biblioteche d'Italia*, vol. 2 (Forlì, 1892)

——, *Inventari dei manoscritti delle biblioteche d'Italia*, vol. 31: *Prato, Vercelli, Novara* (Florence, 1925)

McCulloh, John M., 'Hrabanus Maurus' Martyrology: The method of composition', *Sacris erudiri*, 23 (1978/79), 417-61

——, 'Das Martyrologium Hrabans als Zeugnis seiner geistigen Arbeit', in *Hrabanus Maurus: Lehrer, Abt und Bischof*, ed. Raymund Kottje and Harald Zimmermann (Wiesbaden, 1982), pp. 154-64

McGuckin, John A., 'Poetry and hymnography (2): The Greek World', in *The Oxford Handbook of Early Christian Studies*, ed. Susan Ashbrook Harvey and David G. Hunter (Oxford, 2009), pp. 652-32

McNulty, Patricia M., and Bernard Hamilton, 'Orientale lumen et magistra latinitas: Greek influences on Western monasticism (900-1000), in *Le Millénaire du Mont Athos, 963-1963: Études et mélanges* (Belgium, 1963-64), pp. 181-216

Meckelnborg, Christina, *Mittelalterliche Handschriften im Landeshauptarchiv Koblenz, vol. 1: Die nichtarchivischen Handschriften der Signaturengruppe Best. 701 Nr. 1-190* (Wiesbaden, 1998)

Meeder, Sven, 'Monte Cassino's network of knowledge: The earliest manuscript evidence', in *Writing the Early Medieval West: Studies in Honour of Rosamond McKitterick*, ed. Elina Screen and Charles West (Cambridge, 2018), pp. 131-45

Mockridge, Diane L., 'From Christ's soldier to his bride: Changes in the portrayal of women saints in medieval hagiography' (unpublished doctoral dissertations, Duke University, 1984)

——, 'Marital imagery in six late twelfth- and early thirteenth-century vitae of female saints', in *That Gentle Strength: Historical Perspectives on Women in Christianity*, ed. Lynda L. Coon *et al.* (Charlottesville, VA, 1990), pp. 60-78

Mohlberg, Leo C., *Katalog der Handschriften der Zentralbibliothek Zürich*, vol. 1: *Mittelalterliche Handschriften* (Zurich, 1952)

Morin, Germain, 'Ein zweites christliches Werk des Firmicus Maternus: Die Consultationes Zacchaei et Apollonii', *Historisches Jahrbuch*, 37 (1916), 229-66

Musset, Lucien, 'Recherches sur les pélerins et les pélerinages en Normandie jusqu'à la Première Croisade', *Annales de Normandie*, 12 (1962), 127-50

Muzerelle, Denis, et al., *Catalogue des manuscrits en écriture latine portant des indications de date, de lieu ou de copiste:* vol. 7: *Ouest de la France et Pays de Loire* (Paris, 1994)

Narducci, Enrico, *Catalogus codicum manuscriptorum praeter orientales qui in bibliotheca Alexandrina Romae adservantur* (Rome, 1877)

Neuhaus, H. Joachim, 'Englische Philologie in Münster bis zur Gründung des Englischen Seminars im Jahre 1905' <http://www.anglistik.uni-muenster.de/1905/>

Newton, Francis, *The Scriptorium and Library at Monte Cassino, 1058-1105* (Cambridge, 1999)

de Nicola, Francesco, 'Contributo critico-testuale ed esegetico alla *Passione di San Pansofio*', *Analecta Papyrologica*, 16-17 (2004-05), 247-74

Nolte, Maria E., *Georgius Cassander en zijn oecumenische streven* (unpublished doctoral thesis, University of Nijmegen, 1951)

Nortier, Geneviève, *Les bibliothèques médiévales des abbayes bénédictines de Normandie: Fécamp, Le Bec, Le Mont Saint-Michel, Saint-Évroul, Lyre, Jumièges, Saint-Wandrille, Saint-Ouen* (Paris, 1971)

Novikoff, Alex J., *The Medieval Culture of Disputation: Pedagogy, Practice, and Performance* (Philadelphia, 2013)

Oikonomides, Nicolas, 'The first century of the monastery of Hosios Loukas', *Dumbarton Oaks Papers*, 46 (1992), 245-55

Oldfield, Paul, *Sanctity and Pilgrimage in Medieval Southern Italy, 1000-1200* (Cambridge, 2017)

Oliger, Livarius, 'Johannes Kannemann: Ein deutscher Franziskaner aus dem 15. Jahrhundert', *Franziskanische Studien*, 5 (1918), 39-67

Omont, Henri, *Catalogue général des manuscrits des bibliothèques publiques de France: Départements*, vol. 1: Rouen (Paris, 1886)

Ortenberg, Veronica, 'Archbishop Sigeric's journey to Rome in 990', *Anglo-Saxon England*, 19 (1990), 197-246

Osborne, John, 'Dating medieval mural paintings in Rome: A case study from San Lorenzo fuori le mura', *Roma Felix: Formation and Reflections of Medieval Rome*, ed. Éamonn Carragáin and Carol Neuman de Vegvar (London, 2007), pp. 191-206

Oury, Guy, 'Les pérégrinations de reliques: Saint Révérend de Nouâtre', *Bulletin Trimestriel de la Société Archéologique de Tourraine*, 35 (1968), 279-93

The Oxford Dictionary of the Christian Church, ed. Frank L. Cross and Elizabeth Livingstone (Oxford, 2012)

Pack, Roger A., *The Greek and Latin Literary Texts from Greco-Roman Egypt*, 2nd edn (Ann Arbor, 1965)

Papebroch, Daniel, *Responsio ad exhibitionem errorum*, vol. 1, 2nd edn (Antwerp, 1696)

Papavarnas, Christodoulos, 'The role of the audience in the pre-metaphrastic passions', *AB,* 134 (2016), 66-82

Patrich, Joseph, *Sabas, Leader of Palestinian Monasticism: A Comparative Study in Eastern Monasticism, Fourth to Seventh Centuries* (Washington DC, 1995)

Peeters, Paul, 'La Passion de Saint Pansophios d'Alexandrie', *AB*, 47 (1929), 307-37

——, 'Une légende de Virgile dans l'hagiographie grecque', in *Mélanges Paul Thomas: Recueil de mémoires concernant la philologie classique* (Bruges, 1930), pp. 546-54

Pellegrin, Élisabeth, *et al.*, *Catalogue des manuscrits médiévaux de la bibliothèque municipale d'Orléans* (Paris, 2010)

Peri, Vittorio, 'ΒΙΡΓΙΛΙΟΣ = Sapientissimus: Riflessi culturali Latino-Greci nell'agiografia Bizantina', *Italia Medioevale e Umanistica*, 19 (1976), 1-40

Peristeris, Aristarchos, 'Literary and scribal activities at the monastery of St. Sabas', in *The Sabaite Heritage in the Orthodox Church*, ed. Joseph Patrich (Leuven, 2001), pp. 171-94

Pertz, Georg H., 'Die handschriftliche Überlieferung der lateinischen Dichtungen aus der Zeit der Karolinger I', *Neues Archiv der Gesellschaft für ältere deutsche Geschichtskunde*, 4 (1878), 87-159, 239-322, 511-582

Petitmengin, Pierre, 'Les vies latines de sainte Pelagie: Inventaire des textes publiés et inédits', *Recherches Augustiniennes,* 12 (1977), 3-29

——, 'Les vies latines de sainte Pelagie: Compléments à l'inventaire et classement des manuscrits du texte B', *Recherches Augustiniennes,* 15 (1980), 265-304

Philippart, Guy, *Les légendiers latins et autres manuscrits hagiographiques*, Typologie des sources du Moyen Âge occidental 24-25 (Turnhout, 1977)

——, and Michel Trigalet, 'L'hagiographie latine du xie siècle dans la longue durée: Données statistiques sur la production littéraire et sur l'édition médiévale', in *Latin Culture in the 11th Century: Proceedings of the Third International Conference on Medieval Latin Studies, Cambridge, 9-12 September 1998*, ed. Michael W. Herren *et al.*, 2 vols (Turnhout, 2002), II, pp. 281-301

——, 'Latin hagiography before the ninth century: A synoptic view', in *The Long Morning of Medieval Europe: New Directions in Early Medieval Studies*, ed. Jennifer R. Davis and Michael McCormick (New York, 2008), pp. 111-29

Sinai, Byzantium, Russia: Orthodox Art from the Sixth to the Twentieth Century, ed. Yuri Piatnitsky *et al.* (London, 2000)

Pietersma, Albert, and R. Theodore Lutz, 'Jannes and Mambres', in *Old Testament Pseudoepigrapha*, ed. James H. Charlesworth, 2 vols (New York, 1983-85), II, pp. 427-42

Pilsworth, Clare, 'Vile scraps: "Booklet" style manuscripts and the transmission and use of the Italian martyr narratives in early medieval Europe', in *Zwischen Niederschrift und Wiederschrift: Hagiographische und historiographische Texte im Spannungsfeld von Kompendienüberlieferung und Editionstechnik*, ed. Richard Corrardini *et al.* (Vienna, 2010), pp. 175-96

Poncelet, Albert, 'De magno legendario austriaco', *AB*, 17 (1898), 24-264

——, 'Sancta Catharinae virginis et martyris translatio et miracula rotomagensia saec. XI', *AB*, 22 (1903), 423-38

——, 'Le Légendier de Saint-Felix de Pavie imprimé en 1523', *AB*, 23 (1904), 459-64

——, *Catalogus codicum hagiographicorum latinorum bibliothecarum Romanarum praeter quam Vaticanae* (Brussels, 1909)

——, 'Les biographes de Ste Amalberge', *AB*, 31 (1912), 401-09

——, 'Catalogus codicum hagiographicorum latinorum Bibliothecae Eporidiensis', *AB*, 41 (1923), 326-36

Potts, Cassandra, *Monastic Revival and Regional Identity in Early Normandy* (Woodbridge, 1997)

Professione, Alfonso, rev. Ilo Vignono, *Inventario Manoscritti della Biblioteca Capitolare di Ivrea* (Alba, 1967)

Rambaran-Olm, Mary, 'Medievalism and the "Flayed-Dane" myth: English perspectives between the seventeenth and nineteenth centuries', in *Flaying in the Premodern World: Practice and Representation*, ed. Larissa Tracy (Cambridge, 2017), pp. 91-115

——, 'A wrinkle in medieval time: Ironing out the problems of periodization, gatekeeping, and "others" in Early English studies', *New Literary History*, 52 (forthcoming autumn 2021)

Rayfield, Donald, *The Literature of Georgia: A History*, 2nd rev. edn (London, 2000)

Reames, Sherry L., *The Legenda Aurea: A Reexamination of its Paradoxical History* (Madison, 1985)

Reatz, August, *Das theologische System der* Consultationes Zacchaei et Apollonii*, mit Berücksichtigung ihrer angeblichen Beziehung zu J. Firmicus Maternus* (Freiburg i. Breisgau, 1920)

Restle, Marcell, *Byzantine Wall Painting in Asia Minor*, tr. Irene R. Gibbons, 3 vols (Greenwich, CT, 1969)

Répertoire topo-bibliographique des abbayes et prieurés, ed. Laurent H. Cottineau and Grégoire Poras, 3 vols (Mâcon, 1935-1970)

Reynolds, Leighton D., *et al.*, ed., *Texts and Transmission: A Survey of the Latin Classics* (Oxford, 1983)

Ó Riain, Diarmuid, 'The *Magnum Legendarium Austriacum*: A new investigation of one of medieval Europe's richest hagiographical collections', *AB*, 133 (2015), 87-165

——, 'Neue Erkenntnisse zur Entstehung und Überlieferung des Magnum Legendarium Austriacum', *Mitteilungen des Instituts für österreichische Geschichtsforschung*, 128 (2020), 1-21

Rivet, Antoine *et al.*, *Histoire littéraire de la France*, vol. 4 (Paris, 1738)

Robertson, Elizabeth, *Early English Devotional Prose and the Female Audience* (Knoxville, 1990)

Rochais, Henri, *Un légendier cistercien de la fin du xiie siècle: Le* Liber de natalitiis *et de quelques grands légendiers des xiie et xiiie siècles* (Rochefort, 1975)

Rodley, Lyn, *Cave Monasteries of Byzantine Cappadocia* (Cambridge, 1985)

Roessli, Jean-Michel, 'Catalogues de sibylles, recueil(s) de *Libri Sibyllini* et corpus des *Oracula Sibyllina*', in *Recueils normatifs et canons dans l'Antiquité*, ed. Enrico Norelli (Lausanne, 2005), pp. 47-68

Ross, David J.A., 'Illustrated manuscripts of Orosius', *Scriptorium*, 9 (1955), 35-56

Roubekas, Nickolas P., *An Ancient Theory of Religion: Euhemerism from Antiquity to the Present* (New York, 2017)

Rousseau, Olivier, 'La visite de Nil de Rossano au Mont-Cassin', in *La chiesa greca in Italia dall'VIII al XVI secolo: Atti del convegno storico interecclesiale (Bari 30 apr. – 4 magg. 1969)*, 3 vols (Padua, 1973), III, pp. 1111-37

Ruysschaert, José, 'Costantino Gaetano, O.S.B.: Chasseur de manuscrits. Contribution à l'histoire de trois bibliothèques romaines du XVIIe s.: L'*Anciana*, *L'Alessandrina* et *La Chigi*', *Mélanges Eugène Tisserant*, vol. 7: *Biblioteche Vaticane* (Vatican City, 1964), pp. 261-326

——, 'Trois notes pour une biographie du benedictin C. Gaetano', *Benedictina*, 21 (1974), 215-23

de Saint Paul, Sebastian, *Exhibitio Errorum quos P. Daniel Papebrochius Societatis Jesu suis in notis ad Acta sanctorum commisit* (Cologne, 1693)

Sands, Tracey R., *The Company She Keeps: The Medieval Swedish Cult of Saint Katherine of Alexandria and its Transformations* (Turnhout, 2010)

Sansterre, Jean-Marie, *Les moines grecs et orientaux à Rome aux époques byzantine et carolingienne (milieu du VIe s. – fin du IXe s.* (Brussels, 1983)

——, 'Saint Nil de Rossano et le monasticisme Latin', *Bollettino della Badia greca di Grottaferrata*, n.s. 45, (1991), 339-86

Savio, Fedele, 'Pietro Suddiacono Napoletano agiografo del secolo x', *Atti della R. Accademia delle Scienze di Torino*, 36 (1900/01), 665-79

Sauget, Joseph-Marie, *Premières recherches sur l'origine et les charactéristiques des synaxaires melkites (xie-xviie siècles)*, Subsidia Hagiographica 45 (Brussels, 1969)

Scappaticcio, Maria C., 'Appunti per una riedizione dei frammenti del Palinsesto Virgiliano dell'Ambrosiana', *Archiv für Papyrusforschung*, 55 (2009), 96-120

Schick, Robert, *The Christian Communities of Palestine from Byzantine to Islamic Rule* (Princeton, 1995)

Schill, Peter, *Ikonographie und Kult der Hl. Katharina von Alexandrien im Mittelalter: Studien zu den szenischen Darstellungen aus der Katharinenlegende* (Munich, 2005), <https://edoc.ub.uni-muenchen.de/4091/>

Schlageter, Johannes, 'Franziskanische Theologie des Mittelalters in der Saxonia' in *Von den Anfängen bis zur Reformation*, ed. Volker Honemann, Geschichte der Sächsischen Franziskanerprovinz vol. 1 (Leiden, 2015), pp. 415-520

Schmitz, Wolfgang, *500 Jahre Buchtradition in Köln: Von der Koehlhoffschen Chronik bis zu den Neuen Medien* (Köln, 1999)

Schneider, Karin, 'Die Bibliothek des Katharinenklosters in Nürnberg und die städtische Gesellschaft', in *Studien zum städtischen Bildungswesen des späten Mittelalters und der frühen Neuzeit*, ed. Bernd Moeller *et al.* (Göttingen, 1983), pp. 70-83

Schnekenburger, Gudrun, ed., *Über die Alpen: Menschen, Wege, Waren* (Stuttgart, 2002)

Scull, Christina, and Wayne G. Hammon, *The J.R.R. Tolkien Companion and Guide*, vol. 2: *Reader's Guide* (Boston, 2006)

Ševčenko, Ihor, 'The illuminators of the menologium of Basil II', *DOP*, 16 (1962), 243 + 245-276

Ševčenko, Nancy Patterson, *Illustrated Manuscripts of the Metaphrastian Menologion* (Chicago, 1990)

——, 'The *vita* icon and the painter as hagiographer', *DOP*, 53 (1999), 149-65

——, 'The Liturgical typicon of Symeon of Sinai', in *Metaphrastes, or, Gained in Translation: Essays and Translations in Honour of Robert H. Jordan*, ed. by Margaret Mullett and Robert H. Jordan (Belfast, 2004), pp. 274-86

——, 'St. Catherine of Alexandria and Mount Sinai', in *Ritual and Art: Byzantine Essays for Christopher Walter*, ed. Pamela Armstrong (London, 2006), pp. 129-43

——, 'The Monastery of Mount Sinai and the cult of Saint Catherine', in *Byzantium: Faith and Power (1261-1557)*, ed. Helen C. Evans (New York, 2006), pp. 118-37

——, 'The imperial menologia and the "Menologion" of Basil II', in *The Celebration of the Saints in Byzantine Art and Liturgy*, ed. Ead. (Farnham, 2013), pp. 1-32

Siegmund, Albert, *Die Überlieferung der griechischen christlichen Literatur in der lateinischen Kirche bis zum zwölften Jahrhundert* (Munich, 1949)

Silvestre, Hubert, 'Notes sur les manuscrits de Bruxelles du *De conflictu vitiorum atque virtutum* d'Ambroise Autpert', in *Calames et Cahiers: Mélanges de codicologie et de paléographie offerts à Léon Gilissen*, ed. Jacques Lemaire and Émile van Balberghe (Brussels, 1985), pp. 159-68

Simon, Anne, *The Cult of Saint Katherine of Alexandria in Late-Medieval Nuremberg: Saint and the City* (Farnham, 2012)

Simons, Walter, 'New forms of religious life in medieval Western Europe', in *The Cambridge Companion to Christian Mysticism*, ed. Amy M. Hollywood and Patricia Z. Beckmann (Cambridge, 2012), pp. 80-113

Singleton, Antony, 'The Early English Text Society in the nineteenth century: An organizational history', *The Review of English Studies* n.s. 56, no. 223 (February, 2005), 90-118

De Smedt, Charles, *Principes de la critique historique* (Liège, 1883)

Smith, Katherine A., *War and the Making of Medieval Monastic Culture* (Woodbridge, 2011)

Smith, Julia M.H., 'Old saints, new cults: Roman relics in Carolingian Francia', in *Early Medieval Rome and the Christian West: Essays in Honour of Donald A. Bullough* ed. Julia M.H. Smith (Leiden, 2000), pp. 317-39

Soskice, Janet, *Sisters of Sinai: How two Lady Adventurers Found the Hidden Gospels* (London, 2010)

Soyez, Jean-Marie, 'Les abbayes de Rouen au XIe siècle', in *La Normandie bénédictine au temps de Guillaume le Conquérant (XIe siècle)*, ed. Louis Gaillaird (Lille, 1967)

Spanò Martinelli, Serena, 'Bonino Mombrizio e gli albori della scienza agiografica', in *Erudizione e devozione: Le raccolte di vite di santi in età moderna e contemporanea*, ed. Gennaro Luongo (Rome, 2000), pp. 3-18

van 't Spijker, Ineke, 'Gallia du Nord et de l'Ouest: Les provinces ecclésiastiques de Tours, Rouen, Reims (950-1130)', in *Hagiographies: Histoire internationale de la littérature hagiographique latine et vernaculaire en Occident des origines à 1550*, ed. Guy Philippart, vol. 2 (Turnhout, 1994), pp. 239-90

Stone, Michael W., *The Armenian Inscriptions from the Sinai* (Cambridge, MA, 1982)

van der Straeten, Joseph, *Les manuscrits hagiographiques d'Orléans, Tours et Angers* (Brussels, 1982)

——, 'Le "Grand Legendier Autrichien" dans les manuscrits de Zwettl', *AB,* 113 (1995), 321-29

Suárez de la Torre, Emilio, 'Sibylles, mantique inspirée et collections oraculaires', *Kernos*, 7 (1994), 179-205

Szövérffy, Joseph, *A Guide to Byzantine Hymnography: A Classified Bibliography of Texts and Studies* (Brookline, MA, 1978)

Tilg, Stefan, *Die Hl. Katharina auf der Jesuitenbühne: Drei Innsbrucker Dramen aus den Jahren 1567, 1577, und 1606* (Tübingen, 2005)

Tillyard, Henry W.J., *The Hymns of the Sticherarium for November* (Copenhagen, 1938)

Torre, Christina, 'Italo-Greek monastic typika', in *Greek Monasticism in Southern Italy*, ed. Crostini and Murzaku, pp. 44-77

Trân-Duc, Lucile, 'Les princes normands et les reliques (x^e-xie siècles): Contribution du culte des saints à la formation territoriale et identitaire d'une principauté', *Pecia*, 8-11 (2005), 525-62

——, 'Le culte des saints en Normandie (IXe – XIIe siècle): Enjeux de pouvoir dans les établissements bénédictins du diocèse de Rouen' (unpublished doctoral dissertation, University of Caen Basse-Normandie, 2015), vol. 1

Tristano, Caterina T., 'Scrittura beneventana e scrittura carolina in manoscritti dell'Italia meridionale', *Scrittura e Civiltà*, 3 (1979), 88-150

Tuilier, André, *Histoire de l'Université de Paris et de la Sorbonne*, vol. 1: *Des origines à Richelieu* (Paris, 1994)

Tyler, John E., *The Alpine Passes: The Middle Ages (962-1250)* (Oxford, 1930)

van Droogenbroeck, Frans J., 'Hugo van Lobbes (1033-1053), auteur van de Vita Amalbergae viduae, Vita S. Reinildis en Vita S. Berlendis', *Eigen Schoon en de Brabander* 94, (2011), 649-84
Valente Bacci, Anna Maria, 'Sviluppo e diffusione della *Passio* di S. Caterina di Alessandria nell'area tedesca medievale', *Quaderni Catanesi,* 12 (1984), 435-63
——, 'Testi in volgare', *Quaderni Catanesi,* 13 (1985), 77-134
——, 'La leggenda di S. Caterina di Alessandria: Fonti e diffusione nell'area linguistica tedesca', *Cultura e Sculoa,* 25 (1986), 75-87
Varnhagen, Hermann, *Zur Geschichte der Legende der Katharina von Alexandrien, nebst lateinischen Texten nach Handschriften der Hof.- und Staatsbibliothek in München und der Universitätsbibliothek in Erlangen* (Erlangen, 1891)
Vennebusch, Joachim, *Die homiletischen und hagiographischen Handschriften des Stadtarchivs Köln,* 2 vols (Cologne, 1993-2001)
Vermassen, Valerie, 'Le *Floriarum sanctorum* de Nicolaus Clopper Jr et le martyrologe brabançon de Pièrre de Thimo: Deux martyrologes perdus, deux hagiographes brabançons méconnus', *AB,* 126 (2008), 119-50
Vermeulen, Jan, *Natales sanctorum Belgii et eorundem chronica recapitulatio* (Leuven, 1595)
Vezin, Jean, *Les scriptoria d'Angers au xie siècle* (Paris, 1974)
Violette, Louis, 'Le problème de l'attribution d'un texte Rouennais du XIe siècle: Les *Acta Archiepiscoporum Rothomagensium*', *AB,* 115 (1997), 113-29
Vircillo Franklin, Carmela, '*Pro communi doctorum virorum comodo*: The Vatican Library and its service to scholarship', *Proceedings of the American Philosophical Society,* 146.4 (2002), 363-84
Viteau, Joseph, 'La Légende de Sainte Catherine (Ecaterine)', *Annales de Saint-Louis-des-Français,* 3.1 (1898), 5-23
de Vriendt, François, 'La vie de sainte Renelde, martyre à Saintes (BHL 7082)', in '*Scribere Sanctorum Gesta*': *Recueil d'études d'hagiographie médiévale offert à Guy Philippart,* ed. Étienne Renard *et al.* (Turnhout, 2005), pp. 399-415
Volk, Robert, 'Symeon Metaphrastes: Ein Benutzer des Barlaam-Romans', *Rivista di studi bizantini e neoellenici,* n.s. 33 (1996), 67-180

——, 'Das Fortwirken der Legende von Barlaam und Ioasaph in der byzantinischen Hagiographie, insbesondere in den Werken des Symeon Metaphrastes', *Jahrbuch der Österreichischen Byzantinistik*, 53 (2003), 127-69

Walsh, Christine, *The Cult of St Katherine of Alexandria in Early Medieval Europe* (Aldershot, 2007)

——, 'The Role of the Normans in the development of the cult of St Katherine', in *St Katherine of Alexandria: Texts and Contexts in Western Medieval Europe*, ed. Jacqueline Jenkins and Katherine J. Lewis (Turnhout, 2003), pp. 19-35

Warner, George F., and Julius P. Gilson, *British Museum: Catalogue of the Western Manuscripts in the Old Royal and King's Collections*, vol. 2 (London, 1921)

Waters, Claire M., *Virgins and Scholars: A Fifteenth-Century Compilation of the Lives of John the Baptist, John the Evangelist, Jerome, and Katherine of Alexandria* (Turnhout, 2008)

Watson, Andrew G., *Catalogue of Dated and Datable Manuscripts, c.700-1600, in the Department of Manuscripts, the British Library* (London, 1979)

Watts, Edward J., *Hypatia: The Life and Legend of an Ancient Philosopher* (Oxford, 2017)

Egon Wellesz, *A History of Byzantine Music and Hymnography*, 2nd edn, rev. & enlarged (Oxford, 1961)

White, Carolinne, trans., *Early Christian Lives* (London, 1998)

Wilhelm, Friedrich, 'Lateinische Akten des hl. Psotius', *Münchener Museum für Philologie des Mittelalters und der Renaissance*, 1 (1911), 185-214

Willard, Henry M., and Kenneth J. Conant, 'A project for the graphic reconstruction of the Romanesque abbey at Monte Cassino', *Speculum*, 10 (1935), 144-46

Wilmart, André, *Codices reginenses latini*, vol. 2 (Città del Vaticano, 1937-45)

Wilson van Baak, Nancy, 'English translation of the Latin *Passio Sancte Katerine Virginis*, BHL 1663', in *La festa et storia di Sancta Caterina: A Medieval Italian Religious Drama*, ed. and trans. Anne Wilson Tordi (New York, 1997), pp. 249-91

Winandy, Jacques, 'L'œuvre littéraire d'Ambroise Autpert', *Revue Bénédictine*, 60 (1950), 93-119

Wolff, Robert L., 'How the news was brought from Byzantium to Angoulême; or, the pursuit of a hare in an ox cart', in *Byzantine Style, Religion and Civilization: Essays in Honour of Sir Steven Runciman*, ed. Elizabeth M. Jeffreys (Cambridge, 1979), pp. 139-89

Zervoudaki, Alexandra, 'Θεοφάνης ο Γραπτός: Βίος και έργο' (unpublished doctoral thesis, University of Crete, 2002)

Zolota, Maria, 'A study of Athens, National Library Ms. 74, with an edition of its Menologion (ff. 203-214)' (unpublished M.A. dissertation, University of London, 2000)

GENERAL INDEX

Abbo, Abbot of Fleury 208
Abbotsford Club 14, 15, 17, 19 n. 60
Abbotsford House 14 n. 43,
Abdinghof 272
Achaea 194 n. 30
Acta archiepiscoporum Rothomagensium 155 n. 46
Acta sanctorum, 12-13
Acta sanctorum hiberniae ex codice salmanticensi nunc primum integre edita 22
Adalbero of Verdun 202
Adelperga, wife of Arechis II, Duke of Benevento 112
Ademar of Chabannes 196-7, 198, *Chronicon*, 196-7, 198 n. 39
Admont 250, 254
Ado, *Martyrology* 157 n. 55, 287
Aegidius (Giles), saint 170 n. 81
Agatha of Catania, saint 6, 46
Agathonicus, saint 71
Agati, Maria Luisa 49
Agnes, wife of Geoffrey, Count of Angers 182
Αἰκατερίνα, abbess, Loukas monastery, Thessalonike 83
Αἰκατερίνα, attested in Souda as personal name 84

Ainard, author of a glossary 189 n. 8
Ainard, monk at La-Trinité-du-Mont, Rouen 189-90, 219
Alberic the Deacon 110
Albinus of Angers, saint 171
Alcuin 151, 164
Alderspach 265
Aldhelm, *De virginitate* 153 n. 40
Aleppo 73 n. 141
Alexander II, Pope 101 n. 47
Alexandria 10, 17, 20, 52, 69, 70, 108, 110, 111
Alfanus, Archbishop of Salerno 101-02, 109-10 (hymn on Katherine)
Aligernus, Abbot of Monte Cassino 98, 206 n. 63
Alphege of Canterbury, saint 34 n. 103
Alps 89, 90, 229
Amalberga, virgin, saint 159 n. 58
Amalberga, widow, saint 159-62, 169, 218
Amatus of Monte Cassino, *History of the Normans* 201-02

Amatus of Monte Cassino, *History of the Normans* 201-02

Ambrose Autpert 141, 146; *Conflictus vitiorum et virtutum*, 90, 140, 144, 146-7, 150, 151, 169, 218, 232, 234, 279; authorship of 142, 142 n. 16; manuscripts of 142 n. 17, 146, 219; transmission of 143; *Sermo in purificatione Mariae* 142 n. 17; *Sermo de adsumptione Sanctae Mariae* 146 n. 24

Ambrose of Milan 141, 176

Amiens 157, 185

Amsterdam 294

Analecta Bollandiana 20 n. 63, 31

Anastasius/Athanasius (colophon/purported author of Katherine's Greek passion) 70, 216 n. 94, 247

Anastasius Bibliothecarius 96 n. 32, 231

Anastasius Sinaites 70 n. 128

Anastasius the Stammerer 71-72, 83

Anatolios, archbishop of Thessalonika 63

Anatolios, hymnographer 62-63, 65, 92

Anatolios, pupil of Theodore of the Stoudios monastery 63

Anchin 260

Andrew, bishop of Crete, saint 77 n. 158

Andrew, saint 231 n. 14

Angers 165, 170-72, 174, 175, 185, 218, 255

Anglia: Zeitschrift für Englische Philologie 17 n. 55, 29

Angoulême 139 n. 11, 196, 196 n. 34, 197

Anjou 185

Anthony of Egypt, saint 69, 70

Antioch 74, 193

Apollonia, saint 6

Aprus, abbot of Saint-Èvre, Toul 189 n. 8

Aquileia 261, 294,

Arab attacks 68, occupation 68, conquests 75, raiders 92

Arechis I, duke of Benevento 206 n. 63

Arechis II, duke of Benevento 112, 206 n. 63

Arechis, judge 206 n. 63

Arechis, lay name of Peter, Subdeacon of Naples 205-06, 207, 247

Arechis, son of Iannipertus 206 n. 53

Aristides, *Apology* 42

Arnstein 264

Artemios of Antioch, saint 52-5

Aschaffenburg 255

Asclepius 47, 124

Ashbrook Harvey, Susan xx

Asia Minor 55, 74, 88

Assemani, Giuseppe S. 73 n. 141

General Index

Athanasius I, bishop of Naples 97 n. 35
Athanasius II (translator, Naples) 203
Athanasius, author of life of Anthony the Great 69, 70
Athos, Mount 64, 93, 99
Audoenus, saint, s.v. Ouen
Augsburg 91, 265
Augustine 55, 141 n. 14, 142 n. 16, 163, 164, 182; *Enarrationes in Psalmos* 147, 167-8, 170; *In epistolam Iohannis ad Parthos tractatus x* 179; *Regula secunda et tertia* 287
Aulne 195
Auxerre 152 n. 32
Auzépy, Marie-France 68
Babylas, hymnographer 62-64, 65, 82, 92
Bamberg 255
Bannatyne Club 19 n. 60
Barbara, saint 2 n. 2, 26, 73, 130 n. 140, 176, 222
Barlaam and Ioasaph 42-43, 44-45, 260
Barlaam and Iosaph, saints 42
Baronio, Cesare, *Annales ecclesiastici* 9-10
Bartholomew of Simeri, saint 94, 98
Basil II, emperor xxiv, 40 n. 16, 81, 81 n. 169
Baturich, bishop 143 n. 19
Baumstark, Anton 73

Bavaria xxiv, 88, 90, 143, 219, 229, links with Italy 89
Bayeux 182
Beck, Hans-Georg 63-4
Bede, *Martyrology* 97, 156-7, 158 n. 57, 164; *De tabernaculo* 179
Begga, saint 176
Benedict Biscop 162 n. 63
Benedict IX, Pope 195
Benedict of Nursia, saint 99, 182
Benedict VIII, Pope 195 n. 30
Benediktbeuern 87, 142, 229; contacts with Italy 88, 89, 90
Beneventan script/minuscule 98, 122 n. 105, 202
Benevento 126, 140
Benignus of Dijon, saint 170 n. 81
Berlin 3
Bethlehem 193
Béthune 194 n. 28
BHG 30: 36 n. 6, 37, 38, 39, 40, 41 n. 21, 45, 46-47, 48, 51, 51 n. 58, 61, 65, 68-69, 71, 77, 77 n. 157, 80 n. 166, 83, 84, 104, 206; colophon (Athanasios as author) 70, 206; influence on Latin tradition 91 n. 15, 105, 107 n. 61, 115-17, 119, 123, 127-28, 129, 132; Iannes and Mambres 57-59, 59 n. 88, 91 n. 15; preserved in southern-Italian manuscripts 105

BHG 30a: 37, 38, 39, 40, 43, 45, 46-47, 48, 55 n. 72, 61, early MSS 49-51, 51 n. 58, 65, 66, 68-69, 71, 77 n. 157, 78, 80, 80 n. 166, 82, 83, 84, 85, 104, 206; colophon (Anastasios as author) 70, 206; influence on Latin tradition 91 n. 15, 105, 107 n. 61, 115-19, 123-24, 125-25, 127-28, 132; Iannes and Mambres 57-59, 59 n. 88; preserved in southern-Italian manuscripts 99, 105

BHG 31: 37, 38, 39, 40, 41 n. 21, 43, 45, 59, 61,62, 65, 72, 79, 80 n. 166, 84; used by *Barlaam* author 44; parallels with John Malalas' *Chonography* 41; restricted diffusion 105

BHG 32: 39, 43-44, 45, 59, 62, 80 n. 166; restricted diffusion 105; Symeon Metaphrastes author 39-40, 44, 45

BHL 1657: 91, 102, 107 n. 61, 108, 114-22, 123, 124 n. 110

BHL 1658: 103 n. 52, 108, 109 n. 62, 115, 116, 117, 118, 119, 119 n. 95, 122-28

BHL 1659: 107 n. 61, 132, 191, 191 n. 15, 217, 220, 229, 230, 248 n. 15; attributed to Peter, Subdeacon of Naples 29, 91, 108, 203-04; elevated style 205 n. 58; epilogue 205-07; manuscripts also containing *Translatio et miracula* 208-09; northern French manuscripts 206-07, 210-11, 234; relationship with BHL 1663: 212-16

BHL 1662: 107 n. 61, 108-13, 122

BHL 1662b: 102, 108, 122-32, 212-14, 215 n. 91, 216 n. 96, 230

BHL 1663
allusions to *Aeneid* 162-63, 162 n. 65
dissemination 237-43
earliest manuscripts 170-85
known in England before 1080: 276
localization 151-58, 185, 186 (Map 2), 219-20
parallel with Eugenius of Toledo 163-64
parallel with Eusebius Gallicanus 164-65
parallel with Petrus Chrysologus 165-67
prologue xxi-xxii, 2 n. 3, 25, 26, 30, 133, 133 n. 3, 134, 140, 171, 176, 179, 182, 185, 244, 245, 253, 255, 256, 257, 258, 259, 260, 261, 262, 263, 264, 265, 266, 267, 268, 269, 270, 271, 272, 273, 274, 283
psalm 113 & Augustine 167-68

relationship with *Translatio et miracula* and BHL 1659: 212-16
relationship with *Conflictus vitiorum et virtutum* 140-47
relationship with *Consultationes Zacchei christiani et Apollonii philosophi* 134-40
terminus ante quem 162, 169, 217, 218
terminus post quem 146, 169
use of Orosius 149-50
used by author of BHL 321 (Amalberga, widow) 159-62
BHL 1663a 29, 33, 121, 133-34, 150, 212 n. 86, 238-39, 244-46, 247, 249, 253, 254, 255, 261, 262, 263, 264, 265, 267, 268, 269, 271, 272, 274, 278-80, 278 n. 4, 282 nn. 6 & 7, 293
BHL 1661m xxv, 13, 108, 134, 247, 248, 248 n. 15, 249, 253, 256, 258, 259, 261, 262, 264, 266, 269, 272, 273, 274; date 238-39; divided into readings 276, 291-92; edition 275-375; manuscripts 239, 275-76, 285-90, 293-95; neumed responses 276, 292
Bible
 Exodus 7.10-12: 57
 Exodus 31.18: 70 n. 126
 Psalm 113: 167-8, 170
 Matthew 27.9: 58
 Luke 23.27-28: 282 n. 7

II Timothy 3.8: 57
Biblioteca Alessandrina 11
Biblioteca Aniciana 11, 130
Bidez, Joseph 41
Binggeli, André 77
βιργίλιος, used as noun (rhetor) and adjective (learned, wise) 46-47, 125, 126
Bischoff, Bernhard 88, 113 n. 76
Blasina, James 189-90, 211
Böddeken 267
Bohemia 240, 257, 270
Bolland, Jean 11
Bollandists xviii n. 2, 10, 11, 12, 20 n. 63, 22, 23-24, 27 n. 89, 31, 91, 103, 201 n. 46, 251, 257
Boulogne-sur-Mer 194 n. 28
Bongars, Jacques 255, 294
Boniface IX, Pope 286
Bonitus Neapolitanus, translator 106
bouletée script 49
Bourges 152, 256
Braunschweig 5, 274
Bray, Jennifer 251
Brenner Pass 90
Bressanone 101
Britain, nineteenth-century 14, 14 n. 42
British Library 2 n. 3, 15
British Museum 15, 27 n. 89
Brittany 152 n. 31
Bronzini, Giovanni xxiii
Bruges 8, 256, 285, 293

Brussels 12, 20 n. 63, 22
Burgundy 182, 201
Butler's Lives of the Saints 34
Byzantium xvii, 48, 74, 93, 203 n. 54
Caecilia, saint 6
Caen, council of (1047): 200, 219
Caesarius of Arles 164 n. 71
Calabria 93, 98, 99, 203
Calendar of Naples 97
Calvin, Jean 7
Camaldoli 260
Cambrai 250, 258, 268
Cambron 257
Campania 93, 203 n. 54, 206 n. 63
Canart, Paul 56
Canterbury 34 n. 103, 93 n. 20, 208 n. 70, 258, 266
Capellini, scribe 259, 294
Carmeliano, Pietro, *Numina si veteres* (BHL 1666a) 33 n. 102
Carolingian minuscule 88 n. 3, 158 n. 56, 202-03, 288
Cassander, George 8-9
Cassiodorus 156 n. 59
Catafygiotu Topping, Eva 60
Catharinaria tragoedia 3
Central Greece, Phokis region 222
Chaâlis 269
Chalcedon, Council of 39
Charitina of Amisus, saint xviii
Charlemagne 88

Chartres 258, 259
Cheikho, Louis 78 n. 160
Chemnitz 5, 262
Christ Church, Canterbury 34 n. 103, 258
Christ, Whilhelm 63
Christina of Bolsena, saint 101
Christodoulos of Patmos 80
Cividale 259, 276, 294
Clairmarais 250, 271
Clairvaux 273
Clemence of Barking 7 n. 21, 33 n. 101, 138 n. 9
Clement of Alexandria 55
Clement of Rome, saint 71, 79, 98
Clopper, Nicolaus, *Florarium temporum* 9
codex salmanticensis 22
Collectanea bollandiana 12
Collège de Navarre, library of 243 n. 9, 269
Collegium Gregorianum de Urbe 130
Cologne 1, 2, 2 n. 2, 3, 201 n. 45, 259, 268, 295
Como 121
Computus Gerlandi 285
Constance xx, 119, 259
Constance, Lake 90
Constantine the Great 8
Constantinople 39, 45, 51, 53, 60, 66, 67, 68, 93, 93 n. 20, 95, 99, 192, 201 n. 46 230

Constantinople, Second Council of 39
Constantius of Lyon 211 n. 83
Germanus of Auxerre 162 n. 65, 163, 211
Consultationes Zacchei Christiani et Apollonii Philosophi 135, 140; origin 139; date 139; manuscripts 139
Corbie 143 n. 19, 156, 156 n. 49, 158 n. 56, 185, 218
Corpus Christi, Cologne 259
Corsendonk Abbey 273
Cosmas, travelling companion of Symeon of Trier 194, 196, 197,
Crescentius, painter 231
Crusades xvii; Crusaders xvii, xxiv; Crusader states xvii; Crusader rhetoric (absence of) 218
Cuissy 262
Cyprus 81 n. 168
Cyricus, saint 77 n. 158
d'Achéry, Jean-Luc 140
D'Angelo, Edoardo 203, 205, 206, 207, 208 n. 71, 209
d'Ardenne, Simonne R.T.O. 31, 32; *Liflade ant te Passiun of Sainte Iuliene* 32 n. 99
de Backer, Joseph 22, 30
de Gaiffier, Baudouin 121
de Garaldi, Bernardino 286
de Jerphanion, Gouillaume 221 n. 2

de Saint Paul, Sebastian, *Exhibitio errorum quos P. Daniel Papebrochis …* 13 n. 39
de Salazar, Tamayo de Smedt, Charles 158 n. 57
de Thou, Jacques Auguste 142 n. 17
del Badia, Jodoco, commentary on Battista Mantovano's poem *Parthenice secunda sive Catharinaria* (BHL 1675) 6, 6 n. 18, 33 n. 102
Delehaye, Hippolyte, *Les légendes hagiographiques* 25-26, 69, 89, 134
Demetrios, saint 56
Denis of Paris, saint 182
Der Heiligen Leben 4, 5
Desiderius, abbot of Monte Cassino 100, 101, 102 n. 50, 109, 110, 202
Diesenberger, Maximilian 88
Diessen 265
Diodorus 41
Disticha Catonis 128-29
Doberan Abbey 255
Dobson, Eric J., 31, 32-33, 32 n. 99, 121, 134, 150, 161, 167 n. 77, 171 n. 84, 176, 179, 182, 244, 245, 246, 251, 292, 293, 294
Dolbeau, François 89, 105, 205
Donauwörth 255, 265

Dorothea, saint 2 n. 2, 10, 17 n.52, 24; as Katherine's Christian name 10, 17 n. 52
Durham 276 n. 2, 288
Duyn, Cornelius 257, 294
dyotheletism 68
Dzielska, Marie 21
Early English Text Society 19, 19 n. 60, 32
Eberbach 266
Eberwin of Trier 192, 193, 193 n. 25, 195, 198, 199; author of Life of Symeon of Trier 192, 196; author of Life of Magnericus 195 n. 31; *De calamitate abbatiae S. Martini Treverensis* 195 n. 31
Ebrach Abbey 274
Echternach 195
Edinburgh 14
Edward IV, King 16
Edward the Confessor 208
Egypt xix, 20, 47 n. 45, 53, 55, 58, 73, 74, 89 n. 8, 92, 93, 94, 111, 234
Ehrhard, Albert 40, 46, 50, 79
Eifel 255
Einenkel, Eugen 17-20, 21, 22, 30, 32
Eis, Gerhard 120-21
Elias, scribe of Paris BnF, MS gr 375: 201 n. 45
Ely 16
Émereau, Casimir 63
Emmeline, founder of La-Trinité-du-Mont at Rouen 188, 188 n. 5

Enghien 256
England 155 n. 46, 235 fig. 15, 240, 241, 267, 275, 276, 288, 293
Ennius 152
Ephesus, Council of 39
Erfurt 3, 4, 4 n. 10
Ermoldus Nigellus 152, 153; *In honorem Hludovici imperatoris* 152
Eugenius of Toledo 163-64
Euphemia of Chalcedon (Ephthimia 73), saint xviii n. 3, 92 n. 18
Eupraxia, saint 73, 74
Europe xvi, xvii, xviii, 12, 89, 94, 200-01 n. 45, 238, 240
Eusebius Gallicanus 163; *Homilia II de Pascha* 164, 169
Eusebius 10, 24, 53, 124; *Ecclesiastical History*, Ἐκκλησιαστικὴ ἱστορία 10, 17 n. 52
Eustratios and companions, saints 64
Euthyimios the Georgian 45
Euthymios the Iberian 45
Eutropius, *Breviarium* 112
Evagrius 139
Faral, Edmond 152
Faustus of Riez 164 n. 71
Fawtier, Robert 199, 200 n. 44
Fécamp 148 n. 28, 179, 180, 181, 185, 187, 187 n. 1, 188,

195, 218, 231, 232, 267, 271, 295
Felix, Archbishop of Ravenna 166
Flach, Martin 5 n. 14
Flanders 250
Fleury 139 n. 11, 152 n. 32, 165, 165 n. 71, 165 n. 72, 169, 207, 208, 211, 219, 231
Florus, *Martyrology* 157
Foffano, Tino 119
Francia 90, 154, 156 n. 50, 168, 201 n. 46; Frankish kingdom 139; Frankish saints 88; Frankish legendaries 89
Francis of Assisi, saint 238 n. 3
Frankenthal 273
fratres sancte crucis, Cologne 259
Frazier, Antonia 114, 115, 121-22, 123
Fritzlar 294
Fromund of Cotentin, saint 201 n. 46
Fromund, travels to Rome, Jerusalem, Sinai 201 n. 46
Fulbert, author of BHL 760 (miracle collection of Ouen) 154-55, 168
Fulco of Caldri, healed by Katherine's relics 191, 220
Fulda 152 n. 32, 195
Fulk Nerra, Count of Anjou 172

Fuscianus and Victoricus, saints 156, 157, 158, 158 n. 55, 158 n. 56
Fyodorovich, Tsar Mickhail 34 n. 105
Gaetano, Costantino 10-11, 130-31, 131 n. 141
Galen, author of Armenian Katherine-inscription on Sinai 221
Gallus, saint 148 n. 25
Garitte, Gérard 76
Garsten 263
Gaudentius of Novara, saint 286
Gaugericus, saint 162 n. 65, 163
Gaul 92 n. 17, 139, 164 n. 71
Genulfus, saint 148 n. 25
Geoffrey II, Count of Angers 182
Geoffrey Martel, Count of Anjou 172
George II, King 20 n. 62
George of Cappadocia, saint xviii n. 3, 176, 205
Georgian, language 36, 67 n. 116, 74, 77, 84; manuscripts 55, 75, 75 n. 149, 78; monks 75
Gerard of Crépy, abbot at Saint-Wandrille 189 n. 8
Gerard of Toul 201 n. 45
Germanus of Auxerre, saint 162 n. 65, 166, 211 n. 83
Germany 5, 166, 166 n. 74, 241, 242 n. 8, 274

Gibbs, Henry 21-2, 21 n. 68
Gilissen, Léon 176
Goderan, scribe 176-77
Göreme Valley, Cappadocia 221-2 n. 2
Goscelin of Saint-Bertin 159 n. 58
Goscelin, founder of La-Trinité-du-Mont at Rouen 188, 188 n. 5, 199, 208
Gradulph, monk at La Trinité-du-Mont at Rouen 189 n. 8
Great Domesday Book scribe 275, 276 n. 2, 288 n. 14
Great St Bernard Pass 90
Greece 88, 194 n. 30, 222
Greek East xviii, 47, 83, 99
Greek versions of Katherine's passion s.v. BHG 30, BHG 30a, BHG 31, BHG 32
Gregory of Nyssa, saint 204 n. 56
Gregory of Ostia, saint 11
Gregory of Tours 156 n. 50, 157
Gregory the Great, saint 11, 141 n. 14, 288
Grein 261, 294
Greyff, Michael 5 n. 14
Grimberghen 256
Grosdidier de Matons, José 64, 66-67, 69, 82
Grottaferrata 51, 51 n. 58, 71 n. 129
Guaiferius of Monte Cassino 102, 110
Guarimpotus 203

Guiselgardus, possible lay name of Peter, Subdeacon of Naples 206
Gullick, Michael 190 n. 11, 276 n. 2
Gutenberg, Johannes 1
Haimin of Saint-Waast 153
Hainaut 160, 176, 185
Hali maiðhad (Holy Maidenhood) 18
Halkin, François 50
Hardwick, Charles 16, 19, 20, 22, 24, 25; *An historical inquiry touching Saint Catherine* 16
Harley, Edward 20 n. 62
Harley, Robert 20 n. 62
Harris, James Rendel 42-43, 44
Hautefontaine 271
Heiligenkreuz 250, 261, 294
Heinsberg 256
Heiric of Auxerre 153
Heist, William 22-23
Helena, saint 148 n. 25
Helmarshausen 272
Henschen, Godfrey 12
Hereford 261, 276
Hilarion the Great, saint 69
Hilarius of Arles 164 n. 71
Hildesheim 5
Hiley, David 210, 215
Hincmar, archbishop of Reims 152 n. 32
Holy Land 192, 193, 201, 225, 229

Holy Sepulchre, Church of
  the, Jerusalem 195
Holy Trinity, London 263
Homer 47; *Iliad* 41-42 n. 25
Honorius III, Pope 78 n. 162
Hosios Loukas church 222
Hugh of Flavigny 198-99
Hugo of Lobbes, abbot and
  author of life of Amalberga
  and Raineldis 160 n. 60
humble monk (μόνος
  ταπεινὸς), author of hymn on
  Katherine 51, 64-66, 92
Hus, Jan xix-xx
Hypatia 10, 20-21, 21 n. 67
iconoclast 68-69, 84;
  Iconoclasm 92
iconophile resistance 64;
  stronghold 67, 68
Île-de-France 171 n. 84, 255,
  294
Institut de recherche et
  d'histoire des textes, Paris
  240 n. 4, 251
Ireland 22, 240, 258; Irish
  saints 22, 23 n. 74; Irish 201
  n. 45, 256
Irene, saint 222
Isembert, abbot of La Trinité-
  du-Mont at Rouen 188-89,
  200, 200 n. 44, 212 n. 85
  (tooth-ache/miracle), 219
Isidore of Seville 11, 139, 140,
  141 n. 14
Islamic occupiers in
  Syria/Palestine 68

Ita of Caldri, gift to La Trinité-
  du-Mont at Rouen 191
Italy, connections with
  Northern France 132, 187,
  201-03, 208, 210, 220;
  connections with Byzantium
  93, 94, 203 n. 54,
Jacobins de la rue Saint-
  Honoré 269
Jacobus de Voragine, *Legenda
  aurea* 5 n. 11, 115, 237 n. 1,
  242
Jannes and Mambres 57-59,
  59 n. 88
*Jannes and Mambres, the Book
  of* 58
Jean de Mailly 1, 239 n. 1;
  *Abbreviatio de gestis et
  miraculis sanctorum* 242
Jerome 69, 96 n. 33, 238 n. 3
Jerusalem 67 n. 115, 68, 75,
  76, 93, 99, 192, 194, 194 n.
  30, 195 n. 30, 196, 201 n.
  46, 225 n. 12
Jesuits of Bruges 285, 293
Jesuit seminary, Leuven 23
Jesuits of Trier 272
Jesus College, Oxford 32 n. 99
John II of Jerusalem 43
John the Evangelist 100, 231
  n. 14
John the Almoner, saint 73
John Chrysostom xx
John Malalas 41, 47 n. 45;
  Chronography 41, 43, 45

John of Damascus 42, 43, 45, 52 n. 62, 67, 67 n. 115, 67 n. 116, 71 n. 129
John of Fécamp 188
John of Rhodes 52
John of Salerno 202, 208, 231
John the Deacon, life of Gregory the Great 288
John the Scot 152
John the Theologian, saint 77 n. 158, 80 n. 167
John Zosimos 36 n. 6, 75-76
John, monk, author of *Chronicon vulturnense* 143 n. 18
Jones, Charles 103
Jorius, abott of Sinai, died in Bologne-sur-Mer 194 n. 28
Josephus, *De bello judaico* 176
Jouarre-en-Brie 268
Juliana of Nicomedia, saint 18, 19
Julitta, saint 77 n. 158
Jumièges 143, 187, 207-08, 215, 218, 219, 271, 295
Justinian I, Emperor 41, 95
Kaisheim 255
Kannemann, Johannes 3-4; *Passio Jesu Christi necnon alius tractatus de Christi passione, sive collectura* 3, 5; *De oratione domini* 3,
Katherine
  angels carry body to Sinai 69, 102, 104, 229, 230, 375
  baptism 7
  beheading/decapitation xviii, 61, 82, 212, 373
  birth 8, 107
  conversion xix, 4 n. 10, 7, 8, 22, 30 n. 95, 107
  debate with rhetors xviii, 81 n. 168, 82, 134, 244, 248, 253, 270, 285
  debating champion xx
  educational background xxi
  erudition and intellect xxi, 18
  example xix, 4, 150, 234
  female strength 235
  fifty rhetors xviii, 36, 38, 41 nn. 23 & 25, 63, 81 n. 168, 82, 104, 112, 122, 123, 128, 129, 134, 135, 136, 138, 158 n. 57, 164, 165, 173, 205 n. 58, 244, 245, 248, 280, 303, 307, 311, 313, 315
  flogging 248, 281, 323, 325
  genealogy 8
  learning xx, 26, 37, 67, 134, 136
  marriage to Christ xix, 7, 8
  masculine traits xix
  patron of university of Paris 243 n. 9
  play s.v. *Catharinaria tragoedia*
  prowess, intellectual 232, 235
  public speaker xxi, 46
  speech(es) xx-xxi, 19, 25, 35, 37-38, 41, 43, 65, 107 n. 61, 112, 113, 123, 124, 128, 129, 133, 134, 135, 138, 147, 164,

General Index

168, 205 n. 58, 245, 246, 278
torture(s) 35, 63, 190, 303, 321, 323, 347, 349
volubility 37
wheel(s) xviii n. 3, 16 n. 50, 155, 173, 190, 245 n. 13, 248, 249, 281, 351, 353
wisdom 26
youth 8, 319, 347
Katherine, cult of xxiii, 34, 238, 276
BHL 1663 as promotion 232
body xvii, 12 (discovery of), 74 n. 144 (translation to Sinai), 221, 225, 226 (at Sinai), (prayer) 68-69, 69, 74, 102, 108, 230, (translation to Sinai) 375
cult site xvii
encomium (BHG 32b) 71-72, 77 n. 158, 83
France 220
frescos 222 n. 2, 231 n. 14
Germany 5
graffito, Greek 222 n. 2
Greek East 48, 60, 61, 83-84, 229
hymn/hymns 62, 66;
   'Ave Katherina martyr et regina' 277, 290, 293
   by Alfanus of Salerno 101-02, 109, 110
   by Anatolios (χαρμονικῶς τῇ πανηγύρει) 62-63, 62 n. 98, 92
   by Babylas (βίον ἄϋλον ἐξησκημένη) 63 n. 98, 82, 92
   by the humble monk (χορείαν σεπτὴν) 64, 65-66, 69, 82, 92, 229
   ῥητορεύει σήμερον 70
   σοφίαν θεοῦ ἐκ βρέφους χαριτώσασα 70-71
intercessor xvii, 34, 61, 83
inscription, Armenian 222
Italy 96-99
kanon 66, 66 n. 111, 71
milk 102, 212, 375
miracle(s) 12, 30 n. 95, 31, 102, 107, 169, 200; miracle collection (see also *Translatio et miracula*) 208, 209, 211-12, 211 n. 83, 212 n. 85, 218
monastic office 189-91, 191 n. 15, 211, 219-20
Monte Cassino 100-03
mosaic 222
Normandy 217-18, 219, 225, 233
oil 102, 103, 190, 199, 208, 212, 215, 225, 226, 233, 234, 375
icon 223, 224 fig. 11, 223-25, 227 fig. 12
relic(s) xvii, xxv, 12, 31, 77 (skull) 77 n. 158 (hand & skull), 100, 102, 103, 110, 133, 169, 187, 190, 191, 198-200, 208, 215, 216, 217, 218, 219, 220, 223, 225, 227 fig. 12 (hand & skull), 228

figs 13 & 14 (hand & skull), 229, 230, 233, 234
sequence 'Regi regum decantet' 277, 290
Sinai 221, 222-26
song cycle 210
Katherine, Greek passions s.v. BHG 30, BHG 30a, BHG 31, BHG 32
Katherine Group 18, 32
Katherine, Latin passions s.v. BHL 1657, BHL 1658, BHL 1659, BHL 1662, BHL 1662b, BHL 1663, BHL 1663a, 1661m
Katherine, passion
 Anglo-Norman poem by Clemence of Barking 7 n. 21, 138 n. 9
 Arabic version/translation 31, 36, 39, 62, 78, 84, 105, 128
 French 22, 26
 Georgian version 36 n. 6, 77, 84
 Middle English version/translation xxiii, 15, 17, 18, 19, 31, 32-33
 Picard version 33
 Spanish version/translation 26
Kingsley, Charles, *Hypatia, or the New Foes with an Old Face* 21, 21 n. 67
Kleinmariazell 263
Klostermann, Erich 43-44
Klosterneuburg 262, 276, 287, 293

Knechtsteden Abbey 256
Knust, Hermann 26-28, 29, 30, 31, 33, 34, 150, 162
Koblenz 242
Koehlhoff, Johann, the Elder 1-2, 2 n. 2, 3, 4
Koehlhoff, Johann, the Younger 2 n. 2
Kominis, Athanasios 71
Kosmas the Hymnographer 67, 67 n. 116
Koutloumousianos, Bartholomaios, *Menaion of November* 66
Krausmüller, Dirk 72
La Sapienza, Rome 130
La Trappe Abbey 254
Lambach 273
Lambertus of Maastricht, saint 171
Landfrid, abbot of Benediktbeuren 90, 141, 142 n. 17
Landolfus Sagax 126, 127
Lapidge, Michael 73
Latin versions of Katherine's passion s.v. BHL 1657, BHL 1658, BHL 1659, BHL 1662, BHL 1662b, BHL 1663, BHL 1663a, BHL 1661m
Latium 93
Latros, monastic centre 80 n. 167, 83
Lawrence, saint 231 n. 14
Le Bec 148 n. 28, 232
Lebanon 73 n. 141
Lebanon, Mount 73 n. 141

Lectionary of Jerusalem 76
Legenda aurea 2, 4, 108 n. 61, 115, 128, 133, 237, 237 n. 1, 239, 242, 253
Legendarium flandrense 250, 256, 260, 271
Legendarium magdeburgense 253, 255
Leiden 8
Leo, scribe 98
Leo I, Pope 141 n. 14
Leo VI, Emperor 71
Leo X, Pope 78 n. 162
Leo XIII, Pope 28, 28 n. 91
Leuven 23, 257
Levison, Wilhelm 249
Liber de natalitiis 250-51, 253
Licinius, saint 171
Liège 32 n. 99, 143 n. 21, 144 n. 21, 195, 206, 219, 257, 262
Lilienfeld 250
Lille 257, 294
Limoges 139 n. 11, 143 n. 19, 171 n. 84, 219, 248, 267, 268, 295; (and) Council of, 197
Lisbon 263
Livre Noir 155 n. 46
Lobbes 160, 161, 161 n. 62, 162, 164 n. 69, 169, 176, 177, 178, 179, 179 n. 92, 185, 218, 257, 294
Lobbes Bible 176
Loir, river 185
Loire, river 151, 185 n. 97
Lombardy 206

London 30, 208, 263
Longpont, abbey 164 n. 71
Lorraine 167, 295
Lorsch 113 n. 76
Low Countries 9, 158, 163, 168, 240
Lowe, Elias 89, 109
Lucà, Santo 48, 49, 50
Lucia of Syracuse, saint 6, 171
Lucius Accius 151
Lucretius 163-64
Luke, Gospel of 78
Lupus of Ferrières 151 n. 32
Lutz, Theodore 58
Lyon 182
Lyre 143 n. 19, 143 n. 20, 148 n. 28
MacBain, William 33
Magdeburg 3
Magnericus of Trier, saint 195 n. 31
Magnum legendarium austriacum 1, 120-21, 241, 246, 249, 253, 261, 262, 263, 264, 274
Mainz 1, 262, 263, 264, 266
Manitius, Max 152
Mantovano, Battista, *Parthenice secunda sive Catharinaria* 6, 33 n. 102
Manuel Holobolos 50
Mar Saba 36 n. 6, 60, 63, 66, 67-68, 75, 75 n. 149, 76, 82, 93
Marcella, saint 148 n. 25

Marchiennes 143 n. 21, 153 n. 42, 165, 165 n. 72, 219, 250, 260
Margaret/Marina of Antioch, saint 2 n. 2, 6, 18, 19, 50 n. 89, 205, 289
Maria Laach 165 n. 72
Marinus and companions, saints 175
Marmara, Sea of 50
Marmoutier 166 n. 74
Marne 271
Martial of Limoges, saint 196-97
Martianus Capella 152
Martin of Tours, saint 46, 176, 138 n. 3
Martinengo, Tito 101
Martyrologium hieronymianum 24, 97
Mary of Egypt, saint 26
Mary, Blessed Virgin, saint 6
Mateos, Juan 76
Matthew the Apostle, saint 211 n. 83
Maurilius, saint 171
Mauritius, saint 243 n. 8
Maurus, saint 171
Maxentius 10, 110-11, 111 n. 70, 134, 163 n. 65, 168, 191 n. 15, 216, 216 n. 96, 244, 245
Maximianus 111, 157
Maximinus Daia 10, 110-1, 111 n. 70
Maximinus of Tours, *Sermones de S. Laurentio* 179

Mediterranean xxv, 88, 192, 225, 235
Meeder, Sven 89
Megas Agros monastery 50, 50 n. 56
Melania, saint 73, 74
Melk 142, 250, 264, 288, 293
Melk, anonymous monk of, *De scriptoribus ecclesiasticis* 142
Menologion of Basil 32, 81, 104, 107 n. 61, 111, 229
Mercurius, saint 71, 80, 98, 100, 223
Metallinos George, 72
Methodios I patriarch of Constantinople, 45
Mettlach 272
Metz 139 n. 11, 152, 265, 267, 295
Michael Synkellos 66, 68
Michael, archangel 100
Michael, deacon at Sinai monastery 77
Michaelbeuren 264, 294
Milan 97, 114
Miletus 80 n. 167, 83
Milo of Saint-Amand 152; Life of Amand 153-54; *De sobrietate* 153 n. 40
miracle(s) 53 (Artemios, collection of), 56 (Demetrios), 154 (Ouen, collection), 155 n. 46 (Ouen), 168 (Ouen), 195 (Symeon of Trier), 219 (Ouen), 219 n. 100 (Ouen), 233, 243 n. 8
Moissac 267

Mombrizio, Bonino 91, 108, 114, 123; *Sanctuarium seu vitae sanctorum* 8, 114-15; epic poem in Italian περὶ τῆς Αἰκατερὶνς 7; working methods 114-15, 119-20, 120 n. 96, 122
monophysitism 43, 70 n. 128
Mont Saint-Michel 187
Monte Cassino 11, 90, 93, 95-96, 97, 98, 99, 99 n. 43, 100, 101, 108, 109-10, 115, 122, 122 n. 105, 229, 231, 231 n. 14
Monte Sant' Angelo 202
Mortagne 171 n. 84, 271, 295
Morton, James 15, 15 n. 44, 16, 17, 19, 22
Moselle 267, 295
Moses 57, 58, 70, 70 n. 126, 223
Münster, university of 17
Münstermaifeld 262
Naples 96, 97, 99, 203 n. 54, 209, 215, 230-31
Narbey, C. 23-5, 30
Naumburg Cathedral 262
Neilos of Rossano, saint 51, 94, 98-9
Newton, Francis 109
Nicholas of Bari, saint 94, 103, 171, 172, 233, 243 n. 9
Nicholas the Pilgrim, saint 94
Niederwerth 262
Nienburg 259

Nonius Marcellus 151, 154 ; *De compendiosa doctrina* 151 n. 32, 151-52
Norbertines 256
Norman Conquest 18, 288
Normandy xvii, xviii, xix, xxv, 103, 132, 142 n. 16, 143, 155 n. 46, 185, 186, 188, 190, 193, 195, 198, 201, 202, 203, 204, 210, 215, 216, 217, 219, 220, 225, 230, 231, 232, 233, 234, 235, 293
North Africa 88, 92, 139
north(ern) France xvii, xxv, 140, 143, 146, 148, 154, 158, 163, 164 n. 71, 165, 166, 169, 185, 188, 206, 207, 215, 220, 240, 276
northern Italy 90, 97, 115 n. 81, 148
Northumbria 162 n. 63
Notre Dame de Bonne Espérance 265
Notre Dame, Tongerloo 264
Nuremberg 5 n. 14; convent of St. Katherine 5
Oberaltaich 265
Oderisius, abbot of Monte Cassino 102 n. 50, 109, 110 n. 66
Odo of Cluny 202, 208, 231
Oldfield, Paul 93, 95
Oracula sibyllina 127
Orbán, Arpad 33-4, 34 n. 103
Orderic Vitalis 189, 190
Origen 58

Orosius 148; *Histories* /*Historiarum adversus paganos libri vii*: 148-49, 148 n. 28, 150, 151, 169
Osbern, life of Alphege 34 n. 103
Otto the Great 189 n. 8
Ouen (Audoenus), saint 154, 155 n. 46, 168, 219, 219 n. 100
Oxford 32, 32 n. 99, 275
Paderborn 9, 195
Paldo, Tato, and Taso, saints 142 n. 18
Palestine 26 n. 6, 43, 48, 63, 68, 74-75, 80, 81 n. 168, 84, 92, 93 n. 20, 94, 193 n. 25, 196, 196 n. 34, 202, 230
Pallada, Jeremias 227
Pansophios of Alexandria, saint 52, 55, 56-59, 56 n. 75, 85, 230,
Pantaleon, saint xviii n. 3
Papebroch, Daniel 12, 13 n. 39, 14; *Responsio ad exhibitionem errorum* 13
Paris 20 n. 63, 24, 27 n. 89, 30, 32, 143 n. 19, 146, 161 n. 62, 182, 240, 251, 267, 268, 269, 295
Paris, university of 243 n. 9
Paschasius Radbertus, *Expositio in Matthaeo Libri xii*: 147 n. 24
Passau 263
Patir Monastery, Rossano 98
Patmos 64, 80, 80 n. 167

Patroclus of Troyes, saint 148 n. 25
Paul the Apostle, saint 58, 100, 182
Paul the Deacon 203, 231; *Historia romana* 112, 126
Paul the Younger, saint 83-84
Pavia 269, 285, 286, 293
Peeters, Paul 31, 39, 46, 52, 56, 57, 62, 78, 78 n. 160, 105, 128,
Pelagia, saint 244 n. 11,
Pelplin 255,
Peri, Vittorio 46-48, 50, 51 n. 58, 52
Pershore 266
Person Gobelinus, 9
Peter, saint 182
Peter Calo 237 n. 1
Peter Damian 11, 113
Peter of Alexandria, saint 64, 71, 97, 97 n. 33, 98, 101 n. 49, 198 n. 64
Peter the Deacon 95 n. 28; *Acta S. Placidi* 95; *De viris illustribus casinensibus* 101 n. 49; *Historia romana* 112, 126
Peter of London, *Liber revelationum* 253, 263
Peter, Subdeacon of Naples xxv, 29, 79-80, 91, 91 n. 15, 106, 107 n. 61, 108, 128 n. 130, 132, 203-05; see also BHL 1659
Petrus Chrysologus 166
Philibert of Jumièges, saint 208

Philipp the Apostle, saint 211 n. 83
Philostorgios 53
Photian Council, Acts of 198 n. 39
Photinus of Lyon, saint 182
Picardy 156
Piccolomini-Ammannati, Jacopo 8
Pietersma, Albert 58
Pilsworth, Clare 89
Pintaudi, Rosario 56, 56 n. 75
Pippin, son of Louis 152
Pitra, Jean Baptiste 70,
Pius IX, Pope, *syllabus errorum* 28
Placidus, saint 95
Plutarch 41 n. 23,
Poitiers 182
Poncelet, Albert 31, 200 n. 44, 208 n. 71, 211, 212 n. 85, 286, 286 n. 9
Poppo, archbishop of Trier 194, 195
Porta Nigra 194
Portugal 240
Prudentius, *Psychomachia* 153 n. 40
Psalter of Basil II: 81 n. 169
Pyrenees 156 n. 57, 158
Quentel, Peter 2 n. 2
Quintinus, saint 156
Rabanus Maurus 13: Martyrology 97; *Historia S. Catherinae* (ascribed) 2-3
Radegunda, saint 182

Raineldis, saint 160, 160 n. 60, 176
Radulfus Glaber 195-96, 198
Ravenna 166, 166 n. 74
Red Cloister 257
Reformation 6
Reims 152 n. 32, 270
relic(s) 53 (Artemios), 90 (travel), 219 (Ouen), 233
Remaclus, saint 176
Remiremont 269
Restituta, saint 94
Reutlingen 5 n. 14
Reverentius, saint 182
Rheinau 274, 276, 290, 293
Rhineland 235; Rhine 242; Middle Rhine Valley 243 n. 8; Central Rhine Valley 262
Ricardus 33 n. 102, 34; wrote Latin poems on Katherine & Alphege 34 n. 103
Richard I, Duke of Normandy 187 n. 1
Richard II, Duke of Normandy 187, 193, 193 n. 25, 194, 195
Richard of Saint-Vanne 193, 193 n. 25, 194, 195-96
Rieti 11, 130-31, 130 n. 140, 131 n. 142
Rivet, Antoine 142
Robert I, duke of Normandy 188, 201 n. 46
Robert Champart, abbot at Jumièges, monk and prior at Saint-Ouen, Rouen 208, 208 n. 70

Robert, archbishop of Rouen 188
Rodrigo de Cerrato 237
Roman calendar 26
Romanos the Melode 64, 64 n. 104
Romanos the Neomartyr, saint 75 n. 149
Romantic movement 15
Romanus of Rouen, saint 155 n. 46
Rome 9, 10, 11, 74, 89, 93, 93 n. 20, 96, 162 n. 63, 193, 193 n. 26, 201 n. 46, 208, 230, 231 n. 14, 273
Rossano 51, 51 n. 58, 94, 97, 98, 99
Rouen 107, 134, 154, 155, 155 n. 46, 169, 185, 187, 188, 190, 192, 194, 196, 201, 202, 207, 208, 211, 215, 217, 219, 220, 221, 223, 225, 229, 232, 233, 234, 269; connections with Sinai 195; Katherine's relics at Rouen 198-200, 215, 217
Roxburghe Club 19 n. 60, 21, 21 n. 68
Royal Library, British Museum 27 n. 89
Rufinus, *History/Historia ecclesiastica* 10, 17 n. 52, 24
Sabbas, saint 75 n. 149
Saidnaya, Our Lady of, monastery 73 n. 141
Saint-Amand, abbey, Saint-Amand-les-Eaux 153, 154, 185, 273
Saint-Amand, convent for women at Rouen 188 n. 5, 232
Saint-Arnould, Metz 139 n. 11, 265
Saint-Aubin, Angers 165 n. 72, 171 n. 82, 255
Saint-Augustine, Cumis 271
Saint-Ayoul, Provins 268
Saint-Bénigne, Dijon 187, 265
Saint-Bertin, abbey, Saint-Omer 154, 165, 165 n. 72, 207
Saint-Cybard, Angoulême 139 n. 11, 196
Saint-Denis, Duclair 190
Saint-Dié-des-Vosges 271
Saint-Èvre, Toul 140 n. 11, 189 n. 8
Saint-Évroult 142 n. 16, 143 n. 20, 148 n. 28, 271
Saint-Germain-des-Prés, Paris 143 n. 19, 268, 295
Saint-Ghislain 265
Saint-Hubert, Ardennes 266
Saint-Jacques, Paris 267
Saint-Laurent, Liège 143-44 n. 21, 206 n. 61, 257
Saint-Lo, Rouen 269
Saint-Magloire, Paris 269
Saint-Martial, Limoges 139 n. 11, 143 n. 19, 248, 267, 268, 295

Saint-Martin-des-Champs, Paris 166 n. 74
Saint-Martin, Massay 140 n. 11
Saint-Martin, Tournai 166 n. 74
Saint-Nicolas, Angers 255
Saint-Omer 13, 250
Saint-Père, Chartres 259
Saint-Pierre, Laon 285
Saint-Quentin, Belval 185, 218, 269
Saint-Quentin, Picardy 156
Saint-Remi, Reims 270
Saint-Rictrude, Marchiennes 143 n. 21
Saint-Sauveur d'Anchin 165 n. 72
Saint-Sépulcre, Cambrai 258
Saint-Thierry, Reims 270
Saint-Vanne, Verdun 273
Saint-Victor, Marseille 268, 295
Saint-Victor, Paris 32, 143 n. 19, 161 n. 62, 267, 268, 269, 295
Saint-Vincent, Metz 152
Saint-Waast, Arras 255
Saint-Wandrille 188 n. 7, 189 n. 8, 218
Sainte-Chapelle, Bourges 256
Sainte-Geneviève, Paris 267
Sainte-Trinité, Fécamp 187 n. 1, see also Fécamp
Sainte-Trinité, Vendôme 140, 182, 276 n. 3
Salaberga, saint 148
Salamanca, Irish College 22
Salerno 95, 101, 202
Salzburg 266
Sampadin, Agnes, scribe 263
San Felice, Pavia 269, 286
San Giorgio Maggiore, Venice 264
San Lorenzo fuori le mura Rome, 231 n. 14
San Pietro, Rome 273
San Vincenzo 140
Sappho 165
Saturninus of Toulouse, saint 182
Sauer, Lorenz (Laurentius Surius) 3 n. 8, 39 n. 15
Savio, Fedele 205
Sawles Warde (Guardianship of the Soul) 18
Schäftlarn 143, 143 n. 19, 266
Scott, Sir Walter 14, 14 n. 43
Seckau 261
Sedulius 153
Seeberg, Erich 43-44
Senlis, cathedral 269
Sensenschmidt, Johann 5
Sergius and Bacchus, church of, Bosra 78 n. 160
Servatius of Tongeren, saint 176
Ševčenko, Nancy 223, 225
Shamunith 73
Sibyl 54, 124, 126, 127, 162 n. 65; sibylline oracles 55
Sicily 93, 95
Siegmund, Albert 204

Sigismund, saint 182
Signy, abbey 258
Silvestre, Hubert 143
Simeon of Polirone 195 n. 30
Simon and Judas, saints 211 n. 83
Simon, Anne 5
Sinai convent xvii, 34, 36 n. 6, 70 n. 128, 75, 76, 77, 77 n. 158, 78, 86, 93, 99, 191, 192, 193, 193 n. 25, 194 n. 28, 195, 196, 197, 198, 198 n. 39, 199, 200 n. 45, 201, 201 n. 46, 221, 222, 223, 224, 225, 227-28, 229
Sinai, Mount xvii, 69, 74 n. 144, 77, 78 n. 162, 109, 215, 221, 230, 234
Smith, Agnes 225 n. 12
Smith, Margaret 225 n. 12
Soissons 268
Sokrates 53
Solinus 148 n. 25
Sophocles 41 n. 23
Sophronios, Patriarch of Jerusalem 43, 93 n. 20
Sorbonne 243 n. 9, 269
Souda 84, 84 n. 178
southern France 88, 240
southern Italy xvii, xxiv, 46, 47, 48, 48 n. 47, 49, 50, 51, 51 n. 58, 81 n. 168, 89, 90, 92-4, 96, 97, 98, 99, 100, 105, 201, 203 n. 54, 210, 240
Spanish Inquisition 13 n. 39
Springiersbach 255

St Albans 34 n. 103
St Augustine, Canterbury 266
St Catharina, Muiden 261
St Catherine's College, Cambridge 16
St Gall 90, 195, 271
St George of Rhinia, monastery of 50
St John of Jerusalem, Waterford 287
St John Prodromos, church of 53
St John the Theologian, monastery of 80 n. 167
St Katherine's Hall, Cambridge 16
St Martin, basilica at Monte Cassino 100
St Mary El-Sourian, monastery 73
St Peter, Leominster 261
St. Barbara, Cologne 268, 295
St. Bartholomäus, Frankfurt 260
St. Castor, Karden 262
St. Donatian, Bruges 256
St. Emmeram, Regensburg 90, 142 n. 17, 153 n. 19, 266
St. Eucharius-Matthias, Trier 140, 272, 289, 293
St. Jacob, Würzburg 274
St. Jerome, Utrecht 256
St. Lambrecht 161
St. Martin, Cologne 259
St. Martin, Trier 192, 195 n. 31
St. Mauritius, Altach 163

St. Maximinus, Trier 12-13, 272
St Peter Lobbes 76
St. Pölten 250 n. 19
St. Simeon Trier, 272
Staffarda 272, 276, 286, 293
Stavelot Bible 176
Stavelot, abbey 176
Steinfeld 255
Stephen of Damascus 75 n. 149
Stephen the Sabaite, saint 75 n. 149
Stone, Michael 221
Stoudios monastery 60, 63, 64, 66, 67, 229
Strasbourg 5, 274
Sulpitius of Bourges, saint 211
Syllabus errorum 28
Symeon Metaphrastes 3 n. 8, 38, 39-40, 40 n. 16, 44-45, 105 n. 56
Symeon of Reichenau, saint 194 n. 30
Symeon of Trier, saint 187, 192-200, 200 n. 45, 230
Symeon, abbot of Sinai monastery 78 n. 162, 222
Synaxarion of Constantinople 79, 80 n. 168, 81, 83, 84, 229
Synaxarion of the Coptic Church 75 n. 150
Synesius of Cyrene 20
Syria 48, 55, 68, 73 n. 141, 74-75, 85, 92, 230
Teano, Campania 206 n. 63

Tegernsee 91
Ter Doest 250, 256
Ter Duinen 256
Thecla, saint 73
Theodore Abū-Qurrah 67
Theodore of Tarsus 93 n. 20
Theodore of the Stoudios monastery 63, 64, 66, 67, 229
Theodoretos 53
Theodoros Graptos 66, 68
Theodoros of Heraclea, saint 148 n. 25
Theophanes Graptos 66, 68, 71 n. 129
Theophanes the Confessor 50 n. 56
Theotokos Hodigitria, monastery 49
Theotokos Nea Hodigitria, monastery, Rossano 98
Theotokos, monastery, Mount Sinai 78, 78 n. 162, 223
Theyer, John 264, 288, 293
Thierry de Montgommeri, abbot at Jumièges 208
Thietmar, German cleric 225-26, 229
Thomas Aquinas 289
Thomas Becket, saint 170 n. 81, 253, 267
Tolkien, J.R.R. 32 n. 99
Toscana 166 n. 74
Toul 150 n. 11, 189 n. 8, 201 n. 45
Toulouse 182
Tournai 166 n. 74, 265

Tours 139 n. 11, 151, 219
translation(s) of hagiographic texts 48, 56, 75, 75 n. 149, 89, 94, 96, 96 n. 32, 103, 105-07, 132, 103, 204
Translatio et miracula (sanctae Catharinae) 198-99, 200, 208, 211, 212, 212 n. 85, 215, 216, 217
transmission of hagiographical texts/saints 89, 94, 95-96
Trier 13, 140 n. 11, 192, 193 n. 23, 194, 195, 195 n. 31, 198, 200-01 n. 45, 259, 260, 272, 276, 289, 293
Trinité de Vendôme, s.v. Vendôme
Trinité-du-Mont, Rouen 188, 188 n. 5, 190, 191, 199, 200, 208, 212 n. 85, 219, 232, 233
Tristano, Caterina 202
Turin 286
Typikon of Constantinople 94, 98
Typikon of St Sabbas, Jerusalem 222
Ursinus of Bourges, saint 211 n. 83
Ursula, saint 2 n. 2
Usuard, *Martyrology* 157, 157 n. 55
Utrecht 256, 257
Val Abbey, Val-d'Oise 269
Valenciennes 154 n. 44, 185, 218
Vallelucis monastery 98

Varnhagen, Hermann 28, 29, 29-30 n. 95, 31
Varro 54 n. 70
Vatican 28, 130
Vatican Archives 28
Vatican Council, second 26
Vatican library 10-11, 28 n. 92
Vaucelles 166 n. 74, 250, 256
Vendôme 140, 171 n. 84, 183-84, 185, 219, 268, 276 n. 3, 295
Vercelli 286
Verdun 199 n. 41, 202, 248, 273
Vergil 46, 46 n. 40, 47, 47 n. 45, 52, 54, 71, 80, 80 n. 166, 81 n. 168, 153, 105 n. 60, (*Aeneid*), 6, 162
Verona 90, 90 n. 12
Vezin, Jean 172
Victor of Vita 139
Vienna 153 n. 37, 247, 264
Viking incursions xix, 232, Vikings 233
Vincent de Beauvais (*Speculum historiale*) 115, 237 n. 1
Vincentius of Collioure, saint 158 n. 57
Visconti-Sforza, Bianca Maria, Duchess of Milan 7-8
Visé 263
Vita Haroldi 155 n. 47
Viteau, Joseph 36-39, 41 n. 21, 46, 49, 50, 52 n. 58
Volk, Robert 44-45

von Andernach, Gottfried, scribe 262
von Hunoldesburch, Albertus Saxo, scribe 262
von Uffenbach, Zacharias Conrad 140 n. 11
Vulcanius, Bonaventura 8
Vulganius, saint 155 n. 46
Wagner, Peter 5 n. 14
Walafrid Strabo, life of Gallus 148 n. 25
Waldensian rejection of the saints 3
Walsh, Christine 68, 73-74, 110 n. 68, 200, 217
Waterford, Ireland 258, 287, 293
Weber, Robert 142-43, 143 n. 19, 146, 219
Weihenstefan 266, 289, 293
Weingarten 272
West Country (England) 275, 288
Wiblingen 264, 271

Wilhelm, Friedrich 91
William IV Taillefer, duke of Angoulême 196, 196 n. 33
William Longsword 208
William of Apulia 202
William of Saint-Calais, bishop of Durham 275 n. 1
William of Volpiano 187, 202, 208, 231
William the Conqueror 275
Wimpfen 259
Winchcomb 264
Winchester 208 n. 70, 276, 276 n. 2, 288
Windberg 266
Witten 266
Wolff, Robert 197
Woodlark, Robert 16 n. 50
Ybbs 262, 294
Yohan, author of Armenian inscription on Sinai 221
Zervoudaki, Alexandra 66
Zwettl 250, 274, 295

MANUSCRIPT INDEX

This index does not include manuscripts that appear only in the checklist on pp. 254-274.

Angers, Bibliothèque municipale, MS 144 (136): 165 n. 72
Angers, BM, MS 121 (113): 170, 171 n. 84, 171, 174-75, 218, 255, 275, 276 n. 3
Aosta, Biblioteca Collegiata Sant' Orso, MS 27: 245 n. 13, 254
Athens, National Library of Greece, MS 629: 66 n. 113
Athens, NLG, MS 74, 98
Athos, Lavra, MS Δ 14: 66 n. 113
Athos, Monê Batopediou, MS 1041: 64
Athos, Skêtê Hagiou Andreou, MS 2: 79 n. 163
Augsburg, Universitätsbibliothek, MS I.2.4° 16: 91
Bamberg, Staatsbibliothek, MS Hist. 2 (E. III. 13): 126 n. 121
Bergamo, Biblioteca Civica, MS MAB.64: 119 n. 95
Berlin, Staatsbibliothek zu Berlin Preussischer Kulturbesitz, MS Phill. 1870: 200 n. 41
Berlin, SBPK, MS Theol. fol. 270: 165 n. 72

Bern, Burgerbibliothek, MS 83: 152 n. 32
Bern, BB, MS 133: 170 n. 81, 255, 294
Bern, BB, MS 137: 171 n. 84, 255, 294
Bernkastel-Kues, St. Nikolas Hospital, MS 52: 140 n. 11
Boulogne-sur-Mer, Bibliothèque municipale, MS 106: 165 n. 72
Bourges, Bibliothèque municipale, MS 34: 246, 256
Bruges, Openbare Bibliotheek, MS 404: 250, 256
Brussels, KBR, MS 683 vol. 2: 166 n. 74
Brussels, KBR, MS 944: 107-08 n. 61, 230
Brussels, KBR, MS 1651-52: 164 n. 71
Brussels, KBR, MS 4564-68: 256, 277-83, 285, 293
Brussels, KBR, MS 7461: 250, 256
Brussels, KBR, MS 7672-74: 22, 30, 256
Brussels, KBR, MS 7917: 247, 256
Brussels, KBR, MS 8344-46: 143 n. 21

Brussels, KBR, MS 8690-8702: 257, 294
Brussels, KBR, MS 8714-19: 143 n. 21
Brussels, KBR, MS 8721-28: 153 n. 42
Brussels, KBR, MS 8955-56: 12, 109 n. 63, 257
Brussels, KBR, MS 9120: 257, 294
Brussels, KBR, MS 9361-67: 144 n. 21
Brussels, KBR, MS 9398-99: 144 n. 21
Brussels, KBR, MS 9810-14: 29 n. 95, 206 n. 61, 202 n. 68, 257
Brussels, KBR, MS 14924-34: 179 n. 92
Brussels, KBR, MS 18018: 160 n. 61, 161, 161 n. 62, 176-79, 179 n. 92, 257, 294
Brussels, KBR, MS II.1179: 176
Cambrai, Bibliothèque municipale, MS 543: 166-67, 166 n. 74
Cambrai, BM, MS 863: 170 n. 81, 258
Cambridge, Corpus Christi College, MS 184: 34 n. 103
Cambridge, CCC, MS 375: 34 n. 103
Cambridge, CCC, MS 405: 258, 287, 293
Cambridge, Fitzwilliam Museum, MS McClean 100: 170 n. 81, 258

Cambridge, University Library, MS Mm.5.22: 152 n. 32
Cape Town, South African Library, MS 48b5: 201 n. 68
Cividale, Museo Archeologico Nazionale, MS XII: 259, 294
Cividale, MAN, MS XXI: 259, 294
Como, Biblioteca del Seminario Vescovile, MS 5: 115 n. 82, 121, 122 n. 105, 123
Como, BSV, MS 6: 121
Copenhagen, Det Kongelige Bibliotek, MS 520: 154 n. 42
Douai, Bibliothèque Marceline Desbordes-Valmore, MS 151: 133 n. 3, 247, 256
Douai, BMD-V, MS 201: 165 n. 72
Douai, BMD-V, MS 838: 250, 260
Douai, BMD-V, MS 857: 153 n. 42
El Escorial, Real Biblioteca de San Lorenzo de El Escorial, MS h.I.13: 26 n. 88
El Escorial, RB, MS m.III.14: 152 n. 32
Erlangen, Universitätsbibliothek, MS 712: 30 n. 95
Florence, Biblioteca Medicea Laurenziana, MS Laur. 48.1: 151 n. 32
Florence, BML, MS Sanctae Crucis plut. XXX sin. 2: 166 n. 74

Manuscript Index

Geneva, Bibliothèque publique et universitaire, MS 24: 165 nn. 71 & 72

Geneva, BPU, MS lat. 84: 152 n. 32

Gorizia, Biblioteca del Seminario Teologico, MS 9: 261, 294

Grottaferrata, Biblioteca Statale del Monumento Nazionale, MS Δ.α.27 (gr. 339): 71 n. 129

Harissa, Bibliothèque des Missionnaires de Saint Paul, MS ar. 70: 74, 144

Heiligenkreuz, Stiftsbliothek, MS 14: 246, 250, 261, 294

Herzogenburg, Stiftsbibliothek, MS 57: 261, 294

Hildesheim, Dombibliothek, MS 739f: 5 n. 13, 261

Istanbul, Patriarchikê Bibliothêkê, MS Hagia Trias 99: 72 n. 134

Ivrea, Biblioteca Capitolare, MS 104 (CV): 108 n. 61

Jerusalem, Patriarchikê bibliothêkê, MS Timiou Staurou 40: 79

Karlsruhe, Badische Landesbibliothek, MS Aug. Perg. 15: 165 n. 72

Kassel, Gesamthochschul-Bibliothek, MS 2° Theol. 142: 262, 294

Klosterneuburg, Stiftsbibliothek, CCl 79: 262, 287, 293

Klosterneuburg, SB, CCl 193: 262, 294

Koblenz, Landeshauptarchiv, Best. 701 Nr. 150: 242, 262

Leiden, Universiteitsbibliotheek, MS Voss. Lat. Q. 113: 139 n. 11

Leipzig, Universitätsbibliothek, MS Rep. II 64: 19 n. 59, 30, 263, 295

Leipzig, UB, MS lat. 436: 5 n. 13, 262

London, British Library, MS Add. 28107 (Stavelot Bible): 176

London, BL, Add. MS 28196 (Stavelot Bible): 176

London, BL, Cotton MS Caligula A.viii: 16 n. 48, 19 n. 59, 26, 30, 264, 294

London, BL, Cotton MS Nero A.xiv: 15 n. 45, 17 n. 54

London, BL, Cotton MS Titus D.xviii: 15 n. 45

London, BL, Harley MS 12: 27 n. 89, 264, 275, 276, 287, 291, 293

London, BL, Harley MS 2719: 152 n. 32

London, BL, Harley MS 3685: 153 n. 37

London, BL, Royal MS 12.E.i: 27 n. 89, 264, 288, 293

London, BL, Royal MS 17.A.xxvii: 15 n. 45

Melk, Stiftsbibliothek, MS 222: 264, 288-89, 293

Melk, SB, MS 678: 250, 264

Messina, Biblioteca Regionale Universitaria 'Giacomo Longo', MS S. Salv. 15: 72 n. 134

Metz, Bibliothèque municipale, MS 141: 140 n. 11

Michaelbeuern, Stiftsbibliothek, MS Man. cart. 67: 264, 294

Milan, Biblioteca Ambrosiana, MS D 92 sup.: 51 n. 58

Milan, BA, MS F 144 sup.: 51 n. 58

Milan, BA, MS L 120 sup.: 47 n. 45

Monte Cassino, Archivio della Badia, MS 70: 130

Monte Cassino, AB, MS 117: 115, 122, 122 n. 105, 123 n. 106, 126 n. 119

Monte Cassino, AB, MS 139: 27 n. 89, 109, 109 nn. 64 & 65, 110 nn. 66 & 68

Monte Cassino, AB, MS 149: 109-10, 109 nn. 64 & 65, 110 nn. 66 & 68

Monte Cassino, AB, MS 187: 27 n. 89

Monte Cassino, AB, MS 202: 203

Monte Cassino, AB, MS 230: 98

Monte Cassino, AB, MS 280: 101, 102 n. 50

Monte Cassino, AB, MS 361: 101 n. 49

Monte Cassino, AB, MS 444: 100 n. 43

Monte Cassino, AB, MS Compact. IX, set 10: 122 n. 105

Montmorot, Archives départmentales du Jura, MS 11: 30 n. 95

Montpellier, Bibliothèque de la Faculté de Médecine, MS 1 vol. 1: 207 n. 68

Munich, Bayerische Staatsbibliothek, Clm 4554: 87-92, 92 n. 17, 132, 146 n. 23

Munich, BSB, Clm 4623: 102 n. 50

Munich, BSB, Clm 7954: 30 n. 95

Munich, BSB, Clm 14500: 142 n. 17

Munich, BSB, Clm 14746: 142 n. 17

Munich, BSB, Clm 14757: 143 n. 19

Munich, BSB, Clm 17059: 143 n. 19

Munich, BSB, Clm 21549: 266, 289, 293

Munich, BSB, Clm 23621: 166 n. 74, 167 n. 75

Munich, BSB, Clm 27059: 143 n. 19

Naples, Biblioteca Nazionale, MS VIII.C.4: 10 n. 43

Naples, BN, MS XIII.G.24: 205 n. 61, 206 n. 65, 209, 210

Novara, Biblioteca Capitolare, MS 23: 122 n. 105, 123 n. 106, 126 n. 119

Novara, BC, MS 29: 122 n. 105

Orléans, BP, MS 322: 211

Orléans, Bibliothèque Publique, MS 330: 29 n. 95

Manuscript Index

Orléans, BP, MS 334: 29 n. 95, 207, 208 n. 71, 209, 211, 220
Oxford, Balliol College, MS 163: 166 n. 74, 167 n. 75
Oxford, Bodleian Libraries, MS Bodley 34: 18, 32 n. 99
Paris, Bibliothèque Mazarine, MS 399: 246, 259
Paris, Bibliothèque Mazarine, MS 1713: 243 n. 9, 69
Paris, Bibliothèque nationale de France, MS Coisl. 148: 84 n. 176
Paris, BnF, MS fr. 412: 26 n. 88
Paris, BnF, MS gr. 13: 66 n. 113
Paris, BnF, MS gr. 1180: 44 n. 33
Paris, BnF, MS gr. 1490: 84 n. 176
Paris, BnF, MS gr. 1525: 39 n. 15
Paris, BnF, MS gr. 1538: 50
Paris, BnF, MS gr. 1539: 41 n. 21, 48 n. 47, 49
Paris, BnF, MS gr. 1590: 80 n. 168, 82
Paris, BnF, MS lat. 810: 248, 267
Paris, BnF, MS lat. 1864: 27 n. 89, 267
Paris, BnF, MS lat. 1928: 179 n. 94
Paris, BnF, MS lat. 1970: 27 n. 89, 170-81, 267
Paris, BnF, MS lat. 2145: 166 n. 74, 167
Paris, BnF, MS lat. 2169: 164 n. 71, 165 n. 72
Paris, BnF, MS lat. 2400: 139 n. 11
Paris, BnF, MS lat. 2469: 197 n. 35
Paris, BnF, MS lat. 2628: 164 n. 71
Paris, BnF, MS lat. 2667A: 139 n. 11
Paris, BnF, MS lat. 2731A: 142 n. 17
Paris, BnF, MS lat. 2732: 142 n. 17
Paris, BnF, MS lat. 2811: 165 n. 72
Paris, BnF, MS lat. 2843: 143 n. 19
Paris, BnF, MS lat. 2968A: 139 n. 11
Paris, BnF, MS lat. 3809: 25, 267
Paris, BnF, MS lat. 3809A: 207 n. 67
Paris, BnF, MS lat. 5278: 27 nn. 88 & 89, 29, 30, 276, 295
Paris, BnF, MS lat. 5308: 25, 205, 267, 295
Paris, BnF, MS lat. 5333: 27 n. 89, 267
Paris, BnF, MS lat. 5336: 27 n. 89, 268, 295
Paris, BnF, MS lat. 5343: 25, 171, 171 n. 84, 182-84, 182 n. 96, 268, 276 n. 3, 295
Paris, BnF, MS lat. 5360: 27 n. 89, 268

Paris, BnF, MS lat. 5365: 25, 171 n. 84, 268, 295
Paris, BnF, MS lat. 5371: 27 n. 89, 268
Paris, BnF, MS lat. 5373: 27 n. 89, 207 nn. 67 & 68
Paris, BnF, MS lat. 7667: 152 n. 32
Paris, BnF, MS lat. 8995: 268, 295
Paris, BnF, MS lat. 10400: 144 n. 21
Paris, BnF, MS lat. 10912: 196 n. 33
Paris, BnF, MS lat. 11753: 207 n. 67, n. 68
Paris, BnF, MS lat. 12259: 25, 25 n. 83, 30, 268, 295
Paris, BnF, MS lat. 12598: 158
Paris, BnF, MS lat. 14293: 25, 30, 246, 268, 295
Paris, BnF, MS lat. 14364: 268, 295
Paris, BnF, MS lat. 15149: 32, 161 n. 62, 267, 295
Paris, BnF, MS lat. 16566: 243 n. 9, 269
Paris, BnF, MS lat. 16735: 251, 269
Paris, BnF, MS lat. 16867: 166 n. 74
Paris, BnF, MS lat. 17007: 251, 269, 295
Paris, BnF, MS n.a. lat. 1083: 190
Paris, BnF, MS n.a. lat. 2288: 269, 283

Paris, BnF, MS suppl. gr. 916: 84 n. 176
Paris, Bibliothèque Ste-Geneviève, MS 2657: 113 n. 76
Patmos, Monê tou Hagiou Iôannou tou Theologou, MS 212: 64
Patmos, MS 266: 76, 80, 82, 98
Pavia, Biblioteca del Seminario, fol. G.4v-H.ij: 269, 286, 293
Rome, Biblioteca nazionale centrale, MS Sess. 147: 246
Rome, Biblioteca Universitaria Alessandrina, MS 96: 125, 128 n. 129, 129, 130, 130 n. 140, 132, 212 n. 86
Rome, Biblioteca Vallicelliana, MS 10: 207 n. 68
Rome, BV, MS B.20: 166 n. 74
Rouen, Bibliothèque municipale, MS 204 (A.591): 190
Rouen, BM, MS 231 (A.44): 208 n. 70
Rouen, BM, MS 274 (Y.6): 208 n. 70
Rouen, BM, MS 670 (A.592): 143 n. 20, 190
Rouen, BM, MS 933 (I.60): 143 n. 20
Rouen, BM, MS 1378 (U.40): 143 n. 20
Rouen, BM, MS 1382 (U109): 205 n. 61, 206 n. 65, 207, 209
Rouen, BM, MS 1388 (U.32): 246, 271

Rouen, BM, MS 1394 (U.119): 171 n. 84, 271, 295
Rouen, BM, MS 1399 (U.2): 271, 295
Rouen, BM, MS 1406 (Y.41): 155
Rouen, BM, MS 1410 (U.22): 31, 205 n. 61, 206 n. 65, 207, 208 n. 71, 209
Rouen, BM, MS 1417 (U.45): 179 n. 94
Rouen, BM, MS 1468 (U.136): 144 n. 20
Saint-Omer, Bibliothèque publique, MS 27: 29 n. 95, 207, 207 n. 67, 208 n. 71
Saint-Omer, BP, MS 716 vol. viii: 250, 271
Sinai, Monastery of Saint Catherine, MS ar. 412, 87 n. 143
Sinai, MS ar. 418: 74 n. 144
Sinai, MS ar. 420: 74 n. 144
Sinai, MS ar. 421: 74 n. 144
Sinai, MS ar. 533: 77 n. 158
Sinai, MS ar. 542: 77
Sinai, MS ar. 548: 77 n. 158
Sinai, MS georg. 6: 36 n. 6, 56 n. 73, 76,
Sinai, MS georg. 34: 76
Sinai, MS georg. 37: 76
Sinai, MS georg. 71: 36 n. 6, 76, 76 n. 155
Sinai, MS georg. 91: 36 n. 6, 76, 76 n. 155
Sinai, MS gr. 526: 45
Sinai, MS gr. 925: 64
Sinai, MS gr. 1097: 223
St Gall, Stiftsbibliothek, MS 458: 97 n. 34
Stuttgart, Württembergische Landesbibliothek, HB MS XIV 19: 123 n. 105
The Hague, Koninklijke Bibliotheek, MS L.29 (70.E.21): 247, 261
Todi, Biblioteca communale, MS 107: 166 n. 74, 167 n. 75
Tournai, Bibliothèque du Grand Seminaire, MS 1 (Lobbes Bible): 176
Tours, Bibliothèque municipale, MS 308: 166 n. 74
Trier, Domschatz, MS 72 (143F): 200 n. 45
Trier, Bischöfliche Seminarbibliothek, MS 33: 246, 272
Trier, BS, MS 98: 133 n. 3, 247, 272
Trier, Stadtbibliothek, MS 388/1152 2°: 170 n. 81, 246, 272
Trier, StB, MS 1050/1261 2°: 247, 272, 276, 289, 293
Trier, StB, MS 1155: 207 n. 68
Trier, StB, MS 1413: 195 n. 31
Troyes, Bibliothèque municipale, MS 154: 165 n. 72
Turin, Biblioteca Nazionale, MS D.V.3: 156 n. 49
Turin, BN, MS I.V.36: 272, 286 n. 9

Uppsala, Universitetsbiblioteket, MS C.400: 119 n. 95
Valenciennes, Bibliothèque municipale, MS 414: 153 n. 42
Valenciennes, BM, MS 502: 153 n. 42
Vatican City, Biblioteca Apostolica Vaticana, MS Borgia lat. 211: 100 n. 43
Vatican City, BAV, MS Ottob. gr. 415: 72 n. 134
Vatican City, BAV, MS Pal. lat. 362: 246, 273
Vatican City, BAV, MS Pal. lat. 909: 126 n. 121
Vatican City, BAV, MS Reg. lat. 131: 165 n. 72
Vatican City, BAV, MS Reg. lat. 252: 139 n. 11
Vatican City, BAV, MS San Pietro in Vaticano A5: 207 n. 68
Vatican City, BAV, MS Urb. lat. 585: 99 n. 43
Vatican City, BAV, MS Vat. ar. 696: 78 n. 160, 78 n. 160
Vatican City, BAV, MS Vat. gr. 2: 71 n. 129
Vatican City, BAV, MS Vat. gr. 544: 48 n. 47, 50
Vatican City, BAV, MS Vat. gr. 807: 41 n. 21, 48 n. 47, 49
Vatican City, BAV, MS Vat. gr. 866: 51 n. 58, 99
Vatican City, BAV, MS Vat. gr. 1613: 51 n. 58, 81, 81 n. 169, 82 n. 173, 99
Vatican City, BAV, MS Vat. gr. 1631: 51 n. 58, 99
Vatican City, BAV, MS Vat. lat. 4952: 166 n. 74
Vatican City, BAV, MS Vat. lat. 4958: 100 n. 43
Vatican City, BAV, MS Vat. lat. 9882: 164 n. 71
Vatican City, BAV, MS Vat. syr. 77: 73, 73 n. 141, 74
Venice, Biblioteca Nazionale Marciana, MS gr. 17: 81 n. 169
Vercelli, Biblioteca Capitolare, Fondo Manoscritti MS 12 (alias 68): 273, 286, 293
Verdun, Bibliothèque publique, MS 1: 133 n. 3, 247, 273
Vienna, Österreichische Nationalbibliothek, MS 337: 250 n. 19
Vienna, ÖSB, MS 614: 153 n. 37
Vienna, ÖSB, MS 3759: 166 n. 74
Vienna, ÖSB, MS s.n. 12754: 247, 273
Wolfenbüttel, Herzog August Bibliothek, MS Helmst. 396: 5 n. 13, 274
Zurich, Zentralbibliothek, MS Rh. 18: 274, 276, 290, 293
Zwettl, Stiftsbibliothek, MS 15: 250, 274, 295